Address all correspondence to:

Aaron Blake Publishers[LLC]
15608 S. New Century Dr.
Gardena, CA 90248
(800) 965-5457
(310) 965-0290
www.workingactors.com

ISBN: 0-937609-22-6

Publisher
Aaron Blake Publishers[LLC]

Editor
Kristi Callan

Art Director
Dan Nolte

Research
Kristi Callan

Advertising Manager
Kristi Callan

Advertising Representative
Nicky Sandels

Distributor
SCB Distributors

Table of Contents

Credits I
Table of Contents II
About the Book V
Questionnaire VI
Listing Submission Form VIII

TRAINING

Acting 2
Broadcast Schools 37
Business of Acting 37
Children's Training 40
Classical Training 48
Cold Reading Workshops 50
Combat 56
Comedy & Improv 57
Commercials 63
Crash Courses 68
Dance 72
Make-Up 76
Modeling Schools 77
Movement 77
Music Lessons 79
Musical Theatre 80
Other Industry Training 83
Voice: Accents & Dialects 87
Voice: Singing 91
Voice: Speech 97
Voice: Voice-Over 101
Universities & Colleges 103

MARKETING

Answering Services, Pagers & Cellular Phone Services 106
Audio Demo Production 107
Books, CDs, Tapes & DVDs 112
Clipping Services 121
Computers 121
Costume Sales & Rentals 123
Dancewear 126
Electronics 126
Fax Services & Mail Boxes 128
Game Shows 129
Image Consultants 130
Make-Up Artists & Consultants . . . 131
Marketing Info & Consultants 133
Messenger Services 137
Musical Services: Accompanists, Composers, Arrangers, Etc. . . 138
Periodicals & Trade Publications . . 139
Photo Labs & Reproductions 142
Photo Retouching 146
Photographers 148
Press Releases 167
Printing & Photocopying 168
Professional Make-Up 171
Rehearsal Studios 172

Resume, Bookkeeping & Secretarial Services 176
Sheet Music 178
Showcase Clubs 178
Stationery Stores 179
Theatrical Libraries 180
Video Camera Rentals 182
Video Demos, Duplication, Airchecks & Production 183
Wardrobe Consultants 187
Wigs 188

THE TEAM

Agencies: Quick Reference Chart 192
Agencies: Commercial & Theatrical 199
Agencies: Modeling 213
Agencies: Specialty 216
Attorneys 218
Business Managers 221
Personal Managers 225
Public Relations 233

WORKING

Advertising Agencies 238
Awards 240
Casting Directors: Quick Reference Chart 244
Casting Directors 254
Casting Facilities, Studio Lots & TV Stations 274
Casting Services & Extra Casting . 277
Dance Companies 279
Looping & Voice-Over Groups . . . 281
Miscellaneous 281
Online, CD & Computerized Services 281
Opera, Light Opera & Musical Theatre 283
Organizations 284
Production Accounting 290
Production Companies 291
Student Films 294
Theatres 295
Theatres, Out of State 313
Unions & Guilds 318
Union Pay Rates 330
Variety Work 333
Working Regulations for Children 335

INDEX

Index .337
Index to Advertisers 340

How To Get Listed:

There is no charge to be listed in *The Working Actor's Guide*. If you provide a legitimate service to actors please send details to Aaron Blake Publishers[LLC] using the form on page VIII. Information for the nineteenth edition will be accepted until August 30, 2006. We cannot guarantee inclusion of information sent.

How To Advertise:

Advertisements for the nineteenth edition will be accepted until August 15, 2006. Discounts are offered for early contracts and payments. Paste-up and typesetting is provided, usually for no additional charge.

Where To Buy The Book:

The Working Actor's Guide is available at Amazon.com and sold in most bookstores in the Southern California area, as well as in many Universities and theatrical bookstores nationwide. It is available at Barnes & Noble, Borders Books, B. Dalton Bookseller, Waldenbooks, as well as:

Samuel French Theatre & Film Bookshops
7623 Sunset Blvd.
Hollywood, CA
(323) 876-0570

11963 Ventura Blvd.
Studio City, CA
(818) 762-0535

Larry Edmunds
6644 Hollywood Blvd.
Hollywood, CA
(323) 463-3273

Vroman's Bookstore
695 E. Colorado Blvd.
Pasadena CA
(626) 449-5320

Book Soup
8818 Sunset Blvd.
Hollywood, CA
(310) 659-3110

Skylight Books
1818 N. Vermont Ave.
Los Angeles, CA
(323) 660-1175

For other locations please call our office (800) 965-5457.

Telephone Orders:

Telephone orders are handled by Samuel French Bookstores, at (323) 876-0570.
Or, call our Distributor at (800) 729-6423.

For Distribution Inquiries:

We are distributed by SCB Distributors, 15608 S. New Century Dr., Gardena, CA 90248, (800) 729-6423. Please contact them if you are interested in carrying *The Working Actor's Guide.*

SAVE $$$ ON YOUR NEXT BOOK

Thank you to all our readers who sent back last year's questionnaires. Those readers were all rewarded for their efforts with a significant discount.

If you are interested in receiving a similar discount on the nineteenth edition of The Working Actor's Guide, fill out the following questionnaire and we'll send you a coupon. All information will be kept confidential.

1. Is this the first edition of The Working Actor's Guide that you have purchased?

____

2. Where did you buy this copy of The W.A.G.?

____

____

3. How did you find out about The W.A.G.?

____

____

____

4. Which sections do you use the most? Please list in order of use.

____

____

____

5. How many people use your copy of The W.A.G.?

____

6. Do you have an agent?
   yes___ no___

7. Do you have a personal manager?
   yes___ no___

8. Are you a member of any unions?
   yes___ no___

   If yes, which ones?

____

9. What is your age? _____

10. How long have you been an actor?

____

11. Name some of the photographers that you have worked with.

____

____

____

____

12. What classes have you been involved in? Please list coaches or schools with which you have studied within the last 4 years.

____

____

13. Did you learn about either your acting coach or photographer from The W.A.G.?
   yes___ no___

SAVE $$$$ ON YOUR NEXT BOOK

14. Are there any other services or contacts that you have acquired as a direct result of using the W.A.G.? If yes, please specify.

____

____

____

15. Is there anything not included in the book that you would like or feel you need?

____

____

____

16. How much did you spend last year on acting related expenses? (including hair, makeup, costumes, headshots, acting class, vocal training, travel, car rental, printing, postage, etc.)

____

17. What is your current yearly income from acting?

Less than $500	___	$500-$999	___
$1,000-$1,499	___	$1,500-$1,999	___
$2,000-$2,499	___	$2,500-$2,999	___
$3,000-$3,499	___	$3,500-$3,999	___
$4,000-$4,499	___	$4,500-$4,999	___
$5,000-$6,999	___	$7,000-$9,999	___
$10,000-$14,999	___	$15,000-$19,999	___
$20,000-$24,999	___	$25,000-$29,999	___
over $30,000	___		

18. Do you have another job or source of income?
yes___ no___

If yes, please specify________________________________

19. What is your current yearly income from sources other than acting?

Less than $500	___	$500-$999	___
$1,000-$1,499	___	$1,500-$1,999	___
$2,000-$2,499	___	$2,500-$2,999	___
$3,000-$3,499	___	$3,500-$3,999	___
$4,000-$4,499	___	$4,500-$4,999	___
$5,000-$6,999	___	$7,000-$9,999	___
$10,000-$14,999	___	$15,000-$19,999	___
$20,000-$24,999	___	$25,000-$29,999	___
$30,000-$39,999	___	$40,000 +	___

If you have any additional comments, feel free to enclose those with this questionnaire on a separate sheet of paper. All comments are appreciated and welcome.

In order to receive your coupon for a discount on the nineteenth edition of The Working Actor's Guide, you must include your name and address below:

Name: ____

Address: ____

City, State, Zip: ____

E-mail: ____

SEND QUESTIONNAIRE TO:
Aaron Blake Publishers LLC
15608 S. New Century Dr., Gardena, CA 90248

Listing Submission Form

If you are not listed in this edition and would like to be in the NINETEENTH edition please fill out and mail in to:

Aaron Blake Publishers[LLC]
15608 S. New Century Dr.
Gardena, CA 90248

or log on to:

www.workingactors.com
and submit your own listing

Name of Company ________________________ Contact Person ____________

Address ____________________ City ______________ Zip ________

Phone(s) ________________________ Best Time to Call ____________

Website ________________________ E-mail ______________

Section and Subheading Under Which Your Company or Service Falls

____

Hours of Operation (If Applicable)

____

Using as few words as possible, and keeping adjectives at a minimum, describe your company or service. If you need help, consult sections of the book where similar services are described. Keep in mind that you are not addressing the reader directly in your listing, we, the editors, are. If you would like to address the readers directly, we encourage you to take out a display ad.

____

____

____

____

____

____

Would You Like to Be Contacted Regarding Advertising? ______

PLEASE FILL OUT THIS PAGE AND MAIL BEFORE AUGUST 30, 2006.

ACTING 2
BROADCAST SCHOOLS 37
BUSINESS OF ACTING 37
CHILDREN'S TRAINING 40
CLASSICAL TRAINING 48
COLD READING WORKSHOPS 50
COMBAT 56
COMEDY & IMPROV 57
COMMERCIALS 63
CRASH COURSES 68
DANCE 72
MAKE-UP 76
MODELING SCHOOLS 77
MOVEMENT 77
MUSIC LESSONS 79
MUSICAL THEATRE 80
OTHER INDUSTRY TRAINING 83
VOICE: ACCENTS & DIALECTS 87
VOICE: SINGING 91
VOICE: SPEECH 97
VOICE: VOICE-OVER 101
UNIVERSITIES & COLLEGES 103

Finding a good teacher is not as difficult as you might think, however, you do need to take time to audit a few classes to see who appeals to you the most. If the teacher won't let you audit, consider finding someone else. There's no way to tell from the teacher's hype if the situation is right for you so check it out in person. One other note about teachers: Any teacher is in a powerful position over a student. The teacher is there to lead you and you are there to follow. An acting teacher is more powerful than any other type of teacher because in order to act well, the acting student must be particlularly exposed and vulnerable. Plus, actors like to believe that someone really holds all the answers and thus all the keys to fame, fortune and happiness. The only person who holds all those keys is you. All the information must be filtered through you. Don't blindly follow anyone. I don't care who it is.

— K Callan "The Los Angeles Agent Book" Sweden Press

A NOISE WITHIN CALIFORNIA'S CLASSICAL THEATRE COMPANY (818) 240-0910
234 S. Brand Blvd.
Glendale 91204
www.anoisewithin.org
rasmussen@anoisewithin.org

This acclaimed classical theatre offers the Professional Intern Program, a comprehensive educational experience for emerging theatre artists within a thriving professional repertory company, and ongoing Conservatory Classes. Acting Internships include 60 hours of classwork, minor casting, understudy and technical assignments (tuition:$500). Admission is by audition/interview. Conservatory Classes (tuition for most classes: $350 per 7 week session) include various levels of acting: Shakespeare, classical scene study, voice workshop, teen acting workshop, as well as specialty subjects, and private coaching. Classes taught by A Noise Within Resident Artists, Resident Director Sabin Epstein, and Artistic Co-Directors Geoff Elliott and Julia Rodriquez Elliiot. Most of the faculty are from San Francisco's American Conservatory (ACT).

ACADEMY OF PERFORMING ARTS (619) 282-1884
4580-B Alvarado Canyon Rd. FAX (619) 282-9889
San Diego 92120
www.apastudios.com
kp@apastudios.com

Offers a full range of acting classes that cover scene study, monologues, cold reading, improv, audition technique, picture and resume review, etc. Classes are for all levels and all ages. They also offer classes in singing, dance, and musical theatre. A full scholarship program is available.

ACADEMY OF THEATRICAL COMBAT (818) 364-8420
www.theatricalcombat.com
info@theatricalcombat.com

Classes in acting with weapons are offered. See listing under COMBAT in this section for further information.

THE ACTING PLACE (866) 478-4886 x3
447 N. Larchmont Blvd.
Los Angeles 90014
www.actingplace.com
info@actingplace.com

The Acting Place is a multi-faceted acting school in Los Angeles that offers a safe and nurturing professional environment in which to grow, develop and blossom as a professional working actor or to simply become a more confident, charismatic individual in your everyday personal and professional life. If you want to explore the craft of acting, discover your passion, and honor your talent, The Acting Place is for you.

ACTOR'S DAILY (310) 399-3666
2437 Main St. FAX (310) 399-2898
Santa Monica 90405
www.edgemarcenter.org
actorsdaily@hotmail.com

Actor's Daily is a 90-minute interactive workshop offered several mornings a week for actors designed as a creative jump-start to the day. Exercises are designed as a supplement to auditions, scene study, cold reading and technique breakdown classes. Actors work their craft, flexing their creative muscles each morning with improv games and exercises, sensory work, triggers, psychological gestures, theater games, and breathing/relaxation techniques. Everyone works in each workshop. Actor's Daily is a safe space to practice taking risks, to dive into the unknown and to go beyond limitations. The actor's instrument is their body, yet actors rarely have an opportunity to exercise their instrument in a performance space several times in a week. Actor's Daily provides that opportunity. Classes are held daily, Monday through Friday; Tuition is $150.00 per month for access to unlimited classes.

THE ACTOR'S LAB (310) 621-3900
at the Odyssey Theatre
2055 South Sepulveda Blvd.
Los Angeles 90048
www.theactorslab.com
theactorslab@aol.com

The Actor's Lab is an acting program for the working actor. It combines both work on the craft and guidance in the business aspect of the Industry. It is run by actor/writer/director, J.D. Lewis.

ACTOR'S SANCTUARY (818) 506-6194

Scene study monologue class. Also offers cold reading and audition technique. Affordable rates. Evening classes. Free audits offered. Also offers private coaching.

ACTORS ART THEATRE (323) 969-4953
6128 Wilshire Blvd.
Los Angeles 90048
www.actorsart.com
actorsart@actorsart.com

This is an acting studio which offers private coaching and workshops for all levels. Applicants are interviewed and given a free introductory session. AAT also offers, by audition, an ensemble company for professional actors. The following classes and workshops are taught by the artistic director, Jolene Adams: "A Way To Work" an acting technique workshop that uses scene study to teach script analysis, emotional preparation, rehearsal and performance techniques, improvisation and character work. Class lessons are applied to practical professional working situations and a step by step system is offered to assist the actor to: achieve a receptive state, trust impulses and focus attention in the moment. Jolene teaches her students that when they do all of the work, they can let go and live within the circumstances of the text. She also presents evenings of class members work before invited audiences. Also offered are The Director's Workshop, an On-Camera Audition Workshop and a Solo Show Workshop. Her Small Group Acting, Audition and Directing Workshops are $150 per six sessions. The Solo Workshop is $175 for six sessions. Private coaching is $60 per hour. Admission is by interview and audition.

THE ACTORS CENTER
MICHAEL BUTLER **(310) 459-5064**
www.actorscenter.com **FAX (801) 516-9226**
mike@actorscenter.com

Training as an actor can be a challenging, engaging, and significant experience. Meaningful professional training is not simply a matter of technique, it involves understanding and working with people. It is important to maintain a safe supportive environment to give an actor the room he needs to express his depth and range. Technique involves the ability to make creative choices, based on an understanding of material, and the ability to execute those choices. The Actors Center is a school for actors of every level. Training is rigorous and they believe that one day soon you will get the chance to use every ounce of your training. They offer career development training and seek to make sure that as you develop solid acting skills, you also develop strong business savvy. You will increase your knowledge of how showbusiness works, and learn consistent and creative ways of pursuing it. Acting classes are offered on Friday and Sunday nights. The cost is $150 for 4 classes per month or $200 per month for 2 classes a week, 8 classes a month. The classes are ongoing so you can start at any time.

ACTORS CIRCLE **(310) 837-4536**
4475 Sepulveda Blvd.
Culver City 90230
www.theactorscircle.com
workshops@theactorscircle.com

Film and television workshops are offered for adults 18-80. The workshops cover scene study, cold reading, sensory work, character development, improv, and audition technique. The focus is to bring out the actor's personality through his/her voice, body, emotions, mind, and the five senses. Private coaching also available. Kevin McDermott and Marcie Smolin.

ACTORS CIRCLE THEATRE SCHOOL **(323) 882-6805**
7313 Santa Monica Blvd.
West Hollywood 90046

Uses the Stella Adler technique to teach beg-pro, age 16 through adult. The class covers audition technique, scene study and Shakespeare. They do play readings and develop new plays. An audit is suggested. Requires an 11 week time commitment. Private coaching is available. SEE AD ON PAGE 3.

ACTORS CO-OP **(323) 462-8460**
1760 N. Gower **FAX (323) 462-3199**
Hollywood 90028
www.actorsco-op.org
jcuster@fpch.org

Actors Co-op Actor's Academy is a year round program that provides exceptional training for the actor. Classes for all levels beginner to advanced are taught by working professionals with a curriculum focused on acting, however future directors, producers and writers will also find this program a valuable learning experience. Scene study, improvisation, voice work, movement, character development and technique.

ACTORS CONSULTATION SERVICES (ACS) **(310) 828-7814**
2461 Santa Monica Blvd., #322 **FAX (310) 998-9114**
Santa Monica 90404
www.actorsconsultations.com
jill@actorsconsultations.com

Jill Jaress, career consultant and coach, specializes in teaching new actors how to break into the business and working actors how to increase the number and quality of their bookings. Private consultations are one hour and can be conducted either on the phone or in person. Private coaching is available, especially for audition preparation.

THE ACTOR'S SPOT **(818) 383-8433**
4821 Lankershim Blvd., **FAX (661) 263-0987**
Ste. F, PMB 363
North Hollywood 91601
www.theactorsspot.com
ptreeky@aol.com

The Actor's Spot focuses on moment to moment, or learning to quit acting and start listening, believing, and reacting. Each class is limited to 10-12 students allowing their instructors to provide hands-on work with each and every student. The Actor's Spot was created to encourage people starting out in the entertainment industry, as

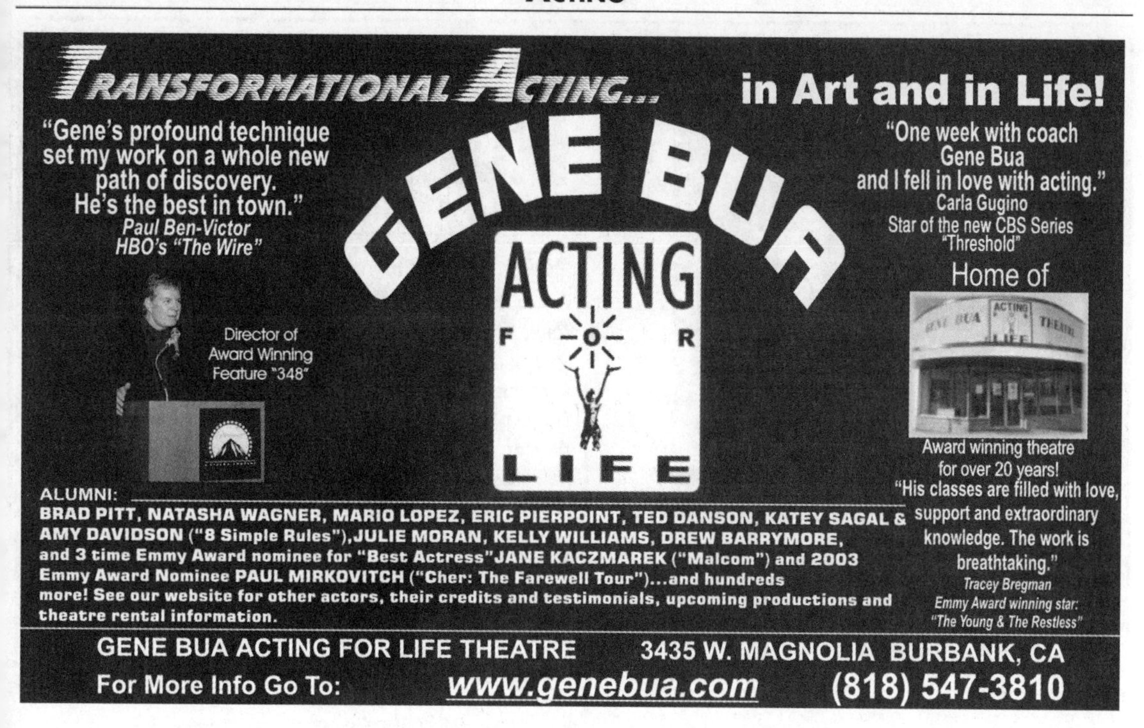

well as to provide a forum for seasoned actors to workout and continue growing. Classes include scene study, cold reading, improvisation and casting directors for ages 7 and up.

THE ACTORS' TEMPLE (323) 930-8986
www.theactorstemple.com

One on one coaching and workshops taught by actress Fabiana Medici, former coach of the Teatro Vittoria resident company in Rome. Ms. Medici has been in the theater field for over twenty years and helps actors build up their confidence while guiding them to gradually develop their own methodology of work, in an open, non-judgmental environment.

ACTORS WORKOUT STUDIO (818) 766-2171
4735 Lankershim Blvd.
North Hollywood 91602
www.actorsworkout.com
info@actorsworkout.com

Professional acting training with Emmy Award-winning acting coach Fran Montano. Acting classes covering Meisner Technique, improvisation, scene study, cold reading, acting company, on-going productions (plays, one acts, showcases, scene nights) & theater rentals.

THE ACTORS WORKSHOP (949) 855-4444
23151 Plaza Pointe Dr. #100
Laguna Hills 92653
www.theactorsworkshop.com
shannonandco@earthlink.net

Now in it's 27th year, this highly respected film/television workshop is Los Angeles and Orange County's oldest acting program. Under the direction of R.J. Adams, classes are conducted twice each week for beginning, intermediate and advanced actors. With co-director Rob Adams and Pete Pastore sessions are conducted in a state of the art digital television studio. Classes include audition/cold reading techniques, on-camera scene work and weekly showcases with major L.A. casting directors. R.J. Adams began his long time teaching career as director/founder of The Actors Workshop/Hollywood in the early 70s with many of his students having risen to starring roles in film and television. R.J. has appeared in more than 60 feature films and television shows in both the U.S. and Europe. Rob Adams has been a working actor since the late 80s with film credits that include "Forrest Gump" and "The Program." The workshop prides itself on the success of the large number of of current and former students working in the film/TV industry.

THE ACTORS' EDGE WORKSHOP (310) 652-4399
7080 Hollywood Blvd., Ste. 306
Hollywood 90028
www.theactorsedgeacademy.com

Using a combination of many methods this casting director teaches from a casting director's point of view. The classes are for beg-pro level children age 6-adult. Cold reading, scene study, audition/interview technique, and a commercial workshop. There is a free audit. Class size is limited to 20 students.

CATLIN ADAMS ACTING LABS (323) 851-8811
The Elephant Theatre
6322 Santa Monica Blvd.
Hollywood 90028

Award winning director Catlin Adams teaches ongoing classes on

Tuesday evenings at the Elephant Theater in Hollywood. Also a professional class on Thursday mornings. Private coach to many stars of film and television, her classes concentrate on teaching to the actor how to develop their craft. The classes cover improvisation, cold reading, monologues, sensory work, camera technique and scene study. Students work in every class. Class size is strictly limited and private coaching is available. Call for information, auditing appointment or class brochure. Interview necessary, auditing allowed.

STELLA ADLER ACADEMY OF
ACTING AND THEATRE COMPLEX (323) 465-4446
6773 Hollywood Blvd., 2nd Fl. FAX (323) 469-6049
Hollywood 90028
www.stellaadler-la.com

Academy director, Irene Gilbert. Call for catalogue and further information. Scene study and script analysis. SEE AD ON THIS PAGE.

AIA ACTOR'S STUDIO (818) 563-4142
1918 Magnolia Blvd., Ste. 204 FAX (818) 563-4042
Burbank 91506
www.aiastudios.com
info@aiastudios.com

AIA Actor's Studio is a nationally recognized acting studio and entertainment company. The Studio has spent the last decade helping actors achieve professional excellence by providing dramatic instruction, career guidance and the opportunity to build relationships with Industry experts. The Studio has successfully integrated the business of acting with both formal and practical training and offers a diverse array of classes and programs taught by working entertainment professionals.

WILLIAM ALDERSON ACTING STUDIO (323) 466-0799
1103 N. El Centro
Hollywood 90028
www.aldersonstudio.com
eefing@pacbell.net

Mr. Alderson, assisted by Don Bloomfield periodically offers a 6-week summer session in "The Meisner Technique." Regular study period is two years of in-depth training in the Meisner technique. Mr. Alderson was the Associate Director to Mr. Meisner at the Neighborhood Playhouse Professional School of the Theater for 20 years. He opened his present studio in Los Angeles in 1995. He formerly headed the acting department at the Neighborhood Playhouse for 10 years while Mr. Meisner was ill. He has been teaching the Meisner technique for 35 years. Former class members include a number of stars including Allison Janney, Kim Basinger, Louise Guzman, Ian Gomez, Dylan McDermott, Jeff Goldblum, Matt McCoy and Jennifer Gray.

ALEXANDER TECHNIQUE & FELDENKRAIS
AWARENESS THROUGH MOVEMENT®
JUDITH STRANSKY (310) 828-5528
stranskyj@aol.com FAX (310) 828-1028

Ms. Stransky applies 42 years experience to teaching freedom of body and self. She specializes in releasing problems and limitations in performance and daily life, by teaching mastery over body and voice through a 'profound' re-education of posture, carriage, movement, breathing, emotional well-being and mental focus. This work is designed to effortlessly achieve optimum ease, freedom, and tension release which allows opening up and perfecting ability in all areas: acting, voice, expression, awareness, movement, suppleness, tone and self confidence as well as alleviating stage

fright, physical pain and stress for both students and professionals. Nina Foch, "With body and voice, the only things that work are techniques that can become a part of your entire life. This is what the Alexander Technique does, better than any other technique I know... Judith Stransky has shown me the way." Clients include stars of stage and screen. Both methods are included world-wide in acting and voice training by foremost teachers, acting companies, drama schools, and universities. Ms. Stransky is a former faculty member of the USC Drama Department, a senior teacher at UCLA Extension and author of "The Alexander Technique: Joy In The Life Of Your Body." SEE AD ON PAGE 11.

ALEXANDER TECHWORKS
JEAN-LOUIS RODRIGUE (310) 209-9023
KRISTOF KONRAD (310) 443-4483
P.O. Box 3194
Beverly Hills 90212
www.alexandertechworks.com
jeanlouisr1@yahoo.com

During the past 25 years Alexander Techworks has provided ongoing group classes, private instruction, and intensive courses offered by AmSAT Certified Teachers. The Alexander Technique helps the actor gain a fundamental awareness, control, and freedom of the whole self. Goals of the technique are effortless movement, increased coordination, a fuller capacity of breath, improvement in the use of voice and speech, increased tonus in the musculature and a stronger sense of the self. Courses are offered in character development through physicalization and period movement. Studio locations in Westwood and Santa Monica. Mr. Rodrigue has been part of the faculty at the UCLA School of Theatre, Film, and Television for the past 15 years. SEE AD ON PAGE 4.

JANET ALHANTI (323) 465-7511

Ms. Alhanti conducts a professional twenty-week technique class and also offers private coaching. Ms. Alahanti studied with Sanford Meisner and Philip Burton and only accepts students by recommendation.

THE AMERICAN ACADEMY OF DRAMATIC ARTS (323) 464-2777
1336 N. La Brea Ave.
Hollywood 90028
www.aada.org
info@ca.aada.org

Director of Instruction: Madonna Young. President – Los Angeles Division: Marguerite Artura. A professional theatre school with 22 instructors on the faculty that offers a 2 year accredited program. During the first year acting, voice, speech, movement, styles, Alexander Technique and theatre history are offered. The second year has advanced courses covering the same material as the first year plus an acting for the camera workshop, Shakespeare, musical theatre, make-up, rehearsal/performance, cold reading, dialect study and a one person show class. Some of their alumni have received (72) Oscar, (55) Tony, and (155) Emmy nominations. Contact the school for an application and audition information.

AMERICAN NATIONAL ACADEMY OF PERFORMING ARTS (818) 763-4431
10944 Ventura Blvd.
Studio City 91604

Director: Dorothy Barrett. Acting classes in scene study, improv, cold

readings, and audition technique. Also offered are classes in ballet, jazz and tap, singing, speech, musical comedy, and pantomime for children, teens, and adults. The Academy is a non-profit organization chartered by the State of California.

JILL ANDRE **(818) 762-3360**

The aim of the work is "to build a personal technique that is always available to you." The work covers scene study, audition preparation, character analysis, monologues, and sensory work. An interview is required. Private coaching available. SEE AD ON PAGE 10.

JOHN ANGELO **(323) 848-6534** **(323) 848-6308**

Mr. Angelo teaches his Theatre Arts and Shakespeare Workshop for adults, youth and children at the West Hollywood Park Auditorium in West Hollywood. He taught previously for the Culver City Department of Parks and Recreation and the Nosotros Theatre as well as for the City of Los Angeles and at Las Vegas high schools. He offers play reading, improvisation, scene study, cold reading for film and stage, projection, theatre games, audition preparation, discipline and self confidence, and also teaches the career minded with respect to photographs and how to get agents. Sessions for children are Saturdays from 11 am to 12:30 pm and teens and adults from 12:30 pm to 2 pm. He also teaches a six-week Shakespeare Workshop. There are public and showcase performances. Auditing is not allowed. John appeared in ten Broadway shows including "Carousel" and "Oklahoma" and was under contract with MGM for ten years, appearing in, among others, "Singing In The Rain," "Silk Stockings" and "An American In Paris." He directs two shows a year for the City of West Hollywood.

JOEL ASHER STUDIO **(818) 785-1551**
www.joel-asher-studio.com **FAX (818) 785-1902**

Joel Asher offers "Acting Unlimited" with no limits on the time you spend learning and doing, no limits on the help you can get to advance your career, and no limits on the methods used to get results – all for one price. The on-camera scene study classes include private coaching to work on scenes for class, audition preparation, or additional work whenever the actor needs help. The classes include script breakdown, character development, improvisation, cold reading, career counseling, etc. Asher provides a wide variety of techniques to help the actor find his/her own methods, relaxation and concentration, exercises to stretch the imagination, plus comedy and camera techniques. Classes are on-going and limited to 12. Periodic workshops are given in "Getting the Job" and "Enhancing Creativity" as well as Industry showcases. Joel Asher Studio also creates state of the art professional demo reels customized to the actor. Joel Asher's expertise on acting comes from many perspectives as a successful actor, director, writer and teacher. Asher has long been known as one of the country's top acting coaches and recognition of his work has extended as far as two TV specials in Japan and even a documentary in this country titled "Joel Asher – Hero." He coaches actors on set and directs for films (most recently Morgan Creek Productions) and television (most recently for Disney Studios). His "Acting on Camera" workshops are in demand nationally and his "Actors at Work" series of videos and DVDs is broadly considered to be one of the best of its kind. Asher also coaches actors privately for auditions and role development, working with beginners and stars individually. See listing for "Actors At Work Series" under BOOKS & TAPES in the MARKETING section for further information. SEE AD ON PAGES 1 & 113.

TONI ATTELL **(818) 787-8685**
www.attell.com
attell@attell.com

Toni Attell's background as an actress, as well as an acting teacher/coach includes a variety of work in TV and film. She has worked with some of the great masters of the performance arts field internationally including: Jean Louis Barroult and Mamako Yoenyama and Marcel Marceau for mime, Carlos Mazzonne for Comedia Del Arte, David Alexander, Nina Foch and Harvey Lembeck for improv, comedy and acting. Toni has performed with the American Conservatory Theater in San Francisco, spent 13 years at Theatre West and has toured over 350 colleges in the United States as a mime-comedienne, winning best act on the circuit for her one-woman shows. Toni also has performed with the improv group "The Committee" and she started "The Comedy Store Players." She has choreographed the clowns at Ringling Bros. and Barnum and Bailey Circus as well as a variety of music videos. She recently toured and taught acting in Japan and China and has started a stand-up comedy group of children called "The Comedy Pups." Current classes include: "Mommy and Me and Show Biz Makes Three" and "Silver Foxes" for adults over 60 who have never worked in acting before. Eighteen of these "Silver Foxes" have already booked their first jobs. Classes for adults, teens, seniors and children include stand up comedy, movement, improv, cold reading techniques and acting on camera for television and movies, as well as commercials. Ms. Attell currently teaches "Acting for Writers" at the USC Cinema School and hosts a talk radio show. Coaches privately, on-set and for businesses. Ms. Attell has pioneered a new technique to use hypnosis and guided meditation to enhance actors' tools and memorization.

THE GARY AUSTIN WORKSHOPS **(818) 753-9000** **(818) 503-3571**
P.O. Box 2320
Toluca Lake 91610
www.garyaustin.net
geneandroy@aol.com

Mr. Austin uses a spontaneous approach to acting using improv technique for the development of characters and material. Free auditing is allowed. He is an alumnus of The Committee and is the creator and original director of The Groundlings.

CYNTHIA BAIN'S YOUNG ACTOR STUDIO **(323) 654-6614**
Laurelgrove Theatre
12265 Ventura Blvd., Ste. 209
Studio City 91604
www.cynthiabain.com
cynthia@cynthiabain.com

Classes are for the young professional and aspiring actor. Cynthia provides young actors with a strong foundation, allowing for individual growth in an inspiring, dynamic, and supportive atmosphere. Classes are primarily scene study with an emphasis on script analysis and improvisation and include exercises and cold reading technique. Cynthia began her professional acting career at age 14 and thus knows firsthand the unique needs of young performers. She was nominated for a Cable Ace Award for Best Actress in a Dramatic Series for her work in HBO's "War Stories" and has had numerous starring roles in feature films, MOWs, miniseries, network pilots, and episodic television. Cynthia received her BA from UCLA in Theater Arts and her many years of study with the legendary acting coach Roy London provides the basis of her instruction. She successfully created, developed, and ran her young actor program at the Cameron Thor Studio for over three years before moving to the Laurelgrove Theatre. The annual show she directs, produces, and co-writes with her students has garnered her much praise and caught the attention of many Industry professionals. These shows have been the primary force in kick-starting the careers of dozens of her students. Class size is limited so every student has an opportunity to work in every class. An eight-week commitment is required; classes are ongoing so a student may join at anytime. Young actor auditors are welcome. Private coaching is available for all ages.

ROBERT BARASH POWER ACTING **(323) 993-8646**
http://members.budgetsurf.net/jbarash@bsn1.net/Acting%20Poster%205-07-04.htm
timberlakepeter@aol.com

Robert Barash teaches acting in Los Angeles after successful classes in New York and Toronto. He was an original member of the Actor's Studio playwright/director's unit in New York studying under Lee Strasberg and is now affiliated with the Actor's Studio in Los Angeles.

ADILAH BARNES CHARACTER DEVELOPMENT WORKSHOP **(818) 752-2225**
Rip Rap Studio Theatre
5755 Lankershim Blvd.
North Hollywood 91601
www.adilahbarnes.com
abpro1@aol.com

Adilah Barnes offers an ongoing multi-level class that utilizes Stanislavski, Uta Hagen and the Spolin techniques. The class focuses on fundamental acting elements including relaxation, imagination, theatre games, object, sensory and improvisation. Through monologue and scene work, it explores character and script analysis. It also includes nuts and bolts of the business and an Industry Night Showcase. The class stresses moment-by-moment listening and truthful communication. Interviews are required and one paid audit is permitted. Private instruction is also available. SEE AD ON PAGE 7.

JOANNE BARON & D.W. BROWN STUDIO **(310) 451-3311**
www.baronbrown.com **FAX (310) 451-1407**
info@baronbrown.com

The Joanne Baron/D.W. Brown Studio has been a wellspring for the theatrical casting and producing community for over twenty years and continues to produce gifted actors, writers, directors and producers who bring their training and talent to all aspects of theatre, film and television. The Studio offers a variety of programs for the professional and select pre-professional actor, writer director and producer. They also produce films utilizing its talent such as the movie "Perfume," which saw its premiere at the Sundance Film Festival. The Studio also does on-set coaching for films and has worked with actors such as Academy, Emmy and Golden Globe Award Winner Halle Berry. This studio is among a handful of select acting schools registered with the California Bureau of Private Post-Secondary and Vocational Education.

TONY BARR'S
FILM ACTORS WORKSHOP (310) 442-9488
2050 S. Bundy Dr., Ste. 100
Los Angeles 90025
www.filmactorsworkshop.com
filmactorsworkshop@earthlink.net

An acting school with a focus on acting for the camera. The approach comes from Mr. Barr's book entitled "Acting for the Camera" and emphasizes the importance of listening and working directly from one's own thoughts and feelings on a moment-to-moment basis. A weekly class with a limit of 14 students all of whom work in every session. Students work on scenes from motion pictures, taking each scene through a cycle of cold reading, rehearsing, taping and recording on DVD in a 3-camera video studio. The workshop has been in continuous operation since 1960. Beginning classes are offered on Tuesday or Thursday, advanced classes offered on Monday or Wednesday. Evening classes are from 7:30 pm to 10:30 pm. The principal instructor, Eric Kline taught with Mr. Barr for over 20 years.

CAROLYNE BARRY'S ACTING
AND IMPROV WORKSHOPS (323) 654-2212
www.carolynebarry.com
carolyne@carolynebarry.com

This complete program for the dedicated professional actor offers beginning, intermediate and advanced improv, on-camera acting/scene study and commercial workshops plus a specialty packaging class and a theater, sit-com, soap and film/TV cold reading workshop. Carolyne Barry, who has trained more than 5,000 working actors, has been teaching for 20 years and casting for 16. Recommended by agents, casting directors, managers and former students, Ms. Barry is recognized as one of the most comprehensive audition teachers and often has a month or two waiting list. She has been featured as an acting authority in The Hollywood Reporter, L.A. Reader, The Examiner, Back Stage West as well as on CNN, KHJ, KTTV and numerous other TV and radio talk shows throughout the country. Recently Ms. Barry was chosen to be the Commercial Audition coach for "E" TV's "Fight For Fame." The workshops are taught Carolyne and a staff of master, professional teachers with programs designed to develop the actor's skills, exercise creativity and freedom, and nurture unique their on-camera personality. Small classes and personalized instruction. Classes range between 6 and 12 weeks; fees vary from $355 to $495 and payment plans are available. Interview and audition required.

MARTIN BARTER MEISNER/CARVILLE
SCHOOL OF ACTING (818) 509-9651
5124 Lankershim Blvd. FAX (818) 763-0049
North Hollywood 91601
www.themeisnercenter.com
info@themeisnercenter.com

The home of the Meisner Technique in Los Angeles. The school was founded by Sanford Meisner in 1987 with James Carville. In 1995 Mr. Meisner turned the school over to Martin Barter, his assistant for 14 years. The studio offers an intensive 2 year program in the reality of doing. It also offers 2 four week summer sessions and there is a working Theatre Company and master classes for graduates. The school now offers screen writing classes as well.

BB'S KIDS (323) 650-5437
www.bbskids.com

Belinda Balaski offers on-camera workshops for kids and teens from age 4 and up. Sessions are on weekends for 8 weeks and cover TV and film acting, commercials, tot's improv, Shakespeare classics, print and runway modeling, music video classes, teen improv, dialects and voice over classes, and auditions with a casting director. With an emphasis on cold reading character study, making choices, improv, commitment and prepared scene work. Progressive and advanced classes are available as is private coaching. 50 years acting experience, 20 years teaching over 3,000 kids in the business. See listing under MUSICAL THEATRE, COMMERCIALS, ACCENTS AND DIALECTS, MODELING and CHILDREN'S TRAINING for further information. SEE AD ON PAGE 41.

JUDY BELSHE (562) 621-0121
www.askjudy.biz
belshecasting@aol.com

Children and adult ongoing on-camera acting classes in Long Beach. For beg-pro. Improv, commercials, theatrical. Guest writers come to classes and teach on theatrical nights.

ANDREW BENNE STUDIO
PROFESSIONAL ACTOR DEVELOPMENT (818) 386-5867
4930 Lankershim Blvd.
North Hollywood 91601
www.andrewbenne.com

The studio specializes in developing actors to be paid working actors. Andrew Benne has been coaching professional actors since 1989 and has a stable of celebrity clientele. Currently several studio members are series regulars on major network shows. The intense training process is rooted in moment to moment work with an emphasis on human behavior, realistic relationships and emotional preparation. The studio offers professional scene study and film style improv, meaning custom improvs with detailed situations written by Benne for his students' breakthroughs. Cold readings, progressive Meisner technique, Industry showcases and private coaching. The studio is suited for serious actors who want to grow. Limited space available. Free audit and interview required for studio membership.

MOLLI BENSON (310) 726-9595
www.mollibensonproductions.com
mollibenson@aol.com FAX (818) 728-6657

Molli Benson conducts master film-acting workshops in Los Angeles. The ongoing film workshops are held one weekend a month Friday 6-10 pm and Saturday and Sunday 9:30 am to 6 pm. Once included in the workshop, all actors participate in periodic 4-day retreats and 4-day, out of state, on location workshops (westerns, police dramas, etc.) Phone interview required.

BERG STUDIO
GREGORY BERGER-SOBECK (323) 822-0152
www.thebergstudios.com
bergstudios@sbcglobal.net

Gregory Berger-Sobeck teaches the Yale School of Drama technique which has trained Meryl Streep, Edward Norton, Sigorney Weaver, Liv Schreiber and Frances McDormand, among others. All students are offered very small classes, giving individualized attention. Class covers scenework, commercial and theatrical auditions, on-camera cold reading technique. Periodic Industry showcases, and guest speakers. Classes meet twice a week. Every actor works every class. Mr. Berger-Sobeck has an MFA from Yale and has worked many years in New York as a teacher and private coach. He has numerous Broadway credits as well as credits in film and television. The technique he teaches is a systematic approach for identifying and personalizing the character's driving need and objectives and engaging the actor's voice, body, mind and spirit in its active pursuit. It is a repeatable step by step process ensuring repeatable returns. Mr Berger-Sobeck recently directed an industry showcase specifically targeting top casting agents and managers coupled with Daryl Marshak Management which was written up in Back Stage West. He recently was the associate casting director on the new network pilot Angel Air.

ALAN BERGMANN (818) 764-0404

Private coaching is offered for beg-adv levels covering audition and camera technique, cold reading, scene study, improv, character analysis, scene breakdown, and monologues. Mr. Bergmann has been a TV actor for 30 years and a TV sit-com director for 15 years, ("Family Ties" and "Night Court.")

BETTER ACTING GROUP
AT MICHAEL CHEKHOV STUDIO (310) 312-4989
www.arta-la.com
info@betteracting.com

Developed and practiced in Russia for over 50 years, now in Los Angeles at the Michael Chekhov Studio: SVC acting system (Stanislavski + Vakhtangov + Chekhov). Find out more information on the website.

BEVERLY HILLS PLAYHOUSE (310) 855-1556
254 S. Robertson Blvd.
Beverly Hills 90212

1816½ N. Vermont Ave.
Los Angeles 90027
www.katselas.com
osman@gameasset.com

A school of comprehensive acting instruction under the artistic supervision of Milton Katselas, an acclaimed director and teacher for over thirty years.

BLACK NEXXUS (323) 467-9987
6472 Santa Monica Blvd., Ste. 203
Los Angeles 90038
www.blacknexxusinc.com
blacknexxus@sbcglobal.net

Cutting edge classes to develop your own method. Vocal workshops, on-camera classes, scene study, and sensory technique geared toward developing the actor's awareness and emotional flexibility through a mixture of imagination and skills.

MICHAEL BOFSHEVER
ENERGY IN MOTION (310) 281-9580
1365 Westwood Blvd.
Los Angeles 90025
mikebofact@aol.com

Michael Bofshever has been profiled as "one of the finest acting teachers in Los Angeles," The Qualified Guide To Acting Coaches: Los Angeles [Smith & Krauss]. Mr. Bofshever is a recognized working actor and author of Your Face Looks Familiar....published by Heinemann Press. He speaks on the topic of how to create and maintain a career as an actor for the Screen Actors Guild Foundation in Los Angeles and New York. He has conducted his highly regarded seminar at AFI, AADA, Players Academy and universities throughout the country. Mr. Bofshever teaches an ongoing exercise and scene study class, Monday nights starting at 6:30 pm. Admission by interview.

JIM BOLT (323) 559-9466

Offers coaching based on the actor honoring the character's experience. Currently specializing in preparing the actor for specific auditions. Valuable for important auditions.

STEPHEN BOOK (323) 461-4263
stephenjbook@yahoo.com

Book's famous workshop in Hollywood is tailored for professionals and teaches Improvisation Technique, the use of improvisation while speaking scripted lines. Book was a longtime faculty member at Juilliard and USC, has taught in London and Moscow, and served as the executive director of the Spolin Theater Game Center. Students have included Val Kilmer, George Carlin, Maura Tierney, Tate Donovan, Marg Helgenberger, and William Hurt, who has been quoted as saying, "Improvisation is essential to acting and Book is a terrific teacher." In the last TV season, 14 current or former students are appearing as regulars in primetime series, three of them in title roles (including David Boreanaz as Angel and Carla Gujino as Karen Sisco). His students have won Oscars, Tonys, and Emmys. He is the author of "Book on Acting: Improvisation Technique for the Professional Actor in Film, Theatre & Television."

IVAN BORODIN (323) 882-1268
1626 N. Wilcox Ave., #490
Hollywood 90028
IvanB83@yahoo.com

Mr. Borodin specializes in private accent reduction/foreign dialect coaching. Coaching actors since 1992, Mr. Borodin also offers on set coaching for accent reduction and foreign and regional dialects.

NORMA BOWLES (323) 953-9036
normabowles@earthlink.net

Offers audition preparation, mask performance training and guidance on the development of original works. She mostly teaches private sessions but will create new classes for groups of 6 or more. Ms. Bowles (BA, Princeton; MFA, CalArts) is the Artistic Director of Fringe Benefits Theatre Company.

RICHARD BRANDER'S ACTING STUDIO (818) 509-1064
12445 Moorpark St.
Studio City 91604

Workshops for all levels covering on-camera, cold reading, scene study, audition and film technique, character analysis and monologues using the Meisner technique. Two classes are offered per week and Mr. Brander has celebrity guest speakers whom he has trained. An audition and an interview are required and there is free auditing.

SEBASTIAN BROOK (323) 876-9103
1435 N. Curson Ave., #5
Los Angeles 90046

A serious and intense approach to the art and craft of acting, which includes one's specific relationship to character, situation, and cognitive self-analysis all resulting from the aggressive and penetrating breakdown of text. The use of monologues, more than most other mediums, reveals the difference between stale imitated attitudes and genuine emotional truth. Sebastian Brook is a native New Yorker, who studied with Stella Adler and the American Theatre Wing, acted on the New York stage and performed Shakespeare at Stratford, Connecticut.

GENE BUA ACTING FOR LIFE (818) 547-3810
3435 W. Magnolia Blvd.
Burbank 91505
www.genebua.com

Transformational Acting for those who dare to become more powerful and spontaneous in their art, and in their lives. Master teacher Gene Bua's profoundly successful method of moving both beginning professionals and seasoned stars to new heights of creativity and joy. "Every artist in the business should have these tools. I used them in take after take and blew Tarentino away." Caitlyn Keats, star of "Kill Bill 2. "After ten years of studying with Gene, his classes never cease to amaze and inspire." Tracey Bregman, Emmy Winner, Best Actress "Young and the Restless." "No waste of time here. With Gene, you hit the ground running." Paul Ben Victor, star of "The Invisible Man" on the SCIFI Channel. "One week with Gene coaching me and I fell in love with acting." Carla Gugino star of "Spy Kids." Classes are ongoing and an interview is required. Films and original plays are cast directly from the classes. Creators of award winning hits: "Pepper Street," "Across from Cindy's Corner," and the current smash hit "Second Wind." The first feature film which Gene directed "348," won the New York International Film Festival and students Caia Coley, and Nino Simone, won Best Actress, and Best New Rising Star. He has been awarded by the White House, the Board of Education, the Senate, the United Nations and six California Mayors. SEE AD ON PAGE 5.

BOB BURGOS (323) 653-5947
www.bobburgosstudios.com FAX (323) 653-5947
bobburgos@comcast.net

Offers classes for all levels at the Sierra Stage in Hollywood. Classes cover all aspects of basic technique, scene study and cold reading. Bob helps you learn your craft and gain confidence while acquiring the skills that prepare you to get the job and deliver an inspired performance. A working professional who writes and directs for television and film, Bob is a member of the Actor's Studio Director's Unit. He has been teaching for over 20 years in New York and Los Angeles in his own classes and at universities and film-schools. Private coaching is available.

RON BURRUS ACTING STUDIO (323) 953-2823
Los Feliz Playhouse FAX (323) 953-2823
4646 Hollywood Blvd.
Los Angeles 90027
www.ronburrus.com
ronburrus@earthlink.net

Complete acting process for film with the creative imagination as a major tool and direct/indirect actions. Taught in four levels: Level 1: Foundation – 6 weeks (4 days a week, 3 hours per day), Level II: Rehearsal/Performance – 3-4 months, Level III: Character/Film Scenes and On-Camera Audition Workshops, Level IV: Business of Acting – 6 week seminar with Burrus/Salazar/D. Aquila camera work, script interpretation and Industry showcases. Interview required. Mr. Burrus was trained by Stella Adler to teach technique in the mid-70s which has resulted in actors learning a craft they enjoy using and skills to play characters. Leonard Salazar, trained by Mr. Burrus heads the evening Foundation and Rehearsal/Performance. SEE AD ON PAGE 7.

MARILIN FOX/GAR CAMPBELL (310) 820-7122
(310) 301-3971
703 Venice Blvd.
Venice 90291
www.pacificresidenttheatre.com

Ms. Fox, an L.A. Drama Critics Circle Award winning actress and director, along with Mr. Campbell, an award winning actor-director, offer three ongoing classes for beginners, intermediate and advanced actors focused on improvisation, film, scene study, cold reading and classical work, including Shakespeare. Ms. Fox is the Artistic Director for Pacific Resident Theatre. Class admittance is by interview, and the attendance fee is $135 per month. Auditing is permitted for $20.

CRAIG CAMPOBASSO (818) 503-2474
craigcampobasso@aol.com

Craig's affordable on-camera classes cover scene study, audition technique, and character development. They meet once a week in 4 week intervals.

ROBERT CARNEGIE
PLAYHOUSE WEST SCHOOL
AND REPERTORY THEATER (818) 881-6520
4250 Lankershim Blvd.
North Hollywood 91602
www.playhousewest.net

Mr. Carnegie is the founding director of Playhouse West and teaches an ongoing program based on his years of work with Sanford Meisner. See listing under Playhouse West School and Repertory Theatre in the this section for further information. SEE AD ON PAGE 9.

MERILYN CARNEY
THIRD STAGE THEATRE **(323) 620-1689**
2811 Magnolia Blvd.
Burbank 91505
www.merilyncarney.com
merilyncarney@earthlink.net

This is a class for actors to stay grounded and creative for auditions and parts or who need a place to build confidence, be challenged, and incorporate all they know. Improvisation, cold reading, and techniques created to get you out of your head and into your body and instincts. Exercises prompt a high level of risk-taking helping the actor to explore new aspects of themselves and find themselves in the part. Wednesday afternoons 1-4 pm, $40 per class or $140 for a series of 4. Call for interview.

SANDRA CARUSO **(310) 476-5113**
scaruso@ucla.edu **FAX (253) 322-6415**

Offers private coaching and audition preparation. Author of "The Actor's Book of Improvisation," and "The Young Actors Book of Improvisation ages 7-11, 12-16." Ms. Caruso trained with Sanford Meisner, Uta Hagen, Lee Strasberg, and Milton Kateselas (master class). She is an experienced teacher/director, and presently teaches for the UCLA School of Theatre, Film and Television.

DIANA CASTLE **(323) 936-6818**
5615 San Vicente Blvd.
Los Angeles 90019
www.2100squarefeet.com
2100sqft@earthlink.net

Ms. Castle's acting classes offer intensive process oriented scene study and cold reading technique. Her private sessions offer monologue work and product work for auditions and current booked projects. Classes meet once a week (Monday and Tuesday during the day and Monday, Tuesday and Wednesday nights) and class size is limited. No auditing. Admittance is by interview/audition only. Private coaching is available 6 days a week.

JUNE CHANDLER'S
ACTORS WORKSHOP **(626) 355-4572**
www.junechandler.com
june@junechandler.com

June Chandler's school teaches the essentials to gain an edge in the Industry and specializes in developing well-rounded actors, helping actors launch their careers and climb up the career ladder. Seventeen different classes are offered for beginning, intermediate and professional levels including basic workshops in Commercials A-Z, Actor's Image, Nuts and Bolts of Acting Techniques, and Cold Reading. Intermediate and professional level ongoing classes in acting, scene study, improv and commercials. Also available are regular showcases, career guidance, Industry seminars, specially priced photo shoots and Industry guest teachers. The Young Actors Division (6-17) offers Acting On-Camera for film, television, and commercials taught by an exceptional staff of Industry professionals. Classes are at Zydeco Studios in Studio City on weekends. Scene Study is also offered onstage at the Sierra Madre Playhouse on Saturdays. Class size is limited, reasonably priced and payment plans are available with credit card options. Private coaching is also available. SEE AD ON PAGES 1 & 43.

VINCENT CHASE WORKSHOP **(323) 851-4819**
7221 Sunset Blvd. **FAX (323) 851-9942**
Los Angeles 90046

Day and evening classes are offered six days a week, including scene study, cold reading techniques and labs, commercial workshops, improv, acting theory, and elements of the Meisner technique and Stanislavski's method, Shakespeare* and the classics. Average class size varies from 6-10 students: beginning, intermediate, advanced and professional levels. 75-80 classes are offered each month and each full-time student can actively participate in a minimum of 35-40 classes per month, plus private coaching is available (for Industry parts, agents, etc.), for one basic fee currently $320 per month. Part time attendance and private coaching are available at prices concurrent with other local coaches. Special subjects include dialects and voice production. Industry referral is requested. More details upon request. *Offered in conjunction with Morgan Sheppard.

SHARON CHATTEN **(213) 486-4229**

Private coaching and ongoing group classes are available covering relaxation, sensory work, scenes, cold reading, improv and pilot season prep. Critiques are by the teacher only. Ms. Chatten coaches major actors in the Industry like Cameron Diaz, Ben Stiller, James Gandolfini, Marg Helgenberger, Vincent D'Onofrio, Matt Dillon and is a member of The Actors Studio and Ensemble Studio Theatre. Classes for teens also available.

LILYAN CHAUVIN **(323) 877-4988**
3841 Eureka Dr.
Studio City 91604

DGA Director. An on-camera class that teaches the transition from stage to film simulating professional circumstances on a real, live set. All props and costumes are available. There is no audition but an audit is required for on-camera class only. Private coaching for auditions is available. Author of "Hollywood Scams and Survival Tactics," "Speak the French You Already Know" and "Discover Yourself in Hollywood." Lilyan is a former Vice President of Women in Film. SEE AD ON PAGES 16 & 255.

SAM CHRISTENSEN STUDIOS (818) 506-0783
10440 Burbank Blvd. FAX (818) 506-8941
North Hollywood 91601
www.samchristensen.com
scsimage@aol.com

Specializes in a non-technical approach that enables actors to "be themselves" in auditions and performances. Limited to 14 students per class, evenings and afternoons. The work is recommended by agents and managers because it specifically addresses maximizing the individual qualities of each actor. Private consultation is also available.

IVANA CHUBBUCK STUDIO (323) 935-2100
7201 Melrose Ave., Ste. 206
Los Angeles 90046
chubbuck@mac.com

Chubbuck has taught such actors as Brad Pitt, Jim Carrey, Charlize Theron, Matthew Perry, Jon Voight, Jake Gyllenhaal, Carrie-Anne Moss, Garry Shandling, Elisabeth Shue, Eriq La Salle, Kate Bosworth, Eva Mendes, Terence Howard, Radha Mitchell, Julian MacMahon, Jessica Biel, Beyonce and she received special thanks from Halle Berry at the Academy Awards for her work with the actor on "Monster's Ball." Instructors Deryl Carroll, Chris Holder, Michael Monks, and Tasha Smith teach the introductory and advanced classes, and Chubbuck teaches the master scene study workshop. Her newest book, "The Power of the Actor," features her own special technique and can be purchased in most bookstores. Auditing is available on Thursday nights by appointment only, but expect a four to five week waiting period.

AN ACTORS WORKSHOP
WITH TIM COLCERI (323) 828-6900
12217 Hartland St.
North Hollywood 91605
colceri@msn.com

Tim Colceri has been an actor for 20 years, and has been teaching for over 10. He will teach you how to use your instrument properly. Tim Colceri is a no-nonsense, in your face coach who tells it like it is. He wants you to be a better actor and will challenge you, and help you meet that challenge. The class curriculum consists of cold reading, scene study, audition technique, on-camera work, and improv which is vital for commercial auditioning. The workshop is Industry driven. As a student you will have the opportunity to become a member of "Full Metal Improv", the bi-weekly improv show which is marketed to casting directors, agents, and managers. Tim is also preparing his students for a bi-monthly Industry showcase.

STEVE NORTH, THE COMEDY COACH (818) 347-5098
22647 Ventura Blvd., PMB 422 FAX (818) 347-5099
Woodland Hills 91364
www.funnycoach.com
steve@funnycoach.com

Classes and private coaching to help students find their comedic character and create the right material for themselves. Beginners to pros are instructed by a working producer/writer/performer who has many national credits. Some classes are on camera. Showcases, Industry nights and touring. Stand up, sketch and sitcom.

JEREMIAH COMEY STUDIOS (818) 248-4104
1648 N. Vine St.
Hollywood 90028
www.jeremiahcomey.com

Videotaped classes in film acting technique and cold reading for beginning to advanced students. Auditing allowed. Classes in Hollywood.

JEFF CONAWAY (818) 921-9287

Study with a working professional with 44 years experience and hundreds of credits. Scene study, cold reading, emotional work, moment to moment. Also private coaching.

CHRISTINA CONCETTA (818) 415-6967

Ms. Concetta offers private coaching in monologues and cold reading, utilizing Uta Hagen's moment-to-moment technique. She is a member of The Actors Studio in N.Y. and studied with Lee Strasberg and Ms. Hagen. Interview required, reasonable fees. Also does actor consultations.

SCOTT CRAWFORD (323) 663-1664

Mr. Crawford teaches intermediate and advanced acting classes at his private studio. Ongoing classes are held afternoons, evenings and weekends with entry at any time following a required one month of auditing. An actor for 40 years, he moved his teaching from N.Y. to L.A. several years ago. His work focuses on scene study, monologue and audition technique, as well as TV commercial acting, plus advice on photos, resumes and agents. Best known for his roles on "As The World Turns" and "All My Children," he has appeared on Broadway, Off Broadway, and in such films as "Annie Hall" and "The Cotton Club."

DEVORAH CUTLER-RUBENSTEIN
NOBLE HOUSE ENTERTAINMENT (310) 943-4378
12210½ Nebraska Ave., Ste. 22
Los Angeles 90025
www.thescriptbroker.com
devo@thescriptbroker.com

Ms. Cutler-Rubinstein has an excellent track record developing those special gifts and unique qualities that will set the actor apart by identifying their special contribution as an artist. Twenty years experience as a private coach with ongoing classes and having produced, directed, written and acted in movies, television and theatre as well as being an executive at Columbia Pictures Television make her uniquely qualified to address any craft or career issue for the actor. Her experience includes working with the actors through the audition process and accompanying them on the set. Available to direct your showcase. "A vibrant innovative director and an inspired acting coach for young people." Jennie Lew Tugend, Producer, "Free Willy." For more information see listing in the BUSINESS OF ACTING.

CAROLE D'ANDREA
A NEW YORK ACTING TEACHER
THE FLIGHT THEATRE (310) 281-7116
6472 Santa Monica Blvd., 2nd Fl.
Los Angeles 90028
www.caroledandrea.com

An ongoing class that meets Wednesdays 11 am to 2 pm and includes scene study, cold reading, monologues and improv. One-on-one coaching is available for dramatic and musical auditions and cold readings.

LISA DALTON STUDIOS (818) 761-5404
www.lisadaltonstudios.com
info@chekhov.net

Lisa Dalton, internationally renowned master teacher, and her staff, offer courses for any actors, teachers, directors, writers who wish to integrate Michael Chekhov's imagination based work. Recommended for all interested in improvisation skills, unique characterization and accessing powerful emotions without involving your personal memory. There is a Master Scene Study for film, television and stage which requires an audition."In Action" Class applies technique to situations such as auditions, on camera, commercials and the "Dalton Gang Ensemble" offers an Actors Workout, cultural events, script readings, film and stage projects and career support group activities. Private coaching in career development, interviews and auditions, headshotology, image and marketing, script coverage, role development. The Chekhov Foundation Course is a prerequisite for joining any of the classes. The structure follows the Chart of Inspired Acting found in the preface of "On the Technique of Acting" by Michael Chekhov which is a prerequisite for training as well. The course is offered in three formats: 5 private or semi-private lessons at any time through out the year in the Burbank/NoHo area; a small group intensive offered about twice yearly in the Pasadena or Studio City area; or at the Chekhov Theatre Institute held at the

University of Southern Maine in June. This program is a ten day intensive for actors or 11 days for the Teacher Certification Program and is team taught with Lisa Dalton, Chekhov Estate executrix, Hollywood Walk of Fame Honoree and long time personal friend Mala Powers as well as Professor Wil Kilroy of the National Michael Chekhov Association.

SAL DANO (877) 592-9410
ACTORS' WORKSHOP (310) 836-4691

A no nonsense scene study class, which has produced many award winning actors, including Tony Award winners Anthony LaPaglia for best actor and Brian Stokes Mitchell for best actor in a musical. One coach, one address for thirty years. By referral only. Audits allowed.

KIM DARBY (818) 985-0666
P.O. Box 1520
Studio City 91614
www.kimdarby.com
kimdarby2003@yahoo.com

Ms. Darby, veteran actress and three time Emmy nominee, two time Golden Globe nominee and a New York Critics Best Actress Award winner, teaches in West Hollywood. Work in the scene study class is filmed and reviewed in weekly cycles. Classes are kept small and admittance is by interview and invitation only.

JOAN DARLING (323) 964-3410

Ms. Darling teaches scene study whenever she is in town, usually 4 or 5 times a year. The class covers audition technique, monologues, sensory work, and scene study. This is a 4 week workshop with a class limit of 35. Auditing is allowed. Over 25 years experience as an actress and director. Writers and directors also welcome.

SONIA DARMEI-LOPES (310) 358-5942
www.screenactorsstudio.com
sonia@screenactorsstucio.com

On-camera acting classes are taught in a positive and caring environment. Students appear in numerous projects including "Malcolm in the Middle," "The Division," "The Guiding Light," "Even Stevens," etc. Private coaching.

CHRIS DE CARLO
SANTA MONICA PLAYHOUSE (310) 394-9779
1211 4th St. FAX (310) 393-5573
Santa Monica 90401
www.santamonicaplayhouse.com
smp@primenet.com

Offers classes for all levels covering inner acting technique, audition technique, character analysis, improv, sensory work and marketabilty. The class is limited to 20, costs $200 for 8 sessions and meets Mondays. Students work in every class. No auditing is allowed and an interview is required. Call for interview information. Mr. DeCarlo has extensive acting experience and has been teaching for over 30 years. He has taught/coached/directed Stuart Pankin, Louise Sorel, Sammy Shore, William Schallert, Priscilla Morrill, George Coe, Debra Harmon and Michael Callan. Private coaching is available.

JACKY DE HAVILAND (323) 691-7077
jdh@sbcglobal.net

Private coaching for new actors and experienced performers covering scene study and monologues, improv, cold reading, character study, Shakespeare, audition techniques: whatever the individual actor needs to improve, polish or gain confidence in. Jacky de Haviland has been directing and coaching actors for 20 years, acting for 35 and is an extremely committed, caring director/teacher thoroughly invested in the success of her actors. Auditing is allowed. Private coaching. Experienced with children.

ZORA DEHORTER, CSA (310) 586-8964
10250 Constellation Blvd. FAX (310) 264-1210
2nd Fl., Ste. 2060
Century City 90067
www.zoradehortercasting.com
zdehorter@mgm.com

Private coaching available for audition preparation. Also teaches through TVI (intermediate and advanced on-camera audition technique) and the John Kirby studio.

DEL MAR MEDIA ARTS (949) 753-0570
15375 Barranca Pkwy., # J-105 FAX (949) 753-0576
Irvine 92618
www.delmarmediaarts.com

Offers a 6 week course for age 4 through adult that covers on-camera work, cold reading, cue card technique, wireless ear plug technique, a teleprompter class, advanced level, 3 camera classes in a full production studio, headshot review and advice, and interview technique. Also offers showcases for agents. There is a voice-over class available. An audition is required. State licensed and approved. See listing under AUDIO DEMO PRODUCTION in the MARKETING section for further information. SEE AD ON PAGE 67.

DELL' ARTE INTERNATIONAL SCHOOL OF PHYSICAL THEATRE (707) 668-5663
P.O. Box 816 FAX (707) 668-5665
Blue Lake 95525
www.dellarte.com
dellarte@aol.com

The Dell' Arte International School of Physical Theatre is the nation's only full-time professional actor training program specializing in physical theatre. The approach stresses that character, speech, thought, and emotion are expressed through the actor's sole instrument: the body. The eight month training program includes studies in mime, mask, yoga, the Alexander Technique, acrobatics, movement, voice, Commedia, melodrama, and clowning. Short term summer workshops in physical theatre offered each year. Dell' Arte also offers MFA in Ensemble-Based Physical Theatre, a two-and-a-half year program designed to train the next generation of ensemble theatre artists. Year One runs concurrently with the one-year Professional Training Program which is based on the work of the actor-creator and includes physical training, F.M. Alexander Technique, movement, physical and vocal improvisation, the study of mask, clown, melodrama, and commedia. Year Two involves composition, devising projects, and the business of ensemble while continuing acting, movement, and vocal studies. Ongoing research and writing assignment cultivate each student's ability to articulate a point of view. Year Three (six months) is divided between an internship with the Dell'Arte Company and an internship with another ensemble chosen by the student.

DEBBIE DEVINE (818) 989-7655
www.24thStreet.org

Acting/improv classes that cover scene study, improv, monologues, character study, and theatre games. These are 8-week sessions and are limited to 12 students. Ms. Devine is the founder and artistic director of Glorious Repertory Company, former president of Women In Theatre, and has taught at The American Academy of Dramatic Arts, Cal Arts, and is head of the Drama Department at Colburn School of Performing Arts.

ANTHONY DI NOVI (310) 490-4761
anthonydinovi@earthlink.net

Private acting coaching to the professional and gifted student. Coaching for specific auditions, character development, and technique for relaxation and concentration to promote creativity and bring forth individual qualities. Meditation, T'ai Chi, Dreamwork. Also works with writers and directors.

JUDY DICKERSON (818) 985-1603

Works with actors to help them prepare and explore the role before they start to shoot the film. Is also available to work on location.

JILL DONNELLAN (818) 879-0486
www.actorsinmotion.com
actorsinmotion@cs.com

Ms. Donnellan conducts her classes in Agoura, covering the entire Conejo Valley, offering cold reading, drama and comedy technique, character development, commercials, improvisation and monologue work. All classes on camera. She has over 20 years of acting experience having appeared in top roles in film, television and theatre and is head of In Motion Management, a management company for actors. She is the author of "All New Scenes for Actors" and "All New Scenes for Young Actors" published by Samuel French and available at their stores. A personal interview is required for children and adults. See website for acting information and casting.

DVORAK & CO., WAYNE DVORAK (323) 462-5328
1949 Hillhurst Ave.
Los Angeles 90027
www.actingcoachdvorak.com

Mr. Dvorak manages and coaches his acting clients using the Meisner technique which is organic foundation work. He has ongoing Industry showcasing at the professional level, and brings several agents each year to see his clients. He offers highly professional career development which includes image consultation for members of the company. Everything in-house.

EAST WEST PLAYERS (213) 625-7000
120 North Judge John Asio
Los Angeles 90012
www.eastwestplayers.org

Acting classes for beg-pro level actors of all ages including fundamentals of acting and scene study.

STEVE EASTIN (818) 980-9828
10107 Camarillo St.
Toluca Lake 91602
www.eastinstudio.com
seastin@aol.com

The Steve Eastin Studio offers intensive film acting training on a weekly basis at their school and video production facility in Toluca Lake. Enrollment is a nice mix of veteran working actors and young up and comers. Classes are all on camera in extreme close up. Students work every class and the Studio provides all material. Select Industry workshops with casting directors and producers are offered every four to six weeks. Audits are allowed. All classes are taught by veteran actor Steve Eastin ("Con Air," "Field of Dreams," "Shawshank Redemption," "Catch Me If You Can," "A Man Apart," "Matchstick Men," "When a Stranger Calls" and "The Black Dahlia." Steve taught at the famous Charles Conrad Studio for nine years before opening his own school in 1998 and is currently working with graduate directors at USC who have cast their thesis films out of the studio. All techniques and exercises are eschewed in favor of the powerful and instinctive handling of dialogue. Some of the more well known actors trained with this approach are Eva Longoria, Susan Sarandon, Michelle Pfeiffer, Veronica Hamel, and Corbin Bernson.

ROBERT EASTON
THE HENRY HIGGINS OF HOLLYWOOD, INC.
THE DIALECT DOCTOR (818) 985-2222

Specializes in characterization, comedy, dialects, accent reduction, and cold reading using the same principles that got him roles in 82 major motion pictures, over 1,700 TV and radio programs and earned his coaching clients Oscars, Emmys, Screen Actor's Guild Awards, and other awards from the Cannes Film Festival and Golden Globes. SEE AD ON PAGE 89.

EDGEMAR CENTER FOR THE ARTS **(310) 399-3666**
2437 Main St. **FAX (310) 399-2898**
Santa Monica 90405
www.edgemarcenter.org
paxjava@hotmail.com

Workshops for kids and teens: acting and improvisation. Courses are designed for both students who are new to acting and these with some experience. Children develop stronger acting skills by creating new characters through improvisation, learning monologues, and writing and acting in their own scenes. Students learn to breakdown a scene, work with intentions and work with a scene partner. 8-week courses through out the year. Ages 7-11 and 12-17. Also adult classes.

DAVID ELLENSTEIN **(323) 466-6485**
www.davidellenstein.com

Classes from time to time at the Los Angeles Repertory Theatre covering external character physicality and internal emotional life. The classes are for beg-pro actors, have a limit of 15 students, and require a 4-week time commitment. A phone interview is required and one class may be audited. There are some showcases and Mr. Ellenstein also directs regional theatre.

THE DENNY EVANS
COMEDY WORKSHOP **(310) 535-6874**
Andrew Benne Theatre
4930 Lankershim Blvd.
North Hollywood 91601

Offers an ongoing improvisational comedy class with a limit of 25 students that is offered Sunday 7 pm to 10 pm. See listing under COMEDY/IMPROV in this section for further information.

FEARLESS CHOICES **(310) 383-0910**
653 Flower Ave.
Venice 90291
www.fearlesschoices.com
fearlesschoices@hotmail.com

Charlotte Cornwell is a leading British actress with 35 years experience in theatre, TV and film, now teaching at USC School of Theatre in Los Angeles.

(323) 953-4000 x2650
SANDY FEDEROFF **(323) 953-4000 x2990**
855 N. Vermont
Los Angeles 90029
www.lacitycollege.edu

Acting workshops that are designed for acting in film, TV, and on-stage. The workshop covers habit forming exercises, memory work, improvisational scenes, and audition and interview techniques and utilizes the "energy-dialogue path and NLP techniques." Classes are offered 5 times per year in 6 week quarters, and meet Monday and Tuesday nights. Fee is $95 per 6 week quarter.

ALAN FEINSTEIN/PAUL TUERPE
ACTING STUDIO **(323) 650-7766**
13273 Ventura Blvd.
Studio City 91604
www.feinstein-tuerpe.com
alfeinstein@msn.com

Offers ongoing classes with the emphasis on freeing the actor's emotions for maximum creative results. The classes cover scene study, emotional exercise work, on-camera, cold reading and audition technique in a safe and supportive environment and are geared towards strengthening each individual's skills. Private coaching is available. Interview required.

OTTO FELIX **(310) 470-1939**
Film Actors Workshop **FAX (310) 470-1795**
10835 Santa Monica Blvd.
Westwood 90024
www.ottofelix.com
ottofelix@aol.com

Classes cover cold reading, self discovery, individuality in film, camera technique, self-confidence, learning to love yourself and your talent. Actors attending the sessions regularly are eligible to participate in Otto's highly acclaimed showcases. Sessions are every Tuesday and Thursday at 7:30 pm at the Film Actors Shop Studios. Free audits. Otto says "Don't waste your talent or your time." Some class members are physically challenged. Otto Felix is the founder/director of Handicapped Artists, Performers and Partners, Inc. (HAPPI) and offers discounted rates to the disabled. He has been teaching for 22 years and was the co-star of "B.J. and The Bear," Peyton Place" and "General Hospital" and he also played the stoned motorcycle cop in the cult film "Up In Smoke." He has also had many guest starring appearances in TV, motion pictures, off Broadway plays and has booked over 300 commercials. Mr. Felix has high standards for admittance to the workshops, but beginners are welcome. He often hires his students for roles in his films. He presently has two films in production "Spirit of Sixty-four" and "Air Wave Thief." He was the original story writer and associate Producer of "South of Heaven, West of Hell" starring Dwight Yoakam (who directed) Billy Bob Thornton, Vince Vaughn, Bridget Fonda, Peter Fonda and Paul Reubens. His film, "Famous Blue Raincoat" made it's way to the Sundance Film Festival and the Great Lakes Film Festival receiving high acclaim. The actors were chosen from Otto's film class sessions.

J.D. FERRANTINO (310) 358-5942
www.screenactorsstudio.com

J.D. Ferrantino combines the method along with his own technique, which he has developed by working as a professional actor and teacher for over 15 years. He uses his training at the Actor's Studio in NYC combined with on-camera technique. This allows the individual to bring a unique creativity to the audition process. Ferrantino offers evening and weekend classes for adults and teens at all levels. All classes include on-camera technique, cold reading, improvisation, sensory work and scene study, with the focus on booking the job. Private coaching is available. One of J.D.'s students has recently been nominated for an Emmy.

HOWARD FINE STUDIOS (323) 951-1221
7801 Melrose Ave.
Los Angeles 90038

By referral only. Private, professional actor's studio offering comprehensive acting classes from fundamentals through various scene study classes, along with Alexander technique, voice production for the actor and private coaching for auditions or specific jobs. A Monday night public audit to observe work and attend an orientation is required. Basic Technique is taught by Howard Fine and Laura Gardner.

NINA FOCH (310) 553-5805
P.O. Box 1884
Beverly Hills 90213

Does consultations and preparation with actors and directors. Professor of USC Graduate Film School teaching directing.

GEOFFREY FORWARD (310) 455-9927
1909 N. Topanga Cyn Blvd.
Topanga 90290
www.shakespeare-usa.com

Mr. Forward is the founder and artistic director of the L.A. Shakespeare Company, a Scholar at Huntington Library, and has been published in the Shakespeare Quarterly. He exclusively conducts Shakespearean role work, voice production, body awareness, and the Alexander Technique at the Actor's Shakespeare Academy. He offers an eight-week basic monologue workshop, and a 12 week performance workshop where a play is rehearsed and performed. His eight-week classes are $295; the 12 week performance workshop is $500. Private coaching services run $100 per hour, and $60 per half-hour. Acting training or experience is required. All classes are conducted outside in a globe style stage. He has been directing and coaching Shakespeare for more than 25 years and was an instructor at the American Academy of Dramatic Arts for seven years.

CHERIE FRANKLIN'S
REACT & RESPOND (818) 762-4658
P.O. Box 5246 FAX (818) 762-4639
North Hollywood 91616-5246
cherolynfranklin@msn.com

Ongoing classes and one-one-one private coaching are offered to prepare the actor for a long-lasting career as well as for those last minute auditions. She also teaches how to make certain your performance is on the audition tape. Focus is on teaching the actor to be in control of their talent at every audition, when on set, and to deliver while remaining open to all direction. Ms. Franklin concentrates on cold-reading for sit-coms, episodics, and feature films, as well as teaching actors to instantly deliver the best work, under pressure, while allowing their choices to be strong, clear and simple. Her main goal is to get the actor's "best work up the first time, every time." She has been an on-set dialogue coach for over 29 years. Ms. Franklin also teaches at AFI, UCLA Extension, the International Film School in Rockport, Maine, The SAG Conservatory, Women In Film, FilmSchule in Cologne, Germany and FOCAL in Zurich, Switzerland.

THE GALLARDO METHOD (661) 250-8530
www.sylvanagallardo.com

Silvana Gallardo shares her powerful and empowering acting technique in her classes. She has developed a way to get in touch with your emotional life by breaking down patterns and habits, connecting you with your infinite possibilities, allowing full, exciting choices to flow freely and openly. Silvana's classes focus on the fine tuning of your instrument. She has created and designed various acting exercises that put you in touch with you. Former students include: Angelina Jolie, Peta Wilson, Amy Jo Johnson and Darren Burrows.

MARLA GAM-HUDSON
THE LOST ACTOR'S WORKSHOP (714) 771-5436
461 N. Citrus
Orange 92868
atheaterdirector@yahoo.com

Specializes in the classics and emergency audition coaching. Regular classes cover accent reduction, audition technique, breathing, character analysis, cold reading, improv, interview technique, headshot review and advice, resume composition, scene study, monologues, sensory work, and story structure. Most of the classes are taught in Orange County. Auditing is by arrangement only.

LAURA GARDNER (323) 957-4764

Ms. Gardner has over 35 years experience as a teacher/actress/coach. She is on the faculty of the Howard Fine Acting Studio in West Hollywood. Ms. Gardner also offers an audition/interview intensive every few months and trained with Uta Hagen and Carol Rosenfeld. Private sessions are available.

KATE GEER (707) 279-2030
SHAKESPEARE SURVIVAL SCHOOL (310) 455-4295
P.O. Box 1606
Kelseyville, CA 95451
shakespearesurvival@mac.com

Covers classical and contemporary monologues and scene study. Beginners lose their fear of Shakespeare and basic skills are taught to lay a strong technical foundation. Intermediate members expand and perfect audition materials and and polish the finer points of speech and technique. Initial interview and audition required. Contemporary monologues also welcome for audition purposes.

THE WILL GEER THEATRICUM BOTANICUM (310) 455-2322
P.O. Box 1222 FAX (310) 455-3724
Topanga 90290
www.theatricum.com
theatricum@earthlink.net

Offers an ongoing class that covers scene and monologue study with an emphasis on classical technique, a summer program which covers Shakespeare and includes monologue and scene study, Linklater voice training, movement, stage combat/fencing, scansion, singing, theatre games, and dialects. The class limit is 15-17 students. There is a summer youth drama program also available. Open auditions for the acting company are held every March.

ELLEN GERSTEIN ACTING WORKSHOP (323) 852-0276

Ellen Gerstein is a writer/producer/director/actress as well as a teacher and coach. Small professional classes for beginning through advanced levels cover exercise work, technique, improvisation, cold readings, auditions and script analysis. Ms. Gerstein uses a technique that focuses on being very specific in your work and the audition technique focuses on what it takes to get the job. Students work every week and receive individual attention. Guest speakers on occasion. Classes for children. Private coaching is available. Ellen Gerstein is a member of the Actors Studio. SEE AD ON PAGE 8.

GLORIA GIFFORD CONSERVATORY (310) 535-4999
FOR THE PERFORMING ARTS (323) 465-4427
289 S. Robertson Blvd., PMB 700 FAX (310) 278-9390
Beverly Hills 90211
jcnagao@yahoo.com

Gloria Gifford shares her numerous years of experience as a teacher and working actor with her students. GGC offers advanced scene study, beginner ("TYRO"), voice production, and cold reading classes and they produce 6-8 showcases every year.

PAUL G. GLEASON (323) 871-8082
6520 Hollywood Blvd.
Hollywood 90028

Offers classical and contemporary theatre training that includes Shakespeare, monologues, scene study, and audition and interview techniques for stage, film, and TV. Uses the Alexander Technique. An interview is required and auditing is by appointment. Mr. Gleason is currently a California State Artist-In-Residence.

BRUCE GLOVER (310) 398-2539

Acting and teaching for 48 years, Mr. Glover has done 70 films, 200 television shows, 100 plays, and 16 Broadway and Off-Broadway productions. Bruce also directs and is currently editing his documentary on the making of a feature film directed by his son, Crispin Glover. Mr. Glover does not teach Meisner, Strasberg or Adler as he feels making early choices can become very confusing strait jackets. Acting is an art which he feels should be out on the dangerous edge. Bruce has "an eye that won't be fooled and if you stink I'll know why and I'll tell you." He helps actors laugh at their fears and, along with inner techniques, he also deals with the conscious craft of comedy. Classes or private coaching available.

MARIA GOBETTI
THE VICTORY THEATRE
THE GOBETTI/ORMENY ACTING STUDIO (818) 841-4404
3326-24 W. Victory Blvd.
Burbank 91505
www.thevictorytheatrecenter.com
victory@thevictorytheatrecenter.org

Basic-adv classes are offered using Meisner basics. The basics class covers how to prepare, repetition exercises, and improvisation with preparation. The intermediate class covers "simple use" scene study. The advanced class covers character, comedy, and audition monologues. Comprehensive special training is offered in defining the unique differences between theatre, TV, and film acting techniques. Special attention to cold readings is provided twice a year and ongoing attention is given to interview techniques and photos. All on-camera classes are limited to 14 students. An interview is required along with a free audit for admission. An audition is required for the adv/pro class. Critiques are by the teacher and student feedback is monitored by Ms. Gobetti who is a member of DGA, AEA, and AFTRA. Private coaching is available. Industry professionals guest lecture and she directs and coaches at the major studios and is the Artistic Co-Director of the Victory Theatre. Students are often used for parts in both theatres. Mr. Ormeny teaches also and these two professional coaches offer a cohesive training with Meisner basics. Mr. Ormeny is the recipient of the LA Stage Alliance Ovation Award for Leadership in Theatre.

GOSCH PRODUCTIONS **(818) 729-0000**
2227 W. Olive
Burbank 91506
www.goschproductions.com
info@goschproductions.com

Taught by working directors Pat Gosch and Giovanni Juarez beginning to advanced actors. Scenework, comedy and improv as well as a class for children and parents where parents count. Parents are invited to the children's classes for ages 7-18. Audition preferred, auditing is allowed. Private coaching as well.

BENNET GUILLORY **(818) 981-4141**
5211 Kester Ave. **FAX (818) 981-4144**
Sherman Oaks 91411
www.robeytheatrecompany.com
robeytcact@sbcglobal.net

Offers an ongoing, 3 hour advanced scene study workshop based in theatre. Uses an eclectic combination of acting methods designed to meet specific needs of each actor. There is a limit of 14 students. Audition and interview are required and auditing is by special arrangement. Private coaching is available. Mr. Guillory has received NAACP Theatre awards for Acting and Directing and he is the current Producing Artistic Director of the award winning Robey Theatre Company.

NIKOLAI GUZOV **(818) 753-0316**
lnguzov@adelphia.net

Mr. Guzov, a Russian-trained actor and director, specializes in teaching the Michael Chekhov technique of acting – an exciting and advanced extension of the Stanislavski system, emphasizing imagination and creativity over cold, dry analysis. His program combines weekly private lessons with group exercises. A commitment of approximately one-year is expected from the student, with time off allowed for professional work. Mr. Guzov's training is unique in that his goal is to teach the actor to continue developing his or her craft on his or her own, as an independent artist. An audition and interview are required.

MARGIE HABER **(310) 854-0870**
971 N. La Cienega Blvd. **FAX (310) 854-0462**
Ste. 207
Los Angeles 90069
www.margiehaber.com

Ongoing, on-camera cold reading classes are offered for adults and cover audition technique and use improv to connect with the scene. The classes are for intermediate and beg-adv, classes are limited to 12 students. An interview is required and private coaching is available.

JANE HALLAREN **(323) 969-8089**

Classes are limited to 10 for all levels and cover sensory and improvisational exercises and scene study. An interview is required as well as a free working audit. Private coaching is available.

HANDICAPPED ARTISTS, PERFORMERS AND PARTNERS, INC. (H.A.P.P.I.) **(310) 470-1939**
Film Actors Workshop **FAX (310) 470-1795**
10835 Santa Monica Blvd.
Westwood 90024
www.ottofelix.com
ottoffelix@aol

Producer, director, actor, Otto Felix conducts his film acting workshop for abled and the disabled at Film Actors Workshop Studios using lots of cold reading from actual film scripts. Some class members are physically challenged. Mr. Felix is the founder of Handicapped Artists, Performers and Partners, Inc. (HAPPI) and offers discounted rates to the disabled. HAPPI is a continuing program of workshops to assist disabled artists seeking careers in film, motion pictures, television, radio and other areas of show business through training and guidance – and to provide a forum for such talent. HAPPI seeks to establish a new awareness of the handicapped community of talent proving that they are capable of working side by side in everyday society and in show business. Ongoing classes allow entry at any time and include guest directors, agents, casting people and producers. Classes are Tuesdays at 7:30 pm. He has been teaching for 23 years and has had co-starring roles on "B.J. and The Bear" and "General Hospital" as well as many guest starring appearances in TV, motion pictures, off Broadway plays and 308 commercials. Mr. Felix has high standards for admittance to the workshops, but beginners are welcome. He uses his students in his films and has two films in pre-production "Wheels" and "The First Real Pirate." He was Associate Producer and Writer for "South of Heaven, West of Hell" starring Billy Bob Thornton, Dwight Yoakum, Vince Vaughn, Bridget Fonda, Peter Fonda and Paul Reubens.

JEANNE HARTMAN
VOICE WITH A HEART PRODUCTIONS **(818) 760-8416**
P.O. Box 2613 **FAX (818) 980-6711**
Toluca Lake 91610
actbelieve@aol.com

Audition/cold reading techniques "Guerrilla acting techniques," one-on-one private coaching and master class available. Recommended by Lawrence Parke in "The Film Actor's Complete Career Guide." Covers different facets in audition vs. the job, big roles vs. small roles, intense script analysis and deals with personal audition problems. Ms. Hartman's background includes a degree from Juilliard, Centre Lyrique Internationale member and professional experience on TV, stage and film. An interview is required. Ms. Hartman has been teaching for over 20 years.

JACK HELLER
LAUREL GROVE THEATRE **(323) 850-6328**

The artistic director of the Laurelgrove Theatre offers private coaching.

LAURA HENRY STUDIO **(310) 399-5744**
1307 Pico Blvd. **FAX (310) 399-0384**
Santa Monica 90405
www.laurahenrystudio.com
lhnrystdio@aol.com

Faculty: Laura Henry, Natsuko O'hama, Julia Caulder, Barbara Bragg, Nan Friedman. Guest teachers: Katherine Gately, Mary Irwin, Ben Furey, Dr. David Kearney, Stephen Hack, Frank Pisco. Offers small classes and training for beg-adv actors. The faculty is dedicated to developing in the actors mastery of emotional, physical and vocal technique. The two-year Meisner conservatory program covers audition technique, advanced scene study and Alexander and Linklater classes. Call for class information and schedules.

JOHN HERZOG **(310) 451-9299** **(323) 464-8542**
6560 Hollywood Blvd., 2nd Fl.
Hollywood 90028
www.larep.org
larep@sbcglobal.net

John Herzog provides a safe and professional environment for actors to push their limitations and expand their artistic horizons. In his ongoing class, he focuses on text analysis, targeted exercises, classical and contemporary scene study and audition preparation. John Herzog has been a professional actor for over 35 years with a career that has encompassed Broadway musicals, regional theatre, feature films and television. A student of famed teacher Robert Ellenstein, he believes in supporting every actor in their quest to strengthen all the acting skills, and helping each actor to develop his own truth through time honored techniques. Admission by interview. Managing Director of the Los Angeles Repertory Company.

DARRYL HICKMAN (818) 344-5796
6514 Lankershim Blvd.
North Hollywood 91601
www.actingandyou.com
actingandyou@aol.com

Mr. Hickman teaches a unique, comprehensive approach to the acting process suitable for film, TV and theater. An interview is required and auditing is allowed by appointment only. Classes are limited to 20 students, and students work in every class. The workshop is taught in ten-week, ongoing sessions, and the fee is $500 per session.

BERNARD HILLER ACTING STUDIO (818) 781-8000
www.berniehiller.com

Bernard Hiller's techniques, which are known worldwide, teach actors to discover their unique quality and overcome any self defeating behavior to achieve success. His classes include monologues, scene study, improv, audition skills, movement and personal exercises. He also incorporates techniques from The Method-Actors Studio, Lee Strasberg to Sandy Meisner. Mr. Hiller believes that success in the Industry is not an accident. He will help you to map out your strategy for a long and successful career. He has worked with Cameron Diaz, Billy Crystal and Richard Dreyfuss. Mr. Hiller often teaches Master Classes in London, Paris, Rome, Spain and Tel Aviv and at the world renowned "Moscow Art Theatre." Beginner to advanced levels accepted. Monthly showcases where actors can meet top directors, producers, agents and casting directors. Interview required. Private coaching is also available.

MARLON HOFFMAN
ACTORS INSTITUTE (818) 878-0242

Before starting his own school in Los Angeles, Marlon Hoffman taught acting for sixteen years at numerous institutions including the Screen Actors Guild Conservatory and the 92nd Street "Y" in New York City as well as at the Center of Contemporary Arts in St. Louis. He is an Equity/SAG actor and director and has coached privately on and off the set around the country. Having studied with Strasberg, Adler, Corey and Morris, Marlon has developed an eclectic technique that empowers students to reach their full potential as performers. His students have gone on to study and/or perform at prestigious educational institutions and in theatre and film. Marlon customizes his work in class to meet the needs of the individual student, so class size is strictly limited. Separate classes are offered for beginners and advanced/professional actors. An audit is required, as is a pre-audit phone interview. Call to request a brochure. Private coaching is encouraged. SEE AD ON THIS PAGE.

HOLLYWOOD ACTING CLASSES (323) 225-1962
5930 Franklin Ave.
Hollywood 90028
aktorchick@ao.com

Classes for beginning through advanced. Adults 7:30-9:30 pm and children 6:30-7:30 pm Monday evenings. Covering cold reading, improv and other excellent unique exercises. Current students have worked on national commercials, music videos, TV and feature films.

HOLLYWOOD ACTORS STUDIO (323) 460-2580 (877) 591-5400
www.actingconnection.com
actorsstudio@actingconnection.com

Eric Stone offers weekly classes, private study and weekend workshops which include cold reading, scene study, improv, commercials, voice-over character development and performance skills for aspiring actors to professional levels including star level. These classes are highly focused on the individual with particular emphasis given to self expression, creativity and getting in touch with feelings as well as self expression, confidence, relaxation, listening, relating, awareness, imagination and concentration. Ongoing classes for adults, teens and children as well as weekend workshops and career seminars on the business of acting for adults, children and teens. Monthly performance series showcase with invited Industry professionals.

MICHAEL HOLMES
THE CHANDLER THEATRE (818) 786-1045
12443 Chandler Blvd.
North Hollywood 91607
holmeshow@cs.com

Offers a basic technique class and a scene study class for basic and advanced students. The classes are limited to 15. Also covers audition technique and on-camera work. Scenes are videotaped and students work in every class. An audition and an interview are required and auditing is by arrangement. There are guest speakers, showcases, and productions that come out of the class. Private coaching is available. Mr. Holmes has taught at UCLA.

SANDY HOLT AUDITION TECHNIQUES
ON-CAMERA COMEDY COLD READING
& IMPROV WORKSHOP (310) 271-8217
FAX (310) 276-1799

Sandy Holt, a Second City Alum, is an acting coach and voice casting director. Sandy casts for Disney, Dreamworks, Warner Bros., etc. and teaches private on-camera, comedy and cold reading workshops for film and TV. Sandy coaches you to: take charge at auditions; stay focused under pressure; get out of your head; create original characters; know what is special about you and use it and get the job. SEE AD ON PAGE 51.

HULL ACTORS STUDIO
LORRIE HULL PH.D. & DIANNE HULL (310) 828-0632
Santa Monica
www.actors-studio.com/hull
hullwshop@hotmail.com

Ongoing classes and 3 to 12 week sessions are offered that cover scene study, monologues, audition techniques, sensory work, emotional work, physical actions, inner actions, relaxation training, improv, cold reading, film technique, Shakespeare, accent reduction, and headshot review. Private lessons and resume composition are also available. Free introductory class offered for beg-adv actors. Workshops for directors, teachers, and writers are also taught. Classes are taught on Wednesday, Thursday and Saturday mornings and Tuesday evenings. Students work in every class and class size is limited to 10-12 students. Students can choose 1, 2, 3 or 4 classes per week. Dianne is an experienced stage, TV and film actress discovered by Elia Kazan and acted for Kazan on stage and film. She has been a member of the Actors Studio since 1971, and played in "The Onion Field" and Spielberg's "Amazing Stories," among other film and TV roles. The Hulls were master teachers at the Stanislavski Conference at Pompidou Centre Paris. Dr. Lorrie Hull is a former college professor, senior faculty member for Lee Strasberg, a 5 year teacher for AFI as well as at her own studio. Seminars and classes are based on Kazan techniques as well as on her book "Strasberg's Method as Taught by Lorrie Hull: A Handbook for Actors, Directors and Teachers" with a foreword by Susan Strasberg. Lorrie and Hull students appear on "The Method" video with Cloris Leachman, Martin Landau, and Shelley Winters. Many well known guest speakers. Private coaching available daily. See listing under BOOKS & TAPES in the MARKETING section for further information.

MARIA JENSON – VISUALIZE THIS (310) 823-9973

Acting From Depth Performance Laboratory. For the intermediate and advanced student. Liberate your imagination and develop confidence in your work. Through script analysis, in-depth scene and character study, improv and exercises, you will learn to make strong choices, to interpret the script to convey the intentions of the characters and to play the subtext instead of dialogue. Periodic workshops are small, informal and dynamic. Entrance is determined by application, resume and available space.

KIMBERLY JENTZEN
LIVING THE ARTS INSTITUTE (818) 779-7770
P.O. Box 4554 FAX (818) 779-1171
Valley Village 91617
www.kimberlyjentzen.net
filmactors@aol.com

Young people put so much of their energy into getting themselves in front of people, and they've got nothing to show, said Jentzen. "They need to invest in themselves." A well respected coach for more than 18 years and award-winning director, Jentzen incorporates Checkov, Adler and Meisner techniques along with insights from her own teachings. Her style is tough, yet encouraging, with on the mark specifics that build confidence in her students. Her classes offer professional training in cold reading, scene work, monologue work, some on-camera training, and improvisation, with an emphasis on individual attention, using techniques to assist actors with their imagination, concentration, emotional range, how to make strong choices and performance consistency. Actors are accepted by interview only. Auditing allowed. Private coaching available. She also holds her popular Cold Reading Weekend Intensive, Essence Weekend Intensive as well as a class for singers who want to improve their presence and acting skills. Ms. Jentzen has been an on-set coach on several feature films as well as a hit TV series. SEE AD ON PAGE 1.

THE ANITA JESSE STUDIO (323) 876-2870
Gardner Stage
www.anitajessestudio.com

Through her classes and her books, Anita Jesse has been providing a practical approach to the actor's creative process since 1978. Ms. Jesse says: "We feel blessed to work with artists, but this town is hard on artists. The truth is you survive here only if you accept the realities of the business. But, why bother if, in the process, you abandon your creative essence? We offer a technique that prepares you to get work in film and television, yet celebrates and nurtures your creative spirit. It's a delicate balance, and we welcome a limited number of fearless and determined actors who are willing to embrace the challenge." Five ongoing classes provide a comprehensive program covering scene study, cold reading, on-camera technique, script analysis, monologues, audition technique, improvisation, exercise work, and career counseling. Limited enrollment guarantees that actors work every week. Critiques by the teacher only. The Studio periodically hosts film festivals to showcase original short films produced by the members. Placement in classes is by audition only. Ms. Jesse is the author of the books, "Let The Part Play You: A Practical Approach To The Actor's Creative Process" and "The Playing Is The Thing: Learning the Art of Acting Through Games and Exercises." See listing under BOOKS in the MARKETING section. SEE AD ON PAGE 15.

JUST BREATHE ACTING WORKSHOP (323) 969-4944
bbenvil@aol.com

Classes consist of auditioning skills, scene-study, cold reading, improv, monologues and conversing with the Industry. The ongoing Monday classes has a limited amount of actors; for the gifted beginner to the working actor. Because of the high demand and bookings privately, a children's class is now underway on Saturday mornings. Barbara Beneville instructs, with Industry professionals dropping in. Call for more information, consultation or individual private coaching.

DAVID KAGEN
SCHOOL OF FILM ACTING (818) 752-9678
www.davidkagen.com

The goals of this class are to prepare students to audition and work confidently in the Industry, help students understand what works for them as an actor and how to do that in the work environment, develop greater emotional freedom, range, and spontaneity, and to solve the student's specific acting problems. Students work twice in every one of these ongoing classes, are video taped each time they work and watch their tape after each time. An interview is required. Private coaching is available. Mr. Kagen has over 30 years experience as a teacher and professional actor and there are other highly trained working actors on faculty.

LESLY KAHN (323) 969-9900
1720 N. La Brea FAX (323) 969-9944
Los Angeles 90046
www.leslykahn.com
lesly@leslykahn.com

Lesly Kahn teaches an instinct-based "non-technique" to enhance actors' raw talent and prior training. Actors learn how to break down and demystify text, their own intuition and the business itself, so that they can consistently and effortlessly perform at their peak. Ms. Kahn sees actors privately for on and off set dialogue coaching, audition preparation, acting tutorials, and diagnostic consultations. She holds intimate acting seminars designed to address the specific needs of the individual through scene study and exercise on film and television as well as theatrical texts, including Shakespeare. She also works with singers, songwriters, comics, writers, dancers and directors. Her clients' film projects include "Bewitched," "Dukes of Hazzard," "Fantastic Four," "The Forty Year Old Virgin," "Happy Endings" and "Wedding Crashers." Ongoing TV projects include: "24," "Boston Legal," "Desperate Housewives," "Entourage," "Closer," "Gilmore Girls, "Gray's Anatomy," "Joey," "The O.C.," "Over There" Six Feet Under," "Will and Grace," "Stargate Atlantis," "Two and a Half Men" and "Without a Trace."

CANDY KANIECKI (818) 753-5393
AKA HERMAN (310) 656-7731
c/o Westend Studios FAX (818) 753-8056
12500 Riverside Dr., #211
Studio City 91607
www.westendstudio.com

Ms. Kaniecki prefers to speak directly with potential students regarding her ongoing acting/audition classes.

MILTON KATSELAS'
BEVERLY HILLS PLAYHOUSE (310) 855-1556
254 S. Robertson Blvd.
Beverly Hills 90211

1816½ N. Vermont Ave.
Los Feliz 90027
www.katselas.com
gabwag@earthlink.net

Milton Katselas' acting classes at the Beverly Hills Playhouse have been providing the theatrical industry with the hottest professionals for over three decades. Call above number to set up an interview.

JANICE KENT (818) 906-2201
www.janicekent.com FAX (818) 906-2974
janicekb@hotmail.com

With more than 30 years of experience as an actor, director and coach, Kent has designed her "life coaching" approach to aid the actor in understanding and identifying the fears and processes that block making risky choices. Her combination of Meisner, Adler and Spolin improvisation techniques, experience and heart encourage confidence with growth in skills. Students are currently appearing as series regulars and in films. Kent offers private coaching, ongoing classes and periodic sitcom intensive workshops four times a year. SEE AD ON PAGE 12.

JUDY KERR'S ACTING WORKSHOP (818) 505-9373
www.actingiseverything.com
judykerr@mindspring.com

A film and television acting coach, formerly the dialogue coach on "Seinfeld" and currently on "All About The Andersons," Judy offers private coaching to strengthen acting and camera techniques and there is scene work and career consulting. She is also the author of the best selling book "Acting is Everything: An Actor's Guidebook for a Successful Career in Los Angeles." Visit the website for information and a sample of her book.

THE KIDZ KOACH (818) 347-5098
22647 Ventura Blvd., Ste. 422 FAX (818) 347-5099
Woodland Hills 91364
www.comedynorth.com
barb@comedynorth.com

Barb offers one-on-one private sessions and small group classes that cover acting, improv, audition technique, cold reading and comedy. She also coaches parents to help them help their kids with auditions and cold readings. Parents may sit in. Phone interview required. Over 25 years experience.

PHILLIP KING (KROOPF) (310) 276-7587

Offers supportive private coaching for beg-pro actors. The emphasis is on speech, "Don't imitate another, create yourself." Teaches the "star method" of self-hypnosis to relax, free and hone your unique talent. Covers Shakespeare through Stanislavski, as he feels that once you master the classics you can play anything. He covers audition, technique, cold reading, scene study, and character analysis. Mr. King has worked for Joe Papp, the Lincoln Center and Carnige Hall. Founder of The Heritage and Amas Repertory Theatre in N.Y.

DAPHNE KIRBY ACTING WORKSHOPS (818) 769-9709
www.daphnekirby.com
daphnekirby@earthlink.net

For the past 18 years Kirby has been an acting coach and caster in Los Angeles. Her classes are referred regularly by agents, and casting directors. Currently, she has combined highly effective cold-reading techniques with expertise gained booking over 100 TV spots into a 6 week on-camera intensive designed to give actors a competitive edge in booking commercials. Open to trained actors only, this weekly class refines skills needed to break through the barriers that sabotage actors during the audition process. Covered: mastering copy, commercial improv technique, nailing callbacks, delivering what the advertising agency wants, successful marketing strategies including fine tuning your look for camera and helping with confidence. She has had great success in turning auditioners into bookers. Class size is limited to 18. Classes meet weekly from 7-10 pm in the Studio City area. Additional information is available in Larry Silverberg's book "The Actor's Guide To Qualified Acting Coaches In Los Angeles."

JOHN KIRBY
AT THE JOHN KIRBY STUDIO (323) 467-7877
1510 N. Las Palmas FAX (323) 467-7897
Hollywood 90028
jkcoaching@sbcglobal.net

One of Hollywood's most prominent acting coaches, John Kirby offers three intensive scene study classes in the evening (Monday, Tuesday and Wednesday) and an upcoming young adult class. These classes are geared towards the working professional as well as the newcomer and are extremely disciplined. Actors work every week with select material and partners are chosen by John Kirby. The classes are structured in the vein of Uta Hagen's teachings and are held at the John Kirby Studio, which gives the actor a sense of working on a film set. Classes are ongoing but set in 12-week commitments. Private coaching is available daily.

IRIS KLEIN (213) 612-5224
Hollywood

Ms. Klein conducts a professional twenty-week technique and scene study class and also offers private coaching. Ms. Klein only accepts students by recommendation.

VERNICE KLIER (310) 392-0064
(011) 33-1-47-38-24-64
www.vermice-klier.com
verniceklier@aol.com

Vernice Klier is an international voice and acting coach specializing in acting in English. She has had 15 years experience coaching privately; and has coached on location on over 25 films including the Academy Award winning The English Patient. Vernice uses a multi-sensory approach (right brain, drawing, writing, mime) to authenticate natural speech and movement. She works on phoenetics, enunciation and vocal work from key words to build self confidence and self knowledge. Extensive work on sense and emotional memory is done. Scene study, monologues, and improvisation (verbal and non-verbal) are all used to aid in accent reduction for film, television and stage and help the actor prepare for auditions and interviews.

DAVID LEHMAN **(818) 845-1549**

Classes are offered covering on-camera work and cold reading. There is a monthly time commitment.

KEN LERNER **(818) 753-7744**
Open Stage West
14366 Ventura Blvd.
Sherman Oaks 91423
www.kenlerner.com
studio@kenlerner.com

Ken brings his experiences as a working actor to the acting classes he has taught for more than 14 years. When not working in films such as "The Story Of Us," "Unlawful Entry" and "Senseless," and TV shows such as "Judging Amy," "Buffy The Vampire Slayer," "Chicago Hope," "NYPD Blue," "E.R.," "The Drew Carey Show" and "Dharma and Greg," Ken coaches and inspires actors, helping them get films, TV shows and pilots. Ken uses methods culled from his own acting experiences as well as his own teachers: Stella Adler, Peggy Feury and Roy London, who handpicked Ken as his first student teacher. Ken's trademarks are his nurturing and positive approach to breaking down scenes and his appreciation of what the actor goes through. Because Ken is out auditioning every week himself, he knows exactly what to do and not to do on auditions and on sets.

CATHLEEN LESLIE **(310) 278-8113**
cathleenleslie@earthlink.net

Ms. Leslie offers private coaching based on her studies with Lee Strasberg/The Method and Stella Adler and being directed by Elia Kazan. She's looking for students who have a true passion and desire to learn their craft. Ms. Leslie taught in Paris and at the School of Visual Arts in N.Y., as well as the Junior Year Abroad of Bennington and Skidmore Colleges. She offers private coaching and an interview is required for admittance to classes. Cathleen is a lifetime member and teaches at the Actor's Studio and is on the Board of Governors of the American Film Institute. She is Artistic Ditrector of La Femme Film Festival, the American version of Le Festival International de Filme du Femmes, a pretigious juried competition that has taken place in Paris France for the past 27 years and she has given master classes as the International Greek Film Festival. Ms. Leslie is a working director.

M.K. LEWIS WORKSHOPS **(310) 826-8118**
(310) 394-2511
1513 6th St., Ste. 203 **FAX (310) 826-6966**
Santa Monica 90401
www.mklewisworkshops.com

Ongoing classes are offered in on-camera acting and are available on three levels: professional, mid-level and master class. Other classes offered are cold reading and film technique. Classes are limited to 14 and all classes are on-camera. Auditing is permitted at no charge. Internationally known acting teacher and author of "Your Film Acting Career." SEE AD ON PAGE 14.

BEVERLY LONG **(818) 754-6222**
11425 Moorpark St.
Studio City 91602
www.beverlylong-casting.com
info@beverlylong-casting.com

An 8 week commitment is required for this class which culminates in a showcase for friends, family and agents. Teens and adults. SEE AD ON PAGE 65.

PETER LOONEY
AT THE DAVID LEHMAN STUDIO **(323) 257-9741**
1819 W. Verdugo Ave.
Burbank 91506

Film acting coach offers classes in scripted cold reading and memorized exercises based on Meisner's and Conrad's work. Professional level class that is limited to 16 students. Auditing permitted. Private coaching available.

LOS ANGELES CITY COLLEGE **(323) 953-4000 x2690**
855 N. Vermont Ave.
Los Angeles 90029
www.lacitycollege.edu

Full and part time matriclated programs in acting. Classes cover all aspects of acting and include voice, scene study, improv, accents and dialects, Shakespeare and classical training, speech and diction. Also offers theatre history, mime, combat, movement for actors, basic theatre, movement, circus techniques, Alexander technique, gymnastics, and an evening non-credit acting workshop. For further information and/or current catalogue call the above number. For non-credit extension program catalogue call Community Service (323) 953-4000 x2650.

LOS ANGELES COMMUNITY ADULT SCHOOL **(323) 931-1026**
4650 W. Olympic Blvd.
Los Angeles 90019

Offers scene study and commercial training for adults 60 and older. Classes are taught by credentialed teachers in many Los Angeles areas. Adrienne Omansky is the Program Director and classes are free for adults over 60.

LOS ANGELES REPERTORY COMPANY **(323) 464-8542**
6560 Hollywood Blvd., 2nd Fl. **FAX (323) 464-6130**
Hollywood 90028
www.larep.org

Specializing in acting for the stage. Scene classes provide for a complete all around grounding in stage and film technique. Instructors include Robert Ellenstein, recipient of the 1994 L.A. Weekly Career Achievement Award, and John Herzog.

THE LOST STUDIO
FORMERLY THE LOFT STUDIO **(323) 933-6944**
130 S. La Brea Ave.
Los Angeles 90036
www.thelostudio.com
loststudio@yahoo.com

Founded by Peggy Feury and William Traylor now currently under the direction of Cinda Jackson. Based on the Stanislavski method, classes are offered that cover sensory work and scene study. Classes are limited to 20 for beg-adv actors and are offered in 8 week sessions. Also offering Les Enfantes Magiques a unique theatre experience for children ages 6-12. Also offering masters class for writers, directors and actors with renowned playwright Donald Freed.

WARNER LOUGHLIN **(310) 276-0555**
www.warnerloughlin.com
warnerloughlin@warnerloughlin.com

Warner Loughlin is a private coach and teacher to many celebrities and award winners. Warner's technique melds several schools of thought with her own unique concepts developed through her experience as an actress, director and teacher. Focus includes on-going and intensive scene study with an emphasis on growth in skills for film and television. Classes are small, with a concentration on a safe environment to create. Students work in every class. Beginners are welcome, with intermediate, advanced and master classes offered. Audits are required and admission is by audition only. Industry referral preferred.

ROSIE MALEK-YONAN **(818) 249-8989**
Glendale Area

Offers classes for adults covering scene study, exercises, and improv. One-on-one sessions available. 25 years teaching.

LILAC PRODUCTIONS
NANCY MALONE **(818) 762-8641**

Ms. Malone's scene analysis class is designed to help the actor develop technique for character interpretation and growth, tune the actor's instrument with technique through performance and reveal the writer's intentions. She provides a technique for getting the job and keeping it.

NED MANDERINO **(323) 860-8790**
P.O. Box 27758
Los Angeles 90027
www.manderino.com

Mr. Manderino offers intensive technique development combined with scenarios to solidify technique results. Enrollment is limited to 10-15 actors and everyone works each session. Mr. Manderino has coached/taught/directed John Amos, Warren Beatty, Bradley Cole, Linda Cristal, Robert Davi, Richard Eden, John Fleck, Pamela Gordon, Angel Tompkins, Cicely Tyson, Russell Wong and other renowned actors. He is the author of "Actor As Artist," "All About Method Acting," and "Stanslavski's Fourth Level." These books are used for the classes to accelerate an actor's technique skills. Mr. Manderino has taught in Great Britain and Europe. Auditing is permitted.

JEFFREY MARCUS **(323) 965-9392**
1415 Carmona
Los Angeles 90019
www.jeffreymarcus.com

Jeffrey Marcus has been teaching acting classes and coaching professional actors in Los Angeles for over 15 years. He receives referrals from agents, managers, and casting directors. Classes are very reasonably priced and it is important to him that each student get up to work every week so classes are intentionally kept to under 15 students. Jeffrey Marcus has been an actor for more than 25 years, having played major roles on Broadway, off-Broadway, in Regional Theatre, TV and film. He came to Los Angeles as a series regular and began teaching at the request of friends whom he had coached for auditions (and they booked them!) His training started at conservatory (Carnegie-Mellon) and proceeded to many wonderful teachers in New York. He studied with proponents of Meisner, Strasberg, Hagen and Adler, and also spent years with Montgomery Clift and Geraldine Page's mentor, Mira Rostova. Accessing information from spiritual-psychology to tantric yoga, Jeffrey is not dogmatic in his approach. Audits are available.

FRANCES MARSDEN
ALEXANDER TECHNIQUE **(818) 760-6454**
www.artofmovement.com
fmarsdenat@aol.com

Frances Marsden trained as an actress at the Royal Scottish Academy of Drama in Glasgow, Scotland, and then trained for three years to become a teacher of the Alexander Technique. She has been teaching for 24 years and has considerable experience working with actors. The Alexander Technique is usually taught in private forty five minute sessions and helps actors become more effective on stage and screen, as tension eases, movement becomes more flexible and emotions more accessible. It's a "hands on" technique, guiding you to a greater awareness of habitual patterns and mannerisms which interfere with your coordination and poise. By learning how to consciously eliminate these habits, you are free to give a more fully alive performance.

MARJI MARTIN **(818) 846-9486**

Open-ended, limited classes that are designed to: teach the hows and whys while exploring comedy beyond improv and stand-up; discover and perfect individual techniques; and channel energies and talent through cold readings and personalized exercises in safe surroundings. Teacher critiques only. Also drama coaching.

KATE MCGREGOR-STEWART **(323) 939-3384**
www.katemcgregorstewart.com
herbalgirl7@aol.com

Private coaching and group classes at all levels from Foundation to MasterClass. Scene study, audition coaching, script analysis, goal-setting, character development and comic timing. Her book, "Freedom in Acting" describes her approach which is "an intuitive balance of mind, body, and spirit." She has many famous clients including Academy Award winners Marisa Tomei, and Nicole Kidman. Ms. McGregor-Stewart has appeared in 4 Broadway shows and over 25 films including "School of Rock," "Father Of The Bride" Parts 1 and 2, "Safe" and "In and Out."

DAWN MCMAHAN **(323) 934-5351**
1054 S. Cloverdale Ave., Ste. 7
Los Angeles 90019
dawn3@attbi.com

Private coaching for film, teleivision, and auditions based on Meisner. Focus on reactive honesty working in both comedy and drama.

MEISNER/CARVILLE
SCHOOL OF ACTING **(818) 509-9651**
5124 Lankershim Blvd.
North Hollywood 91601
www.themeisnercenter.com
info@themeisnercenter.com

The home of the Meisner Technique in Los Angeles. The school was founded by Sanford Meisner 1987 with James Carville. In 1995 Mr. Meisner turned the school over to Martin Barter, his assistant for 14 years. The studio offers an intensive 2 year program in the reality of doing and also offers 2 five week summer sessions. There is a working Theatre Company and there are Master classes for graduates. The school also offers screenwriting classes as well.

HILARY MILLER-BRUCE (818) 990-5324

"Creativity is often stifled in a sea of subtext and acting rhetoric," says Hilary Miller-Bruce, a Los Angeles acting coach since 1982 who has received a university faculty award for excellence. She describes her teaching as a simple, effective approach to understanding the text and presenting it "with abandon and believability." Hilary offers an on-camera class and private sessions to all levels for a reasonable tuition. Commercial acting is also offered.

ALLAN MILLER (818) 907-6262
www.allanmiller.org

Wednesday evening classes. Mr. Miller has taught/coached Meryl Streep, Dustin Hoffman, Barbra Streisand, Geraldine Page, Lily Tomlin, Jeff Goldblum, Judd Hirsch, Dianne Wiest, Rue McClanahan, Peter Boyle, and Ron Leibman among others. He is the author of "A Passion For Acting" and the video "Auditioning."

MIME THEATRE STUDIO
LORIN ERIC SALM (866) 444-MIME
www.mimetheatrestudio.com

The actor has only two tools of expression: words and movement. A well-trained actor must master them both. Mime Theatre training offers the actor awareness of, and control over, physical expression on stage and on screen. It teaches what the body communicates alongside the words, in between them, and in their absence. This study addresses the physical aspects of character, emotion, psyche, and interaction. Lorin Eric Salm trained with world-renowned master Marcel Marceau, and is a graduate of Marceau's Paris International School of Mimodrama. He also studied mime under former assistants of Etienne Decroux, and with Polish master Stefan Niedzialkowski. He has taught mime and character movement to mime artists, actors, dancers, comedians, and animation artists (Disney and DreamWorks); he coaches for film and TV, and is author/administrator of The World of Mime Theatre, the Internet's premier mime website. Class sessions begin every several weeks and run year-round, for beginning through advanced levels.

ERIC MORRIS' ACTORS WORKSHOP
AT THE AMERICAN NEW THEATRE (323) 466-9250
5657 Wilshire Blvd., Ste. 110
Los Angeles 90036
www.ericmorris.com

Mr. Morris uses his own technique in this ongoing class that covers audition technique, character analysis, film technique, improv, interview technique, monologues, sensory work, and scene study. His approach is based on Stanislavski, however he has gone light years beyond the original system. In addition to weekly classes he holds intensives one weekend per month, as well as 4 three day workshops per year and one six day workshop held at the UCLA Conference Center in Lake Arrowhead. Students work in every class, the limit is 20 students. Auditing is allowed and is followed by an interview. Private coaching is available from Mr. Morris or his wife Susana Morris. Mr. Morris has written numerous books on acting. SEE AD ON PAGE 13.

LARRY MOSS ACCENT ON ACTING (310) 395-4284

Classes and private coaching to help actors develop focus, authenticity and intimacy for the camera whether performing in mainstream American or in dialect. The goal: truthful performance without the work showing, i.e., a full-dimensional character speaking with a seamless accent that does not call attention to itself or get in the way of the acting. Through cold reading, improvisation, scenes and monologues, students are guided to: build confidence and trust in their creative process; break through acting blocks and limitations; make creative choices based on an understanding of text; tune up a needed dialect; "give up" the dialect so we hear a flesh-and-blood character instead of a mechanical accent in a vacuum; and—for actors with regional, British or foreign accents—perform convincingly in mainstream American. Students work in a safe, supportive environment conducive to risk taking, breakthrough, and discovery. Classes are on a four-week cycle with an enrollment limit of 12. Interview required. Mr. Moss also coaches privately, as well as on the set, on the looping stage, and on location. A veteran coach with numerous celebrity clients, he has helped shape performances for scores of films including: "In America," "Gladiator," "Barber Shop," "13 Days", "Wayne's World 1 & 2" and "Lethal Weapon 4." For over 30 years he has taught university workshops in acting, dialects, cold reading and voice-over and for several years co-taught workshops with Mel Blanc (cartoon voices and dialect). As a voice-over actor, he has performed character and dialect roles in over 300 feature films and television productions. Note: This is not the teacher of The Larry Moss Studio.

MIKE MUSCAT (818) 904-9494
mustrap@yahoo.com

Offers private lessons that cover acting, cold reading, and commercials. He also coaches for auditions and meets with actors for career guidance and advice. He is an acting and dialogue coach for TV and film. Mike was on-set acting coach for "Terminator 2," "My Girl 2," "Last Action Hero" and "Frazier." The only acting coach in town that gives a money back guarantee.

MYTH-CRAFT (310) 434-9111

Craft any role, scene or film using simple, proven techniques. For actors, writers and directors. Applies to any genre. Interview required. Half-hour or one-hour consultations.

LAUREN PATRICE NADLER (818) 202-0774
lpnclass1@aol.com

A bi-coastal director, coach, casting director, who cast Adrian Brody (Oscar Winner for Best Actor in 2003) in his first lead role, and has coached countless actors in front of and behind the scenes. Originally from New York, Lauren has planted her roots in Los Angeles to share her years of experience. She believes that truthful, creative. dynamic and individual work is the key to success. Having fun is really important to an actor's endurance and that is a focus. Blending business and art, Lauren validates your personal instincts as a most crucial tool. Lauren has also created her own checklist of character building questions to refer to, to help actors develop a personal connection to any role. Using contemporary scenes and improvisation to warm up, students work in every class at least twice. Lauren's philosophy is "you can watch a body builder, and learn about form, but you won't gain one ounce of muscle or tone unless you get up and sweat." These classes are for serious, committed actors who want to enhance their creativity level. Lauren, who is currently in preparation to direct several film projects, is available for private coaching, on-set coaching career counseling and directing projects.

STEPHANIE NASH **(310) 829-9119**
www.nasharts.com
stephanie@nasharts.com

A Yale School of Drama graduate, Stephanie has been an audition and acting coach in Los Angeles for many years. She has taught at USC, the American Academy of Dramatic Art, and presently teaches Directing II at the Art Center Film School in Pasadena teaching directors to work with actors to create the story. She has also taught special workshops at various venues around town. Her focus is on giving the actor tools, techniques and timing that will support him/her in any situation while allowing freedom of spontaneous choices. She emphasizes the permanent growth of the actor, helping them stretch in range, gain confidence in choices, and experience truthful and creative expression of character. Private and small group sessions available. Stephanie has extensive NY and regional theatrical experience in addition to TV, film, and dozens of national commercials. Stephanie also teaches meditation classes in Santa Monica on a regular basis working with pain management and food issues.

THE JULIAN NEIL ACTING WORKSHOP **(323) 954-8811**

Private coaching only. Mr. Neil is a veteran N.Y. director and acting coach who has been training actors for 25 years.

ALLEN NELSON **(818) 786-7154**

Private coaching for film, TV and stage. Coaching for cold reading auditions, working with actors to find and develop prepared audition material; scenes and/or monologues. Accepts beginning actors who lack a foundation and need to develop technique and working actors who need to overcome individual problems in character development and emotional preparation. Allen was administrator/teacher at the acclaimed Tracy Roberts Actors Studio for 21 years and taught all core classes for 10 years. He has been featured in documentaries in Korea and England.

NEW YORK FILM ACADEMY **(818) 733-2600**
100 Universal City Plaza **FAX (818) 733-4074**
Bldg. 9128, Ste. 179
Universal City
www.nyfa.com
munkeeluke@hotmail.com

Acting for Film workshops as well as directing, writing and producing workshops.

THE NEXT STAGE THEATRE **(323) 850-7827**
1523 N. La Brea, Ste. 208-9
Los Angeles 90028

431 N. Brookhurst Ste. 140 **(714) 635-1028**
Anaheim 92801
www.berubians.com

Every creative person has that one script or part they've always wanted to play floating inside of them. The Next Stage has designed a program to allow those dreams to become a reality. With a weekly regimen of workshops in improvisation, sitcom study, cold reading, writing, video scene study, and stand up comedy, participants can go to one or all every week. The end result occurs at the 50 seat theatre where performers play every night except Monday for the public and Industry. Members take advantage of the entire program for $75 a month with a one workshop per week commitment. Auditors for all workshops are welcome, with the first week free. Members are entitled to attend at the The Second Stage in Anaheim and the Tre Stage next door.

OASIS – PIERCE COLLEGE **(818) 710-4163**
6201 Winnetka Ave.
Woodland Hills 91371

Sharon Newman teaches Acting for Fun and Profit at Pierce College on Thursday afternoons. This fun-filled workshop offers a safe environment to enhance your performance and audition skills, creativity and self expression through acting games, improvisation, technique exercises, lively discussion and the study of scenes and monologues. The class also explores the current work opportunities for senior actors.

CLIFF OSMOND **(310) 393-6022**
1526 14th St., Ste. 107
Santa Monica 91404
www.cliffosmond.com

The emphasis in these classes is on scene study, analysis, audition technique, and the application of traditional emotional exercises. The actor is consistently encouraged to develop an honest, open, and exciting instrument, and Mr. Osmond's coaching varies with each actor. All scenes are video taped, and film performance skills are emphasized. The students develop their own personal judgement in evaluating and perfecting their work. Auditing is encouraged.

JIM OTIS **(818) 543-7479**

An actor for over 30 years and an acting coach for 18, Jim Otis works with students to go beyond cold reading to put what's unique about them in to the script. His ongoing six-session private classes are one-on-one, and he allows flexibility in scheduling. Two different courses are offered: a TV and film intensive covering auditions, cold reading, and business strategy, and a monologue intensive emphasizing audition skills and including work with classical, contemporary, and comedy pieces. He takes people at all levels, beginners to pros, works at their pace, and helps them prioritize their goals. Auditing is not permitted.

MARLENE PEROUTKA
ACTING WORKSHOPS **(714) 965-6771**
18910 Mt. Castile Circle
Fountain Valley 92708
showbizpitt@aol.com

Personal manager and television executive producer Marlene Peroutka and her staff offer three levels of classes for all ages of adults: beginner, intermediate and advanced. Admission into intermediate and advanced classes is by audition or instructor permission. Marlene's acting workshops are designed more for San Diego, Riverside and Orange County professional actors, but her students travel as far as from New York to study her successful techniques. Private coaching also available.

PIMLOTT-MEDINA'S **(866) 923-3459**
FILM & TV WORKSHOP **(866) 923-FILM**
955 S. E. St., Ste. F **FAX (909) 884-8904**
San Bernardino 92408
filmtvworkshop@aol.com

Beginning, intermediate and advanced acting workshops for adults and teenagers to help expose natural ability, capture auditions with originality, learn on-set protocol, and learn Industry terminology. Classes cover cold reading, improvisation, commercials, on-camera movement, overcoming stage fright, and monologues. Management, agent and casting director showcases and Industry consultations. Course audits available.

JILL PLACE **(323) 225-9850**
(888) 237-6875
1309 Montecito Dr. **FAX (323) 221-1395**
Los Angeles
www.actingintuitive.com
jill@actingintuitive.com

Jill Place combines the best of 20th Century acting technique with 21st Century intuition into a new type of acting coaching called Act Intuitive. Place honed her acting and intuitive skills through years of intensive training with such illustrious teachers as Lee Strasberg, Uta Hagen, Herbert Berghof, Sanford Meisner, Peggy Feury and Viola Spolin, and in her career as a successful singer, actress and original Groundling. Place is also a medical intuitive and spiritual healer. She can see where actors have emotional or energy blocks that keep them from expressing their craft and can intuit ways to quickly remove these blocks. Jill's students not only become better actors but quickly understand complex acting techniques that have taken her years to learn and they consistently work in films, on stage, and as television series regulars. Jill teaches individual and small-group sessions in a safe, secluded, supportive environment. She also helps actors create their own personal brand because she feels that if you don't create your own brand, someone else will create theirs and steal your TV series, guest star turn or movie lead. Place also regularly contributes to the Now Casting e-zine, Actors Ink. Check out her website for further information and see listing in the BUSINESS OF ACTING section.

PLAYGROUNDS, INK! LLC **(818) 507-1544**
Glendale 91202
www.playgrounds-ink.com
joe@playgrounds-ink.com

Private coaching available. Call for details.

PLAYHOUSE WEST
SCHOOL AND REPERTORY THEATRE **(818) 881-6520**
4250 Lankershim Blvd.
North Hollywood 91602

Playhouse West, The Second Studio
10634 Magnolia Blvd
North Hollywood 91601
www.playhousewest.net

Founding director, Robert Carnegie, and film actor, Jeff Goldblum, have been teaching the Sanford Meisner approach to acting in their own distinctive fashion since 1981. This includes year-round ongoing classes, a theater program with students doing multiple plays in repertory, regular scene nights for the Industry, and feature film projects based on either their own plays or member-initiated projects. Classes are held all week long and weekends at two locations, mornings, afternoons, and evenings for beg-adv level students. Students work in every class and are critiqued by the teacher only. A free audit is allowed and an interview is required. Entry into class can occur anytime during the month. In 1987 Playhouse West became the home of Sanford Meisner's own classes and Mr. Carnegie spent time studying the later teaching methods of Mr. Meisner. SEE AD ON PAGE 9.

THE PLUS WORKSHOPS (ACTING PLUS)
SCOTT BERNSTEIN **(323) 692-0298**

Ongoing one-on-one classes called "Acting Plus" are offered for $120 for 4 weeks. Work is done on monologues, scene study, comedy technique, improv, theatre games, sensory work and character study. Private coaching for auditions and special projects is available for $40 per hour. There are discounts for members of the workshops or for longer projects. Cold reading and script study workshops also available. Take two or three workshops for $175 for 4 weeks. Serious minded actors only. Interview required for admittance. Over 20 years experience.

PROFESSIONAL SCHOOL **(310) 328-SONG**
FOR THE ARTS **(310) 328-7664**
1329 Sartori Ave. **FAX (310) 782-2072**
Torrance 90501
www.psarts.com

Private and group training available for age 6 through adult in singing, musical theatre, dance (tap, ballet, jazz, theatre), acting (classical, commercial, TV, scene study, audition technique, cold reading), and voice (vocal technique, speech, dialects). All instructors are working professionals. They offer ongoing courses and private lessons by appointment as well as frequent masters classes in all areas of training. On-site workshops available.

PROMENADE ACTING CONSERVATORY **(310) 656-8070**
1404 Third Street Promenade **FAX (310) 656-8069**
Santa Monica 90401
www.pierodusa.com
info@pierodusa.com

One of the most prestigious conservatories in the nation; fully equipped with an Equity-approved theatre, The Promenade Playhouse. This training facility is one of the very few that is registered with the California Bureau of Private Post Secondary and Vocational Education. The Conservatory provides artistic excellence with professional acting and writing instruction in the film, television, and theatre industries for a new generation of artists. It has been honored by such legends as Alfred Molina, David Groh, John Savage, and Gary Busey, to name a few, who have inspired graduates at annual festivities. The Conservatory's Programs include: the Meisner Technique, Advanced Acting, Master Performing Class, On-Camera Dynamics, Commercial Auditioning Technique, Advanced Commercial Technique, Auditioning for Film and T.V., Advanced On-Camera Technique, Master Camera and Marketing Technique, Sitcom Technique, Fundamentals of Improvisation, a program for Children and Teens, as well as private coaching in house and on location. The most recent courses that are now offered are the T.O.P. System taught by Nick Mancuso, and the signature technique of the Conservatory, Character Preference, Character Expression, Character Pathology, the writing department's Matrix of Character Preference with Syd Field, and Creating the One Person Show. In addition, the Conservatory has created a complete, full time International Program that offers an Introduction to Meisner & Character Work, Voice & Speech, On Camera Auditioning Techniques, a Performance Workshop & Hollywood Connection Tours that include meetings with Industry Professionals. SEE AD ON PAGES 21 & 297.

THE RANDOLPH STUDIO FOR ACTORS **(323) 882-6669**
www.cc4actors.com
kate@cc4actors.com

Training actors at all levels: beginning, intermediate and professional. A comprehensive approach incorporating the

Stanislavski techniques as taught by Russian master teacher Leonid Anisimov, as well as those taught by Stella Adler, Uta Hagen, and at The London Academy of Music and Performing Arts. Emphasis on externals: articulation, grace of movement, vocal resonance, and breath work along with internal emotional, and motivation work. Kate focuses on ensemble, joy in the work, and support for the partner. Admission by interview only. Reasonable tuition fees.

REEL PROS **(818) 788-4133**
13437 Ventura Blvd., Ste. 220
Sherman Oaks 91423
www.reelpros.com
support@reelpros.com

Reel Pros has three categories for their classes: 1) the Main Arena for professional actors who play 27 and above; membership by audition only; 2) Reel PROs 2 for young professional actors who play 16-26; no audition required; and 3) The Public Access Arena offers classes that are specifically oriented to craft-building and specialty skills like Voice Over, Improv, Audition Technique, How to Book Jobs, How to Be Captivating on Film, etc., and are open to the general public 18 years old and above. The first two classes also offer cold-reading and at times prepared scene workshops with casting directors, producers, directors, and agents.

PAUL E. RICHARDS **(323) 257-2323**

A Broadway actor and teacher for over 40 years, Paul Richards offers classes for actors at his theatre.

ELI RILL WORKSHOP **(818) 384-1607**

With an emphasis on one-on-one private coaching, Mr. Rill uses a combination of Stanislavski, Strasberg, and "eclectic others." His classes cover improv, monologues, scene study, sensory work, Shakespeare, audition technique, and cold reading. An interview is required and auditing allowed by arrangement only. There is a discount for union members.

RIPRAP STUDIOS **(818) 990-7498**
5755 Lankershim Blvd.
North Hollywood 91601
www.riprapentertain.com

Classes are taught on an ongoing basis at Riprap Studio Theatre. Some classes taught by celebrity actors, ncluding "The Art of Acting" taught by Art Evans. Basic, intermediate and advanced performance levels.

ARTHUR ROBERTS **(310) 827-9661**
adr9999@verizon.net

Arthur Roberts teaches actors' survival: all the basics of earning your living as an actor from interview through audition, through performance, converting fear and nervousness to excitement and energy in order to be alive, real and brilliant in the moment. Strong coaching preparation for great auditions. 40 years acting, 30 years coaching.

ALEXIA ROBINSON STUDIOS **(818) 779-1119**
4930 Lankershim Blvd.
North Hollywood 91601
www.alexiarobinsonstudio.com
imaginears@aol.com

Alexia Robinson Studio is a Los Angeles area acting studio for adults and kids that provides ongoing scene study classes, on-camera commercial workshops, audition technique and cold reading classes. All classes are taught by working professionals with extensive film, television and commercial credits. Classes are taught in a supportive and nurturing environment where actors can grow, learn and perfect their craft.

STUART ROGERS **(818) 763-3232**
5267 Lankershim Blvd.
North Hollywood 91601
www.theatretribe.com
theatretribe@hotmail.com

Classes in classical and contemporary styles are offered that cover scene study, cold reading, monologues, text analysis, rehearsal technique, and improv. Emphasis is on building a consistent personal technique. Beginning, intermediate and advanced levels. Private coaching is available. Interview required. Classes held at the Theatre Tribe Studio Theatre. www.stuartrogersstudios.com

RACHEL ROSENTHAL COMPANY **(310) 839-0661**
2847 South Robertson Blvd. **FAX (310) 837-4511**
Los Angeles 90034
www.rachelrosenthal.org
r2co@rachelrosenthal.org

Teaches "The DbD Experience," a 35 hour intensive weekend interdisciplinary performance workshop that explores body, voice extensions, masks, music, sets, costumes, lights, and European stage techniques. The workshop is intended to work as an actor's tuning factory, creating immediate ensemble, and giving the performer a complete instrumental workout. The workshop is held biannually. Ms. Rosenthal also offers ongoing 10 week workshops.

AL ROSSI **(818) 902-1538**
(323) 953-4000 x2975
www.lacitycollege.edu
rossiaa@lacitycollege.edu

Offers classes using a combination of Meisner, Hagen, Strasberg, and Tyrone Guthrie methods for intermediate/advanced levels. These small classes cover scene study, audition material preparation, character analysis, cold reading, emotional release, and Shakespeare. Auditing is allowed by arrangement only. Mr. Rossi is Head of Acting at the Professional School at the LACC Theatre Academy. Actors taught, coached or directed include: Martin Sheen, Joan Van Arc, John Vickery, Dakin Matthews, Scott Glenn, Steve Allen, Cindy Williams, and Diana Canova. Private coaching is available for auditions for theatre, film or TV.

STAN ROTH **(323) 930-1050**
www.stanroth.com
info@stanroth.com

Mr. Roth has taught acting and prepared actors for auditions for the past twenty years, specializing in cold reading technique. Formally an actor for 25 years, he is also an established director with several successful theatre productions to his credit. In addition to conducting private classes he has served on the faculties of the American Academy of Dramatic Arts (12 years), Theatre of Arts Academy, the Denver Center Theatre Academy, South Coast Rep., UCLA, Santa Monica College, Diane Hardin's Young Actors Space, the L.A. County High School for the Arts and the Acting Corps. Among the many actors Stan has taught and directed are Leonardo DiCaprio, Toby Maguire, and Jeremy Davies. Rather than adhere to one particular philosophy or method, his is a no-nonsense, practical approach designed to develop each individual actor's ability and implement reliable, consistent techniques that are applicable in any acting or audition situation. Classes are kept small (6 persons maximum) and actors receive extensive individual attention. Students at all levels of experience are considered by initial interview. Classes are held in his studio in the West Hollywood area. Private coaching for auditions and one-on-one classes are scheduled by appointment.

THE RUSKIN SCHOOL OF ACTING (310) 390-4212
3021 Airport Ave., Studio 113 FAX (310) 455-3821
Santa Monica 90405
www.ruskinschool.com

John Ruskin was Sanford Meisner's apprentice, first studying with the master at the Neighborhood Playhouse School of the Theatre in New York City, continuing in Bequia, West Indies, then teaching with him at the Neighborhood Playhouse and privately during the 1980s. The Ruskin School is the West Coast representative of the Neighborhood Playhouse and all of the teachers were trained directly by Sanford Meisner. Ruskin, who opened his school in Santa Monica in 1987, offers a two year course of study in Meisner's technique, six week introductory courses, and a Master class for those who have completed the two year program. The school also teaches the technique to young adults ages 13-18 and offers classes in Alexander technique, movement, and Comedia dell'Arte. The Ruskin Group Theatre, is located adjacent to the school and is staging ongoing performances as well as an outreach program for children's hospitals, retirement homes, and prisons for both youth offenders and adults. Admission to the school is by personal interview.

CBS COMEDY ACTING &
TV HOSTING WORKSHOPS
WITH PAUL RYAN (818) 788-2190
CBS Studio Center
4024 Radford Ave.
Studio City 91604
www.paulryanproductions.com
paul@paulryanproductions.com

Artistic Director Paul Ryan offers topnotch classes on the CBS lot. See listing under COMEDY & IMPROV in this section for further information.

JOE SALAZAR (323) 882-6433

Mr. Salazar is "only interested in working with those actors who are determined to be the best actors that they can be." The class environment is challenging and geared toward each actor as an individual. Students work in every class. The focus is on scene study, monologues, improv, cold reading, and audition technique. These ongoing classes for beginning-advanced level actors are taught Monday, Tuesday and Wednesday evenings. On-camera technique is taught several times a year in ten week sessions. Auditing is allowed and private coaching is available. Mr. Salazar offers student showcases out of his own theatre in Hollywood, The McCadden Place Theatre.

DIANE SALINGER (323) 512-6062

The greatest gift you have to give is yourself. Bring yourself to the work and become fearless. Salinger has worked with Woody Allen, Clint Eastwood and Tim Burton and is an award winning actress and coach. She offers beginning to advanced classes in technique, scene study and auditioning as well as private coaching. Opportunities to showcase work for agents, casting directors, directors and producers.

SANTA MONICA PLAYHOUSE (310) 394-9779
1211 4th St. FAX (310) 393-5573
Santa Monica 90401
www.santamonicaplayhouse.com
smp@primenet.com

Chris DeCarlo offers classes for all levels that cover inner acting technique, audition technique, character analysis, improv, sensory work and marketability. The class is limited to 20, costs $200 for 8 sessions and meets Mondays. Students work in every class. No auditing is allowed and an interview is required. Call for interview information. Mr. DeCarlo has extensive acting experience, has been teaching for 30 years and has taught/coached/directed Stuart Pankin, Louise Sorel, Sammy Shore, William Schallert, Priscilla Morril, George Coe, Debra Harmon, and Michael Callan. Private coaching is also available.

JOHN SARNO (AND STAFF) (818) 761-3003
www.hollywoodacting.com

Private or group lessons, all levels. Over 30 years teaching. The classes cover cold reading, scene study, commercials and improv. Some of his students have received Academy Award and Emmy nominations. Mr. Sarno himself has received a Golden Globe Award, and a Hollywood Motion Picture Council award for teaching. No auditing.

THE SECOND CITY (323) 658-8190
8156 Melrose Ave.
Los Angeles 90046
www.secondcity.com/training/la

For over 45 years, The Second City has been one of the most influential theatres in the country, turning out some of the world's most beloved actors. Second City has launched hundreds of artists whose careers have changed the face of television, film and theatre with alumni in the current casts of Mad TV, Saturday Night Live and Curb Your Enthusiasm to name a few. A sample of programs offered at The Second City Training Center include Beginning Improvisation, Improv for Actors, Sketch or Sitcom Writing, Musical Improv and the Conservatory Program. Also classes for children and teens.

SECRET ROSE THEATRE (818) 766-3691 x4
11246 Magnolia Blvd FAX (818) 766-3691
North Hollywood 91601
www.secretrose.com
mike@secretrose.com

The Secret Rose Theatre offers a variety of classes including beginning and intermediate technique, professional level scene study, commercial workshops, musical theatre, youth acting classes, play production and playwright workshops. Classes and workshops are offered at different times depending on the theatre's availability. For more information, call the theatre directly. SEE AD ON PAGE 19.

SCOTT SEDITA ACTING STUDIOS (323) 465-6152
526 N. Larchmont Blvd. FAX (323) 465-6202
Los Angeles 90004
www.scottseditaacting.com
scottsedita@aol.com

Sedita, former agent and casting director, has been an acting coach for 20 years, and has worked developing the careers of such talents as Courteney Cox and Christopher Meloni. Scott offers classes in

On-Camera TV and Film Acting, Professional Audition Technique and directs The Showcase Company for invited Industry 3-times a year. Scott Tiler teaches a 10-week comprehensive technique workshop called Nuts and Bolts (a beginning acting class) and the On-Camera TV and Film Drama class (for more advanced actors) as well as "Fall and Fly," a motivational and empowerment workshop open to all actors. Patrick Munoz MFA teaches Acting Through Voice and Speech designed to train actors in articulation, verbal agility and accent reduction. How to Audition for and Book Commercials is taught by Commercial Casting Director Josh Rappaport.

RICHARD SEYD ACTING STUDIO (323) 668-1475
4949 Hollywood Blvd., Ste. 203
Los Angeles 90027
www.seydways.com
studio@seydways.com

A comprehensive lab committed to the art and craft of professional acting training actors for the profession who are in engaged in developing themselves to their fullest potential. They work to create an authentic, intimate, safe environment for the actor to explore and expand the range of their own being so they can experience and express the multifaceted nature of our shared humanity.

PAULA SHAW (604) 684-2424
www.themaxwithpaulashaw.com

Private coaching in Los Angeles and Vancouver. Learning to let go of self-conscious contrived performance choices in favor of genuinely alive, conscious and intentional acting experiences. Lifetime member of Actors Studio, taught at the Strasberg Institute in L.A., and Cal Arts. Private sessions for professional auditions. Leads the MAX weekend intensive in Vancouver and in Big Sur.

SHORT AND SWEET AUDITION CONSULTING (310) 936-9084
jeffreywolf64@yahoo.com

Taking class is great, but what if all you need is a fresh pair of eyes and an honest critique of your audition piece? This is an offer for a straightforward, honest evaluation and help to improve. Either one session or more; whenever the job is complete.

ARETHA SILLS (323) 851-1380
www.paulsills.com/laworkshops
aretha_sills@earthlink.net

Aretha Sills is offering improvisational theater workshops in Los Angeles. Refresh or enhance your performance skills with theater games from Viola Spolin's classic text "Improvisation for the Theater." Actors, teachers, writers, experienced improvisers and beginners welcome. Aretha Sills is the granddaughter of Viola Spolin. She has studied improvisational theater for many years with Paul Sills, and has taught at The Bard College Cabaret, Paul Sills' Wisconsin Theater Game Center and Bay Area Theatresports.

CANDACE SILVERS STUDIOS (818) 755-4609
12215 Ventura Blvd., Ste. 111
Studio City 91604
www.candacesilvers.com

Candace Silvers trained under Roy London for 10 years and has 20 years experience as an actress. Ms. Silvers offers cold reading, career design, foundation, and scene study classes that help free actors while they acquire tools which allow them to enjoy their work and their career. Ms. Silver's coaching encourages discovery of truthful, high-risk choices through an active method of script analysis. She encourages actors to use their own emotional experience when creating characters. Ms. Silvers also makes available an audio cassette which outlines the techniques she teaches.

AUDREY MARLYN SINGER (818) 506-0600
Actors Forum Theatre FAX (213) 465-6898
10655 Magnolia Blvd.
North Hollywood 91601
www.nohoartsdistrict.com
actors4mtheatre@aol.com

This professional workshop for actors and writers is offered on Tuesday, 7:30 pm to 10:30 pm and they present a "Month Of Thursdays," a showcase from the workshop. They also offer 2 shows per year on their mainstage.

CLAIR SINNETT (866) 4 ACTORS
www.clairsinnettcasting.com FAX (310) 606-5626
sinnett@earthlink.net

Ms. Sinnett, head of Clair Sinnett Casting, conducts her TV/Film Audition and Acting Workshops throughout the country, Canada and Europe as well as in Los Angeles. She also career coaches privately. Sinnett has taught at the UC Irvine, South Coast Conservatory, Playwrights Horizon Theater School, American Academy of Dramatic Arts West and NY to name a few. Sinnett presents seminars for Women in Theater, Academy of Televison Arts & Sciences, Women in Film, SAG, AFTRA and numerous other organizations. She has served as Artistic Director for the Actors Company, Hollywood Actors Theater and Real to Reel Productions and is a founding board member of The Black Theater Troupe, The Janus Gay Theater Company and The Actors Company. She conducts her two day weekend intensive in marketing and auditioning: interview and audition techniques, cover letters, who to write to, pics and resumes, script analysis, cold reading, etc. All sessions are videotaped and followed by in-depth critique. Private coaching is by appointment. Sinnett has been teaching for over 25 years during an acting, directing and casting career and trained at NYU, The New School of NY, AADA, Adler, Meisner and Strasberg. Author of "Working Actors: The Actors Guide to Marketing Success."

MELISSA SKOFF (818) 760-2058
11684 Ventura Blvd., Ste. 5141
Studio City 91604

Offers ongoing advanced level acting classes. Entrance is by audition. Ms. Skoff has cast more than 100 feature films and television shows in both comedy and drama.

MILLIE SLAVIN (310) 582-3485
FAX (323) 954-7050

Millie Slavin works to help actors recognize and connect with their uniqueness so they can gain the confidence to risk their best in a highly competitive market. Slavin is a veteran of New York theatre, television and film, a Cable Ace Award nominee for HBO's "Sessions." Her training includes study with Uta Hagen and Roy London and she offers scene study classes as well as private coaching, cold reading, group and individual technique training as well as an eight-week intensive technique course. She frequently teaches acting at UCLA Extension and has been a guest speaker at NYU's Tisch School of the Arts, working with graduate film directors. "A fine actress and a wonderful teacher and coach."—Billy Crystal

ELLA SMITH **(323) 650-0256**

Ms. Smith offers private coaching on a one-to-one basis for theatre, film and television, and specializes in cold reading. An interview is required for acceptance. She has been teaching and directing for over 20 years, she received her MFA in Acting from the Yale School of Drama and she was the acting coach on "Star Search" with 30 winners in one season, and three $100,000 winners, and has taught at various acting schools and universities. Her acting credits are extensive, and she is a member of The Yale Connection.

RON SOSSI THE ODYSSEY THEATRE **(310) 477-2055**
2055 S. Sepulveda Blvd.
Los Angeles 90025
www.odysseytheatre.com

Offers 2 workshops that cover technique/scene study and scene work. The scene study class is ongoing, the technique class is eight weeks and is offered once a year. All classes are limited to 16 students. The workshops cover character analysis, classical drama, improv, monologues, sensory work, theatre games, and Stanislavski and Growtowski techniques as well as other modern theatre techniques. Students work in every class. Mr. Sossi is the Artistic Director of the Odyssey Theatre and former executive, writer and director of network television.

SOUTH COAST REPERTORY ADULT CONSERVATORY/ PROFESSIONAL CONSERVATORY **(714) 708-5500**
P.O. Box 2197 **FAX (714) 545-0391**
655 Town Center Dr.
Costa Mesa 92626
www.scr.org

Director: Karen Hensel. Faculty includes: Greg Atkins, Karen Hensel, Hal Landon, Jr., Cecilia Fannon and Laura Woolery. The Adult Conservatory offers evening courses in the art of acting to students 18 and older of all levels. Coursework is divided into four 9 week sessions. Classes include Fundamentals of Acting: Basic Skills. Fundamentals of Acting: Act II, Intermediate Acting, Actors' Workshop, Beg-Adv Improvisation, Acting for the Camera, and Playwriting. In addition, SCR offers an 8 week summer Professional Conservatory that culminates with a performance lab. Auditions are required for Professional Conservatory. Call for brochures and information.

AARON SPEISER ACTING STUDIO **(310) 399-4567**
1644 S. La Cienega Blvd.
Los Angeles 90035
www.aaronspeiser.com

Classes focuses on training for film and television. Techniques (beginning) offered that develop relaxation, concentration, and imagination through a practical method and process that takes 3 months to complete. Intermediate and advanced scene study classes focus on character development, rehearsal process, techniques, and script breakdown. The Master Class is for advanced and professional actors and is used to further hone, stretch, and develop the actors' instrument and is a great environment to bring in original work, stay sharp between professional jobs and take risks. Invitation or audition only. Mr. Speiser works with beginners as well as professional clients: Jennifer Lopez, Virginia Madsen (Sideways), LL Cool J, Marlon and Shawn Wayans, The Rock, Brook Shields, Flex, etc. SEE AD ON PAGE 17.

STAGE 13 PRODUCTIONS ROBERT BEECHER **(818) 768-3686**
10749 New Haven St., Ste. 15
Sun Valley 91352
www.stage13.com

Private coaching that covers commercials, film, and theatrical acting. Cold reading, audition and cue card technique, and on-camera work are some of the things that are covered. A new comedy class has been added and Robert peppers his teaching with biz of the biz information including headshot and resume advice, agents, generals, etc. Classes are $60 for 4 sessions. There is a required introductory session which is a pre-requisite to joining the regular groups.

DEE WALLACE STONE **(818) 876-0386 ext 3**
www.dwsactingstudio.com
totoent@aol.com

Positive, joyful acting classes held in Burbank. The class is Meisner based and a mix between cold reading, scene study and on-camera. Beginning and advanced classes.

THE LEE STRASBERG THEATRE INSTITUTE **(323) 650-7777**
7936 Santa Monica Blvd.
Los Angeles 90046
www.strasberg.com

Founded by Lee Strasberg, the legendary master of "the Method," the Institute sets the standard by which all other actor training is measured. Intensive full and part time programs are developed upon the world renowned technique that is the foundation for many of the greatest actors of the past century. Instructors are working professionals with years of experience in the Industry and in teaching. In addition to acting technique, available classes include scene study, improvisation, production, acting for the camera, dance, singing, speech and T'ai Chi. Admission is by interview only.

PATRICK STRONG **(310) 721-9479**
The West Hollywood Playhouse
666½ N. Robertson Blvd.
West Hollywood 90069
patrickstrong1@aol.com

Mr. Strong held the position of Assistant to Lee Strasberg for seven years in his Master Classes. Currently conducting classes in his Professional Actors Workshop. Method Acting, with emphasis on emotional preparation, auditions, and scene study. Ongoing classes Tuesdays, 6:30 pm to 10:30 pm are designed to help the trained actor be more creative and relaxed under pressure. Serious beginners are also welcome. $150 per month.

STUDIO 10 PERFORMING ARTS CENTER **(818) 563-4095**

Studio 10 classes are directed by Patricia Bolt, film, commercial, voice over actress, writer and producer. For many years, Ms. Bolt has been an associate of Broadway/TV Star, Allen Fawcett, as Director of Marketing, producer and coach for Mr. Fawcett's acting and production studio in Studio City, in addition to marketing and producing classes and workshops for Actor's Center International in Studio City and One-on-One Productions. Ms. Bolt is also a writer /producer of commercials and special events for prestigious clients like the City of Los Angeles, the Metropolitan Transit Authority and the national Amateur Softball Association, in addition to concerts and theatrical productions, and is currently working on her own feature projects.

KITTY SWINK **(818) 508-9169**

Provides one-on-one training and primarily works to prepare actors for auditions. Also does on-set coaching. Ms. Swink has worked as a dialogue coach for "Dangerous Minds," for Stephen Bochco's "Total Security" and various other shows.

TALENT ACADEMY, INC. **(800) 878-5070**
(310) 962-0414
P.O. Box 1738
Hollywood 90078
www.talentacademy.com
talentacademy@aol.com

Talent Academy, Inc., offers training for stage, film and television actors. The training program called The Essence of Holistic Acting, created by Mr. George Djordjevic, the President of the Talent Academy, has been praised as "the most innovative and effective" approach to developing actors' skills. This program combines the original Stanislavsky System, with American and European acting trends, placing equal attention on actor's mind, body and spirit. In addition, Talent Academy will be the major sponsor of the Los Angeles Actors Showcase scheduled for fall of this year. To learn more or to schedule an interview visit the Talent Academy's website, email or call.

THE THEATRE DISTRICT **(323) 957-2343**
804 North El Centro
Hollywood 90038
www.thetheatredistrict.com
info@thetheatredistrict.com

Macario Gaxiola conducts classes covering scene study, cold reading and audition technique. Also covered: movement and dialects. Private coaching available.

THEATRE OF ARTS (EST. 1927) **(323) 463-2500**
1621 N. McCadden Place **FAX (323) 463-2005**
Los Angeles 90028
www.theatre-of-arts.com

Offers classes in all styles and methods of acting by teachers who are all working professionals. The classes are for beg-pro. This is the oldest acting school west of New York. They offer on-camera work, showcasing of one act and full length plays, and they host Industry events. Also teaches English as a Second Language and accent reduction. State licensed and approved by the Board of Education. Approved for the training of veterans and foreign students. There is an 80 seat theatre.

TOM TODOROFF STUDIO **(310) 281-8688**
1223 Olympic Blvd. **FAX (310) 392-8669**
Santa Monica 90404
www.tomtodoroff.com
todoroff@ix.netcom.com

Tom Todoroff offers classes in acting, voice and speech, directing, producing and writing for students of all levels. Please visit the website for more information.

THE TRAVIS GROUP
MARK W. TRAVIS, DIRECTOR **(323) 737-3223**
2116 Arlington Ave., Ste. 310
Los Angeles 90018
www.travis-johntz.com

Mark Travis is well known nationally and internationally for his development and direction of one person shows. Through Travis-Johntz he offers several opportunities for actors and performers who wish to develop their own shows. Solo Sunday is a one-day immersion into the Solo Process. The Solo Workshop is a weekly workshop where you develop your material in a group environment. The Solo Retreat (Hawaii and Cologne) is a three-day intensive storytelling and writing workshop in a communal remote setting. Solo One-on-One is the most personalized and intensive development process. Free consultations are available by appointment.

MICHELLE TRUFFAUT **(323) 969-0801**

Ms. Truffaut offers private coaching and is the founder and Artistic Director of the San Francisco Repertory and the San Francisco Shakespeare Festival. She received her MFA from AFI and has been teaching acting for theatre and film for more than 20 years. Call for information and interview.

TERI TUNDER **(323) 969-0795**
havemoxie@teritunder.com

Teri offers private coaching and feels you learn by doing and that there is no substitute for doing. Also teaches cold reading and showcasing. Her approach is based on years of training as an actress in New York and San Francisco and being a casting director in Los Angeles. Geared to the individual. Teri says: "Be brave get out there and tell the truth."

MYRA TURLEY **(818) 901-9351**
mtstar@aol.com

Ms. Turley is a New York trained actress and director with an MFA in Theatre Arts from Columbia University and over 25 years teaching experience both on the professional and university levels. Her skill is pinpointing and solving whatever acting problems block you from the success you desire. Classes include instrument work to deepen emotional range and stimulate the imagination, craft tools, scene study and monologues, script analysis, comedy styles, audition and cold reading technique. Hers is an eclectic, theatre-based approach, which she has adapted for film and television. She offers small classes of all levels from beginning to master levels that do not exceed 15 people. Class size is deliberately small so each actor may work more than once every week. Classes are ongoing; commitment is for a minimum of 3 months; new students are added every quarter; no auditing; an interview/audition is required. Private audition coaching and on-set coaching is available. Classes are conducted in the NoHo area. Call for more information.

TVI ACTORS STUDIO **(818) 784-6500**
14429 Ventura Blvd., Ste. 118 **FAX (818) 784-6533**
Sherman Oaks 91423

The Actors Equity Bldg. **(212) 302-1900**
165 West 46th St., 5th Fl.
New York, NY 10036
www.tvistudios.com

Founded in 1986, TVI Actors Studio is the nation's largest resource center for actors, offering dramatic instruction, entertainment industry networking, professional career consultation and marketing support for actors. With full-service centers in Los Angeles and New York and Chicago, weekend programs conducted year-round, TVI is an expanding nationwide network of U.S. cities, and a developing international presence now in Europe, Australia, New Zealand and Canada. TVI merges traditional actor training with the realities of the business. Classes are taught by a core faculty of 35 working Industry professionals, including prominent directors, producers, casting directors and talent agents from both coasts, with course content ranging from cold-reading technique, acting in feature film, sitcoms, primetime and daytime TV, to musical, legit theatre, voice-overs and commercials. Course duration ranges from single one-night workshops featuring different Casting Directors each night of the week to extended 10 week ongoing classes. Auditions are required for most courses. Other benefits of TVI membership include daily free casting director workshops, resume and cover letter consultation with updates as often as you like, mailing labels, one-on-one counseling, use of studio space, and computer workstations with Internet access, all designed to refine the actor's craft, empower the actor with a well-rounded knowledge of the business, and clearly defined career strategy, and maximize an actor's potential in the marketplace. Current and former students include success stories from primetime and daytime television, Academy Award winning feature films, Tony nominees and some of Broadway's rising stars. TVI's experienced management team is comprised of former talent agents, managers, advertising and marketing specialists and university fine arts faculty, which provides a blend of both business-minded practicality and a healthy respect for the actors' craft and process. Outside Greater Los Angeles area call toll-free: 800-884-2772 ext 1 Outside the NY Tri-State area call toll-free: 800-884-2772 ext 2.

UNIVERSITY OF CALIFORNIA LOS ANGELES (UCLA) EXTENSION (310) 825-9064
10995 Le Conte Ave., Rm. 437
Los Angeles 90024
www.ucla.org

Offers courses and workshops for adults taught by Industry professionals from beginning to advanced levels. Some of the courses require an audition. The fee per course varies for these classes that are held mostly evenings and weekends. Courses offered in Stanislavski techniques, creating one person shows, acting for the camera, acting for daytime drama, and many others. Call for the free course catalog. "Professional Studies in the Entertainment Industry."

UNIVERSITY OF SOUTHERN CALIFORNIA (USC) (213) 821-2744
University Park
Los Angeles 90089
www.usc.org

Call for a current catalog and the Theatre School. Cinema/TV School (213) 740-2235.

VAN MAR ACADEMY (323) 650-8823
7080 Hollywood Blvd., Ste. 314 FAX (323) 650-0155
Hollywood 90028

Ivan S. Markota, past president of ACTA (Acting Coaches and Teachers Association) teaches all aspects of film and TV acting in 16 classes. His students have booked 1,034 series (regular and recurring roles). Auditing is required and free.

WALLACE AUDITION TECHNIQUE (323) 960-7852
1532 9th St., #3
Santa Monica 90401

The Wallace Audition Technique is a unique class created by casting directors, agents and producers that offers the actor an opportunity to learn from current Industry professionals. The six week class covers among other things: how to break down material quickly and creatively, make fast and original adjustments, how to identify your own unique qualities and incorporate them into your work and how to eliminate nerves and tension. Class size is limited to 10 people and all classes are on-camera.

RICK WALTERS THEATRE CRAFT PLAYHOUSE (323) 876-1100
7445 1/4 Sunset Blvd.
Los Angeles 90046

Offers ongoing classes for all levels covering cold reading, audition technique, character analysis, classics, improv, monologues, scene study, video promo, and Shakespeare for adults and children.

DOUG WARHIT ON CAMERA SCENE STUDY AND COLD READING (310) 479-5647
www.dougwarhit.com

Classes for beginner through working professional. All work is geared for television and film and is performed on-camera. Classes are kept small because every actor is required to work every week. Once a month an agent or casting director is invited to observe the students' work. In addition to group classes, a 4 week one-on-one workshop is offered, covering cold readings, camera technique, prerequisites for a great audition, commercials and the marketing of the actor. Mr. Warhit is also a licensed psychotherapist, specializing in actor's issues of performance anxiety, self-sabotage, and procrastination. He is the author of "Book the Job: 143 Things Actors Need to Know to Make it Happen," "The Actor's Audition Checklist," and "Warhit's Guidebook for the Actor." See listings under BOOKS in the MARKETING section and SEE AD ON PAGE 2.

DEBRA WATSON (310) 500-6727
Beverly Hills
www.yellowrosesproductions.com

Private coaching specially focused on cold reading techniques to combine natural instincts with practical audition techniques to help create interesting, believable, and rich characters. Beginning actors and working professionals can benefit from these techniques which include character development and script analysis. Learn how to quickly lift your eyes off the page and connect with the casting director while staying in the moment. Cold reading/improv workshops for intermediate to advanced students several times per year.

WEIST-BARRON-HILL (818) 846-5595
4300 W. Magnolia Blvd.
Burbank 91505
www.weistbarronhillacting.com
andlyle@aol.com

Acting classes for film and TV with an emphasis on soap opera technique. Limit of 12 people per class. These ongoing classes are offered Monday, Tuesday, Thursday evenings, and Saturday afternoons for basic and advanced level actors. Students work at least twice per session. Showcases are held for all levels. Critiques are by the teacher only. The cost is $25 per session. Auditing is free.

DAVID WELLS STUDIO (818) 753-5393
12500 Riverside Dr., #211 FAX (818) 753-8056
Studio City 91607
www.westendactingstudio.com

Offers classes in acting, cold reading, and audition technique for beg-pro actors, age 5-21. The classes cover scene study, monologues, theatre games, and improv. Classes are offered days and evenings. Students are encouraged to bring their audition material to class. A parent seminar is offered. There is occasional Industry showcasing. One free introductory class.

Acting

CARYN WEST **(323) 876-0394**
7506 Lexington Ave. **FAX (323) 876-5897**
West Hollywood 90046
qnmaeve@aol.com

Offers classes in audition skills and private coaching for intermediate to working actors. Emphasis in all classes is on preparation, in-depth script analysis, understanding different theatre and camera genres, goal setting, professionalism, creative risk taking, and the freedom to play. Agents and managers refer most of her students. Ms. West is a working actress and director with extensive TV, Broadway, and regional theatre credits. She has taught for 15 years in NYC at Michael Howard Studios, and The School for Film and Television. In L.A. she has taught privately, and formerly at Stella Adler's. 10-12 week class offerings start in late August/early September or late January/early February. One week Audition Intensives offered the last week in November and in late spring. Private coaching available year round. See listing under COLD READING in this section for further information.

JUDITH WESTON ACTING STUDIO **(310) 392-2444**
3402 Motor Ave.
Los Angeles 90034
www.judithweston.com
judyweston@aol.com

Intermediate to advanced coaching for actors. Students work in every class. Interview required. Scene study, technique, improv, cold reading, and Shakespeare. 20 years teaching. Author of "Directing Actors" and "The Film Director's Intuition."

YOUNG ACTORS SPACE **(818) 785-7979**
5918 Van Nuys Blvd.
Van Nuys 91401
www.young-actors-space.com

Classes are offered for children from age 6 through adult. The classes cover improv and scene study, as well as audition and interview skills. No audition or interview is required. "Exploring the joy of acting since 1979."

Broadcast Schools

ACI AMERICAN COMMUNICATIONS INSTITUTE **(323) 462-6166**
3550 Wilshire Blvd., Ste. 1050
Los Angeles 90010
www.network.com

Offers training for DJs, news and sports reporters, and copywriters. Also offers classes in production. All classes are in Spanish.

COLUMBIA COLLEGE HOLLYWOOD **(818) 345-8414**
18618 Oxnard St. **FAX (818) 345-9053**
Tarzana 91356
www.columbiacollege.edu

Offers 2 and 4 year programs in TV and film. There are a small amount of non-credit workshops. They will help with resumes and a limited amount of job placement assistance. This is a licensed, accredited school that awards AA and BA degrees. State and Federal financial aid is available as well as a tuition reduction program.

MVCI (MUSIC VIDEO COMMERCIAL INSTITUTE) **(800) 255-7529**
1655 McCadden Place
Hollywood 90028
www.mvci.tv
mvci@mvci.tv

Music Video and Commercial Film School teaches hands-on workshop courses for directing, producing and editing music videos and commercials on 35mm, 16mm film and digital video. MVCI is a film school where the student can become the director, producer, cinematographer and editor of their own high quality music video or commercial production. Taught by MTV Award winning directors, producers and editors.

Business of Acting

THE ACTOR'S LAB **(310) 621-3900**
at the Odyssey Theatre
2055 South Sepulveda Blvd.
Los Angeles 90048
www.theactorslab.com

A career consulting program helping actors in areas such as union cards, representation, networking, and creation of original projects. See listing under ACTING for further information.

THE ACTORS WORKSHOP **(949) 855-4444**
23151 Plaza Point Dr. #100
Laguna Hills 9653
www.actorsworkshop.com
info@theactorsworkshop.com

Now in it's 27th year, this highly respected film/television workshop is Orange County's oldest acting program. Under the direction of R.J. Adams, classes are conducted twice each week for beginning, intermediate and advanced actors. With co-director R.J., Rob Adams and Pete Pastore sessions are conducted in a state of the art digital broadcast television studio. Classes include audition/cold reading techniques, on-camera scene work and weekly showcases with major L.A. casting directors. R.J. Adams began his long time teaching career as director/founder of The Actors Workshop/Hollywood in the early 70s with many of his students having risen to starring roles in film and television. R.J. Adams has appeared in more than 60 feature films and television shows in both the U.S. and Europe. Rob Adams has been a working actor since the late 80s with film credits that include "Forrest Gump" and "The Program."

ACTORS CONSULTATION SERVICES (310) 828-7814
2461 Santa Monica Blvd., #332 FAX (310) 998-9114
Santa Monica 90404
www.actorsconsultations.com
jill@actorsconsultations.com

Jill Jaress, career consultant and coach, specializes in teaching new actors how to break into the business and working actors how to increase the number and quality of their bookings. She also consults with the parents of children who want to be stars. Private coaching for adults, teens, and children. She specializes in audition preparation, focusing on interviewing for agents and casting directors as well as scene study.

AIA ACTOR'S STUDIO (818) 563-4142
1918 Magnolia Blvd., Ste. 204 FAX (818) 563-4042
Burbank 91506
www.aiastudios.com
info@aiastudios.com

AIA Actor's Studio is a nationally recognized acting studio and entertainment company. The Studio has spent the last decade helping actors achieve professional excellence by providing dramatic instruction, career guidance and the opportunity to build relationships with Industry experts. The Studio has successfully integrated the business of acting with both formal and practical training and offers a diverse array of classes and programs taught by working entertainment professionals.

BB'S KIDS (323) 650-KIDS
www.bbskids.com

Taught by the former Head of Casting for MTV Networks, Dino Ladki. Topics studied include: scene study, cold reading, character breakdown and audition coaching. This is an 8 week opportunity for students to perform and be coached on their actual auditions. Besides class work, students gain a Casting Director's perspective on how "right" their classmates may or may not be for a role. Professional Acting is a business and it is important to know what you're selling, especially when it's yourself. Focus will be on feature films, TV episodics, MOWs, pilots and sitcoms. Age 12 and up. Also available: a parent seminar with Belinda and Rikki to help protect your child and your wallet from common mistakes. Points covered include labor relations, training, the difference between audition/callback/avail/hold, pictures and resumes, the Coogan Law, agency protocol, work permits, differences between agents and managers, contracts and commissions. For more information see listings under ACTING, CHILDREN'S TRAINING, COMMERCIALS, COLD READING, ACCENTS AND DIALECTS, CLASSICAL TRAINING, MODELING, MUSICAL THEATRE and COMEDY AND IMPROV. SEE AD ON PAGE 41.

JIILL PLACE - BRAND ACT (323) 225-9850
BRANDING FOR ACTORS (888) 237-6875
1309 Montecito Dr.
Los Angeles 90031
www.actingintuitive.com
jill@actingintuitive.com

Jill Place, a Los Angeles acting coach has created the BRANDact÷ Branding for Actors e-Book series from going through the process of branding her own successful businesses. First she helps the actor define their acting presence and purpose by developing their branding statement in the BRANDact÷ Branding for Actors interactive e-Book. Next the actor learns how to create dynamite headshots and marketing materials to sell them well. Place feels that in order to truly be successful, one must align all their energies for success so in the Aligning your BRAND÷ e-Book, she teaches how to be a ShowBiz success by learning business strategies that work and then applying them to your acting career. This second e-Book helps you develop an internal acting success consciousness. Place feels that in order to manifest success, you have to define your acting goals, be 100% confident you will achieve them, identify your target market and strategize how to get them to buy what you have to offer. Place feels that building and maintaining lifetime relationships with people in the Industry can get you where you want to go and it is not only important to align yourself with those people who can hire you, it is also important that you initiate and perpetuate these relationships. Place also does in-person and phone branding, career and headshot consulting.

CAREERWORKS
TERRENCE MCNALLY (310) 312-0041
2520 Granville Ave FAX (310) 479-0031
Los Angeles 90064
temcnally@post.harvard.edu

One-on-one sessions cover a wide range of issues as well as acting and audition coaching including goal-setting, the business of a career, personal obstacles to growth and achievement, image clarification and marketing. Mr. McNally has worked as an actor (20 years), producer, writer (Earth Girls Are Easy), director, radio host (KPFK, 90.7 FM), and corporate communications consultant. Terrence says: "Hollywood's like poker, and you're not the only one with a good hand. Let clarity, coaching, and practice be your wild cards." Single sessions or series.

CHRISTINA CONCETTA (818) 415-6967

Provides consultations for actors on the business of acting and career development. A member of the Actor's Studio.

DEVORAH CUTLER-RUBENSTEIN
NOBLE HOUSE ENTERTAINMENT (310) 943-4378
12210½ Nebraska Ave., Ste. 22
Los Angeles 90025
www.thescriptbroker.com
devo@thescriptbroker.com

The CareerWorks Institute is designed to give the entertainment professional a competitive edge. Whether you are an actor trying to get an agent, a producer putting together your first movie, or a director trying to get that important meeting with your star, Devorah Cutler-Rubenstein helps you build a battle plan that gets you where you need to go. Discover where you compete from and break through your blocks. Get your instincts working for you and direct your own career with renewed confidence. She offers penetrating insights, intuitive easy to do craft and career building work and puts her own contacts on the line. CareerWorks is an ongoing workshop that meets once a week with a minimum three month commitment. Devorah Cutler-Rubenstein is uniquely qualified as an Executive Producer of feature films ("The Substitute 1 and 2") and an award winning writer and director (Showtime's "Peacock Blues" and winner of Best Short Film Moondance International Film Festival). "Highly intuitive, she mounts a campaign that challenges personal blocks, and fears are handled with wit wisdom and fun."—Ariel Schoolsky, Development Executive

LISA DALTON: LIFE, CAREER &
NETWORKING CONSULTATIONS (818) 761-5404
www.chekhov.net
chekhov@earthlink.net

Lisa offers guidance on all aspects of the Industry for new and experienced actors ranging from techniques for self promotion, interview and networking skills, how to get set up in Los Angeles, budget for living and developing resume, getting tape, joining unions, etc. Need help coping with the Industry, with maintaining a day job, finding the right classes or a supportive environment, missing family, etc.? Lisa Dalton is a skillful counselor in addition to her vast knowledge of the entertainment industry and has a gentle way of guiding you into feeling wonderful about your love of the Industry and how to use that as a practical tool for happiness, health and success. $75/90 minute sessions. Certified Results Coach, NLP, Hypnosis. See listing under ACTING in this section for further information.

CHRIS DE CARLO (310) 394-9779
1211 4th St. FAX (310) 393-5573
Santa Monica 90401
www.santamonicaplayhouse.com
smp@primenet.com

See listing under ACTING in this section for further information.

WAYNE DVORAK (323) 462-5328
1949 Hillhurst Ave.
Los Angeles 90027
www.actingcoachdvorak.com

Mr. Dvorak manages and coaches his acting clients using the Meisner technique which is organic foundation work. He has ongoing Industry showcasing at the professional level, and brings several agents each year to see his clients. He offers highly professional career development which includes image consultation for members of the company. Everything in-house.

HOLLYWOOD INSIDER EDUCATORS (323) 602-0350
5042 Wilshire Blvd., Ste. 801 FAX (323) 602-0351
Los Angeles 90036
www.hieducators.com
tom@hieducators.com

An intensive eight hours of instruction on such subjects as representation by agents, personal managers, business managers, publicists and attorneys. Instructors discuss self-promotion and marketing issues, from headshots and postcards to submission systems and video reels. Many guest professionals discuss their craft and how their perception affects the careers of actors. There are discussions of union regulations, agency franchise issues, and rates for all media. Residual income from television, film, and commercials are detailed. Finally, the students delve into the casting process, as discussed with a panel of television, film, and commercial casting directors.

HULL ACTORS STUDIO
LORRIE HULL, PH.D. & DIANNE HULL (310) 828-0632
Santa Monica
www.actors-studio.com/hull
hullwshop@hotmail.com

Picture and resume, agent, and work consultations. Showcases for the Industry. Private lessons and coaching available daily. See listing under ACTING in this section for further information.

THE ANITA JESSE STUDIO (323) 876-2870
Gardner Stage
www.anitajessestudio.com

The acting class for intermediate level actors offers a review of headshots and resumes, advice on finding an agent, getting into the unions, choosing showcases, putting together presentation tapes, and tips for avoiding scams. See listing for ACTING in this section for further information. SEE AD ON PAGE 15.

LOS ANGELES
CITY COLLEGE (LACC) (323) 953-4000 x2990
855 N. Vermont Ave. FAX (323) 953-4500
Los Angeles 90029
www.lacitycollege.edu

Call the above number for information and current catalog.

LAUREN PATRICE NADLER (818) 202-0774

A bi-coastal director, coach, consultant and casting director, who cast Adrian Brody (Oscar Winner for Best Actor in 2003) in his first lead role, and has coached countless actors towards successful career choices. Originally from New York, Lauren has planted her roots in Los Angeles to share her years of experience. She believes that dynamic, creative and truthful work is key but knowing your way around and how to communicate effectively in the professional arena is crucial. Lauren helps blend your business and art, validating personal accomplishments to help use them to your advantage by setting up a comprehensive plan of action to move your career beyond the point it is already at. She also teaches acting classes and runs workshops for serious minded, committed actors who want to enhance their creativity level. Lauren, who is currently in preparation to direct several film projects, is available for private coaching, on-set coaching, career counseling and directing projects.

ALEXIA ROBINSON STUDIOS (818) 779-1119
4930 Lankershim Blvd.
North Hollywood 91601
www.alexiarobinsonstudio.com
imaginears@aol.com

Alexia Robinson Studio is a Los Angeles area acting studio for adults and kids that provides ongoing scene study classes, on-camera commercial workshops, audition technique and cold reading classes. All classes are taught by working professionals with extensive film, television and commercial credits. Classes are taught in a supportive and nurturing environment where actors can learn, grow and perfect their craft.

AARON SPEISER ACTING STUDIO (310) 399-4567
1644 S. La Cienega Blvd.
Los Angeles 90035
www.aaronspeiser.com

A series of 5 private sessions or an annual one-day Business of Acting Seminar. Sessions include what you need to do to best succeed in the business, headshots, looks and image, agents, auditioning, identifying your motivation, and much more. Call for more information or visit website for schedule. SEE AD ON PAGE 17.

KELI SQUIRES-TAYLOR (323) 938-7729
6056 Whitworth Dr.
Los Angeles 90019
www.actorsuccess.net
kst1management@earthlink.net

Special marketing for actors. Personal Manager Keli Squires-Taylor works with all acting levels to give honest marketing evaluations, marketing guidance and business advice to help you move on up to the next level(s) quickly.

Business of Acting

THE STEPS TO STARDOM **(310) 659-0262** **(310) 652-4399**
7080 Hollywood Blvd., Ste. 305
Hollywood 90028
www.theactorsedgeacademy.com

The seminar covers the basic business steps that any successful actor has taken to guide his/her career or open the doors for a successful acting career. See listing for The Actor's Edge under ACTING for further information.

SUCCEEDING IN L.A. **(323) 658-6378**
FAX (323) 658-5730

Susan Goldstein, Producer/Personal Manager/Publicist and career coach has given her seminar on actors marketing themselves in L.A. and New York. She works with actors on a one-to-one basis and teaches them how to promote themselves and their project. She has spoken at several universities, Women in Film, and the DGA, SAG Conservatory and several film festivals. She is currently working as a career coach to actors and filmmakers and has represented films as a publicist at the Sundance and Hamptons Film Festivals. Her clients have starred in film, television, theatre and the internet.

THEATRE OF ARTS (EST. 1927) **(323) 463-2500**
1621 N. McCadden Place **FAX (323) 463-2005**
Los Angeles 90028
www.theatre-of-arts.com

See listing under ACTING in this section for further information.

TVI ACTORS STUDIO **(818) 784-6500**
14429 Ventura Blvd., Ste. 118 **FAX (818) 784-6533**
Sherman Oaks 91423
www.tvistudios.com

TVI teaches actors the business of acting with a practical, no-nonsense approach to marketing and promoting yourself as a working actor in a highly competitive marketplace. Founded in 1986, with studios in Los Angeles, New York and Chicago, TVI is a resource center for actors, offering dramatic instruction, entertainment industry networking, professional career consultation and marketing support for actors. In addition to a diverse curriculum of courses taught by leading Industry professionals, TVI provides members with daily free casting director workshops, resume and cover letter consultation with updates as often as you like, mailing labels, one-on-one counseling, use of studio space, and computer workstations with Internet access, all designed to refine the actor's craft, empower the actor with a well-rounded knowledge of the business, and clearly defined career strategy, and maximize an actor's potential in the marketplace.

UNIVERSITY OF CALIFORNIA LOS ANGELES (UCLA) EXTENSION **(310) 825-9064**
10995 Le Conte Ave., Rm. 437
Los Angeles 90024
www.ucla.edu

Courses and workshops for adults taught by Industry professionals. Topics include headshot review and advice, interview technique, image consulting, resume composition, finding/dealing with agents, business managers, lawyers, personal managers, publicists, and getting into unions. Courses in entertainment business and legal affairs also offered. See listing under ACTING in this section for further information.

VAN MAR ACADEMY **(323) 650-8823**
7080 Hollywood Blvd., Ste. 314 **FAX (323) 650-0155**
Hollywood 90028

Ivan S. Markota, past president of ACTA (Acting Coaches and Teachers Association) teaches all aspects of film and TV acting in 16 classes. His students have booked 1,034 series (regular and recurring roles). Auditing is required and free.

DAVID WELLS STUDIO **(818) 753-5393**
12500 Riverside Dr., #211 **FAX (818) 753-8056**
Studio City 91607
www.westendactingstudio.com

A workshop is offered that covers headshot review and advice, resume composition, finding and dealing with agents, personal managers, and publicists, getting into the unions, how to find casting information on your own, working in theatre and student films, and putting together a presentation video.

WORK ACTOR WORK! **(323) 225-1962**
aktorchick@aol.com

Services include advice on resume composition, proven letters to agents, photo resume, etc., and personalized labels for agents, casting directors, managers, and producers. Now offering consultations.

Children's Training

A MINOR CONSIDERATION **(310) 532-1345**
14530 Denker Ave.
Gardena 90247
www.minorcon.org

A Minor Consideration (AMC) is a non-profit organization formed to give aid and support to child actors past, present and future. Some of the previous child actors have bonded together to try to support those who need help and to address the situations that lead up to any difficulties. Through the efforts of organizations like AMC, people are now recognizing the special needs of child actors.

AMERICAN NATIONAL ACADEMY **(818) 763-4431**
10944 Ventura Blvd.
Studio City 91604

The Academy Children's Workshop. Directed by Dorothy Barrett with Catherine Wilkinson, Hana Konupek, Matt Underwood, Lori Travis, and Judiana Castle. A Saturday workshop for children 8-18. This all day session includes: acting, ballet, Jazz, tap, speech, singing, musical comedy, improv, hip hop and career guidance. The teaching staff donate their time to this non-profit organization.

ACTORS CIRCLE **(310) 837-4536**
4475 Sepulveda Blvd.
Culver City 90230
www.theactorscirlce.com
workshops@theactorscircle.com

Kevin McDermott and Marcie Smolin offer classes in cold reading, scene study, improv, interview technique, and character development. These ongoing classes are limited to 12-15 students

per class and are divided by age, 5-7. 8-10, 11-13, 14-19 and 18-26. Classes are offered days and evenings. Private coaching is available. Adult classes are available.

ACTORS CO-OP **(323) 462-8460**
1760 N. Gower **FAX (323) 462-3199**
Hollywood 90028
www.actorsco-op.org
jcuster@fpch.org

The Actors Co-op Young Actor's Academy for ages 10-14 provides a non-competitive environment where your child will increase self confidence and self expression. Classes taught by seasoned professionals. Each acting session concludes with a special showcase performance for parents and friends. Classes cover theatre games, improvisation, scene study and monologue study.

ACTORS CONSULTATION SERVICES **(310) 828-7814**
2461 Santa Monica Blvd., #322 **FAX (310) 998-9114**
Santa Monica 90404
www.actorsconsultations.com
jill@actorsconsultations.com

Jill Jaress, career consultant and coach, specializes in teaching the parents of children who want to be actors, how to break into acting and how to direct your child's career. Private scene study is available for the young actor as well as audition preparation.

THE ACTOR'S SPOT **(818) 383-8433**
4821 Lankershim Blvd. **FAX (661) 263-0987**
Ste. F, PMB 363
North Hollywood 91601
www.theactorsspot.com
ptreeky@aol.com

The Actor's Spot focuses on moment to moment, or learning to quit acting and start listening, believing, and reacting. Each class is limited to 10-12 students allowing their instructors to provide hands-on work with each and every student. The Actor's Spot was created to encourage people starting out in the entertainment industry, as well as to provide a forum for seasoned actors to workout and continue growing. Classes include scene study, cold reading, improvisation and casting directors for ages 7 and up.

STELLA ADLER ACADEMY
OF ACTING AND THEATRE COMPLEX **(323) 465-4446**
6773 Hollywood Blvd., 2nd Fl. **FAX (323) 469-6049**
Hollywood 90028
www.stellaadler-la.com

Academy Director, Irene Gilbert. Youth Program for children age 12-17. Call for catalogue and further information. SEE AD ON PAGE 6.

AIA ACTOR'S STUDIO **(818) 563-4142**
1918 Magnolia Blvd., Ste. 204 **FAX (818) 563-4042**
Burbank 91506
www.aiastudios.com
info@aiastudios.com

AIA Actor's Studio has spent 16 years helping actors achieve professional excellence and has successfully integrated the business of acting with formal training. AIA offers a wide variety of educational opportunities for actors specializing in daytime, primetime television, film, voice-over and commercial audition techniques as well as continuing to provide classes on such topics as screenwriting, directing, and "how to produce your own independent projects." Classes are taught by some of LA's most knowledgeable instructors who work as casting directors, writers, directors, producers and other active and successful entertainment professionals. AIA's mission is to assist actors in maximizing their creative potential and empower them through education to succeed in a competitive marketplace. Children's training combines professional training with creative dramatics in an environment that is both challenging and nurturing. The teaching method used is based on a process that involves the child's individual creative process focusing on cultivating their skills in a natural way.

TONI ATTELL **(818) 787-8685**
www.attell.com
attell@attell.com

Toni Attell has taught stand-up comedy, improvisation, cold reading, and acting technique for TV, movies, and commercials in over 350 universities and schools throughout the United States. She teaches many workshops including "Mommy and Me and ShowBiz Makes Three" which include on-camera techniques for children ages 4-11 in TV, movies, commercials, improvisation, standup comedy and comedy, as well as classes for teens, adults and seniors covering on-camera technique for TV, movies, commercials, improvisation and stand-up comedy. See ACTING listing in this section for further information.

CYNTHIA BAIN'S
YOUNG ACTOR STUDIO **(323) 654-6614**
Laurelgrove Theatre
12265 Ventura Blvd., Ste. 209
Studio City 91604
www.cynthiabain.com
cynthia@cynthiabain.com

Classes are for the young professional and aspiring actor. Cynthia provides young actors with a strong foundation, allowing for individual growth in an inspiring, dynamic, and supportive atmosphere. Classes are primarily scene study with an emphasis on script analysis and improvisation and include exercises and cold reading technique. Cynthia began her professional acting career at age 14 and thus knows firsthand the unique needs of young performers. She was nominated for a Cable Ace Award for Best Actress in a Dramatic Series for her work in HBO's "War Stories" and has had numerous starring roles in feature films, MOWs, miniseries, network pilots, and episodic television. Cynthia received her BA from UCLA in Theater Arts and her many years of study with the legendary acting coach Roy London provides the basis of her instruction. She successfully created, developed, and ran her young actor program at the Cameron Thor Studio for over three years before moving to the Laurelgrove Theatre. The annual show she directs, produces, and co-writes with her students has garnered her much praise and caught the attention of many Industry professionals. These shows have been the primary force in kick-starting the careers of dozens of her students. She has worked with young people of all ages for over 12 years and is dedicated to providing young actors with the kind of training that she desired as a young actor. Class size is limited so every student has an opportunity to work in every class. An eight-week commitment is required; classes are ongoing so a student may join at anytime. Young actor auditors are welcome. Private coaching is available for all ages.

BB'S KIDS **(323) 650-5437**
www.bbskids.com

Belinda Balaski offers 8 week theatrical and commercial workshops on-camera for kids and teens, 4 and up. The workshops are on weekends and the basic TV and film acting class covers theatre games, improv, audition skills and techniques, cold reading, character study and prepared graduation scenes. The Commercial Workshop is offered on Sundays and covers personality slating, improv, doubles, singles, cold and hard copy. The emphasis is on preparing the child for TV, commercials, and film. TV and film classes (8-20), Improv (12-20), Print and Runway Modeling (9-20), Music Video (7-20), Shakespeare (12-20), Dialects and Voice Overs (9-20), Auditions with Casting (12-20). Also a Tot's Acting Class and Fairy Tale Improv class allowing the freedom to stretch the imagination within a loose structure igniting skills used for opening up the creative ability while learning basic acting skills of dialogue and character. Private coaching is also available. Ms. Balaski works individually to bring out the natural talents of her students. 50 years acting experience, 20 years teaching. See listings for ACTING, MUSICAL THEATRE, ACCENTS and DIALECTS, COMEDY AND IMPROV, CLASSICAL TRAINING, MODELING AND COMMERCIALS for further information. SEE AD ON PAGE 41.

JUDY BELSHE **(562) 621-0121**
www.askjudy.biz
belshecasting@aol.com

Children and adult ongoing on-camera acting classes in Long Beach. For beg-pro. Improv, commercials, theatrical. Guest writers come to classes and teach on theatrical nights.

(310) 657-3270
CALIFORNIA YOUTH THEATRE, INC. **(323) 461-7300**
The Ivar Theatre **FAX (310) 657-3272**
1605 Ivar Ave
Hollywood 90028
www.cytivar.org

Workshops are offered periodically which involve young people ages 12-25 in all forms of the performing arts. They produce plays, musicals, dramas, and original shows.

PAMELA CAMPUS CASTING & **(310) 398-2715**
COMMERCIAL WORKSHOP **(818) 897-1588**

Offers commercial classes for children starting at 3½ years of age. See listing under COMMERCIALS in this section for further information.

JUNE CHANDLER'S
YOUNG ACTORS WORKSHOP **(626) 355-4572**
www.junechandler.com
june@junechandler.com

Everything young actors and parents need to know. Professional Saturday classes for kids and teens (6-17) on-camera at Zydeco Casting Studios in Studio City. Step into the Industry is an 8-week commercial workshop where students meet managers and agents. Step Onto the Set is an ongoing study in film, TV and commercial work and students will meet casting directors. "Parent Training" sessions are a bonus. Discounted photo shoots are available. Class size is limited, reasonably priced with credit card options. Ninety percent of our students get representation and work in the Industry. SEE AD ON PAGES 1 & 43.

CONSERVATORY OF PERFORMING ARTS
L.A. UNIFIED SCHOOL DISTRICT **(213) 241-6500**

The Saturday Conservatory offers a unique venue that will effectively provide the serious student with a broad exposure to the performing arts, the discipline required, and the opportunity to develop excellence through performance skill. This program is free to children in third grade and above who attend L.A. Unified Schools. Three areas of the performing arts are covered dance, singing, and theatre with an emphasis on acting. The program is held on the campus of Cal State L.A. on Saturdays, 9 am to 1 pm. Call the above number for information.

CLAIRE CORFF **(323) 969-0565**
www.corffvoice.com

Speaking, singing, and confidence. Provides a fun, safe, and complete vocal technique, following the Bob Corff Voice Method. For children of all ages. SEE AD ON PAGE 90.

DEVOROAH CUTLER-RUBENSTEIN
NOBLE HOUSE ENTERTAINMENT (310) 943-4378
12210 1/2 Nebraska Ave., Ste. 22
Los Angeles 90025
www.thescriptbroker.com
devo@thescriptbroker.com

Ms. Cutler-Rubinstein, has an excellent track record developing those special gifts and unique qualities that will set yourself or your child apart from the brat pack. 20 years experience as a private coach with ongoing classes and having produced, directed, written and acted in movies, television and theatre as well as being an executive at Columbia Pictures Television, make her uniquely qualified to address any craft or career issue for the young actor. Her experience includes working with young actors through the audition process and accompanying them as a coach/guardian on the set. Conducts one showcase for young actors annually or available to direct your showcase. "A vibrant innovative director and an inspired acting coach for young people." Jennie Lew Tugend, Producer, "Free Willy"

SONIA DARMEI-LOPES (310) 358-5942
www.screenactorsstudio.com
sonia@screenactorsstucio.com

On-camera acting classes are taught in a positive and caring environment. Students appear in numerous projects including "Malcolm in the Middle," "The Division," "The Guiding Light," "Even Stevens," etc. Private coaching.

JACKY DE HAVILAND (323) 691-7077
jdh@sbcglobal.net

Private coaching for new actors and experienced performers covering scene study and monologues, improv, cold reading, character study, Shakespeare, audition techniques: whatever the individual actor needs to improve, polish or gain confidence in. Jacky de Haviland has been directing and coaching actors for 20 years, acting for 35 and is an extremely committed, caring director/teacher thoroughly invested in the success of her actors. Auditing is allowed. Private coaching. Experienced with children.

DEL MAR MEDIA ARTS (949) 753-0570
15375 Barranca Pkwy., # J-105 FAX (949) 753-0576
Irvine 92618
www.delmarmediaarts.com

Offers a 6 week course that covers camera work, cold reading, and auditioning skills. SAG agents attend last two sessions. Children and adults. Also offers classes in voice-over, spokesperson (wireless ear prompter/TelePropTer) animation, narration and audio books. Monthly free open-house seminars. State licensed and approved. See listing under VOICE OVERS and AUDIO DEMO PRODUCTION for further information. SEE AD ON PAGE 67.

DEBBIE DEVINE (818) 989-7655
www.24thstreet.org
gloriustheatre@earthlink.org

Creative dramatic workshops and private on-set coaching is offered for children. See listing under ACTING in this section for further information.

DISHU ARTS CONNECTION (818) 755-0049
5051 Lankershim Blvd.
North Hollywood 91602

Teaches children age 8-12 improvisation and acting for theatre, commercial, TV and movies.

EAST WEST PLAYERS (213) 625-7000
120 North Judge John Asio
Los Angeles 90012
www.eastwestplayers.org

Acting classes for beg-pro level actors of all ages including fundamentals of acting and scene study.

EDGEMAR CENTER FOR THE ARTS (310) 399-3666
2437 Main St. FAX (310) 399-2898
Santa Monica 90405
www.edgemarcenter.org
paxjava@hotmail.com

Workshops for kids and teens: intro to on-camera cold reading. Courses are designed for students who are new to being on camera and who want to further develop their basic audition skills working with sides from commercials, film, and television. 8 week courses throughout the year.

FAUNT SCHOOL OF CREATIVE MUSIC (818) 506-6873
12725 Ventura Blvd., Ste. G FAX (818) 508-0429
Studio City 91604
www.musicalskills.com

Lessons are offered for all musical instruments including voice. See listing under MUSIC LESSONS in this section for further information.

J.D. FERRANTINO'S KIDS & TEENS (310) 358-5942
www.screenactorsstudio.com

Sonia and J.D. are professional actors in TV, film and theatre and have coached hundreds of kids, many of whom have gone on to work professionally. They turn the creative potential of the individual student into successful auditions. Beginner, intermediate and advanced commercial and theatrical classes all include on-camera work. There is also a kids and teens theatrical class for professional working actors and a Tiny Tots class for ages 4-6 yrs. Private coaching and adult classes are available.

MEGAN FOLEY (818) 216-9350
11340 Moorpark Ave.
Studio City 91602

One day intensive for children age 4 and up. On-camera commercial workshop.

MARLA GAM-HUDSON
THE LOST ACTOR'S WORKSHOP (714) 771-5436
461 N. Citrus Ave. FAX (714) 289-1906
Orange 92868

Two classes are offered: Introduction to Theatre for age 7-15, with a class limit of 12, and Musical Theatre Workshop, beg-adv for age 7-15, with a class limit of 16. Guest artists are brought in to teach on occasion. An interview is required and private coaching is available.

THE WILL GEER
THEATRICUM BOTANICUM (310) 455-2322
P.O. Box 1222 FAX (310) 455-3724
Topanga 90290
www.theatricum.com
theatricum@earthlink.net

Acting, singing, and theatre games with an emphasis on classical technique. A summer youth drama program is available for kids age 8-14 and there is also a separate program for high school students. The classes work on monologues, scene study, movement, and voice training. Also a fall program for children 8-14 for playwriting and performance class. Young people's camp for ages 5-7 designed to introduce children to the imaginative world of theatre.

ELLEN GERSTEIN (323) 852-0276

Have fun while learning your craft. Ellen Gerstein is a writer/producer/director/actress as well as a teacher and coach. Small professional classes for beginning through advanced levels cover exercise work, technique, improvisation, cold readings, auditions and script analysis. Ms. Gerstein uses a technique that focuses on being very specific in your work and the audition technique focuses on what it takes to get the job. Students work every week and receive individual attention. Guest speakers on occasion. Private coaching is available. Ellen Gerstein is a member of the Actors Studio. See listing under ACTING in this section for further information. SEE AD ON PAGE 8.

GOSCH PRODUCTIONS (818) 729-0000
2227 W. Olive Ave.
Burbank 91506
www.goschproductions.com
info@goschproductions.com

Taught by working director Pat Gosch for beginning to advanced actors. Scene work, comedy and improv as well as a class for children and parents where parents count. Parents are invited to the children's classes for ages 7-18. Audition preferred, auditing is allowed. Private coaching as well.

MARY GROVER, M.A. (818) 787-7664
SINGING TRAINING VOICE THERAPY (800) 787-7731
www.marygrover.com FAX (818) 780-0698
marygrover@aol.com

Singing teacher and medical board licensed singing voice therapist Mary Grover teaches vocal technique, healthy belting, song interpretation, and voice therapy (medical insurance accepted). Polish and perform for the Industry. Individual lessons, on-camera performance, and showcases. Improve audition and performance techniques. Currently on faculty of Los Angeles City College and Pierce College, also guest lecturer at USC and a former faculty member at CSUN, Cal Arts, and UCLA Extension. SEE AD ON PAGE 93.

MARLON HOFFMAN
ACTORS INSTITUTE (818) 878-0242

Marlon Hoffman has taught creative acting classes and summer camps to children age 7-17 for over 20 years. He also works with after school enrichment programs. He and his staff provide a safe, compassionate environment for children focusing on the skills necessary to become an actor and emphasizing imagination and personal growth in the process. Monologue and scene classes as well as one and two week summer camps are offered in Calabasas and North Hollywood. He also offers one week acting camps during winter and spring holiday breaks. Mr. Hoffman is available for all Enrichment programs. Call to request a brochure. SEE AD ON PAGE 23.

HOLLYWOOD ACTORS STUDIO (323) 460-2580
(877) 591-5400
www.actingconnection.com
actorsstudio@actingconnection.com

Eric Stone offers weekly classes and private study and weekend workshops which include cold reading, scene study, improv, commercials, voice-over character development and performance skills for aspiring actors to professional levels including star level. These classes are highly focused on the individual with particular emphasis given to self expression, creativity and getting in touch with feelings as well as self expression, confidence, relaxation, listening, relating, awareness, imagination and concentration. Ongoing classes for adults, teens and children as well as weekend workshops and career seminars on the business of acting for adults, children and teens. Monthly performance series showcase with invited Industry professionals.

HULL ACTORS STUDIO
LORRIE HULL, PH.D. & DIANNE HULL (310) 828-0632
Santa Monica
www.actors-studio.com/hull
hullwshop@hotmail.com

Teaches acting for teens and private coaching for children of all ages. Relaxation, sense awareness, exercises, improv, theatre games, and film work are covered in classes or private coaching. Dianne Hull is a professional actress whose credits include "The Wonder Years," "The New Adventures of Pippi Longstocking," "Highway to Heaven," and "The Arrangement" by Elia Kazan. Lorrie has taught for Lee Strasberg and at colleges and seminars worldwide and is also an author of acting textbooks and video tapes. Private lessons and coaching available daily. See listing under ACTING in this section for further information.

THE JOY THEATRE **(818) 505-9355**
The Raven Playhouse
5233 Lankershim Blvd.
North Hollywood 91601
www.joytheatre.com

Children's community theatre with classes in improv, sketch comedy, standup, and characters.

KIDS ON STAGE **(310) 314-0035**
P.O. Box 3664
Santa Monica 90408
www.kidsonstage.com
kidsonstagela@verizon.net

Classes in acting, movement and music are offered for beg-adv children age 4-16, and are divided into age appropriate groups. The program is designed to enhance self confidence, self esteem, and the natural creative abilities of the students. The class emphasizes student participation in all aspects of theatrical production, such as writing scripts, improv, building props, and directing scenes. The students learn how to interpret scripts, study concentration techniques, and practice proper dialogue delivery. Ask about classes, summer camps, and birthday parties.

THE KIDZ KOACH **(818) 347-5098**
22647 Ventura Blvd., #422 **FAX (818) 347-5099**
Woodland Hills 91364
www.comedynorth.com
barb@funnycoach.com

Barb North offers one-on-one private sessions and small group classes that include acting, improv, audition technique, cold reading, comedy and navigating your way through the business. She also coaches parents to help their kids with auditions, cold reading and understanding the biz. Parents may sit in. Phone interview required. Over 25 years experience.

L.A. CONNECTION **(818) 784-1868**
13442 Ventura Blvd. **FAX (818) 710-8666**
Sherman Oaks 91423
www.laconnectionscomedy.com
madmovies@hotmail.com

A comedy improv group for kids age 5-14 and 11-18. Weekly rehearsal and performance on Saturday and Sunday. Kids also make 25% on box office and have been seen on CBS, CNN, Nickelodeon and the Disney Channel. See listing under COMEDY/IMPROV in this section for further information.

BEVERLY LONG, CASTING DIRECTOR **(818) 754-6222**
11425 Moorpark St. **FAX (818) 754-6226**
Studio City 91602
www.berverlylong-casting.com
info@beverlylong-casting.com

Offers on-camera commercial, improv, TV, film and voice-over classes. There are two groups age 5-11 and 12-17. The classes are limited to 12 students and are for beginners and advanced students. An 8 week time commitment is required. Parents review a tape of the class at the end of each session. Agents attend the class at least once every 8 weeks. Private coaching is available. SEE AD ON PAGE 65.

AMY LYNDON ACTING CLASSES **(818) 760-8501**
www.coldreadingclasses.com

Specializes in actors of all ages who are just starting out and enjoys taking people from scratch and watching them learn the craft of acting and book jobs within a year. Thomas Garner teaches the Intro to the 15 Guidelines in an 8-week Technique Class. The focus is on discipline, respect for the work, extreme specifics, breaking down the scene into three parts, understanding the emotional transitions and putting their own special "spin" on the work. This technique separates the actor from the masses and puts them in the 1% callback/booking category.

TRACY MARTIN
KOACHING KIDS & TEENS **(818) 752-8487**
mstracyco@aol.com **FAX (818) 752-8082**

Ms. Martin is an actress, singer and voice over artist who has been working with and teaching kids for over 10 years. She holds a BFA from NYU's Tish School of the Arts. Since her opening in January 1998, Tracy's students have appeared as series regulars, guest stars, co-stars and leads in TV shows and film. Students have also booked many national and regional commercials. She works with each child individually at whatever level they are at and helps them to be confident when they walk into the audition room. Eight-week audition technique class, private lessons and audition coaching are available for children 5 and up. Ms. Martin holds voice over workshops 4 times per year. All sessions are held in Toluca Lake, "My students work and are real and natural."

STEVEN MEMEL STUDIO **(818) 789-0474**
4760 Halbrent Ave. **FAX (818) 789-0835**
Sherman Oaks 91403

Fun, skill and professionalism are emphasized at the Steven Memel Studio for Voice and Vocal Performance. Your child or teen will learn the same skills the pros learn, but in a way that will make them hungry for more. There are no rigid impositions from the outside and Steven brings out the best in your child while bringing out the joy of the art from the inside. The result is a self-motivated artistic discipline. Areas covered include vocal technique, audition prep, performance technique, movement and gesture, choosing material, working with an accompanist, speech and more. All levels: private lessons, on-camera workshops and showcases. Demo and video production. Credits include: Head of Voice for the Hollywood Acting Workshop, an international training organization for performers; former Head of Voice for the L.A. County High School for the Performing Arts; guest instructor for the Southern California Children's Theater; guest lecturer at USC and UCLA Extension. Clients include SONY E.A.R. Music and Jive Records.

ORANGE COUNTY
COMMERCIAL ACTING WORKSHOP **(714) 832-1895**
222 W. Main St., #201
Tustin 92780
www.occaw.com

Private coaching all year for children starting age 7 and up. See listing under COMMERCIAL training in this section for further information.

MARLENE PEROUTKA ACTING WORKSHOPS **(714) 965-6771**
18910 Mt. Castile Circle
Fountain Valley 92708
showbizpitt@aol.com

Personal manager and television producer Marlene Peroutka and her staff teach three levels of classes for children and teens: beginner, intermediate and advanced. Sessions include a seminar for parents on surviving the Industry. Marlene Peroutka Acting Workshop students have appeared in hundreds of TV shows, feature films and commercials. Intermediate and advanced class placement is by audition or by permission of the instructor. Marlene's workshops are highly recommended by agencies and casting directors. Private coaching also available.

PROFESSIONAL SCHOOL FOR THE ARTS **(310) 328-SONG** **(310) 328-7664**
1329 Sartori Ave. **FAX (310) 782-2072**
Torrance 90501
www.psarts.com

Offers classes in singing, dance, acting, and voice for children starting at age 6. See listing under ACTING in this section for further information.

PROMENADE ACTING CONSERVATORY **(310) 656-8070**
1404 Third Street Promenade **FAX (310) 656-8069**
Santa Monica 90401
www.pierodusa.com
info@pierodusa.com

Saturday classes in the established Sanford Meisner technique, auditioning for film and TV, commercial auditioning technique, fundamentals of improvisation, scene work, tools for once the job is booked, and a final presentation at the end of every semester. SEE AD ON PAGES 21 & 297.

REEL KIDS MARGIE HABER **(310) 854-0870**
971 N. La Cienega Blvd., Ste. 207
Los Angeles 90069
www.margiehaber.com

Reel Kids is an on-camera acting workshop designed for young people that focuses on the audition process for film and television. Students learn how to: have fun with their auditions, use their imagination to create a character, bring their own feelings and experiences into their work and go after what they want in a scene. Kids are encouraged to come from the truth. Students learn a very specific audition technique and work on camera each week. Class size is limited to 12 students. Ages 8-18. Sunday classes.

REEL PROS 2/THE WORKSHOPS FOR YOUNG PROFESSIONAL TALENT **(818) 788-4133**
13437 Ventura Blvd., #220
Sherman Oaks 91423
www.reelpros.com
support@reelpros.com

A Saturday workshop for young professional children who are able to read without help and can be left for an hour and a half without their parents. See listing under COLD READING for further information.

ALEXIA ROBINSON STUDIOS **(818) 779-1119**
4930 Lankershim Blvd.
North Hollywood 91601
www.alexiarobinsonstudio.com
imaginears@aol.com

Alexia Robinson Studio is a Los Angeles area acting studio for adults and kids that provides ongoing scene study classes, on-camera commercial workshops, audition technique and cold reading classes. All classes are taught by working professionals with extensive film, television and commercial credits. Classes are taught in a supportive and nurturing environment where actors can learn, grow and perfect their craft.

SANTA MONICA PLAYHOUSE **(310) 394-9779**
1211 4th St. **FAX (310) 393-5573**
Santa Monica 90401
www.santamonicaplayhouse.com
smp@primenet.com

After school and summer classes covering live performance and audition techniques, musical comedy, improvisation, body movement and voice, writing, costume and make-up design and performance art for children 6-16 and 13-17. Alumni include Kate Hudson, Zooey Deschanel, Rita Mimoun, Keith Coogan, Jason Ritter and Monet Mazur. For fee and interview appointment, contact Education Director Cammy Truong.

THE SCENE STEALERS **(818) 763-4431**
10944 Ventura Blvd.
Studio City 91604

Directors: Dorothy Barrett and Cathy Wilkinson. Classes in acting, ballet, tap, and jazz are offered for children age 3-7. $40 per month.

THE SECOND CITY **(323) 658-8190**
8156 Melrose Ave.
Los Angeles 90046
www.secondcity.com/training/la

For over 45 years, The Second City has been one of the most influential theatres in the country, turning out some of the world's most beloved actors. Second City has launched hundreds of artists whose careers have changed the face of television, film and theatre with alumni in the current casts of Mad TV, Saturday Night Live and Curb Your Enthusiasm to name a few. A sample of programs offered at The Second City Training Center include Beginning Improvisation, Improv for Actors, Sketch or Sitcom Writing, Musical Improv and the Conservatory Program. Also classes for children and teens.

SECRET ROSE THEATRE **(818) 766-3691 x4**
11246 Magnolia Blvd. **FAX (818) 766-3691**
North Hollywood 91601
www.secretrose.com
kaz@secretrose.com

The Secret Rose Theatre offers basic acting technique for ages 8 to 12 and creative "Funshops" for ages 4-7. Through improv and theatre games children explore and create stories and characters, develop self esteem and confidence, use their imaginations and have fun while learning the basics of acting technique. The last class is a performance, and agents and casting directors are invited. SEE AD ON PAGE 19.

SCOTT SEDITA ACTING STUDIOS (323) 465-6152
526 N. Larchmont Blvd. FAX (323) 465-6202
Los Angeles 90004
www.scottseditaacting.com

Jorge Luis-Pallo and Elizabeth Bauman teach on-camera TV and film acting class, speech and voice, scene study and on-camera cold reading for teens and kids.

SOUTH COAST REPERTORY YOUNG CONSERVATORY (714) 708-5510
P.O. Box 2197 FAX (714) 545-0391
655 Town Center Dr.
Costa Mesa 92626
www.scr.org
education@scr.org

Director: Laurie Woolery. Faculty includes: Steve DeNaut, Carrie Gifford, Andrew Levy, Hisa Takakuwa, Patrick Williams, Logan Sledge and Ashley Ward. Offers a 4-year program for children 8-17 designed to build self-confidence while fostering an appreciation for the art of theatre. Sessions are held in fall, winter and spring with an introductory Summer Theatre Workshop offered to new students. Classes cover movement, improv, scene/play performance, speech and Shakespeare. Call for a brochure or more information.

AARON SPEISER ACTING STUDIO (310) 399-4567
1644 S. La Cienega Blvd.
Los Angeles 90035
www.aaronspeiser.com

A comprehensive approach to help young actors. Preparation is where confidence is built and creativity is freed. Through analysis of the character and breakdown of the scene, the class helps young actors sharpen audition skills, make strong choices, understand direction and adjustments, relax and gain confidence, while creating unique and believable characters. SEE AD ON PAGE 17.

THE LEE STRASBERG THEATRE INSTITUTE (323) 650-7777
7936 Santa Monica Blvd.
Los Angeles 90046
www.strasberg.com

Creative training for young people age 7-17 is offered with classes in acting, film, TV, and dance. Plays and productions are performed at the end of every 12 week session. Acceptance to the Institute is by interview only. See listing under ACTING in this section for further information.

TEPPER/GALLEGOS (323) 469-3577
639 N. Larchmont Blvd., # 207 FAX (323) 464-8230
Los Angeles 90004

Offers an on-camera commercial workshop for children that covers audition technique, character analysis, cold reading, cue cards, and interview technique. These 5 week classes are limited to 16, age 6-17, and are divided by age. Students work in every class. No audition or interview is required and no auditing is allowed. You are invited to stop by and see the studio.

BLANCA VALDEZ (323) 876-5700
1001 N. Pointsettia Pl.
Hollywood 90046
www.blancavaldez.com
bvaldez@msn.com

Teaches commercial workshops and voice-over classes in Spanish for children, age 5 through adult.

VOCAL POWER SCHOOL (818) 895-7464
(800) 929-7464
www.vocalpower.com
musicman@borntosing.com

Private coaching in singing and acting for ages 5 and up. Includes singing and song presentation, monologues, commercial copy, stand-up comedy, dialogues, voice-over, voice strengthening, accent reduction and some dialect work. Train under the guidance of Vocal Power director, Howard Austin. Ten Star Search winners including International Junior Grand Champion and eight Broadway leads, quarter finalist on "American Idol" and three "Miss Saigon" title role leads. Also available are self improvement courses, "Born To Sing" on DVD, video, CDs, tapes and books.

VOICES VOICECASTING VOICEOVER WORKSHOP (818) 980-8460
10523 Burbank Blvd., Ste. 202
North Hollywood 91601
www.voicesvoicecasting.com

One day (10 am-1 pm) Saturday seminars in February, March, May, August, October. Teaches your child the basics of voiceover technique: how to breakdown and interpret copy, character development for commercial and animation, and self direction.

DEBRA WATSON (310) 500-6727
Beverly Hills
www.yellowrosesproductions.com

Private coaching specializing in teaching the young actor how to use their natural instincts, which is key in keeping the work real. Basic cold reading and audition techniques that help the student understand how to tackle a role. Children and teenagers have limited life experiences to draw on and also process information differently from adults. Debra recognizes each young actor as an individual and adjusts her lessons according to the age and level of each student.

WEIST-BARRON-HILL (818) 846-5595
4300 W. Magnolia Blvd.
Burbank 91505
www.weistbarronhillacting.com

Workshops for children and teens are offered in commercial and film acting. These on-camera workshops are held on Saturdays for 8 weeks at $250. Students work in every class. Auditing is allowed at no cost. Private coaching is available.

DAVID WELLS STUDIO (818) 753-5393
12500 Riverside Dr., #211 FAX (818) 753-8056
Studio City 91607
www.westendactingstudio.com

Ongoing classes are offered in acting, cold reading, and audition technique. See listing under ACTING in this section for further information.

Children's Training

YOUNG ACTORS SPACE (818) 785-7979
5918 Van Nuys Blvd.
Van Nuys 91401
www.youngactorsspace.com

Classes are offered for children from age 4 through adult and cover improv and scene study, as well as audition and interview skills. No audition or interview is required.

YOUNG VOICES (323) 651-1666

A professional voice-over training class for performers 7-17 years old that incorporates TV and radio commercials, animation, improvisation, theatre games, and technical exercises to create a truly marketable craft. Classes are taught by casting director Alison Stuart (Academy Award Winning animated short "The ChubbChubbs!", Cartoon Network's animated series "SD Gundam Force", commercials, etc.) and director/actor Rick Zieff (hundreds of commercials, TV shows, video games, industrials, etc.)

Classical Training

ACTORS CIRCLE THEATRE SCHOOL (323) 882-6805
7313 Santa Monica Blvd.
West Hollywood 90046

Classes are offered weekly in Shakespeare and period/style movement. SEE AD ON PAGE 3.

STELLA ADLER ACADEMY OF ACTING AND THEATRE COMPLEX (323) 465-4446
6773 Hollywood Blvd., 2nd Fl. FAX (323) 469-6049
Hollywood 90028
www.stellaadler-la.com

Academy director, Irene Gilbert. Call for catalogue and further information. SEE AD ON PAGE 6.

BB'S KIDS (323) 650-KIDS
www.bbskids.com
bbs4kids@aol.com

This 8 week class breaks down and makes accessible the work and fun of Shakespeare with Orlando Seale who studied at the Royal Shakespeare Company in London working with "Hamlet's" Kenneth Brannaugh among others. Utilizing scene study and character work, actors will learn how to approach some of the greatest plays in the world. Performing both soliloquies and scenes, students will discover how rewarding, challenging and fun Shakespeare can be. Class will graduate live and on tape. 12 years and up. SEE AD ON PAGE 41.

VINCENT CHASE (323) 851-4819
7721 Sunset Blvd. FAX (323) 851-9942
Los Angeles 90046

See listing under ACTING in this section for further information.

ANTHONY DI NOVI (310) 490-4761
anthonydinovi@earthlink.net

Private sessions and workshops on line analysis and classical technique for Shakespeare and classical roles.

ROBERT ELLENSTEIN (323) 464-8542
www.larep.org

Robert Ellenstein teaches a Shakespeare class designed to create real characters while expressing the beauty of the language. See listing for Los Angeles Repertory Company for further information.

PROFESSOR LOUIS FANTASIA (213) 383-0648
4221 W. 6th St. FAX (213) 383-1430
Los Angeles 90020

Teaches Shakespeare. These small classes are limited to 8 students and an interview is required. Private coaching is available. Professor Fantasia is an experienced director, actor, and education director of the Shakespeare Globe Center and author of "Instant Shakespeare." See listing in the MARKETING section under BOOKS AND TAPES.

GEOFFREY FORWARD (310) 455-9715
www.shakespeare-usa.com
spchmaftr@earthlink.net

Offers instruction in line analysis and monologues for Shakespearean roles and scene work with an emphasis on voice production, body awareness, and the natural quality of character movement. Private lessons and small classes are available. Mr. Forward is a former instructor at the American Academy of Dramatic Arts, a Shakespearean scholar for the Huntington Library, and is currently the artistic director for the L.A. Shakespeare Company.

THE WILL GEER THEATRICUM BOTANICUM (310) 455-2322
P.O. Box 1222 FAX (310) 455-3724
Topanga 90290
www.theatricum.com
theatricum@earthlink.net

Offers a Shakespeare workshop which includes monologues, scene study, movement, stage combat, voice, scansion, and mime with the emphasis on classical technique. The class limit is 15-17 students. An interview is required for all classes and an audition for the master class.

GLOBE PLAYHOUSE
R. THAD TAYLOR (323) 654-5623
1107 N. Kings Rd. FAX (323) 654-5627
West Hollywood 90069
www.shakespearesocamerica.com

Performs Shakespeare, other classics, and some original material. An audition and an interview are required. Send photo and resume for audition appointment.

HULL ACTORS STUDIO
LORRIE HULL PH.D. & DIANNE HULL (310) 828-0632
Santa Monica
www.actors-studio.com/hull
hullwshop@hotmail.com

Private coaching and lessons available daily. See listing under ACTING in this section for further information.

LOS ANGELES
WOMEN'S SHAKESPEARE COMPANY (310) 453-5069
1158 26th St., #399
Santa Monica 90403
www.lawsc.net

An all female Shakespeare company that offers workshops in voice, text, clowning, and stage combat. 10 three-hour sessions over a five week period. Individual instruction is available. The company produces 2 professional productions each year.

ERIC MORRIS ACTORS WORKSHOP (323) 466-9250
5657 Wilshire Blvd., Ste. 110
Los Angeles 90036
www.ericmorris.com

Mr. Morris deals with classical material from the Renaissance period, Shakespeare, etc. and uses his own technique in this ongoing class. He also covers audition technique, character analysis, film technique, improv, interview technique, monologues, sensory work, and scene study. His approach is based on Stanislavski, however has gone light years beyond the original system. In addition to regular weekly classes, he also offers an intensive that meets one weekend per month, 4 three day weekend workshops at the UCLA Conference Center in Lake Arrowhead and one six day workshop. He offers private coaching sessions as does his wife Susana Morris. Students work in every class, the limit is 20 students. Auditing is allowed and is followed by an interview. Mr. Morris has written numerous books on acting. SEE AD ON PAGE 13.

CLIFF OSMOND (310) 393-6022
1526 14th St., Ste. 107
Santa Monica 91403
www.cliffosmond.com

See listing under ACTING in this section for further information.

PROMENADE
ACTING CONSERVATORY (310) 656-8070
1404 Third Street Promenade FAX (310) 656-8069
Santa Monica 90401
www.pierodusa.com
info@pierodusa.com

Focuses on developing the actor in period text, language, movement, voice, speech, and the emotional tools necessary for bringing such work to life. Courses are included in the Piero Dusa Acting Conservatory 3-year acting program based on the Masters of American Theatre: Meisner, Adler, Strasberg and Dusa's trademark technique, Character Preference. Third year students focus on performances that include works by Chekhov, Ibsen and Shakespeare as well as contemporary one acts and full length plays. Course prerequisites, interview and audition required. SEE AD ON PAGES 21 & 297.

PATRICIA SHANKS (949) 723-4473
www.studioshanks.com
pshanks@studioshanks.com

A private studio facility offering voice instruction and musicianship training for singers ages 12 and over, beginning through advanced. The focus is traditional, educational, foundation-based and fine arts-oriented. Establish a reliable technique and eliminate externally applied cosmetic affectations related to technique (voice production) and performance (presentation). Newport Beach. 28 years experience. Member: NATS, MTAC, AGMA, SCVA.

THE LEE STRASBERG
THEATRE INSTITUTE (323) 650-7777
7936 Santa Monica Blvd.
Los Angeles 90046
www.strasberg.com
admissionsla@strasberg.com

See listing under ACTING in this section for further information.

MARJORY TAYLOR PH.D, ED.D (310) 246-1743
marjorytaylor@netzero.net

Marjory Taylor, Ph.D., Ed.D offers training for Shakespeare and the classical voice. See listing under SPEECH in this section for additional information.

UNIVERSITY OF CALIFORNIA
LOS ANGELES (UCLA) (310) 825-4321
405 Hilgard Ave.
Los Angeles 90024
www.ucla.edu

See listing under ACTING in this section for further information.

UNIVERSITY
OF SOUTHERN CALIFORNIA (USC) (213) 821-2744
University Park
Los Angeles 90089
www.usc.edu

Call for a current catalog.

JUDITH WESTON ACTING STUDIO (310) 392-2444
3402 Motor Ave.
Los Angeles 90034
www.judithweston.com
judyweston@aol.com

Offers a Shakespeare workout for actors and other artists. See listing under ACTING in this section for further information.

ACT NOW! **(818) 285-8522**
14140 Ventura Blvd., Ste. 2
Sherman Oaks 91423
www.actnownetwork.com
actnow4u@aol.com

Act Now! is a networking company that was established with intention of helping actors further their careers, by meeting and performing for Industry professionals including casting directors, directors and agents. Staff provides ongoing guidance and support to help each actor set and meet their professional goals. Audition required.

THE ACTOR'S LAB **(310) 621-3900**
at the Odyssey Theatre
2055 South Sepulveda Blvd.
Los Angeles 90048
www.theactorslab.com
theactorslab@aol.com

Classes in cold reading are conducted by J.D. Lewis. See listing under ACTING for further information.

ACTOR'S SANCTUARY **(818) 506-6194**

Cold reading class that also offers scene study, monologue, and audition technique. Affordable rates. Evening classes. Free audits offered. Also offering private coaching.

ACTORS WORKOUT STUDIO **(818) 766-2171**
4735 Lankershim Blvd.
North Hollywood 91602
www.actorsworkout.com
info@actorsworkout.com

Professional acting training with Emmy Award-winning acting coach, Fran Montano. Acting classes covering Meisner Technique, improvisation, scene study, cold reading, acting company, ongoing productions (plays, one acts, showcases, scene nights), and theater rentals.

THE ACTORS WORKSHOP **(949) 855-4444**
23151 Plaza Point Dr., #100 **FAX (949) 844-4444**
Laguna Hills 92653
www.theactorsworkshop.com
info@theactorsworkshop.com

Orange County's oldest actor's workshop is one of L.A.'s most respected training programs. Cold reading classes concentrate on the casting process from casting director to the Producer/Director. Headshot/resume/Industry guidance are provided and sessions are conducted by working film actors. For further information see listing under ACTING in this section.

STELLA ADLER ACADEMY OF ACTING
AND THEATRE COMPLEX **(323) 465-4446**
6773 Hollywood Blvd., 2nd Fl. **FAX (323) 469-6049**
Hollywood 90028
www.stellaadler-la.com

Academy director, Irene Gilbert. Call for catalogue and further information. SEE AD ON PAGE 6.

AIA ACTOR'S STUDIO **(818) 563-4142**
1918 Magnolia Blvd., Ste. 204 **FAX (818) 563-4042**
Burbank 91506
www.aiastudios.com

AIA makes no promise or guarantee of employment. AIA Actor's Studio has spent 14 years helping actors achieve professional excellence and has successfully integrated the business of acting with formal training. AIA offers a wide variety of educational opportunities for actors specializing in daytime, primetime television, film, voice-over and commercial audition techniques as well as continuing to provide classes on such topics as screenwriting, directing, and "how to produce your own independent projects." Classes are taught by some of LA's most knowledgeable instructors who work as casting directors, writers, directors, producers and other active and successful entertainment professionals. AIA's mission is to assist actors in maximizing their creative potential and empower them through education to succeed in a competitive marketplace.

AMERICAN NATIONAL ACADEMY
OF PERFORMING ARTS **(818) 763-4431**
10944 Ventura Blvd.
Studio City 91604

Director: Dorothy Barrett. The Academy offers workshops in cold reading. A non-profit organization chartered by the State of California. See listing under ACTING in this section for further information.

JOEL ASHER STUDIO **(818) 785-1551**
www.joel-asher-studio.com **FAX (818) 785-1902**

A 6 week on-camera class based on the award winning video "Getting The Part" that covers fast scene breakdown, focusing your imagination, intuition, handling scripts, choices, demo reels, call backs, and interviews. The class is limited to 12 actors. Mr. Asher is a DGA director/producer who has been teaching for over 30 years. See listing under ACTING in this section for further information. Also see listing for "Actors At Work" series of videos under BOOKS & TAPES in the MARKETING section for further information. SEE AD ON PAGES 1 & 113.

BB'S KIDS **(323) 650-5437**
www.bbskids.com
bbs4kids@aol.com

This 8 week class is strictly about cold reading skills and instant choices. How to bring yourself into the room and book the job. Put at least 5 characters in your back pocket and be ready for the new season. This is a "hammers and nails" type course for those who want to book. 10 years and up. SEE AD ON PAGE 41.

BERG STUDIO
GREGORY BERGER-SOBECK **(323) 822-0152**
www.thebergstudios.com
bergstudios@sbcglobal.net

Gregory Berger-Sobeck teaches the Yale School of Drama technique which has trained Meryl Streep, Edward Norton, Sigorney Weaver, Liv Schreiber and Frances McDormand, among others. All students are offered very small classes, giving individualized attention. Class covers scene work, commercial and theatrical auditions, on-camera cold reading technique. Periodic Industry showcases, and guest speakers. Classes meet twice a week. Every actor works every class. Mr. Berger-Sobeck has an MFA from Yale and has worked many years in New York as a teacher and private coach. He has numerous Broadway credits as well as credits in film and television. The technique he teaches is a systematic approach for identifying and personalizing the character's driving need and objectives and engaging the actor's voice, body, mind and spirit in its active pursuit. It is a repeatable step by step process ensuring repeatable returns. Mr Berger-Sobeck recently directed an

Industry showcase specifically targeting top casting agents and managers coupled with Daryl Marshak Management which was written up in Back Stage West. He recently was the associate casting director on the new network pilot "Angel Air."

THE PLUS WORKSHOPS
(COLD READING PLUS)
SCOTT BERNSTEIN (323) 692-0298

Total audition preparation workshop. How to read it right off the page without making it look like you're reading. Simulated casting sessions and all aspects of the audition process. These one-on-one classes cost $120 for a 4 week period. Private coaching for auditions and special projects is available for $40 per hour. There are discounts for members of the Workshops or for longer projects. Acting and script study workshops also available. Take two or three workshops for $175 for 4 weeks. Serious minded actors only. Interview required for admittance. Over 20 years experience.

RON BURRUS ACTING STUDIO (323) 953-2823
Los Feliz Playhouse
4646 Hollywood Blvd.
Los Angeles 90027
www.ronburrus.com
ronburrus@earthlink.net

On-camera cold readings once a week for actors with acting technique but lacking camera experience and process for dealing with lack of partner. SEE AD ON PAGE 7.

CRAIG CAMPOBASSO (818) 503-2474
craigcampobasso@aol.com

Craig's affordable on-camera classes cover scene study, audition technique, and character development. They meet once a week in 4 week intervals.

THE CASTING NETWORK
COLD READING/AUDITION WORKSHOP
MARCIA MORAN (818) 788-4792
12500 Riverside Dr., Ste. 202 FAX (818) 980-6924
Studio City 91604
www.castingnetwork.net
castingnetwork@castingnetwork.net

Bringing Industry professionals together since 1988, the Casting Network offers 5-8 showcases per week with top CDs, agents, and occasionally directors/producers. Actors are given cold reading material generally supplied by the guest. Because of the caliber of their guests, professional training and/or theatre experience is a must. Low discount prices available. Call for free mandatory audition and orientation.

JUNE CHANDLER'S
ACTORS WORKSHOP (626) 355-4572
www.junechandler.com
june@junechandler.com

An 8 week on-camera intensive detailing the audition process in every professional medium. The series includes the 'How To' of cold reading technique, script analysis, film, television and industrial auditions, screen-tests, call backs and acting on the set. Two special career classes deal with the business of acting in regards to auditioning. Classes are taught on Sunday at Zydeco Casting in Studio City. Reasonably priced and class size is limited. SEE AD ON PAGES 1 & 43.

JEFF CONAWAY (818) 921-9287

Study with a working professional with 44 years experience and hundreds of credits. Scene study, cold reading, emotional work, moment to moment. Also private coaching.

CAROLE D'ANDREA – A NEW YORK ACTING TEACHER
THE FLIGHT THEATRE (310) 281-7116
6472 Santa Monica Blvd., 2nd Fl.
Los Angeles 90028
www.caroledandrea.com

Uses a technique that includes "being in the moment" by using and accepting present feelings. Improv technique is included with the cold reading work. Among the areas and exercises covered are "condition" or what the character is feeling, "need" or the character's overall objective, and "intention" or what the character is doing. Private coaching is available.

SONIA DARMEI-LOPES (310) 358-5942
www.screenactorsstudio.com
sonia@screenactorsstucio.com

On-camera acting classes are taught in a positive and caring environment. Students appear in numerous projects including "Malcolm in the Middle," "The Division," "The Guiding Light," "Even Stevens," etc. Private coaching.

ANTHONY DI NOVI (818) 490-4761
anthonydinovi@earthlink.net

Private acting coaching to the professional and gifted student. Coaching for specific auditions, character development, and technique for relaxation and concentration to promote creativity and bring forth individual qualities. Meditation, T'ai Chi, and dream work. Also works with writers and directors

GODEANE EAGLE **(310) 450-5735**

Godeane is a vocal coach with a Masters Degree in speech, her B.A. in theatre and her musical training in private coaching. She teaches singing, speaking voice, stage voice and cold reading.

EDGEMAR CENTER FOR THE ARTS **(310) 399-3666**
2437 Main St. **FAX (310) 399-2898**
Santa Monica 90405
www.edgemarcenter.org
paxjava@hotmail.com

Workshops for kids and teens: Intro to on-camera cold reading. Courses are designed for students who are new to being on camera and who want to further develop their basic audition skills working with sides from commercials, film, and television. 8 week courses through out the year. Ages 7-11 and 12-17

ALAN FEINSTEIN/PAUL TUERPE ACTING STUDIO **(323) 650-7766**
13273 Ventura Blvd.
Studio City 91614
www.feinstein-tuerpe.com
alfeinstein@msn.com

Offers an ongoing class in cold reading and on-camera audition technique. See listing under ACTING in this section for further information.

CHERIE FRANKLIN'S REACT & RESPOND **(818) 762-4658**
P.O. Box 5246
North Hollywood 91616-5246
cherolynfranklin@msn.com

Ongoing classes and one-one-one private coaching are offered to prepare the actor for a long-lasting career as well as for those last minute auditions. She also works with the actor to make sure that your best performance ends up on the audition tape. Focus is on teaching the actor to be in control of their talent at every audition, when on set, and to deliver while remaining open to all direction. Ms. Franklin concentrates on cold-reading for sit-coms, episodics, and feature films, as well as teaching actors to instantly deliver the best work, under pressure, while allowing their choices to be strong, clear and simple. Her main goal is to get the actor's "best work up the first time, every time." She has been an on-set dialogue coach for 29 years. Ms. Franklin also teaches at AFI, The International Film School in Rockport, Maine, The SAG Conservatory, Women In Film, FilmSchule in Cologne, Germany and FOCAL in Zurich, Switzerland.

LAURA GARDNER **(323) 957-4764**

Ms. Gardner has over 35 years experience as a teacher/actress/coach. She is on the faculty of the Howard Fine Acting Studio in West Hollywood. Ms. Gardner also offers an audition/interview intensive every few months and trained with Uta Hagen and Carol Rosenfeld. Private sessions are available.

MARGIE HABER **(310) 854-0870**
971 N. La Cienega Blvd., Ste. 207
Los Angeles 90069
www.margiehaber.com

On-camera cold reading workshops for int-pro adults. They are now offering a class called, "An Introduction To Cold Reading" for adults with little professional experience. An interview is required. The class limit is 10-12 students.

DARRYL HICKMAN **(818) 344-5796**
6514 Lankershim Blvd.
North Hollywood 91601
www.actingandyou.com
actingandyou@aol.com

Mr. Hickman teaches a unique, comprehensive approach to the acting process suitable for film, TV and theater. An interview is required and auditing is allowed by appointment only. Classes are limited to 20 students, and students work in every class. The workshop is taught in ten-week, ongoing sessions, and the fee is $500 per session.

SANDY HOLT ON-CAMERA & COLD READING & IMPROV WORKSHOP **(310) 271-8217**

Sandy Holt, a Second City Alum, is an acting coach and voice casting director. Sandy casts for major studios including Disney, Dreamworks, Warner Bros., etc. She offers private coaching on-camera/cold reading/improv for film and TV talent. Sandy coaches you to: take charge at auditions; stay focused under pressure; get out of your head; create original characters; and know what is special about you and use it. SEE AD ON PAGE 51.

HULL ACTORS STUDIO
LORRIE HULL, PH.D. & DIANNE HULL **(310) 828-0632**
Santa Monica and West L.A.
www.actors-studio.com
hullwshop@hotmail.com

Cold readings are an important part of all classes. Private coaching is available daily, with guest casting directors periodically involved. Students are encouraged to bring audition sides to class for individual coaching and audition techniques are stressed. All agents, casting people, and other Industry people are personally invited free of charge. Taught by Lorrie Hull, Ph.D. and Dianne Hull, actress for Elia Kazan for film and stage. See listing under ACTING in this section for further information.

KIMBERLY JENTZEN
LIVING THE ARTS INSTITUTE **(818) 779 7770**
P.O. Box 4554 **FAX (818) 779-1171**
Valley Village 91617
www.kimberlyjentzen.net
filmactors@aol.com

Jentzen holds frequent cold reading weekend intensives with a maximum of 10 actors per workshop ensuring much individual attention. Focus is on zeroing in on the actor's consistency and empowering the actor in auditions, cold reading technique and much, much more. Interview required. Over 18 years teaching. SEE AD ON PAGE 1.

THE ANITA JESSE STUDIO **(323) 876-2870**
Gardner Stage
www.anitajessestudio.com

Ongoing training in cold reading skills, including on-camera work. See listing under ACTING in this section for further information. SEE AD ON PAGE 15.

CANDY KANIECKI (818) 753-5393
AKA HERMAN (310) 656-7731
c/o West End Studios FAX (818) 753-8056
12500 Riverside Dr., Ste. 21104
Studio City 91604
www.westendactingstudio.com

Ms. Kaniecki prefers to speak directly with potential students regarding her on-going acting/audition classes. Private coaching also available.

JANICE KENT (818) 906-2201
FAX (818) 906-2974

With more than 30 years of experience as an actor, director and coach, Kent has designed her "life coaching" approach to aid the actor in understanding and identifying the fears and processes that block making risky choices. Her combination of Meisner, Adler and Spolin improvisation techniques, experience and heart encourage confidence with growth in skills. Students are currently appearing as series regulars and in films. Kent offers private coaching, ongoing classes and periodic sitcom intensive workshops four times a year. SEE AD ON PAGE 12.

JUDY KERR'S ACTING WORKSHOP (818) 505-9373
www.actingiseverything.com
judykerr@mindspring.com

A film and television acting coach and the dialogue coach on "Seinfeld" and "All About The Andersons." Audition techniques are taught on-camera privately, beginners are welcomed. Actors keep a videotape record of their work as well as Judy's comments and instructions, and she supplies sides for roles you could be cast for. She is also the author of the best selling book "Acting is Everything: An Actor's Guidebook for a Successful Career in Los Angeles." Career coaching is also available. Visit the website for more information and a sample of her book.

DAPHNE KIRBY ACTING WORKSHOPS (818) 769-9709
www.daphnekirby.com
daphnekirby@earthlink.net

For the past 18 years Kirby has been an acting coach and caster in Los Angeles. Her classes are referred regularly by agents, and casting directors. Currently, she has combined highly effective cold-reading techniques with expertise gained booking over 100 TV spots into a 6 week on-camera intensive designed to give actors a competitive edge in booking commercials. Open to trained actors only, this weekly class refines skills needed to break through the barriers that sabotage actors during the audition process. Covered: mastering copy, commercial improv technique, nailing callbacks, delivering what the advertising agency wants, successful marketing strategies including fine tuning your look for camera and helping with confidence. She has had great success in turning auditioners into bookers. Class size is limited to 18. Classes meet weekly from 7-10 pm in the Studio City area. Additional information is available in Larry Silverberg's book "The Actor's Guide To Qualified Acting Coaches In Los Angeles."

DAVID LEHMAN (818) 845-1549

Two levels of classes are offered, covering on-camera work and cold reading. There is a monthly time commitment.

M.K. LEWIS WORKSHOPS (310) 826-8118
(310) 394-2511
1513 6th St., Ste. 203 FAX (310) 826-6966
Santa Monica 90401
www.mklewisworkshops.com

A 12 week on-camera workshop. Mr. Lewis, author of the best seller "Your Film Acting Career," teaches a step-by-step approach to cold readings plus how to handle interviews with casting directors, agents, producers, and directors. Class is limited to 12 and auditing is permitted. SEE AD ON PAGE 14.

AMY LYNDON (818) 760-8501
www.coldreadingclasses.com
coldreadingclasses@yahoo.com

Goes beyond cold reading by providing 15 Guidelines to booking. When taken seriously, these guidelines are proven to help get you the callback or book the job. Lyndon has worked for 14 years to continuously help actors book. She understands the business from her own accomplishments as an actor for over 20 years and as a previous owner of a Personal Management Company for eight. Additionally, Lyndon is also a multi-award winning filmmaker and writer with several projects in development. No auditing allowed. Credit cards accepted.

TRACY MARTIN (818) 752-8487
mstracyco@aol.com FAX (818) 752-8082

Ms. Martin is an actress, singer and voice over artist who has been working with and teaching kids for over 10 years. She holds a BFA from NYU's Tish School of the Arts. Since her opening in January 1998, Tracy's students have appeared as series regulars, guest stars, co-stars and leads in TV shows and film. Students have also booked many national and regional commercials. She works with each child individually at whatever level they are at and helps them to be confident when they walk into the audition room. Eight-week audition technique class, private lessons and audition coaching are available for children 5 and up. Ms. Martin holds voice over workshops 4 times per year. All sessions are held in Toluca Lake, "My students work and are real and natural."

MIKE MUSCAT (818) 904-9494

Offers private lessons that cover acting, cold reading, and commercials. He also coaches for auditions and meets with actors for career guidance and advice. He is an acting and dialogue coach for TV and film. Mike was on-set acting coach for "Terminator 2," "My Girl 2," "Last Action Hero" and "Frazier." The only acting coach in town that gives a money back guarantee.

CLIFF OSMOND (310) 393-6022
1526 14th St., Ste. 107
Santa Monica 91403
www.cliffosmond.com

See listing under ACTING in this section for further information.

PERFORMANCE SHOWCASE
THE SIERRA STAGE (213) 368-8070
1444 N. Sierra Bonita
West Hollywood 90046

Showcase in front of top casting directors, agents and managers in an intimate, professional, and supportive atmosphere. They have a reputation of having very talented actors which is reflected in top Industry guests and the amount of actors called in by them. Also offers individual cold reading showcase evenings, prepared scenes, monologues and agent nights. Yearly membership is also available, offering a 50% discount. Call the 24 hour voice mail for more information. Mention the Working Actors Guide for a discount.

MARLENE PEROUTKA ACTING WORKSHOPS **(714) 965-6771**
18910 Mt. Castile Circle
Fountain Valley 92708
showbizpitt@aol.com

Using Marlene Peroutka's own cold reading technique, she and her staff teach three levels of actors: beginner, intermediate and advanced. The sessions include learning Marlene's technique, mastering the technique and applying it to auditions. Intermediate and advanced students often bring in their own audition sides to prepare for upcoming auditions. Advanced students are all working actors in television, film and commercials.

PIMLOTT-MEDINA'S FILM & TV WORKSHOP **(866) 923-3459** **(866) 923-FILM**
955 S. E. St., Ste. F **FAX (909) 884-8904**
San Bernardino 92408
filmtvworkshop@aol.com

Beginning, Intermediate and Advanced acting workshops for adults and teenagers to help expose natural ability, capture auditions with originality, learn on set protocol, and learn Industry terminology. Classes cover cold reading, improvisation, commercials, on-camera movement, overcoming stage fright, and monologues. Management, agent and casting director showcases and Industry consultations. Course audits available.

PROMENADE ACTING CONSERVATORY **(310) 656-8070**
1404 Third Street Promenade **FAX (310) 656-8069**
Santa Monica 90401
www.pierodusa.com
info@pierodusa.com

A complete film and television program which includes auditioning for film and TV, on-camera dynamics and advanced on camera technique, designed to prepare the actor for the basics as well as challenging emotional scenes. The curriculum covers every aspect of film and TV from booking the job to recreating the set environment by putting the actor on tape. Courses cover: cold reading, monologues, scene work, under fives, day players and contract roles. Techniques focus on script analysis, bull's eye of emotional actions, silent reaction breakdown, emotional presets and Dusa's trademark technique, character preference. The advanced class performs live monologues and taped scenes for agents and casting directors, providing representation and networking opportunities. Courses run 12 weeks and require an interview and audition. SEE AD ON PAGES 21 & 297.

REEL PROS THE WORKSHOP FOR PROFESSIONAL TALENT **(818) 788-4133**
13437 Ventura Blvd., Ste. 202
Sherman Oaks 91423
www.reelpros.com
support@reelpros.com

A workshop for professional actors where the actor hones his/her skills through practice in cold readings, taking adjustments, and interacting with top Industry guests (casting directors, directors, etc.) using prepared work. Entry into the workshop is by a very careful audition process. The focus of the workshop is to prepare the actor for successful auditions and to learn how to strategically market themselves. There is a Saturday workshop for young professionals called Reel Pros 2 for children who are able to read without help and can be left for an hour and a half without their parents. Every class is a showcase. Call for calendar.

ALEXIA ROBINSON STUDIOS **(818) 779-1118**
4930 Lankershim Blvd.
North Hollywood 91601
www.alexiarobinsonstudio.com
imaginears@aol.com

Alexia Robinson Studio is a Los Angeles area acting studio for adults and kids that provides ongoing scene study classes, on-camera commercial workshops, audition technique and cold reading classes. All classes are taught by working professionals with extensive film, television and commercial credits. Classes are taught in a supportive and nurturing environment where actors can learn, grow and perfect their craft.

SCOTT SEDITA ACTING STUDIOS **(323) 465-6152**
526 N. Larchmont Blvd. **FAX (323) 465-6202**
Los Angeles 90004
www.scottseditaacting.com

On-camera TV and film acting class, speech and voice, scene study, on-camera cold reading, comedy improv and audition technique. Studio also offers Nuts and Bolts, a comprehensive technique class for beginners for those who wish to brush up on their technique. Classes are offered days, weekends, and weeknights. Kids and teens classes offered as well.

THE SEENWORK COMPANY JEANETTE O'CONNOR **(818) 225-9851**
4735 Lankershim Blvd. **FAX (818) 225-8123**
Universal City 91608
seenwork@aol.com

Offers ongoing cold reading workshops for the professional actor with a different guest speaker each week. Regular nights on Thursdays at 7:30, and occasional Saturday afternoons are scheduled. Union members or Industry referral only. Auditions by appointment. Also will schedule periodic Industry showcases with prepared scenes. This workshop is intended for educational and networking purposes only. Class fees range from $23 and up if there are multiple teachers. Recommended by casting directors, agents and managers.

MARK SIKES **(818) 759-7648**
www.marksikes.com
marksikes@hotmail.com

Offers an ongoing class in cold reading and auditioning for begint teens and adults. Classes are limited to 8. Private sessions available. Auditing is allowed. Critiques are only by the teacher. Sikes is also a Casting Director.

MELISSA SKOFF **(818) 760-2058**
11684 Ventura Blvd., Ste. 5141
Studio City 91604

Offers ongoing advanced level acting classes. Entrance is by audition. Ms. Skoff has cast more than 100 feature films and television shows in both comedy and drama.

AARON SPEISER ACTING STUDIO **(310) 399-4567**
1644 S. La Cienega Blvd.
Los Angeles 90035
www.aaronspeiser.com

This class teaches you how to audition for film and television roles.

This class is set up like a real audition. The actor is given actual audition sides and has 24 hours to read and work on the material. When their audition comes up the actor leaves the class and comes in and does a "real" auditions. This is a valuable class for actors to get comfortable with the audition process. SEE AD ON PAGE 17.

DEE WALLACE STONE
ACTING STUDIO (818) 876-0386 x3
260 North Pass Ave.
Burbank 91505

Mailing Address:
23035 Cumorah Crest Drive
Woodland HIlls 91364
www.dwsactingstudio.com
totoent@aol.com

Positive, Joyous Acting. Class is Meisner based mixed with Dee's specialty of cold-reading, on-camera and removing blocks so that you move forward in your life and career. Beginning through advanced classes.

STUDIO 10
PERFORMING ARTS CENTER (818) 563-4095

These small, on-camera classes are for beginning to professional actors. Studio 10 classes are directed by Patricia Bolt, film, commercial, voice over actress, writer and producer. For many years, Ms. Bolt has been an associate of Broadway/TV Star, Allen Fawcett, as Director of Marketing, producer and coach for Mr. Fawcett's acting and production studio in Studio City, in addition to marketing and producing classes and workshops for Actor's Center International in Studio City and One-on-One Productions. Ms. Bolt is also a writer/producer of commercials and special events for prestigious clients like the City of Los Angeles, the Metropolitan Transit Authority and the national Amateur Softball Association, in addition to concerts and theatrical productions, and is currently working on her own feature projects.

THE THEATRE DISTRICT (323) 957-2343
804 North El Centro
Hollywood 90038
www.thetheatredistrict.com
info@thetheatredistrict.com

Macario Gaxiola conducts classes covering scene study, cold reading and audition technique. Also covered: movement and dialects. Private coaching available.

TERI TUNDER (323) 969-0795
havemoxie@teritunder.com

Teri offers private coaching and feels you learn by doing and that there is no substitute for doing. Also teaches cold reading and showcasing. Her approach is based on years of training as an actress in New York and San Francisco and being a casting director in Los Angeles. Geared to the individual. Teri says: "Be brave get out there and tell the truth."

TVI ACTORS STUDIO (818) 784-6500
14429 Ventura Blvd., Ste. 118 FAX (818) 784-6533
Sherman Oaks 91423
www.tvistudios.com

One-night workshops with top casting directors are free to TVI members and there is no limit of how many workshops members can attend. Many students have had great success using these cold-reading workshops as a way to meet a different Casting Director each night of the week and learn the ins and outs of each casting office's particular auditioning process. TVI also offers on-going cold reading technique classes designed to sharpen auditioning skills in all styles of acting: feature film, episodic, soap operas, sitcoms, and more. These ongoing classes are taught by prominent Industry professionals casting for daytime, primetime TV, studio and independent feature films. Founded in 1986, with studios in Los Angeles, New York and Chicago, TVI is the nation's largest resource center for actors, offering dramatic instruction, entertainment industry networking, professional career consultation and marketing support for actors. TVI teaches actors the business of acting with a practical, no-nonsense approach to marketing and promoting yourself as a working actor in a highly competitive marketplace. In addition to a diverse curriculum of courses taught by leading Industry professionals, TVI provides daily free casting director workshops, resume and cover letter consultation with updates as often as you like, mailing labels, one-on-one counseling, use of studio space, and computer workstations with Internet access, all designed to refine the actor's craft, empower the actor with a well-rounded knowledge of the business, and clearly defined career strategy, and maximize an actor's potential in the marketplace.

VAN MAR ACADEMY (323) 650-8823
7080 Hollywood Blvd., Ste. 314 FAX (323) 650-0155
Hollywood 90028

Ivan S. Markota, past president of ACTA (Acting Coaches and Teachers Association) teaches all aspects of film and TV acting in 16 classes. His students have booked 1,034 series (regular and recurring roles). Auditing is required and free.

WALLACE AUDITION TECHNIQUE (323) 960-7852
1532 9th St., #3
Santa Monica 90401

The Wallace Audition Technique is a unique class created by casting directors, agents and producers that offers the actor an opportunity to learn from current Industry professionals. The six week class covers among other things: how to break down material quickly and creatively, make fast and original adjustments, how to identify your own unique qualities and incorporate them into your work and how to eliminate nerves and tension. Class size is limited to 10 people and all classes are on-camera.

DOUG WARHIT ON-CAMERA COLD READING
WORKSHOP (310) 479-5647
www.dougwarhit.com

Tools to create a strong emotional core and presence instantaneously, making more exciting choices, character work, pinpointing trouble areas quickly, and projecting power and confidence, whether you're auditioning for a student film or Steven Spielberg. Doug Warhit is the author of "The Actor's Audition Checklist" and "Book the Job: 143 Things Actors Need to Know to Make it Happen." For more information see MARKETING section under BOOKS AND TAPES. SEE AD ON PAGE 2.

DEBRA WATSON (310) 500-6727
Beverly Hills
www.yellowrosesproductions.com

Private coaching specializing in teaching the young actor how to use their natural instincts, which is key in keeping the work real. Basic cold reading and audition techniques that help the student understand how to tackle a role. Children and teenagers have limited life experiences to draw on and also process information differently from adults. Debra recognizes each young actor as an individual and adjusts her lessons according to the age and level of each student.

CARYN WEST
AUDITION SKILLS WORKSHOP (323) 876-0394
7506 Lexington Ave. FAX (323) 876-5897
West Hollywood 90046

Ms. West doesn't believe that any good actor worth his/her salt, given an important audition, would spend only 20 minutes on the materials and try to give a good "cold reading." Jobs are booked by paying close attention to script analysis, grasping the style or genre of the show, being 95% memorized, taking creative risks beyond the skeletal lines, inventing as full a character as you can summon on short notice, staging your audition as imaginably as possible in a small audition office, and investing some real empathy with that character's experience. A positive attitude and knowing how to channel your audition anxiety productively have a big impact too. The class is designed to stimulate and address these conditions. Audition for working pros every 10 weeks. Ms. West is a working director/actress with extensive theater and TV credits. 10-12 week Class offerings start in late August/early September or late January/early February. One week Intensives offered the last week in November and in late spring. Private coaching for auditions or roles is also available.

Combat

ACADEMY OF THEATRICAL COMBAT (818) 364-8420
www.theatricalcombat.com
info@theatrical combat.com

One of the nation's foremost centers for training and choreography in the art of combat, fencing, swordplay, and fight choreography for stage and screen. They have ongoing classes, seminars, and private instruction. Weaponry and fencing equipment sales and rentals are available.

STELLA ADLER ACADEMY OF ACTING
AND THEATRE COMPLEX (323) 465-4446
6773 Hollywood Blvd., 2nd Fl. FAX (323) 469-6049
Hollywood 90028
www.stellaadler-la.com
stellaadler@earthlink.net

Academy director, Irene Gilbert. Call for catalogue and further information. SEE AD ON PAGE 6.

FILM FIGHTING LA (310) 558-1143
2238 Purdue Ave.
Los Angeles 90064
www.filmfightingla.org

Bob Goodwin, a fight/stunt coordinator with over 35 years martial arts training and 20 years experience staging skirmishes, has trained or choreographed fights for Christian Bales, Kristana Loaen, Ving Rhames, The Teenage Mutant Ninja Turtles, The Utah Shakespearean Festival and Regional Theatre and Off-Broadway as well as at universities around the country. Bob served as swordmaster and was a featured role in "Little Hercules." He teaches on-camera classes but private instruction and crash courses are available. Asian and European Weapons: learn Chinese and Japanese sword, rapid and dagger, sword and shield, knives, sticks, staffs, sai, nunchuks and others as seen in swordwork etc. Acting the fight: learn reactions, timing, and vocalization in videotaped sessions. Learn to find the camera and the light. Combat basics: learn foot-falls, kicks, slaps, punches, chokes, and feats. Write ups from the L.A. Times, Sunday Edition, Back Stage West/NY and USA Today.

LOS ANGELES
CITY COLLEGE (LACC) (323) 953-4000 x2990
855 N. Vermont Ave. FAX (323) 953-4500
Los Angeles 90029
www.lacitycollege.edu

Combat classes are offered periodically within the curriculum. The classes primarily consist of Theatre Arts majors with a limit of 30-35 students per class. Private coaching is available. They have a community service program in which karate, wrestling, and some combat is taught. Call the above number for additional information.

LOS ANGELES FIGHT ACADEMY (818) 446-0246
4335 Van Nuys Blvd., #140
Sherman Oaks 91403
www.4lafa.org

The Los Angeles Fight Academy teaches ongoing classes and weekend workshops in theatrical combat for film and stage. Instruction in unarmed combat and various sword styles offered to all ages and levels of ability. Private instruction available on request.

SOUTH BAY GYMNASTICS
SPORTS COMPLEX (310) 328-3136
1275 Sartori Ave. FAX (310) 328-5573
Torrance 90501
www.southbaygymnastics.com
info@southbaygymnastics.com

State of the art gymnastics and martial arts training. Sword play and other weapons for film and stage is also available. High falls, tumbling, mini trampoline, tumble track, and training pit are just a few of the equipment and services they provide. They have high ceilings with a twenty foot cargo net for Galaxy and fitness training as well as the other obstacles in the training course. They also feature aerobic kickboxing. Private lessons and personal trainers available.

SWORDPLAY STUDIO (818) 566-1777
64 E. Magnolia Blvd. FAX (818) 566-4357
Burbank 91502
www.swordplayla.com

Swordplay Fencing Studio, located in the Media City Center (downtown Burbank) is a full training facility for Olympic-style

COMBAT

fencing and theatrical (stage) combat. Swordplay offers classes in traditional fencing, hand to hand combat, stage combat with weapons ranging from broadsword to pole-arms. Whether you're an actor, director, stuntman or sports enthusiast, Swordplay has a class for you! Also available: aerobics and martial arts classes. Children and adults welcome. Owner, Tim Weske.

THEATRE OF ARTS (EST. 1927) (323) 463-2500
1621 N. McCadden Place FAX (323) 463-2005
Los Angeles 90028
www.theatre-of-arts.com

Offers classes in Combat. See listing under ACTING for further information.

COMEDY & IMPROV

ACME COMEDY THEATRE (323) 525-0233
135 N. La Brea Ave.
Los Angeles 90036
www.acmecomedy.com

A state-of-the-art 99 seat theatre designed by renowned architect John Fischer that is host to a critically-acclaimed professional sketch comedy troupe managed by Producer/Director M.D. Sweeney. The Acme Improv and Sketch Comedy School offers classes on five levels beginning with an introduction to the basics of improvisation progressing through advanced sketch comedy writing and offering the potential of moving into Acme's professional performing company. In addition to sketch comedy Acme Comedy Theatre also hosts a wide array of comedy shows including improv, variety and solo performance. Study and perform comedy on the same stage as Wayne Brady, Ryan Stiles, Brad Sherwood, Fred Willard, Wil Wheaton, Adam Carolla, Alex Borstein and Upright Citizens Brigade. Company members who developed their writing skills at the Acme include Emmy-winning writer/producers "Friends," "The Simpsons," "Norm," "3rd Rock From the Sun" and Warner Bros. Animation.

ACTORS CO-OP (323) 462-8460
1760 N. Gower FAX (323) 462-3199
Hollywood 90028
www.actorsco-op.org
jcuster@fpch.org

Actors Co-op Actor's Academy is a year round program that provides exceptional training for the actor. Classes for all levels beginner to advanced are taught by working professionals with a curriculum focused on acting, however future directors, producers and writers will also find this program a valuable learning experience. Scene study, improvisation, voice work, movement, character development and technique.

THE ACTOR'S SPOT (818) 383-8433
4821 Lankershim Blvd. FAX (661) 263-0987
Ste. F, PMB 363
North Hollywood 91601
www.theactorsspot.com
ptreeky@aol.com

The Actor's Spot focuses on moment to moment, or learning to quit acting and start listening, believing, and reacting. Each class is limited to 10-12 students allowing their instructors to provide hands-on work with each and every student. The Actor's Spot was created to encourage people starting out in the entertainment industry, as well as to provide a forum for seasoned actors to workout and continue growing. Classes include scene study, cold reading, improvisation and casting directors for ages 7 and up.

STELLA ADLER ACADEMY OF ACTING AND THEATRE COMPLEX (323) 465-4446
6773 Hollywood Blvd., 2nd Fl. FAX (323) 469-6049
Hollywood 90028
www.stellaadler-la.com

Academy director: Irene Gilbert. Students are invited into the Improv Production class. Call for catalogue and further information. SEE AD ON PAGE 6.

TONI ATTELL (949) 256-0988
www.attell.com
attell@attell.com

Toni Attell has taught stand-up comedy, improvisation, cold reading and acting techniques for TV, movies and commercials in over 350 universities and schools throughout the United States. She holds on-camera workshops teaching acting and improvisation for children, teens, adults and seniors. She is the first acting coach to use hypnosis and guided meditation with acting technique. She teaches at UCLA Extension and at the prestigious USC Lucas School and also privately coaches people in businesses to bring comedy and humor into their presentations. An 8-week online course on standup comedy for children and adults is offered through her website. See ACTING listing in this section for further information.

THE GARY AUSTIN WORKSHOPS (818) 503-3571
P.O. Box 2320
Toluca Lake 91610
www.garyaustin.net
geneandroy@aol.com

Gary Austin provides a safe environment for actors to apply techniques which allow them to portray truthful human behavior in compelling ways, and to create characters and material. He provides workshops for all ages and levels of experience, private coaching, and he develops original projects. Gary created and was original director of the famed Los Angeles based theatrical company, The Groundlings. Mr. Austin is an alumnus of San Francisco's famed The Committee.

BANG IMPROV STUDIO (323) 653-6886
457 N. Fairfax Ave. FAX (323) 653-6266
Los Angeles 90036
www.bangstudio.com
info@bangstudio.com

Bang is an improv conservatory with a five level training program teaching how to create great characters and scenes in the moment. The approach encourages relationship-based, organic comedy over jokes. The second half of the program consists of 7 months of both weekly class workouts and performance every weekend in a primetime Friday night show. Bang is known for high quality classes at an extremely reasonable rate. Tuition starts at $275 for an 8 week term and decreases for each subsequent level ($250, $225, $200, and $100 per month for the performance Master Class level). Bang's teachers are working professionals currently writing, acting, and directing in TV and film. Audits are available for prospective students by appointment. Post graduate work in acting, improv, writing, and performance are also available. Call for a brochure or to register.

CAROLYNE BARRY'S ACTING AND IMPROV WORKSHOPS (323) 654-2212
www.carolynebarry.com
carolyne@carolynebarry.com

This complete program for the dedicated professional actor offers beginning, intermediate and advanced improv, on-camera acting/scene study and commercial workshops plus a specialty packaging class and a theater, sit-com, soap and film/TV cold reading workshop. Carolyne Barry, who has trained more than 5,000 working actors, has been teaching for 20 years and casting for 16. Recommended by agents, casting directors, managers and former students, Ms. Barry is recognized as one of the most comprehensive audition teachers and often has a month or two waiting list. She has been featured as a acting authority in The Hollywood Reporter, L.A. Reader, The Examiner, Back Stage West as well as on CNN, KHJ, KTTV and numerous other TV and radio talk shows throughout the country. Recently Ms. Barry was chosen to be the Commercial Audition coach for "E" TV's "Fight For Fame." The workshops are taught by Carolyne and a staff of master, professional teachers with programs designed to develop the actor's skills, exercise creativity and freedom, and nurture their unique on-camera personality. Small classes and personalized instruction. Classes range between 6 and 12 weeks; fees vary from $355 to $495 and payment plans are available. Interview and audition required.

BB'S KIDS (323) 650-KIDS
www.bbskids.com
BBs4Kids@aol.com

This 8 week class will focus on Improv and Comedy and improve your skills for all those sitcom auditions. Even if you don't think you're funny, you'll realize soon enough we're all pretty hilarious. Learn to combine the elements of improv, clown and Commedia del Arte. Bring joy and sparkle to your work which makes you extremely charming and watchable. Aside from the obvious application to comedy, the skills developed in this class will be of great benefit in all areas of an actor's work from commercials to dramas. This ongoing "workout room" helps to develop the actor's "tool kit." Age 10 and up. SEE AD ON PAGE 41.

JUDY BELSHE (562) 621-0121
www.askjudy.biz
belshecasting@aol.com

Children and adult ongoing on-camera acting classes in Long Beach. For beg-pro. Improv, commercials, theatrical. Guest writers come to classes and teach on theatrical nights.

JUDY BROWN (310) 396-8425
STAND UP COMEDY WORKSHOP
www.judybrown.info
judybrowni@usa.net

Learn how to turn your acting skills and natural sense of humor into a professional stand up act. "Perform at The Improv...by next month." Approaches comedy as an entry into television and films as well as a fun way to make a living. Beginner and advanced. Private coaching is $75 per hour or 5 hours for $250 and includes a performance at the Improv.

CRAIG CAMPOBASSO (818) 503-2474
craigcampobasso@aol.com

Craig's affordable on-camera classes cover scene study, audition technique, and character development. They meet once a week in 4 week intervals.

JUDY CARTER'S COMEDY WORKSHOPS (310) 915-0555
2112 Walnut Ave.
Venice 90291
www.comedyworkshops.com
info@comedyworkshops.com

The LA Weekly calls Judy Carter's class, "LA's best comedy class." Carter's 8-week stand up comedy course teaches actors how to turn problems into punchlines. The course culminates with a showcase at the Hollywood Improv and a digital video of your act. Showcases generally have a large Industry turn out. The course is co-taught by veteran comic Diane Nichols. Private consultations are also available to help "punch up" material. Judy Carter is the author of 3 books, the latest, "The Comedy Bible" (Fireside Books, 2001); as well as audio tapes and CDs on how to write, perform and sell yourself as a comic or comedy writer. Carter, herself is a working comic having appeared on many TV shows including HBO and Showtime comedy specials, and her workshop has been featured on CNN, Good Morning America and Oprah.

JUNE CHANDLER'S ACTORS WORKSHOP (626) 355-4572
www.junechandler.com
june@junechandler.com

Improv taught by well-known actor/teacher Dick Valentine. On-camera training at Zydeco Casting Studios in Studio City. Actors are up many times each session. Small classes and a supportive environment. First improv class is free. Ongoing classes for beginners and advanced levels. Classes are reasonably priced, class size is limited, credit card options. SEE AD ON PAGES 1 & 43.

VINCENT CHASE (323) 851-4819
7221 Sunset Blvd. FAX (323) 851-9942
Los Angeles 90046

Classes that cover basic to advanced improv techniques using exercises developed to stretch the entire acting instrument are taught by John Hindman. See listing under ACTING in this section for further information.

AN ACTOR'S WORKSHOP WITH TIM COLCERI (323) 828-6900
12217 Hartland St.
North Hollywood 91605
colceri@msn.com

Tim Colceri has been an Actor for 20 years, and has been teaching for over 10. He will teach you how to use your instrument properly. Tim Colceri is a no-nonsense, in your face coach who tells it like it is and will challenge you and help you meet that challenge. Tim wants you to be a better actor. Class curriculum consists of cold reading, scene study, audition technique, on-camera work, and improv which is vital for commercial auditioning. The workshop is Industry driven and students have the opportunity to become members of "Full Metal Improv," the bi-weekly improv show which is consistently marketed to casting directors, agents, and managers.

Tim is also preparing his students for a Bi-Monthly Industry Showcase.

COLD TOFU (213) 739-4142
222 S. Hewitt St.
Los Angeles 90012
www.coldtofu.com
coldtofu@hotmail.com

Eight week sessions focusing on improv techniques and games used by the performing cast of Cold Tofu. Geared to help performers and non-performers learn basic improvisation skills and gain confidence in a fun, nurturing environment.

COMEDYSPORTZ (323) 871-1193
8033 Sunset Blvd., #506
Los Angeles 90046
www.comedysportzla.com

Offers improv for adults and teens. Class size is generally 15. No audition is necessary and auditing is allowed. An 8 week time commitment is required.

GREG DEAN'S (310) 285-3799
STAND-UP COMEDY WORKSHOPS (323) 464-4355
P.O. Box 2929
Hollywood 90078
www.stand-upcomedy.com

Offers a six week class for beginning and advanced level students and a workbook written by Mr. Dean is provided. The beginning class is limited to 20 and covers joke writing and performance technique. The advanced class is limited to 12, covers techniques for performance and gives one nightclub performance that is video taped and given to the student. The tape is also reviewed in class. Call for free seminar, free audit, and a free brochure.

THE DENNY EVANS
COMEDY WORKSHOP (310) 535-6874
Andrew Benne Theatre
4930 Lankershim Blvd.
North Hollywood 91601

Offers an ongoing improvisational comedy class with a limit of 25 students. The class is occasionally on-camera. Showcases, public performances, and Industry nights are offered. An audition is required and auditing is allowed. Classes are Sunday, 7 pm to 10:15 pm. Private coaching is available.

THE GOBETTI/ORMENY ACTING STUDIO
AT THE VICTORY THEATRE CENTER (818) 841-4404
www.thevictorytheatres.com FAX (818) 841-6328
victory@thevictorytheatrecenter.com

See listing under ACTING for further information.

THE GROUNDLINGS (323) 934-4747
7307 Melrose Ave.
Los Angeles 90046
www.groundlings.com

Offers 4 levels of comedy classes, basic, intermediate, a writer's lab, and an advanced class as well as an introductory class that does not require an audition. There is a 6 or 12 week commitment and a limit of 12-16 students. An audition is required. Students work in every class.

SANDY HOLT ON-CAMERA COLD READING
AND IMPROV WORKSHOP (310) 271-8217

Sandy Holt, a Second City Alum, coaches on-camera actors privately in cold reading and improv. Sandy casts for all the major studios including Dreamworks, Disney, Warner Bros. etc. Sandy coaches you to: take charge at auditions; stay focused under pressure; get out of your head; create original characters; and know what is special about you and use it. SEE AD ON PAGE 51.

HULL ACTORS STUDIO
LORRIE HULL, PH.D. & DIANNE HULL (310) 828-0632
Santa Monica
www.actors-studio.com/hull
hullwshop@hotmail.com

Comedy and improv taught in classes with a limit of 10 students. Private lessons and coaching available daily. See listing under ACTING in this section for further information.

IDIOTCENTRAL (818) 613-6112
260 N. Pass Ave.
Burbank 91606
www.idiotcentral.com
jw@idiotcentral.com

A fun, safe place to play. Learn improvisation with experienced Industry professionals in a non-competitive environment. Thursday nights. Free audit.

IMPROV OLYMPIC WEST (323) 962-7560
6366 Hollywood Blvd.
Hollywood 90028
www.iowest.com

The IO West offers a six level training program based on its signature long form piece, the Harold. With a heavy focus on performance, the goal is to learn and grow through stage time. Guaranteed performances starting at level 4 and culminating with a class created long form showcase in level 6. Audits are always welcome. Additional workshops are offered in sketch writing, Meisner technique and other related long forms. Call to receive an application by mail or to schedule an audit. Information and applications are also available on the website.

KIMBERLY JENTZEN
LIVING THE ARTS INSTITUTE (818) 779-7770
P.O. Box 4554 FAX (818) 779-1171
Valley Village 91617
www.kimberlyjentzen.net
filmactors@aol.com

Improvisation and developing characters are a regular component of the class and an integral part of Ms. Jentzen's teaching of the necessary tools for the empowerment of an actor. Over 18 years teaching. See listing in the ACTING in this section for further information. SEE AD ON PAGE 1.

KIP KING (818) 784-0544
www.kipking.actorsite.com FAX (818) 784-1809
kip81137@aol.com

One of the original Groundlings and father of Chris Kattan, Mr. King offers ongoing on-camera improv classes for commercials and TV. Workshops and private coaching are available and showcases are included with the tuition. Please call for new location.

L.A. CONNECTION (818) 784-1868
13442 Ventura Blvd. FAX (818) 710-8666
Sherman Oaks 91423
www.laconnectionscomedy.com

Training is offered to members of their repertory company which can be joined after an audition and acceptance into the company. They have several weekly improv, sketch and ongoing shows for live theatre that are cast from the company. They have a stand-up comedy repertory company as well as a children's improv class for ages 5-14 and 11-18. Kids also perform on Saturdays and Sundays and are paid 25% of the profits from the box office. Call for information and an audit. Affiliated with all the unions and guilds. Also dubs movies to funny soundtracks.

HARVEY LEMBECK COMEDY WORKSHOP
HELAINE LEMBECK & MICHAEL LEMBECK (310) 271-2831
FAX (818) 785-1594
www.harveylembeckcomedyworkshop.com

Now in its 42nd year, the workshop has 3 levels but is aimed for the trained/working actor who wants to specialize in comedy. The workshop is designed to teach the actor how to play comedy legitimately in a scene using improv as a tool to enhance comedic skills for sitcoms, TV and film. The students participate on stage 3 or 4 times each night. An interview is required for these ongoing classes and auditing is by arrangement. Critiques are by the teacher only. Classes are often visited by professionals in all areas of the Industry. Former students include: Robin Williams, Penny Marshall, John Ritter, Jenna Elfman, Bryan Cranston, Kim Cattrall, Ted McGinley, John Larroquette, Alan Rachins, Scott Baio, Lenny Clark, Mary Lou Henner and Sharon Stone. SEE AD ON PAGE 59.

BEVERLY LONG (818) 754-6222
11425 Moorpark St.
Studio City 91602
www.beverlylong-casting.com
info@beverlylong-casting.com

An 8 week commitment is required for this class which culminates in a showcase for friends, family and agents. Teens and adults. SEE AD ON PAGE 65.

LOS ANGELES
CITY COLLEGE (LACC) (323) 953-4000 x2650
855 N. Vermont Ave. FAX (323) 953-4500
Los Angeles 90029
www.lacitycollege.edu

Call for a current catalog.

LOS ANGELES THEATRE SPORTS
JOHN RAITT THEATRE (323) 401-6162
1727 N. Vermont
Los Angeles 90027
www.theatresports.com
workshop@theatresports.com

Teaches narrative comedy/improv short and longer form. Ideal for working actors, writers or anyone who wants to learn improv in a supportive and fun environment. Beg-int-adv classes, limit 18. Teaching in Los Angeles since 1988. Repertory company.

MARJI MARTIN (818) 846-9486

Open-ended, limited classes that are designed to: teach the hows and whys while exploring comedy beyond improv and stand-up; discover and perfect individual techniques; and channel energies and talent through cold readings and personalized exercises in safe surroundings. Teacher critiques only. Also drama coaching.

ERIC MORRIS ACTORS WORKSHOP (323) 466-9250
5657 Wilshire Blvd., Ste. 110
Los Angeles 90036
www.ericmorris.com

Mr. Morris uses his own technique in this ongoing class that covers audition technique, character analysis, film technique, improv, interview technique, monologues, sensory work, and scene study. His approach is based on Stanislavski, however he has gone light years beyond the original system. In addition to weekly classes he holds intensives one weekend per month, as well as 4 three day workshops per year and one six day workshop held at the UCLA Conference Center in Lake Arrowhead. Students work in every class, the limit is 20 students. Auditing is allowed and is followed by an interview. Private coaching is available from Mr. Morris or his wife Susana Morris. Mr. Morris has written 5 books on acting. SEE AD ON PAGE 13.

LARRY MOSS' IMPROV WORKOUT
AND DIALECT GYM (310) 395-4284

A creative stretch 'playshop' designed to build confidence and proficiency in the use of voice, dialect, delivery, comedic timing, character development, cold reading and acting technique. Through comedy improvisation and script work, participants are guided to: build trust in their creative process; modify voice, speech or delivery to bring a character to life; break through performance blocks and inhibitions; and develop group consciousness and teamwork. Students work in a safe, supportive climate conducive to risk taking, breakthrough and discovery. Four-week-cycle classes with an enrollment limit of 12. Interview required. Mr. Moss is a veteran dialect/diction/acting coach and voice-over actor. He is also a professional put-on speaker for conventions, banquets and television shows including Jay Leno—introduced to the unsuspecting audience as an expert or authority in their field from another country.

STEVE NORTH THE COMEDY COACH (818) 347-5098
22647 Ventura Blvd., #422 FAX (818) 347-5099
Woodland Hills, 91364
www.funnycoach.com
steve@funnycoach.com

Classes and private coaching to help students find their comedic character as a stand up or actor and create the right material for themselves. Beginning and professional instruction by a working producer-writer-performer who has many national television credits. Some classes are on camera. Also have showcases and Industry nights.

ORANGE COUNTY CRAZIES (714) 550-9890
809 N. Main Street
Santa Ana 92701
www.occrazies.com

Improvisational and sketch comedy workshops, classes and performing groups at basic, intermediate and advanced levels headed by founding member of The Groundlings, Cherie Kerr. A performing element is given to all who take classes at all levels. Always looking for new regular performing members for long and short term.

PIMLOTT-MEDINA'S FILM & TV WORKSHOP (866) 923-3459 / (866) 923-FILM
955 S. E. St., Ste. F FAX (909) 884-8904
San Bernardino 92408
filmtvworkshop@aol.com

Beginning, Intermediate and Advanced acting workshops for adults and teenagers to help expose natural ability, capture auditions with originality, learn on set protocol, and learn Industry terminology. Classes cover cold reading, improvisation, commercials, on-camera movement, overcoming stage fright, and monologues. Management, agent and casting director showcases and Industry consultations. Course audits available.

PROMENADE ACTING CONSERVATORY (310) 656-8070
1404 Third Street Promenade FAX (310) 656-8069
Santa Monica 90401
www.pierodusa.com
info@pierodusa.com

Fundamentals of improvisation prepares the actor to be quick on his feet and creative, as well as providing the tools needed for many commercial auditions, meetings and on-set rehearsals. The course is designed to: sharpen memory, create scenes, improve listening and spontaneity and develop risk taking. The course covers: adding, agreeing, listening, committing, space work, stage movement, dialogue creation, ensemble work, games and characterizations. The company of actors give final performances to showcase their work. SEE AD ON PAGES 21 & 297.

REEL PROS (818) 788-4133
13437 Ventura Blvd., Ste. 220
Sherman Oaks 91423
www.reelpros.com
support@reelpros.com

Reel Pros has three categories for their classes: 1) the Main Arena for professional actors who play 27 and above; membership by audition only; 2) Reel PROs 2 for young professional actors who play 16-26; no audition required; and 3) The Public Access Arena offers classes that are specifically oriented to craft-building and specialty skills like Voice Over, Improv, Audition Technique, How to Book Jobs, How to Be Captivating on Film, etc., and are open to the general public 18 years old and above. The first two classes also offer cold-reading and at times prepared scene workshops with casting directors, producers, directors, and agents.

CBS COMEDY & TV HOSTING WORKSHOPS WITH PAUL RYAN (818) 788-2190
4024 Radford Ave.
Studio City 91604
www.paulryanproductions.com
paul@paulryanproductions.com

Paul Ryan stretches the actor in every way possible to become comedically successful in landing the role, through his innovative comedy/improv situations and revolutionary comedy scene techniques. This helps actors hone their craft and nail the auditions for sitcoms and comedy roles in TV and film. Ryan has been teaching The CBS Comedy Workshops for twelve years, and worked as a comedy consultant and sitcom director in Europe. He performed regularly with Robin Williams, and his previous students include Emmy winner John Larroquette, and Emmy nominee Bryan Cranston ("Malcolm in the Middle"). Paul is now in his sixth year teaching his CBS TV Hosting Intensives, and upon completion, students are eligible to take "Shooting Footage on Location for the Demo Tape." He has hosted/produced 700 TV Talk shows, and recently hosted "Feel Good TV with Paul Ryan & Friends" and "The Art of Comedy," the title of his new book. He also recently produced/directed the TV comedy "Hollywood Alive," using his comedy students in the lead roles.

THE SECOND CITY (323) 658-8190
8156 Melrose Ave.
Los Angeles 90046
www.secondcity.com/training/la

For over 45 years, The Second City has been one of the most influential theatres in the country, turning out some of the world's most beloved actors. Second City has launched hundreds of artists whose careers have changed the face of television, film and theatre with alumni in the current casts of Mad TV, Saturday Night Live and Curb Your Enthusiasm to name a few. A sample of programs offered at The Second City Training Center include Beginning Improvisation, Improv for Actors, Sketch or Sitcom Writing, Musical Improv and the Conservatory Program. Also classes for children and teens.

AARON SPEISER ACTING STUDIO (310) 399-4567
1644 S. La Cienega Blvd.
Los Angeles 90035
www.aaronspeiser.com

Open to actors at all levels, this class is designed to give the actor more intense training in order to gain experience quickly and build confidence to help the actor become more aware and live in the moment through a wide variety of improvisational games and exercises. Students improv comedic as well as dramatic scenes. Work done in this class also helps prepare actors to be more confident and relaxed for auditions. SEE AD ON PAGE 17.

SPOLIN THEATRE GAMES WORKSHOPS (323) 851-1380
www.paulsills.com/laworkshops
aretha_sills@earthlink.net

Refresh or enhance your performance skills with a workshop in the theater games of Viola Spolin, author of Improvisation for the Theater. Side Coach Aretha Sills invites actors, theater students, improvisers, teachers and other players to join in the workshops. These courses are designed with a focus on bringing spontaneity, sensory awareness, physicalization and play to your stage work. Aretha Sills is the granddaughter of Viola Spolin. She has studied improvisational theater for many years with her father, Paul Sills, and has taught at The Bard College Cabaret, The Wisconsin Theater Games Center and Bay Area Theatresports.

STAGE 13 PRODUCTIONS ROBERT BEECHER (818) 768-3686
10749 New Haven St., Ste. 15
Sun Valley 91352
www.stage13.com

Private coaching that covers commercials, film, and theatrical acting. Cold reading, audition and cue card technique, and on-camera work are some of the things that are covered. A new comedy class has been added and Robert peppers his teaching with biz of the biz information including headshot and resume advice, agents, generals, etc. Classes are $60 for 4 sessions. There is a required introductory session which is a pre-requisite to joining the regular groups.

Comedy & Improv

THE LEE STRASBERG THEATRE INSTITUTE (323) 650-7777
7936 Santa Monica Blvd.
Los Angeles 90046
www.strasberg.com
admissionsla@strasberg.com

The Institute offers classes in improvisation. See listing under ACTING is this section for further information.

THEATRE OF ARTS (EST. 1927) (323) 463-2500
1621 N. McCadden Place FAX (323) 463-2005
Los Angeles 90028
www.theatre-of-arts.com

See listing under ACTING in this section for further information.

TVI ACTORS STUDIO (818) 784-6500
14429 Ventura Blvd., Suite 118 FAX (818) 784-6533
Sherman Oaks 91423
www.tvistudios.com

TVI offers classes in Sitcom Technique taught which enable you to sharpen your cold reading and acting skills and refine comic timing when auditioning for sitcoms. The classes teach you the dos and don'ts of auditioning for primetime comedies and provide rare insight into the entire casting process. Founded in 1986, with studios in Los Angeles, New York and Chicago, TVI is a resource center for actors, offering dramatic instruction, entertainment industry networking, professional career consultation and marketing support for actors. In addition to a diverse curriculum of courses taught by leading Industry professionals, TVI provides members with free benefits, including daily casting director workshops, resume and cover letter consultation with updates as often as you like, mailing labels, one-on-one counseling, use of studio space, and computer workstations with Internet access, all designed to refine the actor's craft, empower the actor with a well-rounded knowledge of the business, and clearly defined career strategy, and maximize an actor's potential in the marketplace.

UNIVERSITY OF CALIFORNIA LOS ANGELES (UCLA EXTENSION) (310) 825-4321
405 Hilgard Ave.
Los Angeles 90024
www.ucla.edu

For current catalog call (310) 825-6064.

UNIVERSITY OF CALIFORNIA LOS ANGELES (UCLA) (310) 825-9064
10995 Le Conte Ave., Rm. 437
Los Angeles 90024
www.ucla.edu

Courses and workshops for adults in comic acting, stand-up, improv, sit-coms and person shows taught by Industry professionals. See listing under ACTING in this section for further information.

UNIVERSITY OF SOUTHERN CALIFORNIA (USC) (213) 821-2744
University Park
Los Angeles 90089
www.usc.edu

Call for current catalog.

VAN MAR ACADEMY (323) 650-8823
7080 Hollywood Blvd., #314 FAX (323) 650-0155
Hollywood 90028

Ivan S. Markota, past president of ACTA (Acting Coaches and Teachers Association) teaches all aspects of film and TV acting in 16 classes. His students have booked 1,034 series (regular and recurring roles). Auditing is required and free.

Commercials

ACTORS CONSULTATION SERVICES (310) 828-7814
2461 Santa Monica Blvd., #322 FAX (310) 998-9114
Santa Monica 90404
www.actorsconsultations.com
jill@actorsconsultations.com

Jill Jaress teaches private on camera commercial classes.

THE ACTORS' EDGE WORKSHOP (310) 652-4399
7080 Hollywood Blvd., Ste. 306
Hollywood 90028
www.theactorsedgeacademy.com

Using a combination of many methods this casting director teaches from a casting director's point of view. The classes are for beg-pro level children age 6-adult. Cold reading, scene study, audition/interview technique, and a commercial workshop. There is a free audit. Class size is limited to 20 students.

STELLA ADLER ACADEMY OF ACTING AND THEATRE COMPLEX (323) 465-4446
6773 Hollywood Blvd., 2nd Fl. FAX (323) 469-6049
Hollywood 90028
www.stellaadler-la.com

Academy director: Irene Gilbert. Call for catalogue and further information. SEE AD ON PAGE 6.

MARIKO BALLENTINE (818) 759-8282

On-camera commercial technique from an acting base. Emphasis on truth, believability, and bringing the actor's own personality to the audition. Privates, semi-privates, and one day workshops only. Ms. Ballentine works with Danny Goldman and Associates Casting.

CAROLYNE BARRY'S COMMERCIAL ACTING WORKSHOPS (323) 654-2212
www.carolynebarry.com

This complete program for the dedicated professional actor offers beginning, intermediate and advanced improv, on-camera acting/scene study and commercial workshops plus a specialty packaging class and a theater, sit-com, soap and film/TV cold reading workshop. Carolyne Barry, who has trained more than 5,000 working actors, has been teaching for 20 years and casting for 16. Recommended by agents, casting directors, managers and former students, Ms. Barry is recognized as one of the most comprehensive audition teachers and often has a month or two waiting list. She has been featured as a acting authority in The Hollywood Reporter, L.A. Reader, The Examiner, Back Stage West as well as on CNN, KHJ, KTTV and numerous other TV and radio talk shows throughout the country. Recently Ms. Barry was chosen to be the Commercial Audition coach for "E" TV's "Fight For Fame." The workshops are taught by Carolyne and a staff of master, professional teachers with programs designed to develop the actor's skills, exercise creativity and freedom, and nurture unique their on-camera personality. Small classes and personalized instruction. Classes range between 6 and 12 weeks; fees vary from $355 to $495 and payment plans are available. Interview and audition required.

BB'S KIDS **(323) 650-5437**
www.bbskids.com

Belinda Balaski offers an 8 week on-camera commercial class for children age 4 and up. The class covers personality slating, eating on camera, situation improv, singles, doubles, cold copy, hard copy and call backs. Ms. Balaski originated this class 18 years ago for a casting director and has trained over 3,000 working kids. Private coaching is available. See listing under CHILDREN'S TRAINING for further information. SEE AD ON PAGE 41.

JUDY BELSHE **(562) 621-0121**
www.askjudy.biz
belshecasting@aol.com

Children and adult ongoing on-camera acting classes in Long Beach. For beg-pro. Improv, commercials, theatrical. Guest writers come to classes and teach on theatrical nights.

BERG STUDIO
GREGORY BERGER-SOBECK **(323) 822-0152**
www.thebergstudios.com
bergstudios@sbcglobal.net

Gregory Berger-Sobeck teaches the Yale School of Drama technique which has trained Meryl Streep, Edward Norton, Sigorney Weaver, Liv Schreiber and Frances McDormand, among others. All students are offered very small classes, giving individualized attention. Class covers scene-work, commercial and theatrical auditions, on-camera cold reading technique. Periodic Industry showcases, and guest speakers. Classes meet twice a week. Every actor works every class. Mr. Berger-Sobeck has an MFA from Yale and has worked many years in New York as a teacher and private coach. He has numerous Broadway credits as well as credits in film and television. The technique he teaches is a systematic approach for identifying and personalizing the character's driving need and objectives and engaging the actor's voice, body, mind and spirit in its active pursuit. It is a repeatable step by step process ensuring repeatable returns. Mr Berger-Sobeck recently directed an Industry showcase specifically targeting top casting agents and managers coupled with Daryl Marshak Management which was written up in Back Stage West. He recently was the associate Casting Director on the new network pilot "Angel Air."

TERRY BERLAND **(310) 571-4141**
(323) 969-8200
FAX (310) 820-5408

On-camera commercial audition workshop. The actor has 30 seconds to a minute to give an impressive commercial audition performance. Participants will learn how to immediately create the feeling of a specific environment and show dimensions of his personality. Identifying the space, the beats and moments available to the actor will be completely logical, enabling the actor to make the correct specific choices for a good performance. These workshops are once a week for six weeks and include meeting an agent. Classes limited.

PAMELA CAMPUS CASTING & **(310) 398-2715**
COMMERCIAL WORKSHOP **(818) 897-1588**

Offers commercial training and improv for the camera. The emphasis is on bringing out the actor's inner personality and personalizing his/her auditioning skills. Ms. Campus is a casting director who does theatrical, industrial, and commercial casting.

JUNE CHANDLER'S
ACTORS WORKSHOP **(626) 355-4572**
www.junechandler.com
june@junechandler.com

Beginning, intermediate and advanced level on-camera training. Six week basic workshop (Commercials A-Z) is comprehensive and detailed and concludes with an agent showcase. Intermediate level (The New Pros) focuses on getting the agent and booking the jobs with an agent showcase every six weeks and guest agent seminars. Advanced level (The Old Pros) works to expand the actors' casting range and skills and increase the percentage of bookings. Classes are all on Sundays at Zydeco Casting Studios in Studio City. Reasonable prices and class size is limited. SEE AD ON PAGES 1 & 43.

VINCENT CHASE **(323) 851-4819**
7221 Sunset Blvd. **FAX (323) 851-9942**
Los Angeles 90046

Videotaped classes using actual commercial copy. The class is taught by Vincent Chase. See listing under ACTING in this section for more information.

SONIA DARMEI-LOPES **(310) 358-5942**
www.screenactorsstudio.com
sonia@screenactorsstucio.com

On-camera acting classes are taught in a positive and caring environment. Students appear in numerous projects including "Malcolm in the Middle," "The Division," "The Guiding Light," "Even Stevens," etc. Private coaching.

DEL MAR MEDIA ARTS **(949) 753-0570**
15375 Barranca Pkwy., #J-105 **FAX (949) 753-0576**
Irvine 92618
www.delmarmediaarts.com

Offers a 6 week course that covers camera work, cold reading, and auditioning skills. SAG agents attend last two sessions. Children and adults. Also offers classes in voice-over, spokesperson (wireless ear prompter/TelePropTer) animation, narration and audio books. Monthly free open-house seminars. State licensed and approved. See listing under VOICE OVERS and AUDIO DEMO PRODUCTION for further information. SEE AD ON PAGE 67.

EDGEMAR CENTER FOR THE ARTS **(310) 399-3666**
2437 Main St. **FAX (310) 399-2898**
Santa Monica 90405
www.edgemarcenter.org
paxjava@hotmail.com

Workshops for kids and teens: Intro to on-camera cold reading. Courses are designed for students who are new to being on camera and who want to further develop their basic audition skills working with sides from commercials, film, and television. 8 week courses through out the year. Ages 7-11 and 12-17.

J.D. FERRANTINO'S KIDS AND TEENS (310) 358-5942
www.screenactorsstudio.com

A six week on-camera commercial workshop for kids and adults. Learn how to audition successfully, personality slating, cold reading, improv, use of cue card, handling props and call backs. Last class includes an agent showcase. Theatrical cold reading workshops available.

MEGAN FOLEY
CASTING COMMERCIAL WORKSHOPS (818) 216-9350
11340 Moorpark Ave.
Studio City 91602

Offers an 8-hour workshop that covers all aspects of the commercial audition as well as everything from non-verbal auditions up to and including spokespersons, headshot review, slating, cue cards, and copy. The classes are taught by Megan Foley and Charles Marra for adults 16 and up. Class size is limited and on-camera.

GOSCH PRODUCTIONS (818) 729-0000
2227 W. Olive Ave.
Burbank 91560
www.gosch.net

Taught by working directors Laurie Tubert and Pat Gosch for beginning to advanced actors. Scenework, comedy and improv as well as a class for children and parents where parents count. Parents are invited to the children's classes for ages 7-18. Audition preferred, auditing is allowed. Private coaching as well.

KIP KING (818) 784-0544
www.kipkingactorsite.com FAX (818) 784-1809
kip81137@aol.com

One of the original Groundlings and the father of Chris Kattan, Mr. King offers ongoing on-camera improv classes for commercials, and TV. Workshops as well as private coaching are available and showcases are included with tuition. Please call for new class location.

THE LEARNING ANNEX (310) 478-6677
11850 Wilshire Blvd., #100
Los Angeles 90025
www.learningannex.com

Commercial classes are frequently offered. Schedules vary each term. Call for specific information and current brochure.

BEVERLY LONG CASTING DIRECTOR (818) 754-6222
11425 Moorpark St. FAX (818) 754-6226
Studio City 91602
www.beverlylong-casting.com
info@beverlylong-casting.com

Intense on-camera technique for commercials is offered for a 6 week class. Auditing is allowed. Ms. Long has been training professionals since 1976. SEE AD ON PAGE 65.

LOS ANGELES
CITY COLLEGE (LACC) (323) 953-4000 x2650
855 N. Vermont Ave. FAX (323) 953-4500
Los Angeles 90029
www.lacitycollege.edu

For current catalog call the above number. For additional information call the Cinema, TV Department.

LOS ANGELES
COMMUNITY ADULT SCHOOL (323) 931-1026
4650 W. Olympic Blvd.
Los Angeles 90019

Offers scene study and commercial training for adults 60 and older. Classes are taught by credentialed teachers in many Los Angeles areas. Adrienne Omansky is the Program Director and classes are free for adults over 60.

MIKE MUSCAT (818) 904-9494

Offers private lessons that cover acting, cold reading, and commercials. He also coaches for auditions and meets with actors for career guidance and advice. He is an acting and dialogue coach for TV and film. Mike was on-set acting coach for "Terminator 2," "My Girl 2," "Last Action Hero" and "Frazier." The only acting coach in town that gives a money back guarantee.

MVCI (MUSIC VIDEO
COMMERCIAL INSTITUTE) (800) 255-7529
1655 McCadden Pl.
Hollywood 90028
www.mvci.tv
mvci@mvci.tv

Music Video and Commercial Film School teaches hands-on workshop courses for directing, producing and editing music videos and commercials on 35mm, 16mm film and digital video. MVCI is a filmschool where the student can become the director, producer, cinematographer and editor of their own high quality music video or commercial production. Taught by MTV Award winning directors, producers and editors.

ORANGE COUNTY
COMMERCIAL ACTING WORKSHOP (714) 832-1895
222 W. Main St., Ste. 201
Tustin 92780
www.occaw.com

Evening classes for adults are offered that cover audition and interview technique, cold reading, cue card technique, headshot review and advice, as well as improv and acting technique for TV and film. Private sessions are also offered for children and teens that cover audition and interview technique, cold reading, cue card technique, and headshot review and advice. Individualized treatment and full on-camera work. A guest director is present at the end of the beginning workshop. An audition and interview are required for the advanced class only. Auditing is allowed.

PIMLOTT-MEDINA'S (866) 923-3459
FILM & TV WORKSHOP (866) 923-FILM
955 S. E. St., Ste. F FAX (909) 884-8904
San Bernardino 92408
filmtvworkshop@aol.com

Beginning, intermediate and advanced acting workshops for adults and teenagers to help expose natural ability, capture auditions with originality, learn on-set protocol, and learn Industry terminology. Classes cover cold reading, improvisation, commercials, on-camera movement, overcoming stage fright, and monologues. Management, agent and casting director showcases and Industry consultations. Course audits available.

PROMENADE ACTING CONSERVATORY **(310) 656-8070**
1404 Third Street Promenade **FAX (310) 656-8069**
Santa Monica 90401
www.pierodusa.com
info@pierodusa.com

Full commercial training program available which includes Improvisation Basics, Commercial Auditioning Technique and Advanced Commercial Technique. The curriculum covers every aspect of the commercial, industrial and infomercial auditioning process with emphasis on the callback and bookings. Courses cover all commercial genres, mastering the cue card, script analysis and taking adjustments. Courses run 12 weeks and recreate the audition process, from use of space and scripts to hitting marks and filming. The advanced class invites top agents and casting directors, providing an opportunity for representation and networking. An interview and audition are required. SEE AD ON PAGES 21 & 297.

ALEXIA ROBINSON STUDIOS **(818) 779-1118**
4930 Lankershim Blvd.
North Hollywood 91601
www.alexiarobinsonstudio.com
imaginears@aol.com

Alexia Robinson Studio is a Los Angeles area acting studio for adults and kids that provides ongoing scene study classes, on-camera commercial workshops, audition technique and cold reading classes. All classes are taught by working professionals with extensive film, television and commercial credits. Classes are taught in a supportive and nurturing environment where actors can learn, grow and perfect their craft.

SECRET ROSE THEATRE **(818) 766 3691 x4**
11246 Magnolia Blvd. **FAX (818) 766-3691**
North Hollywood 91601
www.secretrose.com

In the Secret Rose 2-day commercial acting workshop you will learn how to: approach each audition intelligently, identify your strongest tools, dispel myths and misconceptions, protect yourself from scams, and run your career like a successful business. Keisuke Hoashi brings a unique blend of technical, business, and creative approaches to the skill of successful commercial acting. He currently stars in nationally broadcast commercials for Fidelity Investments; IBM; American Express and Sears; other principle roles include 7-Up; UNISYS; Burger King; Sprint; Pontiac; and FedEx, among many others. Keisuke is a genuine working actor, with an actor's perspective on teaching, and has never allowed his "type" or status as a "minority" to get in the way of a successful career. Keisuke will help you to figure out how to make every audition a great one. Call for dates and times. SEE AD ON PAGE 19.

STAGE 13 PRODUCTIONS
ROBERT BEECHER **(818) 768-3686**
10749 New Haven St., Ste. 15
Sun Valley 91352
www.stage13.com

Provides commercial, film and television classes for $60 for 4 sessions. See listing under ACTING in this section for further information.

TEPPER/GALLEGOS CASTING **(323) 469-3577**
639 N. Larchmont Blvd. **FAX (323) 464-8230**
Ste. 207
Los Angeles 90004

Offers on-camera commercial workshops taught by staff casting directors. The classes are held days and/or evenings and culminate with an agent's showcase. Classes are current and updated.

THEATRE OF ARTS (EST. 1927) **(323) 463-2500**
1621 N. McCadden Place **FAX (323) 463-2005**
Los Angeles 90028
www.theatre-of-arts.com

Offers ongoing classes for adults. The class limit is 20 and sessions are 3 hours. See listing under ACTING in this section for further information.

TVI ACTORS STUDIO **(818) 784-6500**
14429 Ventura Blvd., Ste. 118 **FAX (818) 784-6533**
Sherman Oaks 91423
www.tvistudios.com

TVI Actors Studio offers classes in on-camera commercial technique with some of L.A.'s busiest and most respected commercial casting directors, like Mick Dowd and Vicki Goggin. Students also have an opportunity to showcase their work before a panel of commercial talent agents. Founded in 1986, with studios in Los Angeles, New York and Chicago, TVI is a resource center for actors, offering dramatic instruction, entertainment industry networking, professional career consultation and marketing support for actors. In addition to a diverse curriculum of courses taught by leading Industry professionals, TVI provides members with free benefits, including daily free casting director workshops, resume and cover letter consultation with updates as often as you like, mailing labels, one-on-one counseling, use of studio space, and computer workstations with Internet access, all designed to refine the actor's craft, empower the actor with a well-rounded knowledge of the business, and clearly defined career strategy, and maximize an actor's potential in the marketplace.

UNIVERSITY OF CALIFORNIA LOS ANGELES (UCLA) (310) 825-4321
405 Hilgard Ave.
Los Angeles 90024
www.ucla.edu

Call for current catalog (310) 825-6064.

UNIVERSITY OF CALIFORNIA LOS ANGELES (UCLA) EXTENSION (310) 825-9064
10995 Le Conte Ave., Rm 437
Los Angeles 90024
www.ucla.edu

Courses and workshops for adults taught by Industry professionals. Topics include audition and interview technique, cold reading, headshots review and advice, and resume composition. Students work on-camera. See listing under ACTING in this section for further information.

UNIVERSITY OF SOUTHERN CALIFORNIA (USC) (213) 740-2311
University Park
Los Angeles 90089
www.usc.edu

For current catalog call (213) 821-2744.

BLANCA VALDEZ (323) 876-5700
1001 N. Pointsettia Pl.
Hollywood 90046
www.blancavaldez.com
bvaldez@msn.com

Teaches commercial workshops and voice-over classes in Spanish for children, age 5 through adult.

WEIST-BARRON-HILL (818) 846-5595
4300 W. Magnolia Blvd.
Burbank 91505
www.weistbarronhillacting.com
andlyle@aol.com

Offers classes for beginners and advanced level students that cover audition and interview technique, cold reading, cue card technique, headshot review and advice, improv, and resume composition. Students work in every one of these on-camera classes. Classes are limited to 12 and cost $225 for 10 sessions. No audition is required and auditing is allowed at no cost.

Crash Courses

ACCENTS, DIALECTS & SPEECH

IVAN BORODIN ACCENT ELIMINATION (323) 882-1268
202½ N. Cheremoya Ave.
Hollywood 90068

Private instruction helping actors and non-actors lose their foreign or regional accents. An intensive approach geared to develop dialectal mastery. Also offers coaching on all accents.

LILYAN CHAUVIN (323) 877-4988
3841 Eureka Dr.
Studio City 91604

Has taught many top people in Hollywood including Richard Gere and Lauren Hutton for French. See listing under ACTING in this section for further information. SEE AD ON PAGES 16 & 255.

BOB CORFF (323) 851-9042
www.corffvoice.com

Helps his clients to improve their voice and lose or strengthen their accents, fast, clearly and easily. Works in his studio, on the set, or ADR stage. Bob is co-author of the CD and workbook "Achieving the Standard American Accent" and "Accents: The Bob and Claire Corff Method." See listing under BOOKS in the MARKETING section for further information. SEE AD ON PAGE 91.

CLAIRE CORFF (323) 969-0565
www.corffvoice.com

Uses the Bob Corff Method. See her listing under ACCENTS AND DIALECTS for more information. SEE AD ON PAGE 90.

BEN D'AUBERY (818) 783-1951
13002 Riverside Dr., #10
Sherman Oaks 91423

Specializes in emergency and/or crash courses for dialects and accents. Will go to the set, ADR stage, or work with clients over the phone. No phonetics. Private coaching or classes available. See listing under VOICE: ACCENTS & DIALECTS in this section for further information.

JACKY DE HAVILAND (323) 691-7077

Offers private coaching for accents, dialects, and speech. Will teach on location, at her studio, on a set, on the ADR stage or even long distance phone. All American, European, Hispanic and Asian dialects/accents. Especially good for emergencies (like 'be Puerto Rican or Irish or Russian or Vietnamese tomorrow.') Recommended by coach Larry Moss. See listing under ACTING in this section.

THE DIALECT COACH (818) 879-1883
4948 Barbados Court FAX (818) 879-1883
Oak Park 91377
www.thedialectcoach.com
joel@thedialectcoach.com

Dialects taught quickly and easily. Most dialects learned in 1-2 private sessions.

JESSICA DRAKE (323) 662-1831
FAX (323) 662-0288

Offers dialects, Standard American Speech, Shakespeare, and accent reduction for film, TV, and stage. Works on location or her own studio. There is no time commitment. Ms. Drake is a Julliard graduate. She has coached many films including "Catch Me If You Can," "The Green Mile," "Forrest Gump," "L.A. Confidential," "What's Love Got To Do With It," "Path to War" and "Band of Brothers."

ROBERT EASTON
THE HENRY HIGGINS OF HOLLYWOOD, INC.
THE DIALECT DOCTOR (818) 985-2222

Has done crash dialect coaching at airports, in executive jets, in limousines, and over the long-distance phone. His clients have won Oscars, Emmys, Golden Globes, and awards from the Screen Actor's Guild and the Cannes Film Festival, etc. He has often taught dialects for starring roles in films and TV in one or two sessions. SEE AD ON PAGE 89.

STEVEN MEMEL STUDIO (818) 789-0474
4760 Halbrent Ave. FAX (818) 789-0835
Sherman Oaks 91403

Works with clients to reach immediate and emergency deadlines for film, studio work, stage, singing performance and ADR. Coaches at his studio, on set, on the phone or travels to location when needed. Specialties: singing, speech, diction and accent reduction. See additional listings: VOICE: SPEECH, VOICE: SINGING for more information.

LARRY MOSS
THE ACCENT-MINDED PROFESSOR (310) 395-4284

Crash coaching at the office, on the set, or over the phone to quickly learn or tune up a dialect and to meld it with the character. The goal: a full-dimensional character speaking with a seamless accent that does not call attention to itself or get in the way of the acting. Also crash coaching to help actors with regional, British or other accents to perform credibly in mainstream American. Mr. Moss also offers a four-week-cycle acting class with the accent on dialect. A veteran coach with numerous celebrity clients, he has prepped hundreds of actors for scores of films and plays. As an actor himself, he has voiced character and dialect roles in over 300 feature films and television productions.

THEATRE OF ARTS (EST. 1927) (323) 463-2500
1621 N. McCadden Pl. FAX (323) 463-2005
Los Angeles 90028
www.theatre-of-arts.com

See listing under ACTING in this section for further information.

BODY BUILDING

GOLD'S GYM (310) 392-6004
360 Hampton Dr.
Venice 90291
www.goldsgym.com

A fully equipped gym that offers body building and toning.

PRIVATE TRAINERS (818) 766-3317
(818) 679-6756
5530 Vantage Ave. FAX (818) 752-3220
Valley Village 91607
www.privatetrainers.com

Joe Antouri, Mr. USA World Champion Body Builder offers personal private training at your home or on location, including nutrition and weight management guidance. Mr. Antouri holds a Doctorate in Nutrition and Dietetics. Clients include MGM Studios, Warner Bros, HBO, Disney, Penthouse, Playboy, Dreamworks, and many actors and stunt staff. Joe is available to Gold's Gym Venice.

DIALOG COACHES

JUDY DICKERSON (818) 985-1603

Coaches dialects, dialogue, accent reduction, and voice. Extensive experience working with classic text. Has worked at Mark Taper Forum, Seattle Repertory, Intiman Theatre, A Noise Within, Circle X, Kennedy Center and Broadway. Film credits include "Education of Little Tree," "Beautiful Mind," "Master and Commander," "Gladiator," "Cinderella Man," "Lost Souls," "The Contender" and "The Insider." Available for audition preparation and location work. MFA-SMU-certified by Edith Skinner and trained with Authur Lessac.

LESLY KAHN (323) 969-9900
1720 N. La Brea Ave.
Hollywood 90046
www.leslykahn.com
lesly@leslykahn.com

Ms. Kahn works privately with actors on or off the set. See listing under ACTING in this section for further information.

JUDY KERR'S ACTING WORKSHOP (818) 505-9373
www.actingiseverything.com
judykerr@mindspring.com

Available for coaching privately on the set, ADR stage, dressing room, etc. Ms. Kerr is an on-set dialogue coach working on many television series including "Seinfeld" and "All About The Andersons." Visit the website for more information.

REEL ENGLISH (323) 957-4758
Los Angeles 90019
www.reelenglishcoach.com

Standard American dialect specialist Kelly Reiter has been coaching actors in Los Angeles since 1989. Her cutting edge character-study approach gives actors with accents the tools, confidence, and professional voice they need at every step of their career, from getting the agent to getting the part. She works exclusively with regional and non-native speakers of English and has a solid reputation at UCLA where she taught for 11 years. Assessment interview required.

FENCING

ACADEMY OF THEATRICAL COMBAT (818) 364-8420
www.theatricalcombat.com
info@theatricalcombat.com

Offers crash courses in fencing, combat, swordplay, and weaponry. See listing under COMBAT in this section for further information.

SWORDPLAY STUDIO (818) 566-1777
64 E. Magnolia Blvd.
Burbank 91502
www.swordplay.com

Offers private coaching in stage combat as well as crash courses in foil, epee, and saber. See listing under COMBAT in this section for further information.

FIRE ARMS

FIRING-LINE INDOOR SHOOTING & TRAINING RANGE (818) 349-1420
18348 Eddy St.
Northridge 91324
www.firingline.net

Training in the use of hand guns is available. The range is open Monday through Friday, noon to 10 pm and Saturday and Sunday, 10 am to 10 pm.

HORSEBACK RIDING

LOS ANGELES EQUESTRIAN CENTER (818) 569-3666
480 Riverside Dr.
Burbank 91506
www.tes-laec.com

Offers lessons in Western, basics, English, hunters, dressage, etc.

SUNSET RANCH (323) 464-9612
(323) 469-5450
3400 N. Beachwood Dr. FAX (323) 461-3061
Hollywood 90068
www.sunsetranchhollywood.com
sunsetranch3400@aol.com

Home of the famous moonlight dinner ride, open to the public. The ride takes you over the hills of Griffith Park and into Burbank for a Mexican dinner. The return ride brings you back to the stable by 11 pm. Dinner is not included in the price of the ride. Riding lessons are offered, hourly trail rides on 52 miles of trails. A boarding facility under the Hollywood sign has many nice quarter horses for sale. A full old ranch location for movie stills and video.

MARTIAL ARTS

JUN CHONG TAE KWON DO
DANNY GIBSON (818) 769-9308
5223 Lankershim Blvd.
North Hollywood 91601

Private and semi-private lessons in Tae Kwon Do and stage fighting are available for children and adults. Classes are offered days and evenings. Call for further information.

MUSIC

FAUNT SCHOOL OF CREATIVE MUSIC (818) 506-6873
12725 Ventura Blvd., Ste. G FAX (818) 508-0429
Studio City 91604
www.musicalskills.com

Private lessons are offered for all instruments. Call for further information.

GEISLER MUSIC (323) 651-2020
8410 W. 3rd St.
Los Angeles 90048

Mr. Geisler will help any actor, child or adult, play/fake any instrument for film, TV, and stage. See listing under MUSIC LESSONS in this section for further information.

TONY KOL (619) 229-1610
SCHOOL OF PERCUSSION (800) 901-6874
6335 Delbarton St.
San Diego 92120
api@4dcomm.com

Offers crash courses for all percussion instruments, Latin, traps, and ethnic. See listing under MUSIC LESSONS in this section for further information.

HOWARD RICHMAN PIANO (818) 344-3306
18375 Ventura Blvd., #8000
Tarzana 91356
www.soundfeelings.com/products/music_instruction/piano_lessons.htm
howardrichman@soundfeelings.com

He can teach you how to really play, or at least how to look like you've played piano for years, in a hurry. All styles. Also works with singers who need to learn self-accompanying, sight-singing and ear-training. Free introductory lesson.

PATRICIA SHANKS (949) 723-4473
www.studioshanks.com
pshanks@studioshanks.com

A private studio facility offering voice instruction and musicianship training for singers ages 12 and over, beginning through advanced. The focus is traditional, educational, foundation-based and fine arts-oriented. Establish a reliable technique and eliminate externally applied cosmetic affectations related to technique (voice production) and performance (presentation). Newport Beach. 28 years experience. Member: NATS, MTAC, AGMA, SCVA.

SCUBA

BLUE CHEER **(310) 828-1217**
1112 Wilshire Blvd.
Santa Monica 90401

Classes or private instruction in scuba diving are available. Call for further information. There is a pool on the premises.

SINGING

MARA BAYGULOVA **(818) 241-8141**

Teaches private lessons for all types of singing covering range, agility and power. Works with children, teens, and adults of all levels, days, evenings, and weekends. Auditing is allowed. Crash training is available. Ms. Baygulova is a professional musical theatre and opera singer, and teacher of Grammy Nominated singer Duncan Sheik. Also piano and cello lessons.

BOB CORFF **(323) 851-9042**
www.corffvoice.com

Gets results fast. See his listing in this section under SINGING. SEE AD ON PAGE 91.

CLAIRE CORFF **(323) 969-0565**
www.corffvoice.com

A Bob Corff associate who offers crash courses in singing. SEE AD ON PAGE 90.

PATRICIA SHANKS **(949) 723-4473**
www.studioshanks.com
pshanks@studioshanks.com

A private studio facility offering voice instruction and musicianship training for singers ages 12 and over, beginning through advanced. The focus is traditional, educational, foundation-based and fine arts-oriented. Establish a reliable technique and eliminate externally applied cosmetic affectations related to technique (voice production) and performance (presentation). Newport Beach. 28 years experience. Member: NATS, MTAC, AGMA, SCVA.

SKATING

BOBBI MCRAE **(310) 836-7748** **(310) 922-2777**
4545 Sepulveda Blvd.
Culver City 90230
skatermcrae@aol.com

Private instruction for all levels at the Culver City Ice Arena. Has worked with "The Wonder Years," "NYPD Blue," "Party of Five," "ER," and "Jingle All The Way."

DEBBIE MERRILL'S SKATE GREAT USA SCHOOL OF SKATING **(310) 820-1969** **(888) 866-6121**
P.O. Box 3452
Santa Monica 90408
www.skategreat.com

Teaches actors to speak, think, act, skate, and hit their mark at the same time. "Skate to look and feel great." Inline, roller, and ice skating lessons. Private and group classes are available for beg-adv. Ms. Merrill is IISA Certified and a USFSA silver medalist in figure skating. Children starting at age 4 through 84. Has worked with Steve Martin, Melanie Griffith, Geena Davis, Chris Maloney, Kim Delaney, Juliette Lewis, Downtown Julie Brown and former Mayor Richard Riordan. Skating Consultant for "NYPD Blue," "L.A. Story," "White Men Can't Jump," "Party of Five," "Legally Blonde," and "Charlie's Angels" as well The David Letterman Show" etc. Also casts skaters, scouts locations and performs. SAG and AFTRA. Co-host for vegtv.com, Ms. Merrill is an actress, dancer and choreographer and spokesperson. Her new video "Skate to Look and Feel Great at any Age" due out this fall.

NORTHRIDGE SKATELAND **(818) 885-1491**
18140 Parthenia St.
Northridge 91342

Private roller skating lessons are available. The instructor is an SRSTA member and hours are flexible.

VAN NUYS ICELAND **(818)785-2171**
14318 Calvert St.
Van Nuys 91401

Private and group lessons available.

SOCIAL & BALLROOM DANCING

ARTHUR MURRAY DANCE STUDIOS **(310) 274-8867**
262 N. Beverly Dr.
Beverly Hills 90210

4633 Van Nuys Blvd. **(818) 783-2623**
Sherman Oaks 91403
www.arthurmurray.com

Private coaching is available for social and ballroom dancing.

THIRD STREET DANCE **(310) 275-4683**
8558 W. 3rd St.
Los Angeles 90048
www.thirdstreetdance.com

Specializes in all adult Ballroom, Argentine Tango, Salsa, and wedding dances. Private coaching is available.

SPECIALTY VEHICLES – BOATS

CALYPSO **(949) 675-0827**
3300 Via Lido
Newport Beach 92663
www.lidosailingclub.com

Learn to sail in five 3-hour sessions that meet on the weekends. Students can take 3 sessions on one weekend.

SPECIALTY VEHICLES – MOTORCYCLES

MOTORCYCLE TRAINING CENTER **(818) 932-0433**
P. O. Box 10326
Canoga Park 91306
www.motorcycletrainingcenter.com

Offers a beginning safety course and advanced training for the experienced rider. Call for schedule, enrollment procedures, prices, and locations.

CRASH COURSES

TENNIS

GRIFFITH PARK TENNIS INSTRUCTION (323) 662-7772
3401 Riverside Dr.
Los Angeles 90027

Will teach any and all strokes on a crash course basis or in continuing study. They will make you look like a pro.

HILLHURST TENNIS CENTER (323) 661-2769
1600 Hillhurst Ave.
Los Angeles 90027

Will teach any all strokes on a crash course basis or in continuing study. They will make you look like a pro.

TRAMPOLINE & TUMBLING

SOUTH BAY GYMNASTICS
SPORTS COMPLEX (310) 328-3136
1275 Sartori Avenue FAX (310) 328-5573
Torrance 90501
www.southbaygymnastics.com
info@southbaygymnastics.com

State of the art gymnastics and martial arts training. Sword play and other weapons for film and stage is also available. High falls, tumbling, mini trampoline, tumble track, and training pit are just a few of the equipment and services they provide. High ceilings with a twenty foot cargo net for Galaxy and fitness training as well as the other obstacles in the training course make for a full service facility. They also feature aerobic kickboxing.

DANCE

ACADEMY OF PERFORMING ARTS (619) 282-1884
4580 Alvarado Canyon Rd. FAX (619) 282-9889
Ste. B
San Diego 92120
www.apastudios.com
kp@apastudios.com

Teaches modern, jazz, tap, ballet, tumbling, street/hip hop, Irish step dancing, flamenco, and has special master classes. A full scholarship program is available. See listing under ACTING in this section for further information.

STELLA ADLER ACADEMY OF ACTING
AND THEATRE COMPLEX (323) 465-4446
6773 Hollywood Blvd., 2nd Fl. FAX (323) 469-6049
Hollywood 90028
www.stellaadler-la.com

Academy director: Irene Gilbert. Call for catalogue and further information. SEE AD ON PAGE 6.

ALEXANDER TECHNIQUE & FELDENKRAIS
AWARENESS THROUGH MOVEMENT®
JUDITH STRANSKY (310) 828-5528
stranskyj@aol.com FAX (310) 828-1028

Ms. Stransky applies 42 years experience as a specialist in releasing problems and limitations in performance and daily life, through teaching freedom of the body. These methods teach mastery over body and skills through a profound re-education of posture and movement habits and mental focus. They are designed to effortlessly achieve optimum ease, freedom, flexibility, suppleness and tone, leading to opening up and perfecting performance, expression, and self confidence as well as alleviating stage fright, physical pain and stress for both students and professionals. Nina Foch, "With body and voice, the only things that work are techniques that can become a part of your entire life. This is what the Alexander Technique does, better than any other technique I know ... Judith Stransky has shown me the way." Clients include stars of stage and screen. Both methods are included world-wide in dance, movement and acting training by foremost teachers, acting companies, drama schools, and universities. Ms. Stransky is a former faculty member of the USC Drama Dept., a Senior Teacher at UCLA Extension, and author of "The Alexander Technique: Joy In The Life Of Your Body." SEE AD ON PAGE 11.

ALEXANDER TECHWORKS
JEAN-LOUIS RODRIGUE (310) 209-9023
KRISTOF KONRAD (310) 443-4483
P.O. Box 3194
Beverly Hills 90212
www.alexandertechworks.com
jeanlouisr1@yahoo.com

During the past 25 years Alexander Techworks has offered ongoing group classes, private instruction, and intensive courses offered by AmSAT Certified Teachers. The Alexander Technique helps the actor gain a fundamental awareness, control, and freedom of the whole self. Goals of the technique are effortless movement, increased coordination, a fuller capacity of breath, improvement in the use of the voice and speech, increased tonus in the musculature and a stronger sense of the self. Courses are offered in character development through physicalization and period movement. Studio locations in Westwood and Santa Monica. Mr. Rodrigue has been part of the faculty at the UCLA School of Theatre, Film, and Television for the past 15 years. SEE AD ON PAGE 4.

AMERICAN DANCE INSTITUTE
JONETTE SWIDER (818) 385-1382
14374 Ventura Blvd., 7th Fl.
Studio City 91604

Offers a full ballet program for age 3 through adult. Jonette Swider director of school now has a junior ballet company.

ANGELITA'S CONCIERTO FLAMENCO (562) 941-3925
11622 Marquadt Ave.
Whittier 90605

Beg-pro dance training for adults. Flamenco and Spanish. Students are often chosen to be members of their dance company.

ANNESA SCHOOL (818) 752-9829
OF EASTERN DANCE (818) 986-4738
14252 Ventura Blvd.
Sherman Oaks 91423
www.anisadance.com

A variety of classes are offered for adults and children including belly dancing, salsa, ballet, jazz, tango, ballroom, swing, hip hop, East Indian, modern dancing, tap, aerobics and fitness classes. Two studios, 1200 sq. ft. and 900 sq. ft. Both studios have good wooden floors, the larger studio has piano.

ART OF THE DANCE ACADEMY (818) 760-8675
11144 Weddington St. FAX (818) 760-8604
North Hollywood 91601

Offers classes in tap, jazz, ballet, and mommy and me classes. They have a summer performing arts campus group for children and teens. They also offer choreography and dance coaching. Classes are offered 6 days a week. There is a discount for union members and groups.

BALLET ECARTE (310) 477-6414
1365 Westwood Blvd. FAX (310) 265-0938
Los Angeles 90024
www.balletla.com
balletecarte@earthlink.net

Offers classical ballet using the Kirov (Vaganova) Technique. Classes are for beg-pro children through adult. There is no time commitment required. They offer single classes, series, and private lessons. They also offer regular showcases and there are performance opportunities available for all age groups. There is a discount for union members. Call for schedule.

BEACON STREET DANCE PROJECT (323) 633-0466
beaconstdance@earthlink.net

Classes are held weekly and are open to non-company dancers. A modern dance theatre company comprised of dancers, actors and musicians of various backgrounds specializing in collaborative fusion performance works.

DANCECORP (626) 792-4616
100 W. Villa FAX (626) 792-4893
Pasadena 91103
www.lestudiodance.com

Offers ballet, jazz, tap, hip hop, and body conditioning based on the Pilates method for beg-adv children, teens, and adults. They have a professional ballet program.

EDGE PERFORMING ARTS CENTER (323) 962-7733
1020 N. Cole Ave., 4th Fl.
Hollywood 90038
www.edgepac.com

Dance classes ranging from the basics to the professional level that cover ballet, jazz, tap, and hip hop. Call for more information.

GLENDALE COMMUNITY COLLEGE (818) 240-1000
1500 N. Verdugo Rd.
Glendale 91208
www.glendale.cc.ca.us

Classes in jazz, ballet, and modern dance are offered for beg-adv students. They also offer dance workshops, choreography classes, and a Master Class that is taught by top Industry choreographers. A certificate is offered in Choreographic Studies and Dance Techniques. They give several performances at the end of the year.

HOLLYWOOD DANCE CENTER (323) 467-0826
817 N. Highland FAX (323) 467-1525
Hollywood 90038
www.hollywooddancecenter.com

Classes in ballet, tap, ballroom, Argentinian Tango, belly dancing, Flamenco. Studio rentals for auditions, workshops, classes or film and video shoots.

HUNTINGTON ACADEMY OF DANCE (714) 847-6657
16601 Gothard, #A & #B FAX (714) 960-4361
Huntington Beach 92647
www.huntingtonacademyofdance.com

Offers ballet, tap, jazz, song and dance, and modern dance for children, teens, and adults of all levels. They have just added a hula class for age 6 thru adult. An audition is required for some of the classes and auditing is allowed. They have showcases and/or performances for their students. Occasionally students work on-camera. Discounts are given to union members. Home of Ballet Etudes.

JAZZ TAP ENSEMBLE (DRC) (310) 475-4412
1416 Westwood Blvd., #207C FAX (310) 475-4037
Los Angeles 90024
jtensemble@aol.com

Artistic Director: Lynn Dally, Company Manager: Gayle Hooks. Offers rhythm tap classes for all levels. Workshops and master classes taught by Sam Weber, Lainie Manning, and Lynn Dally. They also hold annual holiday workshops that are held Dec 26-31. Private lessons are available.

KATNAP DANCE CENTER (310) 306-7069
12932 Venice Blvd.
Los Angeles 90066
www.katnapdance.net

Director: Kathleen Knapp. Offers classes in ballet, jazz, tap, modern, ballet folklorico, and hip hop for all levels, children through adult. There in no time commitment required. 5-20 students per class. Private lessons are available. Single classes can be purchased or a series for a reduced rate. They offer discounts for union members. Studio space can be rented, and there is a dancewear shop on the premises.

PAUL AND ARLENE KENNEDY'S
UNIVERSAL DANCE DESIGN (323) 938-6508
6009 W. Olympic Blvd.
Los Angeles 90036

Directors Paul and Arlene Kennedy offer classes in all styles of dance including Latino, hip hop, and African dancing. Classes are for beg-adv levels starting at age 2 through adult. They also offer gymnastics yoga for children and adults. Studio rental space available.

ELSPETH KUANG (323) 732-9276

Teaches ballet technique to develop a sense of movement with grace, style, and balance for the actor as well as the dancer. Private instruction and group classes are offered for beg-pro teens, and adults.

MARTIN DANCERS (818) 752-2616
11401 N. Chandler Blvd. FAX (213) 386-6299
North Hollywood 91601

Dance drama and rhythm vocals are performed using the Horton technique and style. The company works with professional level dancers. There is a 6 month-1 year time commitment required for apprentices, and a 2 year commitment required for company members. Auditions are ongoing for company B. Dance classes are available. They hold musical improvs on Sundays with dancers performing to music. A children's company with scholorships is available. Call for audition information.

MILLENNIUM DANCE COMPLEX (818) 753-5081
5113 Lankershim Blvd. FAX (818) 752-8386
North Hollywood 91601
www.millenniumdancecomplex.com

Classes in jazz, ballet, modern dance and hip hop funk for all levels from beg-pro. There is no time commitment. The studios are available for rehearsals, auditions, workshops, and videos.

MILLER ON TAP JANET MILLER (818) 990-6691
millerontap@earthlink.net

Specializing in musical theatre, dance and tap for all levels and every age. Ms. Miller is an experienced director/choreographer. She is available for private consultation and coaching for musical theatre roles. JM is very well known for her "show doctoring" abilities.

ARTHUR MURRAY DANCE STUDIO
BEVERLY HILLS (310) 274-8867
262 North Beverly Dr. FAX (310) 274-8869
Beverly Hills 90210
www.dancestudios.com
arthurmurraybh@aol.com

Classes for adults are offered in all forms of ballroom dancing including: Swing, Salsa, Foxtrot, Waltz, Tango, Cha Cha, Rumba, Samba, Country, Merengue and Disco.

VALENTINA OUMANSKY (323) 850-9497
3433 Cahuenga Blvd. West FAX (323) 876-9055
Los Angeles 90068
www.dramaticdance.org
valentina@dramaticdance.org

Adult classes for dramatic dance on Tuesdays and Thursdays, children for ballet on Saturday mornings. Also a workshop that includes original choreographic works. Dramatic dance techniques.

OUTBACK STUDIO
JENNIFER NAIRN SMITH (323) 938-6836
866 S Bronson Ave. FAX (323) 876-9055
Los Angeles 90005
www.outbackstudios.com

Original Balanchine/Fosse dancer teaches original Fosse choreography; original "All That Jazz" the movie. Private instruction in ballet, tap, and jazz for children and adults. The studio can be rented for rehearsals and auditions. Also teaches Pilates.

PASADENA CIVIC BALLET (626) 792-0873
25 S. Sierra Madre Blvd. FAX (626) 356-0313
Pasadena 91107
www.pcballet.com
inforequest@pcballet.com

Formed in 1980, the Pasadena Civic Ballet Company (PCB) is a not-for-profit organization of pre-professional and professional dancers from ages 10 and up. These are serious, talented ballet students who are accepted by audition or judgment of the director. Referred to as the "Company", the PCB has four divisions: Junior, Teen, Senior, and Chamber Ensemble. The Junior and Teen divisions are for dancers ages 10-15. The members must have a minimum of three classes and one rehearsal per week. The Senior division is for dancers ages 13 and above, and requires at least four technique classes each week; at least three ballet (including Pointe) and one in character, jazz, hip hop or tap. Seniors also have at least one rehearsal per week. The Chamber Ensemble is for selected Senior dancers and older graduates or professional dancers that perform together with the Company and for special engagements. Company members have the opportunity of performing in major productions before large audiences. The Company's original presentations have included "A Christmas Carol", "Hansel and Gretel," and "Cinderella" as well as numerous other presentations. These performances provide a wonderful showcase for all of the dancers, with ensemble and solo opportunities. Dancers also perform in our annual "Solo Fete" and the PCB Center Showcases, as well as invitational events, charity groups, in-studio concerts, and guest appearances.

PASADENA DANCE THEATRE (626) 683-3459
1985 E. Locust St. FAX (626) 683-3559
Pasadena 91107

Offers jazz, ballet, tap and body conditioning for beg-adv children, teens and adults. Discounts are given for series of classes and union members.

BERT PRIVAL SCHOOL OF BALLET (818) 842-9242
San Fernando Valley

Classical ballet classes and private instruction are offered for beg-adv children and adults. There is pre-ballet for children starting at age 4½ and up. Class size limited. Series can be taken for a reduced rate and there is a discount for union members. 63 years in business in the San Fernando Valley. Please call for information.

DENNON AND SAYHBER
RAWLES DANCE INSTRUCTION (818) 709-7542
20314 Lorne St.
Canoga Park 91306

Classes are offered in jazz, tap, and ballet for all levels. The Rawles' are choreographers for film, TV, commercials, and stage and offer private instruction.

DEBBIE REYNOLDS STUDIOS (818) 985-3193
6514 Lankershim Blvd.
North Hollywood 91606
www.drdancestudio.com

Classes for all levels are offered in jazz, tap, and ballet. There is no time commitment and the class size varies. Students can pay per class or by the series. There is a discount for union members in some of the classes. Rehearsal and audition space is available for rental. See listing under REHEARSAL STUDIOS in the MARKETING section for further information.

HILLARY AYN RYAN'S
JAZZTAP DANCE (818) 623-7153
www.hillaryaynryan.com
jazztapdance@hotmail.com

Specializes in Absolute Beginner-Intermediate Broadway style of Tap and Theater Jazz. Classes are taught in 6, 8 and 10 week sessions for adults, children and teens with an emphasis on fun. Classes are small, taught in North Hollywood and on the west side and are supportive. Also available for privates, semi-private lessons and choreography.

SANTA MONICA DANCE STUDIO (310) 319-5339
211 Arizona Ave.
Santa Monica 90401
www.santamonicadancestudio.com

Adult classes: ballet, modern, jazz, hip hop, tap and much more. Check out the website for more information. Pilates: all levels. Children's program, 2 1/2 years and up. Studio rentals available.

THE SOUTH BAY BALLET (310) 532-2703
1261 Sartori Ave.
Torrance 90501
www.southbayballet.org

Artistic Director: Diane Lauridsen.

THE LEE STRASBERG THEATRE INSTITUTE (323) 650-7777
7936 Santa Monica Blvd. FAX (323) 650-7770
Los Angeles 90046
www.strasberg.com
admissionsla@strasberg.com

Offers classes in movement and jazz. See listing under ACTING in this section for further information.

STUDIO A DANCE (323) 661-8311
2306 Hyperion Ave.
Los Angeles 90027
www.studioadance.com

Classes in ballet, jazz, bellydancing, Hawaiian, tap and aerobics are offered. They have classes designed for actors and office workers who have no dance background. Class size is 8-15. They offer series at a reduced rate and there is a discount for union members on the single classes. Studio rental is available. They give a showcase once a year. Has a scholarship program with the Los Angeles City Ballet of gifted children. 99 seat theatre plan.

SYNTHESIS DANCE STUDIO (818) 754-1760
4200 Lankershim Blvd.
Universal City 91602
www.synthesisarts.com
dance@synthesisarts.com

Ballet, jazz, tap, hip hop, modern, ballroom, salsa, and tango for dancers and entertainment. Special program for children and a performing company. All instructors at Synthesis are professionals with extensive and distinguished careers as a performers, choreographers and teachers. Great location for rentals. Renting space available for private lessons, auditions, rehearsals, workshops, music video, filming, etc.

JUAN TALAVERA (562) 699-7595
11018 Loch Lomond Dr.
Whittier 90606
www.flamencobravo.com
juan@flamencobravo.com

Teaches Spanish and Flamenco dancing in ongoing classes for beg-adv teens and adults. Classes held at Santa Ana College, East L.A. College, Rio Hondo College, Step by Step Dance Studio, Palm Springs, and the Center for World Dance, Alhambra, California.

THEATRE OF ARTS (EST. 1927) (323) 463-2500
1621 N. McCadden Place FAX (323) 463-2005
Los Angeles 90028
www.theatre-of-arts.com

See listing under ACTING for more information.

THIRD STREET DANCE (310) 275-4683
8558 W. 3rd St.
Los Angeles 90048
www.thirdstreetdance.com

Offers ballroom dancing for adult. Swing, lindy hop, salsa and tango. Private sessions, single classes, and series are available. They have 5 studios, air conditioning, and parking. There is rental space available for rehearsals and they also offer crash courses.

UNIVERSITY OF CALIFORNIA LOS ANGELES (UCLA) (310) 825-3951
11000 Kinross Ave. FAX (310) 825-7507
Los Angeles 90095
www.ucla.edu

Offers mostly modern dance classes but also classes in world dance, ballet choreography, dance therapy and dance education. For current catalog call (310) 825-6064.

UNIVERSITY OF SOUTHERN CALIFORNIA (USC) (213) 821-2744
University Park
Los Angeles 90089
www.usc.edu

Call for the Theatre School and current catalog.

LULA WASHINGTON DANCE THEATRE (323) 936-6591
5041 W. Pico Blvd.
Los Angeles 90019
www.lulawashington.com
mail@lulawashington.com

Excellence in dance training since 1980. Offers classes in ballet, modern, jazz, hip hop, African and more. Year round classes.

STEFAN WENTA DANCERS STUDIO (310) 836-8036
5772-A W. Pico Blvd.
Los Angeles 90019

Offers classes in classical dance for beg-pro adults. Also offers classical etudes for actors. Single classes and private lessons are available. Offers professional rates.

WESTSIDE ACADEMY OF DANCE (310) 828-2018
1709 Stewart St.
Santa Monica 90402

Offers classes for children, teens, and adults of all levels in ballet, jazz, modern, tap, aerobics, flamenco, and many other styles of dance. There are from 1-20 students in a class although the average is 15. Single classes or a series of classes can be purchased. There is a discount for union members and for children who take the minimum recommended classes. They offer 2 showcases a year.

YWCA (310) 452-3881
2019 14th St. FAX (310) 392-7578
Santa Monica 90405

Frequently teaches modern dance, ballet, aerobics, and yoga classes. Courses vary each session. There are many classes for children and some for teens and adults. There are scholarships available. They also have an improv dance group. Call for further information.

MAKE-UP

AWARD STUDIOS **(310) 395-2779**
www.aawd.net

Free photo sessions with experienced photographer, Amy Ward. She works internationally with Vogue, Vanity Fair, etc. Ms. Ward also trains make-up artists and they need actors and models with clear skin to work on for their portfolios. To find out more about this opportunity, call or visit the website.

JOE BLASCO **(323) 467-4949**
1670 Hillhurst Ave. **FAX (323) 664-1834**
Los Angeles 90027
www.joeblasco.com

A training facility and manufacturer of professional make-up. Offers an 11 week course that includes motion picture, TV, political, print, theatre, music video, old-age, and beauty make-up as well as over 70 phases of character and special effects make-up, prosthetics class, mold making, hair-work classes, making of "bladders," motion picture and TV lighting (in-house studio), lectures by renowned guest make-up artists, and cosmetic compounding. The classes are held 7 hours per day, 5 days per week, days or evenings. A 2 week beauty make-up course is now being offered. There is a theatrical make-up store on the premises in the Los Angeles location only which is within one block of the school. They offer a discount for actors. By appointment only. They also have a make-over service.

CINEMA SECRETS **(818) 846-0579**
4400 Riverside Dr. **FAX (818) 846-0431**
Burbank 91505
www.cinemasecrets.com
cinemasecretsinfo@cinemasecrets.com

Free product demonstration class is available to acting schools. Offers general as well as specific classes in make-up for the actor. Private lessons are also available upon request. Staff make-up artists are available for private makeovers at their facilities for head shots. See listing under PROFESSIONAL MAKE-UP in the MARKETING section for further information.

THE COSTUME SHOP **(619) 574-6201**
2010 El Cajon Blvd.
San Diego 92104
www.thecostumeshop.net
contactus@thecostumeshop.net

Has make-up classes and carries Ben Nye, Mehron, Cinema Secrets, and clown make-up as well as special effects make-up. Discount to actors who are with the Actor's Alliance in San Diego. Monday through Friday, 10 am to 5 pm and Saturday, 9 am to 1 pm. They were moving at the time of publication. Check website or call for new address. See listing under PROFESSIONAL MAKE-UP in the MARKETING section for further information.

ELEGANCE INTERNATIONAL INC. **(323) 871-8318**
1622 N. Highland Ave. **FAX (323) 871-8367**
Los Angeles 90028
www.eleganceacademy.com

Offers 7 make-up courses including beauty, theatre, motion picture and television, prosthetics, special effects, advanced prosthetics, sculpting and drawing, and high fashion photography. Students receive a diploma for completion of all subjects. 5 quarter credits are given for each class, except the motion picture and TV class. Accredited by A.C.C.S.C.T. Most classes are 2 months in length except the motion picture and TV classes which are 4 months in length. Financial aid is available for those who qualify.

LOS ANGELES CITY COLLEGE **(323) 953-4000 x2987**
855 N. Vermont Ave
Los Angeles 90029
www.lacitycollege.edu

Offers one two-unit make-up class during the day per semester.

STUDIO MAKEUP ACADEMY **(323) 465-4002**
1438 N. Gower #14
Hollywood 90028
www.studiomakeupacademy.com

The Studio Makeup Academy is the only school in the world located inside a major film and television studio. The Academy provides the essential training needed to become a professional makeup artist in the entertainment and beauty industries. The Beauty Makeup Artist Course class covers all phases of beauty makeup, Basic Commercial Beauty Makeup, Basic Principles of Photographic Makeup, Makeup for Black and White Photography, Makeup for Color Photography, etc. The Film and Television Special Effect Course covers Makeup for Video and Film—Motion Pictures, Television, Video and Stage Special Effects and Face Casting for Prosthetic Makeup.

UNIVERSITY OF CALIFORNIA
LOS ANGELES (UCLA) EXTENSION **(310) 825-9064**
10995 Le Conte Ave., Rm 437
Los Angeles 90024
www.ucla.edu

The workshops are taught by Industry professionals who cover all types of make-up styles including beauty, corrective, special effects, etc.

WESTMORE ACADEMY
OF COSMETIC ARTS **(818) 562-6808**
916 W. Burbank Blvd., Ste R **FAX (818) 562-6617**
Burbank 91506
www.westmoreacademy.com
westmore@earthlink.net

The ultimate in professional make-up education for spa, salon, fashion, photography, film and television.

Modeling Schools

ADRIAN TEEN MODELS
AGENCY & SCHOOL **(626) 795-2560**
1021 E. Walnut, #101 **FAX (626) 795-9529**
Pasadena 91106

Classes are offered for females only, age 11 through 21. Some of the areas covered are make-up styles, movement, personality development, clothing choices, hair, runway, photographic, tea room, wholesale/retail modeling, TV, and go sees. There are evening classes available. An interview is required. They are a state licensed modeling and talent agency.

BARBIZON MODELING SCHOOL **(562) 799-2985**
4050 Katella Ave., Ste. 213
Los Alamitos 90720
www.modelingschools.com

Classes for children, teens, men, and women are offered in which the students work on acting, modeling, and TV commercials. Students must commit to 34-90 hours of classes that are held evenings and weekends. An interview is required and private coaching is available. State licensed. In business since 1939 with over 90 locations nationally and internationally. They are also a modeling agency.

BB'S KIDS **(323) 650 KIDS**
www.bbskids.com

This cool, hip new 8 week class will focus on the overall modeling experience: print, runway, movement, music videos, spokesmodeling and other modeling opportunities. In addition, self-confidence and unique personal style will be emphasized along with the basics of the fashion industry in both local and international markets. The final performance will feature a mini fashion show; a montage of photo posing and runway catwalk skills. Taught by Liv Boughn. Age 10 and up. SEE AD ON PAGE 41.

TALENT ACADEMY, INC. **(800) 878-5070** **(310) 962-0414**
P.O. Box 1738
Hollywood 90078
www.talentacademy.com
talentacademy@aol.com

Talent Academy, Inc., offers training for stage, film and television actors. The training program called The Essence of Holistic Acting, created by Mr. George Djordjevic, the President of the Talent Academy, has been praised as "the most innovative and effective" approach to developing actors' skills. This program combines the original Stanislavsky System, with American and European acting trends, placing equal attention on actor's mind, body and spirit. In addition, Talent Academy will be the major sponsor of the Los Angeles Actors Showcase scheduled for fall of this year. To learn more or to schedule an interview visit the Talent Academy's website, email or call.

Movement

ACTORS CO-OP **(323) 462-8460**
1760 N. Gower **FAX (323) 462-3199**
Hollywood 90028
www.actorsco-op.org
jcuster@fpch.org

Actors Co-op Actor's Academy is a year round program that provides exceptional training for the actor. Classes for all levels beginner to advanced are taught by working professionals with a curriculum focused on acting, however future directors, producers and writers will also find this program a valuable learning experience. Scene study, improvisation, voice work, movement, character development and technique.

STELLA ADLER ACADEMY OF ACTING
AND THEATRE COMPLEX **(323) 465-4446**
6773 Hollywood Blvd., 2nd Fl. **FAX (323) 469-6049**
Hollywood 90028
www.stellaadler-la.com

Academy director, Irene Gilbert. Call for catalogue and further information. Scene study and script analysis. SEE AD ON PAGE 6.

ALEXANDER TECHNIQUE & FELDENKRAIS
AWARENESS THROUGH MOVEMENT®
JUDITH STRANSKY **(310) 828-5528**
stranskyj@aol.com **FAX (310) 828-1028**

Ms. Stransky applies 42 years experience as a specialist in releasing problems and limitations in performance and daily life, through teaching freedom of the body. These methods teach mastery over body and skills through a profound re-education of posture and movement habits and mental focus. They are designed to effortlessly achieve optimum ease, freedom, flexibility, suppleness and tone, leading to opening up and perfecting performance, expression, and self confidence, as well as alleviating stage fright, physical pain and stress for both students and professionals. Nina Foch, "With body and voice, the only things that work are techniques that can become a part of your entire life. This is what the Alexander Technique does, better than any other technique I know ... Judith Stransky has shown me the way." Clients include stars of stage and screen. Both methods are included world-wide in movement, dance and acting training by foremost teachers, acting companies, drama schools, and universities. Ms. Stransky is a former faculty member of USC Drama Department, a Senior Teacher at UCLA Extension, and author of "The Alexander Technique: Joy in the Life of Your Body." SEE AD ON PAGE 11.

ALEXANDER TECHWORKS
JEAN-LOUIS RODRIGUE **(310) 209-9023**
KRISTOF KONRAD **(310) 443-4483**
P.O. Box 3194
Beverly Hills 90212
www.alexandertechworks.com
jeanlouisr1@yahoo.com

During the past 25 years Alexander Techworks has offered ongoing group classes, private instruction, and intensive courses offered by AmSAT Certified Teachers. The Alexander Technique helps the actor gain a fundamental awareness, control, and freedom of the whole self. Goals of the technique are effortless movement, increased coordination, a fuller capacity of breath, improvement in the use of the voice and speech, increased tonus in the musculature and a stronger sense of the self. Courses are offered in character development through physicalization and period movement. Studio locations in Westwood and Santa Monica. Mr. Rodrigue has been part of the faculty at the UCLA School of Theatre, Film, and Television for the past 15 years. SEE AD ON PAGE 4.

THE AMERICAN ACADEMY OF DRAMATIC ARTS (323) 464-2777
1336 N. La Brea Ave.
Hollywood 90028
www.aada.org
bjustin@ca.aada.org

See listing under ACTING in this section for further information.

CALIFORNIA STATE UNIVERSITY LOS ANGELES (CSULA) (323) 343-3000
5151 State University Dr.
Los Angeles 90032
www.calstatela.edu

Offers voice, movement and musical theatre training. They produce large musicals at various times throughout the year.

ANTHONY DI NOVI (310) 490-4761
anthonydinovi@earthlink.net

Private one-on-one work in various forms of movement for the actor to develop concentration and to work with performance anxiety. Classes include T'ai Chi, Qi Quong, yoga, and meditation.

ANNA DRESDON AT THE RACHEL ROSENTHAL STUDIO (310) 839-0661 (310) 559-8414
2847 S. Robertson Blvd.
Los Angeles 90034
www.annadresdon.com

Anna Dresdon has over 20 experience teaching and performing and offers workshops, private coaching and audition material preparation. She focuses on creating strong movement, precise gesture, a clear image and a commanding presence. "Anna Dresdon is very talented, dedicated and possessed by the spirit of mime... I embrace Anna Dresdon's work with all my heart."–Marcel Marceau

LINDA LACK M.A. TWO-SNAKE STUDIO (310) 273-4797
1637 S. La Cienega Boulevard FAX (323) 932-1441
Los Angeles 90035
www.lindalack.com
lindalack@earthlink.net

The Thinking Body-The Feeling Mind™(SM) is a technique that uses Hatha Yoga and movement therapy for creativity, healing, and spirituality. Lack also offers injury related therapy and help for performance using movement and tension release; technique and teacher training for beginning through advanced actors, dancers and athletes.

LOS ANGELES CITY COLLEGE (LACC) (323) 953-4000 x2990
855 N. Vermont Ave. FAX (323) 953-4500
Los Angeles 90029
www.lacitycollege.edu

Offers basic theatre movement, period movement, circus techniques, Alexander Technique and gymnastics. Curriculum changes each term. For the current catalog call the above number.

LOS ANGELES VALLEY COLLEGE (818) 947-2600
5800 Fulton Ave.
Van Nuys 91404
www.lavc.cc.ca.us

Offers fencing, dance and exercise programs. The curriculum changes each term. Call for the current brochure.

FRANCES MARSDEN ALEXANDER TECHNIQUE (818) 760-6454
www.artofmovement.com
fmarsdenat@aol.com

Frances Marsden trained as an actress at the Royal Scottish Academy of Drama in Glasgow, Scotland, and then trained for three years to become a teacher of the Alexander Technique. She has been teaching for 24 years and has considerable experience working with actors. The Alexander Technique is usually taught in private forty-five minute sessions and helps actors become more effective on stage and screen, as tension eases, movement becomes more flexible and emotions more accessible. It's a "hands on" technique, guiding you to a greater awareness of habitual patterns and mannerisms which interfere with your coordination and poise. By learning how to consciously eliminate these habits, you are free to give a more fully alive performance.

MIME THEATRE STUDIO LORIN ERIC SALM (866) 444-MIME
www.mimetheatrestudio.com

Mime Theatre is actor-centered theatre, where the actor is not only interpreter, but also creator. It is an art that transcends the need for words. Students learn mime as a specialized art of the stage, through the styles of French masters Marcel Marceau, Etienne Decroux, and others. Skills include movement technique, character creation, scene construction, and applying concepts through improvisation and prepared work. This training is excellent for traditional speaking actors, dancers, comedians, and mime artists. Lorin Eric Salm trained with world-renowned master Marcel Marceau, and is a graduate of Marceau's Paris International School of Mimodrama. He also studied under former assistants of Etienne Decroux, and with Polish master Stefan Niedzialkowski. He has taught mime and character movement to mime artists, actors, dancers, comedians, and animation artists (Disney and DreamWorks), and is author/administrator of The World of Mime Theatre, the Internet's premier mime website. Class sessions begin every several weeks and run year-round, for beginning through advanced levels.

THE LEE STRASBERG THEATRE INSTITUTE (323) 650-7777
7936 Santa Monica Blvd.
Los Angeles 90046
www.strasberg.com
admissionsla@strasberg.com

Movement classes (jazz and T'ai Chi) are offered within the Institute's complete training program. See listing under ACTING in this section for further information.

THE THEATRE DISTRICT (323) 957-2343
804 North El Centro
Hollywood 90038
www.thetheatredistrict.com
info@thetheatredistrict.com

Macario Gaxiola conducts classes covering scene study, cold reading and audition technique. Also covered: movement and dialects. Private coaching available.

THEATRE OF ARTS (EST. 1927) (323) 463-2500
1621 N. McCadden Place FAX (323) 463-2005
Los Angeles 90028
www.theatre-of-arts.com

Offers classes to prepare the actor to move in character. Classes are limited to 20. Time commitment varies.

MOVEMENT

UNIVERSITY OF CALIFORNIA LOS ANGELES (UCLA) **(310) 825-4321**
405 Hilgard Ave.
Los Angeles 90024
www.ucla.edu

For current catalog call (310) 825-6064.

UNIVERSITY OF SOUTHERN CALIFORNIA (USC) **(213) 821-2744**
University Park
Los Angeles 90089
www.usc.edu

Specific movement classes and instructors vary each term. Call for a current catalog.

MUSIC LESSONS

WES ABBOTT **(323) 259-0327**
846 N. Avenue 63
Highland Park 90042

Private sessions for all levels and all ages covering vocal interpretation, acting the song, and healthy, free vocal production. See listing under SINGING in this section for further information.

BAXTER-NORTHUP MUSIC CO. **(818) 788-7510**
14534 Ventura Blvd.
Sherman Oaks 91403

Offers instruction in guitar, electric guitar, percussion instruments, piano, organ, flute, wind, string instruments, and voice. Crash courses are available. Private 1/2 hour lessons only for $25. They carry a large selection of sheet music and background music that is useful for lip sync auditions.

COLUMBIA SCHOOL OF PERCUSSION **(619) 229-1610** **(800) 901-6874**
6335 Delbarton St.
San Diego 92120

Teaches private lessons for all percussion instruments, Latin, traps, and ethnic. Lessons are offered on weekdays and evenings. Crash courses are available for actors. There is no time commitment.

EUBANKS CONSERVATORY OF MUSIC AND ARTS **(323) 291-7821**
2975 Wilshire Blvd., Ste. B-1
Los Angeles 90010

Offers lessons in all instruments, voice, and music theory for children, teens and adults. Private and group lessons are available days, evenings, and weekends. Students can earn certificates.

FAUNT SCHOOL OF CREATIVE MUSIC **(818) 506-6873**
12725 Ventura Blvd., #G **FAX (818) 508-0429**
Studio City 91604
www.musicalskills.com

For professional and aspiring musicians, unique flexible schedules. One on one programs which have been producing rave results for 30+ years. Reasonable pay as you go rates. All instruments. All ages. Call for more information.

JUDY GANTLEY **(310) 452-0264**

A piano accompanist for rock, show tunes, and standards. She will make practice tapes, help with learning music, and transpose. She also gives piano lessons.

GEISLER MUSIC **(323) 651-2020**
8410 W. 3rd St.
Los Angeles 90048

Instruction is offered in guitar, electric guitar, piano, flute, woodwind instruments, sax, and clarinet. Also offers work on arranging, composition, improvisation, music theory, and songwriting. Some sheet music. Teaches crash courses for film and TV work. Private lessons only are available for children, teens, and adults. Day, evening, and weekend instruction is available. Has a service department for instrument repair. Mr. Geisler has trained actors for "Mr. Holland's Opus," and "Lost Highway."

GWEN GIRVIN **(626) 287-2452**
6208 N. Oak Ave
Temple City 91780

Teaches voice, piano, accordion, and rhythm instruments for children, teens, and adults. Private lessons are offered days, evenings, and weekends.

MARY GROVER, M.A. SINGING TRAINING VOICE THERAPY **(818) 787-SONG** **(800) 787-7731**
www.marygrover.com **FAX (818) 780-0698**
marygrover@aol.com

Teaches singing, piano, ear training, and sight singing to children and adults. Individual instruction as well as performances. Member of National Association of Teachers of Singing, SAG-AFTRA, is on faculty of Los Angeles City College, guest lectures at USC, and is a former faculty member at, CSUN, Cal Arts, and UCLA Extension. SEE AD ON PAGE 93.

PETER HUME **(818) 363-6281**

Offers guitar lessons in all styles: classical, rock, jazz, folk, etc. Beginners and children welcome. Gentle, patient, nurturing approach. Former faculty member, Berklee College of Music.

HERB MICKMAN **(818) 990-2328**

Accompanist for singers. Formally musical director for Sarah Vaughan. Mr. Mickman teaches popular piano styles and works on jazz improvisation, music theory, and harmony. Private lessons for adults only.

HOWARD RICHMAN PIANO **(818) 344-3306**
18375 Ventura Blvd., #8000
Tarzana 91356
www.soundfeelings.com/products/music_instruction/piano_lessons.htm
howardrichman@soundfeelings.com

He can teach you how to really play, or at least how to look like you've played piano for years, in a hurry. All styles. Also works with singers who need to learn self-accompanying, sight-singing and ear-training. Free introductory lesson.

Music Lessons

UNIVERSITY OF CALIFORNIA
LOS ANGELES (UCLA) **(310) 825-4321**
405 Hilgard Ave.
Los Angeles 90024
www.ucla.edu

See listing in ACTING section or contact the music department for further information.

UNIVERSITY OF CALIFORNIA
LOS ANGELES (UCLA) EXTENSION **(310) 825-9064**
10995 Le Conte Ave., Rm. 437
Los Angeles 90024
www.ucla.edu

Courses and workshops for adults taught by Industry professionals. Fee per course varies. Classes are mostly evenings and weekends. Courses are offered in electronic music, songwriting, the music business, film scoring and recording engineering. Certificate programs are available. Call for a four course catalog. "Professional Studies in The Entertainment Industry."

SENATOR EUGENE J. WRIGHT **(818) 506-7576**
5249 Biloxi
North Hollywood 91601

Specializes in acoustic bass with a focus on position playing and reading. Works with singers to develop their own style. Teaches private lessons for children, teens, and adults during the day, evenings, and weekends. Crash courses are available. A member of the Dave Brubeck quartet the Senator has worked with Marty Alexander, Count Basie, and Carmen McCrae.

YAMAHA MUSIC SCHOOL **(323) 933-2544**
5340 Wilshire Blvd.
Los Angeles 90036

Offers keyboard classes for age 2 through adult. Also offers private lessons for all ages and all instruments. They also sell Yamaha keyboards and music books.

Musical Theatre

ACADEMY OF PERFORMING ARTS **(619) 282-1884**
4580-B Alvarado Canyon Rd. **FAX (619) 282-9889**
San Diego 92120
www.apastudios.com
kp@apastudios.com

Offers a class in musical theatre that includes singing, acting, audition technique, and character study. They have a special scholarship program. See listing under ACTING in this section for further information.

STELLA ADLER ACADEMY OF ACTING
AND THEATRE COMPLEX **(323) 465-4446**
6773 Hollywood Blvd., 2nd Fl. **FAX (323) 469-6049**
Hollywood 90028
www.stellaadler-la.com

Academy director, Irene Gilbert. Call for catalogue and further information. Scene study and script analysis. SEE AD ON PAGE 6.

ALEXANDER TECHWORKS
JEAN-LOUIS RODRIGUE **(310) 209-9023**
KRISTOF KONRAD **(310) 443-4483**
P.O. Box 3194
Beverly Hills 90212
www.alexandertechworks.com
jeanlouisr1@yahoo.com

During the past 25 years Alexander Techworks has offered ongoing group classes, private instruction, and intensive courses offered by AmSAT Certified Teachers. The Alexander Technique helps the actor gain a fundamental awareness, control, and freedom of the whole self. Goals of the technique are effortless movement, increased coordination, a fuller capacity of breath, improvement in the use of the voice and speech, increased tonus in the musculature and a stronger sense of the self. Courses are offered in character development through physicalization and period movement. Studio locations in Westwood and Santa Monica. Mr. Rodrigue has been part of the faculty at the UCLA School of Theatre, Film, and Television for the past 15 years. SEE AD ON PAGE 4.

AMERICAN NATIONAL ACADEMY
OF PERFORMING ARTS **(818) 763-4431**
10944 Ventura Blvd.
Studio City 91604

Academy Children's Workshop directed by Dorothy Barrett presents "A Touch of Broadway" a musical production presented for the public once a year. Children from the Academy participate in this special production.

BB'S KIDS **(323) 650-5437**
www.bbskids.com

BB's Kids offers an 8 week music video class for kids and teens with Siobhan O'Carroll, who besides her lead in Broadway in "Annie" and multiple TV appearances has toured, danced and starred with Bette Midler, Ray Charles, Mary Wells ("My Guy"), Melissa Manchester, Dolly Parton, Mary Wilson (The Supremes), to name a few. Classes will cover a broad variety of musical styles, song selection, light choreography, group numbers, solos and/or duets—they call it the triple threat room. All repertoire building classes culminate in a taped-live performance. 7 years and up. For more information: see listings under, ACTING COMMERCIALS, and CHILDREN'S TRAINING. SEE AD ON PAGE 41.

GENE BUA ACTING FOR LIFE **(818) 547-3268**
3435 W. Magnolia Blvd.
Burbank 91505
www.genebua.com

Transformational acting from the creators and producers of the original hit musicals "Pepper Street" and "Across From Cindy's Corner" as well as the smash hit "Second Wind" and the award winning feature "348." All casting is done from Gene Bua's "Acting For Life" classes. See the listing under ACTING is this section for further information. SEE AD ON PAGE 5.

CALIFORNIA STATE UNIVERSITY LOS ANGELES (CSULA) (323) 343-3000
5151 State University Dr.
Los Angeles 90032
www.calstatela.edu

Offers voice, movement and musical theatre training. They produce large musicals at various times throughout the year.

THE CHAPMANS WILLIAM & IRENE (818) 787-7192

The Chapmans offer a theatre-like studio with stage, lighting and sound equipment. Not only have they trained many of today's stellar Broadway singer-actors, but they've performed among them for over thirty years. Private coaching is available as well as student showcasing. William Chapman was the leading dramatic baritone with the New York City Opera for 25 years and maintains contact with many of the nation's leading opera companies. He is also the author of "Notes For The Singing Actor." For further information see VOICE: SINGING.

BOB CORFF (323) 851-9042
www.corffvoice.com

Bob Corff star of such Broadway shows as "Hair," "Grease" and "Jesus Christ Superstar" offers complete musical performance training including vocal, audition, and performance secrets to help actors get the job and make them stronger in the show, as well as voice technique and performance coaching. Mr. Corff has worked with some of Broadway's biggest stars including Glenn Close and Alan Campbell of "Sunset Blvd," Antonio Banderas in "Evita, The Movie" and Hank Azaria in "Spamalot." SEE AD ON PAGE 91.

CLAIRE CORFF (323) 969-0565
www.corffvoice.com

Singing, auditions, and performance. Specializes in children of all ages. A Bob Corff associate. SEE AD ON PAGE 90.

CAROLE D'ANDREA – A NEW YORK ACTING TEACHER THE COMPLEX (310) 281-7116
6476 Santa Monica Blvd.
Los Angeles 90028
www.caroledandrea.com

A singing performance class offered Tuesdays, 11 am to 2 pm. The class focuses on helping the student find his/her real voice and how to select and present suitable audition material that is appropriate for the individual. Teaches a work process that is applicable to audition and performance and will help the student prepare for theatrical performances, cabaret, concerts, recording, and video. Ms. D'Andrea was a member of the original Broadway cast and the film version of "Westside Story."

MARY GROVER, M.A. (818) 787-SONG
SINGING TRAINING, VOICE THERAPY (800) 787-7731
www.marygrover.com FAX (818) 780-0698

Singing teacher and medical board licensed, singing voice therapist, Mary Grover teaches vocal technique, healthy belting, song interpretation, and voice therapy (medical insurance accepted). Member SAG-AFTRA. Individual lessons, on-camera performance and showcases, all ages. Improve audition and performance techniques. Clients include platinum record and Grammy winners. Currently on the faculty of Los Angeles City College and Pierce College, also a guest lecturer at USC, and a former faculty member of CSUN, Cal Arts, and UCLA Extension. SEE AD ON PAGE 93.

HAKALA-WOLF VOICE STUDIO (323) 514-7851
3671 Midvale Ave.
Los Angeles 90034
www.hakala-wolfvocalstudiolosangeles.info
mdhakala@yahoo.com

Helps you to sing comfortably, correctly and with confidence. Also works on acting and singing at the same time utilizing techniques to help you become strong and believable.

KIMBERLY JENTZEN (818) 779-7770
P.O. Box 4554 FAX (818) 779-1171
Valley Village 91617
www.kimberlyjentzen.net
filmactors@aol.com

"I wouldn't be where I am now without the training, knowledge and confidence I developed in Kimberly's classes." Cristina Fadale – star of "Rent" on Broadway. The one and only class taught by a professional acting coach that celebrates the musical performance, focuses on the skill of acting and strengthens technique for singers. This class is also very inspiring. Guests include a vocal coach and in-house accompanist. Performance styles range from Musical Theatre to Country, Pop to Rap. Scheduled one time a year Class size limited to 16. All singer/actors work every class. Over 18 years teaching. SEE AD ON PAGE 1.

JOHN KIRBY AT THE JOHN KIRBY STUDIO (323) 467-7877
1510 N. Las Palmas FAX (323) 467-7897
Hollywood 90028
jkcoaching@sbcglobal.net

Especially for professional singers/actors in need of a place to fine tune their audition material in addition to building a strong repertoire. John will help the performer define the subtext and physical life of a song.

LOS ANGELES CITY COLLEGE (LACC) (323) 953-4000 x2880
855 N. Vermont Ave. FAX (323) 953-4500
Los Angeles 90029
www.lacitycollege.edu

Offers musical theatre training. Curriculum and instructors vary each term. Call the Music Department for information at the above number.

PEISHA MCPHEE (818) 788-3056

An associate of Seth Riggs, Ms. McPhee specializes in cabaret and musical theatre performance. She works on registration, vocal technique, breathing, improvisation, and audition technique. She and her partner, Mel Dangcil teach the art form of cabaret on different levels. Private coaching and performance workshops are available. Some advanced students are presented in a night club. Ms. McPhee has performed the role of Julie in "Showboat" with Donald O'Connor and Davis Gaines and is a veteran cabaret artist who performs regularly at the Cinegrill. Most recently her students have appeared on Ed McMahon's "Next Big Star" and one student is a four time champion. "After years of performance, the teachers know secrets about every aspect of singing cabaret." Los Angeles Times.

THE STEVEN MEMEL STUDIO (818) 789-0474
4760 Halbrent Ave.
Sherman Oaks 91403

Steven Memel, during his more than 20 years of teaching in the U.S. and abroad, has developed a "no-nonsense" system that gets the job done. Technique work covers expanding range, breathing, stamina, removing "breaks," dynamics, resonance and more. Performance work centers on building a deeper understanding of the story of the song and new techniques for you to use this to create a dynamic result. Integrating your skills and trusting your voice are emphasized. A spontaneous performance that really hits an audience is the ultimate outcome. Other areas covered are audition prep, choosing material, what to do with your hands and body, what to tell the accompanist, and raising the level of your performance in the show. Students are videotaped and both workshops and private classes are available. Call for brochure and client list.

MILLER ON TAP/ JANET MILLER (818) 990-6691
millerontap@earthlink.net

Specializing in musical theatre, dance and tap for all levels and every age. Ms. Miller is an experienced director/choreographer. She is available for private consultation and coaching for musical theatre roles. JM is very well known for her "show doctoring" abilities.

AUDITION WORKSHOP AT THE VOICE STUDIO OF ELIZABETH PRESCOTT (818) 789-8660
Sherman Oaks/New York
www.elizabethprescott.com
prescottvoice@yahoo.com

Workshops fuse the art of acting with singing, moving actors from non-musical theatre into musicals with ease and expertise. The quality of one's singing voice is irrelevant for the workshop. Only the ability to hear pitch and rhythm is needed. Two or more contrasting songs are carefully selected for each actor and then crafted meticulously to top performance level. Performers learn to replace meaningless gestures with a natural physical life timed to the script, as well as everything else they need to know to select material and perfect their auditions. Small classes. Professional accompanist included. Based on the methodology of legendary David Craig. A member of SAG and AEA with extensive theatre and recording credits, Elizabeth Prescott has been teaching vocal and performance technique in New York and Los Angeles for twenty years. Private coaching and singing lessons also available from $40-$90. Private accompaniment from $20 per half hour. SEE AD ON PAGE 95.

PROFESSIONAL SCHOOL FOR THE ARTS (310) 328-7664
1329 Sartori Ave. FAX (310) 782-2072
Torrance 90501
www.psarts.com

Musical theatre audition workshops are available for performers, ages 8 through adult. These vital courses offer the keys to successful music theatre audition, focusing on the selection and performance of the audition song, while also exploring vocal production and basic dance combinations often required at auditions. These workshops are a great introduction for newcomers to musical theatre and an excellent way for experienced professionals to return to the basics and re-examine their auditioning skills and tactics. Introductory courses are taught by Lisa Matsko Hamilton and Gerard Babb, while advanced courses are taught by Hamilton, Babb, and a selection of guest instructors which have included Karen Morrow, Jon Engstrom, Mark Madama, Steven Smith, and others.

PATRICIA SHANKS (949) 723-4473
www.studioshanks.com
pshanks@studioshanks.com

A private studio facility offering voice instruction and musicianship training for singers ages 12 and over, beginning through advanced. The focus is traditional, educational, foundation-based and fine arts-oriented. Establish a reliable technique and eliminate externally applied cosmetic affectations related to technique (voice production) and performance (presentation). Newport Beach. 28 years experience. Member: NATS, MTAC, AGMA, SCVA.

SOUTHERN CALIFORNIA CHILDREN'S THEATRE (310) 456-1763
P.O. Box 1616
Canyon Country 91351

Offers an ongoing training program in musical theatre which provides people of all ages – from five years to infinity – with an opportunity to be active participants in the dramatic process as actors, singers, dancers, and good members of an audience. The class is designed to contribute to personal growth and self-confidence. Instruction is by Industry professionals. This non-profit educational program ends with a full stage Broadway-style spectacular musical drama. The production casts vary from 100 to 300 artists of all ages. Branches in L.A., The Westside, Pasadena, Ventura, and the Santa Clarita Valley.

THEATRE OF ARTS (EST. 1927) (323) 463-2500
1621 N. McCadden Place FAX (323) 463-2005
Los Angeles 90028
www.theatre-of-arts.com

Classes offer voice, dance, production, acting, scene study, audition, interview and performance technique, and movement. Day and evening classes for 16 and over and adults. Showcases, Industry events, and productions are held.

CAROL TINGLE (310) 828-3100
Santa Monica FAX (310) 828-4443

A performer/voice teacher for 35 years, Carol Tingle works with singers of all ages, levels and styles integrating the concepts of excellent vocal technique into the performance of appropriate repertoire. Private instruction, audition preparation, as well as performance workshops are offered at her studio in Santa Monica. Emphasis is placed on the development of the voice and safe, healthy vocal production. A member of the National Association of Teachers, Carol also works with performance anxiety and has completed her CD series "Centering For Performance." SEE AD ON PAGE 94.

UNIVERSITY OF CALIFORNIA LOS ANGELES (UCLA) (310) 825-4321
405 Hilgard Ave.
Los Angeles 90024
www.ucla.edu

For current catalog call (310) 825-6064.

UNIVERSITY OF SOUTHERN CALIFORNIA (USC) (213) 821-2744
University Park
Los Angeles 90089
www.usc.edu

Call for a current catalog.

WHAT'S THE STORY? (310) 392-9186
P.O. Box 1841 FAX (310) 450-1312
Venice 90294
stacie.chaiken@verizon.net

An ongoing solo performance workshop taught by Stacie Chaiken to develop solo work in a group process with writer/performers to try things out in front of a friendly audience on a regular basis. Every six weeks there are private meetings with Ms. Chaiken for an intensive look at what is being created. The class is useful for actors who want to create solo work, writers wrestling with material, and story telling artists (filmmakers, songwriters, poets, directors) who want to bring greater depth and immediacy to their work.

COSTUMES

LOS ANGELES CITY COLLEGE (LACC) (323) 953-4000 x2987
855 N. Vermont Ave. FAX (323) 953-4500
Los Angeles 90029
www.lacitycollege.edu

Courses offered in costume construction, pattern making, fitting, dyeing, costume history and make-up. Two year concentrated program also available. Call the above number for additional information.

DIRECTING

THE ACTOR'S LAB (310) 621-3900
at the Odyssey Theatre
2055 South Sepulveda Blvd.
Los Angeles 90048
www.theactorslab.com
theactorslab@aol.com

Director's work under the direction of J.D. Lewis. See listing under ACTING for further information.

AMERICAN FILM INSTITUTE (AFI) (323) 856-7600
2021 N. Western Ave.
Los Angeles 90027
www.afi.org

Has outreach programs in directing, producing, screenwriting, computer classes, and special effects for film and video makers. Evening and weekend day classes and several lecture series are offered. The school, which is separate from the outreach program, is on the quarter system.

CALIFORNIA INSTITUTE OF THE ARTS (661) 255-1050
24700 McBean Pkwy.
Valencia 91355
www.calrarts.edu

Call for current catalog.

CALIFORNIA STATE UNIVERSITY NORTHRIDGE (818) 677-1200
18111 Nordhoff St.
Northridge 91330
www.csun.edu

Call for current catalog.

LILYAN CHAUVIN (323) 877-4988
3841 Eureka Dr.
Studio City 91604

Former Vice President of Women In Film. See listing under ACTING in this section for further information. SEE AD ON PAGES 16 & 255.

ANTHONY DI NOVI (310) 490-4761
anthonydinovi@earthlink.net

Works with actors privately. On-camera study. For beg-adv directors. Script development, casting, and rehearsal.

DIRECTING YOUR DIRECTING CAREER
K CALLAN
P.O. Box 1612
Studio City 91614
www.swedenpress.com
KCallan@swedenpress.com

Actress-author K Callan's best-selling guide for directors includes an analysis of directing as a realistic career choice, the need to focus one's energies to a particular part of the marketplace, how to know when you are ready to move to New York or Los Angeles, how you can be a working director in your own marketplace, relationships with agents and managers, what agents are looking for and how to go about approaching agents. Callan's books are Industry bibles for writers, actors and directors at all stages of their careers. In addition to Callan's extensive acting career (most visibly Superman's mom in ABC's hit series, "Lois & Clark"), Callan has taught at The American Film Institute, UCLA Extension, South Coast Repertory, is a voting member of The Academy of Motion Picture Arts and Sciences and The Academy of Television Arts and Sciences and a past member of the Board of Directors of The Screen Actors Guild. SEE AD ON THE TRAINING TAB.

HULL ACTORS STUDIO
LORRIE HULL, PH.D. & DIANNE HULL (310) 828-0632
Santa Monica
www.actors-studio.com/hull
hullwshop@hotmail.com

Step-by-step guidance in all stages of directing is offered. Areas covered include general knowledge, preliminary work, script breakdown, identifying units, intentions, casting, production scheduling, and the stages of rehearsal. Continuous training or two-12 week intensives are offered, and also private coaching available taught by Lorrie Hull, Ph.D. and Dianne Hull, actress for Elia Kazan for film and stage. See listing under ACTING in this section for further information.

MILTON KATSELAS WORKSHOPS
BEVERLY HILLS PLAYHOUSE (310) 855-1556
254 S. Robertson Blvd.
Beverly Hills 90211
www.katselas.com

Day and evening classes for actors and directors are offered evenings and mornings throughout the week.

MVCI (MUSIC VIDEO COMMERCIAL INSTITUTE) (800) 255-7529
1655 McCadden Place
Hollywood 90028
www.mvci.tv
mvci@mvci.tv

Music Video and Commercial Film School teaches hands-on

workshop courses for directing, producing and editing music videos and commercials on 35mm, 16mm film and digital video. MVCI is a filmschool where the student can become the director, producer, cinematographer and editor of their own high quality music video or commercial production. Taught by MTV Award winning directors, producers and editors.

NEW YORK FILM ACADEMY (818) 733-2600
100 Universal City Plaza FAX (818) 733-4074
Bldg. 9128, Ste. 179
Universal City
www.nyfa.com
munkeeluke@hotmail.com

Acting for Film workshops as well as directing, writing and producing workshops.

TRAVIS-JOHNTZ (323) 737-3223
2116 Arlington Ave., Ste. 310
Los Angeles 90018
www.travis-johntz.com

Offers a comprehensive series of workshops and seminars covering all aspects of directing for camera and stage. See listing under ACTING in this section for more information.

UNIVERSITY OF CALIFORNIA
LOS ANGELES EXTENSION (UCLA) (310) 825-9064
10995 Le Conte Ave., Rm. 437
Los Angeles 90024
www.ucla.edu

Courses and workshops for adults, taught by Industry professionals. A certificate program is available. Call for a free catalog. See listing under PRODUCTION in the section for further information.

JUDITH WESTON ACTING STUDIO (310) 392-2444
3402 Motor Ave.
Los Angeles 90034
www.judithweston.com
judyweston@aol.com

Offers workshops for directors. Author of "Directing Actors" and "The Film Director's Intuition." See listing under ACTING in this section for further information.

LANGUAGE

REEL ENGLISH (323) 957-4758
www.reelenglishcoach.com

Standard American dialect specialist Kelly Reiter has been coaching actors in Los Angeles since 1989. Her cutting edge character-study approach gives actors with accents the tools, confidence, and professional voice they need at every step of their career, from getting the agent to getting the part. She works exclusively with regional and non-native speakers of English and has a solid reputation at UCLA where she taught for 13 years. Assessment interview required.

MISCELLANEOUS

GOLDSPIRIT FARM (818) 834-1272
12682 Kagel Canyon Rd. FAX (818) 834-1902
Lake View Terrace 91342
www.goldspiritfarm.com

English horseback riding lessons for riders of any level (even those who have never ridden a horse.) Actors and stunt people learn to become comfortable with horses as well as how to ride and jump.

LAST LOOK
ENGLISH LANGUAGE CONSULTANT (323) 653-4555
P.O. Box 641831
Los Angeles 90064
www.iwosc.org

A 3-hour grammar, punctuation, and usage review course for communicators offered by credentialed teacher Flo Selfman, President of Selfman & Others Public Relations firm and President of Independent Writers of Southern California IWOSC). Also proof reads scripts and manuscripts and any documents. See listing under PUBLIC RELATIONS in the TEAM section for further information.

THE PUBLICITY COACH
VICKI ARTHUR (818) 995-8130
P.O. Box 57498
Sherman Oaks 91413
www.hollywoodpublicity.com
vickiarthur@juno.com

Learn how to market and promote your career, your project or your company. Escalate and propel yourself to the next level with Hollywood Publicist, Vicki Arthur. Individual or group coaching and workshops.

PRODUCTION

AMERICAN FILM INSTITUTE (AFI) (323) 856-7600
2021 N. Western Ave.
Los Angeles 90027
www.afi.org

Call for the current catalogue. Directing Women's Workshop and a TV writer's workshop. They also have grants for independent film makers and minority film maker programs.

CALIFORNIA STATE UNIVERSITY
NORTHRIDGE (818) 677-1200
18111 Nordhoff St.
Northridge 91330
www.csun.edu

Call for current catalog.

COLUMBIA COLLEGE (818) 345-8414
www.columbiacollege.edu FAX (818) 345-9053

The school offers classes in TV, film, and motion picture arts and sciences. Some of the classes offered are low budget production, directing, screenwriting, video features, marketing, distribution, etc. Students can earn BA and/or AA degrees at this accredited school.

MVCI (MUSIC VIDEO
COMMERCIAL INSTITUTE) (800) 255-7529
1655 McCadden Place
Hollywood 90028
www.mvci.tv
mvci@mvci.tv

Music Video and Commercial Film School teaches hands-on workshop courses for directing, producing and editing music videos and commercials on 35mm, 16mm film and digital video. MVCI is a filmschool where the student can become the director, producer, cinematographer and editor of their own high quality music video or commercial production. Taught by MTV Award winning directors, producers and editors.

UNIVERSITY OF CALIFORNIA LOS ANGELES (UCLA) (310) 825-4321
405 Hilgard Ave.
Los Angeles 90024
www.ucla.edu

For current catalogue call (310) 825-6064. Call the Theatre, Film and Television Department for further information. (310) 825-5761.

UNIVERSITY OF CALIFORNIA LOS ANGELES EXTENSION (UCLA) (310) 825-9064
10995 Le Conte Ave.
Los Angeles 90024
www.ucla.edu

An extensive variety of courses and workshops for adults, from pre-production to post production, taught by Industry professionals, are offered for entry level to masters. A certificate program in film/TV/video/multi-media, with the specialty of your choice is available. The classes are offered mostly evenings and weekends and the fee per course varies. Call for the free course catalog. "Professional Studies in the Entertainment Industry."

SCRIPT ANALYSIS

THE PLUS WORKSHOPS (SCRIPT STUDY PLUS) SCOTT BERNSTEIN (323) 692-0298

Ongoing classes teach actors how to break down and research movie, TV, and theatre scripts line by line, beat by beat. The class covers how, when, and why to research a role, plot points, style, period, and history. One-on-one private classes for $120 for a 4 week period. Private coaching available for $40 per hour. There are discounts for members of the workshops or for longer projects. Acting Plus and cold reading workshops also available. Take two or three workshops for $175 for 4 weeks. Serious minded actors only. Interview required for admittance. Celebrating over 20 years.

CLIFF OSMOND (310) 393-6022
1526 14th St., Ste. 107
Santa Monica 91404
www.cliffosmond.com

See listing under ACTING in this section for further information.

AMERICAN FILM INSTITUTE (AFI) (323) 856-7600
2021 N. Western Ave.
Los Angeles 90028
www.afi.org

Courses are offered for all levels. See listing under OTHER TRAINING-DIRECTING in this section for further information.

CALIFORNIA STATE UNIVERSITY NORTHRIDGE (818) 677-1200
18111 Nordhoff St.
Northridge 91330
www.csun.edu

Classes are offered evenings and weekends. Call the above number for further information.

DEVORAH CUTLER-RUBENSTEIN SCRIPT BROKER (310) 943-4378
12210 1/2 Nebraska Ave, Ste.22
Beverly Hills 90210
www.thescriptbroker.com
devo@thescriptbroker.ocm

Award winning writer/director and experienced script consultant gets inside your creative work and helps develop, rewrite and complete any writing project. She is uniquely qualified to address any writing issue having not only worked with writers, but is herself a produced feature and television writer and development executive. She has been a Director, Story Department for Marble Arch Productions, in Literary Affairs for Columbia Pictures Television and spearheaded the New York Playwrights Workshop. "Devorah's frank, intelligent appraisal of my work gave me a tremendous boost and the confidence to make changes when I had run out of steam with a grasp of how to make them." Amy Wallace, author "The Book of Lists"

MICHAEL HAUGE (818) 995-4209
P.O. Box 57498 FAX (818) 986-1504
Sherman Oaks 91413
www.screenplaymastery.com
mhauge@adelphia.net

Studio script consultant, story editor, screenwriter and author of "Writing Screenplays That Sell," Michael Hauge offers script consultation and coaching services: hourly consultations, screenplay critique, master coaching program, lectures and intensive weekend screenplay seminars held worldwide.

HOLLYWOOD SCRIPT WRITING INSTITUTE (323) 461-8333 (800) SCRIPTS
1605 N. Cahuenga Blvd., Ste. 216
Hollywood 90028-6201
www.moviewriting.com

Correspondence courses in the art of script writing and a script analysis service. After taking the course they help their students submit their scripts to producers. Monthly screenwriting contest.

HULL ACTORS STUDIO LORRIE HULL, PH.D. & DIANNE HULL (310) 828-0632
Santa Monica
www.actors-studio.com/hull
hullwshop@hotmail.com

Exploration and experimentation with writers' works are covered in a variety of classes. Readings with casts and improvs based on the writings as well as staged scenes and projects presented to the public are some of the things offered. See listing under ACTING in this section for further information.

JEANNE HARTMAN/VOICE WITH A HEART PRODUCTIONS (818) 760-8416
P.O. Box 2613 FAX (818) 980-6711
Toluca Lake 91610
actbelieve@aol.com

Writers can use actors' audition techniques to pitch more effectively. Learn how actors create believable, exciting characters and adapt it to your pitching and your writing. One-on-one sessions. An interview is required.

NEW YORK FILM ACADEMY (818) 733-2600
100 Universal City Plaza FAX (818) 733-4074
Bldg. 9128, Ste. 179
Universal City
www.nyfa.com
munkeeluke@hotmail.com

Acting for Film workshops as well as directing, writing and producing workshops.

RIPRAP STUDIOS (818) 990-7498
5755 Lankershim Blvd.
North Hollywood 91601
www.riprapentertain.com

Writing workshops form year round at minimal costs and those workshops require actors to read new material. Riprap Writer's Playhouse is a free service to writers worldwide wherein professional actors read scripts from selected writers submitted from all over the world. This digital showcase is broadcast in over 1,000,000 homes in Southern California from Santa Barbara to San Diego County. The actor receives credit, tape and priority consideration for upcoming projects at Riprap Studio Theatre.

BARBARA SLOANE (310) 854-3654

Proofreading of scripts, manuscripts, treatments, outlines, etc. Flexible rates. Pick up and delivery available on the westside.

TRAVIS-JOHNTZ (323) 737-3223
2116 Arlington Ave., Ste. 310 FAX (323) 737-3553
Los Angeles 90018
www.travis-johntz.com
info@travis-johntz.com

Mark Travis and Frederick Johntz have been consulting with screenwriters for the past ten years. Working with all writers from beginners to seasoned professionals, they assist the writer in this delicate process of bringing their vision to the page. Free consultations are available by appointment only. See listing under ACTING in this section for further information.

TRUBY'S WRITERS STUDIO (800) 33-TRUBY
(310) 573-9630
664 Brooktree Road FAX (310) 478-6821
Santa Monica 90402
www.truby.com
johntruby@aol.com

Offers workshops, online courses and audio cassettes on screen writing, playwriting, and novel writing. Has the number one rated story coach development software titled "Truby's Block Buster." Call for further information.

UNIVERSITY OF SOUTHERN CALIFORNIA (USC) (213) 821-2744
University Park
Los Angeles 90089
www.usc.edu

Offers evening classes, call (213) 740-2235 for catalogue.

THE WRITERS' COMPUTER STORE (310) 441-5151
2040 Westwood Blvd.
W. Los Angeles 90025
www.writerscomputer.com

See listing under COMPUTERS in the MARKETING section for further information.

SKATING

BOBBI MCRAE (310) 836-7748
(310) 922-2777
skatermcrae@aol.com

Private ice-skating lessons, choreography, and technical advisor. Teaches at Culver City Ice Arena.

DEBBIE MERRILL'S SKATE GREAT USA SCHOOL OF SKATING (310) 820-1969
(888) 866-6121
P.O. Box 3452
Santa Monica 90408
www.skategreat.com

Teaches actors to speak, think, act, skate, and hit their mark at the same time. "Skate to look and feel great." Inline, roller, and ice skating lessons. Private and group classes are available for beg-adv. Ms. Merrill is IISA Certified and a USFSA silver medalist in figure skating. Children starting at age 4 through 84. Has worked with Steve Martin, Melanie Griffith, Geena Davis, Chris Maloney, Kim Delaney, Juliette Lewis, Downtown Julie Brown and former Mayor Richard Riordan. Skating Consultant for "NYPD Blue," "L.A. Story," "White Men Can't Jump," "Party of Five," "Legally Blonde," and "Charlie's Angels" as well The David Letterman Show" etc. Also casts skaters, scouts locations and performs. SAG and AFTRA. Co-host for vegtv.com, Ms. Merrill is an actress, dancer and choreographer and spokesperson. Her new video "Skate to Look and Feel Great at any Age" due out this fall.

STUNT SCHOOLS

THE BEVERLY HILLS KARATE ACADEMY
EMIL FARKAS (310) 275-2661
9085 Santa Monica Blvd.
Los Angeles 90069

Teaches motion picture stunt fighting and all forms of martial arts stunts. Private and group lessons are available. Mr. Farkas is a stunt coordinator and frequently casts stunt people from his classes.

PRIVATE TRAINERS.COM (818) 766-3317
(818) 679-6756
5530 Vantage Ave. FAX (818) 752-3220
Valley Village 91607
www.privatetrainers.com

Joe Antouri, Mr. USA-World Champion Bodybuilder offers personal private fitness training at your home or on location including nutrition and weight management guidance. Mr. Antouri holds a Doctorate in Nutrition and Dietetic Therapy. Clients include MGM Studios, Warner Bros, HBO, Disney, Penthouse, Playboy, Dreamworks, and many actors and stunt staff. Joe is available at Gold's Gym in Venice.

SOUTH BAY GYMNASTICS SPORTS COMPLEX (310) 328-3136
1275 Sartori Ave. FAX (310) 328-5573
Torrance 90501
www.southbaygymnastics.com
info@southbaygymnastics.com

State of the art gymnastics and martial arts training. Sword play and other weapons for film and stage available. High falls, tumbling, mini trampoline, tumble track, and training pit are just a few of the equipment and services provided. They have high ceilings with a twenty foot cargo net for Galaxy and fitness training as well as the other obstacles in the training course. They also feature aerobic kickboxing. Private lessons and personal trainers available.

TEACHING

HULL ACTORS STUDIO
LORRIE HULL, PH.D. & DIANNE HULL (310) 828-0632
Santa Monica
www.actors-studio.com/hull
hullwshop@hotmail.com

Offers a workshop for teachers, and also private coaching available in teaching techniques for all levels and ages including creative dramatics for youth of elementary school age. Dr. Hull has trained and supervised teachers of all levels in colleges, universities, school systems, and for Lee Strasberg and AFI. Taught by Lorrie Hull, Ph.D. and Dianne Hull, actress for Elia Kazan for film and stage. See listing under ACTING in this section for further information.

VOICE: ACCENTS & DIALECTS

STELLA ADLER ACADEMY OF ACTING
AND THEATRE COMPLEX (323) 465-4446
6773 Hollywood Blvd., 2nd Fl. FAX (323) 469-6049
Hollywood 90028
www.stellaadler-la.com

Academy director, Irene Gilbert. Call for catalogue and further information. Scene study and script analysis. SEE AD ON PAGE 6.

THE AMERICAN ACADEMY
OF DRAMATIC ARTS (323) 464-2777
1336 N. La Brea Ave.
Hollywood 90028
www.aada.org
bjustin@ca.aada.org

See listing under ACTING in this section for further information.

ROWENA BALOS (310) 285-8489
rowvoice@aol.com

Offers voice production that covers breathing, strengthening, speech, relaxation, and accent reduction. Individual work is done in these small classes. No interview is required and no auditing is allowed. An introductory workshop is offered periodically. Private coaching is also available.

BB'S KIDS (323) 650-KIDS
www.bbskids.com

This 8 week Dialect and Character Voice Over class includes work on the most asked for dialects: New York, Southern, British and Irish, besides any specific individualized dialect needs. Students will learn how to resource any dialect for any audition and know how to audition for voice over auditions. Classes will culminate in a taped live graduation scene with a dialect or character voice. 8 years and up. SEE AD ON PAGE 41.

BONNIE BIZOZA
ACCENT ON ACCENT (818) 783-0473

Offers accent/dialect training and accent reduction for beginners and established professionals. Ms. Bizoza is a licensed speech therapist and experienced dialect coach who provides private training using a multisensory approach adapted to the students learning style in order to achieve authentic, natural speech pattern. Individual classes and on-set coaching are available.

IVAN BORODIN
ACCENT ELIMINATION (323) 882-1268
1626 N. Wilcox Ave., #490
Hollywood 90028
IvanB83@yahoo.com

Private instruction helping actors with accents. An intensive approach geared to develop dialectal mastery. Especially helpful at reducing foreign and regional dialects. Also offers coaching on all accents. Please note: for committed actors only. Ivan has been coaching since 1992 has taught many actors on many levels, and is only interested in helping actors who are willing to show up more or less on time, commit to the training, and devote the energy necessary to change your speech. On set coaching is offered as well. Mr. Borodin also specializes in coaching actors in foreign and regional dialects.

FRANCIE M. BROWN (818) 999-9124

Private instruction is offered that covers all accents and dialects, plus elimination of regionalisms.

VINCENT CHASE (323) 851-4819
7221 Sunset Blvd. FAX (323) 851-9942
Los Angeles 90046

See listing under ACTING in this section for further information.

LILYAN CHAUVIN (323) 877-4988
3841 Eureka Dr.
Studio City 91604

Has taught many top people in Hollywood including Richard Gere and Lauren Hutton for French. See listing under ACTING in this section for further information. SEE AD ON PAGES 16 & 255.

BOB CORFF (323) 851-9042
www.corffvoice.com

Offers crash courses and private instruction in accent and dialect acquisition and reduction. Works with teens and adults in the studio or on location, days or evenings. Has worked on major films. Bob is co-author of the CD and workbook "Achieving the Standard American Accent" and "Accents: The Bob and Claire Corff Method." See listing under BOOKS in the MARKETING section for further information. SEE AD ON PAGE 91.

CLAIRE CORFF **(323) 969-0565**
www.corffvoice.com

A Bob Corff Associate who offers accent reduction. Claire is the co-author with her husband Bob Corff of the CD and workbook "Achieving the Standard American Accent" and "Accents: The Bob and Claire Corff Method." See listing under BOOKS in the MARKETING section for further information. SEE AD ON PAGE 90.

BEN D'AUBREY **(818) 783-1951**
13002 Riverside Dr., #10
Sherman Oaks 91423
bennjill@sbcglobal.net

Offers dialect and accent acquisition or reduction/removal. Emergency coaching is a speciality. Mr. D'Aubery works to get you ready for an audition or a role quickly. Specialties are British, American, and European accents and dialects stressing melody, rhythm, and believability. No phonetics. Private sessions and ongoing classes available. Recommended by Kimberly Jentzen and Judy Kerr.

JACKY DE HAVILAND **(323) 691-7077**

Teaches dialects/accents and accent removal to adults, teens, and children. Focus on the individual, your uniqueness and the role. Private coaching can be tailored to difficult schedules. Has worked on location and in many crash course situations. Small group lessons can be arranged. Recommended by coach Larry Moss. See listing under ACTING.

THE DIALECT COACH **(818) 879-1896**
4948 Barbados Court **FAX (818) 879-1883**
Oak Park 91377
www.thedialectcoach.com
jgoldes@thedialectcoach.com

Learn any dialect quickly and easily, or learn a neutral American dialect. Coached Jim Broadbent, Jennifer Garner, Mike Myers and hundreds of others. Phone coaching available.

JUDY DICKERSON **(818) 985-1603**

Offers coaching for dialects, accent reduction and Standard American Speech. Ms. Dickerson has served as dialect coach for productions at the Mark Taper Forum, Seattle Repertory, Intiman Theatre, ACT-Seattle, Circle X, the Kennedy Center, Broadway, and on "The Insider," "Gladiator," "Human Nature," "The Contender," Takeshi Kitano's "Brother" and "The Affair of The Necklace." Private sessions, location coaching, and ongoing classes are available. 17 years teaching experience. She has an MFA from SMU, is certified by Edith Skinner, and has trained with Arthur Lessac.

JESSICA DRAKE **(323) 662-1831**

Offers dialects, Standard American Speech, Shakespeare, and accent reduction for film, TV, and stage. Works on location or at her own studio. There is no time commitment. Ms. Drake is a Julliard graduate. She has coached many films including "Catch Me If You Can," "The Green Mile," "Forrest Gump," "L.A. Confidential," "What's Love Got To Do With It," "Haunted Mansion" and "Band of Brothers."

ROBERT EASTON
THE HENRY HIGGINS OF HOLLYWOOD, INC.
THE DIALECT DOCTOR **(818) 985-2222**

Dialect doctor to the stars over the last 40 years, he studied phonetics at University College, London and Trinity College, Dublin and took an advanced dialect course at Cambridge University, and he has taught dialects at USC and lectured on accents at many other universities and the Smithsonian, Washington. He has played dialect roles in 82 major motion pictures and over 1,700 TV and radio programs and he has done extensive dialect research on five continents and Oceania. SEE AD ON PAGE 89.

MARY GROVER, M.A.
THE PROFESSIONAL COMMUNICATOR **(818) 787-7664**
ACCENT REDUCTION **(800) 787-7731**
www.marygrover.com **FAX (818) 780-0698**
marygrover@aol.com

Licensed voice/speech pathologist Mary Grover has over 27 years experience as a voice and speech consultant. She offers accent/dialect reduction/coaching, voice therapy (medical insurance is accepted), voice and speech production, breathing and voice strengthening. Currently is on faculty of Los Angeles City College, guest lecturers at USC, and is a former faculty member at, CSUN, Cal Arts, and UCLA Extension. SEE AD ON PAGE 93.

HULL ACTORS STUDIO
LORRIE HULL, PH.D. & DIANNE HULL **(310) 828-0632**
Santa Monica and West L.A.
www.actors-studio.com/hull
hullwshop@hotmail.com

Separate accent reduction work is done 1/2 hour after each class as well as in private sessions. Private lessons and coaching available daily. See listing under ACTING in this section for further information.

ARTHUR SAMUEL JOSEPH, M.A. **(818) 788-8508**
16815 Moorpark St.
Encino 91436
www.vocalawareness.com
vawareness@aol.com

Mr. Joseph has been teaching for over four decades and has his own trademarked and copyrighted method of instruction called, "Vocal Awareness." This technique creates an awareness of the physical, emotional, and psychological aspects of the voice which allows the participant to more fully integrate the aspects of self through vocal training. Careful attention is paid to subtle details that build confidence, self-esteem, competence, and self-awareness. The work applies to all aspects of voice including all styles of singing, speaking, accent reduction, broadcasting, etc. Mr. Joseph has been a professor of voice at USC, a visiting artist at Yale University and George Washington University, and has taught throughout the U.S., Latin America, Europe, and Japan. He has a book called, "Sound of the Soul: Discovering the Power of Your Voice," and a several CD and DVD series. His latest book is called "Vocal Power" and is available on the website.

VERNICE KLIER **(310) 392-0064**
(011) 33-1-47-38-24-64
www.vernice-klier.com
verniceklier@aol.com

Vernice Klier is an international voice and acting coach specializing in acting in English. She has had 15 years experience coaching privately; and has coached on location on over 25 films including the Academy Award winning "The English Patient."

THE HENRY HIGGINS OF HOLLYWOOD, INC.

ROBERT EASTON

The Dialect Doctor

(818) 985-2222

Has Taught: DON ADAMS, MARK ADDY, JASON ALEXANDER, STEVE ALLEN, FERNANDO ALLENDE, MARIA CONCHITA ALONSO, TRINI ALVARADO, ANTHONY ANDREWS, ANN-MARGRET, ANNE ARCHER, EVE ARDEN, DAVID ARQUETTE, ROSANNA ARQUETTE, ED ASNER, RENE AUBERJONOIS, JEAN-PIERRE AUMONT, HANK AZARIA, JIM BACKUS, DIEDRICH BADER, JOE DON BAKER, TAYLOR BALL, ELIZABETH BANKS, IAN BANNEN, ELLEN BARKIN, DREW BARRYMORE, BILLY BARTY, STEPHANIE BEACHAM, BONNIE BEDELIA, JIM BELUSHI, POLLY BERGEN, PATRICK BERGIN, CRYSTAL BERNARD, KEN BERRY, JACQUELINE BISSET, PETER BONERZ, BARRY BOSTWICK, BRUCE BOXLEITNER, ERIC BRAEDEN, KLAUS MARIA BRANDAUER, EILEEN BRENNAN, BEAU BRIDGES, JEFF BRIDGES, LLOYD BRIDGES, SARA BRIGHTMAN, WILFORD BRIMLEY, JAMES BRODERICK, JAMES BROLIN, PIERCE BROSNAN, BRYAN BROWN, GEORG STANFORD BROWN, IAN BUCHANAN, DELTA BURKE, TOM BURLINSON, CAROL BURNETT, RAYMOND BURR, LEVAR BURTON, RUTH BUZZI, GABRIEL BYRNE, NICOLAS CAGE, HARRY CAREY, JR., GEORGE CARLIN, DAVID CARRADINE, KEITH CARRADINE, ROBERT CARRADINE, NANCY CARTWRIGHT, PATRICK CASSIDY, SHAUN CASSIDY, KIM CATTRALL, MAXWELL CAULFIELD, RICHARD CHAMBERLAIN, STOCKARD CHANNING, JOAN CHEN, CHER, JULIE CHRISTIE, JOHN CLEESE, MICHELLE CLUNIE, JAMES COBURN, IMOGENE COCA, DABNEY COLEMAN, BILLY CONNALLY, ROBERT CONRAD, BARRY CORBIN, ALEX CORD, BUD CORT, BRIAN COX, MICHAEL CRAWFORD, TOM CRUISE, MARIA-GRAZIA CUCINOTTA, ROBERT CULP, JOAN CUSACK, JOHN CUSACK, JIM DALE, JEFF DANIELS, TED DANSON, TONY DANZA, PAM DAWBER, OLIVIA DE HAVILLAND, KIM DELANEY, JULIE DELPY REBECCA DE MORNAY, PATRICK DEMPSEY, BRIAN DENNEHY, ROBERT DE NIRO, BO DEREK, LAURA DERN, WILLIAM DEVANE, DANNY DEVITO, CAMERON DIAZ, BRAD DOURIF, LESLEY-ANNE DOWN, MINNIE DRIVER, HILARY DUFF, DAVID DUKES, LINDSAY DUNCAN, CHARLES DUTTON, ROBERT DUVALL, SHEENA EASTON, AARON ECKHARDT, ANITA EKBERG, SHANNON ELIZABETH, HECTOR ELIZONDO, CARY ELWES, RON ELY, GLORIA ESTEFAN, ROB ESTES, EMILIO ESTEVEZ, MELISSA ETHERIDGE, LINDA EVANS, PETER FALK, SHERILYN FENN, MIGUEL FERRER, LINDA FIORENTINO, PETER FIRTH, JOELY FISHER, FIONNULA FLANAGAN, LOUISE FLETCHER, NINA FOCH, BRIDGET FONDA, JANE FONDA, ROBERT FOXWORTH, TONY FRANCIOSA, JAMES FRANCO, DENNIS FRANZ, KATHLEEN FREEMAN, GEORGE FURTH, SIR MICHAEL GAMBON, JAMES GANDOLFINI, ANDY GARCIA, ALLEN GARFIELD, RICHARD GERE, MEL GIBSON, SIR JOHN GIELGUD, PAMELA GIEN, BRENDAN GLEESON, TRACEY GOLD, TONY GOLDWYN, JOHN GOODMAN, HUGH GRANT, LINDA GRAY, JOEL GREY, RICHARD GRIECO, DAVID ALLEN GRIER, MELANIE GRIFFITH, STEVE GUTTENBERG, SHELLEY HACK, GENE HACKMAN, MICHAEL C. HALL, MARK HAMILL, GEORGE HAMILTON, TOM HANKS, DARYL HANNAH, MARCIA GAY HARDEN, ED HARRIS, MEL HARRIS, RICHARD HARRIS, RUTGER HAUER, MARG HELGENBERGER, MARIEL HEMINGWAY, MARILU HENNER, LANCE HENRIKSEN, BARBARA HERSHEY, HOWARD HESSEMAN, CHARLTON HESTON, JOHN HILLERMAN, EARL HOLLIMAN, LAUREN HOLLY, SIR IAN HOLM, SIR ANTHONY HOPKINS, BO HOPKINS, DENNIS HOPPER, BOB HOSKINS, DJIMON HOUNSOU, FINOLA HUGHES, D.L. HUGHLEY, HELEN HUNT, RACHEL HUNTER, IMAN, JILL IRELAND, KATHY IRELAND, EDDIE IZZARD, KATE JACKSON, GLYNIS JOHNS, KATY JURADO, WILLIAM KATT, JAMES KEACH, HARVEY KEITEL, MARTHE KELLER, SALLY KELLERMAN, MARGOT KIDDER, UDO KIER, VAL KILMER, RICHARD KIND, SIR BEN KINGSLEY, NASTASSJA KINSKI, BRUNO KIRBY, SWOOSIE KURTZ, CHERYL LADD, DIANE LADD, DIANE LANE, STEPHEN LANG, TED LANGE, ANTHONY LAPAGLIA, JOHN LARROQUETTE, LUCY LAWLESS, CLORIS LEACHMAN, JANE LEEVES, EVA LE GALLIENNE, JACK LEMMON, ANNIE LENNOX, JAY LENO, ADRIAN LESTER, MATT LETSCHER, SHARI LEWIS, LUCY LIU, CHRISTOPHER LLOYD, EMILY LLOYD, HEATHER LOCKLEAR, GARY LOCKWOOD, ROBERT LOGGIA, JEREMY LONDON, NIA LONG, LISA LU, DOLPH LUNDGREN, PATTI LUPONE, SARAH MADISON, KARL MALDEN, COSTAS MANDYLOR, KELLEY MARTIN, MARSHA MASON, MARY ELIZABETH MASTRANTONIO, TIM MATHESON, ANDREW MCCARTHY, PEGGY MCCAY, RODDY MCDOWALL, DOROTHY MCGUIRE, MICHAEL MCKEAN, NANCY MCKEON, JULIAN MCMAHON, IAN MCSHANE, JANE MEADOWS, COLM MEANEY, MARIAN MERCER, DINA MERRILL, BETTE MIDLER, REBECCA MILLER, JULIET MILLS, LYNNE MOODY, DEMI MOORE, MARY TYLER MOORE, TERRY MOORE, MICHAEL MORIARTY, PAT MORITA, KATE MULGREW, ARMIN MÜLLER-STAHL, PATRICIA NEAL, LIAM NEESON, SAM NEILL, CRAIG T. NELSON, THANDIE NEWTON, HAING NGOR, DUSTIN NGUYEN, JEREMY NORTHAM, CHRIS NOTH, MICHAEL NOURI, SINEAD O'CONNOR, GAIL O'GRADY, LENA OLIN, SIR LAURENCE OLIVIER, EDWARD JAMES OLMOS, CATHERINE OXENBERG, AL PACINO, JOANNA PACULA, JAMESON PARKER, MANDY PATINKIN, BILL PAXTON, GREGORY PECK, RHEA PERLMAN, BERNADETTE PETERS, MICHELLE PFEIFFER, RYAN PHILLIPE, MICHELLE PHILLIPS, DONALD PLEASENCE, JOAN PLOWRIGHT, AMANDA PLUMMER, MARKIE POST, STEPHANIE POWERS, KELLEY PRESTON, JONATHAN PRYCE, RANDY QUAID, KATHLEEN QUINLAN, BEULAH QUO, DEBORAH RAFFIN, JOHN RAITT, MICHAEL RAPAPORT, DAVID RASCHE, JOHN RATZENBERGER, ROGER REES, CHRISTOPHER REEVE, LEE REMICK, ALEJANDRO REY, JONATHAN RHYS-MEYERS, MICHAEL RICHARDS, JOELY RICHARDSON, NATASHA RICHARDSON, MOLLY RINGWALD, JOHN RITTER, TANYA ROBERTS, KYLIE ROCHA, FREDDY RODRIGUEZ, PAUL RODRIGUEZ, TRISTAN ROGERS, MARION ROSS, JOHN RUBINSTEIN, EVA MARIE SAINT, EMMA SAMMS, FRED SAVAGE, JOHN SAVAGE, JOHN SAXON, GRETA SCACCHI, JACK SCALIA, ROY SCHEIDER, MAXIMILIAN SCHELL, JOHN SCHNEIDER, AVERY SCHREIBER, RICK SCHRODER, ARNOLD SCHWARZENEGGER, MARTHA SCOTT, KYRA SEDGWICK, CONNIE SELLECCA, TOM SELLECK, JANE SEYMOUR, TONY SHALHOUB, NICOLETTE SHERIDAN, YOKO SHIMADA, ROBIN SHOU, RON SILVER, JONATHAN SILVERMAN, GENE SIMMONS, JEAN SIMMONS, CHRISTIAN SLATER, JACLYN SMITH, WILL SMITH, JIMMY SMITS, LEELEE SOBIESKI, MIRA SORVINO, ANN SOTHERN, DAVID SOUL, SISSY SPACEK, JAMES SPADER, BRENT SPINER, SYLVESTER STALLONE, JOHN STAMOS, ROD STEIGER, ANDREW STEVENS, CONNIE STEVENS, FISHER STEVENS, PATRICK STEWART, DEAN STOCKWELL, DEE WALLACE STONE, MADELEINE STOWE, PETER STRAUSS, DONALD SUTHERLAND, KIEFER SUTHERLAND, PATRICK SWAYZE, CHARLIZE THERON, JUSTIN THEROUX, EMMA THOMPSON, JACK THOMPSON, LEA THOMPSON, JENNIFER TILLEY, LILY TOMLIN, LIZ TORRES, CONSTANCE TOWERS, STUART TOWNSEND, JOHN TRAVOLTA, JEANNE TRIPPELHORN, TOMMY TUNE, JANINE TURNER, TWIGGY, CICELY TYSON, ROBERT URICH, BRENDA VACCARO, JEAN-CLAUDE VAN DAMME, CASPER VAN DIEN, DICK VAN PATTEN, JOYCE VAN PATTEN, JIM VARNEY, ROBERT VAUGHN, JON VOIGHT, LINDSAY WAGNER, ROBERT WAGNER, RAY WALSTON, JESSICA WALTER, RACHEL WARD, DAVID WARNER, LESLEY ANN WARREN, DENZEL WASHINGTON, DENNIS WEAVER, RAQUEL WELCH, FOREST WHITAKER, LYNN WHITFIELD, CINDY WILLIAMS, JO BETH WILLIAMS, OWEN WILLIAMS, PAUL WILLIAMS, ROBIN WILLIAMS, BRUCE WILLIS, FLIP WILSON, RITA WILSON, MARIE WINDSOR, JAMES WOODS, JOANNE WORLEY, VIVIAN WU, JANE WYATT, NOAH WYLE, JANE WYMAN, MICHAEL YORK, SUSANNAH YORK, ALAN YOUNG, DAPHNE ZUNIGA, AND OVER 2,600 OTHERS DURING THE LAST 42 YEARS.

HEATHER LYLE (310) 200-0506
15219 Sunset Blvd., Ste. 204
Pacific Palisades 90272
www.vocalyoga.com
vocalyoga@cs.com

Heather Lyle is a speech, accent reduction, singing and Fitzmaurice voice teacher, the leading voice work for actors. She has a bachelor and master's degree in voice and completed a doctoral internship in cutting edge voice research. Heather Lyle operates a private voice studio and has taught voice and acting for L.A. Mission College, the Los Angeles High School for the Performing Arts and at various acting schools in the private sector. She is very effective in helping actors to eliminate undesired accents and vocal patterns. Individual lessons are based on non-regional American dialect, the dialect standard in the entertainment industry. By learning American articulation techniques the actor can make rapid changes in his voice reducing his accent or he can learn to speak American Regional dialect without losing his own unique dialect.

STEVEN MEMEL STUDIO (818) 789-0474
4760 Halbrent Ave. FAX (818) 789-0835
Sherman Oaks 91403

Speaking American English with little or no accent or regional dialect is the focus of these one-on-one sessions with Steven Memel. He helps non-native speakers and people with regionalisms, to gain more range for employment by learning how to speak "General American." Steven Memel is head of the voice program for the Hollywood Acting Workshop, an international training organization that brings actors to the U.S. to study from around the world. Works on set, in studio, on location.

MENTOR LANGUAGE INSTITUTE (310) 887-0777
9744 Wilshire Blvd., Ste 455 FAX (310) 271-9590
Beverly Hills 90212
www.mentoresl.com

Combines acting technique instruction with special English pronunciation and accent reduction exercises. Students work with film scripts and perform a variety of roles in a fun and dynamic learning environment. In addition to mastering basic acting technique, course participants can expect to improve their conversational skills, reduce their accents, and develop self-confidence. Ongoing workshop: Tuesdays and Thursdays from 2:30 to 4:30 pm.

LARRY MOSS
THE ACCENT MINDED PROFESSOR (310) 395-4284

Classes and private coaching to help actors develop focus, authenticity and intimacy for the camera whether performing in dialect or in mainstream American. The goal: truthful performance without the work showing, i.e., a full-dimensional character speaking with a seamless accent that does not call attention to itself or get in the way of the acting. Through cold reading, improvisation, scenes and monologues, students are guided to: build confidence and trust in their creative process; break through acting blocks and limitations; learn or tune up a needed dialect; "give up" the dialect so we hear a flesh-and-blood character instead of a mechanical accent in a vacuum; and—for actors with regional or foreign accents—perform credibly in mainstream American. Students work in a safe, supportive environment conducive to risk taking, breakthrough, and discovery. Classes are on a four-week cycle with an enrollment limit of 12. Interview required. A veteran coach with numerous celebrity clients, Mr. Moss has prepped hundreds of actors for scores of films and plays. As an actor himself, he has voiced character and dialect roles in over 300 feature films and television productions. A university professor for over 30 years, he has taught acting, dialects, voice-over, and accent elimination and for several years co-taught workshops with Mel Blanc (cartoon voices and dialect).

REEL ENGLISH (323) 957-4758
Los Angeles 90019
www.reelenglishcoach.com

Standard American dialect specialist Kelly Reiter has been coaching actors in Los Angeles since 1989. Her cutting edge character-study approach gives actors with accents the tools, confidence, and professional voice they need at every step of their career, from getting the agent to getting the part. She works exclusively with regional and non-native speakers of English and has a solid reputation at UCLA where she taught for 11 years. Assessment interview required.

DEBORAH ROSS-SULLIVAN (626) 795-4767

Accent dialect reduction or acquisition. Over 20 years specializing in accent reduction and all dialects/accents. Also voice strengthening, breathing, and commercial/narration delivery. Uses IPA and tapes for ear training. Private instruction. Monday through Friday.

THE LEE STRASBERG
THEATRE INSTITUTE (323) 650-7777
7936 Santa Monica Blvd.
Los Angeles 90046
www.strasberg.com
admissionsla@strasberg.com

The Institute offers dialect and accent training within its complete program. See listing under ACTING in this section for further information.

THE THEATRE DISTRICT (323) 957-2343
804 North El Centro
Hollywood 90038
www.thetheatredistrict.com
info@thetheatredistrict.com

Macario Gaxiola conducts classes covering scene study, cold reading and audition technique. Also covered: movement and dialects. Private coaching available.

THEATRE OF ARTS (EST. 1927) **(323) 463-2500**
1621 N. McCadden Place **FAX (323) 463-2005**
Los Angeles 90028
www.theatre-of-arts.com

Offers day and evening classes for accent/dialect acquisition or reduction. Also teaches English.

VOCAL POWER SCHOOL **(818) 895-SING**
ACCENTS & DIALECTS **(800) 929-SING**
www.vocalpower.com
musicman@borntosing.com

Private coaching in foreign accents and regional American dialects, accent reduction and voice strengthening. Train under the guidance of Vocal Power Director, Howard Austin. Also offers home study courses for voice training and accent reduction called "VoiceShaping: How to find your million dollar voice" – 7 CDs, 100 page manual and includes "Speak to Influence"; "Speak to Influence – How to unlock the hidden power of your voice" – Book, soft cover, 168 pages; "How to Get Your Voice on TV and Radio Commercials: The Complete Guide to Breaking Into Voice-overs" – 3 audio cassettes.

VOICE: SINGING

WES ABBOTT **(323) 259-0327**
846 N. Avenue 63
Highland Park 90042

Offers private instruction in all styles, classical and commercial, for all levels, and all ages. Also works with small established groups. Works on eliminating the vocal break, concentrating on an even, flexible, healthy production from top to bottom of the range. 30 years Professor of Voice and head of the Voice Program at LACC. Conservatory trained with an MM in Voice. Has professional classical experience.

ACADEMY OF PERFORMING ARTS **(619) 282-1884**
4580-B Alvarado Canyon Rd. **FAX (619) 282-9889**
San Diego 92120
www.apastudios.com
kp@apastudios.com

See listing under ACTING in this section for further information.

TACEY ADAMS **(818) 769-7098**
North Hollywood

Offers private vocal coaching with an emphasis on diaphragmatic breathing, musicality, and performance practice. In addition to having a doctoral degree in music and a masters in voice, she is an accomplished accompanist and will help you find, select and prepare music that suits both your character type and vocal abilities. Affordable prices.

STELLA ADLER ACADEMY OF ACTING AND THEATRE COMPLEX **(323) 465-4446**
6773 Hollywood Blvd., 2nd Fl. **FAX (323) 469-6049**
Hollywood 90028
www.stellaadler-la.com

Academy director, Irene Gilbert. Call for catalogue and further information. Scene study and script analysis. SEE AD ON PAGE 6.

ALEXANDER TECHNIQUE
JUDITH STRANSKY **(310) 828-5528**
stranskyj@aol.com **FAX (310) 828-1028**

Ms. Stransky applies 42 years experience in the Alexander Technique to free body and self. She specializes in releasing problems and limitations in performance and daily life by teaching mastery over body and voice through a profound re-education of posture and movement habits, breathing and mental focus. This method is designed to effortlessly achieve maximum ease and freedom, which allows opening up and perfecting ability in voice, expression, movement, acting and self confidence, as well as alleviating stage fright, physical pain and stress for both students and professionals. Nina Foch, "With body and voice, the only things that work are techniques that can become a part of your entire life. This is what the Alexander Technique does, better than any other technique I know ... Judith Stransky has shown me the way." Clients include stars of stage and screen. The Alexander Technique is included world-wide in voice, acting, and movement training by foremost teachers, acting companies, drama schools, and Universities. Ms. Stransky is a former faculty member of the USC Drama Department, a Senior Teacher at UCLA Extension, participating teacher for the Opera Guild of Southern California and author of "The Alexander Technique: Joy In The Life Of Your Body." SEE AD ON PAGE 11.

ALEXANDER TECHWORKS
JEAN-LOUIS RODRIGUE (310) 209-9023
KRISTOF KONRAD (310) 443-4483
P.O. Box 3194
Beverly Hills 90212
www.alexandertechworks.com
jeanlouisr1@yahoo.com

Private lessons and ongoing classes are offered using the Alexander Technique to re-educate the actor's whole self and his breath coordination. Focus areas of training are effortless breath support, direction of energy in the voice, integration of mind, body and emotion to the text. Practical application to monologues, scenes, and cold readings. Day and evening classes are offered as well private instruction. No auditing. SEE AD ON PAGE 4.

MARA BAYGULOVA (818) 241-8141

Teaches private lessons for all types of singing covering range, agility, and power as well as audition preparation. Works with children, teens, and adults of all levels, days, evenings, and weekends. Auditing is allowed. Crash training is available. Ms. Baygulova is a professional musical theatre and opera singer, and teacher of Grammy Nominated singer Duncan Sheik. Also teaches cello and piano.

BEATRICE (310) 273-5940
FAX (310) 275-6285

Teaches vocal production, musicality, performance technique, range extension, diaphragmatic breathing technique, increasing power and self confidence for auditions. Avoid hoarseness with correct breathing. Teaches all styles. Private coaching. Teacher of two winners of the Heroes and Legends Scholarship Award. See listing under VOICE: SPEECH in this section for further information. SEE AD ON PAGE 93.

BLACK NEXXUS (323) 467-9987
6472 Santa Monica Blvd., Ste. 203
Los Angeles 90038
www.blacknexxusinc.com
blacknexxus@sbcglobal.net

Cutting edge classes to develop your own method. Vocal workshops, oncamera classes, scene study, and sensory technique geared toward developing the actor's awareness and emotional flexibility through a mixture of imagination and skills.

CALIFORNIA STATE UNIVERSITY
LOS ANGELES (CSULA) (323) 343-3000
5151 State University Dr.
Los Angeles 90032
www.calstatela.edu

Offers voice, movement and musical theatre training. They produce large musicals at various times throughout the year.

THE CHAPMANS WILLIAM & IRENE (818) 787-7192

William and Irene Chapman are performers, teachers and lecturers. Their credits include New York City Opera, numerous Broadway productions and concerts throughout the United States and Europe. The structure of singing and its application is what they emphasize in their theater-atmosphere studio. Many of their students are currently appearing in theatres nationwide. William is a veteran of the national company of "Sunset Boulevard." They believe that live theatre, with or without body-mics, is a business of maintaining a constant singing-speaking vocal presence. There should be no register shifting or faking because negotiating eight performances a week takes know-how, not guess work.

WENDY COOPER (818) 385-0442
wendycooper@music.org

The technique you've been looking for – Wendy covers musical theatre, legit and pop as well as voice and speech development for actors.

BOB CORFF (323) 851-9042
www.corffvoice.com

Offers private coaching in all styles covering vocal technique, breathing, relaxation, and removing the "break" through vocal exercises that strengthen the voice to build stamina and increase the vocal range. Bob also teaches singer's performance technique that covers what to do with your face and body, mic technique, how to feel more comfortable and confident on stage, patter between songs, dealing with musicians, and audition technique. Mr. Corff has starred in 3 Broadway shows and is author of "The Bob Corff Singer's Voice Method" tape and CD. See listing under BOOK & TAPES in the MARKETING section for further information. SEE AD ON PAGE 91.

CLAIRE CORFF (323) 969-0565
www.corffvoice.com

Private coaching. Specializes in children of all ages. Follows the breathing, voice, and performance techniques of the Bob Corff Method. SEE AD ON PAGE 90.

STEVEN DAHLKE (310) 995-9659
pdx2lax2@aol.com

Works well with students of all levels to help them feel comfortable producing their voice efficiently and comfortable expressing themselves emotionally. A holistic approach to get your mind out of the way.

DENISE (818) 762-4704

Emphasis is given to proper natural voice production while singing. Her students work on breathing. Lessons are for beg-pro children, teens, and adults in opera, musical comedy, pop, and rock styles. Ongoing lessons with no time commitment. Private instruction only.

GODEANE EAGLE (310) 450-5735

Godeane is a vocal coach with a Masters Degree in speech, her B.A. in theatre and her musical training in private coaching. She teaches singing, speaking voice, stage voice and cold reading.

GWEN GIRVIN (626) 287-2452
6208 N. Oak Ave
Temple City 91780

Works on breath control, pitch, and vocal technique. Classes are offered for beg-adv children, teens, and adults, days, evenings, and weekends. Ms. Girvin always allows auditing. She will assist in the production of an audio tape and teaches her students to accompany themselves. Showcases offered.

GOODRICH VOCAL STUDIO **(818) 766-3030**
3760 Cahuenga Blvd. West **FAX (818) 981-2482**
Studio 107
Universal City 91604
www.goodrichvocal.com
mgvocals@earthlink.net

Michael and Jennifer Winters Goodrich teach the technique the pros use at their Seth Riggs Speech Level Singing Studio.

DEREK GRAYDON **(323) 656-9356**

Derek Graydon uses the Bel Canto Vocal Technique on all styles of singing with immediate results. This technique has been used by Luciano Pavarotti, Placido Domingo, Juan Diego Flores, Renee Fleming, Maria Callas, Alicia Keyes, Kristin Chenowith and Linda Ronstadt. Mr. Graydon is an internationally acclaimed teacher and former Broadway and Opera performer who was on the staffs of the American Musical and Dramatic Academy in New York City and The Academy of Live and Recorded Arts in London. He has taught countless celebrities of stage, film television and opera including Kathryn Grayson and John Travolta. Mr. Graydon is a member of Equity, AEA, SAG, AFTRA, AGMA, AGVA and New York's National Association of Singing Teachers.

MARY GROVER, M.A.
SINGING TRAINING **(818) 787-SONG**
VOICE THERAPY **(800) 787-7731**
www.marygrover.com **FAX (818) 780-0698**
marygrover@aol.com

With over 27 years experience, singing teacher and medical board licensed singing voice therapist, Mary Grover teaches vocal technique, healthy belting, song interpretation, and voice therapy. Individual lessons, on-camera performance, and showcases. All ages, all styles. Improve audition and performance techniques. Clients include Platinum record performing artists and Grammy winners, performers on The Tonight Show, Letterman Show, and major labels such as Columbia Records, BMG, Sony, Warner Bros., and more. Currently on the faculty at Los Angeles City College and Pierce College, also a guest lecturer at USC, Cal Arts, and UCLA Extension. SEE AD ON THIS PAGE.

AMELIA HAAS **(323) 650-4566**
horse3@earthlink.net

Works on vocal technique to build range, volume, and breathing. Teaches all styles of singing. Students range from mid teens through adults of adv-pro levels and students must initially make a 6 week time commitment. Training is then ongoing.

ARTHUR SAMUEL JOSEPH, M.A. **(818) 788-8508**
16815 Moorpark Street
Encino 91436
www.vocalawareness.com
vawareness@aol.com

Mr. Joseph has his own trademarked and copyrighted method of instruction called, "Vocal Awareness." He teaches singing courses and courses for personal empowerment as a singer. See listing under VOICE: SPEECH in this section for further information.

SUZANNE KIECHLE
STUDIO OF VOICE **(818) 769-5880**
4209 Bellingham Ave.
Studio City 91604

Vocal production, coaching, and repair. Teaches all styles. There is

no time commitment required and she offers occasional performance workshops. Level depends on the individual student. No audition is required. Ms. Kiechle is now offering ongoing classes that cover technique and performance, limited to 10 students.

NATHAN LAM (310) 472-4120

Teaches a vocal technique which gives priority to vocal health, longevity of singing, and a practical approach for the professional singer. The technique has proved successful for Broadway, opera, and pop as well as rock and roll singers.

LIS LEWIS
THE SINGER'S WORKSHOP (818) 623-6668
4804 Laurel Canyon Blvd., #123 FAX (818) 753-2065
Valley Village 91607
www.thesingersworkshop.com
lis@thesingersworkshop.com

Private voice lessons in which singers work on developing range, power, and control, on releasing tension and on finding their unique persona. Specializes in rock, R&B, pop, alternative, blues, country, and hip/hop styles. Previous clients include: Gwen Stefani, Britney Spears, Linkin Park, Jack Black and the Pussycat Dolls.

LOS ANGELES
CITY COLLEGE (LACC) (323) 953-4000 x2990
855 N. Vermont Ave. FAX (323) 953-4500
Los Angeles 90029
www.lacitycollege.edu

Call for catalog.

HEATHER LYLE (310) 200-0506
15219 Sunset Blvd., Ste 204
Pacific Palisades 90272
www.vocalyoga.com
vocalyoga@cs.com

Heather Lyle is a singing, speech and Fitzmaurice voice teacher. She has a bachelor's and master's degree in voice and has completed a doctoral internship in cutting edge voice research at Indiana University. She currently operates a private voice studio teaching all styles including classical, musical theatre, R&B, pop and jazz while continuing and to work as a professional singer. She has also taught voice and acting for L.A. Mission College, the Los Angeles High School for the Performing Arts and at various acting schools in the private sector. Lyle specializes in voice technique based on the anatomy and physiology of the voice. She has excellent results with beginners and many of her students have gone on to professional careers. Individual lessons emphasize breath management, register blending, voice strengthening, articulation, increased resonance and range, reduced vocal stress, proper diction and more. Classes as well as private instruction available.

WENDY LEIGH MACKENZIE (818) 753-9111

Private one hour sessions in all styles of music. The students work on breathing, focus, placement, projection, and everything connected to the voice and the singer. Teaches students to get out of their own way when singing. Works with children, teens, and adults at all levels. Students include: Emmy winner Keith David, Melissa Manchester, Lilliath White, and Hattie Winston.

PEISHA MCPHEE (818) 788-3056

An associate of Seth Riggs, Ms. McPhee specializes in cabaret and musical theatre performance. She works on registration, vocal technique, breathing, improvisation, and audition technique. She and her partner, Mel Dangcil teach the art form of cabaret on different levels. Private coaching and performance workshops are available. Some advanced students are presented in a night club. Ms. McPhee has performed the role of Julie in "Showboat" with Donald O'Connor and Davis Gaines and is a veteran cabaret artist who performs regularly at the Cinegrill. Most recently her students have appeared on Ed McMahon's "Next Big Star" and one student is a four time champion. "After years of performance, the teachers know secrets about every aspect of singing cabaret." Los Angeles Times.

SUZAN MEIER (661) 253-9970
suzanmeier@aol.com

Suzan has created and patented a panty that holds a wireless microphone transmitter/receiver pack securely against a woman's body – firmly and inconspicuously in the small of her back. Unlike its elastic belt and holster type predecessors, the MicPac is quite comfortable, secure and discreet. Developed to accommodate the most revealing outfits. Suzan provides personal wardrobe consultation and creation. Also designs and constructs costumes as well as bridal gowns and ensembles. Has a Dramalogue award.

THE STEVEN MEMEL STUDIO (818) 789-0474
4760 Halbrent Ave.
Sherman Oaks 91403

Steven Memel has been helping singers achieve their vocal and performance goals for over 25 years both in the U.S. and abroad. His no-nonsense technique covers expanding range, breathing, stamina, removing breaks, dynamics, resonance and more. Performance work centers on knowing the story of the song, and being able to communicate it while trusting your vocal technique. Other areas covered are: mic technique, what to do with your hands and body, staging, patter, working with musicians, recording techniques and audition prep. Clientele: Broadway, Sony Records, Edel America Recording, Jive Records, tours with Bette Midler, Brenda Russell, TV and film, Linda Hopkins World Tour, and much more. USC guest lecturer, UCLA Extension, extensive credits, film, TV, stage and recording. Offers private, performance workshops, in studio, demo production.

PELAYO VOCAL STUDIOS
DR. HERNON PELAYO (818) 988-2387
13046 Ebell St.
North Hollywood 91605
www.hernanpelayo.com

Private coaching for singing and speech with levels geared to the individual student's needs. Demos are available for an extra fee. A free interview is required and there is no auditing. Dr. Pelayo is one of the few Spanish-speaking vocal coaches in the area. He has performed as the leading baritone for La Scala Opera Company in Milan, Italy, Carnegie Hall and the Metropolitan Opera in N.Y. Dr. Pelayo's fees are $35 for half an hour and $70 for an hour.

LISA POPEIL'S VOICEWORKS (818) 906-7229 (800) 235-8623
Sherman Oaks
www.popeil.com

Offers private voice training in singing and speech in an exciting environment. An expert in all styles including belt, legit, jazz, pop, R&B, country and classical. Ms. Popeil has worked with actors in vocal technique and performance skills for over 20 years. Audition preparation a specialty. Ms. Popeil has an MFA in Voice, is an international lecturer on innovative voice technique and is creator of "The Total Singer" instructional video. Her studio includes a stage, sound system, video as well as digital recording.

THE VOICE STUDIO ELIZABETH PRESCOTT (818) 789-8660
Sherman Oaks/New York
www.elizabethprescott.com
prescottvoice@yahoo.com

Specializing in technical voice training as well as complete singing audition preparation. Private voice lessons apply classically-based techniques to all styles through well-explained exercises. Lessons tailored to each student develop optimal voice quality with healthy, balanced production and seamless transitions between registers. Singers of all ages and levels eliminate unnecessary tension in the tongue, throat, and abdomen with true support and strength, resulting in freedom and power with healthy resonance. Vocal rehabilitation, speech work, musical theater audition workshops and private coaching also available. Piano accompaniment from $20 per half-hour. A seasoned member of S.A.G. and A.E.A with extensive film and television recording credits, Ms. Prescott continues to work professionally in the genres of opera, jazz and musical theater. She has been teaching vocal and audition technique in New York and Los Angeles for over twenty years. SEE AD ON THIS PAGE.

ALLISON PRIVAL (818) 566-4468

New York trained musical theatre voice coach Allison Prival teaches all ages all types of music.

PROFESSIONAL SCHOOL FOR THE ARTS (310) 328-7664 (310) 328-SONG
1329 Sartori Ave. FAX (310) 782-2072
Torrance 90501
www.psarts.com

Study singing in a dynamic and supportive environment. Lessons are available to performers of all ages, at all levels of development working in all styles, from belt to legit. PSA students are have performed in Broadway shows from "Miss Saigon" to "Phantom of the Opera." Private and group lessons are available. Lisa Matsko Hamilton, instructor.

HOWARD RICHMAN (818) 344-3306
18375 Ventura Blvd., #8000
Tarzana 91356
www.soundfeelings.com/products/music_instruction/piano_lessons.htm
howardrichman@soundfeelings.com

Teaches you all the other things you need related to singing: self-accompanying, ear-training, sight-singing, pitch control, songwriting, and piano.

FLORENCE MERCURIO RIGGS
VOCAL TECHNIQUE, VOCAL THERAPY &
CREATIVE SOUNDINGS WORKSHOP (818) 990-1221
Sherman Oaks FAX (818) 990-2151

Works on vocal technique and vocal therapy. The emphasis is given to using the voice as a natural instrument, removing the mystique about middle voice, and balancing resonance as the voice extends through speech connected singing in all ranges. The technique is applicable to any style of singing. Has worked with students in musical theatre, opera, pop, rock, jazz, folk etc.

SUSAN RUMOR (310) 664-9928
West Los Angeles
www.susanrumor.com
susan@susanrumor.com

Ms. Rumor has more than 20 years experience singing professionally for TV, film, and recordings. She offers an extensive training program for aspiring and established singers which includes developing correct voice technique, confidence building, finding a unique style, and studio and live performance coaching. Susan has a masters degree in speech pathology/voice therapy and has lectured in the masters program at Cal State University Long Beach and at L.A. City College. Her vocal technique is based on her extensive experience in voice physiology and focuses on proper breathing, developing power without breaks, correct laryngeal positioning and voice placement. A well known producer, Ms. Rumor has a full digital recording studio available and offers demo production and songwriting training. Clients include Grammy winning, and Platinum selling artists.

PATRICIA SHANKS (949) 723-4473
www.studioshanks.com
pshanks@studioshanks.com

A private studio facility offering voice instruction and musicianship training for singers ages 12 and over, beginning through advanced. The focus is traditional, educational, foundation-based and fine arts-oriented. Establish a reliable technique and eliminate externally applied cosmetic affectations related to technique (voice production) and performance (presentation). Newport Beach. 28 years experience. Member: NATS, MTAC, AGMA, SCVA.

SINGING FOR A LIVING
MARTA WOODHULL (818) 752-0833
www.singingforaliving.com FAX (818) 752-3734
marta@singingforaliving.com

Ms. Woodhull, the author of "Singing For A Living," offers audition preparation and private instruction to help the singer build a repertoire. She also helps with career planning and artistic development providing thorough vocal training to maximize your professional potential. Includes breathing, resonance, vocal style, vocal repair, voice strengthening, and studio technique. She has a digital Pro-Tools compatible studio and offers demo and album vocal production services. Sessions are offered days and evenings. Her website offers free pro tips on vocal health, touring, conditioning, reading lists and Industry links. Also available are the newly released "Singing for a Living" lessons on CD, a workout program in basic to advanced levels. Ms. Woodhull is Juilliard trained and has recorded with Lea Salonga, Brian McKnight, Paula Abdul, etc. Call for complete list of fees and services. SEE AD ON PAGE 97.

THE LEE STRASBERG
THEATRE INSTITUTE (323) 650-7777
7936 Santa Monica Blvd.
Los Angeles 90046
www.strasberg.com
admissionsla@strasberg.com

Classes in singing are offered. See listing under ACTING in this section for further information.

MARJORY TAYLOR, PH.D, ED.D (310) 246-1743
Los Angeles, Beverly Hills
marjorytaylor@netzero.net

Offers private coaching in classical and pop styles and covers voice development for actors, strengthening of weak stage voices, and specializes in repairing damaged voices. Ms. Taylor has a Ph.D. in Voice Science and has California State teaching credentials. 35 years experience teaching.

THEATRE OF ARTS (EST. 1927) (323) 463-2500
1621 N. McCadden Place FAX (323) 463-2005
Los Angeles 90028
www.theatre-of-arts.com

Classes work on breathing, resonance, interpretation, presentation, vocal repair, voice strengthening, audition technique, and character analysis. Singing styles covered are Broadway, cabaret, classical, club, concert, country, jazz, musical theatre, operatic, pop, and rock and are for all levels. These ongoing classes may require an interview. Presents showcases.

CAROL TINGLE (310) 828-3100
Santa Monica FAX (310) 828-4443

A performer/voice teacher for 35 years, Carol Tingle works with singers of all ages, levels and styles integrating the concepts of excellent vocal technique into the performance of appropriate repertoire. Private instruction, audition preparation, as well as performance workshops are offered at her studio in Santa Monica. Emphasis is placed on the development of the voice and safe, healthy vocal production. Member of the National Association of Teachers of Singing (NATS). Carol also works with performance anxiety and has completed her cassette tape series "Centering For Performance." SEE AD ON PAGE 94.

MARY VANARSDEL VOICE STUDIO (818) 559-3659
514 N. Catalina St.
Burbank 91505
www.laurelwood-music.com
mvsings@aol.com

Ms. VanArsdel offers vocal technique for beginning and intermediate students at her Burbank Studio in singing (all styles), voice and speech, and accent reduction. She specializes in working with beginners and people who are scared. Topics covered: vocal anatomy, correct breathing, strengthening exercises for range and power, smoothing vocal "breaks", help with vocal strain, and work with breathiness and nasality. She also provides special help with ear training, reading music and performance coaching, and offers new students a free no-obligation introductory consultation. Ms. VanArsdel has 25 years of professional performing and teaching experience and has received three DramaLogue Awards, and a Los Angeles Drama Critics Circle Award. A Magna Cum Laude graduate of Bowdoin college, she received her vocal training in New York and London and is an active member of two of Los Angeles' premiere companies, Pacific Resident Theatre, and The Musical Theatre Guild.

VOCAL POWER SCHOOL (818) 895-SING
SINGING (800) 929-SING
www.vocalpower.com
musicman@borntosing.com

Private coaching in voice control, power, range and flexibility. All styles and personal style. On stage and on-camera presentation. Train under the guidance of Vocal Power Director, Howard Austin. Ten Star Search Winners, eighteen Broadway leads and a quarter finalist on "American Idol" and three "Miss Saigon" title role leads. Also available are self improvement courses, "Born To Sing" on video, DVDs, CDs, tapes and books.

RICCARDA WATKINS (310) 924-7888
(310) 924-4500
www.thevoicewhisperer.com
riccardaw@yahoo.com

Private coaching available using the Garcia Method. Ms. Watkins has worked with Kanye West as well as with No Authority and Nobody's Angel, actresses Hilary and Haley Duff, E.G. Daily (voice over artist for The Rugrats and The Powerpuff Girls), and TJ Fantini (formerly of the Mickey Mouse Club).

VOICE: SPEECH

STELLA ADLER ACADEMY OF ACTING
AND THEATRE COMPLEX (323) 465-4446
6773 Hollywood Blvd., 2nd Fl. FAX (323) 469-6049
Hollywood 90028
www.stellaadler-la.com

Academy director: Irene Gilbert. Call for catalogue and further information. SEE AD ON PAGE 6.

ALEXANDER TECHNIQUE
JUDITH STRANSKY (310) 828-5528
stranskyj@aol.com FAX (310) 828-1028

Ms. Stransky applies 42 years experience in the Alexander Technique to free body and self. She specializes in releasing problems and limitations in performance and daily life by teaching mastery over body and voice through a profound re-education of posture and movement habits, breathing and mental focus. This method is designed to effortlessly achieve maximum ease and freedom, which allows opening up and perfecting ability in voice, expression, movement, acting and self confidence, as well as alleviating stage fright, physical pain and stress for both students and professionals. Nina Foch, "With body and voice, the only things that work are techniques that can become a part of your entire life. This is what the Alexander Technique does, better than any other technique I know...Judith Stransky has shown me the way." Clients include stars of stage and screen. The Alexander Technique is included worldwide in voice, movement, and acting training by foremost teachers, acting companies, drama schools, and universities. Ms. Stransky is a former faculty member at USC Drama Department, a senior teacher at UCLA Extension, and author of "The Alexander Technique: Joy In The Life Of Your Body." SEE AD ON PAGE 11.

ALEXANDER TECHWORKS
JEAN-LOUIS RODRIGUE (310) 209-9023
KRISTOF KONRAD (310) 443-4483
P.O. Box 3194
Beverly Hills 90212
www.alexandertechworks.com
jeanlouisr1@yahoo.com

Private lessons and ongoing classes are offered using the Alexander Technique to re-educate the actor's whole self and his breath coordination. Focus areas of training are effortless breath support, direction of energy in the voice, integration of mind, body and emotion to the text. Practical application to monologues, scenes, and cold readings. Day and evening classes are offered as well private instruction. No auditing. SEE AD ON PAGE 4.

THE AMERICAN ACADEMY OF DRAMATIC ARTS (323) 464-2777
1336 N. La Brea Ave.
Hollywood 90028
www.aada.org
ca@aada.org

See listing under ACTING in this section for further information.

ROWENA BALOS (310) 285-8489

Coaching for voice production is offered that covers speech, text work, breathing, power, range, relaxation, and the connection of thoughts and feelings into sound. No interview is required and there is no auditing. Offers small ongoing classes and private sessions. Short term voice and a Shakespeare workshop are available. Over 25 years teaching experience. "The Human Instrument" booklet and practice cassettes are available.

BEATRICE (310) 273-5940
FAX (310) 275-6285

Works on voice placement, audition technique, clarity, enunciation, voice levels, range extension, diaphragmatic breathing, and increasing power. See listing under VOICE: SINGING in this section for further information. SEE AD ON PAGE 93.

BONNIE BIZOZA ACCENT ON ACCENT (818) 783-0473

Offers accent/dialect training and accent reduction for beginners and established professionals. Ms. Bizoza is a licensed speech therapist and experienced dialect coach who provides private training using a multisensory approach adapted to the students learning style in order to achieve authentic, natural speech pattern. Individual classes and on-set coaching are available.

FRANCIE M. BROWN (818) 999-9124

Teaches Standard American Speech, elimination of regionalisms, dialects, and Skinner method phonetics. Private lessons by individual appointment.

CALIFORNIA STATE UNIVERSITY LOS ANGELES (CSULA) (323) 343-3000
5151 State University Dr.
Los Angeles 90032
www.calstatela.edu

Offers voice, movement and musical theatre training. They produce large musicals at various times throughout the year.

VINCENT CHASE (323) 851-4819
7221 Sunset Blvd. FAX (323) 851-9942
Los Angeles 90046

See listing under ACTING in this section for further information.

LILYAN CHAUVIN (323) 877-4988

Has taught many of the top people in Hollywood. See listing under ACTING in this section for further information. SEE AD ON PAGES 16 & 255.

WENDY COOPER (818) 385-0442
wendycooper@music.org

The technique you've been looking for – Wendy covers musical theatre, legit and pop as well as voice and speech development for actors.

BOB CORFF (323) 851-9042
www.corffvoice.com

Works on breathing, diction, accents and accent reduction, sibilant "s" and other speech problems, proper placement, lowering your voice, and widening your range. Gives your voice color, strength, and stamina. Small group classes and private sessions are available. Author of the tape and CD, "The Bob Corff Speaker's Voice Method." See listing under BOOKS & TAPES in the MARKETING section for further information. SEE AD ON PAGE 91.

CLAIRE CORFF (323) 969-0565
www.corffvoice.com

A fun, healthy, and complete vocal technique. Follows the Bob Corff Method. SEE AD ON PAGE 90.

JACKY DE HAVILAND (323) 691-7077

Works on breathing, delivery, diction, projection, voice strength, and speech problems such as sibilant "s." Monologues, character work, cold reading accents/dialects, accent reduction, Shakespeare: all tailored to the individual. Fun and productive. Instruction tailored to schedules. Weekends available. Private coaching only. See listing under ACTING.

THE DIALECT COACH (818) 879-1896
www.thedialectcoach.com
info@thedialectcoach.com

Dialect training and accent reduction. Learn any dialect quickly and easily, including a neutral American accent. Coached Mike Meyers in "The Cat in the Hat", NBC's "War Stories", clients have appeared in "Ali", "CSI: Miami", "The Agency", "The Shield", "Finding Nemo" and many others.

JUDY DICKERSON (818) 985-1603

Focuses on an organic approach to voice and speech and works on connecting body to voice, thought, and emotion using contemporary and classical text. Ms. Dickerson has taught professional actor training at UW, Boston U., SMU, Cal Arts, and UC Santa Barbara. Private coaching and ongoing classes are available. She has a MFA from SMU, is certified by Edith Skinner, and has also trained with Arthur Lessac.

JESSICA DRAKE (323) 662-1831

Offers dialects, Standard American Speech, Shakespeare, and accent reduction for film, TV, and stage. Works on location or her own studio. There is no time commitment. Ms. Drake is a Julliard graduate. She has coached many films including "Catch Me If You Can," "The Green Mile," "Forrest Gump," "L.A. Confidential," "What's Love Got To Do With It," "The Haunted Mansion" and "Band of Brothers."

GODEANE EAGLE (310) 450-5735

Godeane is a vocal coach with a Masters Degree in speech, her B.A. in theatre and her musical training in private coaching. She teaches singing, speaking voice, stage voice and cold reading.

ROBERT EASTON
THE HENRY HIGGINS OF HOLLYWOOD, INC.
THE DIALECT DOCTOR (818) 985-2222

Over 40 years experience teaching diction, voice production, dialects and accent reduction. He studied phonetics at University College, London, Trinity College, Dublin, and took an advanced dialect course at Cambridge University. He has done extensive dialect research on five continents and Oceania. He has played dialect roles in 82 major motion pictures, over 1,700 TV and radio programs, and is a former inter-collegiate after-dinner speaking champion. SEE AD ON PAGE 89.

MARY GROVER, M.A. (818) 787-7664
THE PROFESSIONAL COMMUNICATOR (800) 787-7731
www.marygrover.com FAX (818) 780-0698
marygrover@aol.com

Ms. Grover is a licensed voice/speech pathologist with 27 years experience as a voice and speech consultant. Offers accent/dialect reduction, voice therapy (medical insurance accepted), voice and speech production, breathing, and voice strengthening. Currently on faculty at Los Angeles City College and Pierce College, also guest lecturer at USC, and former faculty member at CSUN, UCLA Extension, and Cal Arts. SEE AD ON PAGE 93.

AMELIA HAAS (323) 650-4566
horse3@earthlink.net

Offers private instruction in speech technique that covers voice projection, breathing, diction, speech impediments, accents, and accent reduction using the Alexander Technique. Day, evening, and weekend sessions are available. There is a 1 month time commitment required.

ARTHUR SAMUEL JOSEPH, M.A. (818) 788-8508
16815 Moorpark Street
Encino 91436
www.vocalawareness.com
vawareness@aol.com

Mr. Joseph has been teaching for over four decades and has his own trademarked and copyrighted method of instruction called, "Vocal Awareness." This technique creates an awareness of the physical, emotional, and psychological aspects of the voice which allows the participant to more fully integrate the aspects of self through vocal training. Careful attention is paid to subtle details that build confidence, self-esteem, competence, and self-awareness. The work applies to all aspects of voice including all styles of singing, speaking, accent reduction, broadcasting, etc. Mr. Joseph has been a professor of voice at USC, a visiting artist at Yale University and George Washington University, and has taught throughout the U.S., Latin America, Europe, and Japan. He has a book called, "Sound of the Soul: Discovering the Power of Your Voice," and a several CD and DVD series. His latest book is called "Vocal Power" and is available on the website.

PHILLIP KING (KROOPF) (310) 276-7587

One-on-one classes that cover self-confidence, diction, correction of speech defects/impediments, and regional dialect reduction. Afternoon and evening sessions. Mr. King was the director of the N.Y. School of Announcing and Speech. See listing under ACTING in this section for further information.

VERNICE KLIER (310) 392-0064
(011) 33 1 47 38 24 64
www.vernice-klier.com
verniceklier@aol.com

Vernice Klier is an international voice and acting coach specializing in acting in English. She has had 15 years experience coaching privately; and has coached on location on over 25 films including the Academy Award winning The English Patient.

HEATHER LYLE (310) 200-0506
15219 Sunset Blvd., Ste 204
Pacific Palisades 90272
www.vocalyoga.com

Heather Lyle received her bachelor's and master's degrees in voice specializing in singing, diction and speech science and is also a Fitzmaurice voice teacher, the leading voice work for actors. Ms. Lyle operates a private voice studio and has taught voice and acting for L.A. Mission College, the Los Angeles High School for the Performing Arts and at various acting schools in the private sector. She is the founder of Vocal Yoga, a workshop utilizing yoga techniques to free the voice, and Vocal Archetypes, a workshop for actors to discover the character-type their voices convey. Lyle's Fitzmaurice voice workshops are extremely popular and her individual lessons cover performance skills, voice strengthening, breath management, articulation, increased resonance and range, reduced vocal stress, proper diction and more.

STEVEN MEMEL STUDIO (818) 789-0474
4760 Halbrent Ave. FAX (818) 789-0835
Sherman Oaks 91403

Steven Memel, during his more than 20 years of teaching in the U.S. and abroad, has developed a "no-nonsense" system that gets the job done. The core of the work is building a powerful and flexible technique while at the same time learning how to incorporate it into performance and life. Steven breaks everything down into simple, understandable, attainable elements. The program is designed to be practical and for immediate use. Covers breath, color, tone, power and projection, resonance, music, clarity, stamina, tension release and how to put it all together so it becomes second nature. Mr. Memel is Head of the Voice department for the Hollywood Acting Workshop, an international training organization bringing actors from around the world to the U.S., former head of voice for the L.A. County High School for the Performing Arts, a USC guest lecturer and has taught UCLA Extension classes. His extensive performing credits include film, TV, stage and recording. Call for client list.

LARRY MOSS (310) 395-4284

Private coaching and classes to tune up voice, speech, accent and delivery (on and off camera) for executives, speakers, actors and others in the public spotlight. Attention is given to breath support, clarity, sight reading, spontaneity, image, accent reduction, and performance anxiety. A veteran coach with numerous celebrity clients, Mr. Moss has over 40 years experience as a speech consultant, university professor and dialect/diction/acting coach.

PELAYO VOCAL STUDIOS
DR. HERNON PELAYO (818) 988-2387
13046 Ebell St.
North Hollywood 91605
www.hernanpelayo.com

Private coaching for the singing and speaking voice. There is no time commitment required and there is no auditing allowed. Also coaches people in the Spanish accent. Dr. Pelayo charges $35 for a half hour or $70 for an hour. See listing under SINGING in this section for further information.

REEL ENGLISH **(323) 957-4758**
Los Angeles 90019
www.reelenglishcoach.com

Standard American dialect specialist Kelly Reiter has been coaching actors in Los Angeles since 1989. Her cutting edge character-study approach gives actors with accents the tools, confidence, and professional voice they need at every step of their career, from getting the agent to getting the part. She works exclusively with regional and non-native speakers of English and has a solid reputation at UCLA where she taught for 11 years. Assessment interview required.

DEBORAH ROSS-SULLIVAN **(626) 795-4767**

Over 20 years specializing in accent reduction and all dialects/accents. Also voice strengthening, breathing, and commercial/narration delivery. Uses IPA and tapes for ear training. Private instruction only.

THE LEE STRASBERG THEATRE INSTITUTE **(323) 650-7777**
7936 Santa Monica Blvd.
Los Angeles 90046
www.strasberg.com
admissionsla@strasberg.com

Offers training in phonetics and voice classes. See listing under ACTING in this section for further information.

MARJORY TAYLOR, PH.D, ED.D **(310) 246-1743**
Los Angeles and Beverly Hills
marjorytaylor@netzero.net

Ms. Taylor offers an exclusive technique for power resonance and stamina as well as pitch range and modulation to give every character and nuance of emotion. She helps extend your upper range for pop (scat) or classical and coloratura and can help provide permanent relief from laryngitis or nodes. Ms. Taylor has a unique method for safely lowering the voice three to twelve pitches and helps you achieve crisp, clear diction for stage and film or voice overs. Areas of specialization include: voice therapy, stage and film voices, breath control, clear diction, commercials and accents.

THEATRE OF ARTS (EST. 1927) **(323) 463-2500**
1621 N. McCadden Place **FAX (323) 463-2005**
Los Angeles 90028
www.theatre-of-arts.com

Classes work on breathing, delivery, diction, projection, voice strengthening, speech problems, oral interpretation, monologues, character work, cold reading, voice-over, accents/dialects, and accent reduction. The class limit is 20 and classes are held days and evenings. Also teaches English as a second language. An interview may be required. Theatre of Arts is authorized by Federal law to enroll foreign students for ESL (English as a Second Language) and performing and related arts.

MARY VANARSDEL VOICE STUDIO **(818) 559-3659**
514 N. Catalina St.
Burbank 91505
mvsings@aol.com

Ms. VanArsdel offers vocal technique for beginning and intermediate students at her Burbank Studio in singing (all styles), voice and speech, and accent reduction. She specializes in working with beginners and people who are scared. Topics covered: vocal anatomy, correct breathing, strengthening exercises for range and power, smoothing vocal "breaks", help with vocal strain, and work with breathiness and nasality. She also provides special help with ear training, reading music and performance coaching, and offers new students a free no-obligation introductory consultation. Ms. VanArsdel has 25 years of professional performing and teaching experience and has received three DramaLogue Awards, and a Los Angeles Drama Critics Circle Award. A Magna Cum Laude graduate of Bowdoin college, she received her vocal training in New York and London and is an active member of two of Los Angeles' premiere companies, Pacific Resident Theatre, and The Musical Theatre Guild.

VOCAL POWER SCHOOL: SPEECH **(818) 895-SING** **(800) 929-SING**
www.vocalpower.com
musicman@borntosing.com

Private coaching in presentation of monologues, commercial copy, stand-up comedy, dialogues, voice-over, voice strengthening, accent reduction, some dialect work. Under the guidance of Vocal Power Director, Howard Austin. Also offers home study courses for voice training and accent reduction called "VoiceShaping: – How to find your million dollar voice" – 7 CDs, 100 page manual – and includes "Speak to Influence: How to Unlock the Hidden Power of Your Voice" – Book, soft cover, 168 pages; "How to Get Your Voice on TV and Radio Commercials" – The complete guide to breaking into voice-overs – 3 audio cassettes.

ALISO CREEK PRODUCTIONS (818) 954-9931
P.O. Box 10006 FAX (818) 954-9931
Burbank 91510
www.alisocreek.net

Offers a 6 week class for beg-adv actors. Classes are limited to 5 students and are conducted in a recording studio. All microphone work is recorded for evaluation. Class covers announcing, characters, dialog, and narration. A free consultation is offered prior to class. Also produces demo tapes.

THE ART OF VOICE-ACTING (858) 484-0220
13639 Freeport Rd. FAX (858) 484-7493
San Diego 92129
www.voiceacting.com
jralburger@voiceacting.com

James R. Alburger, author of "The Art of Voice-Acting" and 11-time Emmy winning audio producer, teaches an 8-week workshop and 2-day seminar on the craft of performing for voiceover. See website for complete details. Also offers tele-seminars.

LOUISE CHAMIS (818) 985-0130

Ms. Chamis has been teaching over 27 years and offers private voice-over for adults and children, beg-adv actors. No audition is required and no auditing is allowed. You can hear Louise's voice as the Queen from Snow White in "Fantasmic" at Disneyland and on the TV show "House of Mouse." Referred by many managers and agents. Also produces CD demos. SEE AD ON THIS PAGE.

DEL MAR MEDIA ARTS (949) 753-0570
15375 Barranca Pkwy., #J-105 FAX (949) 753-0576
Irvine 92618
www.delmarmediaarts.com

Offers beginning 6 week class that introduces basic spots, narration, and animation. Also offers advanced classes in narration, audio books, dialects, and spokesperson (wireless ear prompter and TelePrompTer). State licensed and approved. Monthly free open-house seminars. Will assist in the production of a demo tape. See listing under AUDIO DEMO PRODUCTION in the MARKETING SECTION. Also listing in the COMMERCIAL section. SEE AD ON PAGE 67.

DURAN PRODUCTIONS (818) 385-1000
13848 Ventura Blvd.
Sherman Oaks 91423
www.voiceover-demos.com

Specializing in all areas of voice-over demos and jingles. Vocal demos. Career guidance every step of the way. Many clients have gone on to sign with major agencies.

ROBERT EASTON
THE HENRY HIGGINS OF HOLLYWOOD, INC.
THE DIALECT DOCTOR (818) 985-2222

During his 60 years of performing experience, he has done cartoon voices and voice-overs on four continents and has coached many other performers on how to do them. He has been retained as a dialect consultant by many ad agencies for casting sessions and commercial shoots. SEE AD ON PAGE 89.

SANDY HOLT ON-CAMERA COLD READING & IMPROV WORKSHOP (310) 271-8217

Private coaching for on-camera actors. Sandy does voice casting for all major studios including: Dreamworks, Disney, Paramount, Warner Brothers and MTV. She also produces demo tapes in a professional recording studio custom made for your talents. SEE AD ON PAGE 51.

KALMENSON & KALMENSON (818) 342-6499
105 S. Sparks FAX (818) 343-1403
Burbank 91506
www.kalmenson.com
kalmenson@earthlink.net

A leader in the voice-over industry, they offer a full curriculum in the study of voice-over for students/actors at all levels. Courses include Foundations, for beginners; Intermediate for Actors: Working Pro, for the working professional: Kids Voice-Over and more. Based on 50 years of casting and teaching experience, the workshops are conducted using the Kalmenson Method (R), enabling actors to "define their signature."

THE LEARNING ANNEX (310) 478-6677
11850 Wilshire Blvd., Ste. 100
Los Angeles 90025
www.learningannex.com

Offers classes in voice-over. Call for further information.

LOS ANGELES CITY COLLEGE (LACC) (323) 953-4000 x2620
855 N. Vermont Ave. FAX (323) 953-4500
Los Angeles 90029
www.lacitycollege.edu

The Radio and Television Department offers courses in voice-over technique. Call the above number for additional info.

MASTERING VOICEOVER (310) 575-4321
11734 Wilshire Blvd., Ste. 814
Los Angeles 90025
www.masteringvoiceover.com
adan327830@aol.com

Mastering Voiceover is the only voiceover class taught by Dan Balestrero, author of the nationally recognized CD course "Mastering the Art of Voiceovers," and the only voiceover training series that really grounds you in the vocal development techniques all top pros ultimately use. With 18 hours of instruction over 6 weeks, Mastering Voiceover teaches beginners and professionals alike the comprehensive skills they'll need to know to successfully navigate this highly competitive and lucrative Industry.

LARRY MOSS' VOICE-OVER WORKOUT & DIALECT GYM **(310) 395-4284**

A creative stretch workout to tune up acting, dialects, diction, delivery and cold reading. Also to help actors develop new characters, voices and accents and to use them credibly and confidently without the work showing. Four-week-cycle classes are conducted in a safe, supportive climate conducive to risk taking, breakthrough and discovery. Enrollment limit of 12 with interview required. Mr. Moss is a veteran dialect/diction/acting coach and voice-over actor who has coached for scores of films and celebrity clients. He has taught numerous acting, dialect and voice-over workshops at UCLA extension and other universities and for several years co-taught workshops with Mel Blanc (cartoon voices and dialect). As an actor he has voiced character and dialect roles in over 300 feature films and television productions.

NOVA PRODUCTIONS **(323) 969-0949**
3575 Cahuenga Blvd. West **FAX (323) 969-0822**
Ste. 630
Los Angeles 90068
www.novaprods.com
novaprods@aol.com

Offers workshops in the fundamentals of commercial voice-over for beg-adv students. Classes are limited to 8, require a 6 week time commitment, and are held in the evenings. They have an extensive commercial copy library and they will assist in the production of a demo tape. Private instruction is available.

ORIGINAL VOICE BANK **(818) 846-2002** **(800) 500-6661**
www.originalvoice.cs.com

George Crowell a veteran in the voice over field has done sitcoms at Universal and has an extensive resume. Does private coaching and makes digital demos in his studio at reasonable rates.

DICK & CHRIS AT THE RADIO RANCH WORKSHOP **(323) 462-4966**
1140 N. La Brea Ave. **FAX (323) 856-4311**
Los Angeles 90038
www.radio-ranch.com

Dick and Chris offer their famous series of single Saturday voice-over classes. Some half day Saturday, some all day Saturday. Their unique focus is on the essential acting skills needed for booking auditions, finding your own voice, generating energy performance and staying in the creative flow that makes the difference in getting the job. "It's not about the voice." Call for course packet and calendar.

PROMENADE ACTING CONSERVATORY **(310) 656-8070**
1404 Third Street Promenade **FAX (310) 656-8069**
Santa Monica 90401
www.pierodusa.com
info@pierodusa.com

The Voice and Speech Workshop teaches the actor how to integrate a persuasive, resonant, and emotionally effective voice to the craft through physical alignment, relaxation, and breathing. Also available: a bilingual intensive that allows the actor to explore their vocal range, as well as learn how to audition for every style of voiceover, ranging from one-liners to announcers, slice of life characters, animation, PSAs, CD ROMs and narrator copy. The course culminates with a professional demo reel for each student. Taught by the Director of Programs at the Piero Dusa Acting Conservatory, a seasoned professional that has been the voice of numerous campaigns in the English and Spanish markets for over a decade. SEE AD ON PAGES 21 & 297.

REEL PROS **(818) 788-4133**
13437 Ventura Blvd., Ste. 220
Sherman Oaks 91423
www.reelpros.com
support@reelpros.com

Reel Pros has three categories for their classes: 1) Main Arena for professional actors who play 27 and above; membership by audition only; 2) Reel PROs 2 for young professional actors who play 16-26; no audition required; and 3) The Public Access Arena offers classes that are specifically oriented to craft-building and specialty skills like Voice Over, Improv, Audition Technique, How to Book Jobs, How to Be Captivating on Film, etc., and are open to the general public 18 years old and above. The first two classes offer cold-reading and at times prepared scene workshops with casting directors, producers, directors, and agents.

JONI ROBBINS VOICEOVER WORKSHOP **(310) 288-8235**
www.jonirobbins.com

Ms. Robbins, a voiceover director and actress who has done some voiceover casting, holds ongoing 6-week classes held in a recording studio. Classes cover cartoon character voices, commercials, mic technique, etc. Limited enrollment, call for prices.

SCREENMUSIC INTERNATIONAL **(818) 789-3487**
18034 Ventura Blvd., Ste. 450
Encino 91316
www.screenmusic.com

Film and TV music production and licensing and recording studios for voice-overs. Audio post completion services.

SOUND CONCEPTS, INC. **(800) 451-8560**
3485 Meier St. **FAX (310) 391-1165**
Los Angeles 90066
sndcpts@aol.com

Production of affordable, national-quality voice-over demos for voice actors. Commercial, animation, promo, narration, child, dialect, Spanish. Professional direction, scripts, digital recording studio. Mark McIntyre, Producer-Director.

THEATRE OF ARTS (EST. 1927) **(323) 463-2500**
1621 N. McCadden Place **FAX (323) 463-2005**
Los Angeles 90028
www.theatre-of-arts.com

Classes work on audition technique, breathing, delivery, diction, projection, voice strengthening, oral interpretation, accents and dialects, characters, and accent reduction. Will assist in the production of a demo tape. An interview may be required.

VOCAL POWER SCHOOL VOICEOVERS **(818) 895-7464** **(800) 929-7464**
www.vocalpower.com
musicman@borntosing.com

Train under the guidance of Vocal Power Director, Howard Austin.

Voice: Voice-Over

Private coaching in presentation of monologues, commercial copy, stand-up comedy, dialect, voice-over, voice development and strengthening, accent reduction, some dialect work and singing all styles. Also preparation of monologues and copy reading is available. An interview is not required. Also offers home study courses for voice training and accent reduction "VoiceShaping: How to Find Your Million Dollar Voice" – 7 CDs, 100 page manual – and includes "Speak to Influence"; "Speak to Influence: How to Unlock the Hidden Power of Your Voice" – Book, soft cover, 168 pages; "How to Get Your Voice on TV and Radio Commercials: The Complete Guide to Breaking Into Voice-overs" – 3 audio cassettes.

VOICECASTER WORKSHOPS (818) 841-5300
1832 Burbank Blvd.
Burbank 91506
www.voicecaster.com

Offering beginning, intermediate and advanced classes covering every aspect of voiceover.

THE VOICEOVER CONNECTION, INC. (213) 384-9251
www.voconnection.com
doloresdiehl@speakeasy.net

Workshops, seminars, workouts (23 choices), at all levels, beg-pro in commercials, animation, narration, improv, CD Rom, audiobooks, demo tape, also radio drama and comedy production directed by agents, casting directors, producers, and working performers. Evenings and weekends in professional recording studios. Private sessions by phone anywhere in the USA.

VOICES VOICECASTING
VOICEOVER WORKSHOP (818) 980-8460
10523 Burbank Blvd., Ste. 202
North Hollywood 91601
www.voicesvoicecasting.com

They have a five week workshop which meets one night a week, from 7-10 pm. The course provides all the necessary tools needed to begin your career in this highly competitive field. Hosted by a Voices Voicecasting Casting Director, you will learn mic technique, how to break down copy, understanding and interpreting the current trends in the Industry, how to make a killer demo, getting an agent and finding your niche. Also offers a workout session for pros.

WEIST-BARRON-HILL (818) 846-5595
4300 W. Magnolia Blvd.
Burbank 91505
www.weistbarronhillacting.com

Offers classes that work on accent reduction, audition technique, character analysis, and cold reading. There is a 10 week time commitment required for these semi-private classes (limit 4 people) that meet once a week at a cost of $250. The students work in every class.

RICK ZIEFF'S UNBELIEVABLY FUN
VOICE-OVER CLASS (323) 651-1666

Zieff teaches mic technique for TV and radio commercials, animation, narration, and audiobooks. As a busy voice-over director, casting director and actor, he emphasizes the importance of character development, text analysis, and making strong creative choices at the microphone. Zieff guides actors through preparing a demo that will be their calling card to the voice-over world. He voicedirected the acclaimed animated feature "Steamboy" and every episode of "SD Gundam Force" for the Cartoon Network. He also cast the Academy Award winning animated short film "The ChubbChubbs!" Rick's fun, fast-paced style makes him a sought after teacher for adults and children. Group classes or private lessons are available to adults and children at Zieff's studio in West Hollywood.

Universities & Colleges

The following listings are the universities and colleges in the Southern California area that offer classes in all areas of the business including acting, directing, writing, make-up, costuming, etc. Call the individual school for catalogues or information.

CALIFORNIA INSTITUTE OF THE ARTS (661) 253-7853
School of Theatre FAX (661) 255-1050
24700 McBean Parkway
Valencia 91355
www.calarts.edu

CALIFORNIA STATE
POLYTECHNIC UNIVERSITY (909) 869-7659
Department of Theatre and Dance
3801 W. Temple Ave.
Pomona 91768
www.csupomona.edu

CALIFORNIA STATE UNIVERSITY,
DOMINGUEZ HILLS (310) 243-3300
Department of Theatre FAX (310) 243-3696
1000 Victoria
Carson 90747
www.csudh.edu

CALIFORNIA STATE UNIVERSITY,
FULLERTON (714) 278-2011
Department of Theatre and Dance
800 N. State College Blvd.
Fullerton 92634
www.fullerton.edu

CALIFORNIA STATE UNIVERSITY, (323) 343-4110
LOS ANGELES (323) 343-3000
Department of Theatre Arts and Dance
5151 State University Dr.
Los Angeles 90032
www.calstatela.edu

Universities & Colleges

CALIFORNIA STATE UNIVERSITY, NORTHRIDGE (818) 677-1200
18111 Nordhoff St.
Northridge 91330-8320
www.csun.edu

CERRITOS COLLEGE (562) 860-2451
11110 Alondra Blvd.
Norwalk 90690
www.cerritos.edu

EL CAMINO COLLEGE (310) 532-3670 / (866) 352-2646
Marsee Auditorium
16007 Crenshaw Blvd.
Torrance 90506
www.elcamino.cc.ca.us

GLENDALE COMMUNITY COLLEGE (818) 240-1000
Department of Theatre
1500 N. Verdugo Rd.
Glendale 91208
www.glendale.cc.ca.us

LOS ANGELES CITY COLLEGE (LACC) (323) 953-4000
855 N. Vermont Ave. FAX (323) 953-4500
Los Angeles 90029
www.lacitycollege.edu

LOS ANGELES VALLEY COLLEGE (818) 781-1200
Theatre Arts Department
5800 Fulton Ave.
Valley Glen 91401-4096
www.lavc.cc.ca.us

LOYOLA MARYMOUNT UNIVERSITY (310) 338-2839
Theatre Arts Dance
1 LMU Drive, Foley Bldg. MS8210
Los Angeles 90045-8210
www.lmu.edu

OCCIDENTAL COLLEGE (323) 259-2771 / (323) 259-2500
Department of Theatre 1600 Campus Rd.
Los Angeles 90041-3314
www.oxy.edu

PIERCE COLLEGE (818) 710-6488
6201 Winnetka Ave.
Woodland Hills 91371
www.piercecollege.com

POMONA COLLEGE (909) 621-8000 / (909) 621-8186
Department of Theatre and Dance
300 N. College Way
Claremont 91711
www.pomona.edu

RIO HONDO COLLEGE (562) 692-0921
Wray Theatre
3600 Workman Mill Rd.
Whittier 90601
www.rh.cc.ca.us

SANTA MONICA COLLEGE (310) 434-4000
Theatre Department
1900 Pico Blvd.
Santa Monica 90405
www.smc.edu

UNIVERSITY OF CALIFORNIA LOS ANGELES EXTENSION, (UCLA) (310) 825-9064
10995 Le Conte Ave., Rm. 437
Los Angeles 90024
www.ucla.edu

UNIVERSITY OF CALIFORNIA, IRVINE (949) 824-6614
Drama Department 300 Arts
Irvine 92697-2775
www.uci.edu

UNIVERSITY OF CALIFORNIA, LOS ANGELES (UCLA) (310) 825-8787
405 Hilgard Ave.
Los Angeles 90024-1622
www.ucla.edu

UNIVERSITY OF SOUTHERN CALIFORNIA (USC) (213) 821-2744
University Park
Los Angeles 90089-0791
www.usc.edu

Notes

Table of Contents: Marketing

ANSWERING SERVICES, PAGERS & CELLULAR PHONE SERVICES 106
AUDIO DEMO PRODUCTION 107
BOOKS & TAPES 112
CLIPPING SERVICES 121
COMPUTERS 121
COSTUME SALES & RENTALS 123
DANCEWEAR 126
ELECTRONICS 126
FAX SERVICES & MAIL BOXES 128
GAME SHOWS 129
IMAGE CONSULTANTS 130
MAKE-UP ARTISTS & CONSULTANTS 131
MARKETING INFO & CONSULTANTS 133
MESSENGER SERVICES 137
MUSICAL SERVICES: ACCOMPANISTS, COMPOSERS, ARRANGERS, ETC. 138
PERIODICALS & TRADE PUBLICATIONS 139
PHOTO LABS & REPRODUCTIONS 142
PHOTO RETOUCHING 146
PHOTOGRAPHERS 148
PRESS RELEASES 167
PRINTING & PHOTOCOPYING 168
PROFESSIONAL MAKE-UP 171
REHEARSAL STUDIOS 172
RESUME, BOOKKEEPING & SECRETARIAL SERVICES 176
SHEET MUSIC 178
SHOWCASE CLUBS 178
STATIONERY STORES 179
THEATRICAL LIBRARIES 180
VIDEO CAMERA RENTALS 182
VIDEO DEMOS, DUPLICATION, AIRCHECKS & PRODUCTION 183
WARDROBE CONSULTANTS 187
WEB SERVICES 188
WIGS 188

Also see: ELECTRONICS in this section.

A PROFESSIONAL SERVICE (310) 659-2600 / (877) 209-9988
www.aprofessionalanswer.com

Live service with call forwarding, paging, and wake-up calls. Very active in the stunt community. Cost varies according to services.

A SUPER ANSWERING SERVICE (310) 553-6161
400 S. Beverly Dr., Ste. 214 FAX (310) 203-9514
Beverly Hills 90212
www.tel-us.com

Offers live answering service, Beverly Hills mailing address, voice mail, inbound telemarketing and order entries and Internet live backup. 8 week time commitment. Open 24 hours, 7 days a week. Bilingual.

A-1 GILBERT (310) 273-4455 / (800) 698-9172
9304 Civic Center Dr., Ste. 2 FAX (310) 275-4088
Beverly Hills 90210
www.a1gilbert.com
info@a1gilbert.com

24 hour live service, call forwarding, wake-up calls, paging/beeper service, and fax service.

AIRTIME WIRELESS MESSAGING, INC. (818) 776-1999 / (800) 4-AIRTIME
6811 White Oak
Reseda 91335
www.airtimewirelessmassaging.com

Actor owned and operated offering Singular, Nextel, Verizon, Sprint, etc. Lowest cost pager service with free voice mail. Known throughout the Industry for catering to actors. Free delivery. Also, best deals in cellular and P.C.S. phones.

ALERT COMMUNICATIONS (800) 333-7772 / (323) 259-8000
155 Pasadena Ave. FAX (323) 254-6802
South Pasadena 91030
www.alertcom.com

Live service with call forwarding, beeper service, wake-up calls, and voice mail. The oldest service in L.A., in operation since 1949. Offers special out of town rates. 800 inbound telemarketing.

AMERICAN VOICE MAIL, INC. (310) 478-4949 / (800) 847-2861
2310 S. Sepulveda Blvd.
Los Angeles 90064
www.americanvoicemail.com

A voicemail service that offers a private phone number answered 24 hours a day by their computers with your voice. The service is confidential and has unlimited messages for both business and personal use. No credit check. Also offers a fax option.

ANSWER AMERICA (818) 955-7500
348 E. Olive Ave. FAX (818) 841-0171
Burbank 91502
www.answeramerica.com
pba@alists.net

A full service answering service with a family owned feel offering a large variety of budget sensitive plans for the working actor.

AROUND THE CLOCK ANSWERING SERVICE (818) 909-2000
15336 Roscoe Blvd. FAX (818) 782-2016
Van Nuys 91402

Computerized message service with direct pick up, call forwarding, private lines, and unlimited messages. Also has a paging service and wake up calls. 24 hours a day, 7 days a week.

CONCORDE COMMUNICATIONS (310) 854-4411
3699 Wilshire Blvd., Ste. 850 FAX (310) 854-0551
Los Angeles 90010

24 hour live service, also has a paging service and voice mail. 800 numbers, fax service, and conference room available.

DIGITCOM CORP. (310) 358-7000 / (800) DIGITCOM
12923 Venice Blvd. FAX (310) 636-3399
Los Angeles 90066
www.digitcom.net

A voice mail service for $5.95 per month. Can hold up to 100 messages for 30 days. Beeper services available.

ECONOMY ANSWERING & BEEPER SERVICE (323) 878-0680
1335 N. La Brea., Ste. 2 FAX (323) 969-0451
Hollywood 90028

Voice mail for $10 per month. No credit check. Also has beepers and P.O. Boxes available.

EFLS TOTAL COMMUNICATIONS (800) 348-0500
545 8th Ave., Ste. 401
New York, NY 10018
www.efls.net

A bi-coastal answering service for N.Y. and L.A. Also has 800 numbers, voice mail, beepers, fax, and a mail service. Service starts at $10 per month. Nationwide.

EGIX (800) 489-6655
www.egix.com

Nationwide computerized message/pager service with private lines and call forwarding to service lines. Offers voice mail and personal mail boxes. Time commitment and cost varies.

HOLLYWOOD MAIL & MESSAGE (323) 467-5689
1626 N. Wilcox Ave. FAX (323) 467-5845
Hollywood 90028

Private mailbox rentals. Also has answering mail service, mail holding and forwarding, shipping and boxes, and fax and notary services. Monday through Friday, 9 am to 6 pm and Saturday, 10 am to 3 pm. Spanish and English available.

HOLLYWOOD MAIL & MESSAGE SERVICE (323) 467-5689
1626 N. Wilcox Ave. FAX (323) 467-5845
Hollywood 90028

Answering mail service, mail holding and forwarding, shipping and boxes, and fax services. Monday through Friday, 9 am to 6 pm and Saturday, 10 am to 3 pm.

ANSWERING SERVICES, PAGERS & CELLULAR PHONE SERVICES

MANHATTAN CELLULAR **(800) 203-7500**
(800) 203-7500
880 Manhattan Beach Blvd. **FAX (310) 939-1215**
Ste. 101
Manhattan Beach 90266

Sales and service for cellular phones and pagers. Covers the entire Southern California area.

PHONESUSA **(310) 445-3100**
8592 Venice Blvd. **FAX (310) 445-1101**
Los Angeles 90034
www.phonesusa.com

Specializes in cellular headsets, voice mail, cordless phones, low-cost calling VoiP IVX Systems, voice recognition, answering machines, voice and data cabling, silent call announcing, CTI – Computer Telephone Integration, remote maintenance administration, as well as business and residential phone systems. Authorized dealer for a wide range of brands. Also has a service department. Monday through Friday, 9 am to 5 pm and Saturday, 10 am to 2 pm.

POST-TEL BUSINESS SERVICES **(310) 828-8645**
2118 Wilshire Blvd. **FAX (310) 828-0427**
Santa Monica 90403
postel@beachnet.com

Has private voice mail lines in L.A., Beverly Hills, N.Y., San Francisco, and other major cities. They also have a permanent Wilshire/Santa Monica address and will receive mail and parcels and hold them or forward them to your location. Also carries business cards, rubber stamps, packing and shipping materials. With a mail box rental you can receive limited monthly quantities of free fax, photocopy, and notary services.

REX MAIL MESSAGE SERVICE **(323) 461-3127**
1608 N. Cahuenga Blvd.
Hollywood 90028

Private mail boxes. Also offers UPS packaging and shipping, message service, photocopying, answering service, mail holding and forwarding, fax, and passport photos ready in 5 minutes. Their notary public will travel to you. Access hours, Monday through Friday, 9 am to 6 pm and Saturday, 9 am to 3 pm.

TELENET **(310) 253-9000**
3384 Motor Ave. **FAX (310) 253-9800**
Los Angeles 90034
www.telenetusa.net

Has phone systems, and voice mail systems.

VERIZON WIRELESS **(800) 722-8351**
www.verizon.com

Cellular phones, service, and systems. Call the above number for main office. Also offers a long distance service.

VOICE MAIL DEPOT, INC. **(800) 309-8888**
www.voicemaildepot.com **FAX (949) 263-2230**

Voice mail starting at $7.95 per month. The first month and immediate hookup are free.

AUDIO DEMO PRODUCTION

MAKING AN AUDIO DEMO TAPE

By Jill Taggart

The term 'voice-over' means commercial voice work, animation, and ADR or looping. Making a demo tape involves a lot more than simply slapping together some voice recordings. Actors need to know their vocal strengths and locate a recording studio that will work with them. The studio's engineer should be able to help select good material and to direct the actor. If you are not yet ready to work in this lucrative but highly competitive field, the engineer will, hopefully, recommend some workshops or even private study with a speech pathologist. The final recording should consist of several 10-15 second excerpts from longer spots thus allowing for a variety of different sounds on the demo reel while keeping the time to a practical length. Proper music or sound effects are layered in behind the voice, and the spots are arranged to give the tape versatility, variety, and a nice flow. Many studios will advise the actor about different agents that might be receptive to the type of voice you have. DEMO TAPE LENGTH Basically a demo tape should not be longer than 2½ minutes. It is better to make separate tapes for commercial and animation work, although they may be combined as long as it isn't more than 3 minutes. If the actor needs to put both types on one demo tape it is recommended that, following approximately one minute of commercial material, there is a short space then the announcement, "This is the animation segment of the tape" followed with approximately one minute of animation voices. COMMERCIAL MATERIAL Actors are advised to be cautious when selecting material, especially if a major company name is used. For instance, if an actor writes a fake commercial for Reebok and tapes it in a studio with full production values and the tape is later sent to the ad agency that handles Reebok, two things could happen: the ad agency knows it's a fake because they didn't record it, or they get upset about their client being represented in a campaign that isn't theirs. You can always make up a brand name, "I've worn Peppy sneakers all of my professional life," and, if you do it well no one will suspect that it isn't a real brand. And many ad agencies truly don't care. Check with your agent about usable material. Most studios have a library of materials to pick from. It is a good idea to bring in something of your own that you've worked on. You can find good material in magazine ads and the studio engineer can usually help you edit. ANIMATION MATERIAL The best material is an audition script for a cartoon character. These are usually 20-30 second monologues for cartoon characters either in production or development. Another common approach is to tell a story using voices for each of the characters, however this has become cliche and, unless the actor is an excellent writer or a stand-up comic, the results may be less than wonderful. It is probably better to use professionally written material. There are also cartoon scripts available in most sound studios. Try to find one without other characters speaking between your lines, or one that can be easily condensed into one character. COMEDY Stand-up material is best recorded in a club then remixed in a studio. Commercial and animation comedy is best recorded in the studio. A funny bit on a demo tape is usually a plus. COST This will vary from studio to studio but generally is between $50-$100 an hour. Many studios offer package deals that usually range between $300-$700 and often include such extras as career guidance and agent recommendations. ADR or LOOPING This used to be called "group walla," today it is known as "background voices." Whatever it's called, it is high-paying work for actors. It is also a technical specialty and requires exact timing and excellent improv skills. A demo tape should include any real – not cartoon – voices that you do (child, baby, elderly, etc.) as well as any accents, dialects, or foreign languages that you are expert in. This is a highly competitive field, so don't expect a tape that sounds faked, a dialect that you are sort of good in, or a foreign language that you can stumble through to get you any work. You must be letter perfect in dialects and fluent in the foreign language. See LOOPING GROUPS in the WORKING section for the names of some groups. A FINAL WORD The competition in the voice-over field is fierce. Especially since major stars have discovered it. These days we hear James Coburn selling cars, Lauren Bacall touting the joys of a cruise ship, and Tom Bosley selling just about everything. The newest trend seems to be for the character a star plays on a series to do voice-over work, so now Murphy Brown sells a long-distance phone company. Because of this, it is simply good sense to make the best possible tape that you can. Wait until you are ready, take some workshops, and get some microphone experience. There is still a lot of voice work out there, but you have to be good.

48 WINDOWS MUSIC AND MIX **(310) 392-9545**
1661 Lincoln Blvd., Ste. 320 **FAX (310) 392-9445**
Santa Monica 90404
www.48windows.com

ADR, Audio Laybacks, Digital Sound Editing, Dubbing, Foley, Sound FX Library, Synching and Transmission Services, also Composing.

A & T RECORDING **(323) 466-9000**
5301 Rosewood Ave. **FAX (323) 467-6615**
Los Angeles 90004-1305

Produces CDs, DATS, cassettes, etc. Also DVD duplication.

ALISO CREEK PRODUCTIONS **(818) 954-9931**
4106 W. Burbank Blvd. **FAX (818) 954-9931**
Burbank 91510
www.alisocreek.com

Offers full voice-over demo tape production for commercial, narration, and animation. Includes script preparation, recording, music, and sound effects. Also vocal demos for singers and songwriters. Complete jingle and commercial production. Duplication of audio cassettes and CDs. Free consultation.

AMERAYCAN **(818) 760-8733**
5719 Lankershim Blvd.
North Hollywood 91601
www.paramountrecording.com

Two 48 track rooms. Mostly lock-out—some orchestral. Contact through Paramount Recording Studios.

THE ART OF VOICE-ACTING **(858) 484-0220**
13639 Freeport Rd. **FAX (858) 484-7493**
San Diego 92129
www.voiceacting.com
jralburger@voiceacting.com

James R. Alburger, author of "The Art of Voice-Acting," voice-over coach and recipient of 11-Emmy Awards, will produce your voice-over demo. Complete production at their San Diego studio or from work you've done. Call for more information.

AUDIO CD & CASSETTE **(818) 762-2232**
12426½ Ventura Blvd. **FAX (818) 762-3074**
Studio City 91604
www.acdc-cdr.com

Strictly high quality, real time CD and audio tape duplication at competitive rates. Can also make video and DVD copies. Laser printed CD and cassette labels in your choice of colors.

BOOM CHIC STUDIOS **(323) 782-6813**
Beverly Blvd.
Los Angeles 90048
www.boomchic.com
karen@ioproductions.com

Audio production in state of the art Pro Tools recording studio. Voice over recording, sound effects editing, mixing, film scoring, ADR, music production and recording all the way to CD. Compatible with all video formats.

CHANNEL ONE VIDEO **(310) 584-9410**
1406 Innes Place
Venice 90291
www.channelonevideo.com

Fair prices for video and audio tapes. Complete digital audio recording services. Likes to work with actors. See listing under VIDEO TAPE DUPLICATION, AIRCHECKS & PRODUCTION in this section for further information.

CLUB BEVERLY HILLS **(310) 274-6051**
8306 Wilshire Blvd., #279 **FAX (310) 274-7855**
Beverly Hills 90211
www.club-beverlyhills.com
dreams@club-beverlyhills.com

Production and packaging of voice-over demos. They will provide copy or you may use your own. See listing under PUBLIC RELATIONS in the TEAM section and PHOTOGRAPHERS in this section for further information.

DAVE & DAVE INCORPORATED **(818) 508-7578**
4352 Lankershim Blvd. **FAX (818) 508-5830**
Toluca Lake 91602
www.ddicompanies.com
ddi@pacificnet.net

Digital editing specialist in assembly or re-arranging of voice over demos, agent house minutes, final mixes, CD & DVD mastering and miracles. In-house CD & DVD and copies from 1 – 1000, in-house custom graphic designers. Full-color printing of CD & DVD, postcards and business cards. ISDN & MP3 studio too!

DEL MAR MEDIA ARTS **(949) 753-0570**
15375 Barranca Pkwy., #J-105 **FAX (949) 753-0576**
Irvine 92618
www.delmarmediaarts.com

Full service audio demo production house. All pre- and post-production work is done in house and they will help with material, effects, background music, etc. Will help with package design. Can do duplication of recorded work. See listings under ACTING and VOICE OVER in the TRAINING section for further information. SEE AD ON PAGE 67.

DIGITAL JUNGLE (323) 962-0867
6363 Santa Monica Blvd. FAX (323) 962-9960
Hollywood 90038
www.digijungle.com
graphics@digijungle.com

ADR, Audio Laybacks, Digital Sound Editing, Dubbing, Mixing, Sound FX Library, Synching and Transmission Services.

ROBBIE GILLMAN (818) 347-4350
robertgillman@sbcglobal.net FAX (818) 348-4566

Established producer, arranger, composer, and musician creates professional musical background tapes for singers to record their vocals over or to use for live performance and auditions. From simple piano to full orchestral arrangements in any style. See listing under MUSICAL SERVICES in this section for further information.

PETER HUME (818) 363-6281

Independent producer/arranger specializing in customized vocal demo and song demo production. Works with singers and songwriters, novice through advanced, with an emphasis on drawing out the best possible performance. All production elements are handled in his home studio. Has extensive signal processing equipment including digital reverbs, delays, etc. Arranges and plays all instrumental tracks. Offers vocal overdubbing, mixing and editing.

INTERSOUND, INC. (310) 652-3741
962 N. La Cienega Blvd. FAX (310) 652-5973
West Hollywood 90069
www.intersound.com

ADR, Audio Laybacks, Digital, Foley, Mixing, Sound FX Library, Synching and Transfers.

J.E. SOUND PRODUCTIONS (323) 462-4385
1680 N. Sycamore Ave.
Hollywood 90028
www.jesound.com

ADR Dubbing, Mixing, Scoring/Sound Stage, Sound Editing, Synching and Transfers.

JUNIPER STUDIOS (818) 841-1244
801 S. Main St.
Burbank 91506
www.juniperpost.com
info@juniperpost.com

Audio/video post facility. Voice-over, ADR, Video Sweetening, Foley, Music, 24 track capability. Reasonably priced sessions include engineer. They will recommend musicians and can do a special video interlock.

LA STUDIOS, INC. (323) 851-6351
3453 Cahuenga Blvd. FAX (323) 851-0137
Los Angeles 90068
www.lastudios.com

ADR Audio Laybacks, Digital Sound Editing, Dubbing, Mixing, Sound FX Library, Synching, Transfers and Transmission Service.

LARSON STUDIOS (323) 469-3986
6520 Sunset Blvd. FAX (323) 469-8507
Hollywood 90028
www.larsonstudios.com

ADR, Audio Laybacks, Digital Sound Editing, Dubbing, Foley, Mixing, Sound FX Library, Synching and Transfers.

MARGARITA MIX (323) 962-6565
6838 Romaine St. FAX (323) 962-8662
Hollywood 91601

1661 Lincoln Blvd., Ste. 101 (310) 396-3333
Santa Monica 90404
www.lastudios.com

ADR, Audio Laybacks, Digital Sound Editing, Dubbing, Foley, Mixing, Sound FX Library, Synching, Transfers and Transmission Services.

MATCHFRAME VIDEO (818) 840-6800
610 N. Hollywood Way FAX (818) 840-2726
Ste. 101
Burbank 91505
www.matchframevideo.com

ADR, Audio Laybacks, Digital Sound Editing, Dubbing, Foley, Mixing, Sound FX Library, Syncing and Transfers, Telecine, Complete Audio Post Sound Department, Avid, Symphony, Motion Camera, Smoke, Online Clipmail, and ProTools.

MEDIA CITY SOUND (818) 508-3311
12711 Ventura Blvd., Ste. 110 FAX (818) 508-3314
Studio City 91604
www.mcsound.com

Contact: Alan Ett or Scott Liggett. ADR, Audio Laybacks, Digital Sound Editing, Dubbing, Mixing, Music/Sound FX Library, Synching and Transmission Services.

MIKE RECORDING SERVICES (310) 979-0191
2017 S. Westgate Ave. FAX (310) 207-2587
W. Los Angeles 90025
www.mikerecording.com

ADR, Audio Laybacks, Digital Sound Editing, Dubbing, Mixing, Music/Sound FX Library, Synching and Transfers and Flame.

MIX MAGIC POST SOUND (323) 466-2442
839 N. Highland Ave. FAX (323) 463-1677
Hollywood 90028
www.mixmagic.com

ADR, Audio Laybacks, Digital Sound Editing, Dubbing, Foley, Mixing, Music/Sound FX Library, Synching, Transfers and Transmission Services.

MOVIE TECH (323) 467-8491
(323) 467-5423
832 Seward St. FAX (323) 467-8471
Hollywood 90038
www.movietechstudios.net

ADR, Audio Laybacks, Dubbing, Foley, Mixing, Scoring/Sound Stage, Sound Editing, Sound FX Library, Synching and Transfers.

NOVA PRODUCTIONS (323) 969-0949
3575 Cahuenga Blvd. West FAX (323) 969-0822
Ste. 630
Los Angeles 90068
www.novaprods.com
nick@nickomana.com

A commercial production facility that does complete audio demos including music and sound effects. Has DAT, ISDN hook up, digital record/edit, and a wide variety of effects possible. Can email auditions for clients. Copy and director are provided. See listing under VOICE-OVER in the TRAINING section for further information.

NOVASTAR **(323) 467-5020**
6430 Sunset Blvd., Ste. 103 **FAX (323) 957-8707**
Hollywood 90028
www.novastarpost.com

ADR, Audio Laybacks, Digital Sound Editing, Dubbing, Foley, Mixing, Sound FX Library, Synching and Transfers.

ORACLE POST **(310) 449-5550**
3232 Nebraska Ave. **FAX (310) 449-5554**
Santa Monica 90404

4720 W. Magnolia Blvd. **(818) 752-2800**
Burbank 91505
www.oraclepost.com

ADR, Digital Sound Editing, Dubbing, Foley, Sound FX Library and Transfers.

OUTLAW SOUND **(323) 462-1873**
1608 N. Argyle **FAX (323) 957-2733**
Hollywood 90028
www.outlawsound.com
info@outlawsound.com

ADR, Digital Sound Editing and Transmission Services.

P.M. III PRODUCTIONS **(818) 763-3053**
www.pm3prod.com
info@pm3prod.com

A complete demo recording studio with Pro Tools HD and Sound Forge DAW. Has music backgrounds and sound effects. A library of ad copy is available. Rates begin at $35 per hour. See listing under MUSICAL SERVICES in this section for further information.

PACIFICA SOUND GROUP **(818) 845-9930**
919 N. Victory Blvd. **FAX (818) 845-9809**
Burbank 91522

4109 Burbank Blvd. **(818) 845-4100**
Burbank 91505

Post production house. Also does voice-over demos and video demos. They can edit an actor's reel and add special effects.

PARAMOUNT RECORDING STUDIOS **(323) 465-4000**
6245 Santa Monica Blvd. **FAX (323) 469-1905**
Hollywood 90038
www.paramountrecording.com

CD and demo recording including all types of music and voice-over work. Can add effects. Has two 48 track and two 24-track studio rooms. Mixing, Scoring, Stage, Sound Editing, Sound FX Library and Transfers.

PLAYGROUNDS, INK! LLC **(818) 507-1544**
Glendale 91202
www.playgrounds-ink.com
joe@playgrounds-ink.com

Private coaching available. Call for details. Also, a full service production company offering a variety of services for production and talent needs including voice over demo reels.

POP SOUND **(310) 458-9192**
625 Arizona Ave. **FAX (310) 587-1222**
Santa Monica 90401
www.popstudios.com

ADR, Audio Laybacks, Digital Sound Editing, Dubbing, Mixing, Foley, Sound FX Library, Synching and Transfers.

POST LOGIC STUDIOS, INC. **(323) 461-7887**
1800 N. Vine St., Ste. 100 **FAX (323) 461-7790**
Hollywood 90028
www.postlogic.com
info@postlogic.com

ADR, Digital Sound Editing, Dubbing, Foley, Mixing, Sound FX Library and Transfers.

RAVENSWORK **(310) 392-2542**
1611 Electric Ave. **FAX (310) 314-6774**
Venice 90291
www.ravenswork.com

ADR, Audio Layback, Digital Sound Editing, Dubbing, Mixing, Sound FX Library, Transfers and Transmission Service.

GEORGE REICH **(818) 548-7162**
georgereich@charter.net

This 24 track studio is used for jingles, music, demo and master recording, and radio/TV commercials. They can handle digital effects, sound effects, and sweetening. They have drum machines, guitars, pianos, and synthesizers and can create complete instrumental music tracks. Produces digital mix-down and cassette. $35 per hour includes musician, arranger, engineer, and producer. The average session lasts 5-8 hours.

RUSK SOUND STUDIOS **(323) 462-6477**
1556 N. La Brea Ave.
Hollywood 90028

ADR, Audio Layback, Digital Sound Editing, Dubbing, Mixing, Scoring/Sound Stage, Sound FX Library and Synching.

SCREENMUSIC INTERNATIONAL **(818) 789-2954**
18034 Ventura Blvd., Ste. 450 **FAX (818) 789-5801**
Encino 91316
www.screenmusic.com

Film and TV music production and licensing and recording studios for voiceovers. Audio post completion service.

SERIFINE, INC. **(310) 399-9279**
248 Westminster Ave. **FAX (310) 396-0314**
Venice 90291
www.frankserifine.com

Digital Music Production. ADR, Digital Sound Editing, Dubbing, Foley, Mixing, Scoring Stage, Sound FX Library and Synching.

SHORELINE STUDIOS **(310) 394-4932**
1316 Third St., Ste. 109 **FAX (310) 458-7802**
Santa Monica 90401
www.shorelinestudios.com

Contact: Gary Zacuto. Digital sound editing and voice over recording.

SOUND CONCEPTS INC. **(310) 390-7406**
3485 Meier St.
Los Angeles 90066
www.soundconceptsinc.com
sndcpts@aol.com

Mark McIntyre has sound effects and a music library to take you through to a finished demo. Works with voice actors in his hard disk recording studio.

SOUND SERVICES, INC/SSI ADVANCED POST **(323) 874-9344**
7155 Santa Monica Blvd. **FAX (323) 850-7189**
Los Angeles 90046

7165 Sunset Blvd, **(323) 969-9333**
Los Angeles 90028
www.ssi-post.com

ADR, Audio Laybacks, Digital Sound Editing, Dubbing, Foley, Mixing, Sound FX Library, Synching, Telecine, Transfers and Transmission Services.

SIGNET SOUNDELUX STUDIOS **(323) 850-1515**
7317 Romaine St. **FAX (323) 874-1420**
Los Angeles 90046

7080 Hollywood Blvd., 11th Fl. **(323) 603-3200**
Hollywood 90028

ADR, Audio Laybacks, DTS Mastering, Dubbing, Predubbing, Foley, Mixing, Music/Sound FX Library, Restoration, Scoring/Sound Stage, Synching and Transfers.

SOUNDSCAPE PRODUCTIONS **(310) 202-9989** **(310) 202-2974**
3614 Overland Ave. **FAX (310) 202-6088**
Los Angeles 90034
www.dubscape.com

ADR, Audio Laybacks, Digital Sound Editing, Dubbing, Foley, Mixing, Sound FX Library, Synching, Transfers and Transmissions Services.

SOUNDWORKS **(818) 996-1243**
18324 Oxnard St., Ste. 6 **FAX (818) 996-1248**
Tarzana 91356
www.soundworkspost.com
msoundwork@aol.com

ADR, Audio Laybacks, Digital Sound Editing, Dubbing, Foley, Mixing, Sound FX Library and Synching.

STS FOREIGN LANGUAGE SERVICES **(818) 563-3004**
P.O. Box 10213
Burbank 91505
www.stsforeignlanguage.com

ADR, Audio Laybacks, Digital Sound Editing, Dubbing, Foley, Mixing, Scoring/Sound Stage, Sound FX Library, Synching and Transfers.

STUDIO REFERRAL SERVICE **(818) 222-2058**
23480 Park Sorrento, Ste. 223A **FAX (818) 222-6130**
Calabasas 91302
www.studioreferral.com
ellis@studioreferral.com

S.R.S. is a free service that will recommend the studio to meet individual artistic needs. Links artists, producers, film companies, ad agencies, and anyone who uses a recording studio with the individual studios.

THB MUSIC SERVICES INC. **(626) 355-6946**
2340 Hollister Terrace
Glendale 91206

Music production, voice-over, audio for video, sound design and promotion for the Internet, as well as sound mastering.

TODD A-O **(310) 315-5000**
3000 Olympic Blvd., Bldg. #1 **FAX (310) 315-5099**
Santa Monica 90403

2813 W. Alameda Ave. **(818) 840-7225**
Burbank 91505

900 Seward St. **(323) 962-4000**
Hollywood 90038
www.toddao.com

ADR, Audio Layback, Digital Sound Editing, Dubbing, Foley, Mixing, Sound FX Library, Sound Stage, Synching and Transfer.

TREE FALLS **(323) 851-0299**
3131 Cahuenga Blvd. West **FAX (323) 851-0277**
Los Angeles 90068
www.tfsound.com
mike@tfsound.com

Full service audio post production for voice over demos, reels, independent films and shorts. Also provide DVD services and DVD/VHS dubs and transfers.

THE VILLAGE RECORDING **(310) 478-8227**
1616 Butler Ave. **FAX (310) 479-1142**
W. Los Angeles 90025
www.villagestudios.com

ADR, Mixing and Sound FX Library.

VIRTUAL BUSINESS CARDS CYNDIE CARRILLO **(818) 693-0023**
859 Hollywood Way, Ste, 123
Burbank 91505
www.virtualbusinesscards.com

Keep your picture, resume, contact information and either video or audio clip in your pocket. Great for networking.

VOICETRAX WEST CINDY AKERS **(818) 487-9001**
12215 Ventura Blvd., Ste. 205 **FAX (818) 487-9021**
Studio City 91604
www.voicetraxwest.com

A recording studio and a full service commercial demo tape company for voice-over artists. In business since 1981.

WAVES SOUND RECORDERS, INC. **(323) 466-6141**
1956 N. Cahuenga Blvd. **FAX (323) 466-3751**
Los Angeles 90068
www.wavessoundrecorders.com

ADR, Audio Laybacks, Digital Sound Editing, Mixing, Sound FX Library, Synching and Transfers.

AUDIO DEMO PRODUCTION

WEDDINGTON PRODUCTIONS, INC. (818) 980-1506
11036 Weddington St. FAX (818) 980-7832
North Hollywood 91601
www.weddington.com

Digital Sound Editing, Mixing. Sound FX Library and Transfers.

WILD WOODS (323) 878-0400
3575 Cahuenga Blvd. West FAX (323) 878-0444
Ste. 400
Los Angeles 90068
www.wwoods.com

ADR, Audio Laybacks, Digital Sound Editing, Foley, Mixing, Music/Sound FX Library and Transfers.

WILLIAM SOUND SERVICES, INC. (323) 461-5321
1343 N. Highland Ave. FAX (323) 465-8888
Hollywood 90028

ADR, Audio Laybacks, Digital Sound Editing, Dubbing, Foley, Mixing, Sound FX Library, Synching and Transfers.

SINGING FOR A LIVING
MARTA WOODHULL (818) 752-0833
www.singingforaliving.com

Ms. Woodhull has a digital Pro-Tools compatible studio and offers demo and album vocal production services. Sessions are offered days and evenings. Her website offers free pro tips on vocal health, touring, conditioning, reading lists and Industry links. Also available are the newly released "Singing for a Living" lessons on CD, a workout program in basic to advanced levels. Ms. Woodhull is Juilliard trained and has recorded with Lea Salonga, Brian McKnight, Paula Abdul, etc. Call for complete list of fees and services. SEE AD ON PAGE 97.

WORLD DIGITAL STUDIOS (818) 385-1000
13848 Ventura Blvd., Ste. 4D FAX (818) 385-0044
Sherman Oaks 91423
www.voiceover-demos.com
chuck@voiceover-demos.com

Specializing in all areas of voiceover demo production. World Digital works with all the top voiceover agencies. If you're serious about breaking into the voiceover industry, this is the place to go.

RICK ZIEFF'S UNBELIEVABLY FUN
VOICE-OVER CLASS (323) 651-1666

Rick produces demo tapes for TV, radio commercials, animation, narration, and audio books. As a busy voice-over director, casting director, and actor, he knows what the talent agents and advertising producers like to hear. Rick will guide you through preparing a demo that will be your calling card to the voice-over world. Group or private classes at his West Hollywood studio. Also produces demos for kids.

BOOKS & TAPES

Most of the books and tapes listed here can be found at Samuel French Theatre and Film Booksellers. For periodicals, directories, and the Trades, see PERIODICALS & TRADE PUBLICATIONS in this section.

A PASSION FOR ACTING (818) 907-6262
Allan Miller
Dynamic Productions
www.allanmiller.org

An anecdotal book as well as a tech book for beginners and professionals, based on Mr. Miller's experience as an actor and director. Now in its third edition. Available at Samuel French, Drama Bookshop in New York or through the website.

ACCENTS: THE BOB AND CLAIRE
CORFF METHOD (323) 851-9042
Bob and Claire Corff
www.corffvoice.com

Learn an accent with the Bob and Claire Corff method. Bob and Claire will guide you while you learn from people with authentic accents. Available on CD or tape at Samuel French. SEE ADS ON PAGES 90 & 91.

ACHIEVING THE STANDARD
AMERICAN ACCENT (323) 851-9042
Bob and Claire Corff
www.corffvoice.com

Two CDs and an 80 page workbook. Change your accent and keep the true sense of you. Learn the same accent reduction techniques as some of the biggest stars in Hollywood. "The Standard American program really works, I've had great results with it."—Marina Sirtis, Star Trek the Next Generation. "It's not just that I'm learning the Standard American Accent, but every lesson is a joy." Bai Ling, Red Corner. Available at Samuel French Booksellers and Skylight Bookstore. SEE ADS ON PAGES 90 & 91.

ACT RIGHT: A HANDBOOK
FOR PROFESSIONAL ACTORS
www.eringray.com
actright@aol.com

A step-by-step guide by Erin Gray and Mara Purl from the dos and don'ts of auditioning, all the way through set protocol, "Act Right" is filled with personal anecdotes from these well-known actresses, who also interviewed colleagues from every discipline in the film and television business. Filled with practical advice, the book also has a glossary of terms, and is both a manual and a good read. With scores of favorable reviews and hundreds of readers, "Act Right" is available at all Samuel French stores, the New York Drama Book Shop, and may be ordered at any book store or through amazon.com, barnesandnoble.com, borders.com, havenbooks.net, eringray.com, and marapurl.com. Erin and Mara also give Act Right – The Professional Seminar. "Don't make your first job, your last job, learn to Act Right!"

ACTING FROM THE
ULTIMATE CONSCIOUSNESS (323) 466-9250
Eric Morris
www.ericmorris.com

Starting where "Irreverent Acting" left off, "Acting from the Ultimate Consciousness" explores the concept of conscious-unconscious communication as it applies to acting. Believing that 95% of our talent comes from the unconscious, Eric leads the actor into communicating with that "bottomless well of creativity" and piquing responses which will infuse his or her performances with a depth and reality rarely seen on stage or film. In addition to three more "choice approaches," there are also chapters on characterization, ensemble, charts and journals, and rehearsing, with an outline of ten rehearsals which take the actor from the very first reading of a scene to its first performance. A must for all actors. SEE AD ON PAGE 13.

ACTING IN THE MOTION PICTURE BUSINESS (505) 298-0485
David Macklin
www.davidmacklin.com
davidmacklin@yahoogroups.com

Practical, eclectic and candid information germane (geared or specific to) the realities of working in the art and business of motion pictures and television. Preparation exercises that can be done on the soundstage. 300 pages with many photos and illustrations by a professional film actor with hundreds of credits.

ACTING IS EVERYTHING: AN ACTOR'S GUIDEBOOK FOR A SUCCESSFUL CAREER IN LOS ANGELES (818) 505-9373
Judy Kerr
www.actingiseverything.com

Author Judy Kerr shares facts, ideas, and secrets for building and promoting an acting career. Where to go, who to call, what to spend, what not to do. The book is designed to save time and money and to help actors find a better agent, hire a photographer, juggle a part-time job, or keep their instrument in tune for the next big break. Recommended by actors, personal managers, agents, and casting directors throughout the Industry. Available in bookstores throughout the United States and Canada, most online bookstores, or by mail order. Now in its tenth edition, visit the website for an excerpt.

ACTING WORLD BOOKS (818) 905-1345 (800) 210-1197
P.O. Box 3899 FAX (800) 210-1197
Hollywood 90078
www.actingworldbooks.org

Publishes several books for actors including "The Film Actor's Complete Career Guide," "How To Start Acting In Film And Television Wherever You Are In America," "Since Stanislavski and Vakhtangov: The Method As A System For Today's Actor" and "Acting Truth And Fiction" all by Lawrence Parke. Also publishes "The Selective Hollywood Coaches and Teachers Directory." See listing under PERIODICALS & TRADE PUBLICATIONS in this section for further information.

ACTING, IMAGING AND THE UNCONSCIOUS (323) 466-9250
Eric Morris
www.ericmorris.com

Acting, Imaging and the Unconscious is the fifth in a series of books written by Eric Morris on his unique system of acting. His previous works: "No Acting Please," "Being & Doing," Irreverent Acting" and "Acting from the Ultimate Consciousness" have established him among the foremost innovators in the world of acting. In this book the emphasis is on imaging as an acting tool to fulfill material. There is a section on how to program the unconscious and since 95% of your talent lives there, accessing the unconscious crosses the line into that rare state of ultimate consciousness. SEE AD ON PAGE 13.

ACTOR AS ARTIST (323) 860-8790
Ned Manderino
www.manderino.com

Required reading for beginning actors at various colleges and universities. Contains an inspirational collection of essays discussing the origins of acting talent, and progressively outlines its growth through early education, university, and private workshop training. A necessary book for beginning to advanced actors.

THE ACTOR TAKES A MEETING (323) 461-4263
How to Interview Successfully with Agents, Producers, and Casting Directors
Stephen Book
stephenjbook@yahoo.com

Actors are always taking meetings to advance their careers. Seeking representation, management, auditions, or projects, they meet with agents, managers, producers, and casting directors. Many of these meetings are unsuccessful because the actor presents him or herself inadequately. With minimal self-awareness and authenticity, actors frequently conduct themselves in a meeting as victims or manipulators. This leads to being seen as an undesirable working partner, regardless of acting abilities or credits. "The Actor Takes A Meeting" is the first book to address the actor's presentation of him or herself at an interview or meeting. It shows actors how to be the host of the meeting and the initiator of an exciting experience resulting in the interviewer looking forward to seeing them again. This usually results in offers of representation, auditions, and participation in projects. Stephen Book has written a must-read book for actors who don't understand why their career is not advancing or who blame it on lack of effective representation. Published by Silman-James Press.

THE ACTOR'S AUDITION CHECKLIST (310) 479-5647
Doug Warhit
www.dougwarhit.com

A checklist of the specific steps for actors to follow to insure they do their best each and every time. The perfect pocket-size book, not only to help you prepare for your auditions, but to take with you and flip through while you're waiting to go into read. Like having an acting coach in your back pocket. See listing for Doug Warhit in the TRAINING section under ACTING for additional information. SEE AD ON PAGE 2.

THE ACTOR'S BOOK OF IMPROVISATION
Sandra Caruso and Paul Clemmens

Geared for the actor's development, this guide isolates specific aspects of acting utilizing sources from literature, plays, film, novels, and news items on which to base the improvisational exercise. Endorsed by Ed Asner, Arthur Cantor, Nina Foch, Michael Shurtleff, and Lowell Swortzell of Educational Theatre NYU. Publisher, Penguin Paperback.

THE ACTOR'S PICTURE RESUME BOOK (802) 867-2223
P.O. Box 510 FAX (802) 867-0144
Dorset, VT 5251
www.theatredirectories.com

How to put together a professional picture and resume. Available by mail order and at theatre bookstores across the country. 2nd Edition.

THE ACTOR'S ART AND CRAFT (818) 784-8918
Rona Laurie
Empire Publishing Service
P.O. Box 1344
Studio City 91614

Concentrates on the actor's abilities to use voice modulation and movement to develop characterization. Detailed consideration of Shakespeare, comedy, farce and the modern playwrights give extra insights into the genre. The discussion is completed by an evaluation of some of our finest performers including Peggy Ashcroft, Alan Bates, Kenneth Branagh, Judy Dench, John Gielgud and Lawrence Olivier. Available at amazon.com and theatrical bookstores as well as by direct order.

ACTORS AT WORK SERIES (800) 652-7437 (818) 785-1551
Joel Asher
P.O. Box 4223
North Hollywood 91617-4223
www.joel-asher-studio.com

A series of video tapes covering the actor's craft from the first audition through performance. Tape 1) Getting the Part, includes complete cold reading classes with Joel Asher, interview techniques with Casting Director, Joey Paul Jensen, and call backs with actor Robby Benson. Tape 2) Casting Directors: Tell It Like It Is with Joel Asher interviewing casting directors as they tell what they look for in new talent, auditions, call backs, photos, showcases, and more. Tape 3) Agents: Tell It Like It Is with Joel Asher interviewing 5 film, TV, and commercial agents as they tell you how to find the right agent, get him/her to sign you, and then to work for you. Tape 4) Directors on Acting with Joel Asher interviewing 5 important film and TV directors who talk about getting the best out of the actor/director collaboration. SEE ADS ON PAGES 1 & 113.

ACTORS' RESUMES:
THE DEFINITIVE GUIDEBOOK, 2ND EDITION
REVISED AND EXPANDED (818) 784-8918
Richard Devin
Empire Publishing Service
P.O. Box 1344
Studio City 91614-0344

The only book on actors' resumes that asked over 400 casting directors, producers, agents, and directors what it is that they want on your resume. Now in it's second edition (updated and revised), a complete guide to the "perfect resume" for old pros and beginners alike. Recommended by casting directors, agents, producers, directors, actors, and managers. Available at amazon.com and theatrical bookstores as well as by direct order.

ALL ABOUT METHOD ACTING (323) 860-8790
Ned Manderino
www.manderino.com

The first and only guide for actors that brings together the most well-known techniques of Method Acting. Besides basic Method Acting techniques, it includes refinements which were developed in the Ned Manderino Workshop during its beginning months. These were the first basic Method Exercises to go beyond traditional Method Acting and include: a specific and inventive characterization exercise; stimuli exercise (which has demonstrated its effectiveness beyond basic Method sensory technique); the Wandering Personal Object (which has proved itself to give more physicalization to an actor's behavior than the propounded use of temperature sensations). Also included: a long discussion of Method Acting details that are involved in creating a role. The most extensive list available of Actions and Method Acting Choices.

THE ART OF COMEDY (818) 783-7940
Paul Ryan
www.paulryanproductions.com
paul@paulryanproductions.com

The ultimate book on how to be a successful comedy actor. Paul shares the process, step by step to create the best comedy in you. He also covers how to develop sketch comedy characters, learning The Paul Ryan Audition technique, and stretching your acting talent as wide as possible to explore all of your inner comedy talents. Also interviews with some of the legendary comedy greats.

THE ART OF FILM ACTING (818) 248-4104
Jeremiah Comey FAX (818) 249-1751
www.jeremiahcomey.com
comeystudio@aol.com

Acting for film and television do not require and can not tolerate the lengthy rehearsals and speeches of the stage. Film needs a faster, more effective way to work within its limitations. The Art of Film Acting teaches the reader how to become a good film actor. Available at amazon.com as well as Samuel French, Barnes and Noble and Borders.

THE ART OF VOICE-ACTING (858) 484-0220
13639 Freeport Rd. FAX (858) 484-9473
San Diego 92129
www.voiceacting.com
jralburger@voiceacting.com

Considered by many to be the best book on voiceover available. Purchase "The Art of Voice-Acting" by James R. Alburger, direct from the author by visiting the website. All direct orders are autographed by the author.

AUDITIONING (818) 907-6262
Allan Miller
Dynamic Productions
www.allanmiller.org

"Really useful ideas that remind one of how much fun acting really is and why we do it."—John Spencer, actor.

THE BACKSTAGE GUIDE TO CASTING DIRECTORS
Hettie Lynn Hurtes

The first book solely devoted to the art of auditioning for movies, TV, and theatre. It contains over 50 in-depth interviews with top casting directors in every major city in the U.S. Included are Lynn Stalmaster, Juliet Taylor, and Howard Feuer. Published by Watson-Guptill Publications, Inc.

BEING & DOING (323) 466-9250
Eric Morris

This exciting workbook is designed to help the actor integrate the two parts of the process – the instrument and the craft – into a system which gives dimension, spontaneity, and authenticity to his performance. The numerous daily exercises deal with every aspect of acting, including the actor's relationship to the business. Blank pages provide the actor with space to document his own involvement and progress. SEE AD ON PAGE 13.

BOOK ON ACTING
IMPROVISATION TECHNIQUE FOR
THE PROFESSIONAL ACTOR
IN FILM, THEATER & TELEVISION (323) 461-4263
Stephen Book
stephenjbook@yahoo.com

The ability to improvise a skilled performance while speaking scripted and memorized lines is of paramount importance to actors working in today's film and television productions which often allow very little if any rehearsal time. Through his innovative improvisation technique, Stephen Book shows the actor how to create a spontaneous performance by applying improvisation to traditional script-acting for film, theatre and television. "Book on Acting" also contains film and television scenes (with the performance choices) in which Book-coached actors, used his improvisation technique to create their performances. Included are scenes from such TV shows as "Melrose Place," "Star Trek: Voyager," "L.A. Law," "Frasier" and "The Practice." Published by Silman James Press and available at most book stores.

BOOK THE JOB: 143 THINGS ACTORS NEED
TO KNOW TO MAKE IT HAPPEN (310) 479-5647
Doug Warhit
www.dougwarhit.com

Tools to master everything from "Getting in the door without any connections," "Crying on Cue," "Making the Most of your close-up," "Nailing Sitcoms (Even if you don't think you're funny)" to "What makes someone a star." See listing for Doug Warhit in the TRAINING section under ACTING for further information. SEE AD ON PAGE 2.

(818) 895-SING
BORN TO SING: SINGING LESSONS (800) 929-SING
Howard Austin and Elisabeth Howard
www.vocalpower.com
vocalcoach@borntosing.com

Includes: CDs, video and books on Technique/Style/Super Vocals/Sing-Aerobics Exercises. Four CDs with technique/style book in binder album $49.95 Available from the website, this step-by-step voice training program includes: Vocal Technique Course: Breath support, vibrato control, articulation of consonants and vowels, voice placement and resonance for expressive singing, lower and upper register (falsetto, head voice), smoothing out the 'break', volume control and more. Vocal Style Course: Develop your own style, Blues, Pop, R&B, Country, Broadway, Opera; Phrasing, voice coloring and pronunciation are covered as well as how to improvise ('licks') Blues and Pentatonic scales influencing melody; how to build emotional intensity; creating a Broadway character; trill, staccato and cadenza in classical singing, and more. Super Vocals: Takes you even further in developing your artistry in personal style and powerful emotion. Sing-Aerobics: The perfect daily vocal work-out exercise program for continuing to improve your singing.

(310) 571-4141
BREAKING INTO COMMERCIALS (323) 969-8200
by Terry Berland and Deborah Ouellette
www.terryberlandcasting.com

With over thirty-eight years of combined professional experience Terry and Deborah have an everyday, hands-on perspective on what it takes to make it in the business. By collaborating with some of the most respected names in the Industry, they have created a complete framework for making a serious move into commercial work. "Breaking Into Commercials" takes you step-by-step through the entire process of becoming a commercial actor. Special summary pages and commercial exercises will help keep you on track and focused on your goals. See listing for Terry Berland under CASTING in the WORKING section for further information.

COMEDY BIBLE (310) 915-0555
Judy Carter
www.standup411.com

Judy Carter, well known comedian and guru to aspiring comics, delivers the complete scoop on being and writing funny for money and for fun. Using the hands-on workbook format that was so effective in her best-selling book "Stand-Up Comedy: The Book" she offers a series of day-by-day exercises that teach you how to find your "authentic" voice, the true source of comedy.

THE COSTUME TECHNICIAN'S HANDBOOK
THIRD EDITION (800) 225-5800
Rosemary Ingham and Liz Covey
www.heinemanndrama.com

The third edition of this classic book on costuming draws upon the authors' many years of hands-on experience in costume design and technology. For professional costume technicians, students of costume design, or adventuresome home stitchers, this book includes information gleaned across the country from shop managers and staff about their methods, supplemented with images of some of the very best theatrical costume work to be seen today. This a complete guide to developing costumes that are personally distinctive and artistically expressive. Visit the website for a continually updated source list of booksellers, useful publications and addresses, costume societies, and shopping guide.

THE CRAFT OF ACTING (323) 466-9250
Eric Morris
www.ericmorris.com

Recorded live during a three day craft workshop at the Eric Morris Actor's Studio in Hollywood, this collection of five 90-minute tapes contains breakthrough information, vital to anyone seriously interested in acting. Find out exactly what Eric means by "Obligation/Choice/Choice Approach," and listen in on other actors' experiences as Eric guides them through the process, overcoming both the most common and the most difficult obstacles in acting. SEE AD ON PAGE 13.

DIRECTING ACTORS **(310) 392-2444**
Judith Weston
www.judithweston.com
judyweston@aol.com

Judith Weston has written a book for actors and directors which illuminates the difference between "result direction" and "playable direction," describes how to understand and use a scene's "beats" and a character's "spine," and contains chapters on casting, rehearsing, actor's choices, fine tuning between takes, comedy, a short list of action verbs, and five quick fixes.

DISCOVER YOURSELF IN HOLLYWOOD **(323) 877-4988**
Lilyan Chauvin

Available at Samuel French. SEE AD ON PAGES 16 & 255.

DO YOU WANT TO BE AN ACTOR: 101 ANSWERS TO YOUR QUESTIONS ABOUT BREAKING INTO THE BUSINESS
Richard Devin
Empire Publishing
P.O. Box 1344
Studio City 91614

101 questions asked by the neophyte actors that author Richard Devin has posed to agents, casting directors, producers, photographers etc. Available through amazon.com and borders.com.Available at amazon.com and theatrical bookstores as well as by direct order.

THE EIGHT CHARACTERS OF COMEDY **(818) 465-6512**
Scott Sedita
www.scottsedita.com
scottsedita@aol.com

The Eight Characters of Comedy is a Hollywood "How-To" guide for actors and writers who want to break into the world of situation comedy. Renowned acting coach Scott Sedita will teach you how to break down a comedy script, identify different types of jokes and deliver them with comedic precision. You will learn about sitcom history, specific sitcom auditioning techniques and how to market yourself in this competitive Industry. Most importantly, you will be introduced to The Eight Characters of Comedy, eight specific character archetypes that will help you discover your niche in half hour comedy. Who is normally cast as The Logical Smart One? Why do we love The Lovable Loser? Why is The Neurotic such a fun character to play? How can you play The Dumb One smart? Who are the biggest Bitches and Bastards? What drives The Materialistic One? Why is The Womanizer/Manizer so popular? How can you realistically play someone In Their Own Universe? Available at amazon.com, Borders, Barnes & Noble, etc., and through the website.

SUBMISSION TRACKER **(213) 324-5754**
P.O. Box 36862
Los Angeles 90036
www.holdonlog.com
info@holdonlog.com

Submission Tracker Holdon Log helps tracking submissions for: film, TV, commercial, theatre, voice over, industrial, agency, management companies, modeling, internet, print and background. The log contains 200 organizational forms geared specifically for tracking submissions with an evaluation form after every 50 submissions. Also includes contact and vital phone numbers, notes sections, yearly calendar section, convenient storage pockets for submission materials, submission postage and more. Visit the website for more information, product tour and reviews.

ACTOR'S HOLDON LOG **(213) 324-5754**
P.O. Box 36862
Los Angeles 90036
www.holdonlog.com
info@holdonlog.com

Each Actors' Holdon Log tracks 100 auditions and callbacks and allows you to record your audition details and expenses, submission and follow-up information, as well as your thoughts on the audition. It also allows you to chart your successes with a "booked" page, and carry your headshots/resumes and sides. Coil bound with vinyl covers for added durability. Visit the website for more information, product tour and review.

LIVE PERFORMERS' HOLDON LOG **(213) 324-5754**
P.O. Box 36862
Los Angeles 90036
www.holdonlog.com
info@holdonglog.com

Live Performers' Holdon Log is for comedians, singers, musicians, bands, spoken word artists, poets, magicians, and variety acts. 100 organizational pages geared specifically for live performers, contact and information. Pages for important numbers, sections to track venues and days, demo request and follow-up record area, material catalog and convenient storage pockets for promo and performance materials. Visit the website for more information, product tours and reviews.

BOOKED PROJECTS' HOLDON LOG **(213) 324-5754**
P.O. Box 36862
Los Angeles 90036
www.holdonlog.com
tp@holdonlog.com

Booked Projects Holdon Log is for logging and tracking 100 bookings including booking details, contacts, follow-ups, income and expenses, mileage, contracts, headshots/resumes and also has storage pockets for promo materials and call sheets. Visit the website for more information, product tours and reviews.

HOLDON LOG FOR YOUNG ACTORS **(213) 324-5754**
P.O. Box 36862
Los Angeles 90036
www.actortrack.com
info@holdonlog.com

Designed with fun fonts, this log is geared to teach young talent the importance of logging and tracking their audition information and booked projects. The fire engine red log measures 8$^1/_2$ x 11 with a finished coil-bound spine and vinyl front/back covers for durability. The individually numbered audition forms track up to 100 auditions and call-backs with audition details, expenses and mileage for tax purposes. It also allows you to chart your successes with a "booked" page and carry your headshot/resumes and sides and collect contact information and autographs for friends you've made while auditioning and on the set. Visit the website for more information, product tour and reviews.

HOLDON LOG FOR MODELS **(213) 324-5754**
P.O. Box 36862
Los Angeles 90036
www.holdonlog.com
info@holdonlog.com

Now all you need is your Holdon Log for Models and your portfolio to walk in and out of your castings polished, prepared and organized. This log allows you to record and track up to 100 casting and booking details including expenses, agency submission success and your post casting thoughts. Pockets for Comp/Zed Cards and Vouchers. Visit the website for more information, product tour and reviews.

BACKGROUND ARTISTS' HOLDON LOG **(213) 324-5754**
P.O. Box 36862
Los Angeles 90036
www.holdonlog.com
info@holdonlog.com

The Background Artists' Holdon Log logs and tracks up to 100 bookings and contains: a Professional Logging System geared specifically for the Background Artist; easy record keeping of your booking expenses and mileage for tax purposes; a Claims Management Section; pockets for headshots and vouchers; and nationwide background casting registration information for AZ, CA, FL, HI, MD, MA, NV, NY, OR, PA, RI, TN TX and Canada. Visit the website for more information, product tours and reviews.

HOLLYWOOD HERE I COME!
Cynthia Hunter
www.hollywoodhereicome.com

Now the #1 selling acting and modeling book in the world and Irwin Award Winner for Best How-To-Book. This information will launch you ahead of the pack in the competitive world of acting and modeling. A must for show biz parents or anyone who takes their career seriously. This insiders' guide will stuff your head full of personal experience, savvy communication skill and strategies that work. Readers find a new direction for their focus, a very real sense of purpose and a game plan to make goals a reality. Also 400 never before published telephone numbers to help you every step of the way up the ladder to success. To order call (800) 4-DREAMS.

HOLLYWOOD SCAMS AND SURVIVAL TACTICS **(323) 877-4988**
Lilyan Chauvin

Available at Samuel French or call. SEE ADS ON PAGES 16 & 255.

HOW TO SELL YOURSELF AS AN ACTOR
K Callan
P.O. Box 1612
Studio City 91614
www.swedenpress.com
kcallan@swedenpress.com

Actress-author, K Callan's guide teaches you to take your career in your own hands providing nuts and bolts information about how to be more saleable to casting directors, agents, producers and directors. She encourages you to call upon your courage, vision and entrepreneurial skills to stop waiting to be asked to work and presents a way of thinking about the business that will help you retain your sense of humor as well as your sanity. Callan's books are Industry bibles for actors, writers and directors at all stages of their careers. SEE AD ON TRAINING TAB.

IMAGING **(323) 466-9250**
Eric Morris
www.ericmorris.com

Continuing with the exploration of the MegApproaches, Eric takes us into imaging, possibly the most powerful of them all. The many types and techniques of imaging are explored and applied at a Lake Arrowhead two-day workshop. Some of the concepts covered on these tapes include the 11 reasons why we image, the eight imaging techniques and the pragmatic process of the way to image. Listening to these tapes is incredibly informative and a real challenge to the imagination. SEE AD ON PAGE 13.

INSTANT SHAKESPEARE **(312) 787-6262** **(213) 383-0648**
Louis Fantasia **FAX (312) 787-6269**
www.instantshakespeare.com
alexander@ivanrdee.com

A proven technique for actors, directors and teachers in the 21st century, by Louis Fantasia. This book by the American education director of the Shakespeare Globe Center in London demystifies the Bard and allows for performance of his plays in clear, fresh and unpretentious ways. $26.00 Cloth

IRREVERENT ACTING **(323) 466-9250**
Eric Morris
www.ericmorris.com

Irreverent Acting is a craft handbook offering a practical, applicable approach to acting, with specific techniques used to create the emotional life of a character. The craftural process of "Obligation/Choice/Choice Approach" is fully explained in terms of the actor's responsibilities to a piece of material whether it be a monologue, scene, play or film. This book contains 22 of Eric's 30 "choice approaches" and scores of other techniques which make it possible for the actor to fulfill all the obligations of written material from a basis of reality. SEE AD ON PAGE 13.

IT'S A FREEWAY OUT THERE! **(562) 621-0121**
belshecasting@aol.com

A definitive workbook that answers most of the questions parents have about the Industry and their working kids. There is a general overview section including classes, twins/triplets, time management, etc., a section on agencies, pictures, auditions, and even a chapter on the language of the business. This is a hands on tool for the parent. The book also contains scenes, commercials, monologues, and theatre games – anything you would need to test your child at home with. If they don't want to work with the exercises in the book...congrats Mom and Dad...you're done! Don't spend another dime. "The Fry Family Goes To Hollywood Coloring Book" is the first book of it's kind and though it is recommended for grammar school ages, everyone loves to doodle and color. This coloring book has 50 pages of what happens to the Fry Family when they decide to try showbiz. They believe that their French Fry hair is unique and that they are talented and with those two positives why not get into the movies? Even their dog, Curly Fry gets into the act. Both books can be ordered from Judy Belshe@aol.com, Amazon.com and Barnes & Noble.com.

LA FROM A TO Z: THE ACTOR'S GUIDE TO SURVIVING AND SUCCEEDING IN LOS ANGELES **(800) 225-5800**
Tom Mills **FAX (603) 431-2214**
P.O. Box 6926
Portsmouth, NH 3802
www.heinemanndrama.com
pat.carls@heinemann.com

"Actors need the acceptance of unknowing. That's a legitimate job tool." So says Thomas Mills whose twenty years in the profession, eight of them in Los Angeles, have made him something of a philosopher, but even better an insider. Author of the "Tombudsman" and "Working Actor" columns for BackstageWest, Mills knows acting. He knows Los Angeles. And he knows what it takes to survive and even thrive. He now shares his knowledge in LA from A to Z. From A (acting classes, auditions, and agents) to Z (getting enough of them), Mills offers actors a realistic, helpful, and at times bemused guide to life in the big city. Along the way he looks at: attitude: a bad one will earn you the ultimate scarlet letter; boredom: how to deal with that long time between acting jobs; film set etiquette: don't park in Mr. Katzenberg's space, for starters; demo reels: be honest, ask yourself, "Based on this, would I hire me?" Find work. Avoid scams. Cope with your first earthquake. Read Mills and make the most of your LA experience.

LET THE PART PLAY YOU: A PRACTICAL APPROACH TO THE ACTOR'S CREATIVE PROCESS (818) 767-4616
Anita Jesse
www.anitajessestudio.com

Author Anita Jesse provides a concise handbook that covers the actor's craft beginning with the basic skills (including concentration, imagination, and relaxation) through script analysis and performance. The author shares exercises and techniques she has been using in the workshops she has taught in L.A. and throughout the country since 1978. Recommended by professionals such as John Ritter, Bryan Cranston, Eva La Rue and Michael Donovan. Available in bookstores throughout the country or by mail order. Now in its 4th edition. Published by Wolf Creek Press. SEE AD ON PAGE 15.

THE LOS ANGELES AGENT BOOK
K Callan
P. O. Box 1612
Studio City 91614
www.swedenpress.com
kcallan@swedenpress.com

Actress-author K Callan's best selling guide to agents in the Los Angeles area. Learn to be your own first agent until you are ready to attract the agent who is right for you. Based on Callan's face-to-face interviews with Los Angeles theatrical agents, the details in the front of the book prepare readers for the agency profiles in the second half of the book which detail the history of the agencies, the size of their list and a few of their clients. Callan's books are Industry bibles for actors, writers and directors at all stages of their careers. In addition to Callan's extensive acting career (most visibly as Superman's mom in ABC's hit series, "Lois & Clark"), Callan has taught at The American Film Institute, UCLA Extension, is a voting member of The Academy of Motion Picture Arts and Sciences and The Academy of Television Arts and Sciences and a past member of the board of directors of The Screen Actors Guild. SEE AD ON TRAINING TAB.

THE MEGAPPROACHES (323) 466-9250
Eric Morris
www.ericmorris.com

Among the 28 "choice approaches" are five so rich, powerful, and dynamic, that each alone could constitute a whole system of acting. These are "MegApproaches." In this set of tapes, recorded live at a two-day workshop in New York City, three MegApproaches are explored in depth: Sense Memory, Externals and Sub-Personalities. As you listen to these tapes, you will experience the excitement of the actors, their discoveries and breakthroughs as they work with three of the most powerful acting tools ever created. SEE AD ON PAGE 13.

THE METHOD WITH LORRIE HULL PH.D.: BASED ON STANISLAVSKI & STRASBERG (310) 828-0632
1148 17th St., #3
Santa Monica 90403
www.actors-studio.com/hull
hullwshop@hotmail.com

A two hour instructional acting tape with Cloris Leachman, Martin Landau, and Shelley Winters. "The Method II" is due to come out soon. See listing under ACTING in this section for further information.

NEXT!
Ellie Kanner and Paul G. Bens

Next! provides an exceptionally insightful analysis of the often misunderstood audition process. A book for beginning actors who want to learn all about the auditioning process and also for working actors who are having difficulties with auditioning. With a foreword by Matt LeBlanc ("Friends"), Next! serves as a primer for all actors, guiding, educating, and teaching the ins and outs of what a casting director is looking for. According to Director James Burrows ("Cheers") the book "will give you everything but the talent." Available through Lone Eagle, at Amazon.com, Samuel French or Barnes & Noble.

NO ACTING PLEASE (323) 466-9250
Eric Morris
www.ericmorris.com

Often using journal excerpts and actual dialogs from Eric Morris' classes, the book thoroughly explores the "being" state, wherein the actor does no more or less than what he feels. It is a collection of 125 one-of-a-kind exercises created by Eric Morris, which teach the actor to systematically eliminate the instrumental obstacles (tensions, fears, inhibitions) that prevent him from expressing himself moment to moment, and prepare for "real" organic acting and to become a professional experiencer. It also contains a complete step-by-step explanation of Sense Memory. Co-authored by Joan Hotchkis, with excerpts from her journal. SEE AD ON PAGE 13.

THE PLAYING IS THE THING: LEARNING THE ART OF ACTING THROUGH GAMES AND EXERCISES (818) 767-4616
www.anitajessestudio.com

In her second book, author Anita Jesse shares the improvisational games and exercises that are central to the workshops she has taught in L.A. since 1978. Included with the easy-to-learn games and exercises are the author's teaching strategies. Actors, teachers, and directors alike will refer to this resource for tactics that help actors master basic skills such as, concentration, listening, and script analysis. The games and exercises also provide methods for developing spontaneity, ensemble, relaxation, imagination, and emotional freedom. Many of the techniques presented in this guidebook have been developed by Ms. Jesse in workshops and seminars. Whether the reader is looking for help with the basics or interested in honing a performance, this guidebook will provide a useful resource. It is written in the same straightforward and accessible style as Ms. Jesse's earlier book, "Let The Part Play You." Available in bookstores throughout the country or by mail order. Published by Wolf Creek Press. SEE AD ON PAGE 15.

THE POWER OF THE ACTOR (323) 935-2100
Ivana Chubbuck
chubbuck@mac.com

An instructional guidebook from the leading coach and teacher to the stars, whose client roster has included Brad Pitt (Academy Award nominee), Charlize Theron (Academy Award winner), Djimon Honsou (Academy Award nominee), Elizabeth Shue (Academy Award nominee) and Halle Berry (Academy Award winner). The Power of the Actor guides the reader to dynamic and effective results. For many of today's major talents, the Chubbuck Technique is the first choice ˚ the leading edge of acting for the 21st century. Previous generations of actors were steeped in the teaching traditions of Stanislavski, Meisner and Strasberg. Taking the theories of these masters into a new realm of psychological and behavioral study, Industry veteran Ivana

Chubbuck has developed a curriculum that moves acting to the next step: how to utilize the inner pain and emotions, not as an end in itself, but as a way to drive and win a goal. The result recreates human behavior in its most fundamentally accurate and compelling form, taking the reader to the source of what motivates real behavior. In addition to her powerful twelve-step process for becoming and living a character, The Power of the Actor includes fascinating behind-the-scenes accounts of how countless celebrities mastered their craft, offering a trove of tidbits that are inspiring for actors, writers, directors and fans alike; takes classic and contemporary scripts from film, television and theater, and comprehensively breaks them down using Ivana's script analysis process; and provides sections on special acting tools and exercises on how to organically feel drunk or high; creating organic fear; how to organically feel the mindset of a killer; and creating sexual chemistry.

THE SCRIPT IS FINISHED, NOW WHAT DO I DO?
K Callan
P. O. Box 1612
Studio City 91614
www.swedenpress.com
kcallan@swedenpress.com

Actress-author K Callan's best selling resource book and agent guide is the complete marketing guide for scriptwriters filled with details, stories and hard research dealing with actually penetrating the system toward moving their script along the process. Callan encourages you to call upon your vision, courage and entrepreneurial talents to to stop waiting to be asked to work and presents a way of thinking about the business that will help you retain your sense of humor as well as your sanity. Learn to be your own first agent until you are ready to attract the agent who is right for you. Based on Callan's face-to-face interviews with Los Angeles literary agents, the details in the front of the book prepare readers for the agency profiles in the second half of the book which detail the history of the agencies, the size of their list and a few of their clients. Callan's books are Industry bibles for writers, actors and directors at all stages of their careers. In addition to Callan's extensive acting career (most visibly Superman's mom in the hit ABC series, "Lois & Clark"), Callan has taught at The American Film Institute, UCLA Extension, South Coast Repertory, is a voting member of The Academy of Motion Picture Arts & Sciences and The Academy of Television Arts and Sciences, and a past member of the Board of Directors of The Screen Actors Guild. SEE AD ON THE TRAINING TAB.

SANDI SHORE'S SANDBOX
STAND-UP COMEDY HOME STUDY COURSE KIT
www.sandishore.com

Whether you're a beginner, working comic, public speaker or a novelist the 'Sandbox' is for you! Your sandbox comes complete with the workshop workbook, workshop videotape, intro audio tape, "My Daily Workout Journal," bonus video (featuring an interview with Pauly Shore), and a pencil for doodling. Warning! This course will help you to understand and accept yourself. It will definitely increase your ability to communicate in any and all forums whether you are interviewing or being interviewed. Order from the website. $149 + shipping.

SHOWBIZ BOOKKEEPER (802) 867-2223
P.O. Box 510 FAX (802) 867-0144
Dorset, VT 05251-0519
www.theatredirectories.com

A tax record keeping book for those in the arts. Available by mail and at theatre bookstores.

SINGERS VOICE METHOD (323) 851-9042
Bob Corff
www.corffvoice.com

Learn to sing better quickly and easily with the acclaimed "Singers Voice Method" available on CD or audio tape. "Bob is a premiere professor of the performing arts. I have seen the results ... Bob knows how to do it." Louis J. Horovitz, Director of the Academy Awards. "Your success as a singer, actress or speaker will be greatly determined by your vocal skills. Study with a master: Bob Corff." – Reuben Cannon, Casting Director, the Color Purple. Available at Samuel French and Skylight Booksellers. SEE AD ON PAGE 91.

SO YOU WANT TO BE AN ACTOR...
ACT LIKE ONE! (323) 874-1901
Jerry Franks
www.askthecastingdirector.com

Long time casting director Jerry Franks guides you in: how to begin your acting career; creating your own breaks; getting the job; packaging yourself to head shots to image; getting a reputable agent or personal manager; recognizing the pitfalls and cons and how to spot them; beginning with lots of talent and little money; maximizing your look talent; and understanding casting cycles and how they affect you. There is a chapter for parents: "Should my child become an actor?" as well as a new chapter on how to become a successful casting director. Jerold Franks, Independent Casting Director, Lecturer, Educator and Actors' Advocate is responsible for an extraordinary number of television, motion picture, theater, and live show productions and events. Considered one of the foremost experts in guiding talent, Jerry is the former Executive in Charge of Talent and Casting for 20th Century Fox Television, he was also Director of Talent and Casting for Columbia Pictures Television and worked with the Long Beach Civic Light Opera as their Artistic Director. Available through his website and at Samuel French bookstores.

SOUTHERN CALIFORNIA
PERFORMING ARTS VENUES (213) 365-0605
3780 Wilshire Blvd., Ste. 1020
Los Angeles 90010
www.communityartsla.com

A resource book listing over 400 venues/performing spaces including coffeehouses, theatres, galleries, community centers, etc., available to rent in the greater Southern California area for workshops, rehearsals, showcases, productions, fundraisers, or whatever. Describes programming policies, facility features (lighting, sound, seating, etc.) in detail. The book is arranged by area.

SPEAK THE FRENCH
YOU ALREADY KNOW (323) 877-4988
Lilyan Chauvin

Speak the French You Already Know is a 3-hour audio tape series which provides the fastest way to learn French. Lilyan Chauvin has taught top Hollywood people including Richard Gere and Lauren Hutton. SEE AD ON PAGES 16 & 255.

SPEAKERS VOICE METHOD (323) 851-9042
Bob Corff
www.corffvoice.com

Change your speaking voice to one that is solid, powerful and real with this workbook and two CD or two audio tape set. Learn to use a voice that represents you in the best and most positive light. "Creative and stimulating ... I recommend Bob."—Ted Danson, Cheers and Becker. "Since studying with Bob I've become a real woman."—Jenna Elfman, Dharma and Greg. Available at Samuel French and Skylight Booksellers. SEE AD ON PAGE 91.

STANISLAVSKI'S FOURTH LEVEL (323) 860-8790
Ned Manderino
www.manderino.com

A timely book for a world undergoing radical creative challenges guides the actor to a new dimension of personal and creative transformation. Constantin Stanislavski, the great revolutionary of modern acting, envisioned that this higher realm of acting technique could be reached through the use of what he called the superconscious. Years of research during the author's teaching of actors globally led to the successful development of practical Superconscious Exercises. With easy-to-follow guidelines and lists of exercise examples, this book prepares the actor for a journey to a deeper reality and greater truth in acting.

STRASBERG'S METHOD AS TAUGHT BY LORRIE HULL
A PRACTICAL GUIDE FOR ACTORS, TEACHERS AND DIRECTORS
www.actors-studio.com/hull
hullwshop@hotmail.com

This book is the definitive guide to Method Acting and the works of Constantin Stanislavski and Lee Strasberg. "If you ever wondered how some of our better actors arrived at their skills, this book will provide some answers."—Los Angeles Times. "Clear, concise, uncomplicated... just what is needed to explain the method. A must for every beginning actor who wishes to work deeply."—Shelley Winters. The book explains in detail relaxation, concentration and sensory exercises, as well as affective memory work. Also explained is how to use improvisation in actor training, casting, rehearsal, performance and as an aid to the writer. Techniques of preparing and learning the role, as well as the stages of rehearsal are thoroughly explained. Students, teachers and directors world-wide use this book.

STUDENT GUIDE
TO PLAYWRITING OPPORTUNITIES (802) 867-2223
P.O. Box 510 FAX (802) 867-0144
Dorset, VT 05251-0510
www.theatredirectories.com

College and University programs and play development programs around the country. Available by mail order and in bookstores around the country.

SURVIVAL JOBS: 154 WAYS TO MAKE MONEY WHILE PURSUING YOUR DREAMS
Deborah Jacobson

Published by Broadway Books. Available at all major bookstores for $19.00. The book includes 154 detailed part-time ways to make money with job duties, expected salary or income, necessary skills and phone number for major cities listed.

THE ORGANIZED ACTOR
Leslie Becker
www.organizedactor.com
organizedactor@aol.com

The workbook and planner for the serious actor. This the only book you need to organize your career, featuring an audition/submission log, expense tracking, address book, calendar and goal setting. Available at theatrical bookstores or online bookstores. Retails for $17.95.

THE VIDEO DEMO TAPE: HOW TO SAVE MONEY MAKING A TAPE THAT GETS YOU WORK
Larry and Susan Benedict

The authors share their 10 years of experience creating promos for many top stars. Industry professionals learn the secrets of top demo tapes and use money-saving instructions to produce a winner of their own. $34.95 at amazon.com

WARHIT'S GUIDEBOOK FOR THE ACTOR
Doug Warhit
www.dougwarhit.com

Quotes and interviews with actors who have achieved the dream. What you need to know about discipline, success, criticism, and drive. See listing for Doug Warhit in the TRAINING section under ACTING for further information. SEE AD ON PAGE 2.

THE YOUNG ACTOR'S BOOK OF IMPROVISATION DRAMATIC SITUATIONS FROM SHAKESPEARE TO SPIELBERG – AGES 7-11 AND 12-16
Sandra Caruso with Susan Kosoff

With more than two hundred dramatic situations, this book is by far the most extensive source book available for nurturing the creative process in the young actor. Endorsed by Jules Feiffer, Mel Shapiro, Milton Katselas, John B. Welch, Managing Director, Baker's Plays; Professor Robert Colby, Department of Performing Arts, Emerson College. Publisher Heinemann.

YOUR FACE LOOKS FAMILIAR ... HOW TO GET AHEAD AS A WORKING ACTOR (310) 281-9580
Michael Bofshever

In-between the celebrity artist and the struggling actor there is a contingency of working actors in Los Angeles and New York that earn their living in their chosen profession. Michael Bofshever a well respected veteran of stage, film, television and commercials and known as a highly regarded acting teacher shares his insights into how to create and maintain a career as a working professional. There are also interviews with actors from both coasts sharing their valuable experience on such topics as: Getting Started, How To Audition, Life on the Set, Transitioning from Stage to Film, Tools to Deal with Rejection, Unemployment, Success, The Life of the Actor and so much more. Mr. Bofshever conducts a highly regarded seminar on this topic on recurring basis for the Screen Actors Guild Foundation. He has spoken at the American Film Institute, American Academy of Dramatic Arts, The Players Academy and universities throughout the country. Published by Heinemann Press.

YOUR FILM ACTING CAREER (310) 826-2255
M.K. Lewis FAX (310) 826-6966
Gorham House Publishing
2118 Wilshire Blvd., #777
Santa Monica 90403
www.mklewisworkshops.com

The classic bestseller on the business of acting in film and television, now in its 4th edition, gives practical information and career advice with empathy and wit. The authors are internationally known acting teacher M.K. Lewis and writer illustrator Rosemary R. Lewis. Available by mail order and at Samuel French Booksellers, Larry Edmunds, and other bookstores across the country. SEE AD ON PAGE 14.

Clipping Services

Clipping services are an excellent way for actors to obtain printed material of anything that has been written in the media or covered on radio pertaining to their work or to a project they were involved in. Clipping services will also occasionally have copies of television and film work, including overseas productions. These companies will track public relations and publicity. You can also buy a copy of a news broadcast or other special show which is useful for research. Some of these companies work on an international level. Also see VIDEO TAPE DUPLICATION, AIRCHECKS & PRODUCTION in this section.

ALL RESEARCH, INC. (323) 653-1900
8217 Beverly Blvd., Ste. 6 FAX (323) 657-5302
Los Angeles 90048
www.webclipping.com

WebClipping.com is a comprehensive Internet-based monitoring, intelligence gathering and clipping service. Using advanced proprietary searching, verification and database technologies, WebClipping.com helps you meet the Internet monitoring challenge.

ALLEN'S PRESS CLIPPING BUREAU (213) 628-4214
P.O. Box 512761 FAX (213) 627-0889
Los Angeles 90051-0761

657 Mission St., Ste. 602 (415) 392-2353
San Francisco 94105

Provides clippings from magazines and newspapers for both ongoing and one-time events. International service. Offices in San Francisco, Portland, Los Angeles and Seattle. Monday through Friday 8:30 am to 5 pm.

BACON'S INFORMATION, INC. (323) 603-2000
6725 Sunset Blvd., Ste. 450
Los Angeles 90028
www.bacons.com

Provides clippings from newspapers and magazines. A comprehensive service with extensive magazine coverage. Also offers a press release distribution service and publishes a series of magazine directories. 24 hour turnaround. Ongoing work only. Monday through Friday, 8 am to 5 pm.

BURRELLESLUCE (800) 621-1160
INFORMATION SERVICES (818) 817-9600
www.burrelles.com

Provides clippings from magazines and newspapers for both ongoing and one time events. Locations across the country.

CLIP GENIUS (703) 563-4236
5885 Trinity Parkway Ste. 220 FAX (703) 563-4230
Alexandria, VA 22120
www.clipgenius.com

Clip Genius is an online clipping service that searches a variety of news sources on the Internet for your specific search terms. It then emails the results daily so you can stay on top of the news you choose. With Clip Genius, you can keep pace with your competition, follow your Industry, monitor the results of your communications efforts, or stay abreast of a topic that interests you.

SAN DIEGO CLIPPING SERVICE (619) 685-1155
2967 Beech Street FAX (619) 685-1157
San Diego 92102
www.sandiegoclipping.com
info@sandiegoclipping.com

Reads over 140 publications from San Diego County, Tijuana, Baja California. The Los Angeles Times and La Opinion are also read. Delivery is by email, fax or traditional U.S. Postal Service. San Diego Clipping publishes La Fuente Hispanic Media Directory on the Internet.

VIDEO MONITORING SERVICES (323) 993-0111
6430 W. Sunset Blvd., Ste. 400 FAX (323) 762-2038
Los Angeles 90028

Provides tapes and transcripts from radio and TV broadcasts for both ongoing and one-time events. Also tracks public relations work. They have the world's largest collection of TV and radio commercials. Monday through Friday, 8 am to 5:30 pm. See listing under VIDEO TAPE DUPLICATION, AIRCHECKS & PRODUCTION in this section for further information.

Computers

ACTORTRACK
SOFTWARE FOR ACTORS (213) 324-5754
P.O. Box 36862
Los Angeles 90036
www.actortrack.com
info@holdonlog.com

An effective and empowering career tool developed specifically for actors. Log and track auditions and callbacks, manage booked projects, track career income and expenses, organize Industry contacts, schedule career and general appointments, reveals statistics allowing the discovery of trends, and more. Software works with Palm 3, 4, and 5 too!

(800) 851-5145
ALLIANT EVENT SERVICES (909) 622-3306
3260 Pomona Blvd.
Pomona 91768
www.alliantevents.com

Rents computers and peripherals including PCs, notebooks, laser printers, monitors, etc. Equipment may be rented daily, weekly, or monthly and the package includes delivery, installation, 24 hour on-call service, technical assistance/support, and pick-up.

AMERICAN FILM INSTITUTE (AFI) (323) 856-7600
2021 N. Western Ave. FAX (323) 467-4578
Los Angeles 90027
www.afi.com

Has outreach programs for computer classes, directing, producing, screenwriting, and special effects for film and video makers. Evening and weekend day classes and several lecture series are offered.

COMP USA (818) 848-8588
Media City Center FAX (818) 563-5898
761 N. San Fernando Blvd.
Burbank 91502
www.compusa.com

Carries a huge selection of brand name products including

hardware, software, multimedia, and upgrades. They offer a training center and a technical department as well as a special section just for kids. You may try out software before you buy it. There are several locations throughout Los Angeles, call the toll-free number above for the store nearest you.

COMPLETE COMPUTER CURE (818) 986-8770 / (818) 986-5252
15122 Ventura Blvd. FAX (818) 986-5082
Sherman Oaks 91403
www.cccla.com

Factory authorized technicians make repairs at their store or on-site. Monthly, weekly and daily rentals available of laptops, desktops, printers, projectors, monitors, faxes and more.

COMPUTER PALACE (310) 998-1919
2807 Wilshire Blvd. FAX (310) 998-1144
Santa Monica 90403
www.cp4.com

Offers a wide range of IBM compatible and Macintosh products. Also offers repair services.

COMPUTER RENTALS, ETC. (800) 427-2382 / (310) 417-3544
5372 Buckingham Parkway FAX (310) 417-8214
Culver City 90230
www.computerrentals.com

Rents Mac and IBM clones with same day delivery. All deliveries include a technician to set up and get the equipment running. Entertainment Industry specialists. Competitive pricing.

FRY'S ELECTRONICS (818) 526-8100
2311 N. Hollywood Way FAX (818) 526-8118
Burbank 91505
www.frys.com

A discount store that carries a wide range of computers and computer supplies including component parts, printers, and a huge selection of programs. Their prices are extremely low and the staff is knowledgeable. See listing under ELECTRONICS in this section for further information.

HI-TECH COMPUTER RENTAL (818) 841-0677 / (800) 789-7604
172 W. Verdugo Ave. FAX (818) 841-0575
Burbank 91502
www.htcr.net
hitech@htcr.net

Low prices on rental of IBM compatibles or MacIntosh computers, laser printers, notebooks, faxes, etc. Offers on-site maintenance, trained technical support, and delivery and set-up.

HOLLYWOOD COMPUTERS (323) 851-2226
916 N. Formosa
Los Angeles 90038

An authorized repair station for Epson, Okidata, and HP Laser printers. They also sell IBM clones, accessories, and monitors. Monday through Friday, 9:30 am to 6 pm and Saturday, 11 am to 2 pm.

IMAGING PLUS (800) 955-7587 / (949) 341-3355
2 Goddard FAX (949) 341-3375
Irvine 92618
www.imagingplus.com

Color printers for sale, rent, or lease. Same day shipping.

INTERACT! (626) 578-7282 / (800) 479-1323
350 S. Lake Ave., Ste. 112 FAX (626) 683-5639
Pasadena 91101
www.interactcd.com
contact-interact@interact.com

Thousands of new and used CD-ROM titles in stock for both IBM and Mac formats. They buy and sell used CD-ROMs and DVDs. PC and Mac games.

RADIO SHACK (323) 464-4720
1128 N. La Brea
Hollywood 90038

12346 Ventura Blvd. (818) 766-0046
Studio City 91604
www.radioshack.com

Carries IBM computers and accessories, plus many other electrical components including a full supply of video, telephones, and fax machines. There are many locations throughout the Southern California area.

STAPLES THE OFFICE SUPERSTORE (818) 753-6390
12605 Ventura Blvd. FAX (818) 753-6393
Studio City 91604

6450 Sunset Blvd. (323) 467-2155
Hollywood 90027
www.staples.com

Carries most major brands of computer hardware and accessories including monitors, keyboards, printers, modems, and scanners. Also has a large selection of software, computer furniture, and peripherals such as computer covers, wrist rests, copy holders, etc. There are many locations throughout the L.A. area. See listing under STATIONERY STORES in this section for further information.

THOMAS CONSULTING, INC. (805) 497-8004
www.thomasconsultinginc.com FAX (805) 497-8005
shannon@thomasconsultinginc.com

Training at your home or office in Windows, Excel, Word, WordPerfect and BusinessWorks accounting software with certified instructor Shannon Thomas. By appointment.

THE WRITERS' STORE (310) 441-5151
2040 Westwood Blvd.
W. Los Angeles 90025
www.writerscomputer.com

Full service computer store that carries computers, printers, and accessories. Also carries all the software that is current in the Industry including script writing and breakdown programs. Monday through Saturday, 10 am to 9 pm.

Costume Sales & Rentals

ACCENT ON DANCE & BROADWAY COSTUMES (626) 287-0741
9026 E. Las Tunas Dr. FAX (626) 287-9264
Temple City 91780

Carries dancewear from Capezio, Baryshnikov, Danskin and others, shoes are Capezio and Danshuz and they stock Ben Nye make-up. The costume rental collection contains over 6,000 pieces as well as accessories, wigs and masks for sale. Call for discount program details.

ADELE'S OF HOLLYWOOD (323) 663-2231
5034 Hollywood Blvd. FAX (323) 663-2232
Los Angeles 90027

Costumes for all occasions, both rental and sales. Over 2,000 available, also carries all kinds of accessories and children's costumes. Tuesday through Saturday, 10 am to 5 pm.

AMERICAN COSTUME (818) 764-2239
12980 Raymer St. FAX (818) 765-7614
North Hollywood 91605

Costume rentals. Period costumes covering over 200 years of American history from 1770s-1970s including both civilian and military. Has both originals and reproductions. Monday through Friday, 8:30 am to 5:30 pm.

AMERICAN RAG (323) 935-3154
150 S. La Brea Ave.
Los Angeles 90036

Sales only. Carries 30s-70s vintage clothing and accessories both reproductions and originals. Has a large selection of new felt hats for men. Also sells new European clothing for men and women. Monday through Saturday 10 am to 9 pm and Sunday, 11 am to 7 pm.

APPAREL WAREHOUSE, INC. (818) 344-3224
6010 Yolanda St.
Tarzana 91356

Carries dancewear, shoes, and costumes including Halloween and animal costumes, hats, masks, and glitter makeup, gloves, and accessories. Available in quantity to dance companies and studio wardrobe facilities. Wholesale or show prices on all items. See listing for Shelly's Discount Aerobic & Dancewear under DANCEWEAR in this section. Monday through Friday, 8:30 am to 6 pm and Saturday, 8:30 am to 5 pm.

BERGER SPECIALTY (213) 627-8783
413 E. 8th St.
Los Angeles 90014

Carries costume accessories including bindings, rhinestone sequins, and beads. Does not make or carry costumes themselves. Monday through Friday, 9 am to 4:30 pm.

(818) 567-0753
CALIFORNIA COSTUME/NORCOSTCO (800) 220-6915
3606 W. Magnolia Blvd. FAX (818) 567-1961
Burbank 91505
www.norcostco.com
california@norcostco.com

Has a wide variety of clothing and costumes including period, character, uniforms, and animals. Alterations and custom-made costumes available within limits. Also has lighting, props, and an extensive selection of make-up. Monday through Friday, 10 am to 5 pm, Saturday 11 am to 4:30 pm.

CINEMA SECRETS (818) 846-0579
4400 Riverside Dr. FAX (818) 846-0431
Burbank 91505
www.cinemasecrets.com
cinemasecretsinfo@cinemasecrets.com

Complete costume and Halloween shop. Large selection of costumes, also has make-up, masks, facial hair, special effects and accessories. Professional make-up artists are on hand to answer any questions. Industry discounts. See listings under PROFESSIONAL MAKE-UP in this section and MAKE-UP in the TRAINING section for further information.

COSTUME RENTALS CORP. (818) 753-3700
11149 Vanowen St.
North Hollywood 91605

Rentals. Has a large selection of police, military, and security uniforms as well as western wear, hats, sports costumes, tuxedos, and vintage costumes. 30s-60s. Alterations and made-to-order costumes available. Also sells motion picture supplies. Monday to Friday, 8 am to 6 pm.

THE COSTUME SHOP (619) 574-6201
2010 El Cajon Blvd. FAX (619) 574-6268
San Diego 92104
www.thecostumeshop.net
contactus@thecostumeshop.net

Costume sales and rentals. Accessories, hats, wigs, facial hair, special effects, and clown make-up. Has a make-up artist on staff and offers make-up classes. Discount for actors who belong to the Actor's Alliance in San Diego. Monday through Friday, 10 am to 5 pm and Saturday, 9 am to 1 pm. They were moving at the time of publication so call or check the website for the new location.

E.C.2. COSTUMES (818) 506-7695
4019 Tujunga Ave. FAX (818) 506-0772
Studio City 91604

Rentals only. Large selection of beaded gowns, period costumes, showgirl, fantasy costumes, and accessories. No alterations. Monday through Friday, 8:30 am to 5 pm.

EYES ON MAIN (310) 399-3302
3110 Main St., Ste. 108 FAX (310) 399-7682
Santa Monica 90405

Glasses sales and rentals. Many styles available including non-prescription 50s, modern, designer, outrageous, vintage, and custom made. Also an optical boutique. Daily, 10 am to 6 pm.

FULLERTON CIVIC LIGHT OPERA (714) 879-9761
218 W. Commonwealth Ave. FAX (714) 992-1193
Fullerton 92832
www.fclo.com
rentfclo@aol.com

Rentals only. Period, hats, and accessories available. All costumes are from their stage productions and musicals. Monday through Friday, 10 am to 5 pm.

GILBERT OF HOLLYWOOD COSTUMES (818) 506-6668
11345 Chandler Blvd.
North Hollywood 91601

Masquerade and theatrical costume rentals. Carries animal, character, period, uniforms, tuxedos, show girl, and sports costumes. Also has 20s and 30s and 40s-60s clothing, lingerie, accessories, hats, masks, wigs, and hair pieces. Does alterations and custom made costumes and has special rates for theatre productions. Staff has a wide knowledge of theatre history, and most stock characters are available. There is a special rate for actors in a class project or a waiver production. Monday through Friday, noon to 6 pm and Saturday, noon to 3 pm or by appointment. Located in the Haunted Studio, call for directions. Located in NoHo Theatrical District.

GLENDALE COSTUMES **(818) 244-1161**
746 W. Doran St. **FAX (818) 244-8576**
Glendale 91203
www.glendalecentretheatre.com

Rents costumes of all types in excellent condition. Complete stock of theatrical and film costumes including animals, Santas, military uniforms, period clothes, and accessories. Helpful, knowledgeable staff. Also sells theatrical make-up. Tuesday through Saturday, 10 am to 6 pm.

HOLLYWOOD RAGGS, INC. **(818) 760-7166**
11160 Victory Blvd.
North Hollywood 91605

Rentals only. Carries character costumes, many period costumes, uniforms, military, medical, police, accessories, and hats. Will do alterations and custom made costumes are available for shows. By appointment.

HOLLYWOOD TOYS & COSTUMES **(323) 464-4444**
6600 Hollywood Blvd. **FAX (323) 464-4644**
Hollywood 90028
hollywoodtoy@earthlink.net

Vast selection of costumes and accessories. Monday through Friday, 9:30 am to 7 pm, Saturday, 10 am to 7 pm and Sunday 10:30 am to 7pm.

INTERNATIONAL COSTUME **(310) 320-6392**
1423 Marcelina **FAX (310) 320-3054**
Torrance 90501
www.tempcostumes.com

Over 40,000 costumes, also carries wigs, hats, and make-up. Alterations and custom made clothes are available. Can completely costume theatrical productions. You must come at least 45 minutes before closing for any fittings. Monday through Friday, 9 am to 6 pm, Saturday, 10 am to 5 pm. Extended hours start in mid-October. www.platinumcostumes.com

JUNK FOR JOY **(818) 569-4903**
3314 W. Magnolia Blvd.
Burbank 91505

Sales only, no rentals. Carries used garments from many different eras. Also never-worn fashion surplus and accessories from the 60s and 70s. Has accessories and kimonos and they wholesale at trade shows to the costume Industry. Studios shop here. Tuesday through Saturday, noon to 5:30 pm.

KARABEL DANCEWEAR **(818) 955-8480**
3901 W. Magnolia Blvd.
Burbank 91505

Carries dance wear, shoes, and costumes: capes, hats, robes, wings, wands, tiaras, boas, tutus, wigs makeup, teeth, gloves, leotards, tights, unitards, all for sale, no rentals.

LEATHERS & TREASURES **(323) 655-7541**
FAX (323) 655-0449

Studio rentals. Carries vintage clothing including leather. Does custom rock 'n roll tailoring and leather restoration. Also has silver and costume jewelry, 50s sunglasses, western wear, buckles, chaps, boot tips, and props.

MAGIC WORLD **(818) 700-8100**
10122 Topanga Canyon Blvd.
Chatsworth 91311

Costume sales and rental. They have over 10,000 different types of costumes. Adults may rent or buy, children for sale only. Also custom made costumes, balloon imprinting, masks, wigs, theatrical make-up, and magic supplies.

MAKE BELIEVE, INC. **(310) 396-6785**
3240 Pico Blvd. **FAX (310) 396-1936**
Santa Monica 90405

Mostly rentals, some sales. Will custom build costumes and they also carry wigs and special effects make-up. They have stylists, designers, and wardrobe consultants available for work on productions. Monday through Saturday, 10 am to 6 pm and Sunday, 11 am to 5 pm.

SUZAN MEIER **(661) 253-9970**
suzanmeier@aol.com

Suzan has created and patented a panty that holds a wireless microphone transmitter/receiver pack securely against a woman's body – firmly and inconspicuously in the small of her back. Unlike its elastic belt and holster type predecessors, the MicPac is quite comfortable, secure and discreet. Developed to accommodate the most revealing outfits. Suzan provides personal wardrobe consultation and creation. Also designs and constructs costumes as well as bridal gowns and ensembles. Has a Dramalogue award.

MONTANA EYES **(310) 917-4474**
709 Montana Ave.
Santa Monica 90403

Glasses sales and rentals. Many styles available including non-prescription 50s, modern, designer, outrageous, vintage, and custom made. Also an optical boutique. Daily, 10 am to 6 pm.

ONE NIGHT AFFAIR **(310) 474-7808**
1726 Sepulveda Blvd.
Los Angeles 90025
www.onenightaffair.com

Rentals. Specializes in designer evening gowns and cocktail dresses, bridal gowns, bridesmaid dresses, and accessories. Size 2-30. Will do alterations. Now carrying a full line of linens, chair covers, etc., in an array of fabrics. Tuesday through Saturday, 10 am to 7 pm, by appointment only.

PALACE COSTUME COMPANY **(323) 651-5458**
835 N. Fairfax
Los Angeles 90046
www.palacecostume.com

Rents to production companies only. Huge variety of costumes.

REEL CLOTHES AND PROPS (818) 951-7692
Box 4482 FAX (818) 951-7693
Sunland 91040
www.reelclothes.com

Carries wardrobe, set dressing, props and movie memorabilia. No rentals. Monday, Tuesday and Wednesday 10 am to 6 pm, Thursday through Saturday 10 am to 7 pm and Sunday, 12 pm to 5 pm.

ROBINSON BEAUTY (310) 398-5757
12320 Venice Blvd.
Los Angeles 90066

Costume sales and rentals. Complete and varied stock. Will do alterations and made-to-order costumes are available. Monday through Saturday, 9 am to 7 pm and Sunday, 11 am to 5 pm.

SHELLY'S DISCOUNT AEROBIC & DANCEWEAR (310) 475-1400
2089 Westwood Blvd. FAX (310) 470-6125
W. Los Angeles 90025

Sales only. Carries dance costumes, Halloween and animal costumes, lingerie, hats, masks, wigs, hair pieces, accessories, gloves, and special effects and glitter make-up. Available in quantity to dance companies and studio wardrobe facilities. Monday through Saturday, 10 am to 6 pm and Sunday, 11 am to 4 pm. See listing for Apparel Warehouse under DANCEWEAR in this section for further information.

SPORTSROBE (310) 559-3999
8654 Hayden Pl. FAX (310) 559-4767
Culver City 90232

Rents athletic clothing and props. Monday through Friday, 8 am to 5 pm.

THE STUDIO WARDROBE DEPT. (323) 467-9455
1357 N. Highland
Hollywood 90038

Sales only. Has a large selection of vintage clothing from the 1940s-1990s including hats and beaded gowns. Specializes in 1960s clothing. Monday through Saturday, 10 am to 10 pm and Sunday, 10 am to 8 pm.

THE THEATRE COMPANY (909) 982-5736
1400 N. Benson FAX (909) 982-8965
Upland 91786
www.theatreco.com

Over 90,000 costumes in stock. Rentals only for both individuals and groups. Carries period costumes from 1500s to 1900s, and the 1940s through the 1960s and beyond. Many costumes are from musicals. Also has animal costumes, hats, and wigs. Accessories are for sale. Carries Ben Nye stage make-up. Will do alterations. Tuesday through Saturday, 10 am to 5 pm and Monday by appointment.

URSULA'S COSTUMES, INC. (310) 582-8230
2516 Wilshire Blvd. FAX (310) 582-8233
Santa Monica 90403

Party and Halloween costumes. Custom made clothes available, also carries wigs, make-up, masks, accessories, and children's costumes. Will do alterations. Monday through Saturday, 9:30 am to 6 pm.

WESTERN COSTUME CO. (818) 760-0900 (888) 293-7837
11041 Vanowen FAX (818) 508-2190
North Hollywood 91605
www.westerncostume.com

This is the grandmother of costume houses. They carry contemporary, character, uniforms, and period costumes for rent as well as props, accessories, guns and swords. Alterations and made to order costumes, available Monday through Friday, 8 am to 5:30 pm.

YERKES CIRCUS COSTUMES (818) 344-4231 (818) 508-2190
17721 Roscoe Blvd.
Northridge 91325

Having done "Circus of the Stars" for 19 years, Bob has circus style costumes for rent as well as rigging and performers available. By appointment only.

PROP HOUSES

ADSPOSURE (818) 559-6304
209 W. Alameda Ave., Ste. 102
Burbank 91502
www.adsposureadvertising.com

Just give them a call for a customized program to meet your company's needs. Promotional items.

INDEPENDENT STUDIO SERVICES (818) 951-5600
9545 Wentworth St. FAX (818) 951-2852
Sunland 91040
www.issprops.com

Primarily set dressing. Deposit required, cash or check only. Monday through Friday, 8 am to 6 pm.

LAST GRENADIER (818) 848-9144
820 N. Hollywood Way
Burbank 91505
radengeist@aol.com

Carries reference books on military uniforms. Monday through Thursday, 11:30 am to 7 pm, Friday, 11:30 am to 9 pm, Saturday, 11 am to 7 pm and Sunday, 11 am to 6 pm.

OMEGA CINEMA PROPS (323) 466-8201
5857 Santa Monica Blvd.
Hollywood 90038
www.omegacinemaprops.com

Prop rentals. Cash or cashier's check required for deposit. Will establish a credit line for established companies. Monday through Friday, 8 am to 5 pm.

REEL CLOTHES (818) 951-7692
Box 4482 FAX (818) 951-7693
Sunland 91040
www.reelclothes.com

Carries wardrobe, props, set dressing, and movie memorabilia. No rentals. Monday – Wednesday 10 am to 6 pm, Thursday – Saturday, 10 am to 7 pm and Sunday, 12 pm to 5 pm.

Dancewear

ACCENT ON DANCE & BROADWAY COSTUMES (626) 287-0741
9026 E. Las Tunas Dr. FAX (626) 287-9264
Temple City 91780

Carries dancewear from Capezio, Baryshnikov, Danskin and others, shoes are Capezio and Danshuz and they stock Ben Nye make-up. The costume rental collection contains over 6,000 pieces as well as accessories, wigs and masks for sale. Call for discount program details.

APPAREL WAREHOUSE, INC. (818) 344-3224
6010 Yolanda St.
Tarzana 91356

Carries dancewear available in quantity to dance companies and studio wardrobe facilities. Wholesale or show prices on all items. See listing for Shelly's Discount Aerobic & Dancewear under COSTUME SALES & RENTALS in this section. Monday through Friday, 8:30 am to 6 pm and Saturday, 8:30 am to 5 pm.

CAPEZIO DANCE SHOE CO. (323) 465-3744
1779 N. Vine St. FAX (323) 465-9704
Hollywood 90028

Sells dancewear only. Discount for dance teachers. Monday through Saturday, 10 am to 5:30 pm, Thursday 10 am to 7 pm.

CAPEZIO DANCE-THEATRE SHOP (818) 348-4488
7120 Topanga Canyon Blvd. FAX (818) 348-4002
Canoga Park 91303
www.capeziodanceshop.com
info@capeziodanceshop.com

Specializing in children's dancewear. Capezio-Block-Grishko-Sansha-Freed. Experts in fitting all dance shoes. One stop shopping for all dancers. Monday through Saturday 10 am to 6 pm. Sells dancewear only. Discount for dance teachers.

CHAMPION DANCE SHOES (323) 874-8704
3383 Barham Blvd. FAX (323) 656-3256
Los Angeles 90068

Mostly sells ballroom and jazz shoes, some ballet slippers. Discount for full-time professional dance teachers. Monday through Saturday, 9:30 am to 5:30 pm.

THE DANCE STORE (323) 651-4012
421 Rose Ave.
Venice 90291

1446 S. Robertson Blvd. (310) 271-3664
Los Angeles 90038

Carries dance wear, shoes, costumes, capes, hats, robes, wings, wands, tiaras, boas, tutus, wigs, teeth, gloves, leotards, tights, unitards and makeup. No rentals.

DANNY'S WAREHOUSE (310) 837-7511
9443B Venice Blvd.
Venice 90291

Leotards, shoes, skirts— Capezio, Bloch and others. 9 am to 5 pm Monday through Friday.

KARABEL DANCEWEAR (818) 955-8480
3901 W. Magnolia Blvd.
Burbank 91505

Dance wear-workout gear. Leotards, unitards, bike shorts, jazz pants, crop top, tights, flamenco skirts. Dance and ice skating dresses, tutus and knitwear. Huge selection of dance shoes and fairy tale costumes and accessories. Plus sizes.

SUZAN MEIER (661) 253-9970
suzanmeier@aol.com

Suzan has created and patented a panty that holds a wireless microphone transmitter/receiver pack securely against a woman's body—firmly and inconspicuously in the small of her back. Unlike its elastic belt and holster type predecessors, the MicPac is quite comfortable, secure and discreet. Developed to accommodate the most revealing outfits. Suzan provides personal wardrobe consultation and creation. Also designs and constructs costumes as well as bridal gowns and ensembles. Has a Dramalogue award.

SHELLY'S DISCOUNT AEROBIC & DANCEWEAR (310) 475-1400
2089 Westwood Blvd.
W. Los Angeles 90025

Carries dancewear, dance shoes, dance costumes, Halloween costumes, animal costumes, lingerie, hats, masks, wigs, hair pieces, special effects and glitter makeup, gloves, and accessories. Sells in quantity to dance companies and studio wardrobe facilities. Wholesale prices on all items, also special show prices. Monday through Saturday, 10 am to 6 pm and Sunday, 11 am to 4 pm. See listing for Apparel Warehouse under COSTUME SALES & RENTALS in this section for further information.

Electronics

These stores primarily sell or rent electronic items such as fax machines, telephones, cameras, DVD players, and VCRs as well as accessories and components. See COMPUTERS in this section for information about hardware, software, and computer classes and repairs.

ALBEE DISCOUNT APPLIANCES (323) 651-0620
6305 Wilshire Blvd. FAX (323) 651-2678
Los Angeles 90048

Carries phone machines including Sony, Sanyo, Panasonic, and G.E. Also carries video equipment, camcorders, and fax machines. Open Monday through Saturday from, 9 am to 7 pm and Sunday, 11 am to 5 pm.

AMETRON (323) 464-1144
1546 N. Argyle Ave. FAX (323) 871-0127
Hollywood 90028
www.ametron.com
info@ametron.com

Carries audio, video, audio/visual, computer and wireless equipment as well as all kinds of stereo equipment, components, and accessories. Sells blank audio and video tapes, cassettes, and answering machines. Has a wide variety of electronic accessories and does rentals and repairs.

BEL-AIR CAMERA & VIDEO (310) 208-5150
10925 Kinross Ave. FAX (310) 208-7472
Westwood 90024
www.belaircamera.com

Camera and video store with a completely stocked video department. DVD and VCR rentals available with one day advance notice. Also offers digital imaging/restoration of injured photographs. Monday through Friday, 9 am to 7 pm, Saturday, 9:30 am to 6 pm and Sunday, noon to 5 pm.

FRY'S ELECTRONICS (818) 526-8100
2311 N. Hollywood Way FAX (818) 526-8118
Burbank 91505
www.frys.com

A discount store that carries almost everything electronic including telephones, computers, large and small appliances, television sets DVDs and VCRs, printers, and the list goes on. The prices are extremely low and the staff is helpful and friendly. See listing under COMPUTERS in this section for further information. Call for other locations.

HARRY'S CAMERA & VIDEO (818) 763-9750
11851 Ventura Blvd. FAX (818) 985-9836
Studio City 91604

Has one of the largest selections of 35mm cameras, both new and used, in the area. Also carries all accessories and lenses. Rents VHS and 8mm cameras, lighting, stands, and accessories. Also repairs cameras, VCRs, and camcorders. Discount for actors. Monday through Saturday, 9 am to 6 pm. See listing under VIDEO CAMERA RENTAL in this section for further information.

NEXT COM (310) 360-1000 (800) 444-4544
1022 S. La Cienega Blvd. FAX (310) 360-5000
Los Angeles 90035
www.nextcom.net

A communications company providing phone systems, network, and Internet solutions to businesses in the greater Los Angeles area. Founded in 1969, Nextcom is regarded as one of the oldest and most reputable "interconnects." Nextcom specializes in the design, integration, installation, and maintenance of digital key telephones, digital voice/data hybrid, voice mail, and PBX systems. Monday through Friday, 9 am to 5:30 pm.

OFFICE ELECTRONICS (310) 470-5918
8592 Venice Blvd. FAX (310) 470-3943
Los Angeles 90034

Carries phone equipment and answering machines including Code-A-Phone, Panasonic, Phone-Mate, Record-A-Call, Sanyo, Sony, and Takachiho to rent, own or buy. Also carries fax machines and has a service department. Monday through Friday, 8:30 am to 5:30 pm.

PHONESUSA (310) 445-3100
8592 Venice Blvd. FAX (310) 445-1101
Los Angeles 90034
www.phonesusa.com

Specializes in cellular headsets, voice mail, cordless phones, low-cost calling VoiP IVX Systems, voice recognition, answering machines, voice and data cabling, silent call announcing, CTI – Computer Telephone Integration, remote maintenance administration, as well as business and residential phone systems. Authorized dealer for a wide range of brands. Also has a service department. Monday through Friday, 9 am to 5 pm and Saturday, 10 am to 2 pm.

RADIO SHACK
A DIVISION OF TANDY CORP. (323) 464-4720
1128 La Brea Ave. FAX (323) 464-4720
Hollywood 90028

12346 Ventura Blvd. (818) 766-0046
Studio City 91604
www.radioshack.com

Has Compaq computers and accessories, plus many other electrical components including a full supply of video and DVD players, telephones, and fax machines. There are many locations throughout the Southern California area.

SAMY'S CAMERA (323) 938-2420
431 S. Fairfax FAX (323) 937-2919
Los Angeles 90036

585 Venice Blvd. (310) 450-4551
Venice 90291
www.samys.com
samys@samys.com

Rents and sells cameras of all types including video cameras. Carries complete darkroom and film supplies. Also has an electronic imaging department.

TELENET (310) 253-9000
3384 Motor Ave. FAX (310) 253-9800
Los Angeles 90034

Has phone systems, voice mail systems, security systems, computer systems and networking equipment. In business for 23 years. Monday through Friday, 8:30 am to 6 pm.

TRADER JIM'S CAMERA & VIDEO (310) 390-3326
4349 Sepulveda Blvd. FAX (310) 398-5919
Culver City 90230
www.traderjims.com
sales@traderjims.com

Carries photographic and video equipment at competitive prices. Also does all film processing including B&W. Repairs available. Monday through Friday, 9 am to 6:30 pm and Saturday, 10 am to 5 pm.

VCR SERVICE LAB (818) 505-8878
11378 Ventura Blvd. FAX (818) 505-8870
Studio City 91604

Repairs 3/4" and VHS format VCRs as well as stereos and TVs. Offers a discount to actors: show SAG card and mention the WAG (Working Actor's Guide). Monday through Friday, 10 am to 4 pm and Saturday, 8 am to 1 pm.

Fax Services & Mail Boxes

For additional FAX services please see ANSWERING, CELLULAR & VOICE MAIL SERVICES and PRINTING & PHOTO COPYING in this section.

AMERICAN POST'N PARCEL (818) 761-3217
11333 Moorpark St.
Studio City 91602

Mailing and shipping center, fax, notary and packaging. Monday through Friday, 8:30 am to 6 pm and Saturday 10 am to 3 pm.

AMERICAN SHIP & PACK (818) 557-6245
3727 W. Magnolia Blvd.
Burbank 91505

Mailboxes and fax sending and receiving 24 hours.

BEVERLY HILLS MAIL BOX (310) 286-0500
9903 Santa Monica Blvd.
Beverly Hills 90212

24 hour mail box rentals, message service, mail holding and forwarding, fax. Has a mail check call-in service. Monday through Friday 9 am to 6 pm and Saturday 10 am to 3 pm.

BOX BROTHERS (323) 822-0500
8365 Santa Monica Blvd. FAX (323) 822-9405
West Hollywood 90069

16227 Victory Blvd. (818) 904-9234
Van Nuys 91601
www.boxbrothers.com

Fax service available. Also has packaging, UPS, FedEx shipping, and photo copying.

DIGITAL EXPRESS ETC. (310) 402-7528
6404 Wilshire Blvd., Ste. 105
Los Angeles 90048
www.scriptcopier.com
contactus@scriptcopier.com

Box rentals with a prestigious street address, and a suite number. No PMB or post office box designation. Receive parcels from FedEx, UPS, DHL and the post office. Copying services on site.

EFLS TOTAL COMMUNICATIONS (800) 348-0500
(800) WE-ANSWER
545 8th Ave., Ste. 401
New York, NY 10018
www.efls.net

Fax and mail service as well as a bi-coastal answering service for N.Y. and L.A. Also has 800 numbers, voice mail, and beepers.

HOLLYWOOD MAIL & MESSAGE (323) 467-5689
1626 N. Wilcox Ave. FAX (323) 467-5845
Hollywood 90028

Private mailbox rentals. Also has answering mail service, mail holding and forwarding, shipping and boxes, and fax and notary services. Monday through Friday, 9 am to 6 pm and Saturday, 10 am to 3 pm. Spanish and English available.

MAIL BOXES ETC. (818) 623-9988
13029-A Victory Blvd.
North Hollywood 91606

10061 Riverside Dr. (818) 506-4388
Toluca Lake 91602
www.mbe.com

Mailboxes and fax sending and receiving, 24 hours.

THE MAIL SHOPPE (818) 992-9233
7210 Jordan Ave. FAX (818) 703-6087
Canoga Park 91303

Offers packaging and shipping, message service, photocopying, fax, answering service, mail holding and forwarding, key duplication, and rubber stamps. Monday through Friday, 8 am to 6 pm and Saturday 9 am to 3 pm.

PERSONALLY YOURS MAILBOXES (818) 788-0777
13547 Ventura Blvd. FAX (818) 788-0758
Sherman Oaks 91403

Mailboxes, international and domestic fax service. Notary available. Monday through Friday 9:30 am to 6 pm, Saturday, 10 am to 3 pm.

THE PLOST OFFICE (818) 760-6660
12439 Magnolia Blvd. FAX (818) 760-7755
North Hollywood 91607

Offers private mail box rentals, fax, notary, photocopy, laminating, mailing supplies, business cards, and rubber stamps. They will make keys and they are an authorized UPS shipping outlet. They also perform weddings and sell confidential marriage licenses.

POST-TEL BUSINESS SERVICES (310) 828-8645
2118 Wilshire Blvd. FAX (310) 828-0427
Santa Monica 90403
www.posttel.com

A permanent Wilshire/Santa Monica address. Will receive mail and parcels and hold or forward them while you're on location, etc. Also has private voice mail lines in L.A., Beverly Hills, N.Y., San Francisco, and other major cities. Pagers, business cards, rubber stamps, packing, and shipping are available. With a mail box you receive a limited monthly quantity of free fax, copies, and notary services.

POSTAL & PACKING EMPORIUM (818) 762-5555
11288 Ventura Blvd. FAX (818) 762-5554
Studio City 91604

24 hour private mail box rentals. Also offers mail holding and forwarding, UPS, Federal Express, DHL and Airborne shipping, packaging, fax services, notary, voice mail, photocopying, typing, Western Union electronic mailing, gift wrapping, unique gifts, hand made greeting cards and unusual gift wrapping. Also carries packing cartons and office supplies. Monday through Friday, 9 am to 6 pm and Saturday, 9:30 am to 4 pm. See listings under PRINTING & PHOTOCOPYING in this section for further information.

Fax Services & Mail Boxes

REX MAIL MESSAGE SERVICE (323) 461-3127
1608 N. Cahuenga Blvd.
Hollywood 90028

Private mail boxes. Also offers UPS packaging and shipping, message service, photocopying, answering service, mail holding and forwarding, fax, and passport photos ready in 5 minutes. Their notary public will travel to you. Access hours, Monday through Friday, 9 am to 6 pm and Saturday, 9 am to 3 pm.

VILLAGE MAIL-CALL (323) 464-1300
419 N. Larchmont Blvd. FAX (323) 462-3014
Los Angeles 90004

Packaging and shipping, FedEx, UPS, fingerprinting, message service, photocopying, mail box rental, mail forwarding, fax, American Express money orders, and Money Grams, notary public, laminating, and passport pictures. Monday through Friday, 9:30 am to 5:30 pm and Saturday, 9:30 am to 1 pm.

Game Shows

Now here's a great way to make thousands of dollars a half an hour at a time. The upside is that it's nothing but fun, you don't have to be smart, plus you get nationwide exposure. The downside is that it's a short-lived gig and there are no guarantees.

As an actor, there are certain things you should know. Once you are in the Screen Actor's Guild, you're allowed to go on only three game shows in your lifetime. However, if you are not yet a member of SAG, you can appear on as many game shows as possible.

When you single out the shows you want to try out for, be sure to watch the show and know how to play the game well. They look for energetic personalities. When you go to fill out the applications, list either your current job, or the most interesting job you've ever had; don't mention the fact that you are an actor.

– Cynthia Hunter "Hollywood, Here I Come! An Insider's Guide to a Successful Acting and Modeling Career in Los Angeles."

At the time of publication, several new game shows were about to hit the air. Keep an eye on the trades for production information of new and upcoming shows.

BLIND DATE (323) 954-9424
5700 Wilshire Blvd.
Los Angeles 90036
www.blinddatetv.com

Looking for outgoing, fun loving people.

FAMILY FEUD (818) 260-5800
5800 W. Sunset Blvd.
Los Angeles 90028
www.familyfeud.com

What the producers are looking for is a family with plenty of energy, who plays well together and knows the rules of the game very well. Dressing nicely at the interview is suggested, as well as speaking clearly. Most of all, they just ask you to be yourself. Also, the more flexible you and your family are, the better—as they sometimes pick families as late as a week in advance. Family Feud tapes Fridays through Sundays, twice daily, August to February.

JEOPARDY (SYND) (310) 244-4000
Columbia Tristar TV
10202 Washington Blvd.
Culver City 90230
www.jeopardy.com

Wants the best and brightest contestants, 18 and older. You can win cash and prizes and SAG/AFTRA members are welcome. Call Monday through Friday, 10:30 am to 4:30 pm.

THE PRICE IS RIGHT (310) 255-4700
2700 Colorado
Santa Monica 90404
www.cbs.com/daytime/price/
pir@tvc.cbs.com

Wouldn't it be fun to hear Rod Roddy announce your name to "Come on Down?" If you would like to request tickets to "The Price Is Right," please send a self-addressed, stamped envelope, with a note specifying the date you would like to attend. The tickets are free and you can request a maximum of ten tickets. Call: (323) 575-2458. Contestants are chosen randomly from the audience and must be 18 years or older. SAG/AFTRA members are welcome as contestants. You can win cash and prizes.

WHEEL OF FORTUNE (310) 244-4000
10202 West Washington Blvd.
Robert Young Bldg., Ste. 2000
Culver City 90232

They are looking for high energy, outgoing contestants. SAG/AFTRA members are welcome. Applicants must play the game well and contestants can win cash and prizes. Call Monday through Friday, 10 am to 6 pm. To become a contestant, send a postcard.

WHO WANTS TO BE A MILLIONAIRE? (212) 479-7755
30 West 67th St.
New York, NY 10009
www.millionairetv.com

Get on the most popular game show in the world!

CELEBRITY COSMETICS **(323) 466-3100**
1952 Van Ness Ave.
Los Angeles 90068
www.joycelyne.com
jlew@joycelyn.com

Image and make-up consultant. Also does wardrobe consultations, color work and personal wardrobe shopping to help create your own personal style and image. Does studio consultations and has an image consulting salon. By appointment only. Accepts all credit cards. See listing under MAKE-UP ARTISTS in this section for further information.

JUNE CHANDLER'S ACTORS WORKSHOP **(626) 355-4572**
www.junechandler.com
june@junechandler.com

June Chandler's Actors Workshop offers a six week Actors Image Workshop. This course will help you identify your casting and polish your packaging to go to market. There is image consulting by Industry experts on make-up, color, hair, skin care and wardrobe. Commercial print modeling is also covered thoroughly by top print agents. On-camera exercises teach camera technique and help with confidence and presence. The course concludes with a discounted photo shoot by well known photographers. The course is very personalized and enrollment is limited. SEE ADS ON PAGES 1 & 43.

SAM CHRISTENSEN STUDIOS **(818) 506-0783**
10440 Burbank Blvd. **FAX (818) 506-8941**
North Hollywood 91601
www.samchristensen.com
scsimage@aol.com

Specializes in image definition, marketing and career planning for actors. Mr. Christensen has advised major agencies and management companies and offers classes and private consultation for actors wishing to advance their professional standing.

COLOR COMPANY **(818) 760-7798**
www.jillkirschcolor.com
jkirsch@jillkirschcolor.com

Jill Kirsch comes to your home, office, or set and drapes you with all possible colors and picks out the colors that are best for you and makes a chart for you to carry. She works with actors helping them to choose the right colors to dramatically enhance their on-camera appearance. She not only finds colors which make you shine, but will help you find what colors work for different types of character work. Named best color consultant in Los Angeles Magazine. Also does makeup. Many celebrities consult her before attending red carpet ceremonies.

HOLLYWOOD, HERE I COME **(800) 437-3267**
CYNTHIA HUNTER **(800) 4-DREAMS**
P.O. Box 93335
Hollywood 90093
www.hollywoodhereicome.com

Don't just land an agent, get an entire career plan. Cynthia Hunter, CBS Television Star and author of the #1 selling acting and modeling book in the world has designed a mentoring program with all the information necessary for success. Learn from Irwin Award Winner for Best How To Book: Developing an image that sizzles, targeting the shows you are right for, pitching yourself with the 15 second elevator speech, how to approach agents and land the one of your dreams. A full career plan for two hours $125.00. "I took your advice and landed on Desperate Housewives. I'm having a blast, I can't thank you enough for helping me find my way."—Diane Kitchen

KATHY MARSHALL
CERTIFIED IMAGE CONSULTANT **(310) 540-3460**
553 N. Pacific Coast Highway, Ste. 218
Redondo Beach 90277

A professional color analyst. Also offers computer body analysis, make-up lessons, interview technique, personal image enhancement, and wardrobe consulting. By appointment only.

STAR MANAGER IMAGE PRINCIPLES **(310) 273-6508**
280 South Beverly Dr., #203 **FAX (310) 273-6728**
Beverly Hills 90212
www.monroyentertainment.com
comments@monroyentertainment.com

Star Manager Jaime Monroy uses his "Image Principles" to teach actors how to use their talent to market their image. Learn secrets and hear tips on how to stand out and discover your gifts; how to make better use of the money you invest in your career and overcome obstacles you're not aware of.

PERSONAL IMAGE CONCEPTS **(818) 905-0166** **(800) 273-4331**
Sherman Oaks

Guides you toward a personal as well as professional actor's image that will get you work. Sixth generation of an unbroken line of actors, Ms. Gyl Roland has 19 years of experience as a certified image consultant and is past president of the Los Angeles Chapter of The Association of Image Consultants International (AICI). Style classes available once a month. Call for more information.

MARY ROTHSCHILD **(310) 453-0254**
hroth996@aol.com

An image consultant who works on the total look, color, style, make-up and design. Also offers wardrobe consultations, shopping excursions and photo consultations. Will travel to locations.

SARI SHAPIRO, IMAGE CONSULTANT **(310) 575-4154**
FAX (310) 575-4154

Will review and analyze the items you have created to represent yourself—your photos, resumes, bios, audio tapes, DVDs, tapes etc., to better enable you to secure theatrical and/or commercial representation. Also works with musicians.

KELI SQUIRES-TAYLOR **(323) 938-7729**
6056 Whitworth Dr.
Los Angeles 90019
www.actorsuccess.net
kst1management@earthlink.net

Special marketing for actors. Personal Manager Keli Squires-Taylor works with all acting levels to give honest marketing evaluations, marketing guidance and business advice to help you move on up to the next level(s) quickly.

SUCCEEDING IN L.A. **(323) 658-6378**
FAX (323) 658-5730

Susan Goldstein, Producer/Personal Manager/Publicist and career coach has given her seminar on actors marketing themselves in L.A. and New York. She works with actors on a one-to-one basis and teaches them how to promote themselves and their project. She has spoken at several universities, Women in Film, and the DGA, SAG Conservatory and several film festivals. She is currently working as a career coach to actors and filmmakers and has represented films as a publicist at the Sundance and Hamptons Film Festivals. Her clients have starred in film, television, theatre and the internet.

MAKE-UP ARTISTS & CONSULTANTS

Although the make-up artists and hair stylists union will not make specific referrals, they will make a list of make-up artists/hair stylists available. The union can be reached at (818) 295-3933.

SUZETTE ANDREA (818) 415-7697
11271 Ventura Blvd., #169
Studio City 91604
www.suzetteandrea.com
suzette@suzetteandrea.com

Journeyman makeup artist and theatrical hair designer. Makeup artist for the stars and can make you and/or your clients look like stars also. Professionally trained for film, photo shoots, TV, modeling, actors' headshots: hair styling from all periods, beauty application: facial analysis, corrective makeup, rejuvenation makeup, natural beauty techniques, fashion beauty techniques, fantasy makeup, and makeup design. Character makeup: prosthetic application, aging techniques, bald cap application, hair piece application, injury simulation, cuts, bruises, burns, and character conceptualization. See website for resume, celebrities, and photos.

AWARD STUDIOS (310) 395-2779
www.aawd.net

Free photo sessions with experienced photographer, Amy Ward. She works internationally with Vogue, Vanity Fair, etc. Ms. Ward also trains make-up artists and they need actors and models with clear skin to work on for their portfolios. To find out more about this opportunity, call or visit the website.

DALE BACH (310) 614-2414
Santa Monica FAX (310) 452-0714

IATSE Two Emmy nominations. Available to do make-up for actor headshots, etc.

BIANCA BLYTH BEAUTY (323) 549-3100
5225 Wilshire Blvd., Ste. 620
Los Angeles 90036
www.beautyandphoto.com

Make-up artist agent.

JUNE BRICKMAN MAKEUP MATTERS (818) 225-1103

June does make-up for headshots as well as for print, film and TV. She is a licensed cosmetologist.

JENNI BROWN (310) 694-0199

Film, print, video, make-up and brow expert. Available for headshots, will travel to location. Will give makeup lessons. Union.

MICHAEL BURNETT (818) 768-6103
P.O. Box 16627 FAX (818) 768-6136
North Hollywood 91615
www.mbpfx.com

Special make-up effects.

CELEBRITY COSMETICS (323) 466-3100
1952 N. Van Ness Ave.
Los Angeles 90068
www.joycelyne.com
jlew@joycelyne.com

Image and make-up consultant. Does make-up for headshots, TV, video, film, stage, fashion, corrective, make-overs, and period styles. Has own line of cosmetics, and wigs, cuts and styles hair and wigs, and travels to locations. By appointment only. Accepts all credit cards. See listing under IMAGE CONSULTANTS in this section for further information.

CELESTINE AGENCY (310) 998-1977
1666 20th St., Ste. 200B FAX (310) 998-1978
Santa Monica 90404

Represents make-up artists.

JOANNE CERVELLI (310) 395-7770

A make-up artist working in all media. She is a licensed cosmetologist, can make prosthetics, and will travel to locations.

CINEMA SECRETS (818) 846-0579
4400 Riverside Dr. FAX (818) 846-0431
Burbank 91505
www.cinemasecrets.com
cinemasecretsinfo@cinemasecrets.com

Carries their own line of make-up that is formulated for the camera. They also have staff make-up artists available for private sessions at their facility...helpful for photo shoots or awards banquets, etc. See listings under PROFESSIONAL MAKE-UP in this section and under MAKE-UP in the TRAINING section for further information.

CLOUTIER AGENCY (310) 394-8813
1026 Montana Ave.
Santa Monica 90403
www.cloutieragency.com

Hair, make-up, and wardrobe stylists.

COLOR COMPANY (818) 760-7798
www.jillkirshcolor.com
jkirsch@jillkirschcolor.com

Jill is a color specialist and has designed a line of makeup that is based around the right shades for your hair color and skin tone. She can teach you to apply the right colors for you. Many celebrities regularly consult her before red carpet appearances.

COLOR CREATE MAKEUP STUDIO (818) 985-9613

Full service product line. Makeup application for every occasion. Treva Shelley does make-up and hair styling for headshots, special appearances and auditions. Eyebrow styling. Lessons available.

CHARLENE DEL GAUDIO (818) 559-3236

Charlene is a professionally trained make-up artist specializing in make-up for headshot photography. She has worked with many of the top LA headshot photographers. A promotional card with examples of her work is available on request.

DINAIR AIR BRUSH
MAKEUP SYSTEMS, INC. (818) 780-4777
5315 Laurel Cyn. Blvd., Ste. 201
North Hollywood 91607
www.dinair.com

Manufactures air brush make-up air brushes, compressors and equipment and has a school where they teach air brush makeup application. It's fast, flawless, sanitary, and works for the high definition TV that's going to take sheer make-up to work. They also have Glamour and Fantasy make-up and stencils.

MONICA DIVENTI (310) 450-4160

Hair and make-up.

Make-Up Artists & Consultants

FACE TO FACE (323) 913-0312
P.O. Box 39875
Los Angeles 90039

Over 27 years Film, TV and print experience for make-up artistry and hairstyling. Union member.

KATHERINE MILES KELLY (818) 988-7038

Corrective make-up, beauty make-up, and natural make-up (no makeup look.) Also airbrushing and blood and guts.

MARY JO FORTIN (310) 457-6446
29500 Heathercliff Rd., Ste. 214
Malibu 90265

Mostly does hair for union films.

KELCEY FRY (323) 913-0312 (818) 469-0024

A full make-up, hair styling service. Fry works on TV, full feature films and commercials. Does headshots and has over 15 years in the business.

MICHELLE GARBIN (323) 464-1287 (818) 608 0053 FAX (310) 376-0179

Award winning make-up artist. Commercials, film, TV, print. Personal makeup artist for Claudia Christian. Reel and portfolio available. Also a body make-up artist.

MONIQUE HAHN (626) 676-1389 (323) 664-8685
www.moniquemakeup.com
moniquehahn@yahoo.com

Specializes in make-up and hair in all mediums. She is mobile, personable, and reliable, with a great attitude. Does beauty and character make-up and light hairstyling.

LISA HANS (310) 479-2298

Make-up for film, print, video, headshots, and special effects. Will travel to locations. Also does hair.

VALERIE JOSLIA (310) 459-8917

Prefers to work mostly on commercials and specializes in beauty, glamour and fantasy, with some special effects.

JENNIFER LEONARDINI (818) 400-2415
jclmakeup@yahoo.com

Make-up artist for actor's headshots. Will travel to location.

SHERRIE LONG (213) 302-0313
740 N. Alfred St., #202
West Hollywood 90069
sherrielongmakeup@email.com

Makeup and hair for all purposes: photography, film, TV, video, stage and personal. She has been doing makeup and hair for 10 years and does everything from straight makeup, to makeup effects. She also does custom blended makeup, is very professional and sanitary and prides herself in providing the best possible makeup imaginable. Ms. Long comes to you, studio, location, or your home or office. Call to see portfolio and price list.

KERI LYNN MAKEUP (714) 615-2879
www.kerilynnmakeup.com
keri@kerilynnmakeup.com

Portfolio, headshot, media, glamour and bridal.

M.M. GERTZ ENTERTAINMENT (310) 497-7212
3940 Laurel Canyon Blvd., # 222
Studio City 91604
bam411@juno.com

Representing make-up hair and fashion designers.

MAKE-UP ARTISTRY BY PAMELA (818) 519-8405

Specializing in photography, zed cards, film, video, bridal, etc.

MAKE UP BY JC (323) 791-9449
1023 New York Dr.
Altadena 91001
www.makeupbyjc.com
jc@ma2ra.com

Need to look like you, not the make up? JC has 20 years experience and is a veteran of editorial, fashion and TV commercial makeup. Men also need a good grooming to look their best for any photo or video shoot. Checkout the website for a partial sample of his work.

MAKE-UP DESIGNORY (818) 729-9420
129 S. San Fernando Blvd.
Burbank 91502
www.makeupschool.com

Beauty and character make-up, special make-up, special make-up effects. Over thirty years in the business. Modern lab facilities. Gelatin and foam prosthetics. Affordable. Production budget consideration.

MAKEMUP! (818) 241-4685

Freelance make-up and hair artist for commercials, TV and print.

MAKEUP BY SHAWN (323) 856-6105
www.makeupbyshawn.com
shawn2005@verizon.net

Shawn is a professional Makeup Artist with over 15 years experience in all medias. Her warm personality equals her artistic talent and her artistic skills in makeup application help you look your best. Photography, commercials, video, film junkets, Bridal. Free makeup lesson on website.

MAKEUPWERKS (888) 245-4793 (323) 937-9095
5850 W. 3rd St., #207
Los Angeles 90036
www.makeupwerks.com
tania@makeupwerks.com

Portfolio and resume of Los Angeles based makeup artist Tania D. Russell. Providing makeup, hair and men's grooming. Available nationwide.

JENNIFER MANN (310) 291-7593

Headshot make-up as well as fashion, beauty, TV, film and print.

Make-Up Artists & Consultants

REX, INC. **(323) 664-6494**
4446 Ambrose Ave. **FAX (323) 664-6112**
Los Angeles 90027
www.therexagency.com

Represents make-up artists, wardrobe consultants, hair stylists and photographers.

LISA RUCKH **(323) 467-4267**
www.beautybylisa.com

Freelance hair and make-up artist for print, television, commercials and music video. Also specializing in make-up effects, tattoo and body painting and wigs.

ROBERT RYAN **(310) 864-6936**
149 S. Barrington #658
Los Angeles 90049

Headshot make-up for film, TV, print, commercials and some hair.

P.J. STEIER MAKE-UP ARTIST **(323) 662-6044**

Make-up for film, video, fashion, stage, headshots, and print. Also gives make-up lessons. She has worked for People Magazine, Hello, Sony, Comedy Central and TV Guide as a make-up artist and does celebrity make-up for the talk show circuit nationally and internationally. Also does weddings. Hair styling available.

STUDIO MAKEUP ACADEMY **(323) 465-4002**
1438 N. Gower #14
Hollywood 90028
www.studiomakeupacademy.com

The Studio Makeup Academy is the only school in the world located inside a major film and television studio. The Academy provides the essential training needed to become a professional makeup artist in the entertainment and beauty industries. The Beauty Makeup Artist Course class covers all phases of beauty makeup, Basic Commercial Beauty Makeup, Basic Principles of Photographic Makeup, Makeup for Black and White Photography, Makeup for Color Photography, etc. The Film and Television Special Effect Course covers Makeup for Video and Film – Motion Pictures, Television, Video and Stage Special Effects and Face Casting for Prosthetic Makeup.

SUGANO **(323) 663-0414**

Specializes in make-up, hair, barbering, and wig designs. Will travel to locations. Specializing in historical and/or period looks.

PEG THIELEN **(818) 506-6161**

Freelance make-up artist available for TV, commercials or print.

VANITY MAKE-UP STUDIO **(323) 658-9020**
(323) 654-6377
708 N. Gardner (at Melrose)
Los Angeles 90036
www.vanitymakeupstudio.com

Mary Brando and Paule McKenna have been specializing in beauty make-up for men and women since 1985. Will also teach actors how to do their own make-up. Specializing in photography makeup.

ANGIE WELLS GERTZ **(310) 497-7212**
www.angiewells.com
bam411@juno.com

Angie Wells will do headshots. Please see her work on the website and her resume on the IMDB. She is a journeyman with IATSE Local 706 and a member of the Academy of Television Arts and Sciences. Specialties include beauty, special effects, poor skin, eyes and brows, custom foundations, and cutting edge fashion makeup. Angie has worked internationally for 17 years. In addition to her extensive film and television credits, she has worked on music videos and her recent commercial and print work includes, Chrysler Corporation, Pavement Magazine, Incite Magazine, High Street Emporium, Beverly Hills Magazine and Savoy Magazine.

ADAM WINTER **(818) 795-4584**
awinter_makeup@yahoo.com

Adam does a great job and is extremely personable. He will travel to location and his rates are very reasonable.

VERA YURTCHUK **(818) 884-0517**

Freelance make-up artist.

Marketing Info & Consultants

ACT NOW! **(818) 285-8522**
14140 Ventura Blvd., Ste. 2
Sherman Oaks 91423
www.actnownetwork.com
actnow4u@aol.com

Act Now! is a networking company that was established with the intention of helping actors further their careers, by meeting and performing for Industry professionals including casting directors, directors and agents. Staff provides ongoing guidance and support to help each actor set and meet their professional goals. Audition required.

ACTION ADVISOR **(310) 498-3410**
www.actionadvisor.net
cabulliard@hotmail.com

Action Advisor is designed to help professional actors create strategies for success. It is a bicoastal agency that specializes in helping actors take their careers to the next level by focusing on their unique marketability. Action Advisor helps you clarify your goals, create a plan of action, implement that plan and hold you accountable along the way to success and fulfillment. Private sessions are held either in person or over the phone. A complimentary session is offered. Led by MFA actors with extensive training and study in Business Strategy, Finance, Movement/Body Studies and Life Coach training.

THE ACTOR'S LAB **(310) 621-3900**
at the Odyssey Theatre
2055 South Sepulveda Blvd.
Los Angeles 90048

Offers an ongoing program to provide career guidance and to set up a personalized program for pursuing a professional career. See listing under ACTING for further information.

THE ACTOR'S OFFICE **(818) 692-0706**
15353 Weddington St., #D208
Sherman Oaks 91411
www.theactorsoffice.com

The first comprehensive software package designed exclusively for actors to help them manage and market their careers effectively while saving money. Features include: Over 650 agent and casting director addresses, track your auditions and submissions, print cover letters without a mail merge, and print postcards directly from your printer.

ACTORS CONSULTATION SERVICES (ACS) **(310) 828-7814**
2461 Santa Monica Blvd., #322 **FAX (310) 998-9114**
Santa Monica 90404
www.actorsconsultations.com
jill@actorsconsultations.com

Jill Jaress, career consultant and coach, specializes in teaching new actors how to break into the business and working actors how to increase the number and quality of their bookings. Private consultations are one hour and can be conducted either on the phone or in person. Additionally, private coaching is available, especially for audition preparation.

ACTORS PROMO CD **(310) 770-6376**
P.O. Box 974
Beverly Hills 90213
www.actorspromocd.com
david@imediastudios.com

A great marketing tool for actors: the Promo CD contains a demo reel, headshot, resume, a picture gallery and the actor's contact information. Every interactive CD is specifically designed for the individual actor and provides Casting Directors, Agents, Producers, and Directors with instant access to all the information they need.

ACTORS PROMOTIONAL SERVICES, LTD.
ROCK RIDDLE **(323) 462-2777**
6464 Sunset Blvd., Ste. 750
Los Angeles 90028
www.hollywoodsuccess.com
actingwork@aol.com

Advertising, marketing, networking, and promotion for writers, actors, producers, and directors. Also designs resumes. They prefer actors with co-star credits and carry maximum of 100 actors. Has monthly mixers with various Industry people, produces TV series and pilots, and they package and acquire financing for various projects. By appointment only.

ACTORS WEBMASTER **(818) 763-9991**
11684 Ventura Blvd., #999
Studio City 91604
www.actorswebmaster.com
ellen@actorswebmaster.com

Complete web site design and hosting (free updates) service specializing in actors.

THE ACTORS' NETWORK **(818) 509-1010**
11684 Ventura Blvd. **FAX (818) 509-0646**
Studio City 91604
www.actors-network.com
info@actors-network.com

Where the serious actor does business. A business networking group for pro-active actors offering a two-studio space of information and resources regarding auditions, projects, Industry players, and scams. Membership also offers actor Trades, periodicals, an in-house resource library, weekly Industry topical discussions, special guests, networking activities, and four monthly guest speakers which include agents, casting directors, managers, producers, and directors. The Actors' Network assists with an actors' game plan by creating and developing first short term then long term goals. Free monthly orientations. This is not an acting class or CD workshop. $50 per month with a 4 month minimum. Reservations only, limited seating. If possible, checkout the website before calling.

BREAKDOWN SERVICES **(310) 276-9166**
2140 Cotner Ave.
Los Angeles 90025
www.breakdownservices.com

Offers many services for actors including Agents Listing published twice a year and Casting Director Listings published 3 times a year with an update mailed every 2 weeks. Also has self-adhesive mailing labels of L.A. and New York SAG franchised agents and casting directors for sale which are updated constantly. Their Go-Between is a personal messenger service that hand delivers announcements and invitations to every feature film and TV casting director, and every network series producer in L.A. within 72 hours. They also have a service that delivers flyers for 99 Seat Plan productions to agents and personal managers and they will do mailings to advertise a business.

THE CASTING NETWORK
COLD READING/AUDITION WORKSHOP
MARCIA MORAN **(818) 788-4792**
12500 Riverside Dr., Ste. 202 **FAX (818) 986-3311**
Studio City 91604
www.castingnetwork.net
castingnetwork@earthlink.net

Bringing Industry professionals together since 1988. Offers an opportunity to perform (cold reading and/or prepared scenes) for L.A.'s busiest casting directors, agents, producers and directors in a relaxed, non-competitive atmosphere. Their guests offer invaluable inside information. The experienced, trained staff shows the student realistic ways to get connected and/or jump-start his/her career at no cost. Low discount prices. Call for current schedule or visit the website. A great opportunity to work out your audition muscle with other professional actors. Guests offer valuable information on the audition process.

SAM CHRISTENSEN STUDIOS (SCS) **(818) 506-0783**
10440 Burbank Blvd. **FAX (818) 506-8941**
North Hollywood 91601
www.samchristensen.com
scsimage@aol.com

Specializes in image definition, marketing, and career planning for actors. Mr. Christensen advises major agencies and management companies and offers classes and private consultation for actors wishing to advance their professional standing. Easy parking.

CLUB BEVERLY HILLS **(310) 274-6051**
8306 Wilshire Blvd., #279 **FAX (310) 274-7855**
Beverly Hills 90211
www.club-beverlyhills.com
dreams@club-beverlyhills.com

Designs a strategy for the actor, customizes it, and plans a schedule. The strategy is monitored as it progresses while Club Beverly Hills assists with networking. Packaging for film distribution and TV.

Image packaging for actors. See listing under PHOTOGRAPHERS in this section for further information.

COMMUNITY ARTS RESOURCES (CARS) DATABASE SERVICES **(213) 365-0605**
3780 Wilshire Blvd., Ste. 1020
Los Angeles 90010
www.communityartsla.com
mail@carsla.net

Mailing list rentals are available to generate audiences for productions or showcases. The CARS' Database of over 80,000 names is made up of a younger ticket-buying audience that goes to a variety of music, comedy, and theatrical events, etc. Features numerous cross-referencing capabilities to help performers and producers reach the audience they need.

DEVORAH CUTLER-RUBENSTEIN NOBLE HOUSE ENTERTAINMENT **(310) 943-4378**
12210½ Nebraska Ave, Ste. 22
Los Angeles 90025
www.thescriptbroker.com
devo@thescriptbroker.com

Private and group coaching and career counseling for acting and life. Overcoming fear, communication skills, career strategies, and creating a successful life and career plan.

LISA DALTON: LIFE, CAREER & NETWORKING CONSULTATIONS **(818) 761-5404**
www.chekhov.net
chekhov@earthlink.net

Lisa offers guidance on all aspects of the Industry for new and experienced actors ranging from techniques for self promotion, interview and networking skills, how to get set up in Los Angeles, budget for living and developing resume, getting tape, joining unions, etc. Need help coping with the Industry, with maintaining a day job, finding the right classes or a supportive environment, missing family, etc.? Lisa Dalton is a skillful counselor in addition to her vast knowledge of the entertainment Industry and has a gentle way of guiding you into feeling wonderful about your love of the Industry and how to use that as a practical tool for happiness, health and success. $75/90 minute sessions. Certified Results Coach, NLP, Hypnosis. See listing under ACTING in this section for further information.

WAYNE DVORAK **(323) 462-5328**
1949 Hillhurst Ave.
Los Angeles 90027
www.actingcoachdvorak.com

Mr. Dvorak manages and coaches his acting clients using the Meisner technique which is organic foundation work. He has ongoing Industry showcasing at the professional level, and brings several agents each year to see his clients. He offers highly professional career development which includes image consultation for members of the company. Everything in-house.

EWORLD PARTNERS **(213) 715-6161**
1901 Granville Ave.
Los Angeles 90025
www.eworldpartners.com
amanda@eworldpartners.com

Introducing eWorld Business Cards for online email marketing. Send your photo, resume, audio and video demos tapes, press releases and more through your email, all connected to a personalized business card. No attachments, downloads or big email files. All of your information sits on their server and has a link on your business card. Save money on mailings, photo reproductions, video duplications and more. Free basic design, updates and changes for $9.95 per month with the first month free.

SAMUEL FRENCH THEATRE & FILM BOOKSHOPS **(323) 876-0570**
7623 Sunset Blvd. **FAX (323) 876-6822**
Los Angeles 90046

11963 Ventura Blvd. **(818) 762-0535**
Studio City 91604
www.samuelfrench.com
samuelfrench@earthlink.net

Operated by Samuel French, Inc., the world's oldest play publisher. The Samuel French Bookshops contain the largest selection of plays available in the world including plays published by Samuel French, Baker, Dramatist, Methuen, Grove, etc. Also carries a full selection of books on every aspect of film, theatre, the performing arts, and the Motion Picture Industry. Their wide range of titles includes books on acting, directing, music, theatre craft, history and theory, business of film, Industry directories, screenwriting, screenplays, animation, special effects, make-up, costume, cinematography, video, television, radio, and much more. Also available are dialect tapes, vocal selections, casting directories and labels, T-shirts, and mugs. They have a knowledgeable and professional staff. There is a royalty department for licensing amateur and professional productions. World-wide mail order (Visa, MC, AM EX, Discover), fax or email. Samuel French Basic Play Catalogue and Supplement ($5.00 postpaid), also subject book catalogues (acting, monologues and scenes, screenwriting, film Industry, etc.) available free on request. SEE AD ON THE WORKING TAB & PAGE 201.

GMA MARKETING CONCEPTS **(310) 921-6004**
www.getmoreauditions.com
gmamarketing@aol.com

GMA Marketing Concepts (GetMoreAuditions.com) is a headshot submission service, submitting client's headshots to major casting notices and casting directors every week for a low, affordable weekly fee. Over 90% of their clients have booked auditions and/or jobs. Projects their clients have booked and/or auditioned for include: West Wing, CSI: Miami, ER, The Shield, Alias, Without A Trace, CSI: NY, NBC and CBS pilots, House of Sand and Fog, Planet of the Apes, General Hospital, Days Of Our Lives, Passions, Young And Restless, several national commercials (Taco Bell, Doritos, Hertz, Chevrolet, Ford, Amazon.com) and numerous independent, graduate and student films. GMA also supplies clients with a detailed report listing all submissions. GMA was founded in 1997 and is a proud member of the Better Business Bureau.

KIMBERLY JENTZEN **(818) 779-7770**
P.O. Box 4554 **FAX (818) 779-1171**
Valley Village 91617
www.kimberlyjentzen.com
filmactors@aol.com

With an MA in Spiritual Psychology, Kimberly Jentzen teaches the Essence Weekend Intensive, which supports actors with tools on handling the emotional roller coaster of the profession and addresses the challenges in the development of becoming and/or being an artist. SEE AD ON PAGE 1.

MODIFIED STUDIOS (310) 562-1961
www.modifiedstudios.com
greg@modifiedstudios.com

Offers quality graphic and web design services at an actor's rate. Specializing in websites, resumes, zed cards and any marketing materials.

MY DESIGN STUDIO (888) 52-DESIGN (888) 523-3744
www.mydesignprimer.com

My design studio is an advertising services company that works with clients, on an as needed basis, to produce effective marketing materials and collaterals.

LAUREN PATRICE NADLER (818) 202-0774

A bi-coastal director, coach, consultant and casting director, who cast Adrian Brody (Oscar Winner for Best Actor in 2003) in his first lead role, and has coached countless actors towards successful career choices. Originally from New York, Lauren has planted her roots in Los Angeles to share her years of experience. She believes that dynamic, creative and truthful work is key but knowing your way around and how to communicate effectively in the professional arena is crucial. Lauren helps blend your business and art, validating personal accomplishments to help use them to your advantage. Lauren starts by setting up a comprehensive plan of action to move your career beyond the point it is already at. Lauren also teaches acting classes and runs workshops for serious minded, committed actors who want to enhance their creativity level. Lauren, who is currently in preparation to direct several film projects is available for private coaching, on-set coaching, career counseling and directing projects.

THE PUBLICITY COACH (818) 995-8130
P.O. Box 57498
Sherman Oaks 91413
www.hollywoodpublicity.com
vickiarthur@juno.com

One-on-one and group coaching in publicity, promotion, advertising, marketing, and networking for actors, producers, authors, writers and directors who want to propel their career to the next level and beyond. A top Hollywood publicist for over twenty years, Vicki brings winning strategies in an affordable and highly focused service. She specializes in coaching new working actors and other entertainment professionals who want to achieve their goals and accelerate the process.

SAGE MARKETING (310) 234-0116
2140 Westwood Blvd., #213 FAX (310) 234-0117
Los Angeles 90025
www.sage-la.com
info@sage-la

Works with new faces as well as seasoned veterans to assist them in obtaining representation and auditions through a direct mailing service. Sage provides resume and cover letter services, monthly mass-mailing services. "There is only one company in this Industry that gives actors that much needed edge – Sage. Sage not only provides you with the tools you need to succeed, they provide you with the confidence it takes to stay in the business. Whether it is helping you by guiding your career, giving you advice on running your business, or getting you exposed to the right people, Sage is a highly effective tool in the acting market place. An aspiring actor really can't afford to be without the most productive and efficient tool in the Industry. Personally, Sage has helped me acquire theatrical and commercial representation in the last month. I highly recommend Sage to anyone who is serious about the business of acting."—Kim Estes, actor

SMART GIRLS PRODUCTIONS (818) 907-6511
15030 Ventura Blvd., #914 FAX (818) 990-5293
Sherman Oaks 91403
www.smartg.com
smartgirls@smartg.com

Since 1992 Smart Girls has assisted over 4000 actors at all stages of their careers in getting representation with agents and managers and in increasing their number of casting calls. They specialize in composing personalized cover letter mailings and handpicking agents and managers appropriate for you, jazzing up resumes, and creating interesting postcard messages to casting directors for current TV shows, films, and commercials. Starting at under $195 and maintaining an 80% success rate, Smart Girls mailings are a great way for you to create opportunities for yourself to be cast. They also offer Career Plans which include mailings and strategy sessions focused on expanding your confidence, presence, and success in the Industry. Call for a free catalog of services for actors and screenwriters and your very own Lucky Pen! SEE AD ON PAGE 177.

KELI SQUIRES-TAYLOR (323) 938-7729
6056 Whitworth Dr.
Los Angeles 90019
www.actorsuccess.net
kst1management@earthlink.net

Special marketing for actors. Personal Manager Keli Squires-Taylor works with all acting levels to give honest marketing evaluations, marketing guidance and business advice to help you move on up to the next level(s) quickly.

SUCCEEDING IN L.A. (323) 658-6378
FAX (323) 658-5730

Susan Goldstein, Producer/Personal Manager/Publicist and career coach has given her seminar on actors marketing themselves in L.A. and New York. She works with actors on a one-to-one basis and teaches them how to promote themselves and their project. She has spoken at several universities, Women in Film, and the DGA, SAG Conservatory and several film festivals. She is currently working as a career coach to actors and filmmakers and has represented films as a publicist at the Sundance and Hamptons Film Festivals. Her clients have starred in film, television, theatre and the internet.

THE KIDS HOLLYWOOD CONNECTION (949) 851-0920
1151 Dove St., Ste. 225 FAX (949) 851-1902
Newport Beach 92660
www.kidshollywood.com
talent@kidshollywood.com

Consulting agency helping guide and direct parents to place children with top SAG agents.

TVI ACTORS STUDIO (818) 784-6500
14429 Ventura Blvd., Ste. 118 FAX (818) 784-6533
Sherman Oaks 91423
www.tvistudios.com

Founded in 1986, with studios in Los Angeles, New York and Chicago, TVI is a source center for actors, offering dramatic instruction, entertainment Industry networking, professional career consultation and marketing support for actors. TVI teaches actors the Business of Acting with a practical, no-nonsense approach to marketing and promoting yourself as a working actor in a highly competitive marketplace. In addition to a diverse curriculum of courses taught by leading Industry professionals, TVI provides members with free benefits, including daily free casting director workshops, resume and cover letter consultation with updates as often as you like, mailing labels, one-on-one counseling, use of studio space, and computer workstations with Internet access, all designed to refine the actor's craft, empower the actor with a well-rounded knowledge of the business, and clearly defined career strategy, and maximize an actor's potential in the marketplace.

WORK ACTOR WORK! **(323) 225-1962**
aktorchick@aol.com

Services include advice on resume composition, proven letters to agents, photo resume, etc., and personalized labels for agents, casting directors, managers, and producers. Now offering consultations.

GERRIE WORMSER **(310) 277-3281**
2160 Century Park East
Los Angeles 90067

A consulting service. Meet in her office for an hour, bring pictures, resume, and any other marketing materials including tapes, film, and reviews and she will advise on all aspects of career, agents, managers, casting directors, pictures, and projects. You may continue to consult with her on the phone for no additional fee. Should you desire another in-person consultation, another fee is charged. Ms. Wormser is currently a casting director. $100 one-time fee.

Messenger Services

ABSOLUTE MESSENGER **(818) 999-4950**

Same day service, daily, weekly and round-trip specials. Credit cards accepted.

ACTION MESSENGER SERVICE **(323) 654-2333**
(800) 474-2587
P.O. Box 69763 **FAX (323) 654-8889**
Los Angeles 90069
www.actionmessenger.com
info@actionmessenger.com

Offers 3 types of service: Regular: pick-up is within 30 minutes and delivery is made within 2 hours. Exclusive: Pick-up is within 30 minutes, delivery is non-stop to destination and upon delivery they call sender with the name of the person who received delivery and the time of delivery. Economy: Pick-up is within 30 minutes, delivery within 4 hours. Uniformed drivers. Radio dispatched. Daily, 24 hours. Call for further information.

ADCOM EXPRESS **(310) 216-0379**
(877) 288-4416
912 Hillcrest Dock 17-29
Inglewood 90301
www.adcomworldwide.com

Daily, 24 hours. Pick up and delivery world-wide. One hour lead time for pick ups in the Los Angeles area. International Shipping Service.

CHASE MESSENGER **(818) 623-5060**

Daily 24 hour service. The cost is determined by area and there is an extra charge for weekends and nights.

DYNAMEX **(800) 793-9284**
(714) 994-1615
16900 Valley View
La Mirada 90638
www.dynamex.com

Daily, 24 hour service. Delivers to all locations in Southern California. Two hour delivery time in Los Angeles County, and special service is available.

FIRST CLASS MESSENGER **(818) 500-9639**
San Fernando Valley

Rush deliveries, court filings, 24 hours. Accepts credit cards.

THE GO BETWEEN **(310) 276-6266**

Deliveries throughout Southern California. Offers shuttle, rush, and direct service and the cost is based on distance and time. They have a low cost subscription service for entertainment related companies.

GRAF AIR FREIGHT **(323) 461-2719**
(800) 255-6883
5811 Willoughby Ave. **FAX (323) 461-6026**
Los Angeles 90038
www.grafairfreight.com

Open 24 hours, 7 days a week since 1967. Immediate service any weight, anywhere.

MERCURY MESSENGER **(800) 845-5709**
7065-A Havenhurst Ave. **FAX (818) 989-5276**
Van Nuys 91401
www.mercurycourier.com

Serves all of southern California. 24 hour service. Special rates for scheduled runs.

MIDNIGHT EXPRESS **(888) 640-2244**
COURIERS INTERNATIONAL INC. **(800) 643-6483**
300 N. Oak St.
Inglewood 90302

24 hour service. Messenger service covering the entire Los Angeles area, Orange County, and the San Fernando Valley. Special service is available. They also offer complete shipping to all domestic and international locations and they have world-wide courier flights. They specialize in time sensitive material, offer confirmation on all deliveries, and are insured and bonded.

MOBILE MAIL BOX **(323) 969-9853**
1514 N. Formosa Ave. **FAX**
Hollywood 90046

Discounted deliveries to casting directors. Their low rates are due to

Messenger Services

their convenient drop off and delivery mail boxes throughout the L.A. Metro area. Delivery is within 6 hours of drop off.

NOW MESSENGER **(213) 473-1989**
2808 West Temple St., 1st Fl. **FAX (213) 473-1996**
Los Angeles 90026

1301 W. 2nd. St. **(213) 482-1572**
Los Angeles 90026
www.nowlegalservices.com

Rush deliveries by uniformed messengers. Daily, 24 hours.

PACIFIC EXPRESS **(213) 628-3904**
www.pacificcourier.com

Daily, 24 hour service. The cost varies, regular service is 4-6 hours, rush service is 2-4 hours, and priority is 1-2 hours. Office hours are 8 am to 5 pm daily.

ROCKET MESSENGER SERVICE INC. **(323) 469-7155** **(818) 341-9786**
www.rocketmessenger.com

24 hours every day. Same day pick up, delivery within 2-4 hours. Also offers their Rocket service with pick up within 2 hours, and the nonstop service with pick up for immediate delivery. Rates available upon request.

WEST EXPRESS MESSENGER SERVICE **(323) 466-1271**
1800 Century Park West, 6th Fl.
Los Angeles 90067

Daily, 24 hour service. Delivers to locations in the Southern California area.

WESTSIDE EXPRESS MESSENGER **(800) 207-2222**
www.westsidemessenger.com

Guaranteed delivery, state of the art computer technology, global delivery, immediate pick up. Accepts credit cards.

Musical Services: Accompanists, Composers, Arrangers, Etc.

ARTIST ONE PRODUCTIONS **(310) 664-9928**
West L.A.
rumorhasit@excelonline.com

Artist One's creative team specializes in record production, music directing and arranging and vocal production. Works with singers and singer/songwriters to develop their craft. Will collaborate on composing, songwriting, and arranging for recording, live performance, and musical theater. Services include a full digital recording studio, hiring and directing backing musicians, back up singers, musical arrangements from small ensembles to large touring bands, and providing musical direction.

BOOM CHIC STUDIOS **(323) 782-6813**
Beverly Blvd.
Los Angeles 90048
www.boomchic.com
karen@ioproductions.com

Film composer, songwriter, music production services, song demos, voice over demos, etc. Please visit website for more information.

RICHARD FRANKE **(323) 851-9785**

An arranger. He does charts and transposes quickly. Has many show tunes memorized.

JUDY GANTLEY **(310) 452-0264**

A piano accompanist for rock, show tunes, and standards. Judy will make practice tapes, help with learning music, and transpose. She also gives piano lessons.

ROBBIE GILLMAN **(818) 347-4350**
robertgillman@sbcglobal.net **FAX (818) 348-4566**

Professional composer, arranger, sight reader, and transposer will make accompaniment/learning tapes, and/or accompany you to auditions, transcribe music from records, tapes or CDs and create publishing quality computer-generated charts and lead sheets. Over 30 years experience as a vocal accompanist on piano and keyboards in all musical styles. See listing under AUDIO DEMO PRODUCTION in this section for further information.

PETER HUME **(818) 363-6281**

An independent producer/arranger specializing in customized vocal demo and song demo production. He works with singers and songwriters from novice to advanced with an emphasis on drawing out the best possible performance. All production elements are handled in his home studio. He arranges and plays all instrumental tracks including guitars, bass, keyboards, drum machine, etc. Offers vocal overdubbing, mixing, and editing. Has extensive signal processing equipment, digital reverbs, delays, etc.

BONNIE JANOFSKY **(818) 784-4466**
www.bonnieruthjanofsky.com
brjanofsky@sbcglobal.net

A composer/arranger/conductor for film, television, musical theatre, live shows. Scoring, songwriting and arrangements with live musicians and/or MIDI (synthesized) ensembles. Full MIDI/digital audio studio. Also accompanying, transcriptions and copying. By appointment.

HERB MICKMAN **(818) 990-2328**

Former musical director for Sarah Vaughn is available for singer's projects. Services include accompaniment, demo tapes, background music tapes, and lead sheets.

MUSICIANS NETWORK ADMINISTRATOR
AMERICAN FEDERATION **(323) 993-3174**
OF MUSICIANS **(323) 462-2161 x174**
817 Vine St.
Hollywood 90038
www.promusic47.org
network@promusic47.org

A musical reference source offering free coordinating services for all types of acts. Can also hire accompanists for single person performances, groups, and a variety of productions. Locates music teachers. 1000s of musicians available for side-lining.

Musical Services: Accompanists, Composers, Arrangers, Etc.

P.M. III PRODUCTIONS (818) 763-3053
www.pm3prod.com

Specializes in voice over for independent films and full musical production. ProTools HD. Mastering and CD writing. See listing under AUDIO DEMO PRODUCTION in this section for further information.

SCREENMUSIC INTERNATIONAL (818) 789-3487
18034 Ventura Blvd., Ste. 450 FAX (818) 789-5801
Encino 91316
www.screenmusic.com

Offers music productions as well as licensing, provided by award winning film and TV composers and music producers. State-of-the-art recording studios for audio post production and records.

UNIVERSITY OF CALIFORNIA LOS ANGELES (UCLA)
MUSIC DEPARTMENT (310) 825-4761
Box 951616
Los Angeles 90095-1616

Contact the Music Department for a complete list of students and faculty who are experienced accompanists.

UNIVERSITY OF SOUTHERN CALIFORNIA (USC)
KEYBOARD STUDIES (213) 821-2744
University Park FAX (213) 740-1043
Los Angeles 90089
www.usc.edu

Contact the Music Department for a complete list of students and faculty who are experienced accompanists.

Periodicals & Trade Publications

THE ACADEMY PLAYERS DIRECTORY (310) 247-3058
(310) 550-5034
1313 N. Vine
Hollywood 90028
www.playersdirectory.com

The Academy Players Directory is a casting reference known as the Industry standard since 1937. The Players Directory is published January and September as a cooperative service to the players and producers of Hollywood. The Players Directory online is updated continuously. Members of CSA and CCDA receive complimentary copies of the Players Directory. In addition, many production companies, studios and independent film companies purchase the Directory. To be in the Players Directory, actors must be a paid member of an actors union. The printed Directory lists your name, photo and representation information. The online version lists name, photo and representation as well as your resume and additional photos. The cost to be listed in the Directory is $75 per category, per year, which includes your photo in the printed version and on-line version as well as the Now Casting Electronic Submission System. There is an additional cost for extra photos in the Player's Directory Online. For further information, please contact The Academy Players Directory.

ACTING WORLD BOOKS (818) 905-1345
(800) 210-1197
P.O. Box 3899 FAX (800) 905-1345
Hollywood 90078
www.actingworldbooks.org

Publishes "The Agencies – What The Actor Needs To Know" which is updated monthly with a supplement. Available by subscription, $50 per year. Also publishes the quarterly "The Hollywood Acting Coaches and Teachers Directory" which describes the various programs, has bios of coaches, and class information. Both publications are available at Samuel French Bookshops and many other actor-frequented bookstores. "The West Coast Performers Complete Personal Managers Directory" is published quarterly and sells for $15. It lists details for over 600 personal management companies and over 1500 managers. See listing under BOOKS & TAPES in this section for further information.

ADVERTISING AGE (323) 370-2400
6500 Wilshire Blvd., Ste. 2300
Los Angeles 90048
www.adage.com

The 71-year-old flagship magazine of the Ad Age Group, a division of Crain Communications Inc.

ADWEEK (323) 525-2270
5055 Wilshire Blvd., 7th Fl. FAX (323) 525-2392
Los Angeles 90036
www.adweek.com

A weekly publication for advertising executives.

AGENTS' AGENCY
GUIDEBOOK BREAKDOWN SERVICES (310) 276-9166
2140 Cotner Ave. FAX (310) 276-8829
Los Angeles 90025
www.breakdownservices.com

Lists SAG franchised agencies and agents within agencies. Published twice yearly and may be purchased by mail or at their office. Call for prices.

AMERICAN (323) 969-4333
CINEMATOGRAPHER (ASC) (800) 448-0145
1782 North Orange Dr.
Hollywood 90028
www.cinematographer.com

A monthly publication for cinematographers and filmmakers. Available at newsstands, Samuel French, Larry Edmunds, and Waldenbooks.

AMERICAN THEATRE MAGAZINE (212) 609-5900
520 8th Ave. FAX (212) 609-5901
New York, NY 10018
www.tcg.org
tcg@tcg.org

A comprehensive coverage of the theatre scene throughout the country, and monthly schedules of plays appearing at U.S. theatres. Has complete season schedules of some 200 theatre companies, plus a special edition with A Season Overview, published every October. Published by Theatre Communications Group.

BACKSTAGE WEST
THE PERFORMING ARTS WEEKLY (323) 525-2356
5055 Wilshire Blvd., 5th Fl FAX (323) 525-2345
Los Angeles 90036
www.backstagewest.com

Lists casting information for theatre, TV, Film, and student films for the Los Angeles area as well as for San Francisco and elsewhere. Publishes regular spotlights on actors' services and features on craft and business issues. Available on Thursdays at newsstands for $2.75 in L.A. and $3.25 elsewhere, or by subscription. SEE AD ON BACK COVER.

BILLBOARD (323) 525-2300
5055 Wilshire Blvd., 7th Fl. FAX (323) 525-2394
Los Angeles 90036
www.billboard.com

A weekly trade magazine for the music Industry. Sold at newsstands.

BOX OFFICE MAGAZINE (626) 396-0250
155 S. El Molino Ave., Ste. 100 FAX (626) 396-0248
Pasadena 91101
www.boxoffice.com
boxoffice@earthlink.net

Contains advance film information and movie reviews. Also has information for theatre owners regarding current movie theatre technology. Available at major newsstands in L.A. only, or by subscription.

BREAKDOWN SERVICES, LTD
COMMERCIAL EXPRESS (310) 276-9166
2140 Cotner Ave. FAX (310) 276-8829
Los Angeles 90025
www.breakdownservices.com

Information services for talent agents.

THE CD DIRECTORY
BREAKDOWN SERVICES (310) 276-9166
2140 Cotner Ave.
Los Angeles 90025

Casting directors in Southern California are listed alphabetically and geographically with a quarterly update. Sold as a single issue or yearly subscriptions. Call for prices.

CREATIVITY (323) 651-3710
6500 Wilshire Blvd., Ste. 2300 FAX (323) 655-8157
Los Angeles 90048
www.adage.com

Creativity is the magazine that champions creative work and the people behind that work in advertising and related industries. Published ten times a year by the Advertising Age Group, it brings news, features and analysis of the worlds of advertising, production, post-production, design, photography and many other creative disciplines. Featuring pages of work, how that work was created, and profiles of the talents responsible for it, Creativity seeks to identify hot new talent and draw attention to the best work by more established names. Creativity is the forum for all issues related to creative matters in the U.S. and beyond.

DAILY VARIETY (323) 857-6600
(800) 552-3632
5700 Wilshire Blvd., Ste. 120
Los Angeles 90036
www.dailyvariety.com

A trade paper published every weekday. Has information about all aspects of the Industry. Lists film production charts on Friday and TV production charts on Thursday. Also has some casting information.

DGA MAGAZINE (310) 289-2035
(310) 289-2000
7920 Sunset Blvd. FAX (310) 289-5384
Los Angeles 90046
www.dga.org

Published bi-monthly by the Director's Guild.

THE DIRECTORY OF
THEATRE TRAINING PROGRAMS (802) 867-2223
P.O. Box 510 FAX (802) 867-0144
Dorset, VT 5251
www.theatrediretories.com

A biennial guide to theatre programs covering the entire United States and England including colleges, universities, and conservatories for both graduate and undergraduate. Available by mail order and in theatre bookstores around the country.

EMMY MAGAZINE (818) 754-2800
5220 Lankershim Blvd. FAX (818) 761-2827
North Hollywood 91601
www.emmys.org

A bi-monthly magazine that covers all aspects of the TV Industry. Available by subscription and at World Book and News in Hollywood.

EXTRA (310) 289-9400
400 S. Beverly Dr., #307 FAX (310) 277-3088
Beverly Hills 90212
hollywoodos@aol.com

Hollywood OS writes and publishes the 400+ page entertainment directory "Extra" and its quarterly magazine updates which inform and educate Los Angeles' background acting community.

FILM & VIDEO
PRODUCTION MAGAZINE (949) 251-0199
www.filmandvideomagazine.com FAX (949) 251-0809

Covers film, TV, music video, commercial production, special effects, and facilities with emphasis on the technical aspects of filmmaking. Published monthly. Available by subscription, at some newsstands, and at Samuel French Bookshops.

HOLLYWOOD CREATIVE DIRECTORY (323) 308-3490
1024 North Orange Dr. FAX (323) 308-3492
Hollywood 90038

5055 Wilshire Blvd. (800) 815-0503
Los Angeles 90036
www.hcdonline.com
hcd@hcdonline.com

Publishes directories for the Industry including "The Hollywood Creative Directory," "The Hollywood Representation Directory (Agents and Managers)" and "The Hollywood Distributors Directory." These comprehensive, frequently updated reference books are available at major bookstores. Also available: directories for Below the Line Talent, Film Composers, Film Actors, Film Writers, Film Directors.

HOLLYWOOD REPORTER (323) 525-2000
5055 Wilshire Blvd., Ste. 600 FAX (323) 525-2377
Los Angeles 90036
www.hollywoodreporter.com

An Industry trade paper published every weekday. Has information regarding every aspect of the Industry with motion picture production charts listed every Tuesday and TV production charts listed the 1st and 3rd Tuesday of every month.

KID SHOWBIZ MAGAZINE (973) 207-2515
P. O. Box 193 FAX (201) 221-8020
Cedar Knolls, NJ 7927
www.kidshowbizmagazine.com

Focuses on showbiz issues pertaining to kids, teens and parents and seeks to promote healthy and productive methods of pursuing a child's experience in showbusiness. Provides insight into the ever-changing highly competitive entertainment Industry from Industry insiders.

LA 411 (800) 545-2411
5700 Wilshire Blvd., Ste. 120 FAX (323) 965-2052
Los Angeles 90036
www.la411.com
infoagent@la411.com

A complete resource book for commercial and music video production in L.A. Lists services, personnel, and other pertinent information. Available at bookstores, camera stores, and mail order.

LOCATION UPDATE (818) 785-6362
7021 Hayvenhurst Ave. FAX (818) 785-8092
Ste. 205
Van Nuys 91406
www.updatemag.tv

Articles and pictures for productions on location. www.p3update.com

(800) 805-6648
MAKE-UP ARTIST MAGAZINE (360) 882-3488
4018 NE 112th Sve., Ste. D-8 FAX (360) 885-1836
Vancouver, WA 98682
www.makeupmag.com

Make-up Artist Magazine is the only publication specifically for make-up artists. Each issue contains interviews with top makeup artists, Industry news, product news, backstage lab and technique information. Make-up Artist Magazine covers the print and film Industry and brings the world wide web readers the most information in the business. Make-up Artist Magazine also hosts a Make-up and Effects Trade Show at the Pasadena Convention Center.

MYBREAKDOWN.COM, LLC
P.O. Box 54363
Irvine 92619
www.mybreakdown.com
bhoagland@mybreakdown.com

Premier online casting service featuring: membership-specific casting searches, electronic submission capabilities, and state of the art security. The working actor's one-stop marketing resource. Visit the website for more information.

NOW CASTING (818) 841-7165
60 E. Magnolia Blvd., 2nd Fl.
Burbank 91502
www.nowcasting.com
info@nowcasting.com

The most comprehensive up-to-date resource for casting director information. Updated monthly, it includes names, address and phone numbers plus assistants, associates, other CDs in the office, audition likes and dislikes, current and past projects, general notes, background information and more. Available at Samuel French and newsstands throughout Los Angeles. Also available through their website.

PRODUCTION WEEKLY (800) 284-2230
9669 Santa Monica Blvd. FAX (310) 868-2594
Ste. 1177
Beverly Hills 90210
www.productionweekly.com
info@productionweekly.com

A weekly breakdown of projects in pre-production, preparation, and development for film, TV, music videos, commercials, etc.

REGIONAL & OFF-BROADWAY THEATRE GUIDE (917) 689-6774
P.O. Box 231
Adelphia, NJ 7710
www.aclbooks.com
aclbooks@earthlink.net

A tri-monthly comprehensive guide for the 2005-2006 theatre season. Listings include over 250 theatres with seasons and personnel. The big draw is the labels included in the back of the book.

REGIONAL THEATRE DIRECTORY (802) 867-2223
P.O. Box 510 FAX (802) 867-0144
Dorset, VT 5251
www.theatredirectories.com

Year round regional theatres and dinner theatres. Available by mail order and in theatre bookstores around the country.

SCREEN INTERNATIONAL (323) 655-6087
8271 Melrose Ave., Ste. 204 FAX (323) 655-4906
Los Angeles 90046
www.screendaily.com

International trade publication.

SHOOT NEWSWEEKLY (847) 763-9050
P.O. Box 2144
Spokie, IL 60076

A key trade publication for film advertisers. Amusement Business.

THE SUMMER THEATRE DIRECTORY 2004 EDITION (802) 867-2223
P.O. Box 510 FAX (802) 867-0144
Dorset, VT 05251-0519
www.theatredirectories.com

An annual guide to summer theatres covering the entire United States and Canada. Available by mail order and in bookstores around the country.

Periodicals & Trade Publications

VARIETY
VARIETY ON PRODUCTION (323) 857-6600
5700 Wilshire Blvd., Ste. 120 FAX (323) 857-0742
Los Angeles 90036

VIDEOMAKER MAGAZINE (530) 891-8410
(800) 284-3226
P.O. Box 4591 FAX (530) 891-8443
Chico 95927
www.videomaker.com

Camcorders, computers, tools and techniques for creating video.

Photo Labs & Reproductions

Once you've picked a photographer, completed your shoot and chosen your photo, the decision making is done, right? Not completely. You still need to determine a few more things before your headshot is complete. Photolabs and repro centers will need to know what sort of finish to use (glossy, matte, etc.); with border, without border; name printed inside or outside the image area, etc. Any decent repro center will have samples from which to choose, but think about these things ahead of time when you're looking at other people's photos.

A & I COLOR LAB (323) 856-5255
1012 N. Sycamore
Los Angeles 90038

933 N. Highland Ave. (323) 856-5280
Los Angeles 90038
www.aandi.com

E-6 and Kodachrome film processing. Duplicate slides from transparencies or flat art. Type R prints, quick prints, photo CD, and digital services. Also offers C-41 processing and machine prints. Both traditional and digital retouching. Has digital portfolios. Monday through Friday 7 am to midnight. Open weekends at some locations. Check website for more information.

ABC PICTURES, INC. (888) 526-5336
1867 E. Florida St. FAX (417) 869-9185
Springfield, MO 65803
www.abcpictures.com
rodger@abcpictures.com

Produces high quality, low cost B/W and color headshots, composites, postcards, posters, and publicity pictures for the entertainment Industry, actors, models, celebrities, and manufacturers. Serves customers from coast to coast and into Canada. Uses carefully selected inks, a custom made paper and state of the art equipment backed by great customer service. Short turn around. An excellent substitute for costly photographic reproductions. Request a free catalog and samples. Send photograph or digital file with instructions and payment. See website for information of submitting digital files.

ALAN'S CUSTOM LAB (661) 547-5425
(866) 977-5425
333 E. Avenue K FAX (661) 951-7780
Lancaster 93535
www.alanscustomlab.com

A B&W print lab that offers custom printing. Glossies and photographic printing, quantity multiples. No minimum order required. Same day or next day service, and 1 hour rush service is available. Over 30 years in business. Monday through Friday, 8:30 am to 6 pm.

ARGENTUM PHOTO LAB (323) 461-2775
1050 Cahuenga Blvd. FAX (323) 461-2776
Los Angeles 90038
www.argentum.com
custservice@argentum.com

A full service custom lab. B&W, color and digital.

CARD SHARKS (800) 229-1795
PRINTING AND GRAPHICS (818) 300-4525
www.sharksprinting.com
lindley@sharksprinting.com

A good source for innovative marketing tools. Their signature product is Pocket Headshots™, but they also have high-quality, low-cost postcards and business cards. Also available: photo retouching, Pocket Demo Reels™ (your reel on a business card-sized DVD or CD-ROM!), reel production and editing, and entertainer's websites.

CERTIFIED PRINTERS (323) 466-6179
(323) 465-5411
1525 N. Cahuenga Blvd. FAX (323) 467-9100
Los Angeles 90028
www.certprint.com
cp@certprint.com

Custom photographic services, B&W and color digital service bureau. MacIntosh output, four color seps, drum scanning, matchprints, and Cannon fiery. Also color stats, Iris prints, litho negs, color keys, halftones, blow-ups up to 40x60 feet/mounted, transfers, prints, PMT's, stats, transparencies, and slides. 4 color printing and bindry. Does fliers, business cards and brochures. Also does B&W composites, custom photo printing, and glossy and matte finishes. Rush service is available for an extra cost. Cash and check only. Monday through Friday, 8:30 am to 10:30 pm.

CRUSH CREATIVE (213) 380-2980
(818) 842-1121
1919 Empire Ave. FAX (213) 739-6984
Burbank 91506
www.crushcreative.com

Full service lab. Prints and develops both color and B&W. Multiple prints are available. Daily lab, 24 hours. Monday through Friday, 8 am to 4:30 pm.

CUSTOM PRINT SHOP, INC. (323) 461-3001
1644 Wilcox FAX (323) 461-9039
Hollywood 90028
www.customprint.com

A full service B&W and color lab. Monday through Friday, 9 am to 7 pm and Saturday, 10 am to 4 pm.

DIGITAL COLOR (323) 937-3804
5001 Wilshire Blvd., Ste. 111B
Los Angeles 90036
www.netphotolab.net
info@netphotolab.com

Custom printing of color, all types. Type R custom printing is available. Digital retouching and photos. Also scanning pre-press. Monday through Saturday, 9 am to 5 pm.

DRKRM (323) 223-6867
2121 N. San Fernando Rd., Ste. 3
Los Angeles 90065
www.drkrm.com

Full service B&W and color including film processing, prints, and glossy prints in quantity. Rush service is available. No minimums. Digital retouching. Monday through Friday, 8 am to 6 pm.

ELECTRIC SOUP (323) 461-3448
1545 N. Wilcox Ave., Ste. B-5 FAX (323) 461-7430
Hollywood 90028
www.electricsoupstudios.com

Digital photos and photo retouching. Fast service and rush service is available. Monday through Friday, 9 am to 6 pm.

FINAL PRINT (818) 285-6967
5816 Lankershim Blvd., #9
North Hollywood 91601

2050 S. Bundy Dr., Ste. 104 (310) 979-7884
W. Los Angeles 90025

1952 N. Van Ness Ave. (323) 466-0566
Los Angeles 90068-3625 (323) 466-5404
www.finalprint.com FAX (323) 469-7138
headshots@finalprint.com

Final Print specializes in making photo-quality headshots, postcards and business cards. They do zedcards, DVD labels, video boxes, posters, stationery, one sheets, banners, promo items (mugs, magnets, t-shirts) and more. Services include digital design, photos, lithos, 4-color press, and short-run digital color. Custom and specialty orders are welcome. Mail order is available both by e-mail and snail mail. All work is guaranteed and all credit cards are accepted. SEE AD ON THIS PAGE.

FOCUS FOTO FINISHERS (323) 934-0013
138 S. La Brea Ave. FAX (323) 934-9658
Los Angeles 90036

Custom B&W and color printing. Call for rush service. Monday through Friday, 8:30 am to 5:30 pm.

FOTO WORKS (310) 444-1908
11915 W. Olympic Blvd.
Los Angeles 90025

Custom color lab. Will reproduce color or B&W headshots for actors as well. Rush service, and retouching available. Monday through Thursday, 10 am to 6:30 pm, Friday, 10 am to 5 pm and Saturday, noon to 3 pm.

GRAND PRINTS, INC. (818) 763-5743
6143 Laurelgrove Ave.
North Hollywood 91606
www.grandprints.com

Color and B&W lithographic prints, with an unusually low minimum quantity of just 100 copies. Fieries available in even smaller quantities, today's popular choice for modeling composites. Specialize in headshots and other publicity printing, from picture business cards up to posters. Many services are free: including most set-up, most typesetting and logos, cropping, and even UPS delivery throughout the continental U.S. Custom design and digital retouching are also available at good rates. Most orders take about 5 business days in shop. Monday through Friday, 9:30 am to 5:30 pm.

GRAPHIC REPRODUCTIONS (323) 874-4335
(877) 212-6647
1421 N. La Brea Ave. FAX (323) 874-3947
Hollywood 90028
www.graphicreproductions.com

B&W, matte, or gloss finish custom printing. Quantity headshots with a minimum order of 100. Composites, minimum order of 250. Also makes postcards, business cards, and zed cards. Monday through Friday, 9:30 am to 6 pm.

IMAGESTARTER (818) 506-7010
1016 W. Magnolia FAX (818) 506-7017
Burbank 91605
www.imagestarter.com
mikeweis@excelonline.com

No more washed out, grainy lithos. Imagestarter specializes in photo-quality lithographic reproductions which have to be seen to be believed. Other services include: postcards, business cards, resume design, cover letters, mailings, dubs and more. Imagestarter is the working actor's one-stop resource for all the top-quality marketing tools an actor will ever need.

IMAGEXPERTS (323) 874-0624
7095 Hollywood Blvd.
Hollywood 90028
www.imagexperts.com

B&W, color prints, and slides in matte and glossy finishes. Custom printing available and they develop all types of film. Quantity headshots and postcards. 2 hours for E-6 slides, 2 hours for B&W film, 1 hour for color film and 2 days for enlargements. Slide dupes, and copies of negatives. Also has a full digital lab and does digital retouching and composites. Offers Advanced Photo System (APS). Monday through Friday, 9 am to 7 pm and Saturday, 10 am to 6 pm.

KT IMAGE (323) 461-8282
6060 Sunset Blvd., Ste. B FAX (323) 461-8284
Hollywood 90038
www.ktimage.com

E-6 processing, daily. Color prints from negs and slides. 24 hour dupes. Rush service. Pick up available. E-6 counter is open until 8 pm. Last drop for next day pick up is 5 pm.

LAUREL CUSTOM PHOTO LAB (818) 505-8999
5122 Lankershim Blvd.
North Hollywood 91601
www.laurelphotolab.com

B&W and color prints, no lithographs. Custom printing is available. Develops C-41, B&W, and E-6 films. One day service for proofs and prints, rush service is available at 100% extra charge. Digital retouching. Monday through Friday, 8 am to 5:30 pm and Saturday, 9 am to 1 pm.

ISGO LEPEJIAN (818) 848-9001
2220 W. Magnolia Blvd.
Burbank 91506

1145 N. La Brea Ave. (323) 876-8085
Hollywood 90038
www.isgophoto.com

B&W prints and digital imaging. Specializes in custom printing, archive quality prints. Same day proofs, 2-3 days required for prints, and rush service is available. Mass produces headshots, 50% extra charge for next day service, 25% extra charge for 2 day service. Monday through Friday, 9 am to 6 pm. Photographic and lithographic reproductions in B&W and color.

MODEL PRINTING, INC (818) 985-6886
5152 Lankershim Blvd.
North Hollywood 91601
www.modelprinting.com

Full color printing, has a full color Cannon CLC-1000 with Fiery. Full color post cards. B&W post cards, J-cards, CDs, business cards, and lithographs are available. Offers rush service, and makes props for films. 100 color copies for 99 cents.

MODERN POSTCARD (800) 959-8365
(760) 431-7084
1675 Faraday Ave. FAX (760) 431-1939
Carlsbad 92008
www.modernpostcard.com

Modern Postcard provides turnkey promotion by printing and mailing under one roof full color custom postcards from just $125 for 500 copies.

MULTIPLE PHOTO (323) 731-8286
10810 W. Washington Blvd.
Culver City 90232

Digital and B&W and color processing. Glossy and pearl finishes. Makes duplicate slides, custom enlargements, murals, and postcards in color or B&W. $10 minimum order. Will make any number of multiple prints. Normally takes 3 working days for B&W, 4 days for color prints, and same day service is available. Monday through Friday, 9 am to 5 pm.

PAPER CHASE PRINTING, INC. (323) 874-2300
(800) 367-2737
7176 Sunset Blvd. FAX (323) 874-6583
Los Angeles 90046
www.paperchase.net
csr@paperchase.net

B&W and color prints, lithographs only. Custom printing is available. Takes 8-10 working days for proofs and prints. Does quantity printing of headshots and composites. Minimum order of 500 headshots, 500 for composites. Also prints postcards, business cards, makes B&W and color posters, and prints from slides. Retouching is available. Monday through Friday, 9 am to 6 pm. See listing for PRINTING AND PHOTOCOPYING in this section for more information.

PARAGON PHOTO (323) 933-5865
(323) 937-1922
326 S. La Brea Ave.
Los Angeles 90036
www.paragonphoto.com

B&W prints in glossy and matte finishes, also custom prints and digital imaging. Develops all types of B&W film. Has same day service for proof sheets, 1 day for enlargement proofs, 2 days for prints, and rush service is available. Also does quantity runs of headshots and composites. Retouching is available. Also offers color output. Monday through Friday, 8:30 am to 6 pm.

PHOTO GALLERIA (805) 483-3686
2626 Saviers Road
Oxnard 93033

High quality multiple photo reproductions in matte finish up to 300 copies. Also does custom printing and enlargements. 24 hour turnaround.

PHOTO IMPACT (323) 461-0141
931 N. Citrus Ave.
Hollywood 90038

3015 Ocean Park Blvd. (310) 399-9800
Santa Monica 90401
www.photoimpactonline.com

B&W and color multiple printing of headshots. Portfolio printing and custom printing is also available. Also processes film and makes proofsheets. High quality mass production. Digital, C-41 processing and prints.

THE PHOTO LAB AND DIGITAL IMAGING (323) 463-6166
1419 N. La Brea Ave. FAX (323) 463-7865
Los Angeles 90028
www.tphotolab.com
pjdphoto@aol.com

21 Years in Hollywood serving all of the major movie studios.

Complete professional photo and digital lab. Headshot reproduction specials. Call or visit the website for prices and information.

PHOTOMAX LAB (323) 850-0200
7190 Sunset Blvd. FAX (323) 850-0206
Los Angeles 90046
www.photomaxlab.com

Professional B&W and color photo finishing. Also makes custom prints and does quantity reproduction in B&W and color. Color photo reproduction service, digital restoration, and retouching available. Monday through Friday, 9 am to 6:30 pm and Saturday 10 am to 2 pm.

PRINTS CHARM'N, INC. (310) 312-0904
1657 Sawtelle Blvd.
W. Los Angeles 90025

11020 Ventura Blvd. (818) 753-9055
Studio City 91604
www.printscharmn.com

Headshots, 50/$45, 100/$53, 250/$74, 500/$109 on heavy weight paper in soft, medium, or ultra white paper. Photographic color, sepia, and black and white headshot special 100/$69. Price includes one image, type, and agency logos. Composites, ZED cards, photo postcards, photo business cards, and J-cards (cassette inserts). Four working day turnaround. Same day rush available for an additional $35, or next day rush for an additional $25 per side. Digital retouching available, while you watch, $10/10 minutes. Full price list, mail order form and additional information available on the website.

PRO LAB CUSTOM COLOR (310) 204-4608
10325 Jefferson Blvd.
Culver City 90232

Develops and prints headshots in B&W and color. Call for further information. Monday through Friday, 8 am to 6 pm.

PRODUCERS & QUANTITY PHOTO LAB (323) 462-1334 (323) 466-7544
6660 Santa Monica Blvd.
Hollywood 90038
www.pqphoto.com

B&W and color prints as well as digital services including photo CDs. Quantity duplication of headshots and composites. Also does custom printing and retouching. Rush service is available. Monday through Friday, 8 am to 5:30 pm.

QUALITY LAB (323) 938-0174
723 N. Cahuenga FAX (323) 938-7397
Los Angeles 90038
www.qualityphotoreproduction.com

Glossies and matte, specializes in pearl finish, borderless and border prints. Minimum order is 25 pictures. 2 working days for enlargements and 4 days for other services. Rush service available for an extra charge. Monday through Friday, 9 am to 6 pm and Saturday, 10 am to 2 pm.

RAY THE RETOUCHER (323) 463-0555
1330 N. Highland Ave. FAX (323) 856-5335
Hollywood 90028

12345-B Ventura Blvd. (818) 760-3656
Studio City 91604
www.raytheretoucher.com

Full service actor lab. Services include: B&W and color film processing. Retouching, digital archiving, headshot reproductions, custom enlargements as well as digital and resume printing. Acting supplies including: portfolios, books and cases. Able to work with digital files. Headshots and composites available in true black and white photographic paper. High quality lithographs also available. Call for specials.

REPRODUCTIONS (323) 845-9595 (888) 797-7795
3499 Cahuenga Blvd. West FAX (323) 845-0188
Los Angeles 90068
www.reproductions.com

Black and white printing of 8x10 headshots, postcards and business cards for actors and performing artists. Their exclusive Master Print process combines the latest state of the art digital imaging technology with advancements in fine art printing. Digital retouching. Portfolio gallery of L.A.'s finest headshot photographers. Monday through Friday 9 am to 7 pm.

RGB COLOR LAB (323) 469-1959
816 N. Highland Ave.
Hollywood 90038
www.rgbcolorlab.com

Processes and prints 35mm film. Also 16 mm color negative. 8x10 prints in color only. Also does negative processing and 35mm work prints for the motion picture Industry. Monday through Friday 9 am to 5:30 pm.

RICHARD PHOTO LAB (323) 939-8893
8016 Melrose Ave.
Los Angeles 90036
www.richardphotolab.com

Professional B&W and color finishing, digital, and multiple quantity duplicates. Monday through Friday, 9 am to 6 pm.

SCHULMAN PHOTO LAB (323) 466-3343
6677 Sunset Blvd. FAX (323) 466-5019
Hollywood 90028
www.schulmanphotolab.com

All digital services available and everything for the actor. Full service B&W and color custom lab, develops and prints headshots. Also offers conversions from color to B&W and retouching. 3 hour turnaround for proof sheets, 1-2 working days for prints. Monday through Friday, 9 am to 6 pm and Saturdays.

SIGNATURE PRINTING (323) 962-8159
2838 Lakeridge Lane
Westlake Village 91361
www.signaturereproductions.com
rich.tier@earthlink.net

B&W and color reproductions on photographic paper. Also digital and lithographs. Headshots, postcards, composites, business cards, and other services including retouching.

Photo Labs & Reproductions

STILL PHOTO LAB **(323) 465-6106**
1222 N. La Brea Ave.
Hollywood 90038
www.stillphoto.com
info@stillphoto.com

Offers traditional and digital photographic services including retouching. Specializes in theatrical press kits. Headshots in color and B&W. Digital presskits on CD ROM. Monday through Friday, 8 am to 6 pm.

SUN IMAGING CENTER **(323) 654-5556** **(888) 860-4549**
8168 W. Sunset Blvd.
Los Angeles 90046
www.sunimagingcenter.com

Sun Imaging can save you money and time. They provide one-stop shopping with headshot and modeling photography, headshot prints, lithographs, zed cards, business cards, postcards and retouching all available. Also resumes, back side printing and shipping available. Other services include: B/W, slides, slide dupes, print to print (with no negatives), 30 minute color 35mm or advanced photo system. Monday through Friday, 9 am to 7 pm and Saturday 10 am to 4 pm. Satisfaction guaranteed.

SUPER COLOR LAB **(323) 874-2188**
979 N. La Brea **FAX (323) 274-2886**
Los Angeles 90038
www.supercolorimaging.com

B&W and color prints, specializing in color. Custom printing and rush service available. Digital imaging retouching is available. Accepts Visa and Mastercard. Monday through Friday 9 am to 5:30 pm.

DIGITAL SUPERCOLOR **(310) 829-4661**
3200 Olympic Blvd.
Santa Monica 90403
www.digitalsupercolor.com

Does multiple B&W and color 8x10s in 3 days, sooner if needed. No lithographs. See listing under PHOTO RETOUCHERS in this section for further information.

UNIVERSAL PRINT & COPY **(323) 876-3500**
3535 West Cahuenga Blvd. **FAX (323) 876-7141**
Ste. 111
Los Angeles 90068
www.eddietheprinter.com

Full service. Headshots, postcards, business cards, brochures, posters and more. Open daily 9 am to 9 pm.

VARIETY PRINTING **(818) 705-4422**
17618 Sherman Way
Van Nuys 91405

B&W litho printing. Also does photo postcards, business cards, and 2 sided printing.

VIRTUAL BUSINESS CARDS
CYNDIE CARRILLO **(818) 693-0023**
859 Hollywood Way, Ste. 123
Burbank 91505
www.virtualbusinesscards.com

Keep your picture, resume, contact information and either video or audio clip in your pocket. Great for networking.

WEST COAST PHOTO **(323) 465-3506**
1128 N. Las Palmas Ave.
Hollywood 90038

Specializes in duplicate transparencies, also does B&W and color prints in glossy and matte finishes. Custom printing is available and they develop B&W and color film. Next day service for B&W proofs, 2 days for color proofs, 3 days for prints, and rush service is available for an additional charge. Also offers volume prints of headshots and composites. Monday through Friday, 8:30 am to 5:30 pm.

Photo Retouching

ARTIST 2 DESIGN **(323) 856-6105**
www.artist2design.com
shawn2005@verizon.net

Digital retouching. Shawn has over 10 years experience retouching headshots, manually or digitally. Rates begin at $25 for basic clean up on manual touch ups and digital begin at $35, goes up depending on your needs. Turn over time 2-3 days, if you email image turnover is fast.

THOMAS CANNY STUDIO **(323) 653-4421**
7471 Melrose Ave., Ste 14 **FAX (323) 653-2417**
Los Angeles 90046
www.thomascannystudio.com

Over 14 years of expert retouching experience for acting, modeling and the movie Industry. All digital imaging. Illustration and graphics also available. B&W or color, photographs, negatives and transparencies also accepted. Digital files can be sent online to tcanny@pacbell.net.

CARD SHARKS PRINTING **(800) 229-1795**
AND GRAPHICS **(818) 300-4525**
www.sharksprinting.com
lindley@sharksprinting.com

A good source for innovative marketing tools. Their signature product is Pocket Headshots™, but they also have high-quality, low-cost postcards and business cards. Also available: photo retouching, Pocket Demo Reels™ (your reel on a business card-sized DVD or CD-ROM!), reel production and editing, and entertainer's websites.

DIGITAL SUPERCOLOR **(310) 829-4661** **(866) 829-4661**
3200 Olympic Blvd. **FAX (310) 453-9049**
Santa Monica 90403
www.digitalsupercolor.com

Retouching, either by hand or digitally, on matte or glossy finish prints as well as negatives. Also does multiple B&W and color 8x10s. Takes 3 days or sooner if needed. 100% rush charge for 24 hour service.

ELECTRIC SOUP **(323) 461-3448**
1545 N. Wilcox Ave., Ste. B-5 **FAX (323) 461-7430**
Hollywood 90028
www.electricsoupstudios.com
esstudios@earthlink.net

Digital photo retouching, color prints, and transparencies, B&W prints, and air brushing. Fast service and rush service is available. Monday through Friday 9 am to 8 pm.

HOLLYWOOD RETOUCHING **(323) 645-0212**
www.hollywoodretouching.com
valerie@hollywoodretouching.com

Expert digital photo prep and retouching, with 14 years' Photoshop experience. First they prep the photo to give it gorgeous, luminous depth. Then they retouch to make you natural yet polished, not airbrushed-perfect – like you on your best day. SEE AD ON THIS PAGE.

JO LIU PHOTOGRAPHY **(213) 623-2556**
Los Angeles 90013
www.joliuphotography.com
jo@joliuphotography.com

Specializes in digital headshots and promotional pieces for actors, models and entertainers using both studio and natural lighting. Offers proofs online and complimentary retouching.

CAMERON MURLEY **(818) 760-6756**

PhotoShop specialist for 8 years. Digital imaging. Also still does etching, airbrushing, bleach and dye on B&W and color prints in matte or glossy finish. Rush service available. Flexible hours. In the business 22 years. Retouched everyone from the Pope to Andrew Dice Clay. Call for more information.

NICHAN PHOTOGRAPHIC SERVICES **(818) 508-8566** **(323) 467-5638**
5851 Melrose Ave.
Los Angeles 90038

Works with prints and negatives in B&W or color. Does air brushing, bleaching and etching. By appointment only.

RAY THE RETOUCHER **(323) 463-0555**
1330 N. Highland Ave. **FAX (323) 463-4742**
Hollywood 90028

12345-B Ventura Blvd. **(818) 760-3656**
Studio City 91604
www.raytheretoucher.com

Full service actor lab. Services include: B&W and color film processing. Retouching, digital archiving, headshot reproductions, custom enlargements as well as digital and resume printing. Acting supplies including: portfolios, books and cases. Able to work with digital files. Headshots and composites available in true black and white photographic paper. High quality lithographs also available. Call for specials.

GAIL RUDY
MULTI-IMAGE ART STUDIO **(323) 466-1266**
1607 N. El Centro Ave., Ste. 14
Los Angeles 90028
multimage@ispwest.com

Photo restoration, print enhancement, Color and B&W headshot retouching, zed cards. Conventional and digital services are available. Also offers layout and design assistance with brochures, CD covers, cassette jackets, flyers and logos. Personalized consultations. Serving the Industry since 1977.

SIGNATURE PRINTING **(323) 962-8159**
2838 Lakeridge Lane.
Westlake Village 91361
www.signaturereproductions.com

See listing under PHOTO LABS & REPRODUCTION for further information.

SUN IMAGING CENTER **(323) 654-5556** **(888) 860-4549**
8168 W. Sunset Blvd.
Los Angeles 90046
www.sunimagingcenter.com

Sun Imaging can save you money and time. They provide one-stop shopping with headshot and modeling photography, headshot prints, lithographs, zed cards, business cards, postcards and retouching all available. Also resumes, back side printing and shipping available. Other services include: B/W, slides, slide dupes, print to print (with no negatives), 30 minute color 35mm or advanced photo system. Monday through Friday, 9 am to 7 pm and Saturday 10 am to 4 pm. Satisfaction guaranteed.

VTT RETOUCHING **(323) 936-3712**
320 N. Gardner St.
Los Angeles 90036
www.vittiphotography.com
tvphoto@comcast.net

High end digital retouching. You are invited to sit in while your images are retouched the same day. Competitive pricing. Extensive client list available upon request.

WILD STUDIO/IMAGIC **(323) 461-7766**
1545 N. Wilcox **FAX (323) 461-3763**
Hollywood 90028
www.imagicla.com

Electronic and conventional retouching on any size glossy or matte prints in color or B&W. 3 days average time.

You will need pictures for newspapers, casting directors and producers, as well as to introduce yourself to the various organizations in your community. Look at other actors' pictures to see what appeals to you when selecting a photographer. Look at all the other pictures that have ever been taken of you, including snapshots, and isolate what is most interesting about the best ones. If you feel you can't analyze them appropriately, consider taking a photography or art class to develop a more discerning eye. The most important aspect of any picture is that it look exactly like you. It's self defeating to choose a photographer who takes glamour photos if you are a regular person. If a casting director calls you in expecting to see Cindy Crawford and you are Kathy Najimy, he is not going to be pleased. Forget about trying to change people's minds, casting directors are busy.—K Callan "How to Sell Yourself as an Actor" Sweden Press

BOB ABRAMS (760) 228-3042
North of Palm Springs
abramsfoto@aol.com

Studio and location sessions. Specializes in headshots and 3/4 body shots. Bob shoots digital: $125 for 100 shots, actor keeps the disk. 6 changes. Bob works to establish a rapport with the actor, and is great with kids!

ACTOR'S FOTO SERVICE TORY WOLFE (818) 995-1876

Premier photographer born in Los Angeles, shooting working actors for 20+ years including Randy Newman, Ice T, ZZ Top, Sylvester Stallone, Whoopi Goldberg, Rob Lowe, Brian Dennehy, Eric Roberts, Angelina Jolie, Billy Crystal and many more. Advertising clients include: Coke, Pepsi, Honda, Ford, Budweiser, Chevy and Vespa to name a few. Tory shoots as much film as you need. Call to speak directly with him regarding details and prices. SEE AD ON THIS PAGE.

ADRIAAN (818) 222-4828

Both studio and location sessions. Digital headshots and composites. Make-up artist is available. Has specials on occasion.

NICHOLAS ALAN PHOTOGRAPHY (323) 876-0881
(323) 253-4921

Studio and location sessions. Specializes in theatrical and commercial headshots. All work is unconditionally guaranteed and priced competitively. Free consultation and general career guidance. Mr. Alan is a former TV and film agent in both New York and L.A. with over 15 years experience in all areas of entertainment.

PHILIP ALDERTON PHOTOGRAPHY (818) 763-3546
5057½ Cahuenga Blvd.
North Hollywood 91601
www.philipalderton.com
philipalderton@earthlink.net

Studio and location sessions. Theatrical, commercial, publicity, and glamour shots. Does Polaroid testing. Actors keep the negatives. A make-up artist and hair stylist is available. Offers a free consultation and all work is guaranteed. 15 years in business.

THE ANGLE PHOTOGRAPHY (323) 930-2266
5410 Wilshire Blvd., Ste. 608
Los Angeles 90036
www.theanglephototgraphy.com
info@theanglephotography.com

Bradley K. Ross specializes in natural light photography in a relaxed and fun environment. Theatrical, commercial and character headshots catered to your personality. Studio located in the heart of the Miracle Mile District (Wilshire/La Brea.) To view his portfolio, call to schedule an appointment, visit Reproductions (3499 Cahuenga Blvd. West) or visit the website.

ALAN ASCHER (323) 938-9450
www.alanascher.indiegroup.com

Studio sessions. 36 shots, one proof sheet, one 8 x 10, dark room on the premises – actor keeps the negatives. All for $48. Books available for viewing. 24 years experience.

DEBORAH ATTOINESE (310) 657-1220
www.deborahattoinese.com FAX (310) 657-1238
deborah@deborahattoinese.com

Honest, great quality and fair rates. Both studio and location sessions. Headshots, composites, portraits and fashion. Make-up artist is available. Fifteen years experience. Clients include: Vogue Promotions, Charvari, Art Direction Magazine plus many more. Come by, see the work and talk about what you need to get your photographs get you working more.

AW STUDIO (310) 203-7888
www.aw-studio.com
creativeplanet@msn.com

Studio and location headshot and fashion photography. Film and digital. Makeup available for an extra charge. Pays great attention to detail.

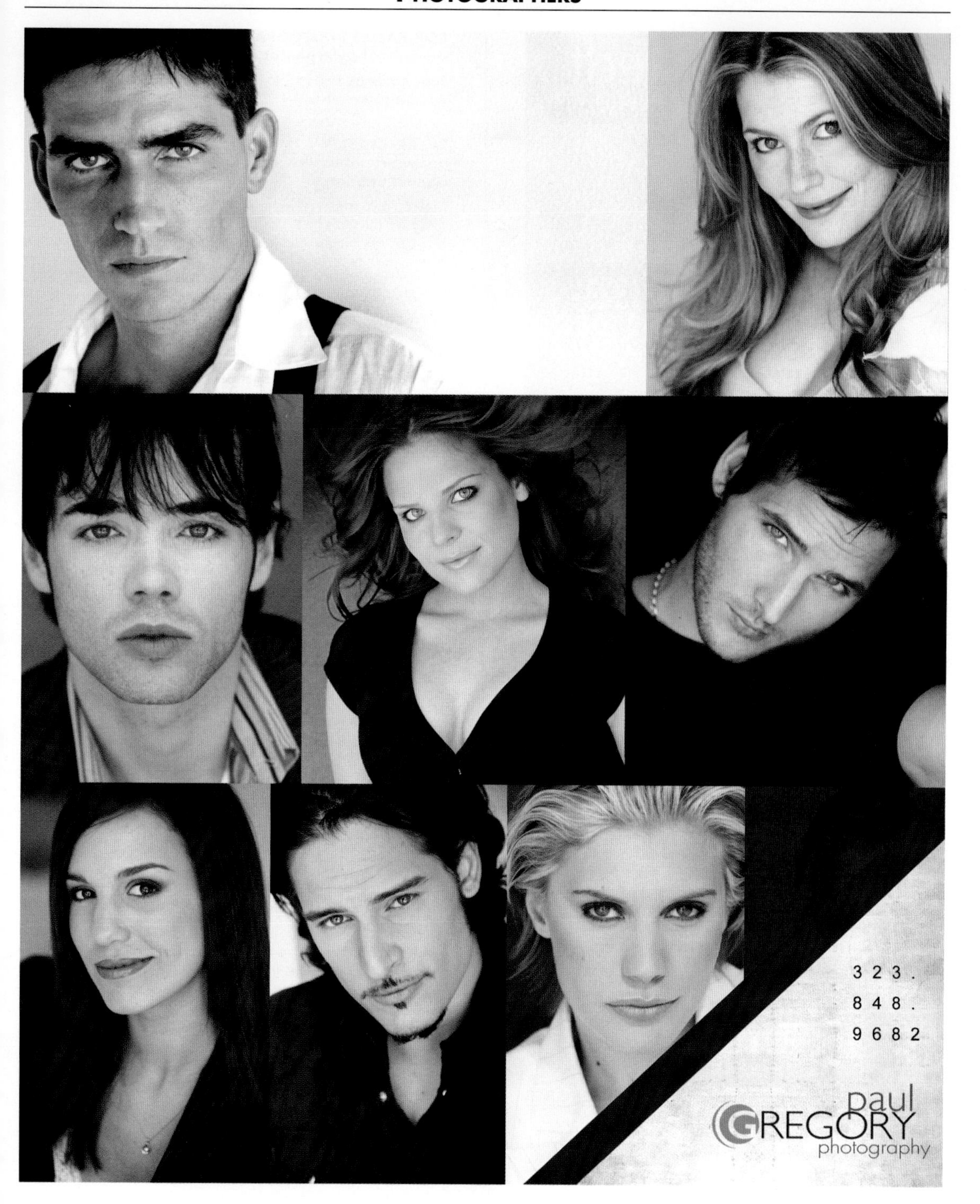
323.
848.
9682
paul
GREGORY
photography

AWARD STUDIOS **(310) 395-2779**
www.aawd.net

Free photo sessions with experienced photographer, Amy Ward. She works internationally with Vogue, Vanity Fair, etc. Ms. Ward also trains make-up artists and they need actors and models with clear skin to work on for their portfolios. To find out more about this opportunity, call or visit the website.

RUSSELL BAER **(310) 452-2705**
www.russellbaer.com

His work has been featured in all forms of media including, television, movie posters, magazine covers and CDs. His images have been displayed in numerous photography shows celebrating Hollywood's top photographers at their artistic best. Russell has also contributed his celebrity portraits to numerous publications. Visit the website to view his portfolio. Call for rates.

SUNNY BAK **(310) 430-2214**
(310) 577-9760
www.sunnybak.com
sunny@sunnybak.com

Celebrity portraiture and actors headshots.

BARIAN STUDIOS **(323) 658-5853**
469 Melrose Ave., Ste. 33
Los Angeles 90038
www.barian-studios.com

Barian was featured in Los Angeles magazine.

BOB BAYLES PHOTOGRAPHY **(818) 997-8518**
www.bobbaylesphotos.com

Basic headshots start at $95 for 80 digital images burned to a CD. All work guaranteed.

BRYAN BEASLEY **(323) 954-8157**
www.bryanbeasley.com
bbeas@attbi.com

Digital Photography – leave the session with headshot in hand. $200 for 80 shots both studio and natural light – leave with CD-ROM of all images and a photo quality printout of the actual headshot. Build your own headshot, pick the border and the font and do retouching – all while you wait. Deluxe package is $325 and also includes 300 headshots delivered to your home within 5-6 business days.

BENNINGTON PHOTOGRAPHY **(323) 655-1929**
www.benningtonphotography.com
markbennington@sbcglobal.net

Mark Bennington insists that he does not take actor headshots, but rather that he takes pictures of real people in character, because casting directors today don't want to see another actor, they want the real thing.

BENVIL PHOTOGRAPHY **(323) 969-4944**
bbenvil@aol.com

Barbara Benvil shoots natural light headshots for actors; in color, black and white or toned. Publicity photos, CD jackets, fashion and portfolio work as well as portraits are available. All work is guaranteed. By appointment only.

LESLEY BOHM PHOTOGRAPHY **(213) 625-8401**
201 S. Santa Fe Ave., Ste. 301 **FAX (213) 928-0948**
Los Angeles 90012
www.bohmphotography.com
lesbohm@mindspring.com

Specializing in natural light, Lesley has been shooting commercial and theatrical headshots in Los Angeles for the last 15 years. She has a spacious studio that helps enhance her relaxed style of shooting. Check out the webpage for a portfolio or come by for a consultation. PR, Portfolios and Fashion. Accepts VISA and MasterCard.

JIM BOYD PHOTOGRAPHY **(310) 418-4528**

Jim captures personality. Location or studio shoots. No website – you must come to see his portfolio in person so you can discuss what you're after. Connections in the casting community mean he knows what casting directors are looking for. Experienced. Competitive rates.

KEVIN BREAK **(323) 221-5129**
1734 N. Main St., 3B
Los Angeles 90031
www.kevinbreak.com

Kevin encourages actors to rest the night before the shoot, bring many changes of clothes and to have fun during the shoot. All digital.

BREE MICHAEL WARNER PHOTOGRAPHY **(323) 788-1190**
4600 Los Feliz Blvd., Ste. 105 **FAX (323) 913-9245**
Los Angeles 90027
www.breemichaelwarner.com
breewarner@earthlink.net

Headshot photography that captures the "real" you. Relaxed environment. Natural light and studio. Both color and black and white available. Digital or film options. Packages include all photos on CD and two images fully retouched and ready for printing. Prices start at $275 with a 10% discount if you mention "The Working Actors Guide." Photography services also available during live shows for bands.

MICHAEL BREWER PHOTOGRAPHY **(323) 227-0307**
Los Angeles
www.mikebrewerphotography.com
mike@mikebrewerphotography.com

Studio and location sessions. Theatrical and commercial headshots, production stills, and publicity shots. Make-up and hair are available. Professional, relaxed working environment. Specializes in bringing out the actor's character. Basic package includes two 8x10s. Digital or film. Mention the Working Actor's Guide for a special discount.

IAN BROOKS PHOTOGRAPHY **(310) 458-6569**
www.ianbrooksphotography.com

Get noticed. Working fashion photographer (Dreamworks, Sony, Warner Bros. PETA, Vogue, Harper's Bazaar, Revlon) will photograph your headshot with a fashion edge. All work guaranteed.

BRAD BUCKMAN DIGITAL PHOTOGRAPHY **(323) 466-2700**
1015 Cahuenga Blvd., #12117
Hollywood 90038
www.bradbuckman.com
brad@bradbuckman.com

Voted one of L.A.'s Top 10 headshot photographers and L.A.'s first digital headshot photographer, Brad offers a shooting experience that is both relaxed and spontaneous while consistently delivering final images that are distinctive and breathtaking. Shooting digital means almost 4x the number of shots, and that means there's no stressing about how many frames you have left or if you blinked in that last one. In addition, the variety of framing and backgrounds, and the careful balance of both natural and studio lighting in Brad's work ensures that you and your representation never have trouble choosing several great shots. SEE AD ON PREVIOUS PAGE.

PHOTOS BY BUNNY **(310) 393-5501**
P.O. Box 367
Santa Monica 90406

Headshot package includes proof sheet, two 8x10s, and all negatives. Three clothing changes and three different looks, ie: commercial, theatrical, and 3/4 body shots. All work is guaranteed. Call for reasonable rates.

LAURA BURKE PHOTOGRAPHY **(818) 759-6767**
www.lauraburkephotography.com
lburkephoto@adelphia.net

Shoots both studio and location headshots, 3/4 bodyshots; whatever is best to represent your personality and character choices. She only

schedules one person a day, so the sessions are fun and relaxed. Ms. Burke is a former New York talent agent and has been in the entertainment business for over 16 years. Call for an appointment and consultation. Reasonable rates for personal service. Shoots digital and film.

KAREN BYSTEDT PHOTOGRAPHY (323) 993-8558
www.karenbystedtphotography.com
osloprod@sbcglobal.net FAX (323) 927-1522

Karen Bystedt is the author and photographer of "The New Breed" and "Before They Were Famous." She has photographed Brad Pitt, Johnny Depp, Keanu Reeves, Sandra Bullock, Djimon Hounsou, and Cuba Gooding Jr., among others. Bystedt specializes in natural light, location, portrait, and headshot photography. All digital. 100 digital shots for $500. Make-up and hair available for an additional fee. SEE AD ON PAGE 150.

CALAS STUDIO DIGITAL HEADSHOTS (213) 804-3116
450½ N. Hayworth Ave.
Los Angeles 90048
www.calasstudio.com
headshots@calasstudio.com

Los Angeles based photographer specializing in professional digital color, black and white actor headshots and portrait photography. Michael favors natural light and enjoys creating a comfortable and relaxed environment, great for newcomers, kids and all types of actors, capturing the best that you can be. Professional hair and make-up is available. Client keeps all digital images. View your photos online the same day.

GLENN CAMPBELL PHOTOGRAPHY (213) 384-1700
3278 Wilshire Blvd., Ste. 804
Los Angeles 90010
www.glenncampbellphoto.com

Celebrity/entertainment photography, capturing images on high resolution digital. Studio or location.

CAVALIER PHOTOGRAPHY (818) 840-9148
CARRIE CAVALIER-AUSTIN (818) 566-8291
www.cavalierphotography.com FAX (818) 840-0142
cecavalier@earthlink.net

Film and Digital. Color and black and white headshots and ¾ length, and full bodyshots. Specializes in adults and children, fashion/editorial, rock and roll, publicity, celebrity, action, sports, comedians, stunts, advertising, and weddings. The emphasis is on the needs of the artist. 22 years experience in the Los Angeles area. 1 roll, $225; 2 rolls, $325; portfolios, including headshots, $450, negatives included. Prints, $16 each. She has children's discounts. Professional hair and makeup available. SEE AD ON PREVIOUS PAGE.

DAN CHAPMAN PHOTOGRAPHY (323) 906-8541
4655 Kingswell Ave., Ste. 206
Los Angeles 90027
www.raytheretoucher.com
chpmd@aol.com

Spacious studio or location sessions. Hair and make-up available at cost. Natural and studio lighting. Film or digital. Studio is air conditioned. Call anytime to review portfolio. Safe free parking.

CHARLAINE BROWN PHOTOGRAPHY (310) 474-8654
P.O. Box 3841 FAX (310) 474-5159
Beverly Hills 90212
www.classicphotos.us

More than 17 years experience, celebrity/fashion photographer she has photographed Christian Slater, Rosanna Arquette, Fabio, and more in personal portrait sessions. Commercial, theatrical and publicity headshots. Fashion portfolios for models who want a 'book' or Zed card. Hair and make-up available. Photographer helps client pick best shots.

SAM CHRISTENSEN STUDIOS (818) 506-0783
10440 Burbank Blvd. FAX (818) 506-8941
North Hollywood 91601
www.samchristensen.com
scsimage@aol.com

A headshot photographers gallery featuring the work of 40 of Hollywood's most sought-after photo artists in an atmosphere of a fine art gallery, with high ceilings and beautiful lighting. This is a free service for actors. Many of the featured photographers offer special discounts to those who visit the gallery. Exhibits change quarterly. See listings also under IMAGE CONSULTANTS in this section and ACTING in the TRAINING section for further information.

JASON CHRISTOPHER PHOTOGRAPHY (818) 889-9559
31584 Agoura Rd. #4 FAX (818) 889-9559
Westlake Village 91361
www.jasonchristopher.com
jason@jasonchristopher.com

Los Angeles based photographer. Great quality and service that is affordable. Digital and film. Location or studio.

CHRIS CLEVELAND PHOTOGRAPHY (818) 817-9522
www.chriscleveland.com
clevelandphoto@aol.com

Specializing in natural light photography. Chris photographs on location or in studio in a comfortable, relaxed atmosphere. Photography ranging from theatrical and commercial headshots to fashion composites and Zed cards. Professional hair and make-up available. Client keeps the negatives and all work is guaranteed.

CLUB BEVERLY HILLS (310) 274-6051
8306 Wilshire Blvd., #279 FAX (310) 274-7855
Beverly Hills 90211
www.club-beverlyhills.com
dreams@club-beverlyhills.com

B&W and color photography. Studio and natural light. Commercial, theatrical, PR, headshots and 3/4 bodyshots. Four B&W packages: A) $219 for 2 rolls, 1 print; B) $275 for 3 rolls, 2 prints; C) $325 for 4 rolls, 2 prints and D) $475 for 6 rolls, 4 prints. Add 10% per package for color. Will split B&W and color rolls. Discount for children. CD ROM available upon request. All packages include proofsheets, negatives, make-up imaging and unlimited changes. Uses ultra fine-grain film. Free consultation. Friendly and relaxed environment. Specializes in directing character photo shoots. By appointment. Newcomers are welcome. Visa, MasterCard, American Express accepted.

MARTIN COHEN PHOTOGRAPHY (310) 396-5587
Santa Monica Area FAX (310) 396-5587
www.martincohenphotography.com
martincohen@earthlink.net

Studio and location sessions for headshots and composites. Actor keeps the negatives. One day rush service available. Over 16 years in business.

KERI COOK PHOTOGRAPHY (310) 476-4573
(323) 791-4533
2467 Nalin Dr. FAX (310) 476-2603
Los Angeles 90077
rubystutu@aol.com

Specializes in natural and studio lighting for commercial and theatrical headshots. Fashion portfolio rates are also available. Relaxed working environment and affordable prices make the photo shoot a great experience.

KATHY COOLEY PHOTOGRAPHY (310) 301-1576
8242 Sunnysea Dr. FAX (310) 302-0040
Playa del Rey 90293
www.kcooleyphoto.com
kathycooleyphoto@hotmail.com

Studio and location sessions. Make-up and styling included. Commercial/theatrical headshots, fashion, and portfolios. Bands, children, women and men. Referred by many agencies. Has worked as a photographer for over 30 years.

JOHN CORBETT PHOTOGRAPHY (323) 654-9427
FAX (323) 656-1195
www.johncorbettphotography.com

Digital and film. Both in the studio and on location. Theatrical, commercial, and publicity headshots as well as 3/4 bodyshots. Professional make-up artist and hair stylist available. Consultation on request. Competitive rates and all work is guaranteed. Over 20 years experience.

SARA CORWIN PHOTOGRAPHY (323) 655-5705
West Hollywood
www.saracorwinphotography.com

Specializing in natural light photography for actors, musicians, dancers and models. Make-up and hair are included in the sessions. Relaxed, private environment with emphasis on allowing the true essence of the individual to be shown. Portfolio is available for viewing. SEE AD ON THIS PAGE.

MARTIN COX PHOTOGRAPHY (213) 482-2676
1634 Sunset Blvd., #211
Los Angeles 90026
www.martincoxphotography.com
photos@martincox.com

Photographer Martin Cox shoots actor's headshots as well as corporate projects, people, landscape, portraits, and maritime. Downtown Los Angeles studio and locations world wide. Some commercial clients include: Rhino Records, Washington Mutual Bank, Los Angeles Contemporary Exhibitions, etc.

GREG CROWDER PHOTOGRAPHY (310) 471-3232
www.gregcrowderphotography.com

Greg shoots location sessions, digital or film. Check out his website to view his portfolio. Call for rates.

MICHAEL J. D'AMBROSIA (310) 444-7391
www.michaeldambrosia.com FAX (310) 444-7391

Shoots digital and film. Commercial and theatrical headshots and 3/4 bodyshots as well as print photography. Hair styling and makeup are available. Actor keeps the negatives or digital disks.

DIANE DA SILVA (323) 871-0447
www.dianedasilva.com
dasilvad1@sbcglobal.net

Studio and natural light headshots. Digital. Actors, musicians, print and models. Shooting since 1990.

DAKOTA HEADSHOTS (877) 721-2667
4646 Scarlet Court
Palmdale 93551
www.dakotaheadshots.com
dakotabphoto@yahoo.com

Dakota Headshots is made up of a team of photographers: Amanda Proffer (formerly LACC – LA CastingCouch Photography), Kirsten Axelsen and Caleb Moody. Studio is located off Doheney just north of Sunset. Sessions are $425 and include up to 6 clothing changes and unlimited shots – they shoot until they get it. All digital – no need to pay for development or get scans of negatives for 8x10 prints. Agent and manager recommended.

JERRY DAY PHOTOGRAPHERS (818) 843-3667
634 N. Reese Pl. FAX (818) 843-3687
Burbank 91506
www.jerryday.com

Air conditioned studio or outdoor location. Film or digital sessions. Mr. Day creates a personalized light and setting based on the client's preferences and takes digital shots for on-the-spot approval. Make-up artists available. Satisfaction guaranteed. Many years experience as photographer and actor.

JERRY DE WILDE (323) 662-6491
www.dewildephotography.com

Studio and location sessions. Cost of headshots and composites vary and the negatives are negotiable. A make-up artist is available as well as retouching at an additional cost. Over 30 years experience.

MARY KATE DENNY (310) 557-2117
W. Los Angeles
www.dennyphoto.com
dennyfoto@aol.com

Both studio and location sessions. Shoots headshots and commercial composites. Specializes in "people photography." Photographer keeps the negatives. Call for details.

DIGITAL HEADSHOTS (323) 791-9449 (626) 794-6439
1023 New York Dr.
Altadena 91001
www.ma2ra.com
jc@ma2ra.com

Quick and easy headshots. Please visit site for samples.

DIGITAL HEADSHOTS LA (562) 292-4031
www.digitalheadshots.la
dpalmer@digitalheadshots.la

Digital Headshots LA operates as a Los Angeles based photography company, specializing in headshots for actors, models, comedians, journalists and executives. If you're an aspiring actor, working actor, agent, manager or reality show contestant, you're going to need a great headshot (for you or your client).

ROBIN DIXON PHOTOGRAPHY (818) 632-4800
www.robindixonphotography.com

Photography that looks into the soul of the actor, singer or model. Shots available in B&W and color. 35mm or digital photography (for instant prints.) Location only. Affordable rates.

KENNETH DOLIN PHOTOGRAPHY (310) 429-2876
www.kennethdolin.com
kenneth@earthlink.net

Your headshot must be an honest representation of your look and must reveal some essential truth about you; your inner-life. For this to happen, you've got to be totally relaxed which is why Kenneth creates a safe, comfortable, fun and positive environment because you're at your most attractive, and your most real, when you're at ease. He begins with a pre-shoot meeting to find out who you are, how you see yourself, and how you wish to be seen. Then he designs a shoot to highlight your special qualities. Kenneth takes about 300 shots and then reviews all the images, editing the shoot down to about 120-200 of the best shots. Studio or location sessions. Digital or film.

PATRICK J. DONAHUE PHOTOGRAPHY (323) 463-4166
1419 N. La Brea FAX (323) 463-7865
Hollywood 90028
www.pjdonahue.com
tphotolab@aol.com

Photography for actors and musicians. Studio photo sessions as low as $195 for headshots includes 4 8x10 prints. The proofs and prints are available the same day Composites, groups, or full length shots from $200.

HEATHER DOTSON PHOTOGRAPHY (323) 243-9778
7510 W. Sunset Blvd., #217
Hollywood 90046
www.heatherdotson.com
htoon@sbcglobal.net

Specializes in natural lighting for commercial and theatrical headshots. Also shoots children, models and musicians. Each roll is $75 with a professional make-up artist available for an additional cost. Call for an appointment to view portfolio.

DOUGLAS M. NELSON PHOTOGRAPHY (310) 567-9045
11501 Venice Blvd., Ste.#1
Los Angeles 90066
www.dmnphoto.com
info@dmnphoto.com

Your headshot is the first impression that you put out. Douglas' philosophy is that "The eyes are the windows to the soul". It is critical that your photo truthfully represents you, while showing your true versatility as an actor. Achieving this in your headshot is most important for actors that want to have that cutting edge with the people that are making the decisions. After all, a picture is worth a thousand words.

RENA DURHAM PHOTOGRAPHY (818) 881-4288
21704 Devonshire St., #166 FAX (818) 881-4288
Chatsworth 91311
www.renadurham.com
rena@renadurham.com

Commercial and theatrical headshots and 3/4 body shots. Studio or location sessions. Fun relaxed atmosphere. They work with children, infants and adults in the film, commercial, television and music industries. Digital imaging for a fast turnaround.

ECM STUDIOS OF HOLLYWOOD (800) 386-7497
1680 N. Vine St., Ste. 1110
Hollywood 90028

Studio and location sessions. Headshots are $125, composites are $195. A make-up artist is available. All work is guaranteed. 22 years in business.

KELSEY EDWARDS (323) 936-6106
633 N. La Brea Ave., 2nd Fl. FAX (323) 936-6107
Los Angeles 90036
www.kelseyedwardsphoto.com
kelsey@kelseyedwardsphoto.com

Studio as well as location. Photographic abilities encompassing theatrical and commercial headshots, composites, zed cards, 3/4 commercial, and fashion as well as musicians for CD covers and promotion. Ms. Edwards specializes in natural light photography. Relaxed atmosphere. Make-up, hair, and retouching is available and all work is guaranteed. SEE AD ON PAGE 153.

HECTOR ELIAS (323) 466-1247

Studio and location. Headshots and 3/4 bodyshots. Make-up, hair styling, and retouching are available. Specializes in natural lighting. Former art director and known actor, Mr. Elias will help you create the perfect image for TV, film, commercials, and print. Free consultation and work is guaranteed. Over 20 years photographing actors.

ELLIOT PHOTOGRAPHY (323) 464-5777
1151 N. La Brea Ave. FAX (323) 876-8827
West Hollywood 90038
www.elliotphotography.com
elliotphotography@sbcglobal.net

Complete digital services. Fully equipped indoor studio plus outdoor locations for natural light. Both can be done in the same photo session. Over 15 years experience photographing actors in

Hollywood. Storefront studio on La Brea (you've probably passed it a million times!) Located next to Isgo Lepejian Custom Lab. For prices, packages, info on make-up and hair styling and more samples of our work check out our website. Consultations are free. Open Monday through Friday 10 am – 5 pm. Saturdays by appointment. See your photos while they're being taken and walk out with your pictures the same day.

FELIX PHOTOGRAPHY **(310) 470-1939**
11000 Wilshire Blvd. **FAX (310) 470-1795**
Box 24225
Westwood 90024
www.ottofelix.com
ottoffelix@aol.com

Award winning photographer. Headshots, theatrical and commercial, album covers, promos, and real estate. Studio or exterior set ups. Otto has shot such celebrities as Dwight Yoakam, Keith Carradine, Billy Bob Thornton, Bo Derek and Tom Selleck. His photos have appeared in Life, Time, People, L.A. Times and Country Music Magazine yet he keeps his rates very reasonable. Member: American Photographers Association and the American Society of Photographers.

PAUL FENTON **(818) 982-3885**
www.fentonphoto.com
fentonphoto@earthlink.net

Studio and location sessions for theatrical headshots and 3/4 shots. Specializes in celebrity, location, and fashion photography. A make-up artist is available and all work is guaranteed.

JEAN FERRO **(323) 462-0121**
www.jeanferro.com

Studio and location sessions for headshots. Specializes in portraits, glamour, and music Industry photography. Actor can negotiate for negatives. Digital and film.

ERIN FIEDLER PHOTOGRAPHY **(818) 415-1533**
www.erinfiedler.com

Capture your unique and most marketable attributes in a comfortable and creative environment. Erin shoots digital or film, color or black and white. CD and/or negatives are yours to keep. Rates are affordable and hair and makeup is available. Check out her website or call for more information.

FLORENZ PHOTOGRAPHY **(323) 848-8447**

Studio and location sessions. Theatrical and commercial headshots and zed cards. Film and digital B&W and color.

LISA FRANCHOT PHOTOGRAPHY **(323) 463-1247**
6183 Glenoak St. **FAX (323) 469-5719**
Los Angeles 90068
www.lisafranchot.com/headshots

As an actress, Lisa spent thousands of dollars on headshots that were beautiful photos but never seemed to capture her. As a photographer it is her goal to capture you, the actor, and what makes you different from everyone else. Lisa shoots one person per day and uses natural lighting and a very comfortable setting to ensure her clients feel as relaxed as possible. Free consultation. Make-up and hair available.

JODY FRANK PHOTOGRAPHY **(818) 763-1545**
4183½ Tujunga Ave.
Studio City 91604
www.jodyfrankphotography.com
jodyfrank@sbcglobal.net

Headshots, publicity, events and theatre. Natural and studio light, digital or film.

FRANTZ PHOTOGRAPHY **(323) 960-4333**
www.frantzturner.com
frantz101@msn.com

Studio and location sessions. All digital 3 hour or half day shoots tailored to suit your personal needs. Headshot packages $400, make-up included. Unconditional money back guarantee. Over 20 years in business.

ERIK FREISER PHOTOGRAPHY **(213) 220-2662**
Hollywood Area
videf@msn.com

Commercial and theatrical headshots and 3/4 bodyshots, as well as fashion photography. Digital still photographer available. Pro Cannon 20D Digital camera. See listing for Orange Video Production under VIDEO TAPE DUPLICATION, AIRCHECKS & PRODUCTION in this section for further information.

FRICK PHOTOGRAPHY **(818) 563-2305**
www.frickphotography.com

Terrence Frick shoots actor headshots with 6-8 looks and unlimited changes. Actor keeps the proofs and negatives. Make-up is extra. Satisfaction guaranteed. If you're not happy with your shots, he'll shoot again for free. He also does fashion photography.

FURNEVEL PHOTOGRAPHY (323) 857-1073
www.furnevelphotography.com
info@furnevelphotography.com

Fun relaxed digital studio shoots. CD available the next business day.

EDDIE GARCIA PHOTOGRAPHY (323) 469-4345
2028 Beachwood Dr.
Hollywood 90068
www.egpictures.com
egarcia1964@sbcglobal.net

Specializes in shooting publicity and production stills for movies and television. Does lots of on-set photography so he understands the needs of actors, producers, and directors. All digital 50 shots for $150 actor supplied with disk and 8 x 11 proof sheet. 100 shots for $150.

JOHN GIBSON PHOTOGRAPHY (323) 662-8884
(800) 241-2769
3346 Wood Terrace
Los Angeles 90027
www.gibsonphotopro.com
photo@gibsonphotopro.com

John does commercial and theatrical headshots for actors and has been recommended by agencies and acting schools for over 20 years. John knows what agents are looking for and how to get that look in your photos.

NANCY JO GILCHRIST (818) 780-0803
www.nancyjophoto.com

Nancy Jo has been serving new and established actors for 20 years. She combines confident experience with up-to-the-minute styling for a fresh, honest and effective photograph that motivates the actor to a higher level of professionalism. Her beautiful, natural light environment and spirited personality make it easy to be open, present and available. Makeup, image consulting, and clear direction are provided, as well as a breathing and relaxation session, before the shoot begins. Check out her website and call for a meeting.

SIMON GLUCKMAN PHOTOGRAPHY (323) 822-0246
www.simongluckman.com FAX (323) 822-0246
simon@simongluckman.com

Originally from England, Simon specializes in actors and celebrities. Working from his Hollywood Hills studio, he mixes natural and studio light in a comfortable and natural setting. Sessions are fun and relaxed, Simon believes an actor's true personality comes out only when they are at their ease. Work is guaranteed. Free consultation. Go to Simon's website to view his work.

DAVID GOLDNER PHOTOGRAPHY (213) 683-1772
2121 E. 7th Pl. #101
Los Angeles 90021
www.davidgoldner.com
photographics@davidgoldner.com

Studio and location. Specializing in special stills for motion pictures and celebrity headshots. Also does fashion, beauty, glamour, advertising and actors' headshots.

PAUL GREGORY PHOTOGRAPHY (323) 848-9682
FAX (213) 382-9158

With 26 years experience in "the business" Paul can give you a shot that not only looks like you, but one that feels like you. Help the Industry know what to do with you. Get a picture that works. Paul shoots mostly natural light and does all his own hair and makeup at no additional charge. The atmosphere at his studio is relaxed and fun loving. All major credit cards accepted and Paul offers a Working Actor's Guide discount. Shoots digital and film (you keep the negatives). SEE AD ON PAGE 149.

WENDY HALL PHOTOGRAPHY (323) 356-2001
2100 N. Main St., Studio A 3
Los Angeles 90031
www.wendyhall.net
info@wendyhall.net

Shooting from a private daylight studio and on location in Los Angeles, Wendy works to make sure that an actor's pictures are what casting directors and agents want to see. Friendly towards budget-conscious performers, digital rolls are $100, film $125, two roll minimum. Retouching, hair, makeup, and wardrobe services also available. Introductory rates for agents. Wendy encourages everyone to look at her online portfolio, full of fashion, editorial and advertising images as well as actor headshots. SEE AD ON PREVIOUS PAGE.

HALPIN-CROYLE PHOTOGRAPHY (323) 874-8500
www.maryannhalpin.com FAX (323) 874-9159

Commercial and theatrical portraiture for the entertainment Industry for 20 years, Mary Ann Halpin is a master photographer and has lectured on the Power of Image and headshots on "Inside Edition," "Extra!" "The View" and has been featured in Life Magazine. Ms. Halpin works with actors to create an image from the inside out based on their personal values and their intrinsic nature. A free consultation is offered when you book the session. Just published: MaryAnn Halpin's "Fearless Women: Midlife Portraits" featuring Joni Mitchell, Erin Brokovich and Shohreh Aghcashloo.

HANDELAND TESORO PHOTOGRAPHY (818) 623-7200
14622 Ventura Blvd., No. 437
Sherman Oaks 91403
www.handelandtesoro.com
info@handelandtesoro.com

Headshot, fashion, and publicity photography. Hair and make-up available. By appointment only.

MICHAEL HELMS (818) 353-5855
www.michaelhelms.com

Commercial and theatrical headshots and 3/4 bodyshots, and fashion photography. Hair styling and make-up are available. Call for details.

JIM HENKEN (818) 988-8612
8538 Paso Robles
Northridge 91325
www.jhpimages.com

Studio and location sessions. Headshots and composites in B&W and color. All ages, also model portfolio work. Reasonably priced. Make-up and hair styling are available.

HIGHLY EFFECTIVE HEADSHOTS BY MARK ROBERT HALPER **(323) 664-7070**
www.highlyeffectiveheadshots.com
headshots@studiomark.com

Mark Robert Halper, an established celebrity and commercial photographer, now offers high-end headshot photography in Los Angeles. Mark brings with him an understanding not only of the craft and art of photography, but an ability to consistently capture who you are and effectively communicate that to people in a position to hire you. He creates highly effective photographic marketing tools for performers by discerning and communicating their individual essence. Rates are on the website.

MICHAEL HILLER **(323) 960-5111**
www.michaelhiller.com

Studio and natural lighting. Digital or film.

RICH HOGAN **(323) 467-2628**
1680 Vine St., Ste. 1110
Hollywood 90028
www.richhogancreative.com
richhoganphotography@hotmail.com

Studio and location. Specializes in headshots, 3/4 bodyshots, commercial and theatrical. A make-up artist is available. Has new specials every couple of months and can design special packages. Actors always keep the negatives. Digital available.

HOLLYWOOD HEADSHOTS **(310) 372-7744**
www.amycantrell.com
amy@amycantrell.com

Amy Cantrell's technical and creative talents as a professional photographer stem from her many years working with celebrities/actors, models, and musicians. Every session is designed to be unique and enjoyable; taking the time and effort necessary to capture personality in the eyes. She uses various lighting styles and backgrounds. Check out our website and call for an appointment to review the portfolios. Satisfaction is guaranteed.

ROBIN HOLLYWOOD PHOTOGRAPHY **(818) 259-2129**
4344 Laurel Canyon Blvd., #7
Studio City 91403
www.robinhollywood.com
robinhollywood@robinhollywood.com

Digital headshot photographer. Robin encourages people to "come have fun and get great shots while you're here."

HOTHEADS PHOTOGRAPHY **(818) 767-8666**

Studio and location sessions. Commercial and theatrical headshots and 3/4 bodyshots. 2 rolls for $150 includes proofsheets and 2 8x10s. Additional prints, $20. Actor keeps the negatives. Digital available. Make-up and hair are available.

ELISA HOWARD PHOTOGRAPHY **(323) 668-2571**

Love your headshots or don't pay! Actors are guaranteed beautiful and natural looking shots. When taking pictures, Elisa looks for sincerity, personality and spirit. She therefore works in a relaxed atmosphere and never rushes her sessions. Hair and make-up available. Studio and natural lighting.

BADER HOWAR PHOTOGRAPHY **(310) 617-5007**
1549 11th St., Ste. 208
Santa Monica 90401
www.baderphoto.com
bader.howar@verizon.net

Bader is a studio and location photographer located in Santa Monica specializing in actors and celebrities. The standard headshot session starts at $400. Digital and film. Private consultation included. Hair/make-up artist available.

JANE HUNT **(323) 874-0134**
Hollywood Hills

Headshots and 3/4 shots that include 3 changes. A make-up artist is available. $350 includes 2 rolls (72 shots), 2 prints, and actor keeps the negatives. A personal planning session precedes each shoot. Ms. Hunt believes casting directors and agents respond to a photo that not only looks like the actor but also conveys his/her own unique presence. Over 20 years in business. Studio located in a beautiful area of the Hollywood Hills.

MARK HUSMANN **(213) 680-9999**
www.greatheadshots.com **FAX (213) 680-1333**

Mark Husmann has been doing headshots for over 20 years, specializing in natural light digital photography in his 6,000 sq. ft. downtown studio. Please visit his website to view the portfolio and state of the art online proof sheets. For rates, to schedule a consultation or to book your headshots, please call. SEE AD ON THE MARKETING TAB.

IDYLLIC PHOTOGRAPHY (310) 226-7110
13819 Riverside Dr.
Sherman Oaks 91423
www.idyllicphotography.com
idyllic2@hotmail.com

Mark Atteberry is an award winning photographer and was voted one of the "Top Three Photographers" by LA Casting Directors and one of the "Top Ten Photographers" by BackStage West. Mark shoots headshots, zed cards and fashion with studio and natural lighting in a relaxed and fun atmosphere. Film and digital.

IGE PHOTOGRAPHY (323) 839-2717
www.igephotography.com

Two rolls, proofs, negatives, wardrobe and makeup consultation for $195.

GREGORY JAMES PHOTOGRAPHER (310) 285-2223

Prefers natural lighting. Works with all types of actors. Keeps his shoots relaxed and affordable. Mr. James has over 10 years in the Industry and welcomes "photographer shoppers" to view his portfolios. Most of his work comes through referrals.

JASHER PHOTOGRAPHY (818) 434-2299
www.jasherphotography.com
jasher@jasherphotography.com

Jeremy Asher does location shoots. Minor retouching included. Hair and makeup available for an additional charge. See website for portfolio and additional information.

KERRY JON PHOTOGRAPHY (661) 259-3198

Studio and location. Fashion, commercial, and theatrical headshots. Works in both B&W and color. Composites and/or portfolios are available. Proofsheets and 8x10s are included, negatives are negotiable. Offers individual packages for actors. All work is guaranteed.

KERRY KARA PHOTOGRAPHY (661) 257-8175
KLS PHOTOS & IMAGING (866) KERRY-KARA
28149 Gibraltar Lane
Santa Clarita 91384
www.kerrykara.com
kerry@kerrykara.com

Film or digital. See website for portfolio and pricing. Shooting headshots is a technique and working actors know that the most important thing, other than studying your craft, is your headshot. Kerry feels it is important that you do not cut corners on your headshots as that always shows in the final product and then you just have to start all over again.

KATAMI DIGITAL PHOTOGRAPHY (818) 421-4544
www.samedayheadshots.com
katami@samedayheadshots.com

The headshot revolution has arrived. KDP uses professional digital equipment to provide the client with same day headshot service. Shoot, instantly review, and take a CD ROM the same day. Forget about contact sheets, waiting for proofs, and several trips in traffic. Get great shots same day. Call for a free consultation and appointments are necessary.

THOMAS KITRELL STUDIOS (213) 738-1904
3978 W. 6th St.
Los Angeles 90020

Studio and location sessions. Specializes in theatrical and commercial headshots with a distinctive style. Also shoots musicians. Make-up artist and retouching is available. $135 for 1 roll, actor keeps the negatives or he can shoot digital and provide a CD. Over 28 years in business.

JACKI KORITO (818) 343-1017
11684 Ventura Blvd., Ste. 717 FAX (818) 343-6252
Studio City 91604
www.jackikorito.com

Studio and location sessions. Theatrical and commercial headshots and publicity photos. Specializes in "people photography." Negatives are negotiable. Also does hand tinting.

ED KRIEGER PHOTOGRAPHY (818) 248-6789

Ed is also a working actor and knows how to work with actors to get good photos. In business for almost 30 years, he specializes in photos for working actors, headshots, 3/4 and productions/publicity photos for theatre and related events. He is currently a contributing photographer to Back Stage West and staff photographer for KCET. Theatre clients include the Music Theatre of Southern California, The Theatre League, The Civic Light Opera of South Bay Cities, The Cabrillo Music Theatre, The Cast, Theatre 40, El Portal Center for the Arts, The Fountain Theatre, Deaf West Theatre Company and The Actors Co-op. Also shoots for SAG, AFTRA, and AEA. Ed tries to keep prices very reasonable and encourages people to get "smaller" shoots but more often.

LA CASTING COUCH
PHOTOGRAPHY AND WEBSITES (877) 721-2667
438 Prospect Ave.
Hermosa Beach 90254
www.laccheadshots.com

Check out their portfolio online or at Reproductions. LA Casting Couch offers three rolls of 36 exposure color or B&W for $350 and you keep the negatives. They also offer affordable prints and Photoshop. Call or go online to schedule an appointment. Credit cards accepted.

MICHAEL LAMONT (818) 506-0285
www.michaellamont.com

Studio and location sessions. Film and digital. Theatrical and commercial headshots, 3/4 bodyshots, and production stills. A full service studio. A member of IATSE Local 600, the International Cinematographers Guild. Rates include make-up and grooming. Call for preliminary consultation. Specializes in working "moment to moment."

PAUL LANDRY PHOTOGRAPHY (818) 399-6899
www.paullandryphotography.com

Studio and location sessions specializing in headshots and 3/4 shots. Also shoots models and portfolios, publicity stills and portraits. Spends a lot of time finding out what the actor's casting is and what your agent expects to get the product you want. Makes sure the actor is comfortable before shooting. Specializes in children, toddlers on up.

HARRY LANGDON PHOTOGRAPHY (310) 859-4900
9244 Wilshire Blvd. FAX (310) 859-9593
Beverly Hills 90210
www.harrylangdon.com
click@earthlink.net

Creative headshots and composites for the experienced actor. Call the studio for prices.

SUZE LANIER PHOTOGRAPHY (323) 460-4060
Studio City 91604
www.suzelanier.com

Studio and location sessions. Digital or film. Specializes in theatrical and commercial headshots, and also shoots Zed cards, high fashion photography and composites. Make-up artist and retouching is available. Also shoots in Dallas and New York.

DIANA LANNES PHOTOGRAPHY (213) 427-8096 (323) 465-3232
650 N. Bronson Ave., Ste. 142
Los Angeles 90004
www.dianalannes.com

Diana has been shooting headshots for the last 10 years in New York and Los Angeles. She shoots in natural light in her garden studio, or on the Raleigh studios lot in Hollywood and specializes in commercial, theatrical and children's shots. Professional make-up is available, the atmosphere is fun and relaxing. Rates are reasonable. Digital and retouching available.

BOB LIBENS PHOTOGRAPHY (323) 876-2977
7188 Sunset Blvd., Ste. 106
Hollywood 90046
www.boblibens.com
bob@boblibens.com

Studio and location sessions. Commercial and theatrical headshots, 3/4 bodyshots, and full-length shots. Digital. Make-up and hair is available. Actor keeps the photo CD. Satisfaction guaranteed.$125 includes 40 pictures on two proof sheets and one 8x10. All pictures on CD ready the same day. Check out the website to view portfolio and pricing information.

LIFE MOMENT PHOTO STUDIO (818) 761-9590 (323) 449-1379
11390 Ventura Blvd. FAX (818) 761-9166
Studio City 91604
www.lifemomentphoto.com
frenkelalex@hotmail.com

Specialists in putting your best face forward. Headshots, portfolios, modeling, dance and any other kind of photo.

LINEAR PHOTOGRAPHY (323) 471-1456
7200 Franklin Ave., #425
Hollywood 90046
michaelconway@hotpop.com

Two-hour digital headshot session regularly $250, $175 for WAG users. Ideal for headshots or ZED card. Each session price includes two 8x10 prints or six 4x6 prints and a CD with JPEG versions of all the pictures available at the end of the session. Sessions vary but usually between 120 – 200 pictures are shot. All pictures in color which can easily be converted to B&W. Photo editing available.

JO LIU PHOTOGRAPHY (213) 623-2556
Los Angeles 90013
www.joliuphotography.com
jo@joliuphotography.com

Specializes in digital headshots and promotional pieces for actors, models and entertainers using both studio and natural lighting. Offers proofs online and complimentary retouching.

PHOTOGRAPHY BY LORENZO (323) 876-9675
www.headshotsbylorenzo.com

Lorenzo specializes in natural light photography. He has built a name for himself shooting much of L.A.'s "up and coming." He believes each shoot should customize itself to the actor and not the photographer's "art" and he doesn't just sit there and do the same thing over and over. Film and digital. Relaxed sessions.

SABI MARKS PHOTOGRAPHY (310) 488-8234
P.O. Box 241025
Los Angeles 90024
www.sabimarks.com
sabi@sabimarks.com

In the Industry for about 20 years, both in front of the lens as a model/actor and behind the lens, Sabi knows what is needed and how to capture it and tries to work within the actor's budget. Now shooting in Los Angeles, San Diego, and San Francisco.

DOUG MAY (818) 763-4433

Natural light photography, 2 rolls for $225, proofs and negatives. 3/4 shots, headshots. 3-4 changes, relaxed atmosphere. Studio City location. Will work with actors to get the best shots.

WES MCDOWELL PHOTOGRAPHY (310) 770-0230
1420 N. Alta Vista Blvd.
Los Angeles 90046
www.wesmcdowell.com
photobywes@aol.com

The Next Generation in Headshot Photography. Working almost exclusively with natural light, Wes specializes in cutting edge headshots that will get you noticed. His contemporary style is perfect for today's actor, and will show not only how you truly look on your best days but also your uniqueness and energy. Check out the website to view his portfolio, or make an appointment to view it at the studio.

KEVIN MERRILL PHOTOGRAPHY (818) 508-4533
www.kevinmerril.com

Studio and location sessions. Specializes in headshots, fashion, and celebrities. Headshots start at $295 and include 3 rolls. Digital or film. All film shoots always include Polaroids and negatives. A make-up artist and retouching is available.

STEVE MESSINA PHOTOGRAPHY (818) 762-7097
5934 Simpson Ave.
Valley Village 91607
www.stevemessina.com
funkycm@pacbell.net

Studio and location sessions. Specializes in quality headshots for actors, dancers, and children. Also shoots 3/4 and full bodyshots. $100 for 1 roll two roll minimum. An actor/dancer himself, he understands the fears and needs of other performers and has an innovative approach to headshots and 3/4 bodyshots. Steve has been in the entertainment business for over 15 years.

ROBERT MILLARD, PHOTOGRAPHER (626) 792-3237
1601 Las Lunas
Pasadena 91106
www.millardphotos.com

Session packages from $350. All digital. All types of publicity portraiture. Make-up, hair, and retouching are available and there is no limit on costume changes. Free consultation and all work is guaranteed. Evening and weekend sessions available. In business since 1982.

MATTHEW MITCHELL PHOTO (310) 488-9134
3416 Glendale Blvd. FAX (323) 664-2909
Los Angeles 90039
www.matthewmitchellphoto.com
matthewmitchellphoto@hotmail.com

Fashion, headshots, editorial, beauty. Digital or film. Studio or location.

DONALD NORRIS PHOTO (818) 693-9114
937 Wilcox Ave., #7
Los Angeles 90038
www.norrisphoto.com
donaldnorris@norrisphoto.com

Relaxed and fun atmosphere. Works great with actors of all ages, beginners, advanced and everything in between. Uses natural light and professional digital equipment. Will consult your agent and help select outfits based on marketability and character type. Hair and makeup available. Retouching available. Prices and packages listed on website. Payment plans, group discounts, and accepts all forms of payment. Book showings and free consultations available. SEE AD ON PAGE 159.

MICHAEL PAPO PHOTOGRAPHY (818) 760-8160
11120 Burbank Blvd., Ste. A
North Hollywood 91601
www.michaelpapo.com
info@michaelpapo.com

26 years of success. Michael shoots new comers, series regulars and stars. He works like a director, not shooting until the client's eyes are speaking to the camera. He does this through nurturing direction, music and an atmosphere where you can be who you are. Michael does most of the make-up for his shoot, using clients' music to enhance the mood and allowing each person to own their negatives or a disc. Includes makeup, negatives/disc and the time to be taken care of. It's a team effort that makes it all work. Check out website for bio, portfolio and pricing.

PERRINE PHOTOGRAPHY (323) 871-1606
(626) 792-3075
www.perrinephotography.com

Studio and location. Does anything and everything from commercial and theatrical headshots to model portfolios. Digital. Same day service.

PHOTO GALLERIA (805) 483-3686
2626 Saviers Road
Oxnard 93033

Photography for actors and musicians. Studio photo sessions as low as $120 for headshots includes 36 exposures, proofs, and three 8x10s. Several different backgrounds available. Proofs available the next day, prints in 24 hours. Make-up available. Composites, groups, or full length shots. See listing under PHOTO LABS & REPRODUCTION in this section for further information.

PHOTO GERARD (818) 762-9115

Studio and location sessions. Headshots or bodyshots starting $250. Also shoots Zed cards. Make-up artist and retouching is available. Quick turnaround time. All work guaranteed. Over 25 years in business.

PHOTOGRAPHY BY LUCIA (818) 771-7733
www.home.earthlink.net/~lucia
lucia@earthlink.net

Studio or location. Theatrical and commercial headshots and 3/4 body shots, composites, model portfolios, musicians. Adults and children. Make-up and retouching available. Air conditioned Hollywood studio has make-up table, private changing room, relaxed atmosphere. Free image and marketing consultation. Quick turnaround. All work is guaranteed. Mention the Working Actor's Guide for a special discount.

PHOTOGRAPHY BY NAOMI (323) 850-5299
naomiyvette@aol.com FAX (323) 851-5156

Mostly studio shoots, some location work. Specializes in glamour, fashion, and mood photography. Headshots and composites for $100 per roll plus the cost of the film. She shoots the rolls of film and gives them to the actor. A make-up artist is available. Over 20 years in business.

THE PICTURE PLACE (818) 757-7803
18399 Ventura Blvd., #17 FAX (818) 735-9919
Tarzana 91356
www.thepictureplace.net
thepictureplace@sbcglobal.net

Digital headshots.

KARL PRESTON (310) 396-9733
2408 2nd St.
Santa Monica 90405
www.karlpreston.com
modelbook@aol.com

Specializes in color headshots. Indoor/outdoor studio and location sessions. Commercial and theatrical headshots, 3/4 modeling portfolios. You keep negatives. $275 for 3 rolls. Takes his time and does not schedule people back to back. A successful actor/model himself for 13 years, and a principal performer in over 100 TV commercials, films, and TV shows. Also the author of a book on modeling, "Modelmania." Lighting is Mr. Preston's specialty.

REX, INC. **(323) 664-6494**
4446 Ambrose Ave. **FAX (323) 664-6112**
Los Angeles 90027
www.therexagency.com

Represents make-up artists, wardrobe consultants, hair stylists and photographers.

ALISON REYNOLDS PHOTOGRAPHY **(818) 788-7757**

Studio or available light in the studio or location sessions. Headshots, character shots, 3/4 bodyshots, or full length. Make-up, help with wardrobe and print retouching on 8x10. Photographer keeps the negatives. Many years experience as a photographer, retoucher, make-up artist and wardrobe stylist. 11 years at a major magazine. Call for prices.

BILL RICH **(310) 207-0722**
www.billrichphotography.com
bill@billrichphotography.com

Studio and location sessions. Theatrical and commercial headshots. Digital or film. Uses actors for brochure and catalogue work.

ROBERT STUDIOS **(323) 653-8888** **(888) 820-9639**
8845 Olympic Blvd., Ste. 103
Beverly Hills 90211
www.robertstudios.com
robertstudios@yahoo.com

Headshots, body and full body shots for modeling, commercial, business, theatrical, portraiture, musician and publicity. Natural light or a mixture designed to bring the best of you. First roll $200, additional rolls are $100 each which includes proof sheets and one 8x10 per roll. Custom in-house printing. Make-up and retouching available. 15 years of experience.

ARTHUR ROBERTS **(310) 827-9661**
Marina Del Rey
adr9999@verizon.net

Studio and location sessions. 2 rolls, $160, actor keeps the negatives. Over 30 years experience in New York and L.A. An actor/model himself, Mr. Roberts knows how actors feel in front of a camera and will bring out the real you. Satisfaction Guaranteed.

DALE ROBINETTE **(310) 455-3040**
P.O. Box 505
Topanga 90290

Studio and location headshot and composite photo sessions. Make-up and retouching is available. Cost varies.

APRIL ROCHA PHOTOGRAPHY **(310) 319-0465**
1633 Oak St.
Santa Monica 90405
www.aprilrocha.com
april@aprilrocha.com

Headshot photography. Studio and location.

BRADFORD ROGNE PHOTOGRAPHY **(310) 497-0642**
1308 Factory Place, #512
Los Angeles 90013
www.photosla.com
bradford@photosla.com

Bradford Rogne is one of L.A.'s premier headshot photographers, as well as an accomplished celebrity make-up artist. Shooting with a simultaneous mix of studio and natural light, his downtown L.A. Loft offers a relaxed and creative environment. All shoots are digital and include make-up as well as a disc of the entire session. An online photo gallery of your session is also posted to the web same day.

JASON ROSE PHOTOGRAPHY **(818) 556-5241**
1513 W. Alameda Ave.
Burbank 91506
www.actorimage.com
jason@actorimage.com

Specializing in headshot and model photography. Check website or call for pricing and information.

MITCHELL ROSE PHOTOGRAPHY **(323) 462-8636**
1142-B Seward St. **FAX (323) 462-6578**
Hollywood 90038
www.mitchellrosephotos.com
mrosephotography@earthlink.net

Studio and location sessions. Make-up artist and hair stylist is available. Free consultations, and referral services. All work guaranteed. Over 20 years in business.

TAMA ROTHSCHILD **(310) 657-1522**

Both studio and location sessions. Ms. Rothschild specializes in theatrical and commercial headshots and 3/4 shots. Make-up artist and hair stylist are available. No charge for consultations. All work is guaranteed and competitively priced. Over 20 years in business.

TIM SABATINO **(213) 840-2220** **(818) 785-7015**
6101 Fulton Ave., #1 **FAX (818) 785-7015**
Valley Glen 91401
www.timsabatino.com
tim@timsabatino.com

Headshot photography for actors. Personalities captured on film. Visit the website for portfolio. SEE AD ON PAGE 161.

ROMAN SALICKI PHOTOGRAPHY **(323) 876-0304**
1310 N. Stanley Ave. **FAX (323) 882-6506**
Los Angeles 90046
www.romansalickiphotography.com
romansalicki@sbcglobal.net

Studio and location sessions. Theatrical headshots as well as publicity and editorial photography. Specializes in people and for many years has been a celebrity photographer. Shoots digital or film. Call for portfolio review. SEE AD ON PAGE 155.

MICHAEL SANVILLE PHOTOGRAPHY **(323) 654-9141**
www.michaelsanville.com

Mr. Sanville works with top agents, managers, casting directors and coaches, all of whom swear by him. He is not a factory photographer. He shoots sessions not per roll shoots. By appointment only.

MARK SAVAGE PHOTOGRAPHER (310) 367-4706
www.marksavage.com
marksavagephoto@aol.com

Works on location throughout Southern California. The standard package is a photo CD for $275. Make-up is extra. Expert digital retouching available for blemishes and wrinkles. Mr. Savage has over 15 years experience photographing hundreds of actors, musicians, performance artists, and personalities.

SCHULTZ BROTHERS PHOTOGRAPHY (323) 634-7004
(714) 540-6544
2949-A Randolph Ave. FAX (714) 540-4393
Costa Mesa 92626
www.schultzbrosphotos.com

Studio and location sessions. Shoots headshots and 3/4 bodyshots. A make-up artist is available. Minor retouching is included in the price and all work is guaranteed. 26 years in business.

CAROL SHERIDAN PHOTOGRAPHY (323) 662-5411
www.carolsheridanphoto.com

Studio or location, digital of film. Carol has a great eye and will capture your essence in a relaxed atmosphere.

THE SHOT PHOTOGRAPHY (323) 850-SHOT
3416 Glendale
Los Angeles 90039
www.theshotphotography.com
shotphotography@aol.com

Features the headshot photography of Jeffrey Nicholson, who has been shooting headshots in Los Angeles, Chicago and New York for over 10 years. He is referred by many of the top agencies and his photography has been described as "fresh" and "original." Sessions are very relaxed with the emphasis always on the eyes. To visit the studio and see more of Jeff's photography, call for a free consultation.

JOHN SKALICKY (323) 933-6771
1025 S. Tremaine Ave.
Los Angeles 90019
www.skalickyphoto.com

Specializes in portraiture that captures the actor's personality rather

CYNTHIA SMALLEY PHOTOGRAPHY (323) 467-4741
www.smalleyphoto.com

Headshots, portraits, "petraits" and commercial advertising. Natural light photography. Digital and film. Also checkout her work on www.wildhorsesandwesternart.com

PAUL SMITH PHOTOGRAPHY (323) 463-8864
www.paulsmithphotography.com
paulsmith@paulsmithphotography.com

Top Australian photographer with over 15 years experience, location and studio sessions. Specializes in commercial and theatrical headshots as well as fashion. Fun relaxed atmosphere with an emphasis on getting the shot and look that's right for the actor. All work is guaranteed and competitively priced. Hair and make-up are available on request.

DAVID SOBEL PHOTOGRAPHY (310) 790-2940
www.davidsobel.com
das28@earthlink.net

David has been shooting for twenty years and is truly an actors' photographer. His shoots are fun, affordable and very specific in capturing exactly what you want in your brilliant new headshot. And he guarantees you'll like your prints or he'll re-shoot you for cost of film and processing. Visit his website or call for more information and price packages.

RON SORENSEN PRODUCTIONS PHOTOGRAPHY (310) 450-7969
5215 Sepulveda Blvd., Ste 9D
Culver City 90230
www.sorensenstudio.com
sorensenstudio@cs.com

Studio and natural light headshots that say "Look at me"! With a degree in marketing and over twenty years shooting actors it's no wonder Ron is one of the most referred photographers in LA. Go to the website and request a free copy of "Playing the Game," the marketing guide for actors that teaches you how to get more auditions.

KELI SQUIRES-TAYLOR (323) 938-7729
6056 Whitworth Drive
Los Angeles 92625
www.kelisquirestaylor.biz
keli@kelisquirestaylor.biz

Personal Manager Keli Squires-Taylor shoots headshots with her new innovative color pictures. Keli also brings her marketing, design and styling expertise as an Industry professional to the photo shoots. Something other photographers just can't do. Works with all acting levels to give honest marketing evaluations, marketing guidance and business advice to help you move on up to the next level(s) quickly. Retouching, graphic design and styling included in packages.

STAR QUALITY PHOTOS (818) 506-6194

Location sessions – natural, soft reflected light. Specializing in theatrical headshots. The number of rolls varies, unlimited changes, and no prints. Actor keeps the negatives and can have whichever prints he likes made up at his own discretion. A make-up artist is available. Reasonable rates, Over 20 years in business.

STOCKWELL PHOTOGRAPHY (818) 754-1126
www.stockwellphotography.com
rickstockwell22@aol.com

Headshots of actors, singers, dancers, models, kids and bands. Studio or location. Competitive rates.

DOREEN STONE (323) 876-2636

Studio sessions. Specializes in headshots, ages 3-21. Relaxed atmosphere. Photos on CD available. Digital and film.

LISA STONICH PHOTOGRAPHY (818) 703-7509

Headshot packages starting at $150. Will do studio theatrical look and outdoor commercial look in the same session on location. Make-up artists available and all work is guaranteed. Call to view portfolio and for more information

SUN IMAGING CENTER (323) 654-5556
8168 W. Sunset Blvd.
Los Angeles 90046
www.sunimagingcenter.com

Sun Imaging can save you money and time. They provide one-stop shopping with headshot and modeling photography, headshot prints, lithographs, zed cards, business cards, postcards and retouching all available. Also resumes, back side printing and shipping available. Other services include: B/W, slides, slide dupes, print to print (with no negatives), 30 minute color 35mm or advanced photo system. Monday through Friday, 9 am to 7 pm and Saturday 10 am to 4 pm. Satisfaction guaranteed.

ALISHA TAMBURRI PHOTOGRAPHER (818) 998-8838
www.atamburri.com FAX (818) 998-6073

Begin your relaxed, fun, safe, sessions with a relaxation exercise. Specializes in actor's theatrical and commercial headshots and 3/4 bodyshots, adults, children, teens, and celebrities. Polaroids are taken before the session and a make-up artist is available. Shoots only two people in a day, never rushed, unlimited wardrobe changes. Your choice of music played. Competitively priced, free consultation. Over 20 years in business.

TRAVIS TANNER (818) 762-8588
(310) 770-7588
10061 Riverside Dr., Ste. 174
Toluca Lake 91602
www.travistanner.com
travistanner@emac.com

Over ten years in Los Angeles, shooting actors, and print models of all types. Check out the website. Prices negotiable according to the specific needs of each client. Travis shoots digital and film, studio and natural light.

TED TRENT (213) 891-9345
www.tedtrent.com
ted@tedtrent.com

Headshot and model photography. Packages start at $50. Studio and location, digital only.

TODD TYLER PHOTOGRAPHY (213) 481-0136
1101 Laveta Terrace #15
Los Angeles 90026
www.laphotospot.com
todd@toddtyler.com

Beautiful color and black and white headshots. Works with actors in all stages of their careers and specialize in creating a relaxed atmosphere to give you that perfect headshot.

MARGO VANN STUDIO (818) 557-8201
134 S. Cordova Unit C
Burbank 91505

Studio sessions. Specializes in actor's headshots and model's portfolios. Headshots range from $200-500. The negatives or CD are negotiable and make-up artist is available. Air conditioned studio. Over 25 years in business for the entertainment Industry. Adults and children. Samples shown by appointment.

LINDA A. VANOFF (310) 550-8430
West Hollywood FAX (310) 550-0148
www.lindavanoff.com
lvanoff@aol.com

Promises the new actor a working headshot. Studio sessions and natural light. Linda A. Vanoff is best known for her advertising and celebrity editorial. Shoots headshots mostly by agency referral. Call for appointment.

RAUL VEGA (213) 387-2058
www.raulvega.com

Available studio and location sessions. Professional hair and make-up are available. Raul has worked with actors and models in the fashion world. Digital services available.

UTE VILLE (323) 658-6574
www.uteville-photography.com
uteville@aol.com

European photographer Ute Ville, has spent more than 15 years creating "special looks" for actors, models, musicians, children, and celebrities. She specializes in theatrical and commercial headshots and location model composites. Each session is complete with make-up and styling.

VITTI PHOTOGRAPHY (323) 936-3712
320 N. Gardner St.
Los Angeles 90036
www.vittiphotography.com
tvphoto@comcast.net

Todd Vitti specializes in commercial and theatrical headshots as well as fashion. He will provide high end digital images the same day. High end retouching also available. Call for rates. Please visit his website.

VLADIMIR STUDIOS (323) 656-3333
5340 Tyrone Ave. FAX (323) 656-6929
Sherman Oaks 91423
www.vladimirstudios.com

Location sessions. Headshots, composites, and digital portfolios. Prices start at $100. Shoots both B&W and color. Make-up artist and retouching is available by request. Over 35 years in business. By appointment only. Also does actors reels.

VOGUE PHOTOGRAPHY (310) 453-0065
2623 Santa Monica Blvd. FAX (310) 453-0407
Santa Monica 90404

Mostly studio sessions but will also do some location. Specializes in fashion, theatrical, and commercial headshots, 3/4 bodyshots, and full length body photography. Big studio with a relaxed atmosphere that includes music and a changing room. 1 roll $220, 2 rolls $320, more for location shots, includes 1 proofsheet and one 8x10 print per roll and actor keeps the negatives. A make-up artist is available. Over 22 years experience.

GLORIA WACO PHOTOGRAPHY (323) 469-2818
Melrose/Highland Studio Location
www.gloriawaco.com

Specializing in the male image. Rated best male photographer in California. Celebrating 26 years of artistic excellence, Gloria has successfully photographed and personally coached thousands of male actors. Headshots, portraits, 3/4 and full body shots, commercial, theatrical, character, comedy, fashion, music, physique, advertising, and PR-celebrity. All ages, newcomers welcome. Gloria is attentive to individual needs and concerns during her prior image/wardrobe/coaching consultation. All sessions are directed, fun-motivated, and reasonably priced. Makeup and hairstyling are also included. Film and digital. Digital retouching available. Studio or location.

KAT WARD PHOTOGRAPHY **(323) 428-9921**
www.katwardphoto.com
katwardphoto@msn.com

Natural light studio. Kat likes to proceed at a relaxed pace in order to develop a rapport with her clients, to have fun (most definitely), and create an atmosphere in which she can capture the personality, character and essence of her clients.

JIM WARREN **(323) 850-1500**

Specializes in publicity shots for the working actor while continuing to provide headshots for all performers. His work has been featured in TV Guide and several other national publications. Call for rates.

KEN WEINGART **(310) 395-4613**
204 Washington Ave., #108 **FAX (310) 395-4618**
Santa Monica 90403
www.kenweingart.com
info@kenweingart.com

The main goal of a shoot with Ken is to get great photos in a relaxing and fun environment which will enhance your portfolio and get the phone ringing for you. He creates photos that capture how you look coming through the door to your audition; photos that show your personality at its best: spontaneous, relaxed, easygoing, natural and elegant. Ken takes photos that have an interesting composition and character spark that makes them compelling and distinct from the other photos of people in your age range and physical type. Check out his website which includes photo galleries, rates and information.

ALAN WEISSMAN PHOTOGRAPHY **(818) 766-9797**
11288 Ventura Blvd. **FAX (818) 766-1742**
Studio City 91604
www.alanweissman.com

Alan is a master of lighting and uses this to bring out each actor's uniqueness resulting in a photo that not only looks like the person, but is the essence of that particular actor. Whether working with Mel Gibson, Jodie Foster or an actor just beginning his or her career, he feels the same excitement. This caring attitude and personal warmth is why many actors refer their friends to him. He is also recognized by casting directors, managers and an extraordinary number of agents for his consistently good work. Alan shoots only two sessions a day to insure the clients' comfort and ease, Digital test shots are taken before each wardrobe or hair change and reviewed by Alan, the client and the make up artist. In addition to a regular session he can provide stylistic lighting to produce an attention-getting postcard. This lighting effect can give you a contemporary working actors portrait like the actors in "People" magazine's 50 Most Beautiful People issue. Alan invites you to make an appointment to look at his books and meet his dog Rex.

WESTSIDE STUDIO **(310) 479-8119**
11316 Santa Monica Blvd.
W. Los Angeles 90025
www.westsidestudio.net

Studio. Natural light available. Headshots, 3/4 bodyshots, full body, and specialty shots individually designed to sculpt your face and bring out the beauty in your eyes. Takes preview Polaroids prior to actual shooting. First roll $200, additional rolls are $125 each which includes proofsheets and one 8x10 per roll. Custom in-house printing. Make-up and retouching available. The studio is open Monday through Friday, 10 am to 6 pm and Saturday, 10 am to 2 pm. They encourage actors to drop by and see their work. Digital available for $100 per hour with a 2 hour minimum.

DICK WIEAND **(818) 788-4746**
www.dickwphoto.com
dickww@sbcglobal.net

Dick Wieand is nationally known as an actor's photographer because he understands the importance of pictures in the casting process. He finds an actor's "castability." Dick shoots in the studio or on location, commercial and theatrical and has an easy and relaxed approach to his sessions. Whether a seasoned professional or a beginning artist, every actor is an individual and has something unique to offer. It's his job to get it on film. Sessions start at $275 whether B&W or color, and actor leaves session with a CD in hand. Make-up is available and encouraged. Film and digital services. Check out his portfolios or see samples at the website.

CRAIG WRIGHT STUDIOS **(323) 860-6525**
1680 N. Vine Street #1110
Los Angeles 90028
www.craigwrightstudios.com
info@craigwrightstudios.com

Craig Wright specializes in shooting fashion, beauty, and publicity shots for actors, models, musicians and the entertainment Industry. His work has appeared in magazines, advertisements and on record album covers and he has worked with a variety of celebrities. Trained by his uncle, an Emmy-nominated cinematographer, his approach is unique and informal, immediately relaxing his subjects. For more information and to review some of his work, visit his website.

DEBRA YOUNG PHOTOGRAPHY **(310) 318-8158**
www.debrayoungphoto.com **FAX (310) 373-3697**
debra@debrayoungphoto.com

Primarily location sessions. Theatrical and commercial headshots and 3/4 bodyshots, also fashion portfolios.

SHANDON YOUNGCLAUS
PHOTOGRAPHY **(818) 766-8389**
www.amazingheadshots.com **FAX (503) 210-7988**
shandon@amazingheadshots.com

Shandon Youngclaus offers a relaxed shooting environment and takes the time to get the shots you need. The digital shoot offers more possibilities, including choice of color or black and white, instant review of your shots in a post-session consultation, online proofsheets for easy sharing, and the ability to quickly adjust the digital file so that your final headshots are more creative and dynamic. Shandon works with the best photo labs in Los Angeles, providing photographic proofsheets and the best reproductions in the Industry.

PHOTOGRAPHY BY ZAREK **(818) 304-0334**
14764 Ventura Blvd.
Sherman Oaks 91403
www.photographybyzarek.com

Capturing pure emotions. Photography for theatrical and commercial. A fresh approach to studio or location headshots (3/4, head and shoulders or both.) Call or visit the website for more information.

Photographers

ZEN TODD (323) 883-0200 / (888) 309-5488
3215 Velma Drive
Los Angeles 90068
www.zentodd.com
zen@zentodd.com

Zen Todd is a master headshot photographer. Using natural light and state of the art digital equipment, Zen has helped thousands of actors from beginners to celebrities get Industry leading headshots. Zen has been a professional actor and photographer for more than 10 years. Based on his extensive experience both in front of and behind the camera, Zen has developed a headshot technique that guarantees dynamic results for actors of all ages and types. Hair and makeup, retouching and free consultations are available. Visa/MC welcome.

Press Releases

If there is something unusual currently going on in your life or in your career, this is an opportune time for you to send out a press release. Since press releases are by their nature designed to be sent to newspapers and magazines, you must have something to say that will capture their attention. Newspapers have pages to fill daily and they are grateful for the help. Whatever you're publicizing should be noteworthy. Look for a hook; find an interesting angle. Press releases must be in a particular format with the following information. 1.. Name of the company sending the release (on their letterhead) 2. Date the release is being sent and when it is to be released. 3. The who, what, why, when and how of the 'event' being publicized. "Hollywood Here I Come! An Insider's Guide to a Successful Acting and Modeling Career in L.A."—Cynthia Hunter

BACK STAGE WEST
THE PERFORMING ARTS WEEKLY (323) 525-2356
Attn: Theatre Openings FAX (323) 525-2354
5055 Wilshire Blvd., 6th Fl.
Los Angeles 90036
www.backstagewest.com
bsweditorial@backstagewest.com

Reviews 99 seat as well as Equity productions. Send one copy of your press kit and they will consider it for review. You may send your press release via email, fax or regular mail. SEE AD ON BACK COVER.

DAILY BREEZE (310) 540-5511
Attn: Jim Farber FAX (310) 540-7581
5215 Torrance Blvd.
Torrance 90505
www.dailybreeze.com

Reviews South Bay productions only.

DAILY NEWS (818) 713-3636 / (818) 713-3000
Attn: Evan Henerson FAX (818) 713-3545
P.O. Box 4200
Woodland Hills 91365
www.dailynews.com

Reviews 99 Seat Plan productions and will list them in the paper's Calendar section. Send two information packets, one to Evan Henderson for review.

DAILY VARIETY (323) 857-6600
Attn: Phil Gallo FAX (323) 857-0742
5700 Wilshire Blvd., Ste. 120
Los Angeles 90036
www.dailyvariety.com
pgallo@reedbusiness.com

Has very few reviewers and does not list productions. They will keep the information as long as the play is running and will send a reviewer as time permits. Send material to Phil Gallo for possible review.

EASY READER (310) 372-4611
Attn: Bondo Wiszpolski FAX (310) 318-6292
P.O. Box 427
Hermosa Beach 90254
www.hermosawave.net

Primarily reviews productions in the South Bay area and a few plays in West Los Angeles.

HOLLYWOOD REPORTER (323) 525-2000
Attn: Ed Kaufman FAX (323) 525-2377
5055 Wilshire Blvd., Ste. 600
Los Angeles 90036
www.hollywoodreporter.com

They prefer that you fax press releases to them.

THE JEWISH NEWS (818) 786-4000
15060 Ventura Blvd., Ste. 210 FAX (818) 380-9232
Sherman Oaks 91403
blazergroup@aol.com

Publishes the opening dates and reviews most San Fernando Valley productions as well as some of those in West Los Angeles and matinees in Hollywood. Send press releases to Bobby.

L.A. WEEKLY (323) 465-9909
Attn: Steven Leigh Morris
6715 Sunset Blvd.
Los Angeles 90028
www.laweekly.com
editorial@laweekly.com

Reviews and lists 99 Seat Plan productions.

LA OPINION (213) 622-8332 / (213) 896-2300
700 S. Flower St., Ste. 3100 FAX (213) 896-2171
Los Angeles 90017
www.laopinion.com

Reviews both English and Spanish language plays. Also has listings in their Calendar section.

LONG BEACH PRESS TELEGRAM (562) 435-1161
Attn: Marlene Greer FAX (562) 499-1232
604 Pine Ave.
Long Beach 90844

Publishes information in their Lifestyle section for the Los Angeles

PRESS RELEASES

and greater Long Beach areas. Will occasionally send a reviewer to productions.

LOS ANGELES INDEPENDENT **(323) 556-5720**
Attn: Marci Santana **FAX (323) 556-5704**
4201 Wilshire Blvd., Ste. 600
Los Angeles 90010
www.laindependent.com
laingroup@aol.com

A group of local community newspapers that lists 99 Seat Plan productions and occasionally reviews them.

LOS ANGELES MAGAZINE **(323) 801-0100**
(323) 801-0075
Attn: R.J. Smith **FAX (323) 801-0105**
5900 Wilshire Blvd., 10th Fl.
Los Angeles 90036
www.lamag.com

They will list 99 Seat Plan productions in their calendar section but they do not review them. Send press releases at least 2 months prior to the opening date.

LOS ANGELES TIMES **(213) 237-7000**
Attn: Don Shirley **FAX (213) 237-7630**
Theatre Calendar Listing
200 W. 1st St.
Los Angeles 90012

FedEx:
130 S. Broadway
Los Angeles 90012
www.latimes.com

Reviews and lists 99 Seat Plan plays in their Calendar section. Send 2 copies of your press release packet which must arrive at least 10 days prior to the Sunday publishing date.

SAN GABRIEL TRIBUNE **(626) 962-8811**
Attn: Jennifer Enrico
1210 N. Azusa Canyon Road
West Covina 91790
www.sgvtribune.com

Press releases should be sent with a cover letter requesting to be reviewed.

PRINTING & PHOTOCOPYING

3R PRINTING **(818) 841-8000**
2921 W. Burbank Blvd. **FAX (818) 841-8088**
Burbank 91505
www.threerprinting.com
threer@pacbell.net

An established printing company since 1983, offering a variety of services from one color to four color printing. Also provides mailing services.

ABC PICTURES, INC. **(888) 526-5336**
1867 E. Florida St. **FAX (417) 869-9185**
Springfield, MO 65803
www.abcpictures.com
rodger@abcpictures.com

Produces high quality, low cost B/W and color headshots, composites, postcards, posters, and publicity pictures for the entertainment Industry, actors, models, celebrities, and manufacturers. Serves customers from coast to coast and into Canada. Uses carefully selected inks, a custom made paper and state of the art equipment backed by great customer service. Short turn around. An excellent substitute for costly photographic reproductions. Request a free catalog and samples. Send photograph or digital file with instructions and payment. See website for information on submitting digital files.

CARD SHARKS **(800) 229-1795**
PRINTING AND GRAPHICS **(818) 300-4525**
www.sharksprinting.com
lindley@sharksprinting.com

A good source for innovative marketing tools. Their signature product is Pocket Headshots™, but they also have high-quality, low-cost postcards and business cards. Also available: photo retouching, Pocket Demo Reels™ (your reel on a business card-sized DVD or CD-ROM!), reel production and editing, and entertainer's websites.

COPY MASTER PRINTING **(323) 467-6111**
1553 Cahuenga Blvd. **FAX (323) 467-6114**
Hollywood 90028

A full service print shop offering full color printing, bindery, typesetting, labels, paper photo reproduction, lithography, composites, stationery, business cards, invitations, invoices and postcards. Also a complete Digital Department. Monday through Friday, 8 am to 5 pm. See listing under PHOTO LABS & REPRODUCTION in the section for further information.

CHAN CHARLIE PRINTING
LOS ANGELES **(213) 380-6121**
3974 Wilshire Blvd.
Los Angeles 90010

8267 Santa Monica Blvd. **(323) 650-7699**
West Hollywood 90069
www.charliechan.com

Specializes in rush Xerox scripts. Full color copying, including the latest Canon color laser, and reduced, enlarged, and oversize copies. Does 8x10 resumes, also stat and velox. Full color offset printing is available.

CMC SCRIPT & COPY **(323) 874-4900**
7516 W. Sunset Blvd. **FAX (323) 874-4026**
Hollywood 90046

Customized service for the Industry including full desktop publishing and computer services. Monday through Friday, 9 am to 7 pm and weekends by appointment.

COLOR IMAGES COPY AND PRINT **(818) 567-2900**
2320 W. Olive Ave. **FAX (818) 567-2999**
Burbank 91506
www.colorimages.com
colorimages@aol.com

Full service copy and print operation. Color and B&W copies, two to four color printing process, inkjet to four color posters and more.

COPY CENTRAL (818) 841-4117
2300 W. Olive Ave. FAX (818) 842-7692
Burbank 94608

330 N. Brand Blvd. (818) 502-0100
Glendale 91203
www.copycentral.com

Full service copying including color copies, scripts, business cards, invoices, and bindery. Self-service is available. Free delivery.

COPY IMPRESS (310) 312-0809
12041 Wilshire Blvd.
Los Angeles 90025
www.copyimpress.com
copyimpressearthlink.net

They sell solutions and services, not just ink on paper. Volume color and B&W discounts, script copies, binding, computer output. Over 50,000 copies the next day. High quality Canon laser color copies, business cards, invoices, typesetting, flyers, and fax services. Pick-up and delivery available. Store hours Monday through Friday, 9 am to 6 pm. Call for a quote. You only have one chance to make a first impression.

COPY MAT (323) 461-1222
6464 Sunset Blvd., Ste. 100 FAX (323) 461-7391
Hollywood 90028
www.copymathollywood.com

Full and self-service printing. Can photocopy headshots and they also have a color laser photocopier. Special rates for script copy.

COPY PLACE (323) 850-8884
1601 N. La Brea Ave FAX (323) 850-8887
Hollywood 90028
copyplace@aol.com

A complete copying and printing store. They laser copy photographs in B&W and color. Also has off-set printing. Monday through Friday, 9 am to 5:30 pm.

COPY VISION (213) 687-9994
123 Figueroa, Ste. 101 FAX (213) 687-9994
Los Angeles 90012
copyvision@pacbell.net

Full service copying including color copies, scripts, business cards, etc. Self-service is available as is free delivery. Open Monday through Friday, 9 am to 6:30 pm.

COPY X-PRESS (310) 444-5577
1609 Westwood Blvd.
Westwood 90024

Full service printing including laser color copies, photo copy, Kodak, binding, custom T-shirt printing, office supplies, and script service. Pick up and delivery available.

DAICOLO CORPORATION (800) 772-9993 ext.103
21203-A Hawthorne Blvd. FAX (310) 316-7867
Torrance 90503

Full color photo business cards and postcards. Monday through Friday 9 am to 5:30 pm.

DIGITAL EXPRESS ETC. (310) 402-7528
6404 Wilshire Blvd., Ste. 105
Los Angeles 90048
www.scriptcopier.com
contactus@scriptcopier.com

A full service print shop offering full color printing, bindery, stationery, business cards, invitations, invoices and postcards. Also website design, post office boxes and more. Upload your files to their website and pick up your finished copies or have them delivered. Fast turnaround.

FINAL PRINT (818) 285-6967
5816 Lankershim Blvd., #9
North Hollywood 91601

2050 S. Bundy Dr., Ste. 104 (310) 979-7884
W. Los Angeles 90025

1952 N. Van Ness Ave. (323) 466-0566
Los Angeles 90068-3625 (323) 466-5404
www.finalprint.com FAX (323) 469-7138
headshots@finalprint.com

Final Print specializes in making photo-quality headshots, postcards and business cards. They do zedcards, DVD labels, video boxes, posters, stationery, one sheets, banners, promo items (mugs, magnets, t-shirts) and more. Services include digital design, photos, lithos, 4-color press, and short-run digital color. Custom and specialty orders are welcome. Mail order is available both by e-mail and snail mail. All work is guaranteed and all credit cards are accepted. SEE AD ON PAGE 143.

GENESIS PRINTING (323) 965-7935
5872 W. Pico Blvd. FAX (323) 965-7875
Los Angeles 90019
www.genesis-printing.com

Genesis Printing, house of model and actor composites.

GREAT GRAPHICS PHOTOSCAN (800) 352-6367
www.ggphotoscan.com

Quality B&W and color headshots and composites. Fast turnaround. Call for a sample, rate card and order form.

IMAGE EXPRESS (323) 874-6940
7300 Sunset Blvd., Ste. C FAX (323) 874-7761
Los Angeles 90046
ieeinfo@aol.com

Laser printing, color copies, and desk top publishing. In-house reproduction facilities. Special rates for actors. Self and same day service. See listing under RESUMES, BOOKKEEPING & SECRETARIAL SERVICES in this section for further information.

KINKO'S (818) 567-1044
4100 Riverside Dr. FAX (818) 567-7363
Burbank 91505

12101 Ventura Blvd. (818) 980-2679
Studio City 91604 FAX (818) 980-9756

5810 Sepulveda Blvd. (818) 780-2123
Van Nuys 91411

1440 Vine St. (323) 871-1300
Hollywood 90028

10924 Weyburn Ave. (310) 443-5501
Los Angeles 90024

601 Wilshire Blvd. (310) 576-7710
Santa Monica 90401 FAX (310) 576-7768
www.kinkos.com

Full and self-service copying and computer services. They offer full color copying, laser typesetting and printing, business cards, script copying, mailing labels, Bradbindery, cutting, folding, and padding. Also carries stationery and office supplies and rubber stamps are available. Has an on-site resume service and does headshot and composite duplication. Pick-up and delivery. Open 24 hours daily.

MODEL PRINTING, INC **(818) 985-6886**
5152 Lankershim Blvd. **FAX (818) 985-2882**
North Hollywood 91601
www.modelprinting.com

Full color printing, full color Cannon CLC-1000 with Fiery. Full color postcards. B&W postcards, J-cards, CDs, business cards, and lithographs are available. Offers rush service, and makes props for films. 100 color copies: 39 cents each.

NEW IMAGE PRINTING **(323) 876-1102**
7109 Sunset Blvd. **FAX (323) 874-8838**
Hollywood 90046
www.newimagegraphic.com

Photocopying, color laser copying, full color printing, typesetting, script copying, oversized color prints, headshots, postcards, business cards, self-service, and lithography. Monday through Saturday, 9 am to 7 pm and Sunday, 9 am to 6 pm.

NU PRINT & GRAPHICS, INC. **(818) 509-0003**
3962 Laurel Canyon Blvd. **FAX (818) 509-8932**
Studio City 91604
www.nuprintinc.com
nuprint@aol.com

Offers full/self service copying, high speed B&W copies for scripts, reductions/enlargements, transparencies, stationery, envelopes, postcards, flyers, duplication from newspaper/magazine/head shots in B&W or color, Canon color laser duplication of slides/transparencies, model zed cards in B&W or color, offset printing, business cards, invitations, resumes, forms, personalized invitations, invoices, composites, labels, rubber stamps, fax service, typesetting sameday/overnight, cutting, stapling, hole punching, folding, velo/spiral/brad/tape binding, laminating, numbering, UPS pick-up and delivery, office supplies, overnight computer printout in B&W or color from CD-ROM and/or oversized copies, and in-house printing. Special rates for Script Writers Network members. Monday through Friday, 8:30 am to 7 pm and Saturday, 10 am to 4 pm.

(323) 874-2300
PAPER CHASE PRINTING, INC. **(800) 367-2737**
7176 Sunset Blvd. **FAX (323) 874-6583**
Los Angeles 90046
www.paperchase.net
csr@paperchase.net

High quality B&W and color printing, geared for the Industry. Composites, lithography, bindery, business cards, invitations. Monday through Friday, 9 am to 6 pm and Saturday, 10 am to 1 pm. See listing under PHOTO LABS & REPRODUCTION in this section for further information.

PLP COPY **(310) 273-2378**
9006 Wilshire Blvd. **FAX (310) 858-0547**
Beverly Hills 90211
www.plpcopy.com
copyandprinting@sbcglobal.net

Color laser copies from prints, slides, and negatives. Also copies of all types including postcards and flyers.

POST-TEL BUSINESS SERVICES **(310) 828-8645**
2118 Wilshire Blvd. **FAX (310) 828-0427**
Santa Monica 90403
www.posttel.com

Carries business cards, color copies, resumes, letterhead, headshots, stationery, and rubber stamps. Also does packing and shipping. With a mail box rental you can receive limited quantities of free fax, copies, and notary services each month. See listings for Post-Tel Business Center under FAX SERVICES/MAIL BOXES and ANSWERING SERVICES/PAGERS in this section for further information.

POSTAL & PACKING EMPORIUM **(818) 762-5555**
11288 Ventura Blvd. **FAX (818) 762-5554**
Studio City 91604

Photocopying, business cards, script copying, office supplies, stationery, rubber stamps, labels, reduced/enlarged copies. Self-service copies and pick-up and delivery are available. Monday through Friday, 9 am to 6 pm and Saturday, 9:30 am to 4 pm. See listings under FAX SERVICES & MAIL BOXES in this section for further information.

(800) 957-5787
POSTCARD PRESS **(310) 715-8811**
18732 Crenshaw Blvd. **FAX (310) 715-8825**
Torrance 90504
www.postcardpress.com

Top quality, full color cards at prices anyone can afford. High glass UV and ultra thick cards.

PRINTING & COPIES UNLIMITED **(818) 985-5235**
12548 Ventura Blvd. **FAX (818) 985-6813**
Studio City 91604
www.printgraph.com
print@printgraph.com

A full service printing center that includes photocopy, bindery, off-set printing, and paper photo reproduction. Pick up and delivery available with a minimum of $25 purchase. Monday through Thursday, 8 am to 7 pm, Friday, 8 am to 6 pm and Saturday, 9 am to 5 pm.

PRINTS CHARM'N, INC.
WEST LOS ANGELES **(310) 312-0904**
1657 Sawtelle Blvd. **FAX (310) 312-0324**
West Los Angeles 90025

11020 Ventura Blvd. **(818) 753-9055**
Studio City 91604
www.printscharmn.com

Offers lithographic and photographic duplications. See listing under PHOTO LABS & REPRODUCTION in this section for further information.

R & R PRINTING & GRAPHIC CORP. **(310) 855-0725**
8505 Santa Monica Blvd. **FAX (310) 855-1361**
Los Angeles 90069

Full commercial printing and full color printing. Monday through Friday, 9:30 am to 6:30 pm and Saturday 10 am to 4 pm. See listing under RESUMES, BOOKKEEPING & SECRETARIAL SERVICES in this section for further information.

Printing & Photocopying

RUSH COPY & PRINTING (323) 462-7874
6095½ Sunset Blvd. FAX (323) 463-5522
Hollywood 90028
rushcopy@primenet.com

Complete printing and copying including laser copies of photos and zed cards. B&W and color. Monday through Friday, 8:30 am to 5 pm.

STAPLES THE OFFICE SUPERSTORE (818) 753-6390
12605 Ventura Blvd. FAX (818) 753-6393
Studio City 91604

6450 Sunset Blvd. (323) 467-2155
Hollywood 90027
www.staples.com

Low cost photocopying in B&W and color. Also carries discount office supplies including paper, telephones, faxes, furniture, pens, envelopes, covers, and has complete computer supplies. There are many locations throughout the L.A. Area. See listing under COMPUTERS in this section for further information.

STUDIO COPY CENTER (818) 766-6161
11839 Ventura Blvd. FAX (818) 766-3131
Studio City 91604

Complete printing and copying including photocopying, offset, full Canon laser color copier and paper photo reproduction, fiery output, and oversized color posters. Self service, pick-up and delivery are available. Monday through Friday, 8 am to 6 pm.

UNIVERSAL PRINT & COPY (323) 876-3500
3535 Cahuenga Blvd. West FAX (323) 876-7141
Ste. 111
Los Angeles 90068
www.eddietheprinter.com

Low cost B&W and color laser copies zed cards. Script copies as low as 2 cents per copy. Headshot and postcard printing. Full service printing center. Free pick-up and delivery. Daily, 9 am to 7 pm.

VIRTUAL BUSINESS CARDS
CYNDIE CARRILLO (818) 693-0023
859 Hollywood Way, Ste, 123
Burbank 91505
www.virtualbusinesscards.com

Keep your picture, resume, contact information and either video or audio clip in your pocket. Great for networking.

WEST HOLLYWOOD PRINTING (323) 650-0107
8132 Santa Monica Blvd.
West Hollywood 90046

They do "anything on paper." Photocopying, typesetting, and offset printing. Color copying is also available. Business cards, postcards, posters, etc. Monday through Friday 9 am to 6 pm and Saturday 10 am to 4 pm.

Professional Make-Up

BALL BEAUTY SUPPLIES (323) 655-2330
416 N. Fairfax Ave. FAX (323) 655-2448
Los Angeles 90036
www.ballbeauty.com

Carries Mehron, Bob Kelly, Rozelle, La Femme, Joe Blasco, and Layla cosmetics. Stocks a complete line of all hair, skin, and manicuring supplies. Sells at professional prices, not retail. In business since 1949. Monday through Saturday, 8:30 am to 5:30 pm.

JOE BLASCO COSMETICS (323) 669-3466
1670 Hillhurst Ave.
Los Angeles 90027
www.joeblasco.com

Carries a full line of Joe Blasco make-up products and does demonstrative makeovers for customers. A training center is available. Monday through Friday, 9 am to 4 pm. See listing under MAKE-UP in the TRAINING section for further information.

CALIFORNIA COSTUME (818) 567-0753
3606 W. Magnolia Blvd. FAX (818) 567-1961
Burbank 91505
www.norcostco.com

Extensive selection of make-up and a wide variety of clothing and costumes including period, character, uniforms, and animals. Alterations are available as are some made-to-order costumes. Also has lighting and props. Monday through Friday, 10 am to 6 pm and Saturday, 11 am to 5:30 pm.

CINEMA SECRETS (818) 846-0579
4400 Riverside Dr. FAX (818) 846-0431
Burbank 91505
www.cinemasecrets.com
cinemasecretsinfo@cinemasecrets.com

Carries their own line of make-up that is formulated for the camera as well as all major brands of theatrical make-up. They also have staff make-up artists available for private sessions at their facility as well as a full service salon. They have private rooms in their store for personal make-up and/or hair sessions, facials, waxing, and electrolysis. See listings under MAKE-UP ARTISTS in this section and under MAKE-UP in the TRAINING section for further information.

THE COSTUME SHOP (619) 574-6201
2010 El Cajon Blvd. FAX (619) 574-6268
San Diego 92104
www.thecostumeshop.net
contactus@thecostumeshop.net

Carries Ben Nye, Mehron, Kroylan, Cinema Secrets, clown make-up, special effects make-up, Jerome Russel colored hairsprays and glitters, wigs, facial hair appliances, and theatrical nail polish. A make-up artist and seamstress are on staff. Also has make-up classes and rents and sells costumes and accessories. Discount to actors who are with the Actor's Alliance in San Diego. Monday through Friday, 10 am to 5 pm and Saturday, 9 am to 1 pm. They were moving at the time of publication so call or check the website for the new address.

Professional Make-Up

FRENDS BEAUTY SUPPLY (818) 769-3834 / (888) 7-FRENDS
5270 Laurel Canyon Blvd. FAX (818) 769-8124
North Hollywood 91607
www.frendsbeautysupply.com

Carries a full line of make-up, both theatrical and street, also hair care products. Mustaches and beards are available. 10% discount to actors. Monday through Saturday, 8 am to 6 pm.

GLENDALE COSTUMES (818) 244-1161
746 W. Doran St. FAX (818) 244-8576
Glendale 91203
www.thecostumeshop.com

Sells theatrical make-up and rents costumes. See listing under COSTUME SALES & RENTALS in this section for further information.

MAKE BELIEVE, INC. (310) 396-6785
3240 Pico Blvd. FAX (310) 396-1936
Santa Monica 90405

Carries Ben Nye, and Mehron make-up as well as some wigs and colored hair spray. Gives referrals to make-up artists. Also carries costumes, mostly rentals, and will custom make costumes. A stylist, wardrobe consultant and costume designer are available for productions. See listing under COSTUMES SALES & RENTALS in this section for further information. Monday through Saturday, 10 am to 6 pm and Sunday, 11 am to 5 pm.

NAIMIE'S FILM & TELEVISION BEAUTY SUPPLY (818) 763-7072
12640 Riverside Dr.
North Hollywood 91607

12801 Victory Blvd. (818) 763-7073
North Hollywood 91606
www.naimies.com

Carries all brands of professional make-up as well as hair care products and nail care supplies. Also hair appliances, wigs, and hair pieces for sale or rent. Consultations are available as are research books. 10% discount for actors and professionals. Monday through Friday, 8 am to 6 pm and Saturday, 8 am to 6 pm.

BEN NYE MAKEUP CO. (310) 839-1984

Manufacturer of professional make-up. Comprehensive line includes theatrical make-up kits, matte foundations, special effects colors, and MagiCake Aqua Paints. Traditional and contemporary shades. Call for a catalog and dealer referral. Monday through Friday, 8 am to 4 pm.

OUTFITTERS WIGS OF HOLLYWOOD (323) 469-9421
6626 Hollywood Blvd. FAX (323) 462-4730
Hollywood 90028

Carries a large selection of wigs and false eyelashes as well as the complete line of Joe Blasco make-up products. Also carries custom jewelry. See listing under WIGS in this section for further information. Monday through Saturday, 10 am to 7 pm.

VANITY MAKE-UP (323) 658-9020
708 N. Gardner
Los Angeles 90036

Wide variety of make-up supplies. Also a make-up training studio.

WEST HOLLYWOOD BEAUTY SUPPLY/SALON (323) 656-6700
8126 Santa Monica Blvd.
West Hollywood 90046

Carries Joe Blasco theatrical make-up as well as regular make-up and supplies. Also has a full service hair salon. Monday through Saturday, 10 am to 6:30 pm.

Rehearsal Studios

Many small theatres are available for classroom or rehearsal rentals. Check under THEATRES in the WORKING section then call the individual theatres for rates and possible schedules.

ACME COMEDY THEATRE (323) 525-0233
135 N. La Brea Ave.
Los Angeles 90036
www.acmecomedy.com

State of the art 99-seat theatre available for rent. Fully equipped, A/C, valet parking available.

ACTORS ART THEATRE (323) 969-4953
6128 Wilshire Blvd.
Los Angeles 90048
www.actorsart.com
actorsart@actorsart.com

This 32 seat theatre is available for rent for casting sessions, classes, workshops and productions. Call for further information.

ACTORS FORUM THEATRE (818) 506-0600
10655 Magnolia Blvd. FAX (213) 465-6898
North Hollywood 91601
www.nohoartsdistrict.com
actors4mtheatre@aol.com

This 49 seat theatre is available for rent and has a light and sound booth. A/C and parking available. Wheelchair accessible. Rents on occasion.

ACTORS WORKOUT STUDIO (818) 766-2171
4735 Lankershim Blvd.
North Hollywood 91602
www.actorsworkout.com
info@actorsworkout.com

Two theatres for rent, classes, productions, casting, and rehearsals. Easy parking, good air conditioning. Call or visit the website for further information.

ALLEY KAT STUDIO (323) 462-1755
1455 N. Gordon St.
Hollywood 90028

Three rooms. Pianos, mirrors, all professional equipment, CDs, tape decks, phonographs, stereos, chairs, air conditioning, and hardwood sprung floors. Low rates.

THE BERUBIANS SECOND STAGE (714) 635-1028
431 N. Brookhurst, St., Ste. 140
Anaheim 92728
www.berubians.com

The 50 seat Second Stage Theater is in the El Rancho Plaza and has a large stage: approx. 16′ x 20′ with three backstage entrances as well as access from the front. The light and sound systems are basic and easy to use. Lots of free parking is available and close. The theater also has easy handicapped access. Most shows can be booked for free with the theater taking the door. Otherwise, straight rental starts at $200 per night. Free rehearsal time can also be arranged with a committed show.

CALIFORNIA YOUTH THEATRE (310) 657-3270 (323) 461-7300
605 N. Ivar Ave. FAX (323) 461-7707
Los Angeles 90038
www.cytivar.org

Three spaces available for rent. The main theatre has 284 seats and is a proscenium style theatre. There is a dance studio rehearsal hall available as well as the Brick Box (like a black box theatre) that can seat up to 100. Digital editing system on the premises. Call or check the website for additional information.

THE CHANDLER STUDIO (818) 786-1045
12443 Chandler Blvd. FAX (818) 780-6517
North Hollywood 91607

A 33 seat, 900 square foot studio with a raised stage. Good sound system, lights on dimmers, A/C, and ample parking. Good for classes. Contact Michael Holmes.

THE COMPLEX (323) 465-0383
6476 Santa Monica Blvd. FAX (323) 469-5408
Hollywood 90038
www.thecomplexhollywood.com

The Complex has 5 rehearsal studios of various sizes plus 5 theaters. All rooms have rehearsal furniture, lights on dimmers and stages. Rehearsal rates from $10-15 per hour. Air-conditioning. Valet parking at night, street parking during the day.

THE CORONET THEATRE (310) 652-9955
366 N. La Cienega Blvd. FAX (310) 652-0718
Los Angeles 90048
www.coronet-theatre.com
staff@coronet-theatre.com

Three beautiful spaces available: The Coronet Studio – Capacity: Seats 49 on cushioned folding chairs. Description: The Studio is located on street level of the Coronet Complex, with side courtyard entrance. The room has soundproofed walls and doors and includes a wooden stage, air conditioning, carpeted seating area and one bathroom and changing room. Upstairs at the Coronet. Capacity: Seats up to 168 on cushioned folding chairs. Description: Upstairs at the Coronet is located on the second floor level of the Coronet Complex, with a balcony entrance above the theatre's courtyard. The room has carpeted floors and one public bathroom and one dressing room with private bathroom. A piano is available for use. The Coronet Theater seats 284. Contact the Coronet Theatre offices for pricing and further information. All spaces available at hourly rates for rehearsals.

EDGE PERFORMING ARTS CENTER (323) 962-7733
1020 N. Cole Ave., 4th Fl. FAX (323) 852-1577
Hollywood 90038
www.edgepac.com

4 rental studios and a production office. Studio E: 134 sq. ft., Studio E2: 1,200 sq. ft., Studio D: 650 sq. ft., Studio G: 1,500 sq. ft., Production office, 115 sq. ft., connected to Studio D. Free parking, professional sound equipment, pianos, floated hardwood and Marley floors, air conditioning, dressing rooms with showers, and free parking. Block rates are available.

ELECTRIC LODGE THEATRE (310) 306-1854
1416 Electric Ave. FAX (323) 306-1117
Venice 90291
www.electriclodge.org

Founder and Artistic Director: Joel Shapiro. Operates under the 99 seat plan. Traditional experimental theatre, dance, music, screenings and performance art. The 1,500 square foot space is available for rent.

GLOBE PLAYHOUSE
SHAKESPEARE SOCIETY OF AMERICA (323) 654-5623
1107 N. Kings Rd. FAX (323) 654-5627
West Hollywood 90069
www.shakespearesocamerica.com

Artistic Director: R. Thad Taylor. A resident theatre under the 99 Seat Plan. Almost exclusively Shakespearian productions. Directors of individual shows do their own casting. There are open calls. Lists casting information in Back Stage West. The 99 seat theatre is available for rent for most theatrical purposes including filming and has its own parking lot.

GOSCH PRODUCTIONS (818) 729-0000
2227 W. Olive Ave.
Burbank 91506
www.goschproductions.com
info@goschproductions.com

1226 square feet studio, fully equipped, air conditioned with make-up area and dressing room, control room, green screen and craft services. Parking available.

HOLLYWOOD DANCE CENTER (323) 467-0826
817 N. Highland FAX (323) 467-1525
Hollywood 90038
www.hollywooddancecenter.com

Studio rentals for auditions, workshops, classes or film and video shoots.

L.A. CONNECTION (818) 784-1868
13442 Ventura Blvd.
Sherman Oaks 91423
www.laconnectionscomedy.com
madmovies@hotmail.com

A/C and parking available. Call for specifics.

**LOS ANGELES
REPERTORY COMPANY (323) 464-8542
6560 Hollywood Blvd., 2nd Fl. FAX (323) 464-6130
Hollywood 90028
www.larep.org**

This historic building in Hollywood has 5 rooms available. 500-1,000 square feet, with A/C, piano and high ceilings. Some have a stage and lights, one has a raised dance floor, two have mirrors. 46 seat theatre with a raised proscenium stage. Paid or street parking.

**THE LOST STUDIO (323) 933-6944
130 S. La Brea Ave.
Los Angeles 90036
www.theloststudio.com**

The 70 seat theatre space is predominantly used for acting classes and is available for rent for production or rehearsal.

**MADILYN CLARK STUDIOS (818) 506-7763
10852 Burbank Blvd. FAX (818) 506-8520
North Hollywood 91601
www.madilynclark.com**

Has 5 studios of various sizes with hardwood sprung dance floors, pianos, mirrors, stereo, microphones, and video equipment. No bands. There is ample parking and a garden in the back which is used for special events and weddings. $15-$30 per hour. Monday through Saturday, 9 am to 10 pm and Sunday when booked.

**MCCADDEN PLACE THEATRE (323) 463-2942
1157 McCadden Place
Los Angeles 90038**

50 seat theatre. Air conditioned, parking, computer light board, mini disc and CD players. 60 lighting instruments. Reasonable rates.

**MILLENNIUM DANCE COMPLEX (818) 753-5081
5113 Lankershim Blvd. FAX (818) 752-8386
North Hollywood 91601
www.millenniumdancecomplex.com**

Seven studios of various sizes and one large dome. Studios have piano, mirrors, and a stereo is available. Monday through Friday, 9 am to 10 pm, Saturday, 9 am to 5 pm and Sunday, 10 am to 6 pm.

**THE NEXT STAGE (323) 850-7827
1523 N. La Brea Ste. 208-9
Hollywood 90028
www.berubians.com**

The Next Stage is a comfortable theater in the heart of Hollywood (above the Lava Lounge) that seats 45 people on padded park benches. Light and sound systems are basic and easy to use and there is a large dressing area with adjacent private bathrooms. Some free parking in the lot; more parking is available on the street (free at night). The stage is approx. 12′ x 16′ and has three backstage entrances as well as access from the front of the theater. There is also a TV monitor on stage with a VCR in the tech booth. The theater can be rented any night but Monday, subject to availability. Most shows can be booked for free with the theater taking the door. Otherwise, straight rental starts at $200 per night. Free rehearsal time can be arranged with a committed show. The Tre Stage and a large rehearsal room share the same address and can be booked for multi-room events.

**NOHO ACTOR'S STUDIO (818) 309-9439
5215 Lankershim Blvd.
North Hollywood 91601
www.nohoactorsstudio.com
stagerentals@aol.com**

This 45 seat theatre is available for rent and also has 2 rehearsal/class spaces. Piano, hardwood floors, parking.

**ODYSSEY THEATRE (310) 477-2055
2055 S. Sepulveda Blvd.
Los Angeles 90025
www.odysseytheatre.com**

Three 99-set theatres available for rent.

**PROMENADE PLAYHOUSE (310) 656-8070
1404 Third Street Promenade FAX (310) 656-8069
Santa Monica 90401
www.pierodusa.com
info@pierodusa.com**

Equity approved, 65-seat theatre ideal for small and large productions, showcases, video/film shoots, screenings, workshops, seminars and castings. Located in the heart of Santa Monica's renowned Third Street Promenade, by the beach with plenty of parking. Also available for rent are The Soho Stage and The Actors Box, all quality venues providing a creative home for a new generation of artists. Call for appointment to view. SEE AD ON PAGES 21 & 297.

**JOHN RAITT THEATRE (323) 871-8082
6520 Hollywood Blvd.
Hollywood 90028
www.acmt.org
pgg@acmt.org**

Available for rent for rehearsal, performance, auditions and film shoots. 2 large rooms. Air conditioned, parking available behind the theatre. Sound system and pianos available. Also available as a screening room for digital films.

**DEBBIE REYNOLDS
PROFESSIONAL REHEARSAL STUDIOS (818) 985-3193
6514 Lankershim Blvd.
North Hollywood 91606**

Has several rooms of various sizes available with pianos, mirrors, and stereo, also parking. $25-$35 per hour. Hours vary.

**PAUL E. RICHARDS THEATRE (323) 257-2323
2902 Rowena Ave.
Los Angeles 90027**

Parking, A/C. This intimate, adaptable space seats between 30-35. Available for classes or productions.

**RIPRAP STUDIOS (818) 990-7498
5755 Lankershim Blvd.
North Hollywood 91601
www.riprapentertain.com**

Riprap Studio Theatre is a 1400 square foot space available for rental for classes, auditions, rehearsals, productions, poetry, meetings and seminars. The theatre is approximately 1000 square feet and seats 60. The stage is approximately 15′X 17′. Back area, dressing area, also doubles as meeting area and is approximately 400-500 square feet. Central air and heat as well as dressing rooms with one unisex bathroom. Plenty of street parking (no meters). Available year round, in whole or in part 7 days a week.

SANTA MONICA PLAYHOUSE (310) 394-9779
1211 4th St. FAX (310) 393-5573
Santa Monica 90401
www.santamonicaplayhouse.com
smp@primenet.com

5 rooms available for rehearsals, auditions, dance, music, vocal, etc. Air conditioned, street or public parking. Contact John.

SCREENLAND STUDIOS (818) 508-2288
10501 Burbank Blvd.
North Hollywood 91601

Two studios with Neo-Shok suspended hardwood floors. The large studio is 30x70 with 14′ ceilings, surround sound, and a production office. There is an easy loading area.

THE SECOND CITY THEATRE (323) 658-8190
8156 Melrose Ave.
Los Angeles 90046
www.secondcity.com/theatre/la

The Second City Studio Theatre is available for rent Tuesday through Saturday. Time slots are 8 pm and 9:30 pm, one hour per show.

SECRET ROSE THEATRE (818) 766-3691
11246 Magnolia Blvd. FAX (818) 766-3691
North Hollywood 91601
www.secretrose.com
kaz@secretrose.com

Available for rent. Full lighting and sound system. Parking lot. Upright piano available. Call for rates and availability. SEE AD ON PAGE 19.

STUDIO THEATRE (323) 850-9497
3433 Cahuenga Blvd. West FAX (323) 876-9055
Los Angeles 90068-1329

This flexible theatre with 50 seats is available for rent for rehearsals, full productions, filming, concerts, dance, and classes. The Studio Theatre is now a historic and cultural landmark of Los Angeles.

THEATRE CRAFT PLAYHOUSE (323) 876-1100
7445 1/4 Sunset Blvd.
Los Angeles 90046

A 60 seat, street level theatre with sound and lights available. Will rent the theatre for rehearsals, full productions, showcases, filming, and classes. Call for rates and further information. Books by appointment, and will vary hours to suit client's needs.

THE THEATRE DISTRICT (323) 957-2343
804 North El Centro
Hollywood 90038
www.thetheatredistrict.com
info@thetheatredistrict.com

Located near Paramount, spacious greenroom, elegant lobby, A/C, parking available one block away, 99 seats, stage is 16′ x 26′ with lighting and sound.

THEATRE OF ARTS (EST. 1927) (323) 463-2500
1621 N. McCadden Place FAX (323) 463-2005
Los Angeles 90028
www.theatre-of-arts.com

Has numerous studios of various sizes and a theatre available for rehearsal, days or evenings with piano. Price is negotiable. Book by appointment.

THEATRE/THEATER (323) 422-6361
5041 Pico Blvd.
Hollywood 90028
www.theatretheater.net
thtrethter@earthlink.net

Artistic Director: Jeff Murray. New works or, at least, new to L.A. A resident theatre operating under the 99 Seat Plan. Accepts pictures and resumes and maintains casting files. Holds open casting calls and lists information in the Trades. Theatre is available for rent.

TU STUDIOS (818) 205-1680
10943 Camarillo St.
North Hollywood 91602

Available for classes, casting sessions, filming, readings, auditions, rehearsals and productions. There is a 53 seat theatre and a carpeted 20 x 23 ft. studio space. Dressing room, restrooms, lights and sound, air conditioning and plenty of parking.

THIRD STAGE (818) 842-4755
2811 West Magnolia Blvd. FAX (818) 842-4267
Burbank 91505
www.thirdstage.org
thirdstage@sbcglobal.net

An intimate 50 seat theater located in the Magnolia Park district of Burbank. Highly regarded by the press and Industry insiders alike. Complete services are available for rent. Contact: James Henriksen.

THIRD STREET DANCE (310) 275-4683
8558 W. 3rd. St.
Los Angeles 90048
www.thirdstreetdance.com

Has 5 rooms of various sizes with hardwood floors, air conditioning, pianos, mirrors and sound systems. Rooms starting $20-$40 per hour. Monday through Saturday, 9:30 am to 10 pm, but will also book by appointment and will open Sunday if needed. Has validated parking.

TRE STAGE (323) 850-7827
1523 N. La Brea, Ste. 209
Hollywood 90028
www.berubians.com

The Tre Stage is a comfortable theater in the heart of Hollywood (above the Lava Lounge) that seats 30 people on benches. Light and sound systems are basic and easy to use and there is a large dressing area with adjacent private bathrooms. Some free parking in the lot; more parking is available on the street (free at night). The stage is approx. 10′ x 12′ and has two backstage entrances as well as access from the front of the theater. The theater can be rented any night but Monday, subject to availability. Most shows can be booked for free with the theater taking the door. Otherwise, straight rental starts at $200 per night. Free rehearsal time can be arranged with a committed show. The Next Stage and a large rehearsal room share the same address and can be booked for multi-room events.

VALLEY CENTER STUDIOS (818) 989-0866
5928 Van Nuys Blvd. FAX (818) 989-3818
Van Nuys 91401

Has 3 soundproofed rooms with PA systems, microphones, air conditioning, and music stands. 42 track capability available with

ProTools and analog. Rents mainly to bands. Day rates start at $15 per hour with a 3 hour minimum. Voice-over studio is available at $55 for 3 hours. Rehearsal space, 11 am to 12:30 am, daily. Recording studio available 24 hours.

THE BIG VICTORY AND THE LITTLE VICTORY THEATRES (818) 841-4404 (818) 841 5421
3324-26 Victory Blvd. FAX (818) 841-6328
Burbank 91505
www.thevictorytheatres.com
victory@thevictorytheatrecenter.com

Both theatres are air conditioned with free parking in a good area. Both the 48 seat theatre and 99 seat theatre are available for productions, casting and classes.

LULA WASHINGTON'S DANCE THEATRE (323) 936-6591
5041 W. Pico Blvd.
Los Angeles 90016
www.lulawashington.com
lulaoffice@aol.com

A 55x45 studio with dressing rooms, piano, mirrors, lobby, TV, microwave, and refrigerator. They are looking for actors or directors with their own classes or workshops. Space is good for video projects including actor's scenes. Bands are welcome. Parking is available.

WEST END STUDIOS (818) 753-5393
12500 Riverside Dr., Ste. 211 FAX (818) 753-8056
Studio City 91607
www.westeendstudio.com

Space for acting class, writing class, script supervision class, etc. Has 21 theatre seats on risers. Parking available. Low rates.

WHITEFIRE THEATRE (818) 687-8559
13500 Ventura Blvd.
Sherman Oaks 91423
www.whitefiretheatre.com
stagerentals@aol.com

99 seat theatre for rent on Ventura Boulevard's restaurant row, available daily, hourly or weekly.

RESUME, BOOKKEEPING & SECRETARIAL SERVICES

Acting resumes are quite different than standard employment resumes. Here are some things to remember when creating yours. Appearance counts, you want to make a good impression. Print it on high grade paper and cut to 8x10 so it will fit on the back of your photo. Remember to put your best credits first since people read from the top down and don't lie! It's a much smaller world than you think and even if you are not caught, you don't want to get a job based on deception. Avoid putting any dates, such as your age, or when your previous work occurred. Dates will 'date' you and your age may bias someone against you. Don't include personal information like your social security number or home phone number; you never know where your resume might end up. List your agent's phone number or use an answering service or voice mail phone number.

THE ACTOR'S OFFICE (818) 692-0706
15353 Weddington St., #D208
Sherman Oaks 91411
www.theactorsoffice.com

The first comprehensive software package designed exclusively for actors to help them manage and market their careers effectively while saving money. Features include: Over 650 agent and casting director addresses, track your auditions and submissions, print cover letters without a mail merge, and print postcards directly from your printer.

ACTORS PROMOTIONAL SERVICES, LTD. ROCK RIDDLE (323) 462-2777
6464 Sunset Blvd., Ste. 750
Los Angeles 90028
www.hollywoodsuccess.com

Designs resumes and cover letters. See listing under MARKETING INFO & CONSULTANTS in this section for further information.

CLUB BEVERLY HILLS (310) 274-6051
8306 Wilshire Blvd., #279 FAX (310) 274-7855
Beverly Hills 90211
www.club-beverlyhills.com
dreams@club-beverlyhills.com

Quality resumes with or without photos as well as biographies, cover letters, and publicity services available. $30 for normal resumes and $5 for additions and deletions of credits thereafter. $65 for biographies. Carefully structured to show a quick profile of your credits and talents. State-of-the-art computer services. Also does scripts, flyers, and press kits and offers advertising assistance. Free consultation. Since 1979. See listings under PUBLIC RELATIONS in the TEAM section and PHOTOGRAPHERS in this section for further information.

CASEY DACANAY DESIGNS (818) 653-2291
6242 Willowcrest Ave.
North Hollywood 91606
only1casey@hotmail.com

Specializes in custom resume design and consultation for actors. Resumes are stored on computer for future updates. Average 24 hour service. Other design services available.

DIGITAL DESIGN L.A. INC. (818) 845-2038
3406 W. Burbank Blvd. FAX (818) 841-6222
Burbank 91502
www.digitaldesignla.com
barbara@digitaldesignla.com

Specializes in resumes for entertainers. Also web design and all graphic services are available.

IMAGE EXPRESS (323) 874-6940
7300 Sunset Blvd., Ste. C FAX (323) 874-7761
Los Angeles 90046
ieeinfo@aol.com

All resumes are typeset quality and computer file retained for future updates. Advice is given on resume composition. In-house reproduction. Special rates for actors. Offers both self and same day service. Also has laser printing, color copies, and desktop publishing.

KINKO'S (818) 567-1044
4100 Riverside Dr. FAX (818) 567-7363
Burbank 91505

12101 Ventura Blvd. (818) 980-2679
Studio City 91604 FAX (818) 980-9756

5810 Sepulveda Blvd. (818) 780-2123
Van Nuys 91411

1440 Vine St. (323) 871-1300
Hollywood 90028

10924 Weyburn Ave. (310) 443-5501
Los Angeles 90024

601 Wilshire Blvd. (310) 576-7710
Santa Monica 90401 FAX (310) 576-7768
www.kinkos.com

Laser printed resumes created on computer and saved to your disc for updates. Also offers graphic design assistance and advice regarding resume composition. In-house reproduction. 24 hour resume service. Script reproduction specialists. Also has desktop publishing, self-service Macintosh computers, and Canon color laser copiers. Full service copying is available. Also does printing, binding, passport photos, laminating, over-sized copies, has fax services, and carries stationery supplies. Free pick-up and delivery. Many locations open 24 hours daily.

BRENDA MARSHALL (818) 766-8735
North Hollywood FAX (818) 762-6225

Resumes on computer that are stored for revisions. Work done while you wait. Will give advice on resume composition. Also writes cover letters and theatre publicity. Script typing to the Industry standard. Professional writing and editing. Has written over 400 published magazine articles, 4 books, and more.

PLP COPY (310) 273-2378
(310) 273-5455
9006 Wilshire Blvd. FAX (310) 858-0547
Beverly Hills 90211
www.plpcopy.com

Designs the format for theatrical and business resumes. Laser printed and saved on computer for future updates. Also does headshot printing. One day and rush services are available.

R & R PRINTING & GRAPHIC CORP. (310) 855-0725
8505 Santa Monica Blvd.
Los Angeles 90069

Full color printing services. Gives advice on resume composition. In-house reproduction. Takes 2 days depending on copy. Also offers typesetting, resumes, business cards, postcards, and fax services. Monday through Friday 9:30 am to 6:30 pm and Saturday, 10 am to 4 pm.

RESUME DOCTOR (323) 461-4332
(818) 505-8791
P.O. Box 931149
Los Angeles 90093-1149

By appointment only.

RESUME WRITERS (323) 658-6378
FAX (323) 658-5730

Resume consultation and analysis. Ms. Goldstein writes a resume that serves as a sales tool and also offers one-on-one consulting on both coasts on how actors should market themselves. She is a producer, publicist, and a personal manager. See listing for "Succeeding in L.A." under BUSINESS OF ACTING in the TRAINING section for further information.

BRUCE SABA - RAPID RESUME (310) 470-8474
10700 Santa Monica Blvd., Ste. 4
Los Angeles 90025
penforhire@verizon.net

Resumes created on computer, laser printed, and maintained on file for future updates. Also writes cover letters.

SMART GIRLS PRODUCTIONS (818) 907-6511
15030 Ventura Blvd., #914 FAX (818) 990-5293
Sherman Oaks 91403
www.smartg.com
smartgirls@smartg.com

Since 1992 Smart Girls has assisted over 4000 actors at all stages of their careers in getting representation with agents and managers and in increasing their number of casting calls. They specialize in composing personalized cover letter mailings and handpicking agents and managers appropriate for you, jazzing up resumes, and creating interesting postcard messages to casting directors for current TV shows, films, and commercials. Starting at under $195 and maintaining an 80% success rate, Smart Girls mailings are a great way for you to create opportunities for yourself to be cast. They also offer Career Plans which include mailings and strategy sessions focused on expanding your confidence, presence, and success in the Industry. Call for a free catalog of services for actors and screenwriters and your very own Lucky Pen! SEE AD ON PREVIOUS PAGE.

VIRTUAL BUSINESS CARDS
CYNDIE CARRILLO (818) 693-0023
859 Hollywood Way, Ste, 123
Burbank 91505
www.virtualbusinesscards.com

Keep your picture, resume, contact information and either video or audio clip in your pocket. Great for networking.

WORK ACTOR WORK! (323) 225-1962
aktorchick@aol.com

Services include advice on resume composition, proven letters to agents, photo resume, etc., and personalized labels for agents, casting directors, managers, and producers. Now offering consultations.

Sheet Music

BAXTER-NORTHUP MUSIC (818) 788-7510
14534 Ventura Blvd.
Sherman Oaks 91403

Carries standards, top 40 and Broadway musicals and has an extensive collection of classical and jazz music. Will special order music for customers. Monday through Thursday, 11 am to 8 pm and Friday through Sunday, 11 am 6 pm.

HOLLYWOOD SHEET MUSIC (323) 850-1075
7777 W. Sunset Blvd. FAX (323) 850-1392
Los Angeles 90046
www.hollywoodsheetmusic.com

Carries standards, top 40, Broadway, opera scores, and instruction books. Also has hard-to-find sheet music. Has a mail service and maintains a large library. Monday through Saturday, 10 am to 6 pm and Sunday, noon to 5 pm.

KEYBOARD CONCEPTS (818) 787-0201
5600 Van Nuys Blvd. FAX (818) 787-1219
Van Nuys 91401

3232 Santa Monica Blvd. (800) 22-PIANO
Santa Monica 90404
www.keyboardconcepts.com

Has an extensive selection including all method books, top 40 single sheets, artists portfolios, and hard-to-find Henle Urtext piano books. They have a large theatrical/singers section as well as the Yamaha Disklaviar software.

Showcase Clubs

THE COMEDY STORE (323) 656-6225
8433 Sunset Blvd.
Los Angeles 90069
www.thecomedystore.com

Potluck Nite Sunday and Monday, 7 pm to 9 pm in the Original Room, anyone can do 3 minutes. Sign up at 6 pm, show at 7 pm.

DIMPLES (818) 842-2336
3413 W. Olive Ave. FAX (818) 842-8483
Burbank 91505
www.showcase.com

Nightly showcases 5 pm to 1:30 am for singers. Soundtracks for over 9,000 songs in all styles. Free audio demo tape of every new singer and video tapes are available. No audition required.

DRESDEN RESTAURANT (323) 665-4294
1760 N. Vermont Ave.
Los Angeles 90027
www.thedresden.com

Open mic for singers at least 21 years old in front of a live audience on Tuesday, 9 pm to midnight. Possible bookings.

GARDENIA (323) 467-7444
7066 Santa Monica Blvd.
Los Angeles 90038

Shows begin at 9 pm, performances daily except Sunday. Singers, comedians, and musicians performing standards and Broadway music. No accompanist is provided. Submit picture, resume, and audio tape for consideration. No live auditions. Acts booked in advance by the owner. Performer keeps cover charge and there is one performer per evening. Open mic nights.

THE ICE HOUSE (626) 577-1894
24 N. Mentor Ave.
Pasadena 91106
www.icehousecomedy.com

Showcase Sundays in the Annex at 7 pm for amateur stand-up comedians and magicians. Open auditions are held the 2nd and 4th Saturday of each month from 4 pm to 5:30 pm.

Showcase Clubs

THE IMPROVISATION **(323) 651-2583**
8162 Melrose Ave. **FAX (323) 655-9050**
Los Angeles 90046
www.improvclubs.com

Books all of their acts through video tape submissions. Send to the attention of Matt Coleman.

LAUGH FACTORY **(323) 656-1336**
8001 Sunset Blvd. **FAX (323) 656-2563**
Los Angeles 90046
www.laughfactory.com

Open mic night is Tuesday, showtime 8 pm. Twenty people are signed up at 6 pm outside the club on a "first come first served basis." Call for information.

Stationery Stores

AAHS **(310) 657-4221**
8878 Sunset Blvd.
West Hollywood 90069

1090 Westwood Ave. **(310) 824-1688**
Westwood 90024

14212 Ventura Blvd. **(818) 907-0300**
Sherman Oaks 91403 **FAX (818) 907-0359**
www.aahs.com

Trendy, fun, and unusual stationery, gifts, balloons, and greeting cards. Novelty items.

THE ACTOR'S OFFICE **(818) 692-0706**
15353 Weddington St., #D208
Sherman Oaks 91411
www.theactorsoffice.com

The first comprehensive software package designed exclusively for actors to help them manage and market their careers effectively while saving money. Features include: Over 650 agent and casting director addresses, track your auditions and submissions, print cover letters without a mail merge, and print postcards directly from your printer.

ANB STATIONERY CORP. **(818) 760-0244**
12338 Ventura Blvd. **FAX (818) 506-8201**
Studio City 91604
www.anbstationery.com

A complete general line of stationery, office supplies, and furniture. Carries spring binders for scripts, fine pens, and gifts. Serving the Industry for over 55 years. Monday through Friday, 9 am to 6 pm and Saturday, 10 am to 5 pm.

ROBIN CAROLL **(818) 788-3396**
16930 Ventura Blvd. **FAX (818) 788-2535**
Encino 91316

Exclusive specialty invitations including play announcements/flyers and stationery. Party planning services are available. Tuesday through Saturday, 11 am to 6 pm.

CORPORATE EXPRESS **(888) 238-6329**
16501 Trojan Way
La Mirada 90638
www.corporateexpress.com

Carries a complete line of office and Industry supplies including furniture and portfolio books. Also has computer equipment, copy machines, and fax machines. Free next day delivery and mail order is available. Monday through Friday, 8 am to 5 pm.

ENTERPRISE PRINTERS
& STATIONERS **(323) 876-3530**
7403 W. Sunset Blvd. **FAX (323) 876-4398**
Los Angeles 90046
www.enterpriseprinters.com
info@entertpriseprinters.com

Carries general stationery supplies, production boards and strips, Industry related software for IBM and Mac (script writing, budgeting), production supplies, and books on TV and film production. Monday through Friday, 9 am to 5 pm and Saturday, 12 am to 5 pm.

ANNE FIEDLER CREATIONS **(310) 358-1177**
333½ S. Robertson Blvd. **FAX (310) 358-1174**
Beverly Hills 90211
www.annefiedler.com
annfiedler@aol.com

Carries handmade party supplies and stationery including thank you notes, custom invitations, packaged invitations decorations. Also custom calligraphy invitations and much much more. Monday through Friday, 10 am to 5 pm and Saturday, 11 am to 4 pm.

KELLY PAPER **(818) 764-0850**
12641 Saticoy St. **FAX (818) 764-4398**
North Hollywood 91605

20800 Lassen Ave. **(818) 718-2298**
Chatsworth 91311
www.kellypaper.com

A paper supply house. Paper by the ream for a good price. Also carries office supplies, fun stationery, and greeting cards. Personalized stationery is available. Free delivery on orders over $250 or more. Monday through Friday, 7:30 am to 5 pm and Saturday, 8 am to 1 pm.

THE OFFICE SUPPLIER **(800) 400-3299**
15237 Sunset Blvd. **FAX (800) 275-1092**
Pacific Palisades 90272
www.theofficesupplier.com
supplier@unidial.com

Carries office and Industry materials including manuscript covers and brads, rubber stamps, computer paper, ribbons, and toner supplies. Personalized stationery is available on order. Specializes in hard to find items. Offers quantity discounts. Free delivery on orders over $100. Monday through Friday, 9:30 am to 5:30 pm.

STATIONERY STORES

STAPLES THE OFFICE SUPERSTORE (818) 753-6390
12605 Ventura Blvd. FAX (818) 753-6393
Studio City 91604

6450 Sunset Blvd. (323) 467-2155
Hollywood 90027
www.staples.com

Discount office supplies including paper, telephones, faxes, furniture, pens, envelopes, covers, and much more. Also does low cost photocopying in B&W and color, and has complete computer supplies. There are many locations throughout the L.A. area. See listing under COMPUTERS in this section for further information.

XPEDX PAPER & GRAPHICS (818) 785-4237
6947 Hayvenhurst Ave. FAX (818) 782-7413
Van Nuys 91406

Excellent prices on bulk purchases of all paper goods including 8x10 photo-mailer cardboard, envelopes, paper in all colors and types including parchment in various colors, and computer paper. Monday through Friday, 7:30 am to 5 pm and Saturday, 8 am to 4 pm.

THEATRICAL LIBRARIES

We have chosen to list the major sources of material for members of the Entertainment Industry. This includes research libraries for actors and producers, as well as Industry oriented libraries. For additional scene material see BOOKS & TAPES in this section. Most colleges and universities have libraries which are open to the public and there are specialty libraries as well. You can find both listed in the Index section of your Yellow Pages.

ACADEMY OF SCIENCE FICTION,
FANTASY AND HORROR FILMS (323) 752-5811
334 W. 54th St.
Los Angeles 90037
www.saturnawards.org

Membership only, call for further information.

ACADEMY OF TELEVISION
ARTS & SCIENCES ARCHIVES (310) 247-3020
Television Library/Doheny Library
Los Angeles 90089-0182

Books and periodicals concerning the Industry as well as a large selection of scripts. They request that you make an appointment if you wish to view their archival collection which includes the history of Hollywood, but you may just walk in if you wish to find a script or periodical.

AMERICAN FILM INSTITUTE (AFI) (323) 856-7600
2021 N. Western Ave.
Los Angeles 90027
www.afi.org

Call for hours. Open to the public but materials are not allowed to be checked out.

GENE AUTRY MUSEUM
OF WESTERN HERITAGE (323) 667-2000
4700 Western Heritage Way FAX (323) 660-5721
Los Angeles 90027
www.autry-musum.org

This private library museum contains information on westerns and cowboys. By appointment only.

BRAND LIBRARY (818) 548-2051
1601 W. Mountain St.
Glendale 91201

Specializes in art and music. Call for further information. Tuesday and Thursday, 1 pm to 9 pm, Wednesday, 1 pm to 6 pm and Friday and Saturday, 1 pm to 5 pm.

BURBANK CENTRAL LIBRARY (818) 238-5600
110 N. Glenoaks Blvd. FAX (818) 238-5553
Burbank 91502
www.burbank.lib.ca.us

Has a selection of scripts available for use in the library.

ARKEL ERB MOUNTAINEERING
MEMORIAL COLLECTION (310) 456-6438
23519 W. Civic Center Way
Malibu 90265

Part of the Malibu Library. This collection has over 2,500 mountaineering books, video tapes, magazines, and maps.

MARGARET HERRICK LIBRARY
ACADEMY OF MOTION PICTURE
ARTS & SCIENCES (310) 247-3020
333 S. La Cienega Blvd.
Beverly Hills 90211
www.oscars.org

Contains clippings, scripts, periodicals, books, and stills from films, also special collections and current film information. Open to the public, be sure to bring a valid picture I.D. Telephone hours, Monday, Tuesday, Thursday and Friday, 9 am to 3 pm. Walk-in hours, Monday, Tuesday, Thursday and Friday, 10 am to 5:30 pm.

HOLLYWOOD FILM ARCHIVE (323) 655-4968
8391 Beverly Blvd., PMB 321
Hollywood 90048

Comprehensive film reference materials available. By appointment only, call between 9 am and 5 pm.

THE HOLLYWOOD
FILM MUSIC LIBRARY (818) 789-2954
18034 Ventura Blvd., Ste. 450 FAX (818) 789-5801
Encino 91310
www.screenmusic.com

World's premier film and television music library. Several hundred volumes available for licensing. Call for free quote and demo.

LAST GRENADIER (818) 848-9144
820 N. Hollywood Way FAX (818) 848-9144
Burbank 91505

Carries reference books on military uniforms. Monday through Thursday, 11:30 am to 7 pm. Friday, 11:30 am to 9 pm, Saturday, 11 am to 7 pm and Sunday, 11 am to 6pm.

LEG-WORK
WRITERS RESEARCH SERVICE (323) 876-1794

Research service that caters to professionals in the Industry.

LOS ANGELES CITY LIBRARY
GOLDWYN/HOLLYWOOD BRANCH (323) 467-1821
1623 N. Ivar Ave. FAX (323) 467-5707
Hollywood 90028
holywd@lapol.org

This branch has extensive material on all aspects of the Industry including the history of both film and theatre. Also has scripts and books on acting.

MOTION PICTURE & TELEVISION
RESEARCH SERVICE ARCHIVES (818) 760-3040
P.O. Box 69434 FAX (818) 766-3889
West Hollywood 90069

Rare research material and information dealing with early Hollywood to the present. By appointment only.

NATURAL HISTORY MUSEUM
OF LOS ANGELES COUNTY (213) 763-3466
900 Exposition Blvd.
Los Angeles 90007
www.nhm.org

There are 3 research facilities at this museum: 1) The Seaver Center for Western History Research contains books, manuscripts, photos, and line drawings of the nation west of the Mississippi, including Hollywood, and a theatre history of Southern California. The material here is a good supplement to the American Film Academy's collection. 2) The Research Library contains a large collection of materials, line drawings, 19th century periodicals, books, and manuscripts that cover military history, industrial history with photos and drawings of period machinery, the Civil War, and children's literature. 3) The Costume Center features photos, drawings, and costumes of early California, plus military uniforms from the late 18th century to 1940.

NON-PROFIT
RESOURCE LIBRARY (213) 623-7080 x44
606 S. Olive St., Ste. 2450 FAX (213) 623-7960
Los Angeles 90014
www.cnmsocal.org

Contains research material regarding private and corporate funding of theatre and the arts, the education of individuals, and non-profit organizations.

NORTH HOLLYWOOD LIBRARY (818) 766-7185
5211 Tujunga Ave. FAX (818) 756-9135
North Hollywood 91601
www.lapl.org

This branch is noted for its large selection of plays as well as books on theatrical history and acting.

PARAMOUNT PICTURES
STOCK FOOTAGE LIBRARY (323) 956-5510
5555 Melrose Ave.
Hollywood 90038
www.paramountstock.com
filmlibrary@paramount.com

Has stock footage and new scenes are added daily.

SIMON WEISENTHAL CENTER (310) 553-8403
9786 W. Pico Blvd. FAX (310) 277-6568
Los Angeles 90035
www.museumoftolerance.com

Contains extensive material regarding World War II and the Nazi death camps. It also has books and photos involving current mistreatment of peoples everywhere. Open to the public however, documentary footage is only available to producers and researchers.

UNIVERSITY OF CALIFORNIA
LOS ANGELES (UCLA)
FILM AND TV ARCHIVE (310) 206-5388
Powell Library, Room 46 FAX (310) 206-5392
Westwood 90095
www.cinema.ucla.edu

Has a large collection of films and TV shows. Researcher must be involved in a project, all viewing takes place at the Powell Library. Monday through Friday, 9 am to 5 pm.

UNIVERSITY OF CALIFORNIA
LOS ANGELES (UCLA)
THEATRE ARTS LIBRARY (310) 825-3817
1400 Pauley Pavilion
Westwood 90024

Catalog Reference (310) 825-7143
www.ucla.edu

Has a large selection of plays and books on theatre. The faculty, staff, students of the University of California, University of California alumni, or donors with a "V" card may check out reference materials. Others must use materials in the library only. You may call the Catalog Reference desk, listed above, to see if they have a particular book. Open daily.

UNIVERSITY OF SOUTHERN CALIFORNIA (USC)
CINEMA TELEVISION &
SPECIAL COLLECTIONS (213) 740-8906
University Park
Los Angeles 90089-0182
www.usc.edu

Contains rare books and American literature. Reading room open Saturday, 9 am to 1 pm. By appointment only. Reference desk open Monday through Friday from 1 pm to 3 pm.

Video Camera Rentals

ADVANCED VIDEO, INC. (323) 469-0707
6757 Santa Monica Blvd. FAX (323) 469-8268
Los Angeles 90038

Rents VHS, SVHS, digital and High 8 cameras. Also has lighting, editing, duplication equipment, and stands and monitors. Monday through Friday, 10 am to 6 pm.

ASTRO AUDIO VIDEO & LIGHTING (818) 549-9915
6615 San Fernando Rd. FAX (818) 549-9921
Glendale 91201
www.astroavl.com
sales@astroavl.com

Rents VHS cameras, stands, monitors, VCRs, and a limited selection of lighting equipment. Monday through Friday, 10 am to 7 pm, Saturday, 10 am to 6 pm and Sunday noon to 4 pm.

CAMERA CRAFT (818) 766-5186
4800 Lankershim Blvd.
North Hollywood 91601
www.cameracraftnh.com

Panasonic VHS cameras and photo flood lighting. Also rents and sells audio-visual equipment. A credit card is required for a deposit. Monday through Friday, 9 am to 6 pm, Saturday, 9 am to 5 pm.

HARRY'S CAMERA & VIDEO (818) 763-9750
11851 Ventura Blvd. FAX (818) 985-9836
Studio City 91604

Rents VHS and 8mm cameras. Also has a repair service for all tape cameras both in-house and on-site. Discounts for actors. Monday through Saturday, 9 am to 6 pm.

ORANGE VIDEO PRODUCTION (213) 220-2662
Los Angeles

Very affordable, complete Betacam SP camera/audio/lighting package for rent. (Camera operator also available-credits include shooting an Emmy award winning documentary, E!, Discovery Channel, Cops, etc.,). Camera: Sony D-30 and B-50/BVV-5 and two PVV-3. Audio: Senheiser 416 mics, Lectrosonic wireless lav. mics, M4A+ =mixer, etc. Lighting: Frezzi focusable camera light; Chimera, Mole fresnels (2k-minimole), Arri Ultralight 4k = 2k soft, Erik Sachtler tripod, etc. Call for low prices.

RENT-A-CENTER (818) 376-0880
6572 Van Nuys Blvd. FAX (818) 376-1466
Van Nuys 91405

6300 Laurel Canyon Blvd. (818) 505-1903
North Hollywood 91606
www.rentacenter.com

Rents electronics, camcorders, DVDs, and VCRs. Also appliances, computers, printers, furniture and more.

SAMY'S CAMERA (323) 938-2420
431 S. Fairfax FAX (323) 937-2919
Los Angeles 90036

585 Venice Blvd. (310) 450-4551
Venice 90291
www.samys.com
samys@samys.com

Rents and sells cameras of all types including video cameras. Carries complete darkroom and film supplies. Also has an electronic imaging department.

VIDEO EQUIPMENT RENTALS CO. (818) 956-1444
912 Ruberta Ave.
Glendale 91204
www.verrents.com

Rents cameras, VCRs and TVs. Also carries audio visual equipment, has editing facilities, and does duplication of demo reels. Delivery is available. Open daily.

WOODLAND HILLS CAMERA (818) 347-2270
5348 Topanga Canyon Blvd.
Woodland Hills 91364
www.telescopecity.com

Rents VHS cameras and lighting equipment. Also carries most visual equipment including still cameras, telescopes, etc. Monday through Saturday, 9 am to 6 pm.

Video Demos, Duplications, Airchecks & Production

Your video demo must be of broadcast quality with your name on the box and the label as well as at the beginning and end of the tape. Put your most impressive credit on the reel first and if you have several clips from well-known shows, pick the one where you are the type of character in which you are the most often cast. You will want to include 3-4 scenes to show your range. The scenes don't have to make any sense, you just want to show a special moment. Keep the tape strong and short, just about 5-8 minutes long, with the running time listed on the label of the tape. Most agents and casting directors say unless you have network quality tape, don't bother, so don't use anything that is staged specifically for a demo.

22GUNS ENTERTAINMENT (818) 981-7500
14320 Ventura Blvd., PMB# 189 FAX (818) 981-7580
Sherman Oaks 91423
www.22guns.com
erikablackwell@scbglobal.net

22Guns Entertainment helps you market yourself in dramatic new ways that are cost-efficient, hip and easy to distribute. They are a cutting-edge developer of custom marketing tools: full-color postcards, digital reels and digital business cards. Anyone can dub your reel, but 22Guns turns it into it a high-tech promotional tool. Start imagining your marketing campaign by visiting their website. Avid and Final Cut Pro editing suites are also available. Visa and MasterCard accepted.

ACTORS VIDEO SERVICES/V4 VIDEO (323) 651-9999
8170 Beverly Blvd., Ste. 106 FAX (323) 655-8672
Los Angeles 90048
www.demoreel.com

Specializes in actors and other below-the-line artists' demo tapes. Can output to any format including DVD.

ADVANCED VIDEO, INC. (323) 469-0707
6757 Santa Monica Blvd.
Los Angeles 90038

Actor's reels. Editing, air checks, duplication, film to tape, and PAL to NTSC standard conversions. Editor provided. Self-service dubbing available. Also rents equipment. Monday through Friday, 10 am to 6 pm.

AUDITIONTAPE, INC. (310) 289-4962
8556 Rugby Dr.
West Hollywood 90069
www.thecastlist.com

AuditionTape provides actors with a venue for professional video taping. Whether you have an audition out of town, or you'd like to add scenes to your demo reel, they provide you with a digital video camera, studio, lighting, a playback monitor, a camera operator/reader, and one complimentary VHS copy. The environment is relaxed, giving you the time and space to review and perfect your work. Other services available include: audition coaching and video dubbing.

BARCON VIDEO (818) 248-9161
3653 Mesalila Lane FAX (818) 249-8884
Glendale 91208
www.barcon.com
barcon@bbs-la.com

Professional Beta cameraman, packages. Documentaries, actors demos, foreign formats. Broadcast quality.

BC EDITORIAL (323) 288-1218
P.O. Box 93415
Los Angeles 90093

6545 Hazeltine Ave., #208 (818) 785-7599
Van Nuys 91401
brian@brianjcavanugh.com

Video demo reels for actors. Reasonable prices.

CARD SHARKS (800) 229-1795
PRINTING AND GRAPHICS (818) 300-4525
www.sharksprinting.com
lindley@sharksprinting.com

A good source for innovative marketing tools. Their signature product is Pocket Headshots™, but they also have high-quality, low-cost postcards and business cards. Also available: photo retouching, Pocket Demo Reels™ (your reel on a business card-sized DVD or CD-ROM!), reel production and editing, and entertainer's websites.

CAREY-IT-OFF PRODUCTIONS (818) 782-4700
7220 Woodman Ave. FAX (818) 782-9944
Ste. 201
Van Nuys 91405
www.carey-it-off.com

Digital and linear editing from 1/2", 3/4", High 8, S-VHS, Betacam and DV CAM, mini DV and DVD. Provides air checks, duplication and one camera shoots. Time base correction, special effects, most format duplication Final Cut Pro and video effects services are available. Air check library from 1996 to present. Will film actors' scenes with multi-camera and edit together. Location shoots available. 24P available. Formerly known as Phase-L Productions.

CHANNEL ONE VIDEO (310) 584-9410
1406 Innes Place
Venice 90291
www.channelonevideo.com

Editing, duplication, and film-to-tape conversion. Works with one, two, or three cameras. Avid, and digital video. The studio is suitable for actors, dancers, and singers. Engineers, operators, and editors are also available. Low prices. See listing under AUDIO DEMO PRODUCTION in this section.

CINEVATIVE (323) 852-8903
8271 Melrose Ave., Ste. 203 FAX (323) 852-0128
Los Angeles 90046
www.cinevative.com
production@cinevative.com

A production company specializing in digital features, shorts, actor demo reels and music videos. Includes full production package, professional lighting, sound, camera, dollies and cranes, etc. Can process your scene to give it a 35mm film look. Edit Beta SP, DV, 3/4 inch, VHS, SVHS, add music, effects, titles, graphics and more. Call for demo. Multiple award winning production company.

DIGIMAX PRODUCTIONS LLC (818) 769-3333 / (888) DIGIMAX
10061 Riverside Dr., #786
Toluca Lake 91602
www.digimaxproductions.com
info@digimaxproductions.com

DigiMax offers a broad range of digital video and post-production services. Services include editing, shooting, DVD authoring, Duplication, video encoding, webdesign and personal website hosting.

DJ EDITORIAL (818) 640-1789 / (818) 753-1044
11136 Hesby St., #312
North Hollywood 91601
www.djeditorial.com
darryljohn@aol.com

Demo reels for actors and other Industry professionals. Design and create a new reel or update and improve an existing one. A calm and creative environment with an emphasis on the unique individual. Digital editing on AVID or Final Cut Pro; all tape formats accepted; ask about custom labels and packaging; VHS and DVD available. Full service professional editing at affordable prices.

ECHO POST (310) 204-7800
FAX (310) 204-7801

Offers post production services for demo reels, shorts, features, etc. Uses the Avid Systems, the leader in digital, non-linear editing. Some clients include Creative Artists Agency, Warner Brothers, and A&M Records. Keith was in the process of moving at the time of publication so please call for new address and website information.

EDIT STUDIO (323) 463-1996
419 N. Larchmont Blvd., Box 90
Los Angeles 90004
www.flamingangelfilms.com
pixelvision@pacbell.net

Fantastic prices with dynamic editors in their all digital studio located in Hollywood. Let them cut your show reel. They support DVCam, miniDV, and VHS and can provide DVCam, DVD and MiniDV masters. Includes free VHS dub.

EZTV (310) 829-3389
1629 18th St., Ste. 6 FAX (310) 829-3409
Santa Monica 90404
www.eztvmedia.com
eztvmedia@aol.com

Located in the 18th Street Arts Complex in Santa Monica. Both studio and location production. They shoot demo tapes at their facility. Editing within all formats. Titles are included in operator assisted editing as are many special effects. Call for special production packages and prices. Mention the Working Actor's Guide and receive a 15% discount. Open Monday through Friday from 10 am to 7 pm and weekends by appointment. Web design and graphic design also available.

GOSCH PRODUCTIONS (818) 729-0000
2227 W. Olive Ave.
Burbank 91506
www.goschproductions.com
info@goschproductions.com

Gosch Productions provides a full service film/video production house and sound stage allowing you to initiate your production seamlessly under one roof. Need a demo reel? Need duplications? Duplications all formats including DVD, their specialty. Digital non-linear editing cuts your editing time by 2/3, yet gives you the highest quality available anywhere. Free consultation.

ROSS HUNT PRODUCTIONS (818) 763-6045 / (818) 980-3812
12440 Moorpark St.
Studio City 91604
www.rosshunthbtv.com

Actors' demo reels. 5 edit bays with non-linear editing. Inexpensive quantity duplication. Also does editing including toaster editing, digital effects, 1/2" and 3/4" with A/B roll. Low prices on blank tape, all formats, all lengths. Worldwide standards conversion. Also webdesign and graphics.

IMAGESTARTER (818) 506-7010
1016 W. Magnolia
Burbank 91506
www.imagestarter.com
customerservice@imagestarter.com

The working actor's marketing source, Imagestarter is the Industry's only one-stop shop for lithos, resumes, videotape packaging, postcards flyers and much more. The original photo resume specialists. Offers a wide variety of formats and guarantees highly innovative and cost-effective marketing tools or your money back. Also offers consultation and advice on resume composition. Free resume updates for every referral. Mail orders welcome. Package pricing available. No appointment necessary. Video demos for actors.

JAN'S VIDEO (323) 462-5511
6381 Hollywood Blvd., Ste. 430 FAX (323) 462-2068
Hollywood 90028
www.demo-reel.com
jansvideo@aol.com

Does all format video duplication, actors' demo tapes, and home video editing. Has many TV shows of the past 15 years on file and pilots from 1980. Once established, clients can phone them to pull an air check. Please call for a free consultation.

M85, INC. (818) 206-8789
www.m85inc.com
jason@m85inc.com

M85 Inc. provides full media web design, graphic design, CD Demo graphics, VHS/DVD reel graphics and does video production and music video production.

MICHAEL'S (310) 828-4313
2402 Wilshire Blvd.
Santa Monica 90403
www.discountproductsandservices.com

Video copies from VHS, S-VHS, 3/4", Betacam SP, 8mm and Hi-8. 3/4" and VHS editing for demo tapes.

MY YOU ME PRODUCTIONS (310) 820-1772
2050 S. Bundy Dr., Ste. 104
W. Los Angeles 90025
www.myyoume.com

My You Me productions is a post facility for all post production needs. They use the Avid digital editing system. It is a superior system allowing editors to edit faster and more precisely, while maintaining the highest resolution. Ninety-six percent (96%) of all television and film productions are edited on Avid. Titles, effects, laugh tracks, applause, etc. For your film needs they have film matchback to convert 24 frames per second (fps) to 30 fps and back and also post production sound with ProTools by Digidesign, a subsidiary of Avid, twenty four tracks of audio and effects. Monday through Friday, 10 am to 6 pm.

ORANGE VIDEO PRODUCTION (213) 220-2662
Hollywood Area
videf@msn.com

Erik Freiser has shot an Emmy winning documentary in 2000, as well as shooting for E!, Rhino Records, HBO, LAPD, Discovery, etc., and has two complete broadcast Betacam SP ENG camera packages and can provide a complete crew. Available for actor demos, documentaries, features, stand-up acts, etc. Can also rent out his camera/audio/light package. Reasonable rates.

PAUL'S VIDEO PRODUCTIONS (323) 851-8825
3493 Cahuenga Blvd., Unit C
Hollywood 90068
paulsvideo@adelphia.net

Paul Norton has nearly 20 years experience editing demo reels. Formerly of Jan's Video, Paul now has his own state-of-the-art digital production facility. Paul's clear-sighted objectivity, relaxed demeanor, and attention to detail make for effective reels that get to the point (without alot of silly effects). That's why he's recommended by top casting directors, agents, managers and actors; just ask around. Editing $80 per hour; DVD Airchecks $25 per hour (actor keeps original); and VHS copies start at $2.50. Audition scenes and monologues shot on DV camera. WebReels and mini CDs, transfer old masters to DVD.

PLANET VIDEO (323) 464-6474
1956 N. Cahuenga Blvd. FAX (323) 464-6476
Los Angeles 90068
www.planet-video.com
pv@planetvideo.com

Started in 1995, Planet Video's philosophy is geared toward creating a specialized demo that promotes your abilities and uniqueness. They work with talented newcomers and seasoned professionals to eliminate the superfluous, and highlight the employable aspects and essences. All demos are archived so any additions or changes to your reel are easy, inexpensive and with no loss of quality.

POINT 360 (323) 957-5500
1220 N. Highland Ave. FAX (323) 466-7406
Hollywood 90038
www.point360.com

Full service duplication and post-production company with 6 Los Angeles locations. All tape format and broadcast standards are available, including digital formats and DVD. Volume discounts available. Hollywood, Burbank and the Westside.

POSITIVE IMAGE (323) 465-5085
1617 El Centro St,, Ste. 17 FAX (323) 465-5085
Hollywood 90028

Actors video demos. Studio/Backgrounds, 3/4" and VHS editing production services. Betacam SP camera, Final Cut Pro editing.

POTTY MOUTH PRODUCTIONS (323) 468-8631
1845 Canyon Dr., #1
Hollywood 90028
www.pottymouthproductions.com

DV Film Production (larger projects upon request.) Digital master, VHS copies, DVD mastering and CD ROMs. Also web design and demo reels.

PRO VIDEO (310) 828-2292
2904-A Colorado Blvd. FAX (310) 828-1808
Santa Monica 90404
www.zyx.org

Professional quality post video services featuring high speed non-linear editing. They edit video demos for actors, comedians, singers, and dancers and provide computer graphics, special effects, titles, music, audience applause, and laugh tracks for a polished performance. Also does DVD and cassette tape duplication.

PROMOTIONAL DESIGN CONCEPTS (310) 210-1533
3388 Centinela Ave., #21
Los Angeles 90066
filmcutter68@hotmail.com

Promotional design for custom, graphics integrated-full color postcards, posters, 8 years experience demo reel editing with Avid, DVD and web applications. All the promotional tools for the serious actor at actor friendly prices.

PSI, INC. (949) 261-6119
18017-H Skypark Circle FAX (949) 250-9018
Irvine 92614
www.psivideoinc.com
psivideo@worldnet.att.net

Edits tapes together for actors. Uses both union and non-union actors for corporate videos and voice-over work. Accepts pictures and resumes and voice tapes.

REEL DEAL DEMOS (818) 679-9117
www.reeldealdemos.com
tom@reeldealdemos.com

Reel Deal Demos specializes in creating professional demo reels for artists, actors and students. See their website for more details.

RSEUMEREELS.COM (818) 769-3333
10061 Riverside Dr., #786
Toluca Lake 91602
www.resumereels.com
troy@digimaxproductions.com

ResumeReels.com is an online video editing company that provides custom edited demo reels. Services include, editing, DVD authoring, video encoding, web design, tape duplication and web hosting.

SHANNON & COMPANY (949) 855-0844
23151 Plaza Pointe, Ste. 110
Laguna Hills 92653

Films and edits actors' reels. Furnishes everything including the script and SAG actors to work with the client. They have state-of-the art broadcast quality equipment. Also shoots documentaries.

DAVID SHINE VIDEOGRAPHER (323) 464-5524
Hollywood
www.davidshine.com

Video tapes all types of performances. Actors, dancers, singers, magicians, etc. Can shoot in any situation with or without tripod. Mr. Shine can create a demo from existing tape as well as shooting one from scratch. Complete editing, titling, effects, and dubbing is available. All formats including PAL transfers. Credit cards accepted. Free consultation.

SHOKUS VIDEO (818) 704-0400
P.O. Box 3125 FAX (818) 701-0560
Chatsworth 91313
www.shokus.com
info@shokus.com

16mm, 8mm, Super 8 film-to-tape transfers, slide and photo transfers to tape and DVD, airchecks, tape, and DVD duplication.

SILVER LINING PRODUCTIONS (303) 485-8989
380 Main St., Ste. 208 FAX (303) 485-9292
Longmont, CO 80501
www.silverliningproductions.net
info@silverliningproductions.net

Silver Lining Productions offers a broad range of digital video and post-production services including, digital video editing/shooting, tape duplication/transfers, DVD authoring and internet media solutions.

SLINGBLADE DIGITAL (323) 785-2504
1149 N. Gower St., Ste. 290
Los Angeles 90038
www.slingblade.com
info@slingblade.com

Slingblade Digital is a full-service multimedia production house offering video production, editing and website development. They shoot demos on DV, cut them on Avid, make VHS or DVD dupes, and/or compress them for the Web. If you don't have an existing website they can get that too. No job is too small. Competitive rates.

SPEEDREELS (323) 931-1712
5225 Wilshire Blvd., Ste. 410
Los Angeles 90068
www.speedreels.com
info@speedreels.com

SpeedReels, are a one minute online talent trailer, hosted at your own web address. They also offer editing and instant demo reels (shoot and edit a high quality demo with them).

STORMMAKER PRODUCTIONS (818) 974-2774
10523 Burbank Blvd., Ste. 104 FAX (818) 985-5165
North Hollywood 91601
www.stormmakerproductions.com
steffanie@stormmakerproductions.com

Edit high quality demo reels. They have surveyed casting directors and know their preferences. The process is collaborative and artistic.

SUNDANCE MEDIACOM (661) 942-2429
44404 N. 16th St., West FAX (661) 942-2729
Ste. 204
Lancaster 93534
www.sundancemediacom.com
rbanis@sundancemediacom.com

Need to make an impact? They can help. Whatever your presentation or product may be, Sundance MediaCom can make sure your message is heard! Their multimedia projects will be ready on time and within budget. They can arrange the start-to-finish production and set-up and tear-down of your video wall, kiosk, or LaserDisc presentation.

TREE FALLS (323) 851-0299
3131 Cahuenga Blvd. West FAX (323) 851-0277
Los Angeles 90068
www.tfsound.com
mike@tfsound.com

DVD mastering/dubs of video demos and clips from many formats including Digibeta, BetaSP, DV, 3/4. DVD, CD, and VHS dubs/transfers. Audio post services and VO demo producing.

VENICE EDIT (310) 714-0433
www.veniceedit.com
info@veniceedit.com

Digital editing of demo reels.

VIDEO EQUIPMENT RENTALS CO. (818) 956-1444
912 Ruberta FAX (818) 241-4519
Glendale 91204
www.verents.com

Rents cameras, VCRs and TVs. Also carries audio visual equipment, has editing facilities, and does duplication of demo reels. Delivery is available. Open daily.

VIDEO MONITORING SERVICES (323) 993-0111
6430 W. Sunset Blvd., Ste. 400
Los Angeles 90028
www.vmsinfo.com

Full editing facility including 3/4" and VHS for actors' reels. Mention the Working Actor's Guide for a special discount. See listing under CLIPPING SERVICES in this section for further information.

VIRTUAL BUSINESS CARDS
CYNDIE CARRILLO (818) 693-0023
859 Hollywood Way, Ste. 123
Burbank 91505
www.virtualbusinesscards.com

Keep your picture, resume, contact information and either video or audio clip in your pocket. Great for networking.

VLADIMIR STUDIOS (323) 656-3333
5340 Tyrone Ave. FAX (323) 656-6929
Sherman Oaks 91423
www.vladimirstudios.com

Studio and location production. One or two cameras, engineer, operator, and editor assistance provided. Also offers audio mixing for voice-overs, demo tapes, editing, A/B rolls, full TBC, digital effects, digital editing, titles, computer graphics, logo design, and DVcam. By appointment only.

Video Demos, Duplications, Airchecks & Production

WEST SIDE MEDIA GROUP (310) 979-3500
12233 West Olympic Blvd. FAX (310) 979-3503
Ste. 152
Los Angeles 90064
westsidedigital@aol.com

A complete broadcast editing facility that does mass video duplication. Can shoot and/or edit actors' demo reels. DVD authoring. Works in all formats. Also does foreign conversions.

WORLD OF VIDEO (310) 659-5147
(866) 900-DUBS
8717 Wilshire Blvd. FAX (310) 659-8247
Beverly Hills 90211
www.wova.com

Editing and duplication, actors' demo tapes, video duplication for all formats, standard conversion, A/B rolls, audio copies, Beta, DVD, digital effects, film-to-tape, and freeze frames. Engineer provided. Volume discounts. Airchecks by request. Video conferencing and voice over reels also available. Monday through Friday, 9 am to 6 pm and Saturday, 11 am to 4 pm.

Wardrobe Consultants

CLOUTIER AGENCY (310) 394-8813
1026 Montana Ave.
Santa Monica 90403
www.cloutieragency.com

Hair, make-up, and wardrobe stylists.

COLOR COMPANY (818) 760-7798
www.jillkirshcolor.com
jkirsch@jillkirschcolor.com

Jill Kirsh comes to your office, set or home and drapes you with all possible colors and picks out the colors that are best for you and makes a chart for you to carry. She works with actors helping them choose the right colors to dramatically enhance on-camera appearance. She not only finds colors which make you shine, but will help you find what colors work for different types of character work. Named best color consultant by Los Angeles Magazine. Regularly requested to consult celebrities before red carpet ceremonies.

JOYCELYNE LEW (323) 466-3100
(213) 613-8785
www.joycelyne.com FAX (323) 469-7138
jlew@joycelyne.com

Wardrobe consultations, color work, and personal wardrobe shopping to create your own personal style and image. Does studio consultations and has an image consulting salon. Will design hair and make-up including wigs to create any character you desire. By appointment only. See listing for Celebrity Cosmetics under IMAGE CONSULTANTS and MAKE-UP.ARTISTS in this section for further information. Accepts all credit cards.

KATHY MARSHALL
CERTIFIED IMAGE CONSULTANT (310) 540-3460
553 N. Pacific Coast Highway, Ste. 218
Redondo Beach

A professional color analyst offers wardrobe consulting and image enhancement as well as computer body analysis and make-up lessons. Will shop for clothes for specific roles as well as for daily wear.

SUZAN MEIER (661) 253-9970
suzanmeier@aol.com

Suzan has created and patented a panty that holds a wireless microphone transmitter/receiver pack securely against a woman's body – firmly and inconspicuously in the small of her back. Unlike its elastic belt and holster type predecessors, the MicPac is quite comfortable, secure and discreet. Developed to accommodate the most revealing outfits. Suzan provides personal wardrobe consultation and creation. Also designs and constructs costumes as well as bridal gowns and ensembles. Has a Dramalogue award.

REX, INC. (323) 664-6494
4446 Ambrose Ave. FAX (323) 664-6112
Los Angeles 90027
www.therexagency.com

Represents make-up artists, wardrobe consultants, hair stylists and photographers.

MARY ROTHSCHILD (310) 453-0254
hroth996@aol.com

An image consultant who works on the total look, color, style, make-up and design. Also offers wardrobe consultations, shopping excursions, and photo consultations. Will travel to locations.

KELI SQUIRES-TAYLOR (323) 938-7729
6056 Whitworth Dr.
Los Angeles 90019
www.actorsuccess.net
kst1management@earthlink.net

Special marketing for actors. Personal Manager Keli Squires-Taylor works with all acting levels to give honest marketing evaluations, marketing guidance and business advice to help you move on up to the next level(s) quickly.

Web Services

ACADEMY PLAYERS DIRECTORY ONLINE (310) 247-3058
1313 N. Vine FAX (310) 550-5034
Hollywood 90028
www.playersdirectory.com
players@oscars.org

The Academy Players Directory is available on-line as well as in a printed version. Known as the "Industry Standard" since 1937, The Players Directory is a cooperative service to the players and producers of Hollywood. To be a part of the Players Directory Online, an actor must be a member of an actor's union. The Players Directory Online is updated continually. It includes your photo(s), name, representation and resume. Casting directors can search for an actor by name, special skills, categories and various other attributes. The cost to be in the Player's Directory Online is $75 per year for one photo and includes your information in the printed version as well as the Now Casting Electronic Submission System. Extra photos online are an additional cost of $10 each. For more information, please contact the Academy Players Directory.

ACTOR SITE CREATOR (888) 583-2499
www.actorsitecreator.com
brooke@actorsitecreator.com

ActorSiteCreator is a web site system that will allow you, the actor, to have an inexpensive, yet professional web site that you maintain yourself. Your ActorSiteCreator website can display your headshots, resume, demo reel, contact information and much more. ActorSiteCreator is a simple and easy way to market yourself. $9.95/month.

ACTORS WEBMASTER (818) 763-9991
11684 Ventura Blvd., #999
Studio City 91604
www.actorswebmaster.com
ellen@actorswebmaster.com

Complete website design and hosting (free updates) service specializing in actors.

CARD SHARKS PRINTING AND GRAPHICS (800) 229-1795 (818) 300-4525
www.sharksprinting.com
info@sharksprinting.com

Web design for actors.

DIGITAL DESIGN L.A. INC. (818) 845-2038
3406 W. Burbank Blvd. FAX (818) 841-6222
Burbank 91502
www.digitaldesignla.com
Barbara@digitaldesignla.com

Specializes in resumes for entertainers. Also web design and all graphic services are available.

INSITEFUL.ORG (310) 359-2536
5118 De Longpre Avenue
Los Angeles 90027
www.insiteful.org
admin@insiteful.org

Fast, reliable, interesting and up-to-date, Insiteful is the place to find great web design and site management for creatives who want to build and manage a successful online presence. Actors, writers, theatre companies have all found their services useful in creating clear, high impact pages that succinctly display CV, photographs, demo reels and business details in one place – often cutting down on, or even eliminating the need to send out expensive headshots. Competitive rates.

MODIFIED STUDIOS (310) 562-1961
www.modifiedstudios.com
greg@modifiedstudios.com

Offers quality graphic and web design services at an actor's rate. Specializing in websites, resumes, zed cards and any marketing materials.

STAND OUT SITES (323) 200-9047
www.stand-out-sites.com
sos@stand-out-sites.com

A full-service web design company specializing in highly affordable as well as high-end and e-commerce websites and demo reels for the entertainment Industry. Organized by artists to help fellow performing artists self-promote and self-publicize themselves. Special prices for websites and reels for performing and creative artists.

Wigs

ACCENT ON DANCE & BROADWAY COSTUMES (626) 287-0741
9026 E. Las Tunas Dr. FAX (626) 287-9264
Temple City 91780

Carries dancewear from Capezio, Baryshnikov, Danskin and others, shoes are Capezio and Danshuz and they stock Ben Nye make-up. The costume rental collection contains over 6000 pieces as well as accessories, wigs and masks for sale. Call for discount program details.

CELEBRITY COSMETICS (323) 466-3100
1952 N. Van Ness Ave.
Los Angeles 90068
www.joycelyne.com
jlew@joycelyne.com

Image and make-up consultant. Does make-up for headshots, TV, video, film, stage, fashion, corrective, make-overs, and period styles. Has own line of cosmetics, and wigs, cuts and styles hair and wigs, and travels to locations. By appointment only. Accepts all credit cards. See listing under IMAGE CONSULTANTS in this section for further information.

CINEMA SECRETS (818) 846-0579
4400 Riverside Dr. FAX (818) 846-0431
Burbank 91505
www.cinemasecrets.com
cinemasecretsinfo@cinemasecrets.com

Carries wigs, costumes, and beauty supplies. Custom wig making is available. 10% discount to SAG members. See listings under PROFESSIONAL MAKE-UP in this section and MAKE-UP in the TRAINING section for further information. Monday through Friday, 8 am to 6 pm and Saturday, 10 am to 5 pm.

GILBERT OF HOLLYWOOD COSTUMES (818) 506-6668
11345 Chandler Blvd.
North Hollywood 91601

Masquerade and theatrical costume rentals. Carries animal, character, period, uniforms, tuxedos, show girl, and sports costumes. Also has 20s and 30s and 40s-60s clothing, lingerie, accessories, hats, masks, wigs, and hair pieces. Does alterations and custom made costumes and has special rates for theatre productions. Staff has a wide knowledge of theatre history, and most stock characters are available. There is a special rate for actors in a class project or a waiver production. Monday through Friday, noon to 6 pm and Saturday, noon to 3 pm or by appointment. Located in the Haunted Studio, call for directions. Located in NoHo Theatrical District.

INTERNATIONAL COSTUME (310) 320-6392
1423 Marcelina FAX (310) 320-3054
Torrance 90501
www.international.com

Carries wigs, make-up, hats, and accessories. Monday through Friday, 9 am to 6 pm and Saturday, 10 am to 5 pm. Extended hours start mid October. See listing under COSTUME SALES & RENTALS in this section for further information.

MAGIC WORLD (818) 700-8100
10122 Topanga Canyon Blvd.
Chatsworth 91311

Costume sales and rental. They have over 10,000 different types of costumes. Adults may rent or buy, children for sale only. Also custom made costumes, balloon imprinting, masks, wigs, theatrical make-up, and magic supplies.

MAKE BELIEVE, INC. (310) 396-6785
3240 Pico Blvd.
Santa Monica 90404
www.makebelieve.com

Mostly rentals, some sales. Will custom build costumes and they also carry wigs and special effects make-up. They have stylists, designers, and wardrobe consultants available for work on productions. Monday through Saturday, 10 am to 6 pm and Sunday, 11 am to 5 pm.

NAIMIE'S FILM & TELEVISION BEAUTY SUPPLY (818) 655-9922
12640 Riverside Dr. FAX (818) 655-9999
North Hollywood 91607

Sales and rentals of wigs and hairpieces in this complete theatrical make-up and beauty supply store. Discounts for actors. Call store for times. See listing under PROFESSIONAL MAKE-UP & BEAUTY SUPPLIES in this section for further information.

OUTFITTERS WIGS OF HOLLYWOOD (323) 469-9421
6626 Hollywood Blvd. FAX (323) 462-4730
Hollywood 90028

Has a large selection of wigs, false eyelashes, and make-up. Specializes in hair extensions and weaving like secret hair. Monday through Saturday, 10 am to 7 pm. Open for 30 years, large selection.

URSULA'S COSTUMES, INC. (310) 582-8230
2516 Wilshire Blvd.
Santa Monica 90403

Party and Halloween costumes. Custom made clothes available, also carries wigs, make-up, masks, accessories, and children's costumes. Will do alterations. Monday through Saturday, 9:30 am to 6 pm.

THE WIG COMPANY (818) 980-3118
12721 Ventura Blvd. FAX (818) 763-5663
Studio City 91604
www.wigsbypierre.com
julie@wigsbypierre.com

Custom wigs for film and TV. Reasonable prices. Has thousands to choose from. Fax or bring in a photo of your chosen wig style. In business since 1959. 10:30 am to 5:30 pm Monday through Saturday.

Wigs

WILSHIRE WIGS & SILHOUETTES
(818) 761-9447
(800) 927-0874
5241 Craner Ave. **FAX (818) 761-9779**
North Hollywood 91603
www.wilshirewigs.com

Carries all major hairgoods manufacturers and a very large selection of costume wigs, hair extensions and supplies. Custom wigmakers and stylists on premises. The men's division, Silhouette Hair for Men, carries fine quality men's products. Special discounts for SAG members. SEE AD ON PREVIOUS PAGE.

CHARLIE WRIGHT, LTD. **(818) 347-4566**
19720 Ventura Blvd., Ste. 106 **FAX (818) 346-1043**
Woodland Hills 91364
www.wrighthair.com

Custom-made hair pieces and wigs. Monday through Friday, 9 am to 5 pm.

Notes

TABLE OF CONTENTS: THE TEAM

AGENCIES: QUICK REFERENCE CHART 192
AGENCIES: COMMERCIAL & THEATRICAL 199
AGENCIES: MODELING 213
AGENCIES: SPECIALTY 216
ATTORNEYS 218
BUSINESS MANAGERS 221
PERSONAL MANAGERS 225
PUBLIC RELATIONS 233

LOS ANGELES AGENTS

Legend: R .... Rarely

NAME OF AGENCY	Theatrical	Commercial	Literary	Voice-Over	Children	Reviews Unsolicited Pic/Res	Reviews Unsolicited Tapes/DVDs	Attends Showcases & Plays	Works w/Non-Union Actors	Will See Newcomers	East Coast Affiliate
ABA TALENT AGENCY	X	X			X	X			X		
ABRAMS ARTISTS	X	X		X	X	X	R	R			X
ACME TALENT & LITERARY	X	X	X	X	X	X					X
ACTORS LA		X				X	X	X			
AFFINITY MODEL & TALENT	X	X	X	X	X	X		X	X	X	X
AGENCY FOR THE PERFORMING ARTS	X		X				X				X
AIMEE ENTERTAINMENT ASSOCIATES	X	X			X	X	X	R			
AKA TALENT AGENCY		X									
ALVARADO/REY AGENCY	X	X		X	X	X		R	X	X	
AMSEL, EISENSTADT & FRAZIER, INC.	X	X			X	X		R	X	X	
ANGEL CITY TALENT	X	X			X	X		X	R	R	
THE ARTISTS AGENCY	X		X			X		X			
ARTISTS GROUP, LTD.	X									R	X
AUSTIN AGENCY	X	X						X			
BADGLEY, CONNOR, SCHIOWITZ & ANKRUM	X					X		X	X	X	
BAIER/KLEINMAN INTERNATIONAL	X					X		X	R	X	
BALDWIN TALENT, INC.		X				X					
BOBBY BALL AGENCY	X	X			X	X		X		X	
BARON ENTERTAINMENT	X	X			X	X		X			
MARC BASS TALENT AGENCY	X										
BAUMAN, REDANTY & SHAUL	X							X	R		
BICOASTAL TALENT, INC.							X	X	X	X	
BONNIE BLACK TALENT AGENCY	X	X	X		X	X		X	X	X	
THE BLAKE AGENCY	X	X		X						X	
BOUTIQUE AGENCY	X	X				X					
BRADY, BRANNON & RICH		X									
SONJIA WARREN BRANDON'S COMMERCIALS UNLIMITED	X	X			X	X			X	X	
BRESLER, KELLY & ASSOCIATES	X					X		X		X	
BRICK ENTERTAINMENT AGENCY	X	X		X	X			X	X	X	
DON BUCHWALD & ASSOCIATES	X		X			X		X			X
BUCHWALD TALENT GROUP	X	X		X	X	X			R	X	
IRIS BURTON AGENCY	X	X			X	X					

LOS ANGELES AGENTS

Legend: R .... Rarely

NAME OF AGENCY	Theatrical	Commercial	Literary	Voice-Over	Children	Reviews Unsolicited Pic/Res	Reviews Unsolicited Tapes/DVDs	Attends Showcases & Plays	Works w/Non-Union Actors	Will See Newcomers	East Coast Affiliate
C.L.I., INC.		X		X		X	X	R	X	X	
CASTLE-HILL AGENCY	X	X		X	X	X		R	R	R	
CAVALERI & ASSOC.	X	X	X		X	X		X		X	
THE CHARLES TALENT AGENCY	X	X				X	X	X	X	R	
CHASIN AGENCY	X		X								
CHATEAU BILLINGS TALENT AGENCY	X	X		X	X	X		R	R		
TORY CHRISTOPHER GROUP	X	X			X	X	R		X	X	
CIRCLE TALENT AGENCY	X	X			X	X		R	X	X	
W. RANDOLF CLARK	X	X			X	X		R	X		
CLEAR TALENT GROUP		X				X	X				
COLLEEN CLER TALENT AGENCY	X	X			X	X		R	X	X	
COAST TO COAST TALENT GROUP, INC.	X	X		X	X	X		X	X	X	
CORALIE JR. AGENCY	X		X		X	X		R	X		
CREATIVE ARTISTS AGENCY (CAA)	X		X					X			
CULBERTSON GROUP	X	X		X						X	
CUNNINGHAM, ESCOTT, SLEVIN, DOHERTY AGENCY		X		X	X	X					X
DANGERFIELD AGENCY		X			X				X		
DIVERSE TALENT GROUP	X	X	X		X	X		R			
DRAGON TALENT	X	X			X	X	X	R			
E.S.I. KIDS	X	X			X	X	X			X	
ELLIS TALENT GROUP	X					X		X		X	
ENDEAVOR AGENCY	X		X								
EQUINOX MODELS & TALENT	X	X	X	X	X			R	X	X	
JAMIE FERRAR ASSOCIATES	X	X			X	X				X	
FERRAR MEDIA ASSOCIATES	X	X				X		X	X	X	
FILM ARTISTS ASSOCIATES	X	X	X		X	X		R		X	X
THE FIRM	X		X			X					
FLICK EAST-WEST TALENTS, INC.		X				X		R			
BARRY FREED AGENCY	X		X			X		X			
ALICE FRIES	X	X				X					
THE GAGE GROUP	X	X	X			X		X		X	X

LOS ANGELES AGENTS

Legend: R .... Rarely

NAME OF AGENCY	Theatrical	Commercial	Literary	Voice-Over	Children	Reviews Unsolicited Pic/Res	Reviews Unsolicited Tapes/DVDs	Attends Showcases & Plays	Works w/Non-Union Actors	Will See Newcomers	East Coast Affiliate
DALE GARRICK INTERNATIONAL TALENT	X	X	X		X	X		R	R	R	
THE GEDDES AGENCY	X					X		X		X	X
LAYA GELFF AGENCY	X		X			X					
DON GERLER AGENCY	X	X	X		X	X	X	X	X	X	
THE GERSH AGENCY	X		X			X		R			X
MICHELLE GORDON & ASSOCIATES	X	X	X					X			
GRANT, SAVIC, KOPALOFF & ASSOCIATES	X							X	X	X	
GREENE & ASSOCIATES	X	X		X	R	X		R	X	X	X
GVA TALENT, INC.	X	X			X	X		X	X	X	
BUZZ HALLIDAY & ASSOCIATES	X	X				X		X		X	
BEVERLY HECHT AGENCY	X	X			X	X	X	X	R	X	
HERVEY/GRIMES TALENT AGENCY	X	X		X	X	X		X	X	X	
HILLTOP TALENT AGENCY		X									
DANIEL HOFF AGENCY	X	X		X	X	X	X	X	X	X	
HOLLANDER TALENT GROUP, INC.	X	X		X	X	X	X	X	X	X	
HOUSE OF REPRESENTATIVES TALENT AGENCY	X				X	X	X	X		R	
HOWARD TALENT WEST	X	X	X		X	X		X		X	
HWA TALENT REPRESENTATIVES	X		X			X		X			X
IDENTITY TALENT AGENCY	X	X			X	X				X	X
IFA TALENT AGENCY	X		X								
INNOVATIVE ARTISTS & LITERARY AGENCY	X		X		X				X		X
INTERNATIONAL CREATIVE MANAGEMENT (ICM)	X	X	X	X							X
JKA TALENT AGENCY	X		X			X					
JS REPRESENTS TALENT AGENCY		X				X	X	R	R	X	
KAZARIAN/SPENCER & ASSOCIATES	X	X		X	X			X		X	
SHARON KEMP TALENT AGENCY	X	X			X	X		X			X
WILLIAM KERWIN AGENCY	X		X			X	X	X		X	
ERIC KLASS AGENCY	X										
PAUL KOHNER, INC.	X		X							X	
VICTOR KRUGLOV & ASSOCIATES	X	X			X	X		X	X	X	
L.A. TALENT	X	X			X	X		X	X	R	X
LANE AGENCY INTERNATIONAL MODELS AND TALENT	X	X	X	X	X	X	X	X	X	X	X

LOS ANGELES AGENTS

Legend: R .... Rarely

NAME OF AGENCY	Theatrical	Commercial	Literary	Voice-Over	Children	Reviews Unsolicited Pic/Res	Reviews Unsolicited Tapes/DVDs	Attends Showcases & Plays	Works w/Non-Union Actors	Will See Newcomers	East Coast Affiliate
THE LEVIN AGENCY	X	X		X	X	X		R	R	X	
JACK LIPPMAN AGENCY	X										
LJ & ASSOCIATES	X	X						X	R	R	X
JANA LUKER'S AGENCY	X	X	X		X	X		X			
L W 1, INC.		X				X			X		
LYNNE & REILLY	X	X	X		X			R			
MADEMOISELLE TALENT AGENCY	X	X				X	X		X		
MALAKY INTERNATIONAL	X	X	R	X	R	X	X	X	X	X	
MAXINE'S TALENT AGENCY		X	X	X				X			
MCCABE/JUSTICE	X					X		X	X		X
MCCARTY TALENT	X	X			X					X	
MEDIA ARTISTS GROUP	X	X	X		X	X					
METROPOLITAN TALENT AGENCY	X		X	R				R	R	R	
MGA TALENT	X	X				X			X	X	
MIRAMAR TALENT		X			X	X				X	
MKS AND ASSOCIATES	X										
MORGAN AGENCY	X	X		X	X	X		X	X	X	
WILLIAM MORRIS AGENCY	X	X						R			
H. DAVID MOSS & ASSOCIATES	X		R			X		X	X	X	
SUSAN NATHE & ASSOCIATES, CPC	X	X				X		X	X	X	
NU TALENT AGENCY	X	X				X	X	X	X	X	
ORANGE GROVE GROUP, INC.	X		X			X	X	X		X	
ORIGIN TALENT AGENCY	X	X			X		X				
CINDY OSBRINK TALENT AGENCY	X	X		X	X	X	R	R	X	X	
DOROTHY DAY OTIS AGENCY		X			X	X	X			X	
PAKULA/KING & ASSOCIATES	X					X		R		R	
PARADIGM TALENT & LITERARY AGENCY	X		X			X		R			X
PARTOS COMPANY		X		X				R	R		
PLAYERS TALENT AGENCY	X	X			X	X		R	X	X	
PRIVILEGE TALENT AGENCY	X	X			X	X		X	X	X	
PROGRESSIVE ARTISTS	X					X				X	
REBEL ENTERTAINMENT PARTNERS	X	X				X		X		X	

LOS ANGELES AGENTS

Legend: R .... Rarely

NAME OF AGENCY	Theatrical	Commercial	Literary	Voice-Over	Children	Reviews Unsolicited Pic/Res	Reviews Unsolicited Tapes/DVDs	Attends Showcases & Plays	Works w/Non-Union Actors	Will See Newcomers	East Coast Affiliate
CINDY ROMANO MODELING & TALENT AGENCY	X	X				X		X			
MARION ROSENBERG OFFICE	X		X								
SAMANTHA GROUP TALENT AGENCY	X	X				X			R		
THE SAVAGE AGENCY	X	X			X	X		R	X	X	
JACK SCAGNETTI TALENT AGENCY	X	X	X	X		X	X		X	X	
SANDIE SCHNARR TALENT				X			X	R		X	
JUDY SCHOEN & ASSOCIATES	X							X	X	X	X
KATHLEEN SCHULTZ	X	X			X	X		X			
SCREEN CHILDREN'S AGENCY	X	X			X	X	R	X	X		
SDB PARTNERS, INC.	X				R			R			
DAVID SHAPIRA & ASSOCIATES	X		X					X			
SHREVE TALENT SOURCE		X					X		X		
JEROME SIEGEL ASSOCIATES	X					X	X				
SILVER, MASSETTI, SZATMARY	X									X	
MICHAEL SLESSINGER & ASSOCIATES	X					X		X	X	R	
SUSAN SMITH & COMPANY	X							R			
SMS TALENT	X							X		X	
SOLID TALENT				X			X				
CAMILLE SORICE AGENCY	X		X								
SPECIAL ARTISTS AGENCY		X		X		X	X	X	X	X	X
STARWIL PRODUCTION TALENT AGENCY	X	X	R	R	X	X		R	X	X	
STEVENS GROUP	X	X				X	X	X	X	X	
STONE/MANNERS	X		X			X				X	
PETER STRAIN & ASSOCIATES	X										
SUITE A TALENT	X	X			X	X			X		
SUPERIOR TALENT AGENCY	X	X			X	X		X	X	X	
SUTTON, BARTH & VENNARI, INC.		X		X		X		X		X	
TALENT WORKS	X	X	X		X	X	R	X		X	X
HERB TANNEN & ASSOCIATES				X							
THOMAS TALENT AGENCY	X	X		X	X	X	X				
ARLENE THORNTON & ASSOCIATES		X		X		X	X	X	X	X	
THE TISHERMAN AGENCY		X		X		X	X	X	X		

LOS ANGELES AGENTS

Legend: R .... Rarely

NAME OF AGENCY	Theatrical	Commercial	Literary	Voice-Over	Children	Reviews Unsolicited Pic/Res	Reviews Unsolicited Tapes/DVDs	Attends Showcases & Plays	Works w/Non-Union Actors	Will See Newcomers	East Coast Affiliate
UNITED TALENT AGENCY	X	X			X	X		X		X	X
VISION MODELS		X				X	X			X	
THE WALLIS AGENCY	X		X	X		X		X	X	X	X
BOB WATERS AGENCY	X					X		X			
ANN WAUGH TALENT AGENCY	X	X	X		X	X		X		X	
RUTH WEBB ENTERPRISES, INC.	X					X					X
SHIRLEY WILSON & ASSOCIATES	X	X			X	X		X	X	X	
WORLD CLASS SPORTS		X									
CRAIG WYCKOFF & ASSOCIATES	X				X	X					
ZANUK, PASSON AND PACE, INC	X	X			X	X	X	X	X	X	

SAN DIEGO/ORANGE COUNTY AGENTS

Legend: R .... Rarely

NAME OF AGENCY	Theatrical	Commercial	Literary	Voice-Over	Children	Reviews Unsolicited Pic/Res	Reviews Unsolicited Tapes/DVDs	Attends Showcases & Plays	Works w/Non-Union Actors	Will See Newcomers	East Coast Affiliate
ARTISTS MANAGEMENT AGENCY		X		X	X	X	X	X		X	
MARIAN BERZON AGENCY	X	X	X	X	X					X	
BRAND MODEL AND TALENT AGENCY	X	X				X	X	X	X	X	
SCOTT COPELAND TALENT	X	X				X					
ELEGANCE TALENT AGENCY	X	X		X		X	X	R	X	X	
SHAMON FREITAS & COMPANY	X	X		X	X	X	X	X	X	X	
JET SET MODELS	X	X			X	X			X	X	
NOUVEAU MODEL TALENT	X	X			X	X				X	
SAN DIEGO MODEL & MANAGEMENT		X			X	X	X				

SAN FRANCISCO/BAY AREA AGENTS

NAME OF AGENCY	Theatrical	Commercial	Literary	Voice-Over	Children	Reviews Unsolicited Pic/Res	Reviews Unsolicited Tapes/DVDs	Attends Showcases & Plays	Works w/Non-Union Actors	Will See Newcomers	East Coast Affiliate
BOOM MODELS & TALENT		X		X	X	X	X	X	X	X	
CAST IMAGES TALENT	X	X		X	X	X				X	
MARLA DELL TALENT AGENCY	X	X			X	X		X		X	
FILM THEATRE ACTORS EXCHANGE	X	X	X	X	X	X		R			X
GENERATIONS MODEL & TALENT	X	X		X	X	X				X	
J.E. TALENT		X			X	X				X	
LOOK MODEL & TALENT AGENCY	X	X		X	X	X	X	X		X	
PANDA AGENCY	X	X	X	X	X	X	X	X	X		
THE STARS AGENCY	X	X		X		X					
TALENT PLUS/LOS LATINOS AGENCY		X		X		X	X	X	X	X	
TONRY TALENT AGENCY	X	X		X	X	X	X	X	X		

The agencies listed in the Quick Reference Chart are all franchised by SAG or AFTRA or both. Before making any submissions from the chart please check the individual listings for details. For example the listing will tell you if the agency prefers headshots or 3/4 bodyshots with a resume, the format of video tapes, the age range they handle or are looking for, the procedures for submissions (mailed or in very rare cases, dropped off), etc. SASE means the submission should be accompanied with a self-addressed, stamped envelope. If the agency has requested no submissions, drop-offs, follow up calls, etc., they mean it. The individual listings also have a few agencies that were not franchised at the time of publication but work with non-union actors. All the information in this book has been verified, but things change and agencies move so please contact each agent or agency you plan to submit to before sending out your picture and resume.

An actor who is a member of one of the performers' unions (Screen Actors Guild, Actors' Equity, American Federation of Television and Radio Artists) must be represented by a franchised agent. He can represent himself anytime he wants, but if an agent conducts business for him, the agent must have signed an agreement with one of the performers' unions. That agreement is called a franchise. To be a franchised agent, the agent must have a license to operate from the state, agree to abide by the Agency Rules and Regulations of the union in question, and have some experience as an agent. Just because an agent is franchised by one of the unions is, however, no guarantee that the agent is ethical, knowledgeable, or effective. He probably is, but you need to do your homework, just in case.

—K Callan "The Los Angeles Agent Book" Sweden Press

ABA TALENT AGENCY **(310) 276-1851**
9107 Wilshire Blvd., Ste. 500 **FAX (310) 276-3517**
Beverly Hills 90210

Theatrical/Commercial/Print: Kimberly Gola and Christina Kurtz. TV/Film: Joseph Le. Children: Chris Ledford. Will accept unsolicited pictures and resumes. Prefers headshots. Union and non-union talent. Primarily handles kids, teens, and young adults. Small agency.

ABRAMS ARTISTS **(310) 859-0625**
9200 Sunset Blvd., 11th Fl. **FAX (310) 276-6193**
Los Angeles 90069

President: Harry Abrams. Theatrical: Peter Novick. Commercial: Mark Measures. Children: Wendi Green and Jennifer Millar. Youth Commercial: Brad Diffley. Voice-over: Mark Quinn. Hosting: Mark Measures. The theatrical department prefers headshots, the commercial department will look at 3/4 body shots and/or headshots. 300 clients, mostly guest stars and established actors. Wide variety of clients. Large agency.

ACME TALENT & LITERARY **(323) 954-2263**
4727 Wilshire Blvd., Ste. 333 **FAX (323) 954-2262**
Los Angeles 90010

Owner/Business Affairs: Adam Lieblein. Adult Talent: Steve Wright and Greg Meyer. Children/Young Adult and Musical Theatre: Molly Sweet. Commercials: Emily Hope. Children's Commercials: Eddie Winkler. No submissions from January to June in Los Angeles. NY office accepts submissions year round.

ACTORS LA **(818) 755-0026**
12435 Oxnard St.
North Hollywood 91606

Patrick Hart accepts pictures and resumes via mail for commercial representation.

AFFINITY MODEL AND TALENT **(888) 252-7000** **(323) 525-0577**
8721 Santa Monica Blvd., Ste. 27
West Hollywood 90069
www.affinitytalent.com
info@affinitytalent.com

Affinity Model and Talent is a licensed, bonded, full-service international SAG-AFTRA agency representing men, women and children throughout its offices in Los Angeles, San Francisco, Chicago and New York. They provide models, actors, musicians, writers and entertainers for the film, television, video, fashion, advertising, trade show, promotion and special event industries. They will accept submissions via email only and do not want drop offs or follow up calls. They will call if interested.

AGENCY FOR THE PERFORMING ARTS (APA) **(310) 888-4200**
9200 Sunset Blvd., Ste. 900 **FAX (310) 888-4242**
Los Angeles 90069

Over 20 agents in L.A., also handles DGA, WGA, and AFM talent, mostly deals with established actors. Prefers headshot submissions. They will review pictures and resumes, and tapes by request or with referral. Karen Forman, Tyler Graham, Mike Wilson, Jeff Howard and Tim Scally are new additions to their long list of agents.

AIMEE ENTERTAINMENT ASSOC. **(818) 783-9115**
15840 Ventura Blvd., Ste. 215 **FAX (818) 783-8308**
Encino 91436

Joyce Aimee, Helen Barkan and Sharif Ali. Union talent only. Specializes in character actors. Will look at mailed submissions (3/4 bodyshots) and resumes, and VHS tapes. No drop-offs. Small agency.

AKA AGENCY **(323) 965-5600**
6310 San Vicente Blvd. **FAX (323) 965-5601**
Ste. 200
Los Angeles 90048
aka@akatalent.com

Doug Ely, Pamela Porter, Mike Abrams, Noreen Konkle and Robin Spitzer represent adult actors commercially. They accept pictures and resumes via mail and will call if interested.

ALVARADO/REY AGENCY **(323) 655-7978**
8455 Beverly Blvd., Ste. 410
Los Angeles 90048

Owner/agent: Nikkolas Rey. Youth Division: Andre Samewil. Commercials: Alex Lara. They specialize in Latinos, Europeans, and ethnic types and children. Will see non-union and young people who have had good training. DVDs and tapes only if requested. No preference on photos. Contemporary scenes. Small agency.

AMSEL, EISENSTADT & FRAZIER, INC. **(323) 939-1188**
5757 Wilshire Blvd., Ste. #510 **FAX (323) 939-0630**
Los Angeles 90036
michael@aeftalent.com

Theatrical: Mike Eisenstadt, John Frazier and Gloria Hinojosa. Youth Theatrical and Commercial: Carolyn Thompson Goldstein and Nicole Jolley. They prefer headshot submissions by mail and will call you after 2-3 weeks if they are interested. Medium sized agency.

ANGEL CITY TALENT (818) 760-9980
4741 Laurel Canyon Blvd., #101
Valley Village 91607

Mimi Mayer, Lincon Dabagia and Vicki Miller represent children, teens, young adults and adults for commercial and theatrical. Pictures and resumes accepted by mail, no unsolicited tapes. No drop offs or deliveries.

ARTISTS AGENCY (310) 277-7779
1180 S. Beverly Dr., Ste. 400 FAX (310) 785-9338
Los Angeles 90035

Jimmy Cota and Mike Livingston primarily handle established actors, WGA and DGA talent, but will see newcomers by referral only. Will review headshots and resumes but no DVDs, tapes or manuscripts.

ARTISTS GROUP, LTD. (310) 552-1100
2049 Century Park East FAX (310) 277-9513
Ste. 460
Los Angeles 90067

Handles only union celebrities, established actors and some newcomers. Prefers headshots. Medium sized agency with 6 agents. Has East Coast and European affiliates.

THE AUSTIN AGENCY (323) 957-4444
6715 Hollywood Blvd., Ste. 204
Hollywood 90028

Represents actors for TV/film and theater. Actors' submissions strictly by referral. Has a new commercial division.

BADGLEY, CONNOR,
SCHIOWITZ & ANKRUM (323) 463-7300
1680 N. Vine St., Ste 1016
Hollywood 90028

Erin Connor, Josh Schiowitz and David Ankrum represent actors for television and theatre. They accept pictures and resumes from union actors. Also literary.

BAIER/KLEINMAN INTERNATIONAL (323) 874-9800
3575 Cahuenga Blvd. West FAX (323) 874-4828
Ste. 500
Los Angeles 90068

Joel Kleinman handles newcomers as well as established adults and will view headshots or 3/4 bodyshots, which may be mailed or dropped off at the receptionist's desk. They will call if interested. DVDs and VHS tapes only by request. Has a separate division for international talent.

BALDWIN TALENT, INC. (310) 827-2422
8055 W. Manchester Ste. 550
Playa Del Rey 90293

A small agency representing commercial clients. Mainly handles sports figures, stuntpeople, circus and rodeo for commercials.

BOBBY BALL AGENCY (818) 506-8188
4342 Lankershim Blvd. FAX (818) 506-8188
Universal City 91602
www.bobbyballagency.com

Patti Grana-Miller reviews headshots and resumes, but no DVDs or tapes from adults and children. Commercial and theatrical representation.

BARON ENTERTAINMENT, INC. (323) 936-7600
5757 Wilshire Blvd., Ste. 659
Los Angeles 90036
www.baronentertainment.com
rod@baronentertainment.com

Rod Baron, Mike Sutton and Gar Lester represent infants through adults commercially and theatrically and will accept pictures and resumes. Please allow two weeks before calling to follow up. They will attend showcases and screenings.

MARC BASS TALENT AGENCY (310) 278-1900
415 N. Crescent Dr., Ste. 320 FAX (310) 281-0900
Beverly Hills 902120
mba-agency.com
mlbass@mba-agency.com

Marc Bass represents adult actors theatrically. By referral only.

BAUMAN REDANTY & SHAUL (323) 857-6666
5757 Wilshire Blvd., Ste. 473 FAX (323) 857-0368
Los Angeles 90036

David Shaul, Adam Lazarus and Colleen Schlegel handle mostly celebrities and established actors, but will see newcomers through recommendation. Actors must be SAG. Headshots and resumes, DVDs and VHS tapes by request only. Medium sized agency.

BICOASTAL TALENT, INC. (818) 845-0150
210 N. Pass Ave., Ste 204
Burbank 91505
www.bicoastaltalent.com

Handles children and adults for TV, film, and print. Will accept pictures and resumes via mail, no phone calls or drop offs. Has a literary division.

BONNIE BLACK TALENT AGENCY (818) 753-5424
12034 Riverside Dr., Ste. 103
Valley Village 91607
blabon@pacbel.net

Bonnie Black and Frank Black represent talent for commercials, MPTV and literary. Franchised members of SAG, AFTRA and WGA. They handle both adults and children. Mailed submissions only. DVDs and VHS tapes must have SASE.

THE BLAKE AGENCY (310) 899 9898
1327 Ocean Ave., Ste. J FAX (310) 899-3858
Santa Monica 90401

Merritt Blake only handles union adults and does not accept unsolicited submissions.

BOUTIQUE AGENCY (818) 753-2385
10 Universal City Plaza
Universal City 91608

Handles adults for commercial and theatrical work. Mailed submissions only, no drop-offs, or follow up calls.

BRADY, BRANNON & RICH (323) 852-9559
5760 Wilshire Blvd., Ste. 820
Los Angeles 90036

David Brady, Pat Brannon and Judy Rich handle adults for commercial and voice-over and prefer mailed headshot and resume submissions. They will accept audio tape and CD submissions by referral only. No drop-offs and no follow up phone calls. Medium sized agency.

SONJIA WARREN BRANDON'S COMMERCIALS UNLIMITED, S.W. **(310) 278-5123**
190 North Cannon Dr., Ste. 302
Beverly Hills 90210

Accepts pictures and resumes but no follow up calls. Works with union and non-union adults and children.

BRESLER KELLY & ASSOCIATES **(310) 479-5611**
11500 W. Olympic Blvd., Ste. 352
Los Angeles 90064

Sandy Bresler and John Kelly accept headshots and 3/4 bodyshots and will review DVDs and tapes only when there has been a very strong recommendation. Small agency.

BRICK ENTERTAINMENT **(818) 784-2000**
13321 Ventura Blvd. **FAX (818) 986-8730**
Sherman Oaks 91423
www.brickentertainment.com
barryrick@brickentertainment.com

Represents actors/actresses, athletes, broadcasters, children, comedians, ethnic/foreign types, hand/body part models, infants/babies, models (male and female), musicians, performers with disabilities, singers, spokespersons, teens/young adults for animated series/features, CD-ROMs, interactive, commercials, films, industrials, infomercials, music videos, print advertising, soaps, sound recordings, promotional announcements, TV, and voice-overs. Please no visits, interviews are by appointment only. DVDs, CDs, audio and video tapes are accepted by mail only. Open to attending showcases, plays and screenings.

DON BUCHWALD & ASSOCIATES **(323) 655-7400**
6500 Wilshire Blvd., Ste. 2200 **FAX (323) 655-7470**
Los Angeles 90048

Mailed submissions (headshots) and resumes are accepted, but tapes and DVDs by request only. Handles adults and has a Youth Department. Open to some SAG newcomers. Has a New York office.

BUCHWALD TALENT GROUP **(323) 852-9555**
6500 Wilshire Blvd., Ste. 2210
Los Angeles 90048

Accepts mailed submissions only. No follow up calls. Handles children and young adult voice-over talent. Specializes in infants through young adults in their early 20s. They have no photo preference for submissions and do not require a headshot for kids.

IRIS BURTON AGENCY **(310) 288-0121**
1450 Belfast Dr.
Los Angeles 90069

Iris Burton handles children from age 5 but no infants. Will review pictures and resumes.

C.L.I. INC. **(323) 461-3971**
843 N. Sycamore Ave. **FAX (323) 461-1134**
Los Angeles 90038

Owner/principal agent: Leanna Levy. On-camera: Richard Ohanesian. Represents established names and celebrities for TV and radio commercials, print and industrials. Mailed audio tapes and CDs are accepted for voice-over. Children and adults. Headshots or 3/4 bodyshots are OK. 2 agents. SAG franchise only.

CASTLE-HILL AGENCY **(323) 653-3535**
1101 S. Orlando Ave.
Los Angeles 90035

Leigh Castle handles SAG, AFTRA, AEA, AFM, variety artists, and print. Will review pictures and resumes (headshots or 3/4 bodyshots). Small agency.

CAVALERI & ASSOCIATES **(818) 955-9300**
178 S. Victory Blvd., Ste. 205 **FAX (818) 955-9399**
Burbank 91502

Ray Cavaleri, Cinthia Becks and Al Choi handle actors as well as literary and directors. They prefer established talent but will see some newcomers. Will see tapes or DVDs by their request only.

THE CHARLES TALENT AGENCY **(818) 761-2224**
11950 Ventura Blvd., Ste. 3 **FAX (818) 761-5761**
Studio City 91604

Bert Charles and James Kelly. Mailed submission only. No drop-offs. If interested they will call you. Tapes and DVDs by request only.

THE CHASIN AGENCY **(310) 278-7505**
8899 Beverly Blvd., Ste. 716 **FAX (310) 275-6685**
Los Angeles 90048
chasin@pacbell.net

Scott Penney, Tom Chasin and Kelly Duncan represent actors, directors, producers, screenwriters and writers. Not accepting any new clients at this time. Submissions by referral only.

CHATEAU BILLINGS TALENT AGENCY **(323) 965-5432**
8489 W. Third St.
Los Angeles 90048

Kay Billings, Guy Chateau, and Jessica Biscardi handle commercial and theatrical actors from age 4 through adult. They prefer 3/4 bodyshots and resumes to be mailed not dropped off. No follow up calls. Also a Print Department.

TORY CHRISTOPHER GROUP **(323) 436-0891**
7920 Selma Ave., #12 **FAX (323) 850-6985**
West Hollywood 90046
www.torychristopher.com
tory@torychristopher.com

Currently looking for ages 9-19. Will accept non-union children but adults should be union. Modeling and print. Tory Christopher and Brad DeVore specialize in developing talent, primarily from pre-teens to young adults. No new submissions are sought, except for the commercial department. Please do not send unsolicited photos, resumes, DVDs, tapes or scripts. Commercial department is known for extreme sports and edgy young actors. The motion picture and television roster is set with established clients.

CIRCLE TALENT AGENCY **(310) 285-1585**
433 N. Camden Dr., Ste. 400
Beverly Hills 90210

Theatrical and commercial: Jennifer Lee Garland. Specializes in character types and young adults age 7 and up. Prefers headshot submissions. DVDs and tapes by request only. Small agency.

W. RANDOLPH CLARK **(818) 385-0583**
13415 Ventura Blvd., #3
Sherman Oaks 91423

Randolph Clark and Arlene Tsurutani and handle children age 3-16 and some below-the-line people (production designers, DPs, etc.) The agency is receiving submissions for their senior division for professional men and women over 55 who are union members. They must be available for commercial and theatrical work. Headshots, 3/4 bodyshots, or snapshots are fine. No personal deliveries and no follow up calls.

CLEAR TALENT GROUP **(818) 509-0121**
10950 Ventura Blvd.
Studio City 91604
www.cleartalentgroup.com

President Tim O'Brien. A full service talent agency with offices in Los Angeles and New York, representing actors, dancers, choreographers and artistic directors for all aspects of the entertainment Industry. Submissions by mail only, no drop offs, no emails.

COLLEEN CLER TALENT AGENCY **(818) 841-7943**
178 S. Victory Blvd., Ste. 108 **FAX (818) 841-4541**
Burbank 91502
www.colleencler.com
colleen@colleencler.com

Craig Schulze, Colleen Schulze and Tamar Papirian handle newborns through young adults for commercial, theatrical and print. Will accept snapshots for submissions with SASE and they will let you know if they are interested.

COAST TO COAST
TALENT GROUP INC. **(323) 845-9200**
3350 Barham Blvd **FAX (323) 845-9212**
Los Angeles 90068

Theatrical/Children: Meredith Fine. Theatrical/Adult: Elyah Doryon and Dana Edrick. Commercial/Adult: Hugh Leon. Commercial/Children: Renata Dobrucki. Will handle newborns through adults. Mailed submissions only, they will call if interested.

CORALIE JR. AGENCY **(818) 766-9501**
4789 Vineland Ave., Ste. 100
North Hollywood 91602
coraliejr@earthlink.net

Stewart Edward. Literary, Theatrical and Commercial. Also a print, modeling, variety and literary agency. Specializes in character actors and handles age 5 to 105. Prefers headshots for submissions and they will call if interested. The literary department will accept query letters only. Medium sized agency.

CREATIVE ARTISTS AGENCY (CAA) **(310) 277-4545**
9830 Wilshire Blvd.
Beverly Hills 90212

A large agency that handles established actors and celebrities, directors and producers. They will see SAG newcomers by referral only. No preference for submission photos.

CULBERTSON GROUP **(323) 650-9454**
8430 Santa Monica Blvd., Ste. 210
West Hollywood 90049

Edward Culbertson, Eliane Ellison and Lorri Herman. Handles adults only. Accepts submissions by referral. Union only. No unsolicited tapes or DVDs and no follow up calls please.

CUNNINGHAM, ESCOTT,
SLEVIN, DOHERTY AGENCY **(310) 475-2111**
10635 Santa Monica Blvd. **FAX (310) 475-1929**
Ste. 130
Los Angeles 90025

257 Park Ave. South, #900 **(212) 477-1666**
New York City, NY 10010
www.cesdtalent.com

Also handles print and fashion models and theatrical for children. They prefer headshots for theatrical submissions and for commercial representation a 3/4 bodyshot and a theatrical resume. Voice-over submissions accepted by CD or via your website or an FTP site. Children's department: (310) 475-3336, Print/fashion department: (310) 475-7573. They represent actors, comedians, dancers, choreographers, models, new media, sports personalities, variety artists, voice over artists and children. Agents: Adrienne Berg, Linda Jenkins Dedra Galiher and David Ziff.

THE DANGERFIELD AGENCY **(818) 766-7717**
4063 Radford Ave., Ste. 201C
Studio City 91604

Handles adults for TV and film and accepts pictures and resumes via mail only. Please, no drop offs or phone calls.

DIVERSE TALENT GROUP **(310) 556-4343**
1875 Century Park East **FAX (310) 201-6572**
Ste. 2250
Los Angeles 90067

Premiere and CNA merged to become Diverse Talent. Christopher Nassif, Tom Harrison, Susan Sussman and others handle actors aged 5 through adult, producers, directors, composers and editors. They prefer headshot and resume submissions by mail. No unsolicited manuscripts.

DRAGON TALENT INC. **(323) 653-0366**
8444 Wilshire Blvd., Penthouse
Beverly Hills 90211
www.dragontalent.com

A full service agency handling commercial and theatrical for adults and children. Accepts pictures and resumes by email only. No drop offs and no follow up calls please.

E.S.I. KIDS **(323) 653-0366**
6310 San Vicente Blvd., #340
Los Angeles 90048

Specializes in development and placement of babies thru teens in the realm of commercials, print, film and TV. Accepts unsolicited pictures and resumes.

ELLIS TALENT GROUP **(818) 980-8072**
4705 Laurel Canyon Blvd., Ste. 300
Valley Village 91423

Pamela Ellis-Evenas, Gabrielle Allabashi, Andy Coleman and Jeremy Jones handle adults and emancipated teens for commercial, theatrical, and legitimate theatre. Also comedians. By referral only. Non union seen for commercial only.

ENDEAVOR AGENCY **(310) 248-2000**
9601 Wilshire Blvd., 3rd Fl. **FAX (310) 248-2020**
Beverly Hills 90210

Represents established actors, directors, producers and writers. By referral only.

EQUINOX MODELS AND TALENT (323) 951-7100
8455 Beverly Blvd., Ste. 304
Los Angeles 90038

Represents adults and teenagers for commercial and print. No height requirements for models and no open calls. Accepts pictures and resumes but no tapes and DVDs.

JAIME FERRAR ASSOCIATES (JFA) (818) 506-8311
4741 Laurel Canyon Blvd., Ste. 110
Valley Village 91607

Represents children from age 5 and up and adults for TV, film, and commercials. Mailed headshot and resume. No follow up calls.

FERRAR MEDIA ASSOCIATES (323) 654-2601
8430 Santa Monica Blvd., Ste. 220
Los Angeles 90069
fma2@earthlink.net

Tony Ferrar handles actors and comedians and accepts mailed submissions (3/4 bodyshots and resume) but no tapes or DVDs, no drop-offs and no follow up calls. They will call you if interested. Most clients come through referral.

FILM ARTISTS ASSOCIATES (818) 386-9669
4717 Van Nuys Blvd., Ste. 215
Sherman Oaks 91403

Pen, Martha and Cris Dennis handle adults 18 and up for commercials. Headshots or 3/4 bodyshots accepted by mail only. VHS tapes and DVDs by request only.

THE FIRM (310) 860-8000
9465 Wilshire Blvd., 4th Fl.
Beverly Hills 90212
rfrank@firmentertainment.net

A literary, talent and animation agency that will accept newcomers by referral only. SAG and AFTRA franchised.

FLICK EAST-WEST TALENTS, INC. (310) 271-9111
9057 Nemo St., Ste. A
West Hollywood 90069

Tina Kiratsoulis handles mostly established leading actors, but will handle some young adults starting at age 18. They have no photo preference on submissions.

BARRY FREED COMPANY (310) 860-5627
468 N. Camden Dr., #201
Beverly Hills 90212

Barry Freed handles adults and some children with good credits for TV, and film. Will accept pictures and resumes via mail only. No drop offs, phone calls or faxes. No manuscripts accepted but query letters are fine.

ALICE FRIES (323) 464-1404
1927 Vista Del Mar Ave.
Los Angeles 90068

Handles adults for commercial and theatrical. By referral only.

THE GAGE GROUP (818) 905-3800
14724 Ventura Blvd., Ste. 505
Sherman Oaks 91403

Martin Gage, Gerry Koch, Jonathan Westover, Mark Fadness, Sharon Moist, and Kitty McMillan handle actors and some directors. They see newcomers by referral only. Submissions can be mailed (headshot or 3/4 bodyshot). Will represent young adults age 18 and up but no children. A boutique agency.

DALE GARRICK INTL. TALENT (310) 657-2661
1017 N. La Cienega Blvd., Ste. 109
West Hollywood 90069

Dale Garrick, Cynthia Lynn, Alexander Dale and Tony Tenecelli handle actors and children from age 6 and up. Mailed submissions only, they prefer headshots. No tapes. No literary submissions. No form letters.

THE GEDDES AGENCY (323) 848-2700
8430 Santa Monica Blvd., Ste. 200
West Hollywood 90069
www.geddes.net
ag@geddes.net

Ann Geddes and Richard Lewis represent actors of all levels age 18 and above. They will see newcomers only by referral. Mailed submissions only (Headshots or 3/4 bodyshots.) No drop-offs and no follow up calls. Chicago affiliate.

LAYA GELFF AGENCY (818) 996-3100
16133 Ventura Blvd., Ste. 700
Encino 91436

Literary and Talent agency. SAG, AEA, AFTRA, DGA, WGA. Note to actors: Very small select list. No children or models. Note to writers: Query letter only with self addressed stamped envelope. Do not phone or visit without appointment.

DON GERLER AGENCY (323) 850-7386
3349 Cahuenga Blvd. West, Ste. 1
Los Angeles 90068

Don Gerler and Doug Bennet handle newcomers and established actors age 16 and up for television and film. Don handles the more established actors and Doug is very open to developing new talent and will accept mailed submissions (headshots or 3/4 bodyshots). SAG preferred.

THE GERSH AGENCY (310) 274-6611
232 N. Canon Dr.
Beverly Hills 90210

Handles guest stars, established actors, celebrities, and top stars. They see newcomers only by referral. They will accept DVDs, tapes, headshots or 3/4 bodyshots only by referral. Large agency. East Coast affiliate.

MICHELLE GORDON & ASSOCIATES (310) 246-9930
260 S. Beverly Dr., Ste. 308
Beverly Hills 90212

Michelle Gordon handles actors who are at least 18 years of age and all ethnicities including Caucasians. She likes actors who have strong stage credits and have done a series lead or a lead in a major feature film. Submissions only through Industry referral (headshot or 3/4 bodyshot, resume, and a cover letter). No tapes, DVDs, and no unsolicited manuscripts but a query letter is fine. No drop-offs. She will call you within two weeks if interested.

GRANT, SAVIC,
KOPALOFF & ASSOCIATES (323) 782-1854
6399 Wilshire Blvd., Ste. 414
Los Angeles 90048

Larry Metzger handles actors but accepts mailed submissions by referral only. Open to attending showcases, plays and screenings.

GREENE & ASSOCIATES **(323) 960-1333**
7080 Hollywood Blvd., Ste. 1017 FAX (323) 960-8560
Hollywood 90028
www.greenetalent.com
michaelgreene@greenetalent.com

Michael Greene, Azeem Chiba, and Matt Cronrod handle mostly established, well trained character types for film and television. Jaclyn Raymundo and Jim Lighte handle commercial talent and are looking for young people age 18 and up especially minorities. Submissions by Industry referral only. Michael worked with and represented Sanford Meisner and is very interested in Meisner trained actors.

GVA TALENT, INC. **(310) 278-1310**
9229 Sunset Blvd., Ste. 320 FAX (310) 888-1290
Los Angeles 90069
gvaassistant@aol.com

Tony Martinez, Geneva Bray, Brett Carducco and others represent actors theatrically. Mailed submissions only.

BUZZ HALLIDAY & ASSOCIATES **(310) 275-6028**
8899 Beverly Blvd., Ste. 715
Los Angeles 90048
buzzagent@earthlink.net

Buzz Halliday and Gail Honeystein handle teens through adults. Mailed submissions (headshot or 3/4 bodyshot) only. No tapes or DVDs. No drop-offs and no follow up calls. Carries a very small select list of clients. Rarely takes on non-union actors. Also AEA franchised.

BEVERLY HECHT AGENCY **(818) 505-1192**
12001 Ventura Pl., Ste. 320 FAX (818) 505-1590
Studio City 91604
www.beverlyhecht.com

Teresa Valente handles featured and above and will see newcomers by referral. Mailed submissions can be headshot or 3/4 bodyshot. No drop-offs, no follow up calls. They also handle children from age 6 and up and have been in business for 28 years.

HERVEY/GRIMES TALENT AGENCY **(818) 340-8402**
10561 Missouri #2
Los Angeles 90025

Pam Grimes and Marsha Hervey handle children from age 3 through adults. Some newcomers. Prefers mailed submissions. No phone calls or drop-offs. No unsolicited tapes or DVDs.

HILLTOP TALENT AGENCY **(310) 727-2642**
Raleigh Manhattan Beach Studios
1600 Rosecrans Bldg. 1B, Ste. 208
Manhattan Beach 90266
www.hilltoptalent.com

Hilltop handles children, young adults and adults theatrically and commercially. Mailed submissions are fine but they prefer union actors.

DANIEL HOFF TALENT AGENCY **(323) 932-2500**
5455 Wilshire Blvd., Ste. 1100
Los Angeles 90036
www.danielhoffagency.com

Commercial: Daniel Hoff. Theatrical: Nancy Abt. Children: Debra Manners. Mailed submissions only. No drop-offs or follow up calls. DVDs, VHS, CDs and audio tapes are accepted but will not be returned. Also a voice-over division.

HOLLANDER TALENT GROUP, INC. **(818) 382-9800**
14011 Ventura Blvd., Ste., 202
Sherman Oaks 91423

Vivian Hollander and Stefane Wetherholt handle infants through young adults for commercial and theatrical with some print. Mailed picture and resume, no drop-offs, no follow up calls, and no DVDs or VHS tapes accepted.

THE HOUSE OF REPRESENTATIVES TALENT AGENCY **(310) 772-0772**
400 South Beverly Dr., Ste. 101
Beverly Hills 90212

Ginger Lawrence, Pam Braverman and Denny Sevier handle age 5 through adults. Union only. They prefer mailed submissions but drop-offs are fine. If they are interested they will call you within two weeks and they will look at DVDs and tapes only when requested. Any unrequested DVDs or tapes will be returned unopened.

HOWARD TALENT WEST **(818) 766-5300**
10657 Riverside Dr.
Toluca Lake 91602

President/Agent: Bonnie Howard. Commercials: Lynn Eriks. They handle established performers. Children from infants on up. Will review mailed submissions only. No personal deliveries and no follow up calls. Also AEA and DGA franchised.

HWA TALENT REPRESENTATIVES **(818) 972-4310**
3500 W. Olive, Ste. 1400
Burbank 91505

Patty Woo handles adults and will accept mailed headshots and resumes, but no drop-offs or follow up calls. The literary department will accept a query letter with a synopsis but no manuscripts. They will call if they are interested.

IDENTITY TALENT AGENCY **(323) 469-1100**
7080 Hollywood Blvd.
Los Angeles 90029
idtalent@aol.com

Erik DeSando, Rob D'Avola, Fran Tolstonog and Peggy Rudman handle adults and children for commercial and theatrical representation. Pictures and resumes are accepted by mail only. No drop-offs, faxes or follow up calls. Union only.

IFA TALENT AGENCY **(310) 659-5522**
8730 Sunset Blvd., Ste. 490
Los Angeles 90069

Eileen Feldman, David Lillard, Wendy Murphy, Tony Zimmerman and Christy Hall handle established union actors. Young adults through adult. No submissions. They are not taking any new clients at this time.

INNOVATIVE ARTISTS & LITERARY AGENCY **(310) 656-0400**
1505 10th St. FAX (310) 656-0456
Santa Monica 90401

Scott Harris, David Rose, Nevin Dolcefino, Adena Chawke and Craig Shapiro handle actors age 8 and up. Submissions accepted only by request and/or recommendation. Medium sized agency.

INTERNATIONAL CREATIVE MANAGEMENT (ICM) **(310) 550-4000**
8942 Wilshire Blvd. **FAX (310) 550-4100**
Beverly Hills 90211

Handles only established actors. Also handles directors. They want no submissions. A very large agency.

JKA TALENT AGENCY **(818) 980-2093**
8033 Sunset Blvd., Ste. 115
Los Angeles 90046

Represents actors, writers, and producers. By referral only.

JS REPRESENTS TALENT AGENCY **(323) 462-3246**
6815 Willoughby Ave., Ste. 102 **FAX (323) 654-2510**
Los Angeles 90038

Handles age 8 through adult commercially. Mailed submissions only. No drop-offs or phone calls.

KAZARIAN/SPENCER & ASSOCIATES **(818) 769-9111**
11969 Ventura Blvd., 3rd Fl.,
Box 7409
Studio City 91604
www.ksawest.com

Also handles dancers, choreographers, and print work. Clients are infants through adults. Mailed submissions only. No drop-offs or follow up calls. They will call if interested. Open calls for print representation on Wednesdays from 3-5 pm. Youth Department: Jody Alexander and Bonnie Ventis. Performers with Disabilities: Riley Day. Print: Jenny Vavra. Theatrical: Mara Santino.

SHARON KEMP TALENT AGENCY **(310) 858-7200**
447 S. Robertson Blvd., Ste. 204
Beverly Hills 90211

Sharon Kemp handles adults and children from age 6 up, twins and triplets from any age. Headshots and resumes are accepted via mail only and will not be opened if they are sealed. Commercials and print.

WILLIAM KERWIN AGENCY **(323) 469-5155**
1605 N. Cahuenga Blvd., Ste. 202
Los Angeles 90028

Bill Kerwin will see newcomers and is looking for actors with strong stage training. Will accept headshots or 3/4 bodyshot submissions. They will view DVDs and VHS tapes with self addressed return envelopes. Small agency with 35-40 clients.

ERIC KLASS **(310) 274-9169**
139 S. Beverly Dr., Ste. 331
Beverly Hills 90212

Eric Klass does not actively seek new clients. Please do not call or visit.

PAUL KOHNER INC. **(310) 550-1060**
9300 Wilshire Blvd., Ste. 555
Beverly Hills 90212

Pearl Wexler, Stephen Moore, Samantha Crisp, Brian Dreyfuss, Amanda Glazer and Sheree Cohen do not accept unsolicited literary material and submissions by actors are by request only. Newcomers by recommendation and request only. Theatrical and literary.

VICTOR KRUGLOV & ASSOC. **(323) 934-7007**
7461 Beverly Blvd., Ste. 303 **FAX (323) 934-7030**
Los Angeles 90036
www.victorkruglov.com

Handles actors 18 and older. Mailed submissions only and no follow up calls. Will review tapes or DVDs by request only. They attend several performances per week.

L W 1 INC. **(323) 653-5700**
7257 Beverly Blvd., 2nd Floor
Los Angeles 90046

Sean Robinson represents adults 18-90 of all types. Mailed submissions only, headshots or 3/4 bodyshots. No open calls, drop-offs, or follow up calls. SAG franchised. Commercials.

L.A. TALENT **(323) 436-7777**
7700 Sunset Blvd. **FAX (323) 436-7788**
Los Angeles 90046
www.latalent.com

Mostly handles union actors and some non-union. Submissions by mail only. No follow up calls please.

LANE AGENCY INTERNATIONAL MODELS AND TALENT **(310) 275-1455**
9903 Santa Monica Blvd., #756
Beverly Hills 90212
www.laneagency.com
info@lane-agency.com

Handles talent, models, spokespersons, athletes, hosts and hostesses for conventions, trade shows, print, infomercials, videos, industrials, voice over, theatre, TV and film. Uses union and non-union talent of all ages and accepts P&R.

THE LEVIN AGENCY **(323) 653-7073**
8484 Wilshire Blvd., Ste. 750
Beverly Hills 90211

Sid Levin specializes in character types, ethnics, and children starting at age 7. Mailed submissions only, they prefer 3/4 bodyshots. No drop-offs and no follow up calls. Carries 60 people.

JACK LIPPMAN AGENCY (JLA) **(310) 276-5677**
9151 Sunset Blvd.,
West Hollywood 90069

Jack Lippman handles established actors for TV and film. No submissions. No DVDs or tapes. No follow up calls.

LJ AND ASSOCIATES **(818) 345-9274**
5903 Noble Ave.
Van Nuys 91411

Represents adults for commercial and theatrical. By referral only.

JANA LUKER'S AGENCY **(310) 441-2822**
1923 1/2 Westwood Blvd., Ste. 3
Los Angeles 90025

Jana Luker, Gigi Schell and Kathy Keeley. The children's division handles 4 and up. They prefer mailed submissions, no drop-offs and no follow up calls.

LYNNE & REILLY **(818) 755-6434**
10725 Vanowen St., Ste. 113 **FAX (818) 755-6444**
North Hollywood 91605
lynneandreilly@aol.com

Julie Lynne and Teresa Reilly handle guest level talent of all ages including children and young adults. They accept submissions only by referral.

MADEMOISELLE TALENT AGENCY (310) 441-9994
10835 Santa Monica Blvd. FAX (310) 441-9988
Ste. 204A
Los Angeles 90024

Won Lee and Alan Siegel handle teens and adults. Mailed headshots and resumes, DVDs or VHS tapes. No drop-offs and no follow up calls. SAG franchise only.

MALAKY INTERNATIONAL (310) 234-9114
10642 Santa Monica Blvd., Ste. 103
Los Angeles 90025

They handle adults and children aged 6 and up. They will accept mailed headshot and resume. DVDs and VHS tapes accepted with SASE. No drop offs. They will call back if they are interested. Looking for all ethnicities for commercials, print, TV and film.

MAXINE'S TALENT AGENCY (818) 986-2946
4830 Encino Ave.
Encino 91316

A full service agency that handles adults only. They want submissions only by request. "No children please."

MCCABE JUSTICE (323) 650-3738
8285 Sunset Blvd., Ste. 1
Los Angeles 90046
www.atalentagency.com

Todd Justice and Brian McCabe handle very established actors and newcomers by referral. Medium sized agency, 200 clients.

MCCARTY TALENT (818) 556-5410
www.mccartytalent.com FAX (800) 494-7587
agent@mccartytalent.com

Represents primarily established adult actors and select newcomers. Small agency with a focus on film, TV and commercials. Mailed headshots and resumes only. SAG Franchise. They were moving at the time of publication. Check their website for their new address.

MEDIA ARTISTS GROUP (323) 658-5050
6300 Wilshire Blvd., Ste. 1470
Los Angeles 90048

Raphael Berko handles children 4 and up. They look at newcomers only with a very strong recommendation. SAG franchised only.

METROPOLITAN TALENT AGENCY (323) 857-4500
4526 Wilshire Blvd. FAX (323) 857-4599
Los Angeles 90010

Christopher Barrett handles actors, directors, writers, and producers. Adults only. They will occasionally see SAG newcomers by referral. All submissions are by referral only. Medium sized agency.

MGA TALENT (818) 763-8400
4804 Laurel Canyon Blvd., Ste. 592
Valley Village 91607
www.mgatalent.com

Represents adults and children for theatrical, commercial and print. Unsolicited pictures and resumes accepted but email and DVDs by request only. Open to attending showcases and screenings.

MIRAMAR TALENT (323) 934-0700
7400 Beverly Blvd., Ste. 220
Los Angeles 90036

Handles children age 5-16 and established young adults and adults age 18-35. Handles actors and models. They have added a print department. They will review headshots or 3/4 bodyshots and resumes. No drop-ins or phone calls. No open calls. SAG franchised only.

MKS AND ASSOCIATES (310) 838-1200
8695 W. Washington Blvd. FAX (310) 838-1245
Ste. 203
Culver City 90232
www.mksagency.com
mks@mksagency.com

Represents actors theatrically by Industry referral only. Mitchell K. Stubbs, Ray Moheel and Carrie Johnson.

MORGAN AGENCY (323) 469-7100
(800) 656-1120
7080 Hollywood Blvd. FAX (323) 469-7122
Ste. 1009
Hollywood 90028
www.themorganagency.com

President: Keith Lewis. The agency handles stars, experienced actors and exceptionally qualified children. Mailed pictures and resumes are accepted but DVDs and tapes only by referral and no drop-offs, faxes or follow up calls. Print, commercial, theatrical, children, promotions, literary and voice-over.

WILLIAM MORRIS AGENCY (310) 274-7451
151 El Camino Dr.
Beverly Hills 90212
www.wma.com

A very large agency with world wide associates. They do not accept submissions and discourage newcomers.

H. DAVID MOSS & ASSOCIATES (323) 465-1234
733 N. Seward St., Penthouse FAX (323) 465-1241
Hollywood 90038

H. David Moss handles adults and young adults. All levels and all types. Also handles a select few writers, spokespersons, and directors. Has no photo preference. DVDs and tapes by request only.

SUSAN NATHE & ASSOC., (323) 653-7573
8281 Melrose Ave., Ste. 200
Los Angeles 90046
susannathe@pacbell.net

Susan Nathe and Liz Quintero handle young adults 18 and above, adults, and character types. Will see newcomers. Also does print and commercial.

NU TALENT AGENCY (310) 385-6907
117 N. Robertson Blvd., Ste. A
Los Angeles 90048

Represents adults commercially and theatrically and accepts headshots and resumes via mail only, no drop offs or follow up calls.

ORANGE GROVE GROUP, INC. (818) 762-7498
12178 Ventura Blvd., Ste. 205 FAX (818) 762-7499
Studio City 91604
www.orangegrovegroup.com
agent@orangegrovegroup.com

Gregory D. Mayo handles young adults and adults. Prefers submissions be on DVD or VHS tape and by referral only. Both headshots and 3/4 bodyshots are accepted.

ORIGIN TALENT AGENCY (818) 487-1800
4705 Laurel Canyon Blvd., Ste. 306
Studio City 901607

Mark Chancer, Annie Schwartz, Robin Spitzer and Janet Shaw represent children and adults for commercial and theatrical. Mailed picture and resume is fine, but no drop offs, no follow calls and no faxes.

CINDY OSBRINK TALENT AGENCY (818) 760-2488
4343 Lankershim Blvd., Ste. 100
North Hollywood 91602

Handles infants from 14 days old through young adults. Also a modeling agency. Has a new voice-over department. Mailed submissions (headshot or 3/4 bodyshots) only, no drop-offs and no follow up calls. They will view DVDs and VHS tapes only by recommendation. They do handle non-union newcomers for commercials.

DOROTHY DAY OTIS AGENCY (323) 782-0070
8322 Beverly Blvd., Ste. 301 FAX (323) 782-0111
Los Angeles 90048
www.ddoagency.com

Theatrical, commercial, dance and print agency that handles established actors and newcomers. They require previous training but accept pictures and resumes with no follow up calls.

PAKULA/KING & ASSOCIATES (310) 281-4868
9229 Sunset Blvd., Ste. 315
Los Angeles 90069

Joel King, Hillary Steinberg and Lee Haspel accept mostly referrals and only mailed submissions. DVDs and tapes by request only.

PARADIGM TALENT &
LITERARY AGENCY (310) 288-8000
360 N. Crescent Dr. FAX (310) 288-2000
North Building
Beverly Hills 90210

Handles mostly established actors but will handle well-trained or established young adults by referral only. No phone calls please.

PARTOS COMPANY (310) 458-7800
227 Broadway St., Ste. 204
Santa Monica 90401
www.partos.com

Walter Partos handles young adults and adults, but is not looking for any new people. Mainly they handle directors and below-the-line. No drop-offs and no follow up calls.

PLAYERS TALENT AGENCY (818) 528-7444
7700 Sunset Blvd. FAX (818) 528-7457
Los Angeles 90046

Joe Kolkowitz accepts mailed submissions only and handles adults and young adults. No drop-offs or follow up calls. SAG franchise only. Union only except for athletes.

PRIVILEGE TALENT AGENCY (818) 386-2377
14542 Ventura Blvd., Ste. 209 FAX (818) 386-9477
Sherman Oaks 91423

Danielle Milkes, Carol Oleesky and Melanie Raymundo handle infants to adults. Headshots or 3/4 bodyshots are OK for submissions. They require a solid theatrical background for actors. Mailed submissions only, no phone calls, no drop-offs. Also a modeling agency. SAG franchised only.

PROGRESSIVE ARTISTS (310) 553-8561
400 S. Beverly Dr., Ste. 216
Beverly Hills 90212

Bernard Carneol and Belle Zwerdling handle mostly established talent but do handle a few newcomers. Submissions can be headshots or 3/4 bodyshots and resumes. Adults and young adults from age 18 and up. DVDs and tapes only by request. No phone calls.

REBEL ENTERTAINMENT PARTNERS (323) 935-1700
5700 Wilshire Blvd., Ste. 456 FAX (323) 932-9901
Los Angeles 90038
www.reptalent.com

President: Richard Lawrence. Hosting: Susan Haber. Reality show hosting. Established union actors mostly, full range of types, they do call actors in from submissions on occasion. They prefer 3/4 bodyshots. Must have hosting experience.

CINDY ROMANO
MODELING & TALENT AGENCY (760) 323-3333
P.O. Box 1951 FAX (760) 327-6666
Palm Springs 92263
www.crtalent.com

Cindy, Charis and Rick Romano handle established talent only. Mailed submissions: resume and headshot, no follow up calls or drop offs. They attend showcases, plays, and screenings on occasion.

MARION ROSENBERG OFFICE (323) 822-2793
P.O. Box 69826
Los Angeles 90069
www.marionrosenberg.com

Primarily handles established actors. Submissions are by referral only.

SAMANTHA GROUP TALENT AGENCY (626) 683-2444
300 S. Raymond Ave., Ste. 11 FAX (626) 683-2451
Pasadena 91105

Adults only. Commercial and theatrical. Looking for all ethnicities, 18 and over to play younger. "Beauties that can talk." Union only. Will accept mailed pictures and resumes, but no tapes or DVDs.

THE SAVAGE AGENCY (323) 461-8316
6212 Banner Ave.
Los Angeles 90038

Judith Savage, Jennifer Mahland, Stella Alext and Barbara Divisek handle children age 3-18, young adults age 18-25 who look younger and are union members with credits. Mailed submissions are OK, but no follow up calls, they will call you if interested. Please do not seal envelopes. Commercial and theatrical. Senior citizens are considered commercially.

JACK SCAGNETTI TALENT AGENCY (818) 762-3871
5118 Vineland Ave., Ste. 102
North Hollywood 91601

Jack Scagnetti handles actors and models. Headshots or 3/4 bodyshots are fine. When making mailed submissons, please do not seal the envelope. No drop offs or follow up calls. Over 20 years in business.

SANDIE SCHNARR TALENT (310) 360-7680
8500 Melrose Ave., Ste. 212
West Hollywood 90069

Sandie Schnarr and Melissa Grillo. A voice-over agency. Will see newcomers if they have a referral. Accepts mailed voice-over CDs. No drop-offs. They will call if they are interested.

JUDY SCHOEN & ASSOCIATES (323) 962-1950
606 N. Larchmont Blvd., #309 FAX (323) 461-8365
Los Angeles 90004
jsatalent@aol.com

Jinny Raymond, Joy Keller Cynthia Land and Jon Williams specialize in young adults. They accept headshots and resumes for submissions. New people are seen by recommendation only. No DVDs or tapes.

KATHLEEN SCHULTZ (818) 760-3100
6442 Coldwater Cyn, Ste. 206 FAX (661) 253-3493
Valley Glen 91606

Kathleen Schultz handles a small number of teens and adults. All levels and all types. All their actors have theatrical backgrounds. They prefer headshot submissions and will accept DVDs and tapes only by request. Over 35 years in business.

SCREEN CHILDREN'S AGENCY (818) 846-4300
4000 Riverside Dr., #A
Burbank 91505

Irene Gallagher only handles children and young people from 15 days up to 18 years. Will accept pictures and resumes (non-returnable snapshots are fine.) In business for 67 years.

SDB PARTNERS, INC. (310) 785-0060
1801 Avenue of the Stars FAX (310) 785-0071
Ste. 902
Los Angeles 90067
www.sdbpartners.com

Susie Schwarz, Ro Diamond, Louis Bershad, and Steven Jang handle children through adults, established actors. Submissions by their request only and with a strong Industry recommendation.

DAVID SHAPIRA & ASSOC. (310) 967-0480
193 N. Robertson Dr.
Beverly Hills 90211
www.dsa-agency.com
ds@dsa-agency.com

David Shapira sees actors by referral only. Headshots and resumes for submissions. Adults only. No drop-offs and no follow ups.

SHREVE TALENT SOURCE (760) 327-5092
(760) 327-5855
1701 N. Palm Cyn Dr., Ste 6
Palm Springs 92262

Also a modeling agency. Handles non-union people of all levels. Headshots or 3/4 bodyshots are fine for submissions.

JEROME SIEGEL ASSOCIATES, INC. (323) 466-0185
1680 N. Vine St., Ste. 613
Los Angeles 90028

President Jerome Siegel will review mailed photos and resumes, no follow up calls.

SILVER, MASSETTI & SZATMARY (310) 289-0909
8730 W. Sunset Blvd., Ste. 440
West Hollywood 90069
www.smsla.com
donna@smsla.com

Donna Silver, Marilyn Massetti, Charles Szatmary, and Greg Mehlman represent adults theatrically. By Industry referral only.

MICHAEL SLESSINGER & ASSOC. (310) 657-7113
8730 Sunset Blvd., Ste. 270
West Hollywood 90069

Michael Slessinger and Billy Miller accept submissions by referral only.

SUSAN SMITH AND COMPANY (323) 852-4777
121 A North San Vicente Blvd. FAX (323) 852-9605
Beverly Hills 90211
susansmithco@email.com

Represents established actors theatrically. By referral only. No unsolicited submissions.

SMS TALENT, INC. (310) 289-0909
8730 Sunset Blvd., Ste. 440
Los Angeles 90069

Handles adults theatrically, all levels and all types. Prefers headshot and resume submissions by referral only. No drop-offs and no follow ups.

SOLID TALENT (323) 978-0808
6860 Lexington Ave. FAX (323) 978-0810
Hollywood 90038
www.solidtalent.com
mikesoliday@solidtalent.com

Mike Soliday represents voice over talent by referral only.

CAMILLE SORICE AGENCY (818) 995-1775
13412 Moorpark St., #C
Sherman Oaks 91423

Mainly handles adult actors and will accept submissions from performers only when there is a recommendation but will accept a query letter with a synopsis from writers.

SPECIAL ARTISTS AGENCY (310) 859-9688
9465 Wilshire Blvd., Ste. 890
Beverly Hills 90212

Liz Dalling handles established adults only. Voice-over and celebrities. They very seldom take on any new people. Prefers headshot submissions. DVDs, VHS tapes, CDs and audio tapes are accepted by request only.

STARWIL PRODUCTION TALENT AGENCY (323) 874-1239
433 N. Camden Drive, 4th Fl.
Beverly Hills 90210
starwil@earthlink.com

Starwil Reed, Gwen Reed, Lon Miles, Gregory Porter and Tony Jackson handle all levels of actors, composers, musicians, variety acts, singers, and children starting at age 4. They will see union and non-union newcomers and young adults and review pictures and resumes and tapes by request. They require DVDs or video tapes from music acts. SAG franchised only.

STEVENS GROUP (818) 528-3674
14011 Ventura Blvd., Ste. 201
Sherman Oaks 91423

Steven R. Stevens Sr. and Jr. are looking for talented people of all sizes, all ages. They accept mailed pictures and resumes. DVDs and tapes will not be returned.

STONE/MANNERS (323) 655-1313
6500 Wilshire Blvd., Ste. 550
Los Angeles 90048

Scott Manners, Glenn Salners, Mark Perara, Bobby Moses and Holly Shelton handle established talent and celebrities specializing in theatre actors. Submissions should be mailed and include a headshot and resume plus references from actors. Literary submissions are by referral only to Mike Sweeney. No follow up calls. They have affiliates in London and New York.

PETER STRAIN AND ASSOCIATES (323) 525-3391
5455 Wilshire Blvd., Ste. 1812
Los Angeles 90036
www.peterstrainla.com
pstrain@peterstrainla.com

Represents established union adults only. Submissions by referral only.

SUITE A MANAGEMENT
TALENT AND LITERARY AGENCY (310) 278-0801
120 El Camino Dr. FAX (310) 278-0807
Beverly Hills 90212
suitea@juno.com

Serving actors, producers, directors and writers. Primary emphasis is on movies of the week and low to mid budget features. All submissions: Lloyd Robinson.

SUPERIOR TALENT AGENCY (818) 508-5627
11712 Moorpark St., Ste. 209
Studio City 91604

Handles adults and children for theatrical, commercial and print. Accepts unsolicited pictures and resumes but DVDs by request only.

SUTTON, BARTH & VENNARI INC. (323) 938-6000
145 S. Fairfax Ave., Ste. 310 FAX (323) 935-8671
Los Angeles 90036
www.sbvtalentagency.com

Rita Vennari, Anna Rodriguez, Mary Ellen Lord, Cynthia McLean, Mike O'Dell and Pam Sparks handle established talent and some SAG newcomers. Adults only. Mailed submissions can be headshots or 3/4 bodyshots and resumes. They will call if they are interested. Voice-over CDs are accepted only by referral. No DVDs or VHS tapes.

TALENTWORKS (818) 972-4300
3500 W. Olive Ave., Ste. 1400 FAX (818) 955-6411
Burbank 91505

Adult/Theatrical: Harry Gold, Suzanne Wohl, Patty Woo (at HWA), Joe Dean and Marian Campbell. Youth/Theatrical: Bonnie Leidtke, Thor Bradwell and Brandy Gold. Handles established union talent. They prefer headshot submissions, DVDs and tapes by request only. No unsolicited manuscripts or screenplays. They only see newcomers (children and young adults) for commercial representation. NY Affiliate.

HERB TANNEN & ASSOC. (310) 446-5802
10801 National Blvd., Ste. 101
Los Angeles 90064

Herb Tannen handles voice-over only. CDs accepted only by request.

THE THOMAS TALENT AGENCY (310) 665-0000
6709 La Tijera Blvd., #915 FAX (310) 665-0070
Los Angeles 90045
agent007tta@aol.com

Venus Thomas represents a carefully selected clientele of actors for film, TV and commercials. Currently accepting submissions from adults of all ages and types. Seeking actors looking for commercial representation. She maintains a close working relationship to actors with focus on career building. Interviews are by appointment only, no personal deliveries. SAG only. Mail photo and resume, she will call if interested. DVDs and VHS tapes by request only. Small agency. Carries 35-40 actors.

ARLENE THORNTON & ASSOC. (818) 760-6688
12711 Ventura Blvd., Ste. 490 FAX (818) 760-1165
Studio City 91604
www.arlenethornton.com
arlene@arlenethornton.com

The agency specializes in voice-over work but also has a strong camera department. Will consider SAG newcomers. Handles adults and young adults. Prefers headshots and resumes, will also listen to CDs.

THE TISHERMAN AGENCY (323) 850-6767
6767 Forest Lawn Dr., Ste. 101
Los Angeles 90068
www.tishermanagency.com
tishermanvoices@yahoo.com

Steve Tisherman, Malcolm Cassell, and Vanessa Gilbert. Full service commercial and voice-over agency. Prefers union talent but will consider non-union people. Accepts headshot and resume submissions and CDs or audio tapes for voice-over. Mailed submissions only.

UNITED TALENT AGENCY (310) 273-6700
9560 Wilshire Blvd., Ste. 500 FAX (310) 247-1111
Beverly Hills 90212

Handles writers, producers, actors, directors, below-the-line people (CPs and editors). Please do not send unsolicited material. They see new people by referral only.

VISION MODELS (310) 275-0067
9250 Wilshire Blvd., Ste. 200 FAX (310) 205-3431
Beverly Hills 90212
www.champagnetrott.com

A commercial and print agency that is open to newcomers. Will accept pictures and resumes by mail but no drop offs and no follow up calls. Does attend showcases and screenings. Union only. No tapes or DVDs. Francine Champagne.

WALLIS AGENCY (818) 953-4848
4444 Riverside Dr., Ste. 105
Burbank 91505
www.wallisagency.com
kristenewallis@wallisagency.com

Kristene Wallis represents actors for commercial, theatrical and voice over by referral only. Seeking native speakers of foreign languages, submissions should have Attn: Foreign Language Division on the outside of the envelope. No drop-offs.

BOB WATERS AGENCY (323) 965-5555
4311 Wilshire Blvd., Ste. 622
Los Angeles 90010

Handles union adult actors for television and film. Mailed headshot submissions are fine but no drop offs or follow up calls. DVDs by request only.

ANN WAUGH TALENT AGENCY **(818) 980-0141**
4741 Laurel Canyon Blvd., Ste. 200
Valley Village 91607

John Hugh, Connie Hamilton and Shelly Pang. Literary: Larry Benedick. Handles established actors and some young newcomers, union only. Headshots or resumes are accepted. They are looking for new people at this time, but the literary department is not looking for material.

RUTH WEBB ENTERPRISES, INC. **(323) 874-1700**
10580 Des Moines Ave.
Northridge 91326

Ruth Webb handles established actors and celebrities. Children 6 and up. Submissions are fine but no drop-offs or follow up calls, they will call if they are interested. She also handles reality show stars.

SHIRLEY WILSON & ASSOCIATES **(323) 857-6977**
5410 Wilshire Blvd., Ste. 510 **FAX (323) 857-6980**
Los Angeles 90036
son4shirl@aol.com

Shirley Wilson primarily represents adult union actors but will handle some non-union children starting at age 4. Headshots or 3/4 bodyshots are fine for submissions. Small agency.

WORLD CLASS SPORTS **(310) 535-9120**
880 Apollo St., Ste. 337
El Segundo 90245
wcsagent@pacbell.net

Don Franken and Andrew Woolf handle sports celebrities for commercials, personal appearances, and print. They only handle athletes with competitive backgrounds and real athletes who have played sports at a collegiate or national level. No non-athletes. Will see pictures and sports resumes. SAG franchised only.

CRAIG WYCKOFF & ASSOCIATES **(818) 752-2300**
11350 Ventura Blvd., Ste. 100
Studio City 91604

Craig Wyckoff handles children and adults. Mostly established actors. Headshots are fine for submissions. No tapes or DVDs.

ZANUCK, PASSON AND PACE, INC. **(818) 783-4890**
4717 Van Nuys Blvd., Ste. 102 **FAX (818) 501-8857**
Sherman Oaks 91403

Zanuck, Passon and Pace is a full service, state licensed theatrical agency representing actors for film, TV, commercials and print. Jerry Pace heads the commercial and print division and Michael Zanuck heads film and TV. Barry Rick assists in film and TV. All the agents at Zanuck, Passon, Pace have 20+ years. Each agent has background as a music and comedy agent before representing actors.

SAN DIEGO & ORANGE COUNTY AREAS

ARTIST MANAGEMENT AGENCY **(619) 233-6655**
835 5th Ave., Ste. 411 **FAX (619) 233-5332**
San Diego 92107

261 Bush Street **(714) 972-0311**
Santa Ana 92701
www.artistmanagementagency.com
nanci@artistsmanagementagency.com

Artist Management has been representing models, actors and voice-over talent for over 32 years in San Diego. Areas include fashion, print, commercial, industrial, film and voice-over. All submissions are accepted through the mail with a self-addressed-stamped envelope. No open calls. Please submit via U.S. mail only; no emails, faxes or phone calls.

MARIAN BERZON AGENCY **(949) 631-5936**
336 E. 17th St. **FAX (949) 631-6881**
Costa Mesa 92627
www.berzon.com
marian@berzon.com

Marian Berzon represents talent for theatrical, commercial, industrial, voice-over, look-alikes, print, literary, and high fashion work. Also handles children, twins, and triplets age 5 and up. They have no preference regarding style of photo. DVDs and VHS tapes only if requested.

BRAND MODEL AND TALENT AGENCY **(714) 850-1158**
1520 Brookhollow Dr., Ste. 39 **FAX (714) 850-0806**
Santa Ana 92705
www.brandmodelandtalent.com

President: Patty Brand. Adult Commercials: Lisa Marie. Print: Marlene Fairmont and Linda Schmidt. Plus Size: Lisa Burdick. Trade shows and Conventions: Dana Ross and Kelly Louch. Kids: Chrissie Hawke and Aubrey Green. Also handles print, industrial films, conventions, and models. Will look at 3/4 bodyshots and headshots. DVDs and VHS tapes must have SASE.

SCOTT COPELAND
CONSERVATIVE MANAGEMENT **(858) 456-9189**
1255 Coast Blvd.
La Jolla 92037
www.scottcopelandtalent.com
newfaces@scottcoplandtalent.com

Scott Copeland and Andrew Taft are open to mailed or emailed submissions and handle talent through all phases of their careers.

ELEGANCE TALENT AGENCY **(760) 434-3397**
2763 State St.
Carlsbad 92008
www.eletalent.com
eletalent@aol.com

Handles adults and young adults as well as models for fashion print. Headshots or 3/4 bodyshots and resume should be mailed for submissions. No drop-offs. They will call if they are interested. DVDs and CDs with SASE will also be accepted. SAG and AFTRA franchised.

SHAMON FREITAS & COMPANY **(858) 549-3955**
9606 Tierra Grande., Ste. 204 **FAX (858) 549-7028**
San Diego 92126
www.shamonfreitas.com

President: Carol Shamon Freitas. Also a modeling agency. They are open to newcomers and non-union talent. Handles infants through adults. They will review submissions (headshots or 3/4 bodyshots are fine), and DVDs and voice-over CDs. All submissions must have SASE. No material will be returned, will mail response (be patient). No drop-offs and no follow up calls.

JET SET MODELS **(858) 551-9393**
2160 Avenida de la Playa **FAX (858) 551-9392**
La Jolla 92038
www.jetsetmodels.com

This groovy agency represents young adults and children for print, commercials and theatrical. Also representing surfers, skaters and snowboarders. Mail photo and resume along with a self-addressed stamped envelope. Interviews by appointment only.

NOUVEAU MODEL AND TALENT (858) 456-1400
909 Prospect St., #230 FAX (858) 456-1969
La Jolla 92037
www.nouveaumodels.com

Nouveau represents adults, young performers and children starting at age 3 for theatrical, commercial and print. Mail headshot and resume along with a self-addressed, stamped envelope. No material will be returned. No phone calls please!

SAN DIEGO MODEL MANAGEMENT (619) 296-1018
438 Camino del Rio South FAX (619) 296-3422
Ste. 116
San Diego 92108
www.sdmodel.com

Represents adults and children from age 4 for commercials and print. P&R accepted with SASE. Open call Mondays from noon to 2 pm and Wednesdays from 2 pm to 4 pm. Height requirements: women 5′8″, men: 6″. Bring pictures. No open call for children, but pictures and resumes are accepted with SASE to Jennifer.

SAN FRANCISCO BAY AREA

BOOM MODELS & TALENT (415) 626-6591
2325 3rd St., Ste. 223 FAX (415) 626-6594
San Francisco 94107
www.boomagency.com
boommodels@aol.com

Co-owners Kristen Usich and John Hutcheson have over 25 years combined experienced in all facets of the model and talent Industry. Full service agency. They will accept mailed pictures and resumes and DVDs and CDs, but all submissions should have SASE. No drop-offs or follow up calls. They handle children from 6 months through adult seniors.

CAST IMAGES (916) 444-9655
2530 J St.
Sacramento 95816
www.castimages.com
info@castimages.com

Chandra Bourne is President of Cast Images, a full service licensed talent agency servicing Northern California in business for twelve years representing top notch professional models, actors and children in the areas of fashion print and runway, TV, film, local and national commercials, commercial print, voiceovers, trade shows and promotions. Headshot and resume submissions accepted by email of regular mail.

MARLA DELL TALENT AGENCY (415) 563-9213
2124 Union St., Ste. C FAX (415) 563-8734
San Francisco 94123
www.marladell.com

Also represents SAG and AFTRA actors for print and commercials. They specialize in children, infants to teenagers. They are also interested in mom, dad and grandparent types. Call or visit the website for submission procedures.

FILM THEATRE ACTORS EXCHANGE (415) 379-9308
3145 Geary Blvd., #752 FAX (415) 387-3656
San Francisco 94118
craigjones185@comcast.net

Craig Jones handles mostly established actors and some newcomers. Mailed submissions only (headshots or 3/4 bodyshots) and resumes, DVDs and tapes only by request. Include a self addressed stamped envelope. No follow up calls, they will call if they are interested. Also a print agency and AEA and WGA franchised.

GENERATIONS MODEL & TALENT (415) 777-9099
340 Brannan St., Ste. 302
San Francisco 94107
www.generationsagency.com

Full service, SAG and AFTRA franchised agency representing infants to early teens, as well as adults and seniors for TV, film, radio, CD-ROM, Internet, commercials and print. Submit a recent snapshot or professional headshot, color preferred with self addressed stamped envelope. Call the hotline for complete submission information (650) 366-5301.

J.E. TALENT (415) 395-9475
323 Geary St., Ste. 302
San Francisco 94102
www.jetalent.com
jetalent@pacbell.net

This full service SAG franchised agency represents children and adults for voice-overs, commercials and print. Accepts pictures and resumes with a self addressed stamped envelope. Please, no follow up calls.

(415) 781-2841
LOOK MODEL & TALENT AGENCY (415) 781-2822
166 Geary Blvd., Ste. 1406 FAX (415) 781-5722
San Francisco 94108
www.looktalent.com

A full service agency that handles children age 3 through adult. They will accept picture and resume, DVDs, VHS tapes, CDs and audio tapes with SASE only by mail and all submissions must have a cover letter. Send to the attention of Joan Spangler. Also a fashion model agency. Height requirements for models are 5′8″ for women and 6′ for men.

PANDA TALENT AGENCY (707) 576-0711
3721 Hoen Ave. FAX (707) 544-2765
Santa Rosa 95405

Audrey Grace also handles some animals. Specializes in minorities and handles infants through senior citizens. They will look at mailed submissions. Send a headshot or 3/4 bodyshot and resume. Also accepts DVDs and VHS tapes. All submissions should have SASE. Small agency with 1 agent. In business for over 20 years. SAG, WGA, AFTRA, AEA franchised.

STARS, THE AGENCY (415) 421-6272
23 Grant Ave., 4th Fl.
San Francisco 94108
www.starsagency.com

Also handles models for print and runway work. They want mailed submissions only (and with a self addressed, stamped envelope). No follow up calls. They now have a children's division for commercials (infants and up). Also a dance division. Open calls are held Monday through Friday from 2 pm to 4 pm. Height requirements: women 5′8″, men: 6″. Plus size models are welcome.

AGENCIES: COMMERCIAL & THEATRICAL

TALENT PLUS/LOS LATINOS AGENCY (831) 443-5423
2801 Moorpark Ave., Ste. 11 Dyer Bldg.
San Jose 95128

Gail Jones. All submissions should be sent with SASE. Headshots and resumes, CDs, and DVDs are accepted. Mail submissions and they will respond within two weeks if they are interested. They have a Hispanic division called "Los Latinos Agency" for work in the Spanish market. Established in 1981. SAG and AFTRA franchised. Specializing in commercials, print, trade shows, corporate and educational videos, television and film and ethnic voice overs. Serving the entire San Francisco Bay area.

TONRY TALENT AGENCY (415) 543-3797
885 Bryant St., Ste. 201 FAX (415) 957-9656
San Francisco 94103
www.tonrytalent.com
tonry@mindspring.com

Mary Tonry handles variety artists, comedians, character types, children, teens, and young adults. Will review headshots and resumes, CDs, and DVDs. All submissions must be by mail and be accompanied with cover letter and SASE. No drop-offs. 15 years in business. Small agency with 1 agent. SAG, AFTRA, and AEA franchised.

AGENCIES: MODELING

A.S.A. TALENT &
MODELING DIVISION (323) 662-9787
4430 Fountain Ave., Ste. A
Hollywood 90029
www.asatalent.com/models

Print and fashion modeling. Represents non-union and AFTRA models. They review unsolicited pictures and resumes and prefer that submissions are mailed and, if they are interested, they will call and schedule an interview.

ABRAMS ARTISTS AGENCY (310) 859-0625
9200 Sunset Blvd., 11th Fl. FAX (310) 276-6193
West Hollywood 90069

Will accept mailed submissions for commercials and print via mail. No phone calls, drop offs or follow up calls.

ADRIAN TEEN MODELS
AGENCY & SCHOOL (626) 795-2560
1021 E. Walnut., Ste. 101 FAX (626) 795-9529
Pasadena 91106

Handles young women 11-21. Commercial and print work. Will work with all ethnics. Will review unsolicited pictures and resumes. They offer training at the facility, but it is not required. With 55 years in the business they are the oldest modeling agency in California.

AFFINITY MODEL AND TALENT (888) 252-7000
(323) 525-0577
8721 Santa Monica Blvd., Ste. 27
West Hollywood 90069
www.affinitytalent.com
info@affinitytalent.com

Affinity Model and Talent is a licensed, bonded, full-service international SAG-AFTRA agency representing men, women and children throughout its offices in Los Angeles, San Francisco, Chicago and New York. They provide models, actors, musicians, writers and entertainers for the film, television, video, fashion, advertising, trade show, promotion and special event industries. They will accept submissions via email only and do not want drop offs or follow up calls. They will call if interested.

ARTIST MANAGEMENT AGENCY (714) 972-0311
261 Bush St.
Santa Ana 92701
www.artistmanagementagency.com

A print, fashion, and runway agency that mostly offers work in the Orange County area. Will represent non-union models. Height requirements for runway models only are women, 5'9" and men, 6'-6'2" and petite is 5'2"-5'4". No age requirement. Will review unsolicited pictures and resumes. Please mail any submissions. No drop-ins and no phone calls.

BOBBY BALL AGENCY (818) 506-8188
4342 Lankershim Blvd. FAX (818) 506-8588
Universal City 91602
www.bobbyballagency.com

Christine Tarallo, Wendy Bogdan and Tracee Roderick handle the print and modeling division for commercial, fashion, and print. Minimum height requirements are women 5'9", men 6'. Open calls are Thursdays from 3 pm to 5 pm and they require a professional high fashion portfolio.

BARBIZON MODELING AGENCY (562) 799-2985
4050 Katella Ave., Ste. 213
Los Alamitos 90720

A commercial, print, and runway modeling agency that handles non-union children age 4½ and older. State approved modeling curriculum and commercial classes are offered at the facility. A 3 to 9 month part-time commitment is required for classes. In business since 1939.

MARIAN BERZON AGENCY (949) 631-5936
336 E. 17th St. FAX (949) 631-6881
Costa Mesa 92627
www.berzon.com
marian@berzon.com

Books models for commercials, industrials, print, and theatrical work. They represent men, women, children, character types, and look-alikes. There are no minimum height requirements. They will review pictures and resumes (headshot or ¾ bodyshot). VHS tapes and DVDs by their request only. Over 20 years in business. Open calls Tuesdays, Wednesdays and Thursdays from 1:30 pm to 3:30 pm.

BLEU MODEL MANAGEMENT (310) 854-0088
8564 Wilshire Blvd. FAX (310) 854-0033
Beverly Hills 9021
www.bleumodels.com
info@bleumodels.com

Matthew Schwartz. No open calls. Height requirements: women 5'9" and men 6'.

BOOM MODELS & TALENT (415) 626-6591
2325 3rd St., #223 FAX (415) 626-6594
San Francisco 94107
www.boomagency.om
boomodels@aol.com

Co-owners Kristen Usich and John Hutcheson have over 25 years combined experienced in all facets of the model and talent Industry. Also a print agency. Will accept mailed pictures and resumes, DVDs, CDs, VHS and audio tapes. All submissions should have SASE. No drop-offs or follow up calls. They handle children from 6 months through adult. No height requirements or open calls.

BRAND MODEL AND TALENT AGENCY (714) 850-1158
1520 Brookhollow Dr., Ste. 39 FAX (714) 850-0806
Santa Ana 92705
www.brandmodelandtalent.com
brand@deltanet.com

Print and commercial print. They represent non-union talent and also handle models for non-union commercials. Height requirement for women is 5'8" and for men, 6'. Plus Size models need to be 5'9". They handle children from age 4 through adults. Open call for models only is held each Wednesday from 3 pm to 4 pm for ages 16 and above. SAG and AFTRA franchised.

BRICK ENTERTAINMENT (818) 784-2000
13321 Ventura Blvd. FAX (818) 986-8730
Sherman Oaks 91423
www.brickentertainment.com
barryrick@brickentertainment.com

Represents actors/actresses, athletes, broadcasters, children, comedians, ethnic/foreign types, hand/body part models, infants/babies, models (male and female), musicians, performers with disabilities, singers, spokespersons, teens/young adults for animated series/features, CD-ROMs, interactive, commercials, films, industrials, infomercials, music videos, print advertising, soaps, sound recordings, promotional announcements, TV, and voice-overs. Please no visits, interviews are by appointment only. CDs, DVDs, audio and video tapes are accepted by mail only. Open to attending showcases, plays and screenings.

CASSELL-LEVY,INC./CLI (323) 461-3971
843 N. Sycamore Ave. FAX (323) 461-1134
Hollywood 90038

Talent and voice-overs. Print, commercial, industrials, etc. Open to mailed headshots and resumes or zed cards or CDs.

COLLEEN CLER FOR KIDS (818) 841-7943
178 S. Victory Blvd., Ste. 108 FAX (818) 841-4541
Burbank 91502
www.colleencler.com
colleen@colleencler.com

Represents children and young adults for print work and commercials. Will accept photo and resume with SASE and will let you know whether they are interested or not. Over 15 years in business. SAG and AFTRA franchised.

CLICK MODELS OF LOS ANGELES, INC. (310) 246-0800
9057 Nemo St. FAX (310) 858-1357
Hollywood 90069
www.clickmodelsla.com

Print and modeling for fashion. Pictures and resumes accepted with a stamped self addressed envelope. Height requirements 5'9" for females, 6' males. Open calls on Thursdays from 3 to 4 pm.

CORALIE JR. AGENCY (818) 766-9501
4789 Vineland Ave., Ste. 100
North Hollywood 91602
coraliejr@earthlink.net

A print agency that handles character types. There is no height requirement. Prefers headshot submissions and VHS tapes or DVDs with SASE. Previous training and/or experience is required. The agency receives 10% commission. Over 50 years in business. 3,000 clients. WGA, SAG and AFTRA franchised.

CREATIVE ARTISTS AGENCY (CAA) (310) 288-4545
9830 Wilshire Blvd.
Beverly Hills 90212

Union only, not interested in unproven talent.

CUNNINGHAM, ESCOTT, SLEVIN, DOHERTY AGENCY (310) 475-7573
10635 Santa Monica Blvd. FAX (310) 475-6146
Ste. 135
Los Angeles 90025

257 Park Avenue South (212) 477-1666
New York City, NY 10010
www.cesdtalent.com

Handles models for fashion, catalog and product print, as well as runway. The modeling agency does not handle infants or children, or theatrical. They have a separate children's division for babies and kids.

DDO ARTISTS AGENCY (323) 782-0070
8322 Beverly Blvd.
Los Angeles 90048
www.ddoagency.com

The agency handles "lifestyle" models 16 and up for print, and commercials. They have no scheduled open calls and there are no height requirements.

DRAGON TALENT (323) 653-0366
8444 Wilshire Blvd., Penthouse FAX (323) 653-0367
Beverly Hills 90211
www.dragontalent.com
dragonsubmit@hotmail.com

Robin Harrington and Chaim Magnum represent actors, models, young adults and teens. They prefer emailed submissions but accept submissions by mail. No faxes, drop offs or phone calls. Tapes, CDs and DVDs by referral only.

ELITE MODEL MANAGEMENT (310) 274-9395
345 N. Maple Dr., Ste. 397 FAX (310) 278-7520
Beverly Hills 90210
www.elitemodels.com

Handles women, age 13-21 for modeling including high fashion, print, and runway. Send submissions (headshot and a bodyshot) ATTN: New Faces. Minimum height for models is 5'9". General interviews are given Mondays and Thursdays from 3:00 to 3:30 pm. Large agency, carries 60 models plus an international group. Affiliates all over the U.S. and internationally. SAG franchised.

EQUINOX MODELS AND TALENT (323) 951-7100
8455 Beverly Blvd., Ste. 304
Los Angeles 90038

Represents adults and teenagers for commercial and print. No height requirements for models and no open calls. Accepts pictures and resumes but no tapes or DVDs.

FORD MODELS, INC. **(310) 276-8100**
8826 Burton Way **FAX (310) 276-9299**
Beverly Hills 90211
www.fordmodels.com

A fashion print agency that has an open call Tuesdays from 2:30 pm to 4 pm. Minimum height requirement for women is 5'8" and 6" for men. They will accept pictures and resumes (headshots or 3/4 bodyshots). Has affiliates worldwide.

FRESH MODEL MANAGEMENT **(323) 934-7007**
7461 Beverly Blvd., Ste. 303 **FAX (323) 934-7030**
Los Angeles 90036
www.victorkruglov.com

A commercial, print, and fashion agency that only handles women. Minimum height is 5'5" and the age range is 18-27. Open calls are Monday through Friday from 3 to 5 pm. SAG franchised.

HERVEY/GRIMES **(818) 340-8402**
10561 Missouri Ave., #2 **FAX (310) 475-2010**
Los Angeles 90025

Pam Grimes and Marsha Hervey handle children from age 3 through adults. Some newcomers. Prefers mailed submissions. No phone calls or drop-offs. No unsolicited tapes.

IDENTITY TALENT AGENCY **(323) 469-1100**
7080 Hollywood Blvd.
Los Angeles 90029
idtalent@aol.com

Erik DeSando, Rob D'Avola Fran Tolstonog and Peggy Rudman handle adults and children for commercial and theatrical representation. Pictures and resumes are accepted by mail only. No drop-offs, faxes or follow up calls. Union only.

INTERNATIONAL CREATIVE MANAGEMENT (ICM) **(310) 550-4000**
8942 Wilshire Blvd. **FAX (310) 550-4100**
Beverly Hills 90211
www.icmtalent.com

No submissions.

J.E. MODELS **(415) 395-4777**
323 Geary St., Ste. 302
San Francisco 94102
www.jemodels.com

This new division of J.E. Talent is looking for women 5'8" and above, and men 6" and over for print and commercial work. Call for open call schedule.

KAZARIAN/SPENCER & ASSOCIATES **(818) 769-9111**
11969 Ventura Blvd., 3rd Fl. **FAX (818) 769-9840**
Box 7409
Studio City 91604
www.ksawest.com

Handles adults only for print work. Send submission to the Print Department. Models are seen at the open call on Wednesday from 3 to 5 pm. Over 30 years in business. SAG and AFTRA franchised.

L.A. MODEL AGENCY **(323) 436-7777**
7700 Sunset Blvd. **FAX (323) 436-7755**
Los Angeles 90046
www.lamodels.com

A commercial and print agency that handles established models and newcomers. They require previous training for people in their commercial department. Character types only for commercials. Height requirements for models are women, 5'9" and men 6'. They hold open calls Tuesdays and Thursdays from 2:30 pm to 4:00 pm. Large agency.

LANE AGENCY **(310) 275-1455**
9903 Santa Monica Blvd. #756
Beverly Hills 90212
www.laneagency.com

Full service modeling and talent agency. No walk ins, submissions accepted with a self addressed envelope. No open calls or height requirements.

MCCARTY TALENT **(818) 556-5410**
www.mccartytalent.com **FAX (800) 494 -7587**
talent@mccartytalent.com

Requirements: women, age 19 to 35; height 5'7" to 5'11" with weight and build proportionate to your height; Men: age 19 to 35; height 5'11" to 6'1" with weight and build proportionate to your height. Please mail or email a headshot, full body shot and contact information and McCarty's Talent Director will contact you directly.

SUSAN NATHE & ASSOC. C.P.C. **(323) 653-7573**
8281 Melrose Ave., #200
Los Angeles 90046
susannathe@pacbell.net

Handles all levels of union actors and models and they will see newcomers. They prefer 3/4 bodyshots and resumes for submissions. No DVDs or tapes. No children. SAG and AFTRA franchised.

NEXT MANAGEMENT CO. TALENT AGENCY **(323) 782-0010**
8447 Wilshire Blvd., #301
Beverly Hills 90211
www.nextmodelsusa.com

Handles adults for modeling, print, commercial, and theatrical representation. Height requirements for women 5'9", for men 6'. Will look at mailed headshot and resumes. Open call for women on Tuesdays from 11 am to noon and for men on Wednesdays from 11 am to noon.

NOUVEAU MODEL MGMT., INC. **(858) 456-1400**
909 Prospect St., #230 **FAX (858) 456-1969**
La Jolla 92037
www.nouveaumodels.com

Handles children from 3 years through adults for modeling, theatrical, and commercial representation. They prefer mailed submissions and if they are interested they will call you in for an interview. SAG and AFTRA franchised.

CINDY OSBRINK TALENT AGENCY **(818) 760-2488**
4343 Lankershim Blvd. **FAX (818) 760-0991**
Ste. 100
North Hollywood 91602

Handles infants from 14 days old through young adults. Height requirement for men and women 5'10" and above. Mailed submissions (headshots or 3/4 bodyshots) only, no drop-offs and no follow up calls. They do handle non-union newcomers for commercials. They are also a theatrical and commercial agency. SAG and AFTRA franchised.

PEAK MODELS AND TALENT (661) 288-1555
25852 McBean Parkway, #190 FAX (323) 969-0401
Valencia 91355
www.peakmodels.com

Height requirements: Male 6', Female 5'8'. No open calls. Adults only. Pictures, resumes and zed cards accepted by mail only.

PRIVILEGE TALENT AGENCY (818) 386-2377
14542 Ventura Blvd., Ste. 209 FAX (818) 386-9477
Sherman Oaks 91403

Represents all ages for commercial and print work, SAG, AFTRA and non-union talent. They will see newcomers and review unsolicited pictures and resumes (headshots or 3/4 bodyshots). The minimum height requirement for women is 5'8", for men 6'. Open calls are held Wednesdays from 2 pm to 3 pm. No drop-offs or phone calls. They look for high fashion, the European look, or California types. SAG franchised.

Q MODEL MANAGEMENT (310) 205-2888
8618 W. 3rd St.
Los Angeles 90048
www.qmodels.com

Open call for print on Tuesdays from 10 am to 11 am. Height requirements: women 5'9", men 6".

CINDY ROMANO
MODELING & TALENT AGENCY (760) 323-3333
P.O. Box 1951 FAX (760) 322-6666
Palm Springs 92263
www.crtalent.com

Handles union talent for commercials and print work. They handle children age 6 through adults. Models should send a composite and a resume and then call for open call times which are held once a month. SAG franchised.

SAN DIEGO MODEL MANAGEMENT (619) 296-1018
438 Camino del Rio South FAX (619) 296-3422
Ste. 116
San Diego 92108
www. sdmodel.com
sdmm@eciti.com

A commercial, print, and runway modeling agency that represents SAG, AFTRA, and non-union talent. They have many out of town clients. Works with all ages, infants to seniors The height requirements for women are 5'8"-5'11" and for men 6'. They will review pictures and resumes that are sent by mail. Open calls are held Mondays from noon to 2 pm., and Wednesdays from 2 pm to 4 pm, bring a photo. SAG and AFTRA franchised.

SCREEN CHILDREN'S CASTING (818) 846-4300
4000 Riverside Dr., #A FAX (818) 846-3745
Burbank 91505

Talent only. Children through 18 years or over 18 years but look younger.

DOROTHY SHREVE AGENCY (760) 327-5855
(760) 327-5092
1701 N. Palm Cyn Dr., Ste 6
Palm Springs 92262

Represents models for commercial, print, and runway work. Handles standard model types, ethnics, children, and character types. Submissions can be headshots or 3/4 bodyshots and resumes. Training offered at the facility, but it is not required.

STARS, THE AGENCY (415) 421-6272
23 Grant Ave. FAX (415) 421-7620
San Francisco 94111
www.starsagency. com

A commercial, theatrical, and print agency that handles union and non-union models for fashion and runway work. Height requirement for women is 5'8", 13 and older and for men, 6', 15 and older. Open calls are held Tuesdays from 2 pm to 4 pm. SAG and AFTRA franchised.

AGENCIES: SPECIALTY

BALDWIN TALENT, INC. (310) 827-2422
8055 W. Manchester Ste. 550
Playa Del Rey 90293

A small agency representing commercial clients. Mainly handles sports figures, stuntpeople, circus and rodeo for commercials.

BOBBY BALL AGENCY (818) 506-8188
4342 Lankershim Blvd. FAX (818) 506-8588
Universal City 91602
www.bobbyballagency.com

The agency represents SAG, AFTRA, and AEA dancers, singers, and sports people. They will review pictures and resumes (prefers headshots). No tapes or DVDs. Auditions about every three months, and they vary seasonally, call for information. They will attend showcases and screenings and will see acts in the office only by their request.

BLOC (323) 954-7730
5651 Wilshire Blvd., Ste. C FAX (323) 954-7731
Los Angeles 90036
www.blocagency.com

A dance/choreography agency in Los Angeles whose unique approach to representation involves artist development and career expansion of each client as an individual. With an elite roster of top working dancers, they remain personable and intimate with a boutique-like feel. They handle dancers of all ages for commercials, television, film, music videos, industrials, tours and live shows. Currently they are accepting new clients by referral or through photo submission. SAG franchised. New York office.

BRICK ENTERTAINMENT (818) 784-2000
13321 Ventura Blvd. FAX (818) 986-8730
Sherman Oaks 91423
www.brickentertainment.com
barryrick@brickentertainment.com

Represents actors/actresses, athletes, broadcasters, children, comedians, ethnic/foreign types, hand/body part models, infants/babies, models (male and female), musicians, performers with disabilities, singers, spokespersons, teens/young adults for animated series/features, CD-ROMs, interactive, commercials, films, industrials, infomercials, music videos, print advertising, soaps, sound recordings, promotional announcements, TV, and voice-overs. Please no visits, interviews are by appointment only. CDs, DVDs, audio and video tapes are accepted by mail only. Open to attending showcases, plays and screenings.

THE CHASIN AGENCY (310) 278-7505
8899 Beverly Blvd., Ste. 716 FAX (310) 275-6685
Los Angeles 90048
chasin@pacbell.net

Directors/Packaging: Tom Chasin. Primarily a directors and literary agency. They are not looking for new clients. SAG franchised.

CORALIE JR. AGENCY (818) 766-9501
4789 Vineland Ave., #100
North Hollywood 91602
coraliejr@earthlink.net

Represents all variety performers, circus, look-alikes, nightclub acts, comedians, unusual, oddball acts, wrestling, sports figures, little people, twins, triplets, actors in their 80s and 90s, vaudeville acts, musicians, and animal acts and their trainers. Overseas bookings. Over 40 years in the business. Also modeling, commercial and theatrical.

CROFOOT GROUP, INC. (818) 223-1500
23632 Calabasas Rd., Ste. 104 FAX (818) 223-1599
Calabasas 91302
crofoot@pacbell.net

Terry Crofoot and Andrew Crofoot handle on-air news talent and program hosts.

MARLA DELL TALENT (415) 563-9213
2124 Union St., Ste. C FAX (415) 563-8734
San Francisco 94123
www.marladell.com

A SAG/AFTRA talent agency specializing in children and also representing adult actors for commercial print, as well for all media. Will accept pictures and resumes with SASE.

DYTMAN AND ASSOCIATES (310) 274-8844
9200 Sunset Blvd., Ste. 809
Los Angeles 90069

A literary agency only. Submissions only by referral. SAG franchised.

THE FIRM (310) 860-8000
9465 Wilshire Blvd., Ste. 600
Beverly Hills 90210

A literary, talent and animation agency that will accept newcomers by referral only. SAG and AFTRA franchised.

MITCHELL J. HAMILBERG (310) 471-4024
11718 Barrington Court #732
Los Angeles 90049

A literary agency. They accept query letters SAG and AFTRA franchised.

IMPACT TALENT GROUP (818) 557-7754 (818) 753-4040
244 N. California
Burbank 91505

Represents actors theatrically by Industry referral only.

THE KAPLAN–STAHLER–GUMER–BRAUN AGENCY (323) 653-4483
8383 Wilshire Blvd., Ste. 923
Beverly Hills 90211

The agency handles TV writers and directors only. No unsolicited manuscripts. SAG and AFTRA franchised.

KEN LINDNER & ASSOC. (310) 277-9223
2049 Century Park East FAX (310) 277-5806
Ste. 3050
Los Angeles 90067
www.kenlindner.com

Ken Lindner handles TV broadcast people (reporters, announcers, etc.) and game show hosts. Adults only. They prefer video submissions. More than 10 years in business.

LUCKY ENTERTAINMENT
BERT EPSTEIN (310) 277-9666
10271 Almayo Ave., Ste. 101
Los Angeles 90064

Represents union and non-union variety acts, mimes, circuses, look-alikes, puppeteers, musicians, and little people. They will review pictures and resumes. Mr. Epstein auditions performers in the office, call for an appointment. Established 1966.

OMNIPOP INC. (818) 980-9267
10700 Ventura Blvd., 2nd Fl. FAX (818) 980-9371
Studio City 91604
www.omnipop.com

A theatrical and commercial agency that only handles stand-up comics, union and non-union. They will review mailed pictures and resumes, DVDs and VHS tapes of performers with TV credits. No follow up calls. The best time to approach them is during the summer and late fall. They will attend showcases. They have an east coast office and affiliate.

PERIWINKLE PRODUCTIONS (714) 776-5820
P.O. Box 2486 FAX (714) 635-1711
Anaheim 92814

Circus, variety acts and magic!

REBEL ENTERTAINMENT PARTNERS (323) 935-1700
5700 Wilshire Blvd., Ste. 456
Los Angeles 90036
www.reptalent.com

Hosting: Susan Haber. A full service agency that handles reality hosts of all levels. By referral only. Over 25 years in business. SAG and AFTRA franchised.

SHAPIRO-LICHTMAN (310) 859-8877
8827 Beverly Blvd.
Los Angeles 90048

Literary agency. Actors for theatrical only. They accept no unsolicited scripts, will accept pictures and resumes. SAG franchised.

RON SMITH'S
CELEBRITY LOOK-ALIKES (323) 467-3030
928 N. San Vicente Blvd., Penthouse #210
West Hollywood 90069
www.entertainmentforhire.com

Represents look-alikes and sound-alikes of any age for theatrical and print work. They are especially interested in young starlet types. They will review photos (headshots or 3/4 bodyshots) and resumes, DVDs and VHS tapes. If they are interested they will call you. A large agency with offices worldwide that has been in business for over 20 years.

SONJIA WARREN
BRANDON'S COMMERCIALS UNLTD. (310) 278-5123
190 N. Cannon Dr., Ste. 302
Beverly Hills 90210

Handles union projects. Age range is 20 and under. Non-returnable mailed submission (3/4 bodyshots/resumes) only.

STARWIL PRODUCTION
TALENT AGENCY (323) 874-1239
433 N. Camden Dr., 4th Fl.
Beverly Hills 90210
starwil@earthlink.com

Starwil Reed, Gwen Reed, Vesta Robertson, Gregory Porter, Tony Jackson. A commercial, theatrical agency that handles all levels of actors, composers, musicians, variety acts, and singers. They will see union and non-union newcomers, children from age 4 to young adults. They will review pictures and resumes, and tapes by request and require video tapes from music acts. SAG franchised.

TALENT PLAN (818) 752-9474
11824 Oxnard St.
North Hollywood 91606
www.talentplan.com

Represents look-alikes, variety acts, spokesmodels, dancers, and actors, with customized comedy roasts for corporate events, conventions, and overseas commercial bookings. Reviews pictures and resumes and DVDs. Especially interested in celebrity, political, or historical look-alikes. Attends showcases but does not see acts in the office.

THE THOMAS TALENT AGENCY (310) 665-0000
6709 La Tijera Blvd., Ste. 915 FAX (310) 665-0070
Los Angeles 90045

Venus Thomas represents a carefully selected clientele of actors for film, TV and commercials. Currently accepting submissions from adults of all ages and types. She maintains a close working relationship to actors with focus on career building. Interviews are by appointment only, no personal deliveries. Mail photo and resume, she will call if interested. VHS tapes by request only. Small Agency carries 35-40 actors.

VISION ART MANAGEMENT (310) 888-3288
9200 Sunset Blvd., Penthouse #1
Los Angeles 90069

Scott Schwartz runs this literary agency handling writers for TV and film. Industry referral only.

WICKED TALENT (818) 237-5477
www.wickedtalent.com

Wicked Talent is the oldest and most respected modeling and movie extra referral service for alternative talent in the world. They offer goths, glam, pierced, punk, tattooed and all around circus-freaks to the entertainment Industry. Not an agency, Wicked Talent is a not for profit company. They do not charge casting or booking fees to utilize their site nor do not they take percentages of talent work and do not interfere in your work. Through networking events year-round, Wicked Talent is helping to build relationships and set new standards for professionals.

STELLA ZADEH & ASSOCIATES (818) 424-2226
1187 Coast Village Rd., #123
Santa Barbara 93108

Stella Zadeh represents writers and producers of reality television shows.

ATTORNEYS

Actors really do not need attorneys since their contracts are standard Screen Actors Guild contracts and any problems would easily be addressed by SAG. However, if you negotiate a fee significantly overscale or your contract is somehow unique you may need an attorney. Some larger agencies will have lawyers in residence that can assist, otherwise ask around for recommendations, interview a few different attorneys and be very clear on what they will charge. Entertainment lawyers are very expensive and their compensation will be the deciding factor for most actors.

ABRAMS, GARFINKLE,
MARGOLIS, BERGSON, LLP (310) 300-2900
9229 Sunset Blvd. FAX (310) 300-2901
Los Angeles 90069
www.agmblaw.com

The partners have proven legal experience representing production companies, writers, directors, actors, musicians and models, as well as many other clients in the entertainment Industry. Their partners have negotiated various issues on behalf of the entertainment Industry's trade unions. The firm's expertise in negotiating and drafting agreements for motion picture, television, music productions and live theater productions is enhanced by its ability to provide complete accounting and management services for all members of the entertainment Industry.

AKIN, GUMP, STRAUSS, HAUER & FELD, LLP (310) 229-1000
2029 Century Park East, 2400 FAX (310) 229-1001
Los Angeles 90067
www.akingump.com

The firm represents studios and personalities, but mainly does contract work for actors. They believe actors need an attorney when they are becoming established. A fee is charged for the initial interview. Fee structure is hourly.

RAYMOND ASHER (310) 277-4510
1801 Avenue of the Stars, Ste. 340
Los Angeles 90067

Handles negotiations, contracts, and litigation primarily for producers but they also handle and package established actors with credits. Over 25 years in business.

STEPHEN BARON LAW OFFICE (310) 260-6060
1299 Ocean Ave., Ste. 312 FAX (310) 260-6061
Santa Monica 90401

Specializes in entertainment law working with actors, musicians, writers, producers, and directors. Mainly negotiates contracts for actors. They believe actors need legal advice on specific projects. They package actors with other entertainment clients on occasion. There is no fee for an initial interview. Fee structure is either hourly, by percentage, or a flat fee. A small firm that has been in business for more than 23 years.

LAW OFFICES OF MARK B. BEAR (818) 567-6488
3800 W. Alameda Ave., Ste. 1150
Burbank 91505

Bankruptcy, family law, wills and trusts, and corporate/business law.

BECK & CHRISTIAN (949) 855-9250
23041 Mill Creek Dr.
Laguna Hills 92653

Specializes in estate planning (wills, trusts, probate) and taxation (tax planning, negotiation with IRS and corporate/business law). Fees are reasonable so that actors can afford to protect their families with estate planning services (wills, trusts) specifically tailored to meet their unique needs.

ARTHUR T. BERGGREN (310) 392-3088
2727 Main St., Ste. F
Santa Monica 90405

Represents actors, writers, musicians, and producers specializing in representing actor/writer deals. Mr. Berggren believes actors need an attorney when they have an established reputation or are consistently working. Fees are hourly.

BERKOWITZ & BLACK (310) 275-3600
9401 Wilshire Blvd., Ste. 1100 FAX (310) 724-8340
Beverly Hills 90212-2924

Handles production, distribution, intellectual properties and financing.

EDWARD BLAU (310) 556-8468
1901 Avenue of the Stars FAX (310) 282-0579
Ste. 1900
Los Angeles 90067

Works with actors and others in the entertainment Industry specializing in entertainment law.

BLOOM, HERGOTT & DIEMER (310) 859-6800
150 S. Rodeo Dr., 3rd Fl. FAX (310) 859-2788
Beverly Hills 90212

This firm works with actors and others in the entertainment Industry specializing in entertainment law. They take on new clients by personal referral only.

BOBBITT & ROBERTS (310) 315-7150
1620 26th St., Ste. 150 South FAX (310) 315-7159
Santa Monica 90404

The firm works with actors and others in the entertainment Industry specializing in entertainment law.

LAW OFFICES OF STUART L. CARROLL (310) 785-6655
1033 Gayley Ave., Ste. 107 FAX (310) 785-3925
Los Angeles 90024

Assists independent producers, performers, developers, and designers of unique content in navigating the legal obstacles involved in the financing, production, and distribution of their works.

GARY S. DIAMOND (805) 985-1803
3844 West Channel Island Blvd., PMB 224
Oxnard 93035

Specializing in entertainment law, Mr. Diamond works with actors, writers, directors, producers and musicians. He represents clients in contract negotiations and agreements. There is no fee for initial consultation and fees are hourly or contingency depending on circumstances.

DONALDSON & HART (310) 273-8394
(310) 273-5370
9220 W. Sunset Blvd., Ste. 224
Los Angeles 90069
www.donaldsonhart.com
info@donaldsonhart.com

This firm specializes in TV, stage, and motion picture law. Michael Donaldson and Joseph Hart believe actors have need of an attorney when they are in a pilot, a series, or make $35,000+ per year. They occasionally package actors with other entertainment clients. There is no fee for the initial interview. Fee structure varies with individual situation.

FEIG MORRIS, LLP (310) 275-0562
9454 Wilshire Blvd., Ste. 850 FAX (310) 275-5370
Beverly Hills 90212

Eric J. Feig is an entertainment attorney licensed to practice law in California, New York, and New Jersey and represents actors, writers, directors, producers and filmmakers in film, television, multimedia and theater. Feig is a graduate of New York University and earned his law degree in 1991 at Fordham University Law School in New York City.

GIPSON, HOFFMAN & PANCIONE (310) 556-4660
1901 Avenue of the Stars FAX (310) 556-8945
Ste. 1100
Los Angeles 90067

This firm's specialties include motion picture and TV transactional work, production, distribution, and financing. The entertainment department covers almost every aspect of the entertainment business, frequently assisting actors in motion picture packages. They represent all types of talent in the entertainment Industry and believe an actor needs an attorney when he/she stops working for scale. They package actors with other entertainment clients. There is no fee for the initial interview. Fee structure varies.

GREENBERG, GLUSKER, FIELDS, CLAMAN, MACHTINGER & KINSELLA LLP (310) 553-3610
1900 Avenue of the Stars FAX (310) 553-0687
Ste. 2100
Los Angeles 90067
www.ggfirm.com

Works with actors, writers, producers, and directors. The firm's entertainment lawyers handle a broad range of legal and business matters.

WILLIAM HARRIS (626) 441-9300
1499 Huntington Dr., #403
South Pasadena 91030

They only work with established actors and deal mostly with agreements and contracts. They package actors with other entertainment clients. There is a fee charged for initial interview. A personal referral is usually required before scheduling an appointment. Fee structure varies. A small firm that has been in business for more than 13 years.

PETER L. KNECHT (310) 652-2532
9000 Sunset Blvd., Ste. 1115
Los Angeles 90069

A business management firm that also provides attorney services in the area of entertainment law.

A. MORGAN MAREE (310) 824-5599
1145 Gayley Ave., Ste. 303 FAX (310) 443-1997
Los Angeles 90024

Hugh Duff Robertson negotiates contracts for actors and directors.

LAW OFFICES OF WILLIAM MITCHELL MARGOLIN (818) 999-4529
16255 Ventura Blvd., Ste. 1008
Encino 91436
legalhelpforyou@msn.com

Mr. Margolin works with actors and production companies on forming contracts, negotiations and general practice. He works in both the entertainment law and litigation area.

MITCHELL, SILBERBERG & KNUPP (310) 312-2000
11377 W. Olympic Blvd. FAX (310) 312-3100
Los Angeles 90064
www.msk.com

A general practice as well as entertainment law firm that works mostly on general contracts and agreements. Their clients include actors, directors, and producers. New clients are accepted by referral only.

MYMAN, ABELL, FINEMAN, GREENSPAN & LIGHT (310) 820-7717
11601 Wilshire Blvd., 200 FAX (310) 207-2680
Los Angeles 90025

Specializes in entertainment law working with actors, writers, producers, directors, and production companies. They mostly work on contracts and negotiations for actors. The fee for the initial interview depends on individual circumstances.

NACHSHIN & WESTON L.L.P. (310) 478-6868
11601 Wilshire Blvd., Ste. 1500 FAX (310) 473-8112
Los Angeles 90025
www.nwdivorce.com

The firm specializes in high profile clients including entertainment executives, celebrities and sports figures. Best known for their victory in the precedent-setting Barry Bonds prenuptial case, Nachshin and Weston assist actors, writers, directors, producers, musicians and other entertainment Industry types in all matters dealing with family law, including custody, child and spousal support orders and modifications, premarital and postnuptial agreements, palimony and paternity cases. Fees vary.

O'MELVENY & MYERS (213) 430-6000
400 S. Hope St. FAX (213) 430-6407
Los Angeles 90071
www.omm.com

Specializes in working with studio and actor contracts. Believes actors need an attorney at the time of their first picture and when negotiating contracts. No fee is charged for the initial interview. The fee structure is hourly. A large firm that has been in business for over 100 years. They have offices nationwide.

SAM PERLMUTTER (323) 931-1017
5757 Wilshire Blvd., Ste. 636 FAX (323) 857-1351
Los Angeles 90036

Specializes in entertainment law and litigation working with actors, musicians, writers, producers, and directors. They feel talent needs an attorney when negotiating contracts. Initial interview is over the phone.

GERALD F. PHILLIPS (310) 277-7117
2029 Century Park East FAX (310) 286-9182
Ste. 1200
Los Angeles 90067

Phillips, who has been involved in legal matters in the entertainment Industry for four decades, handles Alternative Dispute Resolution matters relative to all disputes in film, television, theatre and music. Through negotiation, mediation and ADR sessions, Phillips assists his clients in resolving matters outside the courtroom. The author and keynote speaker specializes in the film Industry.

LAW OFFICES OF REUBEN & NOVICOFF (310) 777-1990
1100 Glendon Ave., 10th Fl. FAX (310) 777-1989
Los Angeles 90024

Timothy D. Reuben is a trial attorney who handles many civil disputes relative to contracts, employment issues and production deals. The firm handles both personalities and entities and offers its entertainment legal services not only in the courtroom, but also through mediation and alternative dispute resolution sessions as well.

RICHMAN, MANN, CHIZEVER, PHILLIPS & DUBOFF (310) 274-8300
9601 Wilshire Blvd., Penthouse
Beverly Hills 90210

This firm works with actors, musicians and writers. New clients by referral.

ROSENFELD, MEYER & SUSMAN (310) 858-7700
9601 Wilshire Blvd., 4th Fl. FAX (310) 271-6430
Beverly Hills 90210

This is a general practice law firm that specializes in entertainment law. They work with actors, musicians, writers, producers, and directors mainly negotiating contracts for actors. They believe actors need a lawyer when they're close to signing contracts. There is usually no fee charged for the initial interview. The fee structure is hourly or on a percentage basis. A medium sized firm that has been in business over 40 years.

OWEN J. SLOANE
LAW OFFICES OF BERGER KAHN **(310) 821-9000**
4215 Glencoe Ave., 2nd Fl. **FAX (310) 578-6178**
Marina Del Rey 90292
www.bergerkahn.com

Sloane, best known for his work in the music Industry for the past 30 years representing well-known artists, songwriters, composers, bands and record companies, also handles actors, writers, directors and producers in television and film. In addition to these areas, Sloane also handles contracts and negotiations dealing with the entertainment in multimedia and the Internet. Fees are charged on an hourly basis. Sloane, licensed to practice law both in California and Tennessee, is an honors graduate of both Yale and Cornell, and frequently teaches at major universities and entertainment Industry seminars and conferences.

STANBURY FISHELMAN **(310) 278-1800**
9200 Sunset Blvd., Penthouse 30
Los Angeles 90069

Represents actors, musicians, writers, radio personalities, and production companies. They also practice family law and civil litigation. They mostly deal with contract negotiations, but they also handle intellectual properties such as ideas for screenplays and movie rights. Their specialty is entertainment law. They believe actors need an attorney for any transaction that goes beyond the scope of minimum guild requirements.

STEIN & FLUGGE **(323) 936-1455** **(310) 275-5351**
6100 Wilshire Blvd.. Ste. 1250
Los Angeles 90048

Specializes in film and TV law and often works on contract disputes for actors. They feel actors need an attorney at every stage of their careers. Usually there is no fee for the initial interview and their fee structure is hourly. Over 50 years in business.

TERRAN T. STEINHART **(323) 933-8263**
4311 Wilshire Blvd., Ste. 415 **FAX (323) 933-2391**
Los Angeles 90010-3713
www.steinhartlaw.com
terran@steinhartlaw.com

Litigation firm that handles business, entertainment, intellectual property, real estate and personal injury litigation, trials and appeals. Most cases taken on hourly fee basis, some on contingency. Small firm, in business since 1965.

LAW OFFICE OF DUANE C. STROH **(818) 502-1912**
144 N. Glendale Ave., Ste. 202
Glendale 91206

Works with actors, musicians, writers, producers, and production companies specializing in civil litigation. They frequently work on contract negotiations for actors. They feel an actor needs an attorney before signing anything and they occasionally package actors with other entertainment clients. The initial contact with an actor is over the phone to determine whether an attorney is needed.

LAW OFFICES OF
PAULA S. TESKE & ASSOCIATES **(310) 391-6800**
3415 S. Sepulveda Blvd. **FAX (310) 391-1725**
Ste. 660
Los Angeles 90034
www.teskelaw.com
teskelaw@earthlink.net

West Los Angeles firm with over 60 years of combined experience in the following areas: business, civil litigation, bankruptcy, and family law.

LAWRENCE J. TURNER **(310) 273-4026**
9200 Sunset Blvd., Ste. 701
Los Angeles 90069

Specializes in business and contract negotiations primarily helping actors deal with contracts and taxes. No fee is charged for the initial interview. Fees are on an hourly basis. Mr. Turner is also a business manager and a CPA. See listing for Turner Accountancy under BUSINESS MANAGERS in this section for further information.

MARVIN LOUIS WOLF **(310) 285-1550**
433 N. Camden Dr.
Beverly Hills 90120

Specializes in general entertainment law frequently working with actors and directors on reviewing contracts and drafting negotiations. Mr. Wolf feels an actor should have an attorney look over any contract before signing. Packages actors with other entertainment clients. There is no fee charged for an initial interview. Fee structure varies.

BUSINESS MANAGERS

Some actors are not interested in this aspect of the business. If you are this type, be very selective in choosing your professional advisor. There are no regulations for financial managers so they really have free rein. You will sign your money over and trust they will do the right thing. Your hard earned money could be gone – we have all heard the horror stories of business managers running off with their clients' money. On the other hand, most actors with money have been guided by financial consultants and managers. Since there are no regulatory bodies or other ways to check on financial decisions, ask your accountant, attorney, agent, manager, successful actor friend or any other trusted friends in the business for their recommendations. When you reach a point in your career where you are ready to seek a financial manager you want to make a wise decision.—"Acting is Everything" by Judy Kerr

ABRAMS, GARFINKLE,
MARGOLIS, BERGSON, LLP **(310) 300-2900**
9229 Sunset Blvd., Ste. 710
Los Angeles 90069
www.agmblaw.com
info@agmblaw.com

The partners at AGMB have proven legal experience representing production companies, writers, directors, actors, on-air television personalities, musicians and models, as well as many other clients in the entertainment Industry. Their partners have negotiated various issues on behalf of the entertainment Industry's trade unions. The firm's expertise in negotiating and drafting agreements for motion picture, television, music productions and live theater productions is enhanced by its ability to provide complete accounting and management services for all members of the entertainment Industry.

ACCOUNT MANAGEMENT GROUP (818) 983-2448
5440 Katherine Ave. FAX (818) 989-4944
Sherman Oaks 91401-4921

Trisha Pitsch. Personal and business assistance. Accounting.

AMERICAN EXPRESS FINANCIAL ADVISORS (949) 863-9400
2 Park Plaza, Ste. 1100 FAX (949) 724-9910
Irvine 92614
www.americanexpress.com

Can provide a one-stop service for both personal and business planning. They work with other professional advisors, such as your accountant and attorney, to help assure that all of your financial concerns are addressed as a whole.

VINCENT ANDREWS MANAGEMENT CORP. (310) 557-2552
315 S. Beverly Dr., Ste. 208 FAX (310) 557-1231
Beverly Hills 90212

Household and/or business financial management including investments and insurance. Takes clients by referral and personal interview. Affiliates in California, Connecticut, and New York.

BAMBERGER BUSINESS MANAGEMENT (310) 475-1222
10850 Wilshire Blvd., Ste. 575 FAX (310) 475-1014
Los Angeles 90024

Works with actors, writers, directors, producers, musicians, and composers. Personal financial management including investments, real estate, insurance, and banking. The best time to approach them is after tax season. They believe actors need a business manager when they earn (or have prospect of earning) $250,000 or more per year. Small firm. 50 years in business.

BASH, GESAS AND CO. (310) 205-2300
9401 Wilshire Blvd., Ste. 700 FAX (310) 278-2031
Beverly Hills 90212
www.bashgesas.com

An accounting firm that works with musicians, writers, directors, producers, and a few actors. They pay bills, set up corporations (working with an attorney), handle investments, and set up tax shelters. Percentage or fee depends on client, also hourly basis available for simple accounting needs. Will take tax-only clients. They believe the need for an actor to have a business manager is determined by the extent of business being done. Medium sized firm.

BERNSTEIN, FOX, WHITMAN & COMPANY (310) 277-3373
2029 Century Park East FAX (310) 785-9035
Ste. 500
Los Angeles 90067
www.bfwco.com

The firm has a business management and a CPA division. They will take tax-only clients. Mostly works on a percentage basis. Medium sized firm.

CBIZ MAYER HOFFMAN MCCANN (310) 268-2000
11601 Wilshire Blvd., 23rd Fl. FAX (310) 268-2001
Los Angeles 90025
www.cbiz.com

Business management and accountants. They work with actors and all Industry professionals. A full service firm that offers, financial planning, taxes, business management, and investments. Contact them any time except tax time. Usually work on a fee basis and occasionally on a percentage basis. Will take tax-only clients.

LISA MITCHELL CLAUS (310) 453-3985

Production accounting and personal business manager. Lisa manages finances for individuals.

CROSBY & ASSOCIATES, CPA (323) 871-2978
1800 N. Highland Ave., #604
Los Angeles 90028

Handles accounting, tax planning, business management, and financial management for performers, musicians, writers, producers, and directors. The charge for an initial consultation depends on the needs of the client at the time and they work on a percentage or fee basis, depending on the individual situation. They will take tax-only clients. They have been business for over 20 years specializing in the entertainment Industry.

DELOITTE TOUCHE TOHMATSU (213) 688-0800
350 S. Grand Ave., Ste. 200 FAX (213) 688-0100
Los Angeles 90071
www.deloitte.com

A full service CPA firm with a business management office that works with actors and others in the Industry. The typical income of their clients is $500K yearly. Will take tax-only clients. A large international company, over 50 years in business.

ELKINS & ELKINS (818) 789-3644
16830 Ventura Blvd., Ste. 300 FAX (818) 501-7733
Encino 91436

A full service business management firm that works mostly with Industry professionals. If a client prefers to handle his/her own business, they will work on taxes for an hourly fee. Their accountants are qualified for check signing authority at the client's request.

ERNST & YOUNG (818) 703-4700
21800 Oxnard St., Ste. 500 FAX (818) 347-9325
Woodland Hills 91367

725 S. Figueroa St., 5th Fl. (213) 977-3200
Los Angeles 90017
www.ey.com

Offers personalized service for actors and professionals in other industries. They specialize in business management and tax work. They will take tax-only clients. A large firm with over 300 locations worldwide.

FRANCIS & ASSOCIATES (310) 277-7351
501 S. Beverly Dr., 3rd Floor FAX (310) 556-0253
Beverly Hills 90212

Offers general business management and investment counseling. Large firm, over 25 years in business.

FRANKEL, LODGEN, LECHER, GOLDITCH, SARDI & HOWARD (818) 783-0570
16530 Ventura Blvd., Ste. 305
Encino 91436

This CPA firm has business management and tax divisions. They work with musicians and actors who have an annual income of at least $100K. They specialize in personalized financial management and investment. They work on a percentage basis. They will take tax-only clients. Medium sized firm, over 15 years in business.

FREEDMAN, BRODER & COMPANY (310) 449-6700
2501 Colorado Ave., Ste. 350 FAX (310) 449-6791
Santa Monica 90404
www.fbcpa.com

They offer entertainment business management, accounting, etc. A medium sized firm, over 30 years in business.

GLOBAL BUSINESS MANAGEMENT (818) 385-3100
15250 Ventura Blvd., Ste. 710 FAX (818) 385-3110
Sherman Oaks 91403
www.gbmi.com

Works specifically with actors offering tax planning, personal and/or business financial management including bills, insurance, pensions, investments, etc. They will take tax-only clients. Medium sized firm, over 20 years in business.

GLWG, INC. (310) 473-2266
10960 Wilshire Blvd., Ste. 2150 FAX (310) 473-8846
Los Angeles 90024

A business management and CPA firm that works with actors and others in the Industry. The yearly income of their clients varies. Over 35 years in business. Will take tax only clients.

GUILD MANAGEMENT CORP. (310) 277-9711
9911 W. Pico Blvd. FAX (310) 785-9280
Penthouse #A
Los Angeles 90035

They offer complete financial management for actors and others in the Industry. Medium sized firm.

HALPERN & MANTOVANI (818) 385-0111
16530 Ventura Blvd., Ste. 611
Encino 91436

Primarily works with people in the Industry specializing in financial planning, taxes, investments, etc. Will take tax-only clients. Small firm.

SAL IANNOTTI (818) 547-1733
322 Raymond St., Ste. 12
Glendale 91201
saliannotti@att.net

Sal Iannotti, Financial Representative teaches at UCLA and UC Santa Barbara. Business management and some taxes. Helps purchase, sell, exchange and manage real estate and retirement plans.

JACQUELINE KEEHN (818) 501-7496
15300 Ventura Blvd., Ste. 315 FAX (818) 501-5054
Sherman Oaks 91403

CPA firm that specializes in business management. Works with actors, musicians, writers, producers, and directors. Also does financial planning, taxes, and investments. They will take on income tax-only clients. They can be approached any time of the year.

HAROLD B. KERN, CPA (310) 205-2333
9401 Wilshire Blvd., Ste. 700
Beverly Hills 90212

This business management and CPA firm specializes in business management for actors with a yearly income of $500K. Will take tax-only clients. Small firm, over 35 years in business.

KUCHER AND COHEN, LLP (818) 999-9200
21031 Ventura Blvd., #210 FAX (818) 999-5344
Woodland Hills 91364
www.kucherandcohen.com
info@kucherandcohen.com

Business managers, income tax preparation, tax and estate planning.

LAGNESE, PEYROT AND MUCCI, INC. (323) 938-7900
5750 Wilshire Blvd., Ste. 580
Los Angeles 90036

Works with actors, musicians, writers, producers, directors, and others in the Industry. They offer full service business management including extensive financial planning, bills, taxes, investments, etc. Personal attention.

LONDON & COMPANY (310) 478-5151
11601 Wilshire Blvd., Ste. 2040 FAX (310) 478-3696
Los Angeles 90025
www.londonco.com

This business management and CPA firm offers business management, financial planning, taxes, and investments. Their clients earn $200K annually. They will take tax-only clients. Usually works on a percentage basis. Medium sized firm.

A. MORGAN MAREE JR. & ASSOC., INC. (310) 824-5599
1145 Gayley Ave., Ste. 303 FAX (310) 443-1997
Los Angeles 90024

This business management and CPA firm works with actors, musicians, writers, producers, and directors. They specialize in taxes, investment advising, and financial planning and can be approached any time except tax time. They work on a percentage basis and will take tax-only clients. A small firm with over 50 years in business.

MARTINDALE MANAGEMENT (818) 700-2988
18915 Nordhoff St., Ste. 5 FAX (818) 700-2989
Northridge 91324

This business management and CPA firm works with actors and others in the Industry. They work on a percentage basis. Medium sized firm, 35 years in business.

H. ROY MATLEN & ASSOCIATES (818) 506-5911
10862 Fruitland Dr.
Studio City 91604

Works with actors, musicians, writers, directors, and producers. They offer full service business management including financial planning, bills, taxes, investments, and contract review. They work on a percentage basis.

SAMUEL B. MOSES, C.P.A. (310) 395-9922
429 Santa Monica Blvd. #710 FAX (310) 395-3385
Santa Monica 90401
smosescpa@aol.com

Offers complete business management and tax services to actors and other persons in the Industry. Also offers accounting and consulting services. Mr. Moses began his career with Arthur Andersen & Co.

NANAS, STERN, BIERS, NEINSTEIN & CO., LLP (310) 273-2501
9454 Wilshire Blvd., 4th Fl. FAX (310) 859-0374
Beverly Hills 90212
www.nsbn.com

A business management and accounting that firm works with actors and other Industry professionals. Will take tax-only clients.

OWEN & DE SALVO COMPANY (818) 754-6370
5141 Colfax Avenue FAX (818) 763-6556
North Hollywood 91601

Works with Industry professionals providing accounting, business management, and financial planning. Services range from simple tax returns to full business management, including paying bills, preparing financial statements, coordinating insurance, maintaining "loan out" corporations, financial records, and tax returns. Fees are structured on an hourly basis and a percentage basis.

HERSH PANITCH & COMPANY, INC. (818) 999-2530
21243 Ventura Blvd., Ste. 101 FAX (818) 999-6935
Woodland Hills 91364

They handle Industry professionals who have an income of at least $100K per year. Full managerial services that include payment of bills, tax returns, investments, etc. Small firm, over 20 years in business. They have an east coast office.

PERRY & NEIDORF (310) 550-1254
9720 Wilshire Blvd., 3rd Fl. FAX (310) 550-2039
Beverly Hills 90212

This full service business management firm takes on new clients by referral only. They work on a percentage basis. Medium sized firm, over 25 years in business.

PRICE WATERHOUSE COOPERS (213) 356-6000
350 S. Grand Ave., 49th Fl. FAX (213) 830-8490
Los Angeles 90071
www.pricewaterhousecoopers.com

This business management and CPA firm's clients usually have very high incomes. The charge for the initial consultation depends on the situation and the fee structure is generally based on the time expended. They will sometimes take tax-only clients. Large firm, over 100 years in business. Branches world-wide.

RODGERS ACCOUNTANCY CORPORATION (310) 201-6523
10100 Santa Monica Blvd. FAX (310) 201-6589
Ste. 1060
Los Angeles 90067

They offer customized financial management for people in the Industry that includes bill payments, investments, and other personal care. Will take tax-only clients. Medium sized firm.

SHAPIRO AND CO. (310) 278-2303
9229 Sunset Blvd., Ste. 607 FAX (310) 278-2306
Los Angeles 90069

This full service firm specializes in business management. Services include bookkeeping, tax returns, and accounting. They work on a percentage basis and will take tax-only clients. Small firm, over 18 years in business.

SINGER, LEWAK, GREENBAUM & GOLDSTEIN (310) 477-3924
10960 Wilshire Blvd., Ste. 1100 FAX (310) 478-6070
Los Angeles 90024
www.slgg.com

This full service business management and CPA firm that does tax work, and post production accounting. No charge for the initial consultation. Branches in Santa Ana and Ontario, CA.

JERRY B. SWARTZ ACCOUNTANCY CORP. (310) 278-9944
9595 Wilshire Blvd., Ste. 1020
Beverly Hills 90212

Full service business management and accounting services are offered. They will sometimes take tax-only clients. Small firm.

TROUBLESHOOTERS INC. (310) 454-6001
881 Alma Real Dr., Ste. 203
Pacific Palisades 90272

A full service business management firm with certified financial planners that offers portfolio advisement and goal planning. An initial meeting is required to determine compatibility and the degree of management needed. They offer short-term planning as well as long-term.

TURNER ACCOUNTANCY (310) 273-4858
9200 Sunset Blvd., Ste. 701
Los Angeles 90069

This business management firm works with actors, musicians, writers, producers, and directors. They can be approached anytime of the year. Fees are on a percentage basis.

LEONARD WEISSBACH RIFF ENTERTAINMENT GROUP (818) 349-7763
17127 Gledhill FAX (818) 349-9399
Northridge 91325
www.business-affairs.com
lenacct@earthlink.net

Business management, financial planning, and real estate investment are offered. They believe the most common mistake actors make in regard to their finances is improper budgeting and not having a business manager to advise them. They feel an actor needs a business manager when they are making $100K annually. Will take tax-only clients.

WHITE, ZUCKERMAN, WARSAVSKY, LUNA & WOLF (818) 981-4226 (310) 276-7831
14455 Ventura Blvd., 3rd Fl. FAX (818) 981-4278
Sherman Oaks 91423
www.wzwlw.com
gmgab@wzwlw.com

Offers Management/Wealth Management services to actors, musicians, writers, producers, directors and composers to assist in managing their financial resources (personal and family goals). Services include personal bookkeeping and bill paying services, cash management services, investment advisory services, insurance, retirement and estate planning and traditional tax and accounting services emphasizing tax minimization.

Business Managers

WISEMAN AND BURKE (818) 247-1007
206 S. Brand Blvd. FAX (818) 247-1861
Glendale 91204
www.wiseman-burke.com

Wiseman and Burke is a small full service financial management company focusing on highly personalized services primarily to actors, actresses, directors, producers and musicians. They work on a percentage basis, hourly fee or retainer.

WOOD & FREEMAN BUSINESS MANAGEMENT (323) 469-5196
2018 N. Vine St.
Hollywood 90068

This firm specializes in business management, taxes, and investments. Small firm, 70 years in business.

Personal Managers

Personal managers are most useful to an actor who works regularly, though the right manager could be beneficial to an actor just starting out. Your manager may be responsible for overall career guidance, but you should have clear, defined goals and keep them on track. Find out who manages actors whose career choices you admire or ask colleagues for recommendations and try to interview at least three for contrast. You want a manager with sound judgment and the respect of the agents, casting directors and producers they work with. Be sure to discuss compensation. Typically mangers take a 15% commission from your earnings but this can vary. Watch out for anyone asking for money up front or insisting you only use their teachers or photographers. Unfortunately, state law does not govern personal managers so you need to be very careful with your selection and diligent about staying on top of their activities.

ACRONYM ENTERTAINMENT (310) 247-9119
8899 Beverly Blvd., Ste. 510
Los Angeles 90048

Laina Cohn and Emily Bugg handle actors, children, comedians, voice-over artists, models, musicians and producers. Submissions by referral only.

ALLMAN RAY MANGEMENT (310) 440-5780
141 S. Barrington, Ste. E
Los Angeles 90049

Danielle Allman handles actors by referral only.

ARTIST CIRCLE ENTERTAINMENT (310) 275-6330
8955 Norma Pl.
Los Angeles 90069

Represents established actors. Not looking for new actors at this time. No unsolicited submissions.

ARTISTS INTERNATIONAL (800) 350-1602 089/2311 3873
23151 Plaza Pointe Dr. #110
Laguna Hills 92653
shannonandco@earthlink.net

Management and packaging of actors/actress 18-35. Accepts photo/resume submissions by mail only from both union and non union. No phone calls please.

ASSOCIATED ARTISTS (323) 852-1972
6399 Wilshire Blvd., Ste. 211 FAX (323) 852-0141
Los Angeles 90048
www.associatedartistsmgmt.com

Melissa Birnstein develops, maintains and accelerates the actor's career. She asks for a referral prior to interviewing and has an emphasis on marketing and publicizing the career of the actor. Looking for unstoppable, highly motivated and creative actors.

MARILYN ATLAS MANAGEMENT (310) 278-5047
8899 Beverly Blvd., Ste. 704 FAX (310) 278-5289
West Hollywood 90048

Works with established actors and up and coming actors with credits by Industry recommendation only. She also handles established writers and directors. Submissions are by recommendation only. Ms. Atlas and/or Elizabeth Lopez keep a small client list but do attend plays and attend showcases if and when time permits. No soliciting.

DAVID BELENZON MANAGEMENT, INC. (COPM) (619) 462-6400
P.O. Box 3819
La Mesa 91944
www.belenzon.com

Specializes in variety artists, some actors, union and non-union talent of all levels. Accepts pictures and resumes, DVDs and tapes. Does not see scenes in the office but does attend showcases, screenings, and occasionally plays.

IRA BELGRADE (323) 938-3800
5850-E W. Third St.
Los Angeles 90036

Will accept tapes and DVDs nothing is returnable. He will call if interested. Finds young people and helps develop them.

JAY BERNSTEIN PRODUCTIONS (310) 851-2126
P.O. Box 1148 FAX (310) 858-1607
Beverly Hills 90213
www.jaybernstein.com

Handles all levels of union actors including newcomers. Sees new people through recommendation only. Prefers that actors approach them by sending a picture and resume in the mail. Attends showcases, screenings, and plays on occasion. Over 20 years in business, small company, 1 manager. DGA, WGA, AMPAS, Television Academy, Publicists Association, AFTRA, SAG and Producers Guild member.

SUE BERNSTEIN MANAGEMENT (818) 502-8195
2552 N. Vermont
Los Angeles 90027
bernsteinmgt@earthlink.net

Sue Bernstein handles mostly established actors/actresses or established up and coming adults. Photos and resumes are welcome by mail. No drop-offs. Also handles children.

BLACKWOOD ENTERTAINMENT (818) 264-1932
17555 Ventura Blvd., Ste. 200 FAX (818) 264-1938
Encino 91316

7928 Owensmouth Ave.
Canoga Park 91304
www.talentmanagers.org
blkwoodent@aol.com

Management and Production – Music, Film and TV represents actors, singers, models and writers. Accepts mailed submissions and attends showcases, plays and screening.

JANE BLOOM & ASSOC. (760) 200-1199

Handles select list of young adults/adults, well trained, theatre experience preferred. Referrals preferred. Will accept mailed submissions. No tapes or DVDs. Will attend plays, showcases, and screenings. Ms. Bloom also directs and coaches. Please no sealed envelopes! Also handles writers. Union only.

BREAKTHRU MANAGEMENT (323) 874-1648
3575 Cahuenga Blvd. West Ste. 360
Los Angeles 90068

Represents actors commercially and theatrically. Lin Milano asks that submissions be made via mail only, no phone calls. She is seeking talent with recent TV/film credits only.

BRILLSTEIN/GREY
ENTERTAINMENT CO. (310) 275-6135
9150 Wilshire Blvd., Ste. 350 FAX (310) 275-6180
Beverly Hills 90212

Handles established union talent, actors, comedians, and some writers. Sees new people through recommendation only. Does attend showcases, screenings, and plays on occasion.

THE BROKAW CO. (310) 273-2060
9255 Sunset Blvd., Ste. 804 FAX (310) 276-4037
Los Angeles 90069
www.brokawcompany.com

Primarily works with musicians, TV personalities, and established union actors. Does not accept submissions unless an actor has exceptional professional experience. Will attend showcases and plays. Places emphasis on public relations and immediate publicity. Over 20 years in business, small company.

BUTTERKNIFE ENTERTAINMENT (310) 289-1700
8721 Santa Monica Blvd., Ste. 37
West Hollywood 90069
www.butterknife-ent.com

Handles recording artists and actors. Will attend screenings and showcases and sees new people by referral only. Union only.

CALLIOPE (323) 343-9823
TALENT MANAGEMENT COMPANY (310) 244-1744
101 N. Victory Blvd., Ste. L-267
Burbank 91502
www.calliopetalent.com
calliopesa@sbcglobal.net

Calliope specializes in representing trained, skilled professional talent and secures agency representation for nearly all. Calliope regularly produces showcases for its talent with agents and casting directors. The CEO of Calliope has an M.A, B.A., A.A. and A.A.S. in TV/film. Calliope also has an office in Texas.

CENTRAL ARTISTS (818) 557-8284
3310 W. Burbank Blvd. FAX (818) 557-8348
Burbank 91505
www.centralartists.com
centralartists@centralartists.com

Management company licensed by the state of California to represent talent for Print, Commercial and Theatrical.

CHANCELLOR ENTERTAINMENT
BOB MARCUCCI (310) 474-4521
10600 Holman Ave., Ste. 1 FAX (310) 470-9273
Los Angeles 90024
www.chancellorentertainment.com
info@chancellorentertainment.com

Reviews unsolicited pictures and resumes and VHS tapes. Attends showcases, plays, and screenings. Will see monologues and scenes in the office. All ages and ranges.

CHEATHAM, GREENE & COMPANY (323) 769-5561 (323) 463-0420
P.O. Box 27742
Los Angeles 90027

Handles all levels of union actors and a select group of writers, authors, directors, musicians and comedians. This small company (two managers) sees new people through recommendation only though they attend screenings, showcases and plays on occasion.

VINCENT CIRRINCONE ASSOCIATES (310) 854-0533
8721 Sunset Blvd., Ste. 205
Los Angeles 90069
www.vincentcirricione.com

Vincent Cirrincione and Anna Liza Recto represent actors, writers and young adults. They accept mailed submissions and are open to attending showcases.

CLUB BEVERLY HILLS (310) 274-6051
8306 Wilshire Blvd., #279 FAX (310) 274-7855
Beverly Hills 90211
www.club-beverlyhills.com
dreams@club-beverlyhills.com

Established in 1979 by Robert and Rose Clements. CBH represents actors and entertainers between the ages of 18 to 91+. Prefers union actors, but will accept non-union actors, if the actor is in the process of obtaining his union membership. CBH represents less than 20 people and they will attend showcases, plays and screenings and also review demo tapes. CBH offers a complete imaging and development program; and provides a full publicity, public relations, advertising and marketing system, including photography, resumes, bios, voice-over production, ad design, press releases and press kit for their clients. They will act as your spokesperson and provide free consultation. CBH takes pride in their ability to give that personal touch and a family environment that is necessary for the success of their client's careers. CBH has direct contact with agents, producers and directors. They are dedicated and expect the same. Unsolicited pictures and resumes accepted. Will see people by appointment only.

CONNECTION III
ENTERTAINMENT CORP. (323) 653-3400
8489 W. 3rd. St.
Los Angeles 90048

Represents talent for music, TV and film specializing in young performers age 4-21 for all areas. They handle comedians and writers for TV and film, and bands, solo artists, and songwriter/producers for music. Open to non-union actors 21 or younger. They will review unsolicited photos, resumes, and audio and video tapes with SASE. They attend showcases, screenings, plays, and clubs. Will see monologues and scenes in the office.

COPPAGE COMPANY (818) 980-8806
5411 Camellia Ave.
North Hollywood 91601
coppage@aol.com

Represents actors and writers by Industry referral only.

MGC/CUSHMAN ENTERTAINMENT GROUP (818) 980-6215
10947 Bloomfield Ave., Ste. 205 FAX (818) 980-1803
Studio City 91602
mgc-ceg@juno.com

Works with union actors (teens, young adults and adults) as well as writers and singers (pop, country, R&B). Actors must have very strong network credits (co-starring and above), be a member of SAG and have agent representation. Clients mostly by referral. Looking for Latinos and African Americans (mainly female leading lady types) 18-21. Actors who meet the criteria may submit pictures and resumes or CDs. They will attend certain Industry showcases and plays. Former two-term president of C.O.P.M. (now known as Talent Managers Association (T.M.A.)

MARV DAUER MANAGEMENT (310) 207-6884
11661 San Vicente Blvd., Ste. 104
Los Angeles 90049

Marvin Dauer handles established actors of all ages. Referrals preferred. Accepts submissions by mail only, no phone calls or faxes.

BEVERLEE DEAN MANAGEMENT (310) 652-7436
FAX (310) 652-9350

Primarily represents established union talent. Reviews unsolicited pictures and resumes and VHS tapes. Attends showcases, plays, and screenings and will see scenes and monologues in the office on occasion.

RON DEBLASIO MANAGEMENT (323) 933-9977
740 N. La Brea, 1st Fl. FAX (323) 933-0633
Hollywood 90038
www.sdmmusic.com

Works with established union actors. Prefers written submissions only. Sees prospective clients through referral only.

RICHARD DELANCY & ASSOC. (818) 760-3110
4741 Laurel Canyon Blvd. FAX (818) 760-1382
Ste. 100
Valley Village 91607
www.delancy.com

Handles all ages and levels of union actors. Reviews unsolicited submissions from late teenagers and young adults, union and non-union. Sees new people strictly by referral. Reviews DVDs and tapes by request only. Sees scenes and monologues and attends showcases, screenings, and plays.

DIROSA TALENT MANAGEMENT (310) 967-5285
311 N. Robertson Blvd., #505
Beverly Hills 90211
thelawyeractor@yahoo.com

Represents actresses and models between the ages of 18-30 for film, television, commercials, print, industrials, and documentary. Prefers SAG/AFTRA talent but will occasionally represent non-union talent. Accepts unsolicited pictures and resumes by mail or email and also attend plays and showcases. Louis DiRosa, Jr., worked as an actor and entertainment lawyer before becoming a personal manager. "The qualities I look for most are: beauty, enthusiasm, individuality, and presence."

DUPUY MANAGEMENT (COPM) (818) 241-6732
P.O. Box 9271 FAX (818) 957-2038
Glendale 91226

Pedro Dupuy handles established actor/writers who know exactly where they want to go in the business and on rare occasion he sees newcomers. Mr. Dupuy works only with powerful, business-minded artists who are uncompromising in what they give to the Industry. He accepts pictures, resumes and cover letters, but accepts tapes, DVDs, scripts and synopses by request only.

EDMONDS MANAGEMENT (323) 769-2444
1635 N. Cahuenga Blvd., 5th Fl.
Los Angeles 90028
www.edmondsent.com

Mainly handles established actors/actresses and celebrities as well as directors, screenwriters and television writers. Open to newcomers with excellent training. Prefers to see prospective clients through referral but will review unsolicited pictures and resumes. Attends showcases, plays and screenings. No drop-offs. No faxing over photos.

ENVOY ENTERTAINMENT (310) 689-9800
1640 S. Sepulveda Blvd. FAX (310) 689-9801
Ste. 530
Los Angeles 90025

Barbara Gale, Peter Donaldson, Elaina Deutsch and Amy Macnow handle actors, directors, producers and writers. Submissions by referral only.

MARTY ERLICHMAN (323) 653-1555
5670 Wilshire Blvd., Ste. 2400 FAX (323) 653-1593
Los Angeles 90036

Handles top celebrities, sees new people through recommendation only and rarely accepts submissions though he does attend plays and screenings on occasion.

ESI KIDS (310) 888-1128
6310 San Vicente Blvd., Ste. 340 FAX (310) 888-1127
Los Angeles 90048
www.theesinetwork.com

Works with top 10 Los Angeles agents specializing in babies, kids and teens. Will accept headshots and interested in clients fluent in Spanish and all ethnicities, babies through seniors.

FIRE COMM MANAGEMENT (818) 343-4202
17366 Chase St.
Northridge 91325

Rusty Feuer handles union actors under 20 years old of all levels. Reviews unsolicited pictures and resumes. DVDs and tapes by request only. Will see monologues and scenes in the office if interested.

THE FIRM (310) 860-8215
9465 Wilshire Blvd.
Beverly Hills 90212

By referral only.

FUTURE STARS MANAGEMENT **(818) 787-8685**
www.attell.com
hypnosis4you.net

A pipeline for children entering the field, Toni has placed many children including Jerry Messing ("Adams Family," "Freaks and Geeks," "Even Stevens," "Malcolm in the Middle" as well as 15 Jay Leno appearances) and Jill Spurgeon (12 national commercials and she's the Polaroid girl). Toni handles ages 5-24. She is looking for children with improvisational and comedic skills but who also have a flair for drama. A very small, select management company. Toni regularly writes a column called "The Biz."

JEFF GITLIN ENTERTAINMENT **(310) 553-0951**
1801 Avenue of the Stars **FAX (310) 553-0953**
Ste. 525
Los Angeles 90067
www.jeffgitlin.com

Jeff Gitlin represents actors, comedians, screenwriters and television writers. He accepts mailed submissions and prefers referrals. Jeff is open to attending showcases.

PHILLIP B. GITTELMAN **(323) 656-9215**
1221 N. Kings Rd. **FAX (323) 656-9184**
Penthouse Ste. #405
West Hollywood 90069
phildinner@earthlink.net

Handles all levels of union talent, open to newcomers. Works with actors, writers, producers and directors. Reviews unsolicited pictures, resumes, and DVDs and tapes.

MARIANNE GOLAN MANAGEMENT **(323) 653-1232**
651 N. Kilkea Dr. **FAX (323) 653-2326**
Los Angeles 90048

Handles actors. Some newcomers, but primarily has an established clientele. Rarely takes on non-union actors. Prefers not to receive unsolicited submissions, primarily works through referrals. Sees scenes and monologues on occasion. Will attend showcases, screenings and plays. She is more likely respond to an invitation than cold mailing. Actors would do best to approach her by referral. Over 15 years in business. Small company, 1 manager.

GOLDSTEIN MEDIA GROUP **(323) 658-6378**

Represents literary and theatrical talent as well as directors. New and established actors for film, television, and theatre. Collaborates with clients on creating successful. Incorporates producing experience and extensive background as a publicist. Happily attends plays professional mounted and performed.

JOAN GREEN MANAGEMENT **(323) 878-0484**
1836 Courtney Terrace
Los Angeles 90046

Works with all levels of union actors. Accepts pictures and resumes and, if they are interested, they will request a tape. Prefers submissions through the mail. Will see scenes or monologues on occasion and attends showcases, screenings and plays.

GSC MANAGEMENT **(310) 274-1694**
1905 N. Beverly Dr. **FAX (310) 274-1697**
Beverly Hills 90210

Geraldine S. Chuchian represents actors and young adults. Mailed submissions are accepted, please no phone calls, emails or faxes. Referrals preferred.

HALPERN MANAGEMENT **(310) 837-5566**
5225 Wilshire Blvd., #401
Los Angeles 90036

Joann Halpern and Chris Sherman handle adult actors and accept mailed submissions only. Headshot or 3/4 bodyshot and a resume. No tapes or DVDs.

HAND PRINT ENTERTAINMENT **(310) 481-4400**
1100 Glendon Ave., Ste. 1000 **FAX (310) 481-4419**
Los Angeles 90024

Handles union actors and some writers. Reviews unsolicited pictures and resumes, DVDs and tapes, they do not return tapes but they can be picked up. Prefers that actors approach them by mailing submissions. They will attend showcases, plays, and screenings and will only view monologues and scenes in the office if necessary to see an actor's work.

MICHAEL HARRAH JLO WEST **(818) 760-1895**
P.O. Box 8569
Universal City 91618

Michael Harrah handles all levels and ages from children through young adult who can play under 18. Open to talented newcomers, union and non-union. Usually sees prospective clients through referral. Written submissions with picture and resume, and DVDs and VHS tapes are accepted. No phone calls. Sees scenes and monologues in office on occasion. Attends showcases and plays. Over 35 years in business, 1 manager.

HECHT/HARMAN/VUKAS **(323) 654-6061**
P.O. Box 69919
Los Angeles 90069

Will not consider clients unless they have a minimum of three co-starring credits in episodic television.

HHR MANAGEMENT **(310) 474-3305**
8306 Wilshire Blvd., #533
Beverly Hills 90211
www.hhrmanagement.com
info@hhrmanagement.com

Specializing in career development. Accepts pictures and resumes via mail only. No drop offs or phone calls.

HIT AGENCY MANAGEMENT GROUP **(310) 470-1939**
www.ottofelix.com
ottoffelix@aol.com

HAPPI (Handicapped Artists, Performer & Partners, Inc.) International Talent (HIT) was formed because of the growing number of disabled performers. Hundreds of HAPPI members disabled and able-bodied alike have been discovered and employed in numerous film, radio, television and stage productions by performing in HAPPI showcases. Jack Francis and Jan Thompson, managers are open to talented newcomers.

IMPACT TALENT GROUP **(818) 557-7754** **(818) 753-4040**
244 N. California
Burbank 91505

Represents actors theatrically by Industry referral only.

INDUSTRY ENTERTAINMENT **(310) 954-9000**
955 S. Carrillo Dr., Ste. 300
Los Angeles 90048

Highly select client list includes Angelina Jolie. No submissions. By referral only.

JAMES/LEVY/JACOBSON MANAGEMENT (818) 955-7070
3500 W. Olive Ave., Ste. 1470 FAX (818) 955-7073
Burbank 91505

Handles union actors of all levels. Accepts pictures and resumes. DVDs and tapes by request only. Attends showcases, screenings and plays and will accept flyers and invitations.

JDS TALENT MANAGEMENT (661) 298-4050
15901 Condor Ridge Rd. FAX (661) 298-8655
Santa Clarita 91387
jdstalent@aol.com

Specializing in children 4-12 All levels, union and non-union. Will attend showcases, screenings and plays. Accepts mailed submissions only. No phone calls.

K.S.T. MANAGMENT (KELI SQUIRES-TAYLOR) (323) 938-7729
P.O. Box 361521
Los Angeles 90036
www.actorsuccess.net

Keli Squires Taylor maintains a small, very selective client list. Currently not taking on any "development" clients. Will accept submissions from union talent with substantial guest star, series regular and film credits. Also professional comedy and improv actors.

KID STUFF MANAGEMENT (310)-770-1821
P.O. Box 2172 FAX (818) 761-9269
Toluca Lake 91602
kdixonla@aol.com

Kevin Dixon handles children age 6-17, accepts mailed submissions and is open to talented newcomers. Kevin attends showcases, plays and screenings.

KJAR AND ASSOCIATES (818) 760-0321
10732 Riverside Dr., Ste. 222
Toluca Lake 91602

Handles established actors with credits, some newcomers, children, and young actors under 21. Prefers mailed submissions for actors.

EILEEN KOCH AND COMPANY (310) 441-1000

Handles all levels of established union talent specializing in young adults age 6-18. Will only review mailed pictures and resumes, DVDs and tapes. Will see monologues and scenes in the office and they attend showcases, screenings, and plays. Also does Public Relations and has a musical division.

L.A. KIDZ (818) 766-4441
4924 Vineland Ave.
North Hollywood 91601

Handles from age newborn to age 17 and will accept pictures. Looking for twins and triplets.

LAPIDES ENTERTAINMENT ORGANIZATION (818) 986-8040
14724 Ventura Blvd., Penthouse
Sherman Oaks 91403

Handles established, union talent only and specializes in comics and hosting Accepts pictures and resumes and DVDs by referral only. Prefers to be approached by mail. Open to attending showcases, plays and screenings.

LEMACK & COMPANY MANAGEMENT (323) 655-7272
221 S. Gale Dr., Ste. 403
Beverly Hills 90211
blemack@thebusinessofacting.com

Represents a roster of established actors.

LHB MANAGEMENT (818) 506-4774
8033 W. Sunset Blvd., Ste. 1057
Los Angeles 90046
www.lhb-mgt.com

Represents great-looking, talented actors. For ten years LHB has focused on young talent in television and film. Exceptional talent with contemporary looks and attitudes, and the firm guidance of top management people combine to provide a unique environment for talent growth and a reliable, upbeat resource for the television, film, and media Industry. LHB guides the careers of the cutest, talented and brightest kids, teens and the hottest, youngest looking young adults in the Industry today. LHB talent is working in national commercials, television sitcoms, feature films and doing voiceovers in animation series. Lola H. Blank personally works to ensure that "no stone is left unturned" in finding the perfect marriage of ability and skill, looks and energy, that conveys the messages and needs of the director and producer.

KATHY LYMBEROPOULOS (661) 297-8000
P.O. Box 803205
Los Angeles 91380

Works with celebrities, guest stars, established talent, children and recording artists. Will rarely develop new talent. Reviews unsolicited pictures and resumes and VHS tapes and attends showcases, plays and screenings occasionally.

TAMI LYNN MANAGEMENT AND PRODUCTION (COPM) (818) 888-8264
20411 Chapter Dr. FAX (818) 888-8267
Woodland Hills 91364
tamilynn@webtv.net
tamilynn8264@aol.com

Producer and Manager: Tami Lynn. Producer and Writer: Kim Marriner and Marc Alexander. Tami is past president of the Conference of Personal Managers. No submissions.

LEE MAGID MANAGEMENT (LMI PRODUCTIONS) (323) 463-5998
P.O Box 532
Malibu 90265

Will consider all levels of union and non-union talent. Accepts pictures and resumes and non-returnable audio or video tapes. Occasionally attends showcases and plays. Specifically looking for musical and comedic talent.

MAIER MANAGEMENT (310) 860-0099
117 N. Robertson Blvd. FAX (310) 860-0098
Los Angeles 90048
www.maiermanagement.com

Ted Maier has been in the entertainment business for 10+ years. Jacque Pedersen has extensive experience in film, TV, commercials, print, infomercials and music videos.

MANAGEMENT 360 (310) 272-7000
9111 Wilshire Blvd. FAX (310) 272-0084
Beverly Hills 90210

Manages actors and directors and works with all ethnic groups.

They attend plays and showcases and accept mailed photos and resumes, but no dropffs and no follow up calls.

THE MANAGEMENT TEAM (310) 276-7173
9507 Santa Monica Blvd. FAX (310) 276-5811
Ste. 304
Beverly Hills 90210

Works with newcomers. Call first and then submit picture and resume and a tape. Attends showcases, screenings and plays.

THE MARCELLI CO. (818) 760-8008
11246 Valley Spring Lane FAX (818) 760-8005
Studio City 91602

Handles all levels, union and non-union. Reviews pictures and resumes and VHS tapes. Attends showcases, plays and screenings.

M.E.G. MANAGEMENT (323) 932-6500
15303 Ventura Blvd., Ste. 900 FAX (323) 932-6599
Sherman Oaks 91403

Representing working actors. Age range emancipated to 35 years. Small roster, highly selective. Looking for young actors with star potential, will accept unsolicited pictures and resumes but prefers a recommendation. Will request a tape if interested.

MIDWEST TALENT MANAGEMENT, INC. (818) 765 3785
4821 Lankershim Blvd. FAX (818) 765 2903
Ste. F, # 149
North Hollywood 91601
www.midwesttalent.com
talktous@midwesttalent.com

Betty McCormick Aggas is the founder. Agent for 17 years and a manager for 8 years. Betty is First Vice President of the Talent Managers Association. Mark Blake is an Associate Manager. Internship programs are available. Betty and Mark look for talent that is positive, enjoys life and dedicated to their craft. They attend showcases and review pictures, resumes and demo tapes weekly. Please no follow up calls. If they do not call you, your submission is passed on to other managers in the Talent Managers Association. More information can be found on their website.

APRIL MILLS MANAGEMENT (818) 667-9529
P.O. Box 1983
Burbank 91602
millsmgnt@aol.com

Handles all levels of actors; including children. Will see newcomers. Accepts pictures, resumes, and VHS tapes. Does attend showcases, screenings, and plays with invitations through the mail. Prefers not to cross age. No phone calls. Will call if interested.

MMC ENTERTAINMENT DANCE DIRECTIONS (818) 769-6316
P.O. Box 46544
Los Angeles 90046

Handles choreographers, actors, singers and dancers for theatre, film and TV. Teenagers through young adults. Will accept mailed pictures and resumes but tapes by request only. No follow up calls. Does attend showcases, plays and screenings.

JAIME MONROY (310) 273-6508
280 S. Beverly Dr., #203 FAX (310) 273-6728
Beverly Hills 90212
www.monroyentertainment.com

A 25 year veteran of the TV Industry, Jaime focuses on comedic actresses and represents stars and model types with a flair for comedy.

CAROL MORRIS MANAGEMENT (619) 390-6710

Carol Morris has been a manager for over 29 years and is open to theatrically trained newcomers. She also handles comics, writers and directors and has a very select list of actors. No children or minors, union only. Must be trained and in class.

MP MANAGEMENT (714) 965-6771
showbizpitt@aol.com

Marlene Peroutka and Associates created MP Management over 20 years ago. MP Management is comprised of a staff with backgrounds in casting, agenting, producing and personal management. They represent working children and teens with a few celebrity adults. Clients have starred in thousands of feature films, television shows, Broadway productions, made for television movies and commercials. Marlene Peroutka is also the executive producer of three television series.

NEBULA MANAGEMENT (323) 664-8244
P.O. Box 29490 FAX (323) 372-3784
Los Angeles 90027
www.nebulamanagement.com
info@nebulamanagement.com

Clients include actors, actresses, newscasters, comedians, voice-over talent, models and writers. TMA member. Submit pictures and resumes by mail only. Please, no phone calls.

NIAD MANAGEMENT (818) 981-2505
15030 Ventura Blvd., #19-860 FAX (818) 386-2082
Sherman Oaks 91403
www.niadmanagement.com
queries@niadmanagement.com

Wendy Niad handles writers, directors and actors and will see newcomers by Industry referral only.

ON BOY ENTERTAINMENT (310) 689-9800

Works with established actors and stars. Reviews submissions by referral only. Attends showcases, plays and screenings.

PAGE MANAGEMENT (TMA) (818) 703-7328 (818) 725-3483
P.O. Box 573040
Tarzana 91357
jeanpage@earthlink.net

Handles children ranging in age from infancy through teenagers. Twins, triplets, all ethnics. Submit picture or snapshot with SASE. Conducts general interviews one Saturday or Sunday every other month.

PATCO/PAT LYNN (310) 472-7950
1551 S. Robertson Blvd.
Los Angeles 90035

Handles actors who are age 65 or over who have a minimum of 20 years stage experience including work in Waiver theatre. No longer takes new clients.

PERSONAL MANAGERS

RAW TALENT (310) 246-1100
9615 Brighton Way, Ste. 300 FAX (310) 246-2345
Beverly Hills 90210

Handles union actors, writers and directors.

LINDA REITMAN MANAGEMENT (323) 852-9091
(323) 259-3611
859 Sierra Bonita FAX (323) 852-9094
Los Angeles 90046

Linda Reitman handles actors, experienced writers, producers and directors. Actors should have film and/or TV experience with tape. She will accept mailed pictures, resumes and tapes if there is a SASE. No unsolicited scripts and follow up calls only when requested. She occasionally attends plays, showcases and screenings.

RIBISI ENTERTAINMENT GROUP (213) 388-2118
3278 Wilshire Blvd., Ste. 702
Los Angeles 90010

Very select client list. No submissions. Not looking for any new clients.

GLEN ROSE PERSONAL MANAGEMENT (310) 788-0519
8899 Beverly Blvd., Ste. 918
Los Angeles 90048

Handles established talent. No submissions. Sees newcomers by referral only. No children but will handle young adults. Attends showcases, screenings and plays.

BILL SAMMETH ORGANIZATION (310) 275-6193
9255 Sunset Blvd., Ste. 600 FAX (310) 441-5111
Los Angeles 90069

Works primarily with established artists. Prefers no submissions.

SARI SHAPIRO PERSONAL MANAGEMENT (310) 575-4154
FAX (310) 575-4154

Handles actors, musicians, artists, painters, and writers by recommendation only. Will work with both union and non-union. New clients through referral only – no phone calls. See listing under IMAGE CONSULTANTS in the MARKETING section.

BOOH SCHUT AGENCY (818) 760-6669
11365 Sunshine Terrace
Studio City 91604

By referral only.

RICHARD SCHWARTZ MANAGEMENT (818) 783-9575
2934½ Beverly Glen Circle., Ste. 107
Bel Air 90077

Richard Schwartz and Stephen Arenholz primarily handle actors and some writers, directors, producers and musicians who are union and non-union. He will accept unsolicited pictures and resumes, DVDs and VHS tapes, but prefers mailed submissions with recommendations. He regularly attends plays, showcases and screenings.

SCREEN ARTISTS (818) 755-0026
12435 Oxnard St. FAX (818) 755- 0027
North Hollywood 91606

Patrick Hart has a long and varied show business background: he owned a legitimate theatre and produced over 120 productions and owned Screen Artists Agency for many years. He accepts pictures and resumes by mail only (please no drop offs) and will call if interested. Attends showcases.

SEEKERS MANAGEMENT (818) 225-0065
4909 Reforma Road
Woodland Hills 91364
seekersmgt@yahoo.com

Joe Fikes represents actors, bands, solo artists, comedians, screenwriters and television writers. He accepts electronic submissions from formally trained artists with a passion for their craft and dedication to success. Will attend showcases and screenings.

SHAPIRO/WEST & ASSOC., INC. (310) 278-8896
141 El Camino Dr., Ste. 205
Beverly Hills 90212

Howard Shapiro, George West, Amy Hyatt, and Shelly Turner-Banks accept pictures and resumes. If they are interested they will request a tape. The tape can consist of commercials, taped stage performances, and/or film or TV. They attend showcases and plays.

SHARK ARTISTS, INC.
DEBBIE DESTETEFANO (310) 503-2121
P.O. Box 88225
Los Angeles 90009

Reviews submissions by Industry referral only. Works with established actors, directors, writers, musicians and stars. Represents unstoppable, highly motivated and creative individuals to deepen and accelerate the career. No unsolicited submissions. Innovative drive, caring and creative leadership, intensely focused.

ALAN SIEGEL ENTERTAINMENT (310) 278-8400
345 N. Maple Dr., Ste. 375 FAX (310) 278-8498
Beverly Hills 90210

Open to new talent, but is extremely selective. Requests that there be no phone calls. Will accept mailed submissions and if interested they will contact you. Submissions will not be returned but will be kept on file. Sees clients mostly through referrals.

BLAIR SILVER & COMPANY ENTERTAINMENT MANAGEMENT (310) 546-4669
P. O. Box 3188
Manhattan Beach 90266
blairsilver@aol.com

True personal career management for dedicated professionals: actors, animators, athletes, composers, directors, martial artists, models, multimedia gaming artists, producers, screenwriters. Considers name talent to union newcomers. Submit photo, resume, calls OK.

STEIN ENTERTAINMENT GROUP (323) 822-1400
11271 Ventura Blvd., PMB 477
Studio City 91604

1351 Crescent Heights Blvd., #312
West Hollywood 90048
www.steinentertainment.com
info@steinentertainment.com

President: T.J. Stein. Representing children through young adults for film, TV and commercials, they attend plays and showcases regularly with invitations through the mail and they view tapes and DVDs through referrals only. Visit the website for more information.

STERLING/WINTERS CO. (310) 557-2700
10900 Wilshire Blvd., Ste 1550 FAX (310) 557-1722
Los Angeles 90024

Handles mostly established actors and is open to newcomers. Written submissions with picture and resume and tape. Will discuss seeing scenes at time of follow up. Attends showcases and plays.

STUDIO TALENT GROUP (310) 393-8004
1328 12th St. FAX (310) 393-2473
Santa Monica 90401
www.studiotalentgroup.com
stgactor@gte.net

STG is a unique combination of a caring talent manager with the ability to submit and book talent as a licensed California talent agent. As a past director of the Talent Managers Association, Phil Brock and his staff have provided caring personal talent management to their clients for over seven years and represent performers for the MP/TV/Theatre/Commercial areas. As a former actor and member of the Academy of Television Arts and Sciences, Phil brings empathy and an immense amount of knowledge to his representation of STG clients. STG clients work on Broadway, N.Y. and L.A. soaps, guest star and series regulars on many series and local theatre. In addition STG clients book many commercials through Studio Talent representation. Union submissions are preferred however talented newcomers may also submit their packages by mail or e-mail with no follow up submissions. You may obtain further information by accessing the STG website.

THE SUCHIN COMPANY (818) 505-0044
12747 Riverside Dr., Ste. 208 FAX (818) 505-0110
Valley Village 91607-3333

Handles actors with some credits. Mostly referrals. Prefers written submissions with picture and resume and DVD. Handles actors for theatrical commercial and some children, comedians and models.

TALENT MANAGERS ASSOCIATION (310) 205-8495
4804 Laurel Canyon Blvd., #611 FAX (818) 765-2903
Valley Village 91607
www.talentmanagers.org
info@talentmanagers.org

Not for profit organization started in 1954. This group of professional managers are dedicated to being ethical and abide by the TMA code of ethics.

STACEY TESTRO INTERNATIONAL (323) 848-7848
8265 Sunset Blvd., #102 FAX (323) 848-7868
West Hollywood 90046
www.sti.com.au

Management/Production Company with International offices. Will consider talented newcomers, but no personal dropoffs, deliveries or follow up calls.

THIRD HILL ENTERTAINMENT, INC. (310) 786-1936
195 S. Beverly Dr., Ste. 400 FAX (310) 786-1939
Beverly Hills 90212

Toni Benson and Amanda Hendon handle actors, screenwriters and young adults. They accept unsolicited mailed submissions only, no phone calls or faxes.

ROZ TILLMAN MANAGEMENT (TMA) (818) 985-3514
11054 Ventura Blvd., Ste. 289 FAX (818) 505-0481
Studio City 91604
roztill@pacbell.net

Primarily handles adult union actors, but is open to talented non-union newcomers age 12-24. Accepts pictures and resumes. DVDs and tapes with SASE by request after a written submission. Attends showcases and plays. Please, no faxes.

RONALD WALDEN & ASSOC., INC. (310) 552-3174
2 Century Plaza, Ste. 1080
Los Angeles 90067

Handles all levels of union and non-union actors and models. Accepts pictures and resumes, DVDs and tapes. Sees scenes and attends showcases or plays occasionally. Also has a TV/film production subsidiary.

MICHAEL WALLACH MANAGEMENT (310) 820-9926
res181cw@verizon.net

A firm specializing in the representation of actors, casting directors, producers and writers. Mr. Wallach's former positions include Director of Business Affairs at Columbia Pictures Television; Associate Counsel in the Legal Department of Motown Records and Capital Records and Associate Director of Business Affairs at RCA Records in New York City. He is a licensed California talent agent.

MIMI WEBER MANAGEMENT LTD. (310) 474-0594
10717 Wilshire Blvd., Penthouse
Los Angeles 90024

Established actors only. Not accepting any new clients. Prefers no submissions. New clients are mostly through referrals.

DAVID WESTBERG MANAGEMENT (323) 874-5544
1604 N. Vista St. FAX (323) 874-7757
Hollywood 90046

Works with actors of all levels. Reviews unsolicited pictures and resumes. DVDs and tapes by request only. Prefers to be approached initially with a phone call. Attends showcases, plays, and screenings.

WHITTAKER ENTERTAINMENT (818) 766-4441
4924 Vineland Ave.
North Hollywood 91601

This management company handles adults only for theatrical, commercial and some literary projects. They require a 1-year commitment.

DAN WILEY MANAGEMENT (323) 876-5824
2341 Zorada Ct.
Los Angeles 90046

Primarily handles comedians and some working actors through referral only. No submissions of any kind are accepted.

WILLIAMS UNLIMITED
HOLLY WILLIAMS (818) 905-1058
5010 Buffalo Ave. FAX (818) 995-1904
Sherman Oaks 91423
hollyarts@aol.com

Primarily handles children 6 to 25 years of age. Accepts mailed pictures and resumes and tapes of children. They keep submissions on file. Does attend showcases and plays.

BONNIE YOUNG PERSONAL MGT. (323) 969-0162
1534 N. Formosa Ave., Ste. 6
Hollywood 90046

Handles union actors of all levels and accepts pictures and resumes but no tapes. Will see scenes and monologues in the office and does attend showcases, screenings and plays.

Public Relations

No one knows who you are or what you are doing without publicity. A publicists' basic responsibilities include preparing written biographies of their client to send to the press; keeping contacts in the media aware of any favorable newsworthy developments in their client's lives; taking requests from newspapers, magazines and TV talk shows that want to interview their clients; and pitching story ideas about clients to these same requesters. The publicist can also decide how the public should see the client and proceed accordingly to create that image. When selecting a publicist, as in other business choices, choose by reputation, personality and a mutual agreement on the way you want to be represented.

—"Acting is Everything" by Judy Kerr

ALINE MEDIA (310) 576-1808
1460 4th St., Ste. 205 FAX (310) 576-1809
Santa Monica 90401
www.alinemedia.com
411@alinemedia.com

Aline media is a full service public relations firm with expertise in the development and execution of media coverage, event planning, artist representation and brand marketing. They will work with new and emerging talent on a monthly retainer.

ARSLANIAN & ASSOC. (323) 465-0533
6671 Sunset Blvd., Ste. 1502 FAX (213) 465-9240
Hollywood 90028

Handles established talent. They prefer to be approached by mail. Over 20 years in business.

VICKI ARTHUR PUBLIC RELATIONS (818) 995-8130
P.O. Box 55728 FAX (818) 986-1504
Sherman Oaks 91413
www.hollywoodpublicity.com
vickiarthur@juno.com

Top Hollywood publicist and publicity consultant for over twenty years, and former Vice President of the Publicists Guild of America, Vicki Arthur specializes in promotion and publicity for producers, directors, actors, production companies, motion pictures, authors and entertainment professionals. Her clients have included: Hector Elizondo, Jodie Foster, Jessica Lange, Jane Curtin, Peter O'Toole, Edward James Olmos, American Playhouse, HBO, Universal Pictures, Paramount, MGM, Warner Brothers and many others. Full service agency, one-on-one consultations, publicity and promotion training and workshops.

JANE AYER PUBLIC RELATIONS (310) 581-1330
3205 Ocean Park Blvd. FAX (310) 581-1335
Ste. 240
Santa Monica 90405
www.janeayerpr.com
japr@janeayerpr.com

A full service entertainment and corporate public relations company.

BENDER/HELPER IMPACT (310) 473-4147
11500 W. Olympic Blvd. FAX (310) 478-4727
Ste. 655
Los Angeles 90064
www.bhimpact.com

Corporate and home entertainment only.

THE BLAINE GROUP (310) 360-1499
8665 Wilshire Blvd., Ste. 301 FAX (310) 360-1498
Beverly Hills 90211
www.blainegroupinc.com

A full service entertainment and corporate public relations company.

BLOCK KORENBROT
PUBLIC RELATIONS (323) 655-0593
8271 Melrose Ave., Ste. 115 FAX (323) 655-7302
Los Angeles 90046

Handles actors at various levels.

HENRI BOLLINGER ASSOCIATES (818) 784-0534
P.O. Box 57227 FAX (818) 789-8862
Sherman Oaks 91413
www.bollingerpr.com
info@bollinger.com

Will consider newcomers, but prefer that the actor have a current project. Specializes in working with individuals and TV and film projects. Contact them by phone. They mostly work on a monthly retainer basis, but can make arrangements on a per project basis if necessary.

MICHELLE BOLTON & ASSOCIATES (818) 990-4001
boltonpr@pacbell.net FAX (818) 990-5010

Public relations, marketing and special events.

BRAGMAN NYMAN CAFARELLI (310) 854-4800
8687 Melrose Ave., 8th Floor FAX (310) 854-4848
Los Angeles 90069
www.bncpr.com
info@bncpr.com

BNC is one of the leading marketing communications firms operating within the entertainment and lifestyle/pop culture arena. With offices in Los Angeles and New York and a staff of 130, BNC executes brand-based marketing programs, integrating such core competencies as event marketing, celebrity/influencer marketing and outreach, product integration, sponsorships, PR, promotion and total project management.

THE BROKAW COMPANY (310) 273-2060
9255 Sunset Blvd., Ste. 804 FAX (310) 276-4037
Los Angeles 90069
www.brokawcompany.com
brokawc@aol.com

They work with established name actors who have a current project and prefer to be approached by mail. They will accept phone calls if representation is needed for a specific project, but only on an emergency basis. Fees are per project. They believe actors need a publicist when they need to be promoted. Also a personal management firm.

DICK BROOKS UNLIMITED (760) 778-4246
1120 San Jacinto Way FAX (760) 778-1436
Palm Springs 92262
dick71@earthlink.net

Specializes in motion picture and television actors and productions, but will consider any level actor. A current project is not necessary but they prefer an actor to have previous theatrical work experience. Contact them by sending a picture and resume, a tape, or an invitation to a performance. The fee structure is flexible, and no time commitment is required. They believe actors need a publicist when they are working or have worked professionally.

BUMBLE WARD & ASSOCIATES (323) 655-8585
8383 Wilshire Blvd., Ste. 340 FAX (323) 655-8844
Beverly Hills 90211
www.bumbleward.com

A full service entertainment and corporate public relations company.

BURSON-MARSTELLER (310) 226-3000
1800 Century Park East FAX (310) 226-3030
Ste. 200
Los Angeles 90067
www.bm.com

Mostly handles well-established actors but will work with non-established actors if they have a specific project. The company specializes in corporate, sports and entertainment public relations. Fees are monthly and they prefer a 6 month time commitment. A full service agency with 8 publicists and 20-40 clients. Over 40 years in business.

BWR PUBLIC RELATIONS (310) 248-6105
9100 Wilshire Blvd., 6th Fl.
Beverly Hills 90212
www.ogilvypr.com

BWR Public Relations, a subsidiary of Ogilvy Public Relations Worldwide, handles well established actors, television shows, events, motion pictures and more.

ESME CHANDLEE (323) 962-5704
2967 Hollyridge Dr.
Los Angeles 90068

Works with established personalities.

CLUB BEVERLY HILLS (310) 274-6051
8306 Wilshire Blvd., #279 FAX (310) 274-7855
Beverly Hills 90211
www.club-beverlyhills.com
dreams@club-beverlyhills.com

Specializes in promotion, spokesperson, public relations and publicity for film, TV and actors. Photos and resumes accepted. The fee varies according to project. They feel actors need a publicist from the beginning of their careers. All accounts are handled personally but they will delegate specific areas to other experts. There is no consultation fee. They are also involved with a marketing and advertising networking within the Industry. Serving the Industry since 1979. See listing under PHOTOGRAPHERS in the MARKETING section for further information.

COSTELLO & COMPANY
PUBLIC RELATIONS (818) 842-9604
3604 W. Clark Ave. FAX (818) 558-3799
Burbank 91505
ccostello9@compuserve.com

They prefer actors who have a current project and specialize in all areas of entertainment PR, including junket tours and promotions. Contact by phone or fax. The company works on a monthly retainer fee basis.

DEVORAH CUTLER-RUBENSTEIN
THE ARTIST'S WORKSPACE (310) 943-4378
12210½ Nebraska Ave, Ste. 22
Los Angeles 90025
www.thescriptbroker.com
devo@thescriptbroker.com

As a former Columbia Pictures Studio Executive, Vice President of Marketing and Promotion, Executive Producer ("The Substitute 1 and 2") she will help you distinguish what is special about you and look to find how to utilize that in the marketing of your career. Together you will create a logo, letterhead, portfolio of your work and PR package that sizzles. In addition, you will launch a battle plan designed to get you your dream job. She puts her contacts on the line for presentations in meetings, self-promotion and audition/interview settings. "Devorah knows the 'scene' and has developed a strong reputation for launching careers and revitalizing passion when burnout has set in." Dolores Diehl, author, actor and improvisation teacher.

LORI DEWAAL & ASSOCIATES (323) 462-4122
7080 Hollywood Blvd. Ste. 515 FAX (323) 463-3792
Los Angeles 90028

Will work with all levels of actors. They take on people that they feel have potential. A current project and a monthly retainer are required.

FILM ADVISORY BOARD (323) 461-6541
Janet Stokes FAX (323) 469-8541
Executive Director
P.O. Box 9258
North Hollywood 91609

Handles established talent only. They prefer actors to approach them by mailing a picture and resume. Ms. Blythe is also the president of the Film Advisory Board.

GOLDSTEIN MEDIA GROUP (323) 658-6378
FAX (323) 658-5730

Works with actors, writers, directors and production personnel specializing in PR for movies. Handles all levels of union and non-union actors from newcomers to established. She prefers that actors approach by phone. Charges are either an hourly consulting fee or a monthly retainer. The time commitment required varies with individual clients. Ms. Goldstein has previously worked in New York and she is one of the few publicists whose clients work in 99 Seat Plan theatres as well as film and television. She also assists with resume composition and works with actors as a career coach. She has spoken at universities, Women in Film, the SAG Conservatory, DGA, and film festivals. Ms. Goldstein also has publicized films at the Sundance and Hamptons film festivals. 16 years in business. See listing for "Succeeding in L.A." under BUSINESS OF ACTING in the TRAINING section for further information.

GUTTMAN & ASSOCIATES (310) 246-4600
118 S. Beverly Dr., Ste. 201 FAX (310) 246-4601
Beverly Hills 90212

Works with actors, variety artists, singers, comedians, writers and directors. Will handle actors with a specific film or TV project and prefers the role to be above the 3rd or 4th lead on a typical show, but will consider all levels of talent. They prefer to be approached by agent or manager. Fees are on a monthly basis only and they generally require a 3 month commitment. Specific areas of an account are handled by experts. They also have a TV division and handle special events, art galleries, and books. Over 20 years in business.

HANSON & SCHWAM P.R. (310) 248-4488
9350 Wilshire Blvd., Ste. 315 FAX (310) 248-4499
Beverly Hills 90212

They work with all levels of actors and prefer to be approached by referral. A well established firm that has been in business for over 30 years.

I D PUBLIC RELATIONS (323) 822-4800
8409 Santa Monica Blvd. FAX (323) 822-4880
West Hollywood 90069
www.id-pr.com

Provides PR for actors. Call for more information.

JONAS PUBLIC RELATIONS (310) 656-3355
240 26th St., Ste. 3 FAX (310) 656-3365
Santa Monica 90402

Works with actors, variety artists, and specializes in working with comedians. Contact them by phone or mail. An actor should have a part in a feature or a TV role. 19 years in business.

EILEEN KOCH AND COMPANY (310) 441-1000
www.eileenkoch.com
staff@eileenkoch.com

A full service public relations firm that does special events and works with all types and levels of the entertainment business. They prefer to be approached by phone. Fees are monthly retainers and they prefer a 6 month time commitment. Over 13 years in business.

LEMACK & COMPANY PUBLIC RELATIONS/MANAGEMENT (323) 655-7272
221 S. Gale Dr., Ste. 403
Beverly Hills 90211
blemack@thebusinessofacting.com

Specializes in personality public relations.

EDWARD P. LOZZI & ASSOCIATES (310) 922-1200
9454 Wilshire Blvd., Ste. 600
Beverly Hills 90212
www.lozzipr.com
elp@lozzipr.com

A full service entertainment PR firm that works with all levels of performers and, under special circumstances, some newcomers. Also handles writers, directors, producers, authors, political campaigns, packaging, unit publicity, film and TV publicity and premiere events. They can be approached by phone or by mail. A specific project is helpful but not required. A monthly retainer is required as well as a 3 month time commitment. They believe an actor needs a publicist when a job comes up. Over 24 years in business. They have offices in Beverly Hills at CBS Studio City, and in New York and London. They were the press advance office for the White House from 1989-1993.

MUCH & HOUSE (323) 965-0852
8075 W. 3rd. St., Ste. 500 FAX (323) 965-0390
Los Angeles 90048
www.muchandhousepr.com

Works with actors, singers, comedians, writers, directors, choreographers and producers. They handle consistently working actors only. There is a minimum 3 month commitment and fees are on a monthly retainer basis. A medium sized firm with 5 or 6 accounts per executive. Over 20 years in business.

PARKER PUBLIC RELATIONS (818) 990-2252
5068 Amestoy Ave.
Encino 91316

Handles actors, comedians, athletes, artists, writers, musicians and producers of all levels. Contact them by phone. Actors do need to have a current or upcoming project. Charlotte believes it is important to take advantage of every opportunity to build your career. Over 15 years in business.

PATRICOLA/LUST, PUBLIC RELATIONS (323) 655-5150
8383 Wilshire Blvd., Ste. 530 FAX (323) 655-7223
Beverly Hills 90211

Works with actors, writers, directors, and producers of all levels. They prefer actors who have a substantial role in a play, series, movie of the week or film and prefer to be contacted through agents. They require a 3 month commitment and fees are month-to-month. A medium sized firm with 4-5 account executives on staff and they usually have 60 clients. A full service firm that has been in business for 17 years.

PMK HBH, INC. (310) 289-6200
700 N. San Vicente Blvd. FAX (310) 289-6677
West Hollywood 90069

Works with all levels of actors, also handles directors, producers and legit theatre projects. Can be approached by phone or mail. Actors should have a current project. They work with established TV, film, and theatre actors and require a monthly retainer. Over 20 years in business. East coast affiliate.

THE ROBBINS GROUP (818) 776-1244
18425 Burbank Blvd., Ste. 706 FAX (818) 776-1174
Tarzana 91356
www.robbinsgrp.com

A full service firm that works primarily with established actors, specializing in special events, talent, sports and corporate public relations. Send pictures and resumes or a tape. They require a minimum commitment of 1 year.

ROGERS & COWAN (310) 854-8100
Pacific Design Center FAX (310) 854-8101
8687 Melrose Ave., 7th Fl.
Los Angeles 90069
www.rogersandcowan.com

Works with actors, singers, writers, directors and producers. They will consider newcomers, but in most cases it is better to have a current or upcoming project. They prefer a 6 month time commitment and fees are on a monthly retainer basis. They deal with all media forms. Over 37 years in business. Offices in New York and London.

Public Relations

STAN ROSENFIELD & ASSOCIATES **(310) 286-7474**
2029 Century Park East **FAX (310) 286-2255**
Ste. 1190
Los Angeles 90067
www.srapr.com
sra@srapr.com

Prefers actors with a current or upcoming project. Primarily handles established performers. Fees are on a monthly retainer basis and a 6 month commitment is desired. They deal with all forms of media. A medium sized firm. 35 years in business.

SELFMAN & OTHERS
PUBLIC RELATIONS **(323) 653-4555**
P.O. Box 641831
Los Angeles 90064

Works with actors, production companies, authors, theatre productions, events and special projects. Actors must have an important role in a film or play or a recurring role or better in a TV series. Prefers a 3-month minimum commitment. Works on a monthly retainer basis or project fee. Hourly consultations are available. Contact by phone. 20 years in business. Personalized campaigns. Listed in "Who's Who In Entertainment." Full service firm.

SHARP & ASSOC. **(310) 652-7770**
8721 Sunset Blvd., Ste. 208 **FAX (310) 652-1037**
Los Angeles 90069
sharpassociates@aol.com

Works with actors of all levels from newcomer to established, also singers, stand-up comedians, screenwriters, directors and authors. There is no time commitment required. A boutique agency with individualized attention.

THE SHEFRIN COMPANY **(323) 931-8200**
808 S. Ridgeley Dr. **FAX (323) 939-5799**
Los Angeles 90036

Works with a wide spectrum of clientele including actors, literary talent, singers, comics, directors and producers. They prefer that actors have some credits and clients are accepted through referral. They will accept invitations to performances. They require a monthly retainer and a minimum 3 month time commitment but they prefer a 6 month commitment. 40 years in business.

KELI SQUIRES-TAYLOR **(323) 938-7729**
6056 Whitworth Dr.
Los Angeles 90019
www.actorsuccess.net
kst1management@earthlink.net

Special marketing for actors. Personal Manager Keli Squires-Taylor works with all acting levels to give honest marketing evaluations, marketing guidance and business advice to help you move on up to the next level(s) quickly.

VELASCO & ASSOCIATES **(323) 466-8566**
c/o Raliegh Studios **FAX (323) 466-8540**
650 N. Bronson Ave., Ste. 102
Los Angeles 90004
www.nosotros.org

Works with actors, singers, and film and TV promotion. Contact by phone or mail. There is no time commitment required. They believe actors and artists need a publicist anytime they have a worthwhile project. Over 25 years in business.

Notes

Table of Contents: Working

ADVERTISING AGENCIES 238
AWARDS 240
CASTING DIRECTORS: QUICK REFERENCE CHART .. 244
CASTING DIRECTORS 254
CASTING FACILITIES, STUDIO LOTS & TV STATIONS . 274
CASTING SERVICES & EXTRA CASTING 277
DANCE COMPANIES 279
LOOPING & VOICE-OVER GROUPS 281
MISCELLANEOUS 281
ONLINE, CD & COMPUTERIZED SERVICES 281
OPERA, LIGHT OPERA & MUSICAL THEATRE 283
ORGANIZATIONS 284
PRODUCTION ACCOUNTING 290
PRODUCTION COMPANIES 291
STUDENT FILMS 294
THEATRES 295
THEATRES, OUT OF STATE 313
UNIONS & GUILDS 318
UNION PAY RATES 330
VARIETY WORK 333
WORKING REGULATIONS FOR CHILDREN 335

There are many advertising agencies in Los Angeles that cast commercials. Typically they work through an agent, but some will listen to your voice-over tape and look at your reel. Be sure to call first and find out who to send your package to and be sure to follow up.

ABERT/POINDEXTER (310) 798-3383
2615 Pacific Coast Highway FAX (310) 798-3386
#218
Hermosa Beach 90254
www.abertpoindexter.com

AD2, INC (310) 356-7600
1990 E. Grand Ave., Ste. 200
El Segundo 90245
www.ad2.com

Keeps P&R and tapes on file. Send to Jenny Whitley.

ADLHOCHCREATIVE, INC. (323) 460-4089
646 N. Cahuenga
Los Angeles 90004
www.adlhochcreative.com

Full service agency/design firm. Casting: Beverly Castaldo-Brown.

ADMARKETING INC. (310) 203-8400
1801 Century Park East, Ste. 2000
Century City 90067
www.admarketing.com

Union and nonunion. Send voice-over tapes to Anne Marie Lasher.

ADVILLE/USA (626) 397-9911
44 S. Mentor Ave.
Pasadena 91106
www.adville-usa.com

Send tapes to Mark Schiozaki.

B & A DESIGN GROUP (661) 253-9876

Union and non-union. Primarily print. Maintains casting files. Submit P&R to Barry Anklam.

BBDO/LOS ANGELES (310) 444-4500
10960 Wilshire Blvd., Ste. 1600
Los Angeles 90024
www.bbdo.com

They work through casting agents.

BEAR MARKETING GROUP (818) 865-6464
32121 Lindero Canyon Rd. FAX (818) 865-6499
Ste. 200
Westlake Village 91361-4207
www.bearemg.com

Pictures and resumes and audio tapes or CDs can be sent Attention: Production.

BERT BERDIS & CO. (323) 462-7261
1956 N. Cahuenga Blvd.
Hollywood 90068
www.bertberdisandco.com

Prefers CDs for voiceover submissions. Submit to Jason.

LEO BURNETT CO., INC. (310) 443-2000
6500 Wilshire Blvd., Ste. 1950
Los Angeles 90048
www.leoburnett.com

JON BYK ADVERTISING (310) 476-3012
140 S. Barrington Ave. FAX (310) 476-3016
Los Angeles 90049
www.bykadvertising.com

Audio submissions can be sent to Tim Byk.

CAMPBELL-EWALD/WEST (310) 231-2900
11444 Olympic Blvd., 11th Fl.
Los Angeles 90064
www.campbell-ewald.com

Full service agency. Submit P&R, CDs or tapes to Monica Torres.

CASANOVA & PENDRILL (949) 474-5001
275-A McCormick Ave., Ste. 100
Costa Mesa 92626

Union. P&R, CDs or audio tapes to Ana Wilkinson.

CASTELLS & ASSOCIADOS (213) 688-7250
865 S. Figueroa, 12th Fl.
Los Angeles 90017
www.adamericas.com

Union. Looks for Spanish-speaking Hispanic models and actors. Send P&R, CDs and audio tapes to John Trusso.

CLUB BEVERLY HILLS (310) 274-6051
8306 Wilshire Blvd., #279 FAX (310) 274-7855
Beverly Hills 90211
www.club-beverlyhills.com
dreams@club-beverlyhills.com

Entertainment advertisers. Print, TV, radio media, plays, motion pictures, and events. Specializes in design and copy and has state-of-the-art computer capabilities. Accepts pictures, resumes, DVDs and tapes. Has in-house casting and maintains casting files. Union and non-union. See listing under PUBLIC RELATIONS in the TEAM section for further information.

COLBY & PARTNERS (310) 586-5800
2001 Wilshire Blvd., Ste. 600
Santa Monica 90403
www.colbyandpartners.com

Send P&R and tapes to Mike Davison.

CRUZ/KRAVETZ:IDEAS (310) 312-3630
11858 LaGrange Ave., 2nd Fl.
Los Angeles 90025
www.ckideas.com

Send pictures, resumes and voice over CDs and tapes to Gilda Zevallas.

DAILEY & ASSOCIATES (310) 360-3100
8687 Melrose Ave. FAX (310) 360-0810
West Hollywood 90069
www.daileyads.com

Mostly casts through agents.

DAVISELEN (213) 688-7000
865 S. Figueroa, 12th Fl. FAX (213) 688-7288
Los Angeles 90017
www.daviselen.com

Union. Voice-over CDs and tapes to John Trusso.

DDB LOS ANGELES **(310) 907-1500**
340 Main St. **FAX (310) 907-1992**
Venice 90291
www.ddb.com

P&R, CDs and tapes to Judy Riha.

DGWB **(714) 881-2300**
217 N. Main St., Ste. 200
Santa Ana 92701
www.dgwb.com

Union and non-union. P&R, CDs and voice-over tapes to Anne Coleran.

DSLV/LAWLOR ADVERTISING **(626) 449-0021**
150 S. Los Robles **FAX (626) 795-5987**
Pasadena 91101

Pictures, resumes and audio to Dennis Haig.

ERICSON SOTO AGENCY **(323) 461-4969**
1020 C Mission St. **FAX (626) 799-2404**
South Pasadena 91030

Union and non-union. Print ads. Primarily interested in models. P&R to William Ericson.

FMS DIRECT **(818) 708-7814**
18618 Oxnard St.
Tarzana 91356
www.fmsdirect.com

Union and non-union. P&R, CDs and audio tapes to Rodney Buchser.

FOOTE, CONE & BELDING/MCELROY **(949) 851-3050**
17600 Gillette Ave.
Irvine 92614
www.fcb.com

B.D. FOX & FRIENDS INC. ADVERTISING **(310) 399-9101**
2800 28th St., Unit 222
Santa Monica 90405
www.bdfox.com

Advertising for the Industry. Pictures and resumes to Jeff Farrow.

GREY ADVERTISING **(323) 936-6060**
6100 Wilshire Blvd., 9th Fl.
Los Angeles 90048
www.grey.com

Union. P&R, CDs and voice-over tapes to Miranda Candelaria.

HSR ASSOCIATES **(818) 757-7152**
18829 Paseo Nuevo Dr.
Tarzana 91356
www.hsrassociates.net

Primarily interested in models. P&R, CDs and audio tapes to Steve Goodman.

INTER-MEDIA **(818) 995-1455**
15760 Ventura Blvd., Ste. 110 **FAX (818) 995-6093**
Encino 91436
www.intermedia-advertising.com

Union and non-union. P&R, CDs, DVDs, video and audio tapes to Oscar Bassinson.

KALIS & ASSOCIATES **(310) 459-4499**
17383 Sunset Blvd., Ste. 270
Pacific Palisades 90272

Send voice-over CDs or tapes and P&R to Murray Kalis.

KOVEL FULLER **(310) 841-4444**
9925 Jefferson Blvd.
Culver City 90292
www.kovelfuller.com

Mostly casts through agents. Audio can be sent to James Smith.

LA AGENCIA DE ORCI & ASSOCIADOS **(310) 444-7300**
11620 Wilshire Blvd., Ste. 600
Los Angeles 90025
www.laagencia.com

Exclusively Hispanic advertising. Mostly works through casting agents.

MATSUNO DESIGN GROUP **(818) 247-4200**
719 W. Broadway
Glendale 91204
www.matsunodesign.com

Sometimes uses models for print ads and movie posters. P&R to Mark Matsuno.

MCCANN/ERICKSON INC. **(323) 900-7100**
5700 Wilshire Blvd., Ste. 225
Los Angeles 90036
www.mccann.com

Pictures and resumes to Elena Karrerna.

EDWARD J. MCELROY ADVERTISING **(310) 822-4300**
4223 Glencoe Ave., Ste. C215
Marina Del Rey 90292

Union and non-union. P&R to Eve Bonanomi.

MENDELSOHN/ZEIN **(310) 444-1990**
11111 Santa Monica Blvd., Ste. 2150
Los Angeles 90025
www.mzad.com

Union. P&R to Bridget Merrill.

MENDOZA, DILLON & ASSOC., INC. **(949) 754-2000**
7535 Irvine Center Dr.
Irvine 92618
www.mendozadillon.com

Hispanic advertising exclusively. P&R and voice-over CDs and tapes to Nari Johnson.

MUSE COMMUNICATIONS **(323) 954-1655**
6100 Wilshire Blvd., 16th Fl. **FAX (323) 954-9171**
Los Angeles 90048
www.musecordero.com

Union and non-union. P&R and voice-over CDs and tapes to Sharon Jones.

OGILVY & MATHER **(310) 280-2200**
3530 Hayden Ave.
Culver City 90232
www.ogilvy.com

Primarily casts through agents.

Advertising Agencies

PASADENA ADVERTISING (626) 584-0011
51 W. Dayton., Ste. 100
Pasadena 91105
www.pasadenaadv.com

Print, broadcast, newspaper, outdoor and digital advertising as well as web design and packaging. Send pictures, resumes and audio demos to Corrinne.

REALITY 2 (310) 826-5662
12100 Wilshire Blvd., Ste. 1800
Los Angeles 90025

Union. P&R, CDs and audio tapes to Jorge Alonso.

REGBERG & ASSOCIATES (310) 475-5735
10850 Wilshire Blvd., Ste. 301
Los Angeles 90024
www.regberg.com

Union and non-union. P&R, CDs and voice-over tapes to Scott Regberg.

RUBIN, POSTAER & ASSOC. (310) 394-4000
2525 Colorado Ave. FAX (310) 917-2540
Santa Monica 90404
www.rpa.com

Usually works through a talent agent.

SAATCHI & SAATCHI PACIFIC (310) 214-6000
3501 Sepulveda Blvd. FAX (310) 214-6160
Torrance 90505
www.saatchila.com

Union. Voice-over tapes to Darian Stevens.

SOUND CONCEPTS INC. (310) 390-7406 (800) 451-8560
3485 Meier St.
Los Angeles 90066
www.soundconceptsinc.com

Radio commercials. Voice-over tape to Mark McIntyre.

RON TANSKY ADVERTISING CO. (818) 990-9370
14852 Ventura Blvd., Ste. 111
Sherman Oaks 91403

Small agency. Projects are usually cast by producers.

TBWA CHIAT/DAY INC. (310) 305-5000
5353 Grosvenor Blvd. FAX (310) 305-6000
Los Angeles 90066
www.twbachiat.com

Mainly goes through agents.

TEAM ONE ADVERTISING (310) 615-2000
1960 E. Grand Ave., 7th Fl.
El Segundo 90245
www.teamoneadv.com

J. WALTER THOMPSON (310) 309-8200
2425 Olympic Blvd., Ste. 200 FAX (310) 309-8101
Santa Monica 90404
www.jwt.com

Mainly goes through agencies.

Awards

ACADEMY OF MOTION PICTURE ARTS & SCIENCES AWARDS (310) 247-3000
8949 Wilshire Blvd. FAX (310) 859-9351
Beverly Hills 90211
www.oscar.com
ampas@oscar.org

This is the Oscar. Presented annually, these awards are given for outstanding achievement in film based on a vote by members of the Academy.

THE AMERICAN CINEMATHEQUE AWARD (323) 466-3456 (323) 461-2020
6712 Hollywood Blvd. FAX (323) 461-9737
Hollywood 90028
www.americancinematheque.com
amcin@msn.com

Presented annually to an extraordinary artist currently making a contribution to the art of the moving picture. The award is presented at an award ceremony dinner called the "Annual Moving Picture Ball."

AMERICAN FILM INSTITUTE'S LIFE ACHIEVEMENT AWARD (323) 856-7600
2021 N. Western Ave. FAX (323) 467-4578
Los Angeles 90027
www.afi.com

Annual presentation of the motion picture industry's highest honor recognizing a lifetime body of work. Award winners are selected by the American Film Institute's Board of Trustees.

AMERICAN MUSIC AWARDS (818) 841-3003
Dick Clark Prods. FAX (818) 954-8609
3003 W. Olive Ave.
Burbank 91505
www.dickclarkproductions.com

Awards are given for the public's favorite albums, singles, male and female vocalists, group/duo of the year, and new artists in 7 areas. Nominees are determined by music business trade sources and anyone with a hit song on the charts during the year is eligible. Presented annually in January since 1974. To attend call TicketMaster.

ANNIE AWARDS (818) 842-8330
2114 Burbank Blvd. FAX (818) 842-5645
Burbank 91506
www.annieawards.org

The Annie Awards are the highest honor given for excellence in animation. Each year, Annie Award trophies are awarded for the year's best productions including feature film, short subject. home video, television production; as well as individual achievement by artists, writers and voice talent. The most prestigious awards given at the annual award ceremonies are the June Foray award, presented for special service to the artform; and the Winsor McCay award for a lifetime of achievement in animation.

ANTOINETTE PERRY AWARDS (TONYS) **(212) 764-2929**
226 W. 47th St., 5th Fl. **FAX (212) 302-3721**
New York City, NY 10036
www.tonys.org

Awarded for outstanding achievement in the New York legitimate theatre and regional theatre. Presented annually since 1946.

ARTIOS AWARDS
CASTING SOCIETY OF AMERICA **(323) 463-1925**
606 N. Larchmont Blvd., Ste. 4B
Los Angeles 90004
www.castingsociety.com

The Artios Awards are presented annually to recognize outstanding achievement in casting by CSA members in film, theatre and television.

ASCAP **(323) 883-1000**
(323) 883-1049
7920 Sunset Blvd., Ste. 300 **FAX (323) 888-0849**
Los Angeles 90046
www.ascap.com

The American Society of Composers, Authors, and Publishers presents the Pop Awards, established in 1984 for the most performed works in the ASCAP repertory. Eligibility is determined by the number of performances, including the most performed standards of the previous 10 years. Awards for the publisher, songwriter, and song of the year are presented at a black tie awards dinner ceremony. The Film and Television Music Awards honors writers and composers of songs for television and motion pictures as well as songs from motion pictures and feature film classics.

BMI **(310) 659-9109**
8730 Sunset Blvd. 3rd Fl. W. **FAX (310) 657-6947**
Los Angeles 90069-2211
www.bmi.com

There are two annual awards. The Motion Picture and Television award honors BMI principal composers of the top-grossing motion picture of the previous year as well as songwriters of film songs that received the most airplay during the eligibility period. The Pop Music Award honors BMI songwriters and music publishers whose songs receive the greatest amount of airplay on American radio and television during the eligibility period.

BRITANNIA AWARD
BRITISH ACADEMY OF FILM & TV ARTS
LOS ANGELES **(310) 652-4121**
8533 Melrose Ave., Ste. D **FAX (310) 854-6002**
West Hollywood 90069
www.baftala.org
info@bafta.org

The Britannia Award is BAFTA/LA's highest accolade, a celebration of achievement honoring individuals and companies who have dedicated their careers or corporate missions to advancing the entertainment arts. The Awards are presented annually at a gala dinner, where peers and colleagues celebrate the work and accomplishments of the distinguished honorees.

CINDY AWARDS **(760) 358-7012**
P.O. Box 250 **FAX (760) 358-7569**
Ocotillo 92259

57 W. Palo Verde Ave. **(760) 358-7000**
Ocotillo 92259
www.cindys.com

CINDY, an acronym for "Cinema in Industry," began in 1959 as an industrial film competition. It was originally created by the Industry Film Producers Association (IFPA), an American professional organization. Later, this group became the Informational Film Producers of America and, in 1984, the Association of Visual Communicators (AVC). Today the twice-a-year Cindy Awards are proudly presented by the International Association of Audio Visual Communicators (IAAVC), a non-profit group representing theatrical, broadcast, non-broadcast, and interactive media professionals throughout the world.

CLIO AWARDS **(212) 683-4300**
220 5th Ave., Ste. 1500 **FAX (212) 683-4796**
New York City, NY 10001
www.clioawards.com

The awards are given for television, radio, and print advertising as well as for packing design and worldwide websites.

CRYSTAL AWARDS **(310) 657-5144**
Women in Film **FAX (310) 657-5154**
8857 West Olympic Blvd., Ste. 201
Beverly Hills 90211
www.wif.org

Honors outstanding individuals who, through their endurance and the excellence of their work, have helped to expand the role of women within the Entertainment Industry. The recipients are chosen for both the diversity of their accomplishments and their contributions to the support and advancement of women within the Industry. Presented annually in June.

DIRECTORS GUILD OF AMERICA AWARDS **(310) 289-2000**
7920 Sunset Blvd. **FAX (310) 289-2029**
Los Angeles 90046
www.dga.org

Established in 1949 the awards are presented annually to DGA members for outstanding directorial achievement in motion pictures, TV, and commercials based on a vote by the membership. The presentation banquet is usually held in March.

EMMY AWARDS **(818) 754-2800**
5220 Lankershim Blvd. **FAX (818) 761-2827**
North Hollywood 91601
www.emmys.org

Presented annually since 1948 by The Academy of Television Arts and Sciences. Awards are given for outstanding comedy, drama, mini-series, variety show, children's program, technical crafts, creative arts including animated programs, daytime, and the local L.A. awards. Nominees are chosen by their peers, winners are determined by a Blue Ribbon Panel. The ceremonies are held in September, May, and June. Contact academy for tickets and further information.

EMMY AWARDS FOR NEWS AND DOCUMENTARY PROGRAMS (212) 586-8424
111 W. 57th St., Ste. 600 FAX (212) 246-8129
New York City, NY 10019
www.emmyonline.org

Presented annually in New York.

FILM ADVISORY BOARD AWARD OF EXCELLENCE (323) 461-6541
Janet Stokes – Executive Director FAX (323) 469-8541
P.O. Box 9258
North Hollywood 91609
www.filmadvisoryboard.org
fabfamaoe@medione.net

Presented to family oriented motion pictures, television programs, CD-ROMs, DVD, and home videos. An award also honors celebrities for outstanding contributions to the Industry and there is an award for inventions that pertain to the Industry. Past winners include Bob Hope, Jack Lemmon, Liza Minnelli, Ted Turner, Bette Davis, and Jack Haley, Jr.

THE GOLDEN BOOT AWARD (818) 876-1888
The Motion Picture & Television Fund FAX (818) 876-1940
23300 Mulholland Dr.
Woodland Hills 91364
foundation@mptvfund.org

Presented to actors and other film professionals who have made their mark in western film history. Nominees and winners are selected by a committee of volunteers, mostly entertainment professionals.

NOSOTROS GOLDEN EAGLE AWARDS (323) 465-4167
650 N. Bronson Ave., Ste. 102 FAX (323) 465-8540
Hollywood 90004
www.nosotros.org

These awards are presented to entertainment figures who help the Hispanic cause or image. Management companies, studios, and other Industry professionals select the nominees. The categories include Male and Female Performers, Television Actor and Actress, Most Promising Actor/Actress, Lifetime Achievement Award, Humanitarian Award, Legend Award, and Special Tribute Award.

THE GOLDEN GLOBE AWARDS (310) 657-1731
646 N. Robertson Blvd. FAX (310) 657-5576
West Hollywood 90069
www.hfpa.org
info@hfpa.org

Sponsored by the Hollywood Foreign Press and presented annually since 1943. Winners are selected by members of the Hollywood Foreign Press Association representing 100 million readers in 50 countries. Awards banquet is in January, by invitation only.

GRAMMY AWARDS (310) 392-3777
National Academy of Recording Arts & Sciences FAX (310) 399-3090
3402 Pico Blvd.
Santa Monica 90405
www.grammy.com

Grammys are awarded by votes of the Academy's active members, individuals directly involved in the creative process of recording including singers, musicians, producers, and songwriters. An artist whose recording has been released in general distribution for the first time during the eligibility year can be nominated. Award ceremony is usually in February.

INDEPENDENT FEATURE PROJECT/WEST (310) 432-1200
8750 Wilshire Blvd., 2nd Fl. FAX (310) 432-1203
Beverly Hills 90211
www.ifp.org

Hosted annually on the Saturday before the Oscars, the IFP Independent Spirit Awards is the yin to the Oscars' yang – a celebration honoring filmmakers of independent vision. It is televised in millions of homes and covered internationally.

INTERNATIONAL BROADCASTING AWARDS FOR BEST COMMERCIAL IN RADIO & TV AROUND THE WORLD (818) 789-1182
13701 Riverside Dr., Ste. 205 FAX (818) 789-1210
Sherman Oaks 91423
www.hrts.org

Sponsored by the Hollywood Radio and TV Society, the awards are presented annually for the best international radio and TV commercials.

INTERNATIONAL EMMY AWARDS NATAS (212) 489-6969
888 Seventh Ave., 5th Fl. FAX (212) 489-6557
New York City, NY 10019
www.iemmys.tv
icouncil@iemmys.tv

Presented annually in New York for International television achievement.

L.A. WEEKLY THEATRE AWARDS (323) 465-9909
6715 Sunset Blvd. FAX (323) 465-3220
Hollywood 90028
www.laweekly.com

Rewards work done in 99 seat theatres. Award ceremony is usually in April.

MEDIA ACCESS AWARDS VERDUGO JOBS CENTER (818) 409-0448
1255 S. Central Ave. FAX (818) 507-4819
Glendale 91204 TTY (818) 753-3427
www.disabilityemployment.org

Presented annually in the fall by the California Governor's Committee on employment of people with disabilities. Awards are given for outstanding media contributions, drama, comedy, and magazine shows, for non-stereotypical portrayals of persons with disabilities. Anyone seen in a role which positively and realistically shows a person with a disability may be nominated.

NAACP IMAGE AWARDS (323) 938-5268
4929 Wilshire Blvd., Ste. 310
Los Angeles 90010
www.naacp.org

Awarded annually to people and programs that portray positive images of African-Americans and individuals who have given outstanding performances in the fields of film, TV, music, and literature. Winners are selected by membership vote. Submissions of recordings, video tapes, and screenings of films are considered for nomination.

NATIONAL ASSOCIATION OF THEATRE OWNERS AWARDS (NATO) (818) 506-1778
4605 Lankershim Blvd. FAX (818) 506-0269
Ste. 340
North Hollywood 91602
www.natoonline.com
nato_inc@earthlink.net

Awards recognizing achievement for the past year are presented at the annual convention for the National Association of Theatre Owners. Honored are Stars of The Year, Director of The Year, Producer of the Year, Screenwriter of the Year, and Stars of Tomorrow. Special awards are also presented to exhibitors who represent the motion picture theatre industry. The Sunshine Group organizes these awards and can be contacted at (646) 654-7680 for additional information.

NEW YORK FILM CRITICS CIRCLE AWARDS
745 Fifth Ave.
New York City, NY 10151
www.nyfcc.com

Presented annually since 1935. Categories include best picture, best actor, and best actress.

SATURN AWARDS (323) 752-5811
334 W. 54th St.
Los Angeles 90037
www.saturnawards.org

Sponsored by the Academy of Science Fiction, Fantasy, and Horror Films. These are annual awards for outstanding achievement in film. The winners are selected by membership vote and the date of the awards presentation is determined by the Board of Directors.

SCREEN ACTORS GUILD AWARD (323) 954-1600
5757 Wilshire Blvd.
Los Angeles 90036
www.sag.org

These awards are presented for excellent achievement in acting during the past year in TV and film.

SOUTHERN CALIFORNIA MOTION PICTURE COUNCIL (323) 931-8110
P.O. Box 3672
Hollywood 90078

These awards are presented annually in December, to motion picture, television, and the professional arts as well as television and film productions for their contribution to high standards in the Entertainment Industry. S.C.M.P.C. is a non-profit organization founded in 1936 by Jean Doran.

STUDENT FILM AWARDS (310) 247-3000
Academy of Motion Picture Arts & Sciences FAX (310) 859-9351
8949 Wilshire Blvd.
Beverly Hills 90211
www.ampas.org

These awards were established to encourage outstanding achievement in film production by college and university students with no previous professional experience. The categories are Animation, Documentary, Narrative, and Alternative.

WOMEN IN THEATRE (W.I.T.) (818) 763-5222
11684 Ventura Blvd., #444
Studio City 91604
www.nohoartsdistrict.com/womenintheatre
womenintheatre@aol.com

The Red Carpet Awards are presented during an annual program.

WRITERS GUILD AWARDS (323) 951-4000
7000 W. 3rd St. FAX (323) 782-4800
Los Angeles 90048
www.wga.org

Screenwriting awards given to motion picture, radio, and television writers. Voters consist of Writers Guild members. The annual awards banquet is usually held in March and is open to the public. Contact the Writers Guild for further information.

YOUNG ARTIST AWARDS (818) 761-4007
5632 Colfax Ave. FAX (818) 761-6671
North Hollywood 91601
www.youngartistawards.org
contact@youngartistawards.org

Presented annually to recognize deserving young actors and actresses and to promote wholesome entertainment. Young actors and actresses age 5-18 who perform in motion pictures, TV, and theatre are eligible. The awards are presented at an invitational ceremony and banquet every spring. Scholarships awarded for outstanding performances in the performing arts.

CASTING DIRECTORS: QUICK REFERENCE CHART

Legend:
F............Features
C............Commercials
Tv..........Television
S............Stage
Vo..........Voice Overs
O............Other
R............Rarely

		Will See Non-Union	Accepts Pictures & Resumes	Accepts Tapes/DVDs	Sees Scenes & Monologues	Does Generals	Teaches	Attends Showcases	Attends Plays	Attends Screenings	Sees Non-Represented
A FACE IN THE CROWD CASTING	CFTvSVoO		X	X				X	X	X	
MELISSA ABESERA	FCTvSVoO	X	X	X				X	X	X	
STACY ALEXANDER	FTv		X			X					X
ANTHONY & ASSOCIATES	TvC	X	X					X	X	X	X
AQUILA/WOOD CASTING	F		X								
MAUREEN ARATA	FTv		X					X	X	X	
ARTZ/COHEN CASTING	FTv	X	X	X				R	R	R	
ASG CASTING	CTv										
JULIE ASHTON	FTv		X								
AUTOMATIC SWEAT	FCTvO	X	X					X	X	X	X
ROE BAKER	CF	X					X	R	R	R	X
RISE BARISH	CF		X					R	R	R	
BARRY/GREEN-KEYES	FCTvO		X					R	R	R	
DEBORAH BARYLSKI	FTv	X	X			X			X	X	X
PAMELA BASKER	Tv	R	X			R		R	R	R	
BEACH/KATZMAN CASTING	FTv	X	X					X	X	X	X
EYDE BELASCO	FTv	X	X	X	R	R		R	R	R	
JUDY BELSHE	COF	X	X		X			R	R	R	X
LINDA BERGER CASTING	FTv		X					X	X	X	
TERRY BERLAND CASTING	CVoTv	X	X				X	X	X	X	X
AMY JO BERMAN – HBO	Tv										
CHEMIN BERNARD & ASSOCIATES	FTvC	X	X			R		X	X	X	X
BARBARA BERSELL	FOC	X						R	R	R	X
BESTROP/YANKLOWITZ CASTING	FTv	X	X	X		R		X	X	X	X
BETTY MAE, INC.	TvF										
TAMMARA BILLIK CASTING	FTvCO	X	X					X	X	X	X
JAN BINA	FTv		X				X				
TONY BIRKLEY	Tv		X					X	X	X	
JOE BLAKE CASTING	C	R	X	R							
BARBIE BLOCK	TvF		X					X	X	X	
BLUESTEIN/ST. CYR CASTING	Tv										

Casting Directors: Quick Reference Chart

Legend:
F............Features
C............Commercials
Tv...........Television
S............Stage
Vo...........Voice Overs
O............Other
R............Rarely

Name	Type	Will See Non-Union	Accepts Pictures & Resumes	Accepts Tapes/DVDs	Sees Scenes & Monologues	Does Generals	Teaches	Attends Showcases	Attends Plays	Attends Screenings	Sees Non-Represented
EUGENE BLYTHE	Tv		X	X	X			X	R	R	
ANNIE BOEDECKER	Tv		X					X	X	X	
DEEDEE BRADLEY	Tv	X	X	X				R	R	R	X
MEGAN BRANMAN	FTvO	R	X								
KATE BRINEGAR	Tv	R	X					R	X	R	X
JACKIE BRISKEY	TvCO	R	X	X				R	R	R	R
ANDREW BROWN	FTv		X			R		R	R	R	R
BROWN/WEST CASTING	FTv		X			R		R	R	R	X
MARY BUCK	FTv		X			X		R	R	R	
PEGGY BULLINGTON	TvFC		X					X	X	X	
BURROWS/BOLAND CASTING	FTv		X					R	R	R	
TWINKIE BYRD	C	X	X					X	X	X	X
CRAIG CAMPOBASSO	Tv		X				X				
PAMELA CAMPUS	TvOFC	X			R		X	R	R	R	
REUBEN CANNON & ASSOCIATES	F		X	X				X	X	X	
BLYTHE CAPPELLO	Tv		X					X	X	X	
CATHI CARLTON	C		X								
CARNES & COMPANY	CO		X					X	X	X	
MEGAN CARRAFIELLO	CTvF		X				X				
CARSEY-WERNER-MANDABACH	Tv										
FERNE CASSEL	Tv	X	X					X	X	X	
ALICE CASSIDY	C		X								
CASTING BY CHRISTINA	FTv		X				X				
THE CASTING COMPANY	F		X			X		X	X	X	
THE CASTING COUCH	TvCF		X								
LUCY CAVALLO	Tv		X					X	X	X	X
LINDSAY CHAG	F		X					X	X	X	
DENISE CHAMIAN	FTvCO		X					X	X	X	
FERN CHAMPION	FTvCO	X	X					X	X	X	X
SHARON CHAZIN-LEIBLEIN	TvCO	X	X					X	X	X	X
KAREN CHURCH	Tv		X								

Casting Directors: Quick Reference Chart

Legend:
F............Features
C............Commercials
Tv..........Television
S............Stage
Vo..........Voice Overs
O............Other
R............Rarely

Name	Type	Will See Non-Union	Accepts Pictures & Resumes	Accepts Tapes/DVDs	Sees Scenes & Monologues	Does Generals	Teaches	Attends Showcases	Attends Plays	Attends Screenings	Sees Non-Represented
JOANNA COLBERT	FTvSCVo		X			X					
AISHA COLEY	F							X	X	X	
ANNELISE COLLINS CASTING	FCTvO	R	X			X	X	X	X	X	R
RUTH CONFORTE CASTING	FTvCO	X	X					X	X	X	X
ALLISON COWITT	FTv		X								
ELAINE CRAIG VOICE CASTING	Vo		X	X	R			R	R	R	X
CRYSTAL SKY COMMUNICATIONS	F	X	X	R	R	R		X	X	X	X
CURRENTLY CASTING	FTv	X	X					X	X	X	X
JOE D'AGOSTA	FTv		R	R				X	X	X	X
BILLY DAMOTA	FCTv	X	X		X	X	X	X	X	X	X
COLLIN DANIEL	Tv		X					X	X	X	
ANITA DANN	FTv		X					X	X	X	R
AYO DAVIS	Tv		X		R	R					
DAVIS BADDELEY CASTING	TvC		X								
ERIC DAWSON	FTv							X	X	X	
TRISHA DEBSKI	FTvC		X					X	X	X	
ZORA DEHORTER CASTING	FTVoO					X	X	X	X	X	X
RICHARD DELANCY & ASSOCIATES	FTv	X	X		X	X	X	X	X	X	X
JOANNE DENAUT	S		X			X					
LESLEE DENNIS	CO	X	X					R	R	R	X
ELINA DE SANTOS	Tv	X	X	X	X	X	X	X	X	X	X
DICKSON ARBUSTO CASTING	FTvCO	X	X				X	R	R	R	X
RON DIGMAN - 20TH CENTURY FOX TV	Tv										
PAM DIXON	F		X			R	X	X	X		R
DONOVAN CASTING	FTvCS	X	X		R	R	X	X	X	X	X
CHRISTY DOOLEY	FTvCO		X				X	R	R	R	R
BRIAN DORFMAN	Tv		X	X				X	X	X	
MICK DOWD CASTING	C		X					X	X	X	
MARY DOWNEY	Tv	X	X					X	X	X	X
DORIAN DUNAS	FTvC										
EDELMAN CASTING	Tv		X			X			X		

Casting Directors: Quick Reference Chart

Legend:
F............Features
C............Commercials
Tv...........Television
S............Stage
Vo...........Voice Overs
O............Other
R............Rarely

		Will See Non-Union	Accepts Pictures & Resumes	Accepts Tapes/DVDs	Sees Scenes & Monologues	Does Generals	Teaches	Attends Showcases	Attends Plays	Attends Screenings	Sees Non-Represented
KATHRYN EISENSTEIN	Tv		X								
STEVEN ERDEK CASTING	TvFVoC		X								
DANIELLE ESKINAZI	TvCOF	X	X	X				X	X	X	X
LESLEE FELDMAN	FTv		X			X					
FENTON/COWITT CASTING	FTv		X				R	R	R	R	
LISA FIELDS – CASTING CAFE	C		X	X	X						
FINN HILLER CASTING	F		X					X	X	X	
MALI FINN CASTING	TvF	X	X					X	X	X	X
FIORENTINO/MANGIERI CASTING	TvF		X								
FIREFLY CASTING	FTvS		X					X	X	X	
MEGAN FOLEY CASTING	CF	X	X				X	X	X	X	X
KIMBERLY FOSTER CASTING	Tv	X	X					X	X	X	X
NANCY FOY	FTv		X	X		X		X	X	X	
DELIA FRANKEL – SONY	FTv		X								
LISA FREIBERGER	COTV	X	X					X	X	X	X
JEAN FROST	FTv	X	X			X	R	X	X	X	X
NICOLE GARCIA	Tv		X	X							
RISA BRAMON GARCIA	FCO		X						X		
CASTING BY JEFF GERARD	FTvSOC		X				X	X	X	X	X
DAN GIBSON – E ENTERTAINMENT	Tv	X	X	X		R		X	X	X	X
JAN GLASER	F		X			X		X	X	X	X
LAURA GLEASON CASTING	FTvS		X	X				X	X	X	X
CHARISSE GLENN CASTING	TvVoC							X	X	X	
VICKI GOGGIN & ASSOCIATES	C		X					R	R	R	
GAIL GOLDBERG – DISNEY	F		X	X		X		X	X	X	
PETER GOLDEN – CBS	Tv	X	X			X		X	X	X	X
DANNY GOLDMAN & ASSOCIATES	CVo	X	X			X		X	X	X	X
LOUIS GOLDSTEIN & ASSOCIATES	FCO		X			X					
GOLDWASSER/MELTZER	FTvS		X					R	R	R	
MARSHA GOODMAN – DIC	Vo		X	X				X	X	X	
MARILYN GRANAS	FCTv		X								

Casting Directors: Quick Reference Chart

Legend:
F............Features
C............Commercials
Tv..........Television
S............Stage
Vo..........Voice Overs
O............Other
R............Rarely

		Will See Non-Union	Accepts Pictures & Resumes	Accepts Tapes/DVDs	Sees Scenes & Monologues	Does Generals	Teaches	Attends Showcases	Attends Plays	Attends Screenings	Sees Non-Represented
JEFF GREENBERG & ASSOCIATES	FTvS	X	X	X		X	R	X	X	X	X
AARON GRIFFITH	F		X			R		X	X		
AL GUARINO	FS	X	X	X	X	R		X	X	X	X
PAMELA RACK GUEST	Tv		X					R	R	R	X
SHEILA GUTHRIE	Tv		X					X	X	X	X
MILT HAMERMAN	Tv	X	X	X	X			R	R	R	X
ROBERT HARBIN	Tv	X	X	X		X		X	X	X	X
SUSAN HAVINS	FCTvO	X	X					X	X	X	X
PATTI HAYES	TvF	X	X								X
RENEE HAYNES	FTv	X	X			R		X	X	X	
CATHY HENDERSON-MARTIN	TvF		X					X	X	X	
DAWN HERSHEY	Vo	X		X							X
MARC HIRSCHFELD	Tv		X					R	R	R	
HISPANIC TALENT CASTING OF HOLLYWOOD	FCO	X	X		R	R					X
ALYSON HORN	FTv		X								
BOB HUBER	Tv							R	R	R	
VICTORIA HUFF & ASSOCIATES	TvCO	R	X	X		R		X	X	X	R
JULIE HUTCHINSON	Tv		X			X		X	X	X	X
DONNA ISAACSON	F		X	X		X					X
JOHN JACKSON	FTvCO	X	X				X	X	X	X	X
RICK JACOBS	Tv		X	X		R					
JOEY PAUL JENSEN	FTv	R	X								X
ELIZABETH JERESKI	TvF		X								
TARA-ANNE JOHNSON	Tv		X			R		X	X	X	R
KALLES/JAMES CASTING	Tv		X								
CHRISTIAN KAPLAN	F		X	X				X	X	X	
TRACY KAPLAN	TvCO		X					X	X	X	
SARAH KATZMAN	FTv		X				X	X	X	X	
LORA KENNEDY	FO		X					X	X	X	
BETH KLEIN	Tv	R	X				R	X	X	X	
SHARON KLEIN	FTv		X								

Casting Directors: Quick Reference Chart

Legend:
F............Features
C............Commercials
Tv..........Television
S............Stage
Vo..........Voice Overs
O............Other
R............Rarely

		Will See Non-Union	Accepts Pictures & Resumes	Accepts Tapes/DVDs	Sees Scenes & Monologues	Does Generals	Teaches	Attends Showcases	Attends Plays	Attends Screenings	Sees Non-Represented
THOM KLOHN	Tv		X								
NANCY KLOPPER	F		X								
EILEEN KNIGHT	FTvC		X			R		R	R	R	X
KATHY KNOWLES	C	X	X	X	R	R		R	R	R	X
KOBLIN HARDING CASTING	F		X								
ANNAMARIE KOSTURA - NBC	Tv	X	X					X			
DEBORAH KURTZ CASTING	FTvCO	X	X					X	X	X	X
LA PADURA/HART CASTING	Tv										
KATE LACEY	F		X								
ROSS LACY	TvFCO	X	X		X			X	X	X	X
DINO LADKI	FTv		X								
JUDY LANDAU	CTvF	X	X					X	X	X	X
LANDSBURG/FIDDLEMAN CASTING	TvF		X			X		X	X	X	
MEREDITH LAYNE	TvF	X		X				X	X	X	
GERALDINE LEDER	TvCOF	X	X	X	X			X	X	X	X
KELI LEE	Tv		X	X	X		X	X			
CAROL LEFKO CASTING	CFTvO	X	X					X	X	X	X
KATHLEEN LETTERIE - WB	Tv										
JOHN LEVEY - WARNER BROS.	Tv		X			X					
GAIL LEVIN	TvF		X					X	X	X	R
HEIDI LEVITT	F		X					R	R	R	
LIBERMAN/PATTON CASTING	Tv	X	X				X	X	X	X	
AMY LIEBERMAN	S							X	X		
MICHAEL LIEN & DAN COWAN CASTING	CO	R	X	X		R	X	X	X	X	R
TRACY LILIENFIELD	CTv		X	X				R	R	R	
MARCI LIROFF	S							X	X	X	
LESLIE LITT	Tv	X	X			R		R	R	R	X
BEVERLY LONG & ASSOCIATES	FC		X	X			X				
MOLLY LOPATA	Tv		X			X		X	X	X	
LINDA LOWY	VoTv		X	X							
BOB MACDONALD	F		X						X	X	

Casting Directors: Quick Reference Chart

Legend:
F............Features
C............Commercials
Tv...........Television
S............Stage
Vo...........Voice Overs
O............Other
R............Rarely

		Will See Non-Union	Accepts Pictures & Resumes	Accepts Tapes/DVDs	Sees Scenes & Monologues	Does Generals	Teaches	Attends Showcases	Attends Plays	Attends Screenings	Sees Non-Represented
MACKIE/SANDRICH	FTv	X	X								X
MAGIC CASTING	FCO	X	X	X		X					
FRANCINE MAISLER	F	X	X					X	X	X	X
SHEILA MANNING	CFTv	X	X	X		X		X	X	X	X
MARY & KAREN MARGIOTTA	FTv	X	X	X							X
MINDY MARIN	F	X	X		X	R			X	X	X
MELISSA MARTIN CASTING	C		X								
TONY MARTINELLI	FTv		X								
LIZ MARX	TvCO	X	X					X	X	X	X
MASLAR/LIEM CASTING	TvF		X								
VALERIE McCAFFREY	Tv		X					X	X	X	
JEANNE McCARTHY	FTv		X			R					
CYDNEY McCURDY	FTv		X								
KELLY McDONALD-AARON SPELLING PRDS	Tv							R	R	R	
ROBERT McGEE	FTv		X					X		X	
JEFF MESHEL - NBC	Tv		R	R	R						
D LYNN MEYERS	TvCF		X					X	X	X	X
JOSEPH MIDDLETON	Tv		X					R	R	R	
KEVIN MILLER	TvCO	X	X					R	R	R	X
RICK MILLIKAN	Tv	R		R		R		R	R	R	R
LISA MIONE	FTv		X					X	X	X	
RICK MONTGOMERY	FTv	R	X			R		X	X	X	R
BOB MORONES CASTING	FTv	X	X	X		X		X	X	X	X
DONNA MORONG	F		X					R	R	R	
MICHELLE MORRIS-GERTZ	FTv										
JOHN MULKEEN	COVoF	X	X					X	X	X	X
ROGER MUSSENDEN	TvF	X	X			X			X	X	X
NASSIF & BACA	FTv	X	X		X		R	R	R	R	X
NANCY NAYOR	FTv		X								X
DEBRA NEATHERY	F		X				R				
BRUCE NEWBERG CASTING	TvFS	R	X								R

Casting Directors: Quick Reference Chart

Legend:
F............Features
C............Commercials
Tv...........Television
S............Stage
Vo...........Voice Overs
O............Other
R............Rarely

		Will See Non-Union	Accepts Pictures & Resumes	Accepts Tapes/DVDs	Sees Scenes & Monologues	Does Generals	Teaches	Attends Showcases	Attends Plays	Attends Screenings	Sees Non-Represented
KRIS NICOLAU, CSA - SKIRTS CASTING	C	X	X	X		X		X	X	X	X
SONIA NIKORE	Tv	X	X	X							X
MARJORIE NOBLE	TvF		X					X	X	X	
PATRICIA NOLAND	FTv		X					X	X	X	
SARAH NOONAN	Tv		X					X	X	X	R
WENDY O'BRIEN	Tv		X								
PAULINE O'CON	Tv		X								
GILLIAN O'NEILL	Tv		X					X	X	X	
LORI OPENDEN	Tv	X	X		X		R	X	X	X	X
GREG ORSON CASTING	FTv										
JESSICA OVERWISE	FCTvS	R	X	X	X		R	X	X	X	X
MARVIN PAIGE CASTING	FTv		X				X				
MARK PALADINI	FTvCO	X	X	X				X	X	X	X
PANTONE CASTING	TvC		X								
JENNIFER RUDIN PEARSON	Vo			X							
MARSHALL PECK	FTv		X						X		
PEMRICK/FRONK CASTING	F	X	X	X		X	R	X	X	X	X
MERCEDES PENNEY	SVoCFTvO	X	X	X	X	X		X	X	X	X
NANCY PERKINS	COTv	X	X					X	X	X	X
KARI PEYTON	FTv										
LINDA PHILLIPS-PALO	FTv		X			R	X	X		X	X
BONNIE PIETILA	Tv		X								
POWELL MELCHER CASTING	FTv		X								
PRIME CASTING	FCTv	X	X					R	R	R	X
LYNN QUIRION	TvC	X	X								X
MARK RANDALL CASTING	TvC	X	X								X
JOHANNA RAY	TvF	X	X								X
TINA REAL	CFO	X	X			R	X	X	X	X	
AMY REECE	FTv	X	X					X	X	X	X
ROBI REED & ASSOCIATES	Tv		X								
BARBARA REMSEN	FTv		X					X	X		

Casting Directors: Quick Reference Chart

Legend:
F............Features
C............Commercials
Tv...........Television
S............Stage
Vo...........Voice Overs
O............Other
R............Rarely

		Will See Non-Union	Accepts Pictures & Resumes	Accepts Tapes/DVDs	Sees Scenes & Monologues	Does Generals	Teaches	Attends Showcases	Attends Plays	Attends Screenings	Sees Non-Represented
JOAN RENFREW	C	X	X								X
GRETCHEN RENNELL COURT	F		X			X					
RODEO CASTING	C		R			R					R
ROMANO/BENNER CASTING	Tv		X					X	X	X	
VICKI ROSENBERG	Tv		X					R	R	R	
DONNA ROSENSTEIN	Tv		X								
MARCIA ROSS	F		X				R	R	R	R	
JAMI RUDOFSKY	F		X								
ELIZABETH RUDOLPH	FTv		X								
PATRICK RUSH	TvFC		X								
MARNIE SAITTA CASING	TvCO	X	X	X				X	X	X	X
GAIL SALUS CASTING	FTv		X					X	X	X	
TESS SANCHEZ	Tv										
GABRIELLE SCHARY	C	X						R	R	R	X
LAURA SCHIFF	TvF		X								
ARLENE SCHUSTER-GOSS	CO		X	X			R	R	R	R	
WENDY SCHWAM	F		X								
KEVIN SCOTT	Tv		X			X	R	X	X	X	
JAY SCULLY	FTv	X	X	X				X	X	X	X
TINA SEILER CASTING	FTvVoO		X								
LILA SELIK CASTING	CTvFO	X	X								
TONY SEPULVEDA	Tv	X	X			R		X	X	X	X
PAMELA SHAE	Tv		X			X					R
SHANER/TESTA CASTING	FTvSC		X								
SARI SHAPIRO	FC	X						X	X	X	
MANDY SHERMAN	Tv		X								
AVA SHEVITT	CTv	X	X					X	X	X	
SHOOTING FROM THE HIP CASTING	FTvCSVoO		X								
MONICA SHULMAN	Tv										
MARK SIKES	F	X	X				X				X
CLAIR SINNETT	CFO		X	X			X				

CASTING DIRECTORS: QUICK REFERENCE CHART

Legend:
F............Features
C............Commercials
Tv...........Television
S............Stage
Vo...........Voice Overs
O............Other
R............Rarely

Name	Type	Will See Non-Union	Accepts Pictures & Resumes	Accepts Tapes/DVDs	Sees Scenes & Monologues	Does Generals	Teaches	Attends Showcases	Attends Plays	Attends Screenings	Sees Non-Represented
MELISSA SKOFF	FTv		X			X		X	X	X	
SLATER BROOKSBANK	Tv		X								
STEPHEN SNYDER	FCOTv	X	X								X
SHARON SOBLE	FTv		X								
SOBO CASTING	OFTvSC		X	X			X				
LYNN STALMASTER & ASSOCIATES	FTv		X			R					
DAWN STEINBERG	FTv		X					X	X	X	
SALLY STINER	TvF		X					X	X	X	
ANDREA STONE CASTING	CFTv	X	X						X	X	X
STUDIO TALENT GROUP	F		X	X							
LORI SUGAR CASTING	TvF		X					X	X	X	
MONICA SWANN	TvF	X									
T.L.C. BOOTH, INC.	C	X	X								X
YUMI TAKADA	CF	X	X	X				X	X	X	X
JAMES TARZIA	TvF		X					X	X	X	
JUDY TAYLOR - DISNEY	Tv										
RACHEL TENNER	FTv	X	X					X	X	X	X
TEPPER/GALLEGOS	CTvF		X				X				
MARK TESCHNER	Tv		X				X				
DANA THEODORATOS - UPN	Tv		X								
MARK TILLMAN	F		X					X	X	X	
JOY TODD	FTv		X						X	X	
TONDINO/WARREN			X			X					
TRIPLE THREAT CASTING	CFTvO		X								
ULRICH/DAWSON/KRITZER CASTING	TvCO		X								
BLANCA VALDEZ	CFTvVo	X	X	X		X	X	X	X	X	X
VALKO-MILLER	FTv		X					R	R	R	
MINA VASQUEZ	Tv		X					X	X	X	
THE VOICECASTER	Vo			X							
VOICES VOICECASTING	Vo		X								
DAVA WAITE	Tv		X			X	X				

Casting Directors: Quick Reference Chart

Legend:
- F............Features
- C............Commercials
- Tv...........Television
- S............Stage
- Vo...........Voice Overs
- O............Other
- R............Rarely

		Will See Non-Union	Accepts Pictures & Resumes	Accepts Tapes/DVDs	Sees Scenes & Monologues	Does Generals	Teaches	Attends Showcases	Attends Plays	Attends Screenings	Sees Non-Represented
ALEX WALD	FTv		X					X	X	X	
KATY & CO./KATY WALLIN	TvCOF	X	X			R	X	X	X	X	
SAMUEL WARREN	FC	R	X		X		X			X	R
PAUL WEBER CASTING	TvF		X					X	X	X	
APRIL WEBSTER	Tv		X								
WILSHIRE CASTING	Tv	X	X					X	X	X	X
KEITH WOLFE	FCVo		X					X	X	X	X
GERALD WOLF	TvF	R	X								R
JASON WOOD	FTv		X								
GERRIE WORMSER	SCTvF		X								X
BARBARA WRIGHT	Tv		X			R		R	R	R	
G. CHARLES WRIGHT	Tv		X					X	X	X	
RHONDA YOUNG	FTvC		X					X	X	X	
DEBRA ZANE CASTING	Tv		X								
ZANE/PILLSBURY CASTING	Tv		X					X	X	X	
LISA ZAROWIN	FTv		X					X	X	X	
GARY ZUCKERBROD	FTv		X								
DORI ZUCKERMAN CASTING	FTv	X	X					X	X	X	X

Casting Directors

If you are planning to do a casting director mass mailing first check the Quick Reference Chart and narrow down the people you want to submit to, then check the listing for each one and follow the information. Also, if the listing below says, "no phone calls" that's exactly what it means. Some casting directors who are members of CSA have requested that we list the CSA address and phone number as that is the most permanent address and most reliable way to contact them. CSA will forward mail to casting directors and take messages for them as well. Check out the Casting Society website at www.castingsociety.com for additional listings. Be sure to check ALL addresses before submitting anything. We strive for the most current information available, but casting directors often move around with each project they cast, so verify that the address is correct before submitting anything.

A FACE IN THE CROWD CASTING **(310) 458-1100** **(310) 720-3117**
1216 Fifth St.
Santa Monica 90401

Maryclaire Sweeters does commercial casting as well as casting for cable, direct-to-video, independent, industrials, informercials, mini-series, print, music videos, shorts, reality programming, theatre, variety and voice casting/animation. She accepts submissions by mail only. Please no drop offs, follow up calls or faxes. Attends showcases. Was in the process of relocating at press time. Please call for further information.

MELISSA ABESERA **(323) 931-1782**
400 N. Orange Dr.
Los Angeles 90036

Melissa Abesera casts TV, film, radio, sports, theatre, variety, voice casting, animation, commercials and extras. Submissions by mail only, no drop ins or phone calls.

STACY ALEXANDER, CSA VH-1 (310) 752-8345
2600 Colorado Ave.
Santa Monica 90404

Gives general interviews if appropriate. Mailed submissions only. No follow up calls.

ANTHONY & ASSOCIATES (818) 655-4154
4024 Radford Ave., Trailer 800
Studio City 91604

Jill Anthony is open to mailed submissions from union, non-union, represented and non-represented actors. She is also open to attending showcases, plays and screenings.

AQUILA WOOD CASTING (323) 460-6292
1680 Vine St., #806
Hollywood 90028

Union only. No drop offs or walk-ins. Accepts DVDs and tapes by request only. Features. Mary Tricia Wood and Debra Aquila.

MAUREEN ARATA (323) 463-1925
c/o CSA
606 N. Larchmont Blvd., Ste. 4B
Los Angeles 90004

Accepts mailed pictures, resumes and invitations to showcases, plays and screenings.

ARTZ & COHEN CASTING (323) 463-1925
c/o CSA
606 N. Larchmont Blvd., Ste. 4B
Los Angeles 90004

Mary Gail Artz and Barbra Cohen mainly cast features but also do cable, network and independent films. They will accept submissions by mail, but no drop offs and no follow up calls.

ASG CASTING (818) 762-0200
10200 Riverside Dr., Ste. 205
Toluca Lake 91602

Casts for commercials and television, predominantly union and by referral only.

JUILIE ASHTON (323) 856-9000
6715 Hollywood Blvd., Ste. 203 FAX (323) 856-9010
Hollywood 90028

Prefers written submission and maintains casting files. Please, no phone calls, faxes or drop offs.

AUTOMATIC SWEAT INC. (323) 934-5141
5541 W. Washington Blvd.
Los Angeles 90016

John Papsidera is open to union and non-union as well as non-represented. Submissions are accepted by mail only, no drop offs, faxes or follow up calls. DVDs and tapes are accepted by request only and are not returned. Casts for TV and film.

ROE BAKER (818) 705-2278
FAX (818) 986-3636

Accepts mailed submissions from union and non-union actors. Call first to get address from Ms. Baker. She gives seminars on occasion and casts for commercials and features.

MARIKO BALLENTINE

See listing for DANNY GOLDMAN & ASSOCIATES.

RISE BARISH (310) 456-9018
(310) 458-1100
1216 5th St. FAX (310) 456-9718
Santa Monica 90401
www.risebarishcasting.com

Casts commercials and features. Union. Accepts photos by mail only.

CAROL BARLOW (323) 962-0377

See listing for PRIME CASTING.

BARRY/GREEN-KEYES (818) 759-4425
4924 Balboa Ave., #37
Encino 91316

Matthew Barry and Nancy Green-Keyes cast features and accept mailed pictures and resumes only. No drop offs and no follow up calls.

DEBORAH BARYLSKI (323) 463-1925
c/o CSA FAX (323) 463-5753
606 N. Larchmont Blvd., Ste. 4B
Los Angeles 90004

Deborah Barylski, CSA. Cast "Home Improvement," "Just Shoot Me" and "Costello." Also casts MOWs. Wants photos to look like the actor. Wants to see credits, likes resumes on postcards.

PAMELA BASKER, CSA **(323) 463-1925**
c/o CSA
606 N. Larchmont Blvd., Ste. 4B
Los Angeles 90004

Casts TV. Will see DVDs and tapes only by request for a particular role. Prefers a postcard for follow ups.

LISA BEACH
BEACH/KATZMAN CASTING **(323) 468-6633**
606 N. Larchmont Blvd., #311
Los Angeles 90004

Lisa Beach and Sara Katzman cast features and TV and accept mailed submissions only. Please no phone calls, drop offs or faxes. They will attend showcases.

EYDE BELASCO **(213) 388-1475**
3780 Wilshire Blvd., 7th Fl. **FAX (310) 369-1496**
Los Angeles 90011

Accepts mailed submissions from union and non union actors. Will attend showcases and screenings and conducts generals when time permits.

JUDY BELSHE – THE GREAT BALBOA **(562) 621-0121**
3317 E. 10th St.
Long Beach 90804
belshecasting@aol.com

Casts: industrials, CD ROMs, commercials and features. Prefers to be approached by email. Under BOOKS & TAPES in the MARKETING section for further information.

LINDA BERGER CASTING **(310) 271-2690**
9200 Sunset Blvd., Penthouse 20
Los Angeles 90069

Casts for television and features. Mailed pictures and resumes are accepted. No drop offs or follow up calls.

TERRY BERLAND CASTING **(323) 969-8200**
www.terryberlandcasting.com

Will only accept mailed submissions. Please no drop-ins or phone calls. Follow ups by note or postcard are welcome. Ms. Berland teaches a class in "Acting In TV Commercials" and casts commercials, independent films, voice overs and animation. Moving at time of publication. Call or check website for more information.

AMY JO BERMAN – HBO **(310) 201-9537**
Director of Features Casting
2500 Broadway Ste. 400
Santa Monica 89494

Accepts agent submissions only. Please no phone calls or faxes.

CHEMIN BERNARD & ASSOCIATES **(213) 507-7400**
c/o CSA
606 N. Larchmont Blvd., Ste. 4B
Los Angeles 90004

Chemin Sylvia Bernard, CSA. No photo preference in mailed submissions. Please, no follow up calls. Actors may call for current address for submission purposes only.

BARBARA BERSELL **(310) 470-1670**

Does not want any unsolicited submissions. Prefers to work through an agent. Will accept a written follow up. Please no unsolicited phone calls.

BESTROP/YANKLOWITZ CASTING **(818) 508-7451**
11336 Camarillo St., Ste. 301
W. Toluca Lake 91602

Juel Bestrop and Seth Yanklowitz cast features and accept mailed submissions only. No faxes, drop offs or phone calls.

BETTY MAE, INC. **(310) 396-6100**
1023 1/2 Abbot Kinney
Venice 90291

Mary Vernieu does TV and film casting. Agent submissions only.

TAMMARA BILLIK CASTING **(818) 623-1631**
13547 Ventura Blvd., Ste. 688
Studio City 91604

Tammara is open to non-union and non-represented and accepts submissions by mail only. No drop offs and no follow up calls. Attends showcases.

JAN BINA

See listing for MICHAEL LIEN/DAN COWAN & ASSOCIATES. Jan teaches workshops on occasion.

TONY BIRKLEY – WARNER BROS. **(818) 954-7648**
Manager of Casting
300 Television Plaza, Bldg. 140, Ste. 141
Burbank 91502

Accepts mailed unsolicited pictures and resumes from union actors. No phone calls or drop offs.

JOE BLAKE CASTING **(323) 954-0007**
200 S. La Brea
Los Angeles 90038

Commercial casting. Accepts submissions by mail only, no phone calls, drop offs or faxes. They go not give Generals or classes. Was in the process or moving at press time. Please call for further information.

BARBIE BLOCK **(323) 453-1925**
c/o CSA
606 N. Larchmont Blvd., Ste. 4B
Los Angeles 90004

BLUESTEIN/ST. CYR CASTING **(323) 468-4562**
1438 N. Gower, Bldg. 35, Ste. 156
Los Angeles 90028

Casts for television. Agent submissions only.

EUGENE BLYTHE ABC TELEVISION **(818) 460-7313**
Executive Vice President of Casting
500 S. Buena Vista, ABC Bldg.
Burbank 91522

Union only, accepts DVDs, tapes, and will attend showcases. No calls, don't visit.

ANNIE BOEDECKER – E! NETWORK **(323) 954-2400**
Vice President of Casting
5700 Wilshire Blvd.
Los Angeles 90036

Accepts mailed pictures and resumes. No phone calls or faxes please.

LOREE BOOTH

See listing for T.L.C. BOOTH.

DEEDEE BRADLEY, CSA (818) 977-8956
6767 Forest Lawn Dr., Ste. 100
Los Angeles 90068

Casts for television. Will see DVDs and tapes by her request only. Prefers mailed submissions. Agent referral only.

MEGAN BRANMAN (323) 463-1925
c/o CSA, 606 N. Larchmont Blvd., Ste. 4B
Los Angeles 90004

Accepts mailed submissions only. No drop offs, phone calls or faxes. Union only.

KATE BRINEGAR (323) 463-1925
c/o CSA
606 N Larchmont Blvd., #4B
Los Angeles 90004

Will accept pictures and resumes via mail only.

JACKIE BRISKEY, CSA (818) 655-5601
CBS Studio Center
4024 Radford Admin Bldg., Ste. 280
Studio City 91604

Jackie Briskey and Dana Olson accept mailed submissions only. No phone calls or faxes. They are open to attending showcases and screenings.

ROSS BROWN

See listing for BROWN/WEST CASTING.

BROWN/WEST CASTING (323) 938-2575
7319 Beverly Blvd., Ste. 10
Los Angeles 90036

Partners: Ross Brown, Mary West. DVDs and tapes are seen by request only and actor must pick them up within 2 weeks. Follow up calls are accepted.

ANDREW S. BROWN
DIRECTOR OF CASTING, MOTION PICTURES
PARAMOUNT STUDIOS (323) 956-5480
5555 Melrose Ave. FAX (323) 862-1371
Bob Hope Bldg., Ste. 206
Los Angeles 90038

Casts features. Will accept pictures and resumes by mail only. No DVDs or tapes. No drop-offs and no follow ups.

MARY BUCK, CSA – WARNER BROS. (818) 954-7645
Senior Vice President of Talent/TV
300 Television Plaza, Bldg. 140, 1st Fl.
Burbank 91505

Will review mailed pictures and resumes. Please no drop off and no tapes or DVDs. Generals are scheduled through agents.

PEGGY BULLINGTON (323) 463-1925
c/o CSA
606 N. Larchmont Blvd., Ste. 4B
Los Angeles 90004

Will accept mailed pictures and resumes only. No drop offs, faxes, or phone calls.

BURROWS BOLAND CASTING (310) 587-3596
bbcasting@aol.com

Victoria Burrows and Scot Boland cast features, cable, direct to video, studio independents, made for TV movies, miniseries and network. They do not accept unsolicited materials. Email for their current mailing address as they move from project to project.

TWINKIE BYRD (818) 623-2336
6044 Farmdale Ave.
North Hollywood 9160

Open to working with non-union actors on occasion. Accepts mailed submissions only. No drop-offs or follow up calls.

IRENE CAGEN

See listing for LIEBERMAN/PATTON CASTING.

CRAIG CAMPOBASSO CASTING, CSA (818) 503-2474
c/o CSA
606 N. Larchmont Blvd., Ste. 4B
Los Angeles 90004

2425 Colorado Ave., Ste. 208
Santa Monica 90404
craigcampobasso@aol.com

Nineteen year veteran Casting Director for film and television. Emmy Nominated for Outstanding Casting for a Series for "Picket Fences" on CBS. Also recently cast "Sky Captain and the World of Tomorrow."

PAMELA CAMPUS CASTING (818) 897-1588 (310) 398-2715

Casts commercials, industrials, film, and soaps. Only accepts submissions through agents. Prefers to see composites and 3/4 bodyshots as she wants to see both the face and body of an actor. Will accept follow ups from agents only. Does not accept phone calls or drop-ins.

REUBEN CANNON & ASSOCIATES (323) 939-3190
5225 Wilshire Blvd., Ste. 526 FAX (323) 939-7793
Los Angeles 90036

Reuben Cannon, CSA. Casts animated features. Prefers mailed submissions. Will not accept follow up calls, prefers a note.

BLYTHE CAPELLO (310) 752-8000
Director of Casting, Spike TV
2600 Colorado Blvd.
Santa Monica 90404

Accepts pictures, resumes and invitations to showcases, plays and screenings.

CATHI CARLTON (310) 248-5296

Cathi Carlton casts commercials and will accept pictures and resumes by mail only. No faxes, drop offs or phone calls. Was in the process of moving at press time. Call number for forwarding information.

CARNES & COMPANY (818) 445-0996

Thomas Carnes casts commercials and industrials and accepts pictures and resumes via mail only. He is open to attending workshops and showcases. Call for current address.

MEGHAN CARRAFIELLO

See listing for TEPPER/GALLEGOS.

CARSEY WERNER MANDABACH (818) 655-5598
4024 Radford Ave., Bldg. 3 FAX (818) 655-6189
Studio City 91604

Agent submissions only.

FERNE CASSEL (323) 463-1925
c/o CSA
606 N. Larchmont Blvd., Ste. 4B
Los Angeles 90004
fcassel@earthlink.net

Ferne casts made for TV movies, as well as studio and independent projects. She accepts submissions by mail only from union and non-union talent. No drop offs or phone calls. She attends showcases and workshops and asked that we list the CSA contact information as she is constantly moving from project to project.

ALICE CASSIDY, CSA (323) 931-4381
c/o CSA
606 N. Larchmont Blvd., Ste. 4B
Los Angeles 90004

Alice Cassidy accepts submissions through agents or managers only.

CASTING BY CHRISTINA (310) 652-4399
7080 Hollywood Blvd., Ste. 305
Hollywood 90028
www.theactorsedgeacademy.com

Prefers 3/4 bodyshots and mailed submissions. Christina looks for stats and film/TV credits on resumes and she casts feature films, and TV pilots. A written note or postcard is fine for follow up. Please, no phone calls or walk-ins. Also teaches classes.

THE CASTING COMPANY (818) 487-5600
12750 Ventura Blvd., Ste. 102
Studio City 91604

Janet Hirshenson, CSA. Jane Jenkins, CSA and Michelle Lewitt will see requested tapes only. Uses the Academy Players Directory "all the time." Absolutely no phone calls.

THE CASTING COUCH (818) 907-6999
13731 Ventura Blvd., Ste. C
Studio City 91423

Sande Alessi casts for television, commercials and film. Mailed submissions are accepted, but no follow up phone calls or faxes.

LUCY CAVALLO – CBS (323) 575-2335
VP of Drama Casting
7800 Beverly Blvd.
Los Angeles 90036

Agent submissions only.

LINDSAY CHAG (818) 501-0260
14611 Hartsook St.
Sherman Oaks 91403

Casts film. Open to showcases, plays and screenings.

DENISE CHAMIAN (323) 858-6765
c/o CSA
606 N. Larchmont Blvd., Ste. 4B
Los Angeles 90004

FERN CHAMPION, CSA (323) 650-1280
8255 Sunset Blvd.
Los Angeles 90046

Accepts mailed submissions only. Please no drop offs or follow up calls. Open to non-represented and non-union. Attends showcases, plays and screenings.

SHARON CHAZIN LEIBLEIN
NICKELODEON (310) 752-8402
2600 Colorado Ave., 2nd Fl.
Santa Monica, CA 90404 90066

Accepts mailed submissions from actors whether they are union, non-union, represented or without representation.

KAREN CHURCH – CBS (323) 575-2335
VP of Comedy Casting
7800 Beverly Blvd., Ste. 284
Los Angeles 90036

Will see tapes and DVDs by her request and only with a SASE. Please, no follow ups.

JOANNA COLBERT CASTING (310) 777-3104
9720 Wilshire Blvd., 4th Fl.
Beverly Hills 90202

Independent casting director. Will accept mailed pictures and resumes but no follow faxes or phone calls.

AISHA COLEY (323) 882-4144

Prefers to be approached by agents only.

ANNELISE COLLINS CASTING (310) 586-1936
3435 Ocean Park Blvd. FAX (310) 586-1100
Ste. 112
Santa Monica 90405
www.annelisecast.com
annelisecast@earthlink.net

Annelise casts features films, television, independent films, industrials, miniseries and commercials. Will accept mailed headshots and resumes and is open to attending showcases, plays and screenings.

RUTH CONFORTE CASTING (818) 771-7287
P.O. Box 2637
Toluca Lake 91610

Ruth Conforte, CSA. Casts feature films, TV and commercials. Has no photo style preference for mailed submissions. Suggests that actors keep in touch through the mail via postcards or new photos. Ruth will accept invitations to showcases and screenings and is open to non-union and non-represented.

ALLISON COWITT, CSA (818) 345-3434
P.O. Box 570550
Tarzana 91357

See listing for FENTON/COWITT CASTING.

ELAINE CRAIG VOICE CASTING (323) 469-8773
6464 Sunset Blvd., Ste. 1150
Los Angeles 90028
www.elainecraig.com
ecvc@elainecraig.com

Casts voice-overs. Cassette tapes, CDs accepted by mail only, no drop offs or follow up calls.

CRYSTAL SKY COMMUNICATIONS (310) 843-0223
1901 Avenue of the Stars. FAX (310) 553-9895
Ste. 605
Los Angeles 90067

Dorothy Koster. Primarily casts features. Will occasionally accept agent-submitted tapes or DVDs and wants follow ups to be done only by agents. No generals.

CURRENTLY CASTING INC. **(818) 613-7703**
16311 Ventura Blvd., Ste. 1180
Encino 91436

Michelle Metzner casts for TV and film and accepts pictures and resume via mail only. No drop offs, faxes or phone calls. DVDs by request only.

JOE D'AGOSTA **(310) 652-8123**

Casts primarily independent films, some features and MOWs. Will accept headshot submissions and tapes only from an agent or with a recommendation. Only sees actors when casting a specific project. Please, no calls.

BILLY DAMOTA CASTING **(818) 243-1263**
www.castboy.com
castboy@castboy.com

Cast the film, "Reflection in the Dark" with Mimi Rogers, and other independent films. Cast films and commercials. Gives occasional Generals.

COLLIN DANIEL, CSA **(323) 463-1925**
c/o CSA
606 N. Larchmont Blvd., Ste. 4B
Los Angeles 90004

ANITA DANN, CSA **(310) 278-7765**
8665 Wilshire Blvd., Ste. 309 **FAX (310) 652-7663**
Beverly Hills 90211

Accepts submissions by mail only. No drop offs and no follow up calls.

AYO DAVIS – ABC **(818) 460-6425**
Exec. Director of Casting for Drama and MOWs
500 S. Buena Vista, ABC Bldg.
Burbank 90067

Accepts headshot submissions. Follow up calls are not encouraged.

DAVIS BADDELEY CASTING **(323) 465-9999**
1641 N. Ivar Ave.
Hollywood 90028

Accepts unsolicited submissions and maintains casting files. Please, no phone calls.

ERIC DAWSON, CSA

See listing for ULRICH/DAWSON/KRITZER CASTING.

ELINA DE SANTOS **(310) 829-5958**
P.O. Box 1718
Santa Monica 90406-1718

Prefers mailed submissions and wants to see "a spark of life" in pictures. Prefers written follow ups, and asks that there be no drop-ins. In addition to Ms. De Santos' ongoing scene study class and her monthly workshop, she also teaches a 25 hour intensive workshop, "You Are The Pilot," and several classes at UCLA Extension. Currently directing several shows.

LIZ DEAN

See listing for ULRICH/DAWSON/KRITZER CASTING.

TRISHA DEBSKI **(310) 234-5035**
Viacom
10880 Wilshire Blvd., Ste. 1500
Los Angeles 90024

Casts for television and film. Mailed headshots and resumes only. Please no drop offs, faxes or phone calls.

ZORA DEHORTER CASTING, CSA **(310) 586-8964**
10250 Constellation Blvd. **FAX (310) 264-1210**
2nd Fl., Ste. 2060
Century City 90067
www.zoradehortercasting.com
zdehorter@mgm.com

Casts features, TV, theatre and music videos. Agent referral only. Also teaches.

RICHARD DELANCY & ASSOC. **(818) 760-3110**
4741 Laurel Canyon Blvd. **FAX (818) 760-1382**
Ste. 100
Studio City 91604
www.delancy.com

Has no photo style preference "as long as a phone number is on the resume somewhere." Will accept DVDs and tapes by request only and auditions are by appointment only. No drop-offs, no walk-ins. A postcard is a good idea for a personal update, new agent, new phone number, etc. Mr. Delancy is also a personal manager.

JOANNE DENAUT
SOUTH COAST REPERTORY THEATRE **(714) 708-5500**
655 Town Center Dr. **FAX (714) 545-0391**
Costa Mesa 92626

P.O. Box 2197
Costa Mesa 92628
www.scr.org
sberry@scr.org

Works with Equity actors. Mailed submissions should be headshots and resume. No follow up calls. Will also look at agent submissions. Gives Generals twice a year at the theatre for people she has called from their submissions.

LESLEE DENNIS **(323) 463-1925**
c/o CSA
606 N. Larchmont Blvd., Ste. 4B
Los Angeles 90004

Casts for commercials. Accepts mailed pictures and resumes but tapes by request only. Union only.

DICKSON/ARBUSTO CASTING **(213) 739-0556**
3875 Wilshire Blvd., Ste. 701
Los Angeles 90010

Joy Dickson and Nicole Arbusto accept mailed submissions from union, non-union and non-represented but ask that there be no drop offs, faxes of follow up calls. They cast for TV, film and commercials.

RON DIGMAN
20TH CENTURY FOX TELEVISION **(310) 369-2121**
10201 W. Pico Blvd.
Los Angeles 90035

Television casting through agents. By referral.

PAM DIXON, CSA (310) 432-4852
10351 Santa Monica Blvd., Ste. 200
Los Angeles 90025

Prefers mailed submissions. Please, no walk-ins. Prefers to meet actors for specific projects. Follow up should be through an agent.

MICHAEL DONOVAN CASTING (323) 655-9020
8170 Beverly Blvd., Ste. 105
Los Angeles 90048

Michael Donovan has an extensive background in the entertainment field including numerous feature films, television series, theatre productions, and commercials. Michael Donovan started in the business as an actor and director, and has now been casting for over 12 years. He accepts pictures and resumes from union, non-union and non-represented actors via mail. No drop offs, faxes or follow up calls.

CHRISTY DOOLEY (323) 575-4501
CBS Television
7800 Beverly Blvd., #3371
Los Angeles 90036

Casts soaps and TV. Union. Mailed headshots and resumes are accepted by mail only, but please no phone calls or drop offs.

BRIAN DORFMAN – ABC TELEVISION (818) 460-6547
500 S. Buena Vista, ABC Bldg., Ste. 9218
Burbank 91521-4643

Vice President of Casting, Comedies, for ABC Television. Union only. Accepts tapes, and will attend showcases. No phone calls or drop ins.

MICK DOWD CASTING (323) 665-1776
200 S. La Brea, 2nd Fl.
Los Angeles 90048

Mick Dowd casts commercials. Likes both 3/4 bodyshots and headshots. Submit by mail only, no walk-ins. Also accepts invitations by mail and sees plays and showcases often. Frequently casts actors he's seen.

MARY DOWNEY (818) 563-1200
705 N. Kenwood St.
Burbank 91505

Casts TV. Prefers mailed submissions. Please, no follow ups. Is interested in discovering new talent, so she accepts invitations and goes to plays and showcases often. Believes that many excellent actors and performers are without representation.

DORIAN DUNAS, CSA (323) 463-1925
c/o CSA
606 N. Larchmont Blvd., Ste. 4B
Los Angeles 90004

SUSAN EDELMAN CASTING CO. (818) 977-1820
6767 Forest Lawn Dr., Ste. 210
Los Angeles 90068

Susan Edelman, CSA casts pilots and MOWs as well as mini-series. Prefers mailed submissions. Will accept written follow ups and gives Generals by referral and does not teach classes.

KATHRYN EISENSTEIN (323) 463-1925
c/o CSA
606 N. Larchmont Blvd., Ste. 4B
Los Angeles 90004

STEVE ERDEK (310) 770-7226

Maintains casting files and accepts pictures and resumes from union actors via mail only. Casts TV, film, commercials and voice over. Was in the process of relocating at press time. Please call number for forwarding information.

DANIELLE ESKINAZI (323) 465-9999 x2
1641 N. Ivar
Hollywood 90028
www.daniellecasting.com

Accepts mailed submissions from union, non-union and non-represented actors. Please no phone calls, faxes or drop offs. Film, TV, and commercial casting.

LESLEE FELDMAN (818) 733-6411
100 Universal City Plaza, Bldg. 5135
Universal City 91608

Gives general interviews when arranged by an agent. Supervises talent casting for network TV, feature film and animation at Dreamworks. No follow ups, if she's interested she will pass a P&R on to a casting director for a particular project.

FENTON/COWITT CASTING (818) 345-3434
P.O. Box 570550
Tarzana 91357

Associates: Mike Fenton, CSA. Allison Cowitt, CSA. Prefers mailed submissions and follow ups by agents although they will accept mailed follow ups from actors.

LISA FIELDS – CASTING CAFE (310) 274-9909
9000 Santa Monica Blvd.
West Hollywood 90069

Currently casting commercials and features. Maintains casting files. Will see scenes in the office only when casting for a specific part. Please no follow ups and no phone calls, and no drop offs. Mainly interested in agent submissions, non-union OK.

FINN HILLER CASTING (323) 460-4530
588 N. Larchmont Blvd.
Los Angeles 90004

Randy Hiller and Sarah Halley-Finn will accept unsolicited pictures and resumes with a follow up postcard. No DVDs or tapes, no drop-offs and no follow up calls. Cast "Crash."

MALI FINN CASTING (323) 848-3737
8284 Santa Monica Blvd. FAX (323) 822-3465
West Hollywood 90046

Mali Finn and Lauren Bass accept submissions by mail only. No phone calls, faxes or drop offs. Open to union, non-union and unrepresented.

SARAH HALLEY FINN

See listing for FINN HILLER CASTING.

FIORENTINO/MANGIERI CASTING (323) 671-4700
4151 Prospect Producers Bldg, 1st Fl.
Los Angeles 90027

Cast for TV and features. Pictures and resumes accepted by mail only. No drop offs or follow up calls.

FIREFLY CASTING **(323) 857-1699**
5225 Wilshire Blvd., Ste. 502
Los Angeles 90036

Richard Hicks and David Rubin cast for film, television and theatre. They prefer mailed submissions and will accept invitations. No follow up calls.

MEGAN FOLEY CASTING, CCDA **(818) 216-9350**
11340 Moorpark Ave.
Studio City 91602

Prefers mailed submissions. Does not want to see DVDs or tapes. A written thank you note is fine, but no telephone follow ups.

KIMBERLY FOSTER CASTING **(323) 634-5207**
5700 Wilshire Blvd., #575
Los Angeles 90036

Kimberly Foster casts "Charmed" and accepts pictures and resumes from union and non-union as well as non-represented actors by mail only. No drop offs and no follow up calls. Her Associate is Karen Morris.

NANCY FOY, CSA **(323) 463-1925**
CSA, 606 N Larchmont Ave., Ste. 4B
Los Angeles 90004

Accepts submissions by mail only.

DELIA FRANKEL
SONY PICTURES TELEVISION **(310) 202-3257**
Director of Casting
9336 W. Washington Blvd.
Culver City 90232

Submissions by agent referral only.

LISA FREIBERGER, CSA **(818) 990-9956**
c/o CSA
606 N. Larchmont Blvd., Ste. 4B
Los Angeles 90004

Casts for TV and film and accepts pictures and resume by mail only.

DEAN E. FRONK

See listing for PEMRICK/FRONK CASTING.

JEAN FROST **(323) 634-8181**
c/o CSA
606 N Larchmont Blvd., Ste. 4B
Los Angeles 90004

Prefers to use the CSA address for submissions. Will call if interested. DVDs and tapes by request only.

DENNIS GALLEGOS

See listing for TEPPER/GALLEGOS CASTING.

NICOLE GARCIA **(323) 860-8975**
c/o MADtv
Hollywood Center Studios
1040 North Las Palmas, Bldg. 3
Hollywood 90038

Accepts pictures and resumes by mail only. Do not fax or visit.

RISA BRAMON GARCIA, CSA **(323) 463-1925**
c/o CSA
606 N. Larchmont Blvd., Ste. 4B
Los Angeles 90004

CASTING BY JEFF GERRARD **(818) 752-7100**
www.jeffgerrard.com **FAX (818) 782-0030**
thebigdaddy@adelphia.net

Jeff Gerrard casts TV, voice, stage, radio and commercials. He accepts pictures and resumes by mail only. No drop offs or follow up calls. Open to seeing non union and non represented. Call for address.

DAN GIBSON E! ENTERTAINMENT TV **(323) 954-2446**
Director of On-Air Talent and Casting
5750 Wilshire Blvd., 2nd Fl.
Los Angeles 90036

Prefers mailed submissions. A postcard follow up is fine but no phone calls. DVDs and tapes, with a SASE, are welcome.

JAN GLASER

See listing for GERALD WOLF AND ASSOCIATES.

LAURA GLEASON CASTING, CSA **(818) 881-6643**
19528 Ventura Blvd., #370
Tarzana 91356

Casts for theatre, film and TV. Mailed submissions from union actors only. A postcard follow up is OK.

(818) 735-7372
CHARISSE GLENN CASTING **(310) 656-4600 x9**
www.cgcasting.com
cgcast@flash.net

Accepts agent submissions only.

VICKI GOGGIN & ASSOCIATES CASTING **(310) 492-6540**
Chelsea Studios
451 N. La Cienega Blvd.
Los Angeles 90048

Commercial casting. Accepts mailed pictures and resumes.

GAIL GOLDBERG DISNEY PICTURES **(818) 560-7509**
500 S. Buena Vista St., Frank Wells Bldg., Ste. 1088
Burbank 91521

Will see actors through agents. Prefers headshots for mailed submission and written follow ups. Does not accept any phone calls.

PETER GOLDEN, CSA – CBS **(323) 575-2335**
Exec. Vice President **FAX (323) 575-2279**
of Talent & Casting
7800 Beverly Blvd., Ste. 284
Los Angeles 90036

Oversees the casting for CBS. Does no actual casting himself. Pictures and resumes are accepted but no tapes or DVDs.

DANNY GOLDMAN & ASSOCIATES **(323) 463-1600**
1006 N. Cole Ave. **FAX (323) 463-9566**
Los Angeles 90038

Associates: Danny Goldman, Alan Kaminsky, Mariko Balentine, Josh Rapparot. Primarily casts commercials and voice-overs. Video tapes are not encouraged. Follow ups are accepted and they prefer a postcard. They also prefer to work through agents.

LOUIS GOLDSTEIN & ASSOCIATES CASTING **(805) 646-2957**

Louis Goldstein and Diane Goldstein. Casts industrials, print work, and voice-overs on occasion. Prefers mailed submissions and will accept written follow ups. Has Generals as time permits. Call for address.

GOLDWASSER/MELTZER CASTING (323) 762-7114
5800 W. Sunset Blvd., Bldg. 11, Ste. 201
Los Angeles 90028

Carol Goldwasser and Howard Meltzer cast for TV and film. They accept pictures and resumes by mail, no drop offs or follow up calls.

MARSHA GOODMAN
DIC ENTERTAINMENT (818) 955-5400
Senior Vice President of Talent FAX (818) 955-5696
4100 W. Alameda
Burbank 91505

Casts voice-overs for all of DIC's animated series. Will listen to voice tapes from actors submitted by agents only. CDs and tapes should be no longer than 3 minutes and should have a wide range of voices including many character voices.

MARILYN GRANAS (310) 278-3773
220 S. Palm Dr. FAX (310) 278-5359
Beverly Hills 90212

Casts films, TV, and commercials. Does not look at tapes and does not accept follow up calls. Please, no phone calls.

JEFF GREENBERG & ASSOC. (323) 956-4886
Paramount Studios FAX (323) 862-1368
5555 Melrose Ave.
Swanson Bldg., Ste. 10
Los Angeles 90038

Jeff Greenberg does not appreciate walk-ins, prefers mailed submissions. Will not accept phone calls but a postcard follow up is fine. Several of the associates teach classes.

AARON GRIFFITH (323) 654-0033
8440 Santa Monica Blvd., Ste. 200
West Hollywood 90069
www.castingdirector.nu

Cast the features, "Jeepers Creepers Part 2", "Pavilion of Women," and "Speedway Junkie." Prefers mailed submissions and mailed follow ups are fine. Maintains casting files. Please, no phone calls and no drop-ins.

AL GUARINO (310) 829-6009
2118 Wilshire Blvd., Ste. 995
Santa Monica 90403

Will see DVDs and tapes with a SASE. Please, no phone calls or drop-ins.

PAMELA RACK GUEST (323) 463-1925
c/o CSA
606 N. Larchmont Blvd., Ste. 4B
Los Angeles 90004

SHEILA GUTHRIE (323) 956-5578
Senior Vice President of Casting, Paramount
5555 Melrose Ave., Bludhorn Bldg. #128
Los Angeles 90038

Shelia casts for television and accepts mailed pictures and resumes but no drop offs or phone calls are accepted.

MILT HAMERMAN, CSA (323) 463-1925
c/o CSA
606 N. Larchmont Blvd., Ste. 4B
Los Angeles 90004

ROBERT HARBIN (323) 463-1925
c/o CSA
606 N. Larchmont Blvd., Ste. 4B
Los Angeles 90004

Miled submissions only. Please no drop offs or follow up calls.

NATALIE HART, CSA

See listing for LA PADURA/HART CASTING.

SUSAN HAVINS (310) 492-6500
Chelsea Studios
451 N. La Cienega Blvd.
Los Angeles 90048

Casts commercials music videos and print. Cast the feature "Dog Fight." Prefers to work with agents but will accept P&R submissions and postcard follow ups from actors. Will see tapes and DVDs only by request. Open to union, represented actors as well as non-union and non-represented actors.

PATTI HAYES (323) 933-0116
419 N. Larchmont Bl., #249
Los Angeles 90004
pattisan2@hotmail.com

A full service casting supervisor. Prefers mailed submissions, the 8 x 10 photo should not be folded and put into a business envelope. Ms. Hayes will look at DVDs and tapes only at her request. A postcard with a photo on it is welcome as long as she knows or has spoken to the actor. She maintains a casting file.

RENE HAYNES, CSA (818) 842-0187
1314 Scott Rd.
Burbank 91504

Full service casting director who does specialized talent searches such as the casting for "Into the West," the Native American movies "Skins," "The New World" and "Dream Keeper." She accepts pictures and resumes by mail only, DVDs and tapes by request and she is open to non-represented actors. Union projects.

CATHY HENDERSON–MARTIN, CSA (805) 773-2256
205 Five Cities Dr., Ste. 134
Pismo Beach 93449

Accepts pictures and resumes via mail only. No drop offs or phone calls.

DAWN HERSHEY (818) 414-9854
8335 Sunset Blvd., Ste. 303
West Hollywood 90069

Accepts mp3s for voiceover.

RANDI HILLER

See listing for FINN HILLER CASTING.

MARC HIRSCHFELD, CSA NBC (818) 840-3774
3000 W. Alameda Ave., Ste. 225
Burbank 91523

Accepts unsolicited pictures and resumes from union actors.

JANET HIRSHENSON, CSA

See listing for THE CASTING COMPANY.

HISPANIC TALENT CASTING OF HOLLYWOOD (323) 934-6465
P.O. Box 46123
Los Angeles 90046

Bill Hooey. Casts TV commercials. Also casts industrials. Prefers headshots and finds mailed follow ups important whenever your look changes. When submitting your headshot please include email address as they will notify by email.

BILL HOOEY

See listing for HISPANIC TALENT CASTING OF HOLLYWOOD.

ALYSON HORN (323) 874-8764
1015 N. Orange Dr.
Los Angeles 90038

Accepts pictures and resumes by mail only. No drop offs or follow up phone calls. No tapes or DVDs.

BOB HUBER FOX BROADCASTING (310) 369-1000
Senior Vice President of Fox Talent and Casting
10201 W. Pico Blvd. FAX (310) 369-1914
Executive Bldg., Ste. 4010
Los Angeles 90035

Agent referrals only. Union.

VICTORIA HUFF & ASSOCIATES (323) 634-1260
5700 Wilshire Blvd., Ste. 500N FAX (323) 634-1266
Los Angeles 90036

Accepts agent submissions only.

JULIE HUTCHINSON, CSA (818) 777-8327
100 Universal City Plaza, Bldg. 2160, Ste. 8A
Universal City 91608

Prefers mailed submissions. Interested in comedic talent. Follow up postcards, faxes, etc., are welcome. Union.

DONNA ISAACSON, CSA
20TH CENTURY FOX (310) 369-1824
Exec. Vice President Features FAX (310) 369-1496
10201 W. Pico Blvd., Bldg. 12, Rm. 201
Los Angeles 90035

Casts two or three projects a year herself, otherwise she oversees the process. Has no preference for photo styles in mailed submissions and a post card follow up is fine. Please, no phone calls and no drop-ins.

JOHN JACKSON (310) 429-42552
c/o CSA
606 N. Larchmont Blvd., Ste. 4B
Los Angeles 90004

Independent. Casts for TV, commercials and film and will accept submissions by mail only, no faxes, drop offs or follow up calls. Will attend showcases, plays and screenings.

RICK JACOBS LIFETIME TELEVISION (310) 556-7564
2049 Century Park East, Ste. 840
Los Angeles 90067

Accepts pictures and resumes from actors but its better if they come through an agent. No phone calls or drop offs. Rarely gives generals.

JANE JENKINS, CSA

See listing for THE CASTING COMPANY.

JOEY PAUL JENSEN, CSA (323) 860-3306
1040 N. Las Palmas, Bldg. 33, 2nd Fl.
Hollywood 90028

Independent. Casts for Disney "That's So Raven" and "Phil of the Future" among many other projects. Accepts unsolicited pictures and resumes by mail only. DVDs and tapes by request. Uses non-union on rare occasion. No phone calls please!

ELIZABETH JERESKI (310) 393-3141
c/o CSA
606 N. Larchmont Blvd., Ste. 4B
Los Angeles 90004

Casts for TV and film and accepts unsolicited pictures and resumes via mail. Please no drop offs, faxes or follow up calls.

TARA-ANNE JOHNSON (818) 470-1291
c/o CSA
606 N. Larchmont Blvd., Ste. 4B
Los Angeles 90004

Casts for television and uses the CSA address and phone number for submissions which are then forwarded to the office she is working out of. Open to headshot submissions and invitations to showcases and screenings.

KALLES/JAMES CASTING (310) 467-7971
1801 Avenue of the Starts, Ste. 611
Los Angeles 90067

Pictures and resumes accepted by mail only. No phone calls and no drop offs. DVDs accepted by request only.

ALAN KAMINSKY

See listing for DANNY GOLDMAN & ASSOCIATES.

CHRISTIAN KAPLAN, CSA
VP OF FEATURE CASTING
20TH CENTURY FOX (310) 369-1883
10201 W. Pico Blvd. FAX (310) 369-1496
Bldg. 12., Rm. 201
Los Angeles 90035

Oversees feature casting at Fox. Prefers mailed submissions. Interested in comedic talent. Follow up postcards, faxes, etc., are welcome.

TRACY KAPLAN CASTING (310) 559-3306
c/o CSA
606 N. Larchmont Blvd., Ste. 4B
Los Angeles 90004

Accepts mailed pictures and resumes as well as invitations to showcases and screenings.

SARAH KATZMAN
BEACH/KATZMAN CASTING (323) 468-6633
606 N. Larchmont Blvd., Ste. 311
Los Angeles 90004

Features and TV casting. Accepts mailed submissions only. Please no phone calls, drop offs or faxes. They will attend showcases.

LORA KENNEDY WARNER BROS. (818) 954-4191
Senior Vice President of Talent Features
4000 Warner Blvd. FAX (818) 954-4082
Bldg. 103, Ste. 117
Burbank 91522

Does not accept phone calls, and doesn't want any unsolicited tapes. Submissions by agents only.

LEE SONJA KISSIK

See listing for MAGIC CASTING.

BETH KLEIN SHOWTIME (310) 234-5035
10880 Wilshire Blvd., Ste. 1101
Los Angeles 90024

Casts MOWs and cable TV. Prefers mailed submissions. No drop-offs or phone calls. Postcard follow ups are accepted. Union only.

SHARON KLEIN
20TH CENTURY FOX TV (310) 369-2121
Sr. VP of Talent and Casting
10201 W. Pico Blvd., Bldg. 88, Rm. 243
Los Angeles 90035

Only accepts agent submissions.

THOM KLOHN (323) 463-1925
c/o CSA
606 N. Larchmont Blvd., Ste. 4B
Los Angeles 90004

NANCY KLOPPER (323) 463-1925
c/o CSA
606 N. Larchmont Blvd., Ste. 4B
Los Angeles 90004

Features casting. Cast "Ray."

ELLEN KNIGHT (818) 753-9585
12031 Ventura Blvd., Ste. 4
Studio City 91604

Accepts mailed pictures and resumes only, please no drop offs, faxes or phone calls. Eileen casts for television, film and commercials.

KATHY KNOWLES (310) 394-4145
1216 5th St.
Santa Monica 90401

Casts commercials only. Prefers mailed submissions. Please no phone calls and no follow ups. Open to union, non-union, represented and non-represented.

KOBLIN HARDING CASTING (310) 785-9779
P.O. Box 7156
Beverly Hills 90212

Prefers to be approached by agents.

DOROTHY KOSTER

See listing for CRYSTAL SKY COMMUNICATIONS.

ANNAMARIE KOSTURA NBC (818) 840-4410
Vice President of Daytime Casting
3000 W. Alameda Ave., Ste. 304
Burbank 91523

Vice President of Daytime Casting for NBC TV works with AFTRA actors but will see non-union actors. Strongly prefers headshots. A written follow up is welcome but not necessary.

CAROL KRITZER, CSA

See listing for ULRICH/DAWSON/KRITZER CASTING.

DEBORAH KURTZ CASTING (310) 477-6555
11751 Mississippi Ave., Ste. 140
Venice 90291

TV, film and commercial casting. Accepts pictures and resumes from union, non-union, represented and non-represented via mail only. Please no drop-offs, faxes or follow up calls. Open to attending showcases, plays and screenings.

LA PADURA/HART CASTING (818) 733-4735
100 Universal City Plaza, Trailer 6149
Universal City 91608

Jason La Padura and Natalie Hart accept submissions only by referral. They are open to attending showcases, plays, and screenings.

JASON LA PADURA, CSA

See listing for LA PADURA/HART CASTING.

KATE LACEY (818) 560-6950
500 S. Buena Vista St.,
Frank G. Wells Bldg., Ste. 1088
Burbank 91521

Casts for features. Union talent only. Mailed submissions only. No drop offs or follow up calls.

ROSS LACY (323) 954-0007
c/o Casting Studios
200 S. La Brea
Los Angeles 90036

Accepts unsolicited pictures and resumes by mail but no drop offs, faxes or follow up calls.

DINO LADKI (310) 289-4962
8556 Rugby Dr.
West Hollywood 90069

Please no submissions unless from agents. Casts for TV, and film.

JUDY LANDAU CASTING (310) 458-1100
1216 Fifth St.
Santa Monica 90401

Accepts mailed pictures and resumes but does not follow up phone calls or faxes.

LANDSBURG FIDDLEMAN CASTING (818) 981-4995
13455 Ventura Blvd., Ste 214
Sherman Oaks 91423

Submissions can be headshot and resume or a postcard. No follow ups and no fax submissions. Shana Landsburg and Teri Fiddleman cast for television and film.

MEREDITH LAYNE, NICKELODEON (818) 736-3275
231 W. Olive Ave.
Burbank 91502

Casts for television. Accepts pictures and resumes but mainly works through agents. Please, no phone calls.

GERALDINE LEDER (323) 463-1925
c/o CSA
606 N. Larchmont Blvd., Ste. 4B
Los Angeles 90004

Submissions should be headshots and resumes. Maintains casting files. Will sometimes see actors without agents and non-union actors. Casts for features and television

KELI LEE ABC (818) 460-6308
2300 Riverside Dr.
Burbank 91521

Union only. Accepts DVDs and tapes, and will attend showcases. No calls, don't visit.

CAROL LEFKO CASTING **(310) 888-0007**
P.O. Box 84509
Los Angeles 90073

Casts features, TV, commercials and theatre. Carol accepts pictures and resumes via mail from union, non-union, represented and non-represented actors. She is open to attending showcases, plays and screenings.

KATHLEEN LETTERIE
WB TV NETWORKS **(818) 977-6016**
Head of Casting **FAX (818) 977-6336**
4000 Warner Blvd., Bldg. 34r, Ste. 161
Burbank 91522

Agent referrals only.

JOHN LEVEY, CSA WARNER BROS. **(818) 954-4080**
Senior Vice President of Casting
300 Television Plaza Bldg. 17, Ste. 106
Burbank 91505

Casts "ER" and pilots. Generals are given when there is time and interest. Agent submissions should be headshots and resumes only.

GAIL LEVIN PARAMOUNT STUDIOS **(323) 956-5444**
Senior Vice President of Talent
5555 Melrose Ave., Bob Hope Bldg., Ste. 206
Los Angeles 90038

Feature Casting. No follow up calls. Postcards are accepted from time to time. Prefers to see someone on stage or in a film rather than in the office. Prefers headshot submissions.

HEIDI LEVITT CASTING **(323) 525-0800**
7201 Melrose Ave., Ste. 203 **FAX (323) 525-0843**
Los Angeles 90046
www.heidilevittcasting.com

Heidi Levitt accepts pictures and resumes by mail only. Please no drop offs, faxes of phone calls.

MEG LIBERMAN, CSA

See listing for LIBERMAN/PATTON CASTING.

LIBERMAN/PATTON CASTING **(323) 462-9175**
6464 Sunset Blvd., Ste. 707
Los Angeles 90028

Meg Liberman, Cami Patton, Irene Cagen and others. Cast "Las Vegas," "King of Queens," "Invasion" and "Medium" and many other television shows. Agent submissions only. No follow up calls and no generals.

AMY LIEBERMAN CASTING **(213) 972-7374**
601 W. Temple St. **FAX (213) 972-7645**
Los Angeles 90012

Associate: Erika Sellin. They accept invitations to plays and showcases as well as headshots with a cover letter. They do not accept tapes or DVDs. No follow up call please. They cast productions at the Mark Taper Forum, Kirk Douglas Theatre and the Ahmanson Theater. For further details regarding auditions call the Hot Line at (213) 972-7235 for Equity actors only.

MICHAEL LIEN & DAN COWAN
CASTING **(323) 937-0411**
7461 Beverly Blvd., Ste. 203 **FAX (323) 937-2070**
Los Angeles 90036

Associate: Jan Bina. Mostly casts commercials, some TV, and features. No follow up calls. Rarely sees non-union and non-represented people. No submissions will be returned. No faxes.

TRACY LILIENFIELD, CSA **(818) 655-5652**
4024 Radford Ave., Sound Shop Second Fl.
Studio City 91604

Casts for television and accepts unsolicited pictures and resumes.

MARCI LIROFF **(818) 784-5434**
P.O. Box 57948
Sherman Oaks 91413

Casts for TV and film and accepts submissions from agents only. Does attend showcases, plays, and screenings.

LESLIE LITT **(323) 463-1925**
c/o CSA
606 N. Larchmont Blvd., Ste. 4B
Los Angeles 90004

Will accept pictures and resumes but no tapes, DVDS or follow up calls. A follow up postcard is OK. Casts for TV.

BEVERLY LONG AND ASSOC. **(818) 754-6222**
11425 Moorpark St. **FAX (818) 754-6226**
Studio City 91602
www.beverlylong-casting.com
info@beverlylong-casting.com

Owners: Beverly Long and Debra-Lynn Sindon. Will accept pictures (3/4 bodyshots or "a recent photo that looks like the actor") and resumes. Tapes or DVDs are accepted, four minutes in length or less, and only if dropped off and left for a few days and then picked up. No follow up calls. Will accept a note or a postcard. Teaches commercial workshops. See listing under COMMERCIALS in the TRAINING section for further information. SEE AD ON PAGE 65.

MOLLY LOPATA, CSA **(818) 788-0673**
13731 Ventura Blvd., Ste. A
Sherman Oaks 91423

Will look at headshots and resumes by mail only. Absolutely no DVDs, tapes or phone calls. Casts for television. Union only.

LINDA LOWY **(323) 671-5438**
4151 Prospect, Cottages Room 105
Los Angeles 90027

Linda Lowy accepts unsolicited pictures and resumes via mail only, no drop offs, phone calls or faxes please. TV and film casting, no generals.

BOB MACDONALD **(323) 463-1925**
c/o CSA
606 N. Larchmont Blvd., Ste. 4B
Los Angeles 90004

Prefers to use the Casting Society address for submissions.

MACKIE/SANDRICH **(310) 449-4009**
3000 Olympic Blvd., Ste. 2323
Santa Monica 90404

Cathy Sandrich Gelfond and Wendy Weidman accept mailed submissions only.

MAGIC CASTING **(805) 688-3702**
1660 Cougar Ridge Rd.
Buellton 93427

Lee Sonja Kissik. Also casts industrials and union and non-union extras. Will view DVDs or VHS tapes, actors must pick up the tape 2 weeks after delivery. Generals are given on a project-by-project basis.

FRANCINE MAISLER, CSA (310) 244-6945
Sony Pictures
10202 W. Washington Blvd.
Jimmy Stewart Bldg., Rm. 207
Culver City 90232

Open to union, non-union, represented and non represented depending on the project. Accepts mailed pictures and resumes only. No drop offs, faxes or follow ups please.

SHEILA MANNING (323) 852-1046
332 S. Beverly Dr. FAX (323) 852-1013
Beverly Hills 90212

Casts commercials, television and features. Will look at headshots and resumes that are mailed. Gives Generals when time permits. Will not attend showcases if they are "paid situations." DVDs and voice CDs and tapes accepted. No follow up calls.

MARY AND KAREN MARGIOTTA CASTING (310) 288-2502

Mary and Karen cast for television and features and accept mailed submissions only. Please no phone calls, faxes or drop offs.

MINDY MARIN, CSA CASTING ARTISTS INC.
BLUEWATER RANCH (310) 395-1882
1433 6th St.
Santa Monica 90401

BlueWater Ranch Entertainment + Casting Artists Inc. Accepts pictures and resumes by mail but DVDs and tapes by request only. Open to non-union and non-represented and occasionally gives generals.

MELISSA MARTIN CASTING (323) 860-8256
6565 Romaine St., Bldg. 30
Los Angeles 90038
www.martincasting.com

Accepts pictures and resumes by mail only. No DVDs or tapes unless requested. Commercial casting.

TONY MARTINELLI
20TH CENTURY FOX TV (310) 369-2121
Director of Casting
10201 W. Pico Blvd.
Los Angeles 90035

Works through agents. By referral only.

LIZ MARX (323) 463-1925
c/o CSA
606 N. Larchmont Blvd., Ste. 4B
Los Angeles 90004

MASLAR-LIEM CASTING (818) 769-6800
4130 Cahuenga Blvd., Ste. 108
Universal City 91602
www.maslarliem.com

Casts for television and film. Accepts mailed submissions only. No drop offs, follow up calls or faxes.

VALERIE MCCAFFREY, CSA (818) 785-1886
4924 Balboa Blvd., Ste. 172
Encino 91316

Valerie McCaffrey and Steve Rhodes prefer headshot submissions via mail only. No follow up calls and no drop-offs. They cast for television and accept invitations to showcases, plays and screenings.

JEANNE MCCARTHY CASTING (310) 820-5250
12340 Santa Monica Blvd., Ste. 233
Los Angeles 90025

Casts features and pilots. Primarily goes through agents but mailed pictures and resumes are OK. No DVDs, tapes, CDs or follow up calls.

CYDNEY MCCURDY (818) 569-3055
2460 North Lake Ave., Ste. 111
Altadena 91001

Accepts pictures and resumes via mail only. No drop offs or follow up phone calls.

KELLY MCDONALD
AARON SPELLING PRODUCTIONS (323) 965-5789
Executive Director of Talent FAX (323) 634-3604
5700 Wilshire Blvd., Ste. 575
Los Angeles 90036

Agent submissions only.

ROBERT MCGEE (323) 463-1925
c/o CSA
606 N. Larchomnt Blvd. Ste. 4B
Los Angeles 90004

JEFF MESHEL, CSA NBC (818) 840-4729
Vice President of Casting FAX (818) 840-4412
3000 W. Alameda Ave., Ste. 225
Burbank 91523

Only occasionally does any casting. Does look at mailed headshots and resumes. Will look at tapes or DVDs by request only.

D. LYNN MEYERS (818) 681-5780
P.O. Box 11028
Burbank 91510-1208

Accepts pictures and resumes via mail only.

JOSEPH MIDDLETON (323) 463-1925
c/o CSA
606 N. Larchmont Blvd., Ste. 4B
Los Angeles 90004

Open to mailed headshots and resumes, do not phone or visit. Interviews by appointment only.

MONICA MIKKELSEN (310) 396-6100

See listing for BETTY MAE CASTING.

KEN MILLER

See listing for VALKO/MILLER.

KEVIN MILLER (310) 492-6500
Chelsea Studios
451 N. La Cienega Blvd.
Los Angeles 90048

Casts for TV, commercials, music videos, etc. Accepts pictures and resumes from union, non-union, represented and non-represented via mail. Please no phone calls, faxes or drop offs.

RICK MILLIKAN, CSA (310) 244-3188
10202 W. Washington Blvd., Bldg. 80
Culver City 90232

Has no preference for photo styles although it should look like the actor. All follow ups should be made by an agent, a thank you note is appreciated. Currently casting "The Guardian."

LISA MIONIE, CSA (213) 300-4905
c/o CSA
606 N. Larchmont Blvd., Ste. 4B
Los Angeles 90004

Prefers to use the CSA address for submissions. Mostly casts TV pilots and is open to invitations to plays, showcases and screenings.

RICK MONTGOMERY (310) 841-5969
10820 W. Washington Blvd. FAX (310) 841-2600
Culver City 90232

Rick Montgomery casts features and is open to seeing actors who do not have agents or non-union actors on occasion.

BOB MORONES CASTING (323) 465-8110
4130 Cahuenga Blvd., Ste. 309
Universal City 91602

Casts for TV and film. Accepts pictures, resumes and DVDs or tapes from union, non-union, represented and non-represented actors. Open to attending showcases, plays and screenings and gives Generals as time permits. His associate Dori Keller teaches workshops.

DONNA MORONG
DISNEY/TOUCHSTONE (818) 560-7875
Vice President of Features Casting
500 S. Buena Vista St.
Frank G. Wells Bldg., Ste. 1088
Burbank 91521

Oversees the casting process. Agent referrals only.

MICHELLE MORRIS-GERTZ, CSA (323) 463-1925
c/o CSA
606 N. Larchmont Blvd., Ste. 4B
Los Angeles 90004

Casts mainly features, some television. Agency referrals only.

JOHN MULKEEN (323) 463-1925
c/o CSA
606 N. Larchmont Blvd., Ste 4B
Los Angeles 90004

John Mulkeen casts commercials, series, cable and voice over. He accepts mailed submissions only from union, non-union, represented and non-represented actors and is open to attending showcases, plays and screenings.

ROGER MUSSENDEN CASTING (310) 559-9522
10536 Culver Blvd., Ste. C
Culver City 90232

Accepts mailed pictures and resumes from union, non-union, represented and non-represented. Interested in comedic talent. Follow up postcards, faxes, etc., are welcome.

NASSIFF & BACA (818) 528-2080
c/o CSA
606 N. Larchmont Blvd, Ste. 4B
Los Angeles 90004

Cast motion pictures, MOWs, pilots, series, theatre. Photos and resumes by mail only. No phone calls. Occasionally gives casting workshops. No Generals.

ROBIN STOLTZ NASSIF, CSA

See listing for NASSIF & BACA.

NANCY NAYOR CASTING (323) 857-0151
6320 Commodore Sloat, 2nd Fl.
Los Angeles 90048

Casts for features and television and will accept mailed headshots and resumes from union actors. Please no follow up calls.

DEBRA NEATHERY (818) 506-5524
4820 N. Cleon Ave.
North Hollywood 91601

Appreciates a cover note with submissions. Follow up calls are accepted only after an audition. Teaches workshops on occasion.

BRUCE H. NEWBERG CASTING (323) 468-6633
606 N. Larchmont Blvd., Ste. 311
Los Angeles 90004

Bruce will accept unsolicited mailed submissions but rarely uses non-union, non-represented actors. TV, film and theatre casting.

KRIS NICOLAU, CSA
SKIRTS CASTING (323) 650-9899
P.O. Box 480026 FAX (323) 650-0198
Los Angeles 90048

Will accept mailed submissions and/or DVDs with SASE. They will call if interested.

SONIA NIKORE, CSA
DIRECTOR OF CASTING NBC (818) 840-3835
3000 W. Alameda., Ste. 225 FAX (818) 840-4412
Burbank 91523

Will see non-union and non-represented actors. Reviews unsolicited headshots and resumes. Tapes ok. No follow up calls.

MARJORIE NOBLE (310) 488-8399
c/o CSA
606 N. Larchmont Blvd., Ste. 4B
Los Angeles 90004

Accepts pictures and resumes by mail only. No drop offs and no follow up calls.

PATRICIA NOLAND, CSA (323) 463-1925
c/o CSA
606 N Larchmont., Ste. 4B
Hollywood 90004

SARAH NOONAN – NICKELODEON (818) 736-3508
231 West Olive Ave.
Burbank 91502

Television casting. Mailed submissions only. No follow up calls or faxes.

WENDY O'BRIEN
AUTOMATIC SWEAT **(310) 271-2650**
221 N. Robertson Blvd., Ste. F
Beverly Hills 90211

Casts for features and television. Accepts agency referrals only.

PAULINE O'CON
FOX BROADCASTING **(310) 369-3849**
Senior Vice President of Casting
10201 W. Pico Blvd.
Executive Bldg. 100., Ste. 4030
Los Angeles 90035

Vice President of Casting for Fox Broadcasting. Oversees casting but does no actual casting.

GILLIAN O'NEILL, CSA **(323) 463-1925**
c/o CSA
606 N. Larchmont Blvd., Ste. 4B
Los Angeles 90004

LORI OPENDEN, CSA – UPN **(310) 575-7000**
Senior VP Talent and Casting, UPN
11800 Wilshire Blvd.
Los Angeles 90025

Casts for television and accepts unsolicited pictures and resumes via mail only.

GREG ORSON CASTING **(323) 469-6464**
6464 Sunset Blvd., Ste. 970
Los Angeles 90028

Greg Orson and Lesli Gelles cast for features and television and accepts submissions by referral only.

JESSICA OVERWISE, CSA **(310) 459-2686**
17250 Sunset Blvd., Ste. 304 **FAX (310) 459-0961**
Pacific Palisades 90272

Will review unsolicited photos (no preference) and resumes. Mailed submissions only. No drop-offs and no phone calls. Occasionally teaches casting director workshops.

MARVIN PAIGE CASTING, CSA **(818) 760-3040**
P.O. Box 69434 **FAX (818) 766-3889**
West Hollywood 90069

Marvin Paige, CSA. Accepts mailed pictures (headshots) and resumes. No follow up calls. Teaches workshops on occasion.

MARK PALADINI **(323) 613-3982**
c/o CSA
606 N. Larchmont Blvd., Ste. 4B
Los Angeles 90004

Open to all submissions. Prefers receiving pictures for specific roles he is casting and encourages actors to send him postcards.

LINDA PHILLIPS PALO **(323) 463-1925**
c/o CSA
606 N. Larchmont Blvd., Ste. 4B
Los Angeles 90004

Linda Phillips Palo, CSA. Will see newcomers as time permits. Will review submissions (headshots and 3/4 bodyshots). To schedule an interview, send a photo and resume and they will call you if they are interested. Offers workshops on occasion.

PANTONE CASTING **(310) 360-9936**
On Your Mark
451 N. La Cienega Blvd., #12
Los Angeles 90048

Lisa Pantone casts commercials and accepts mailed headshots and resumes. No drop offs, phone calls or faxes.

JENNIFER RUDIN PEARSON **(818) 460-9565**
Walt Disney Feature Animation
500 S. Buena Vista St.
Burbank 91505

Does voice casting for feature film animation.

MARSHALL PECK **(310) 497-3279**
9663 Santa Monica Blvd. **FAX (323) 954-0933**
Beverly Hills 90210

DVDs and tapes only by request. Casts TV and film. Mailed submissions only. No drop-offs or follow up calls. Will accept invitations to plays.

PEMRICK/FRONK CASTING **(818) 325-1289**
14724 Ventura Blvd., Penthouse
Sherman Oaks 91403
www.pfcast.com

Donald Paul Pemrick, Dean E. Fronk. Submissions by mail only. No phone calls or follow ups. Open to non-union and non-represented.

MERCEDES PENNEY **(818) 842-2270**
224 E. Olive Ave., Ste. 215 **FAX (818) 842-2279**
Burbank 91502
epaainc@aol.com

Independent. Accepts P&R and voice-over CDs, DVDs and tapes viewed if time permits. Casts voice-overs for Disney. Also casts independent films, features, commercials, industrials, training films and videos, documentaries, and stage. Gives Generals. Postcards and notes are accepted. Will accept flyers and invitations. No-drops offs.

NANCY PERKINS **(818) 777-1000**
Head of Casting
100 Universal City Plaza, Bldg. 1320 Ste. 4M
Universal City 91608

Nancy Perkins casts for television and accepts unsolicited pictures and resumes via mail only, no phone calls, faxes or visits.

KARI PEYTON **(323) 462-1500**
1145 N. McCadden Place
Los Angeles 90038

Casts for TV and films and does not accept unsolicited submissions.

BONNIE PIETILA **(310) 369-3632**
10201 W. Pico Blvd. Trailer 730, Rm. 2
Los Angeles 90035

Casts "The Simpsons." Does not work with non-union and non-represented actors. Will accept headshot and resume submissions.

GAYLE PILLSBURY

See Listing for ZANE/PILLSBURY CASTING.

POWELL MELCHER CASTING **(323) 956-4260**
5555 Melrose Ave., Swanson Bldg., Rm. 107
Los Angeles 90038

Casts for film and television. Pictures and resumes accepted by mail only. No drop offs or phone calls.

PRIME CASTING **(323) 962-0377**
6430 Sunset Blvd., Ste. 425
Hollywood 90028

Associates: Carol Barlow and Peter Alwazzan. They will accept mailed submissions for specific projects. No follow up calls, drop-offs, or faxes and tapes are accepted by request only.

LYNNE QUIRION **(310) 492-6500**
Chelsea Studios
451 N. La Cienega Blvd.
Los Angeles 90048

Casts for commercials and television. Accepts pictures and resumes by mail only. No phone calls or faxes.

MARK RANDALL CASTING **(323) 465-7553**
1811 N. Whitley Ave., #401
Los Angeles 90028

Casts for commercials and television. Accepts pictures and resume by mail only. No follow up calls or faxes.

JOHANNA RAY, CSA & ASSOCIATES **(310) 652-2511**
1022 Palm Ave., Ste. 2 **FAX (310) 652-4103**
West Hollywood 90069

Johanna Ray, CSA casts television and features and accepts submissions by referral only.

TINA REAL **(619) 298-0544**
3108 5th Ave., Ste. C **FAX (619) 298-1766**
San Diego 92103-5829
www.tinarealcasting.com
tnreal@aol.com

Casts commercials, films, industrials, print jobs, principals and extras. Ms. Real prefers 3/4 bodyshots for commercial and head shots for theatrical and commercial submissions. Please call before submitting anything and do not submit via email.

AMY REECE CASTING **(310) 889-1660**
500 S. Sepulveda Blvd., Ste. 310
Los Angeles 90049

Casts feature films and television. Accepts pictures and resumes by mail only. Please no drops offs, faxes or phone calls. DVDs and tapes by request only. Open to attending showcases, plays and screenings.

ROBI REED AND ASSOCIATES **(323) 463-6350**
6605 Hollywood Blvd., Ste. 100
Los Angeles 90028

Casts voice over and television. Accepts submissions by mail only, please no phone calls, faxes or visits. Does not accept invitations to showcases, plays and screenings.

BARBARA REMSEN **(323) 463-1925**
c/o CSA
606 N. Larchmont Blvd., Ste.4B
Los Angeles 90004

Accepts pictures, resumes and invitations via mail only.

JOAN RENFREW
ONYX PRODUCTIONS **(323) 692-9830**
2331 Wilshire Blvd., Ste. 401
Los Angeles 90064

Casts commercials and accepts pictures and resume by mail only. No drop offs, faxes or follow up phone calls.

GRETCHEN RENNELL COURT **(805) 565-1675**
c/o CSA
606 N. Larchmont Blvd., Ste. 4B
Los Angeles 90004

Accepts pictures and resumes but no tapes or DVDs. Gives Generals on occasion. Casts for film.

RODEO CASTING **(323) 969-9125**
7013 Willoughby Ave. **FAX (323) 874-7729**
Hollywood 90038

Britt Enggren casts print and commercials including the Energizer Battery Cowboy commercial. Mailed submissions are accepted. No follow up calls, they will call you if they are interested.

ROMANO/BENNER CASTING **(818) 623-1880**
12655 Riverside Dr., 1st Fl.
Valley Village 91607

Brett Benner and Debbie Romano cast "Scrubs". Union preferred. Will accept mailed submissions and is open to attending showcases, plays and screenings.

VICKI ROSENBERG **(310) 369-3448**
20th Century Fox
10201 W. Pico Blvd., Bldg. 80, Room 10
Los Angeles 90035

Casts for TV, no drop offs. They don't want you to phone or visit but they will accept unsolicited mailed submissions from union actors.

DONNA ROSENSTEIN
WALT DISNEY STUDIOS **(818) 560-7837**
500 S. Buena Vista
Old Animation Bldg. 3A-11
Burbank 91521

Casts for television. Unsolicited pictures and resumes are accepted by mail only. No drop offs and no follow up calls. Tapes are by request only.

MARCIA ROSS, CSA
DISNEY/TOUCHSTONE PICTURES **(818) 560-7510**
Senior Vice President – Casting **FAX (818) 563-3719**
500 S. Buena Vista Wells Bldg. 1088
Burbank 91521

Marcia Ross, CSA. Accepts headshots and resumes only from agents. Has taught classes for UCLA. Will see some non-represented people.

JAMI RUDOFSKY – JAM CASTING **(818) 954-7192**
Warner Bros.
4000 Warner Blvd., Bldg. 136, Rm. 127
Burbank 91522

Works through agents. Will accept pictures and resumes by mail only. No drop offs or phone calls.

ELIZABETH RUDOLPH **(323) 463-1925**
c/o CSA
606 N. Larchmont Blvd., Ste. 4B
Los Angeles 90004

Casts for television.

PATRICK RUSH, CSA
WARNER BROS. **(818) 954-5126**
300 Television Plaza., Bldg. 140 Room 134
Burbank 91505

Accepts mailed pictures and resumes, please no drop offs or phone calls.

MARNIE SAITTA CASTING **(323) 575-2803**
7800 Beverly Blvd., 3305
Los Angeles 90036

Marnie Saitta casts "The Young and the Restless." Agent submissions or by referral.

GAIL SALUS CASTING **(818) 783-5717**
12953 Moorpark St., Ste. 4
Studio City 91604

Pictures & resumes by mail only. No drop offs and no follow up calls.

TESS SANCHEZ
WB TELEVISION NETWORK **(818) 977-5000**
Director of Casting
4000 Warner Blvd.
Burbank 91505
tess.sanchez@thewb.com

Agency referrals only.

GABRIELLE SCHARY **(310) 450-0835**
2601 Ocean Park Blvd., #120 **FAX (310) 450-7794**
Santa Monica 90405

Accepts submissions from agents only. Does not do generals.

LAURA SCHIFF **(818) 954-5781**
4000 Warner Bros. Blvd., Bldg. 17, Ste. 104
Burbank 91522

Casts features and episodics. Through agents only. Interviews by appointment. Pictures and resumes accepted via mail, no drop offs, faxes or phone calls.

ARLENE SCHUSTER-GOSS, CCDA **(818) 762-0200**
10200 Riverside Dr., Ste. 205 **FAX (818) 753-9322**
Toluca Lake 91602
adg@wavenet.com

Accepts submissions from agents only. Does not do generals.

WENDY SCHWAM - DREAMWORKS **(818) 733-6007**
100 Universal City Plaza **FAX (310) 575-7007**
Bldg. 5125
Universal City 91608

Works via agents with union actors only.

KEVIN SCOTT - CBS **(818) 655-6379**
4024 Radford Ave., Bldg. 5. Rm. 205
Studio City 91604

Agent referral only.

JAY SCULLY **(310) 656-9366**
1531 14th St.
Santa Monica 90404

Mailed submissions only. A postcard follow up is fine. Maintains casting files. No drop offs or follow up calls.

TINA SEILER CASTING **(818) 628-1953**
P.O. Box 2001
Toluca Lake 91610
tinacasting789@yahoo.com

Tina does film, television, reality, voice-over, and some extra casting. She is open to all submissions via mail only.

LILA SELIK CASTING, CCDA **(310) 556-2444**
1551 S. Robertson Blvd., Ste. 202
Los Angeles 90035

Casts principals, extras and models of all types for features, TV, industrials, and commercials. SAG, AFTRA, and non-union. Absolutely no phone calls and no general interviews. Agent referral only. There is no fee.

TONY SEPULVEDA, CSA
WARNER BROTHERS TELEVISION **(818) 954-7639**
Director of Casting **FAX (818) 954-7478**
300 Television Plaza Bldg. 140, Room 140
Burbank 91505

Casts MOWs. Prefers mailed headshot and resume submissions. DVDs and VHS tapes accepted only by request. No drop-offs and no phone calls.

PAMELA SHAE
AARON SPELLING PRODS. **(323) 965-5718**
Vice President of Talent and Casting
5700 Wilshire Blvd., Ste. 575 **FAX (323) 634-3604**
Los Angeles 90036

Oversees all casting for Aaron Spelling. Mailed headshot and resume submissions only. No follow up calls. Generals given when arranged by agent or manager referral. Will see non-represented actors very rarely. Occasionally teaches seminars.

SHANER/TESTA CASTING **(213) 382-3375**
3875 Wilshire Blvd., Ste. 700
Los Angeles 90010

Dan Shaner and Michael Testa accept mailed pictures and resumes. Union only, no drop offs, will accept tapes by request only.

SARI SHAPIRO **(310) 575-4154**
FAX (310) 575-4154

Casts independent features and commercials. Union and nonunion. Accepts pictures and resumes by request only.

MANDY SHERMAN
APRIL WEBSTER CASTING **(818) 526-4242**
800 S. Main St., #309
Burbank 91506

Prefers written submissions and maintains select casting files. Please no calls or drop offs.

AVA SHEVITT, CCDA **(310) 656-4600**
Village Studios **FAX (310) 656-4610**
519 Broadway
Santa Monica 90401

Casts commercials, film and television. Will review mailed submissions, headshots and resumes. No DVDs or tapes. Will work with non-union actors. No drop-offs.

SHOOTING FROM THE HIP CASTING (818) 506-0613
Zydeco Studios, FAX (818) 506-8858
11317 Ventura Blvd.
Studio City 91604

Francene Selkirk-Ackerman casts for film, television, theatre, commercials, voice-over, music videos, etc. She accepts all mailed pictures and resumes, please no phone calls, faxes or emails.

MONICA SHULMAN
20TH CENTURY FOX TV (310) 369-2121
Exec. Vice President of Casting
10201 W. Pico Blvd.
Los Angeles 90035

Casts for television through agents. By referral only.

MARK SIKES, CSA (818) 759-7648
www.marksikes.com
marksikes@hotmail.com

Accepts headshots and wants follow ups from agents only. Will see non-union and non-represented actors. Teaches cold reading and audition technique classes.

CLAIR SINNETT (310) 606-0813
531 Main St, #1135 FAX (310) 606-0823
El Segundo 90245
www.clairsinnett.com
sinnett@earthlink.net

Casts industrials, features and commercials. Will accept submissions (headshots, DVDs, or VHS tapes) but prefers phone contact from agents or managers. Likes to see original material. Teaches TV/Film Marketing and Auditioning and TV/Film Acting throughout the U.S., Canada and Europe. Author of "Working Actors: The Actors' Guide to Marketing Success."

MELISSA SKOFF, CSA (818) 760-2058
11684 Ventura Blvd., Ste. 5141
Studio City 91604

Prefers mailed headshots and resumes. Agent phone calls only. Generals given when arranged through an agent if time permits. Has cast more than 100 feature films and television shows in both comedy and drama.

SLATER BROOKSBANK CASTING (818) 777-6572
100 Universal City Plaza, Bldg. 1440, 14th Fl.
Universal City 91608

Mary Jo Slater and Steve Brooksbank are open to mailed headshots and resumes.

STEPHEN SNYDER (323) 465-4241
1801 N. Kingsley Dr., Ste. 202 FAX (213) 465-3446
Hollywood 90027

Stephen Snyder primarily casts principals and day players, independent feature films, commercials, music videos, etc. Mailed headshot and resume submissions with a cover letter. Will see non-represented and non-union actors. Tapes only by request. No drop-offs and no phone calls.

SHARON SOBLE (323) 463-1925
c/o CSA
606 N. Larchmont Blvd., Ste.4B
Los Angeles 90004

SOBO CASTING (310) 248-5296
Castaway Studios
8899 Beverly Blvd. Lobby Level
Los Angeles 90048

Amy and Jane Sobo accept mailed submissions and ask that the envelope not be sealed.

LYNN STALMASTER AND ASSOC. (310) 552-0983
500 S. Sepulveda Blvd., Ste. 600
Los Angeles 90049

Submissions accepted through the mail only. No follow up calls. Generals given rarely.

DAWN STEINBERG
COLUMBIA TRISTAR TELEVISION (310) 202-3444
Senior VP of Talent and Casting FAX (310) 202-3531
9226 W. Washington Blvd.,
Bldg. C, Room 207
Culver City 90232

Pictures and resumes accepted by mail only, please no phone calls, faxes or visits. DVDs and tapes by request only.

SALLY STINER (310) 392-3197
c/o CSA
606 N. Larchmont Blvd., Ste. 4B
Los Angeles 90004

Sally is open to unsolicited submissions and invitations to plays, showcases and screenings.

ANDREA STONE (323) 463-1925
c/o CSA
606 N. Larchmont Blvd., Ste 4B
Los Angeles 90004

Accepts pictures and resumes by mail at this address.

GILDA STRATTON (323) 463-1925
c/o CSA
606 N. Larchmont Blvd., Ste. 4B
Los Angeles 90004

STUDIO TALENT GROUP (310) 393-8004
1328 12th St. FAX (310) 393-2473
Santa Monica 90401
www.studiotalentgroup.com
stgactor@gte.net

Phil Brock is a veteran actor turned manager who specializes in casting low budget independent features and festival bound films. Several films that he cast have been exhibited in numerous festivals over the past ten years.

LORI SUGAR CASTING (310) 482-3216
5933 W. Slauson Ave.
Culver City 90230

Accept pictures and resumes, DVDs and tapes via mail only. Open to attending showcases and screenings.

MONICA SWANN (818) 977-5888
6767 Forest Lawn Dr., Ste. 100
Los Angeles 90068

Accepts pictures and resumes by mail only. No phone calls, drop offs or faxes. DVDs and tapes by request only. Casts for TV and film.

T.L.C. BOOTH, INC. **(323) 464-2788**
6521 Homewood Ave. **FAX (323) 464-3472**
Los Angeles 90028
tbooth1255@aol.com

Associates: Loree Booth and Leland Williams. Mailed submissions are not encouraged. Please, agent follow ups only.

YUMI TAKADA **(310) 372-7287**
2105 Huntington Lane Ste. A **FAX (310) 937-4813**
Redondo Beach 90278

Primarily casts different ethnic groups. Does theatrical and commercial. Accepts mailed headshots, resumes and tape, or DVD submissions.

JAMES F. TARZIA CASTING **(323) 547-0888**
11312 ½ Huston St.
North Hollywood 91601
www.jamestarzia.com

Casts for television and film. Union only, through agents. No phone calls, faxes or visits.

JUDY TAYLOR – VP OF CASTING **(818) 973-4086**
3800 W. Alameda Blvd., Ste. 2126
Burbank 91505

Casts for the Disney Channel. Union only.

RACHEL TENNER **(323) 463-1925**
c/o CSA
606 N. Larchmont Blvd., Ste. 4B
Los Angeles 90004

Sees union and non-union actors. No phone calls. Also accepts invitations to showcases, plays, and screenings.

TEPPER/GALLEGOS CASTING **(323) 469-3577**
639 N. Larchmont Blvd. **FAX (323) 464-3577**
Ste. 207
Los Angeles 90004

Dennis Gallegos and Meghan Carrafiello accept pictures and resumes. They also teach classes and workshops. See listing under COMMERCIALS in the TRAINING section for further information.

MARK TESCHNER, CSA
ABC PROSPECT **(818) 863-7777**
4151 Prospect Ave., Stage #4
Los Angeles 90027

Casts "General Hospital." Will review headshots and resumes. Teaches soap technique classes on rare occasion.

DANA THEODORATOS – UPN **(310) 575-7027**
Manager of Casting
11800 Wilshire Blvd.
Los Angeles 90025

Casts for television mainly through agents. Mailed pictures and resumes accepted. No drop offs or phone calls.

PAM THOMAS

See listing for ROGER MUSSENDEN CASTING.

MARK TILLMAN **(323) 463-1925**
c/o CSA **FAX (310) 724-8970**
606 N. Larchmont Blvd., Ste. 4B
Los Angeles 90004

Accepts pictures, resumes and invitations to showcases, plays and screenings.

JOY TODD, CSA **(323) 463-1925**
c/o CSA
606 N. Larchmont Blvd., Ste. 4B
Los Angeles 90004

Casts mostly in New York and occasionally in L.A.

GENNETTE TONDINO

See listing for TONDINO/WARREN CASTING.

TONDINO/WARREN CASTING **(818) 843-1902**
2550 N. Hollywood Way **FAX (818) 225-8123**
Ste. 204
Burbank 91505
tw2cast@aol.com

Casts independent features. Accepts pictures and resumes and occasionally will do Generals, but prefers readings for projects.

TRIPLE THREAT CASTING **(818) 415-7450**
11684 Ventura Blvd., #117
Studio City 91604
tripletcasting@earthlink.net

Specializes in casting for Dance, Music and Choreography related job opportunities i.e: music videos, live shows, tours, industrials, commercials, film and television. Also reality television.

ULRICH/DAWSON/KRITZER CASTING **(818) 623-1818**
4705 Laurel Canyon Blvd., Ste. 301
Valley Village 91607

Robert Ulrich, Eric Dawson, Carol Kritzer and Shawn Dawson accept submissions by referral only. Please no phone calls. Open to attending showcases, plays and screening.

ROBERT ULRICH, CSA

See listing for ULRICH/DAWSON/FRITZER CASTING.

BLANCA VALDEZ **(323) 876-5700**
1001 N. Pointsettia Pl. **FAX (323) 876-5297**
Hollywood 90046
bvaldez@msn.com

Specializes in bilingual casting, primarily Spanish language jobs and a few jobs in English and Portuguese for commercials, films, voice-over and independent films. Will accept V/O tapes and video tapes.

VALKO MILLER CASTING **(310) 727-2360**
1600 Rosecrans Blvd., Bldg. 1-A, 1st Fl.
Manhattan Beach 90266

Kenneth Miller and Niki Valko cast union only. Mailed submissions accepted, no phone calls, faxes or visits.

MINA VASQUEZ **(323) 669-1723**
8306 Wilshire Blvd., Ste. 1918
Beverly Hills 90211

Mina casts for television and submissions are accepted by Industry referral only but she is open to attending showcases, plays and screenings.

MARY VERNIEU

See listing for BETTY MAE, INC.

THE VOICECASTER (818) 841-5300
1832 W. Burbank Blvd. FAX (818) 841-2085
Burbank 91506
www.voicecaster.com
casting@voicecaster.com

Huck Liggett and Martha Mayakis cast voice-overs. Commercials, animation, narration, industrials and film. They will accept CD and audio tape submissions by mail only. Please, no drop-offs, and no follow up calls.

VOICES VOICECASTING (818) 980-8460
10523 Burbank Blvd., Ste. 202 FAX (818) 789-8462
Sherman Oaks 91423
www.voicesvoicecasting.com
voices@voicesvoicecasting.com

Casts for animation, infomercials, radio, interactive multimedia, etc. Unsolicited submissions are accepted by mail only. Please no drop offs or phone calls.

DAVA WAITE, CSA (818) 655-5050
c/o CSA
606 N. Larchmont Blvd., Ste. 4B
Los Angeles 90004

Gives Generals when arranged by agents. Headshot submissions. No drop-offs and no follow ups. Occasionally teaches workshops. Casts television.

ALEX WALD (323) 463-1925
c/o CSA
606 N. Larchmont Blvd., Ste. 4B
Los Angeles 90004

Accepts pictures and resumes and invitations.

KATY WALLIN CASTING, CSA
MYSTIC ART PICTURES (818) 563-4121
1918 Magnolia Blvd., Ste. 206 FAX (818) 563-4318
Burbank 91506
www.katywallin.com
katy@katywallin.com

Also has full casting facilities that are available for rent on a daily basis. Casts for TV, film, and commercials, accepts unsolicited photos, invitations for plays, shows, and screenings.

SAMUEL WARREN, CSA (619) 264-4135
SAMUEL WARREN AND ASSOCIATES (323) 462-1510
2244 4th St., Ste. D
San Diego 92101
www.samuelwarrenandassociatescasting.com

Prefers that unsolicited submissions be sent by postcard. Postcards are kept in a file. No phone calls. Will see non-represented and non-union talent. Teaches film acting classes in San Diego.

TED WARREN

See listing for TONDINO/WARREN CASTING.

PAUL WEBER – MGM (310) 449-3685
10250 Constellation Blvd., Ste. 2060
Los Angeles 90067

Accepts submissions by referral only. Please no phone calls, faxes or visits. Will accept invitations to showcases, plays or screening. Casts television and features.

APRIL WEBSTER CASTING, CSA (818) 526-4242
800 S. Main St. #309
Burbank 91506

Accepts mailed submissions only. No drop offs or follow up calls please.

MARY WEST

See listing for BROWN/WEST CASTING.

LELAND WILLIAMS

See listing for T.L.C. BOOTH, INC.

WILSHIRE CASTING (818) 623-9200
11684 Ventura Blvd., #118
Studio City 91604

Catherine Wilshire accepts mailed pictures and resumes. Submissions from union actors submitted by agents are preferred but Catherine is open to non-union and non-represented. Currently seeking young adults 18-22.

KEITH WOLFE CASTING (323) 469-5595
1438 N. Gower #39 FAX (323) 957-1872
Hollywood 90028
www.hollywoodaccess.com
silverscreen@earthlink.net

Casts features, commercials, videos, industrials, voice-overs and pilots. Written submissions accepted.

GERALD WOLFF & ASSOCIATES (818) 382-2006
14242 Ventura Blvd., #201
Sherman Oaks 91423

Union and represented actors only. Mailed headshot and resumes only. No drop-offs and no phone calls. Jan Glaser and Christine Joyce.

JASON WOOD CASTING (323) 969-9588
8205 Santa Monica Blvd., 1-187
Los Angeles 90046

Jason Wood casts for television and film and accepts pictures and resumes from actors by mail only. No drop offs or follow up calls.

GERRIE WORMSER (310) 277-3281
2160 Century Park East
Los Angeles 90067

Pictures (no preference) and resumes are accepted as well as voice-over tapes. No follow up calls. Also does consultations for a fee. See listing under MARKETING CONSULTANTS in the MARKETING section for further information.

BARBARA WRIGHT (818) 783-6305
c/o CSA
606 N. Larchmont Blvd., Ste. 4B
Los Angeles 90004

Only looks at agent submissions. Gives general interviews on occasion for specific projects.

G. CHARLES WRIGHT CASTING (818) 655-6092
4024 Radford Ave., Bldg. 1, Rm. 114
Studio City 91604

G. Charles Wright casts "That 70s Show" and accepts submissions by mail only. No drop offs or phone calls.

Casting Directors

RHONDA YOUNG **(213) 461-1925**
c/o CSA
606 N. Larchmont Blvd., Ste. 4B
Los Angeles 90004

Accepts mailed pictures and resumes. Will contact sender if interested.

DEBRA ZANE CASTING **(323) 965-0800**
5225 Wilshire Blvd., #601
Los Angeles 90036

Debra accepts pictures and resumes by mail only, but no tapes, faxes, drop offs or phone calls.

ZANE/PILLSBURY CASTING **(323) 769-9191**
585 N. Larchmont
Los Angeles 90004

Bonnie Zane and Gayle Pillsbury mostly cast for television and accept all submissions online or by mail only. Open to attending showcases, plays and screenings.

LISA ZAROWIN **(323) 461-1925**
c/o CSA
606 N. Larchmont Blvd., Ste. 4B
Los Angeles 90004

Accepts pictures and resumes but no DVDs or tapes. No drop offs or follow up calls, a follow up postcard is fine.

GARY ZUCKERBROD, CSA **(323) 463-1925**
c/o CSA
606 N. Larchmont Blvd., Ste. 4B
Los Angeles 90004

Accepts unsolicited pictures and resumes.

ZUCKERMAN CASTING **(818) 788-8909**
16161 Ventura Blvd., Ste. 106
Encino 91436

Dori Zuckerman accepts pictures and resumes only by mail. Will accept tapes and DVDs by request only and a written follow up is welcome. Please no phone calls.

Casting Facilities, Studio Lots & TV Stations

For individual casting directors please check the Casting Director Chart and/or the listings under Casting Directors in this section. To find a studio lot, a television studio, or an independent casting facility or to check the parking at one of the above, read on.

1 SILVER LAYNE CASTING STUDIOS **(323) 468-6888**
1161 N. Las Palmas **FAX (323) 468-8811**
Hollywood 90038
www.silverlayne.com
tori@silverlayne.com

Work out of the newest, state-of-the-art casting facility in Hollywood. Four spacious, fully-equipped stages available for all your casting needs. Each stage includes: a private office with a color monitor to view casting sessions, a comfortable in-stage viewing area for clients (callbacks), also with a color monitor, two 3/4" decks, one 1/2" deck, DVD camera with one-button remote access to all three decks, and a shared off-line editing bay. They provide catered lunches for all casting directors, assistants, and camera operators. Snack at will in their fully-stocked kitchen. Remote location camera packages also available. The friendly staff has the knowledge and experience to help you get the job done right. Tori Silvera has over six years of experience running a successful Hollywood casting facility while working on the side as a casting director. Layne Girvin has seven years of experience in the commercial casting world. She has been the primary assistant to several major casting directors and knows how to cater to clients. Comfortable surroundings, state-of-the-art equipment, experienced staff and affordable rates.

20TH CENTURY FOX STUDIOS **(310) 369-1000**
10201 W. Pico Blvd.
Los Angeles 90035
www.foxstudios.com

Mailed submissions to a specific person/office are accepted. Permission is required to enter or park on the lot, but the company you audition for can call in a parking pass for you if you ask. There is non-metered, two hour street parking located one block west of the main gate on Fox Hills Dr. or you can park for a limited time on Motor Dr., Rancho Park, or in the Fox Plaza garage. Expect to walk quite a distance to the main gate. Century Park West garage is available, a shuttle bus will take you to the studio, check with the front gate for directions. Allow plenty of time for parking and getting back to the studio.

ABC **(818) 863-7777**
4151 Prospect Ave.
Los Angeles 90027

500 Circle Seven Drive
Glendale 91201
www.abc.com

All submissions should specify a casting person. Mailed submissions are preferred although they will accept drop-offs at the first guard gate only, and submissions are kept on file. Appointments are required for admittance into the studio and on-lot parking is only allowed with a pass, but there is street parking available in the vicinity.

CASTAWAY STUDIOS **(310) 248-5296**
8899 Beverly Blvd. **FAX (310) 248-5297**
Los Angeles 90048
www.castawaystudios.com
info@castawaystudios.com

A civilized way to cast, Castaway provides closed circuit monitoring of studios, complete editing services, a fully stocked gourmet kitchen, a comfortable conference room and private restrooms.

THE CASTING SUITE **(818) 755-0524**
4705 Laurel Canyon Blvd., Ste. 202
Valley Village 91607
www.castingsuite.com

Does not accept any actor-submitted submissions. An appointment is required for admittance and the building has a parking lot.

THE CASTING UNDERGROUND **(323) 465-9999**
1641 N. Ivar Ave.
Hollywood 90028

No submissions are accepted and an appointment is required for admittance. There is metered street parking, or lot parking nearby.

CBS STUDIO CENTER (818) 655-5000
4024 Radford Ave.
Studio City 91604
www.cbssc.com

Submissions to a specific casting director or production company will be accepted by mail or at the Colfax gate. An appointment and/or clearance is required for entrance onto the lot. Meter parking is available on Radford and parking is available in the lot structure (at a cost.)

CBS TELEVISION CITY (323) 575-2345
7800 Beverly Blvd.
Los Angeles 90036
www.cbs.com

Submissions addressed to a specific casting director may be mailed or dropped off at the artist's entrance. Clearance is required for entrance into the studio. Parking is available on the lot with validation.

CHANNEL 11–KTTV (310) 584-2000
1999 S. Bundy Dr.
W. Los Angeles 90025
www.fox11la.com

CHANNEL 13–KCOP (310) 584-2000
1999 S. Bundy Dr.
Los Angeles 90025
www.kcop.com

CHANNEL 18–KSCI (310) 478-1818
1990 S. Bundy Dr., Ste. 850 FAX (310) 479-8118
Los Angeles 90025
www.kscitv.com

CHANNEL 2–KCBS (323) 460-3000
6121 Sunset Blvd.
Hollywood 90028
www.kcbs.com

CHANNEL 22–KWHY (818) 409-5200
1100 Air Way Ave.
Glendale 91201
www.kwhy.com

CHANNEL 28–KCET (323) 666-6500
4401 Sunset Blvd. FAX (323) 665-6067
Los Angeles 90027
www.kcet.org

CHANNEL 34–KMEX (310) 216-3434
6701 Center Dr. West, 15th Fl.
Los Angeles 90045

CHANNEL 4–KNBC (818) 840-4444
3000 W. Alameda Ave.
Burbank 91523
www.knbc.com

CHANNEL 40–KTBN (714) 832-2950
P.O. Box A
Santa Ana 92711
www.tbn.org

CHANNEL 5–KTLA (323) 460-5500
5800 Sunset Blvd.
Los Angeles 90028
www.ktla.com

CHANNEL 50–KOCE (714) 895-5623
15751 Gothard St. FAX (714) 895-0852
Huntington Beach 92647
www.koce.org

CHANNEL 52–KVEA (818) 840-4444
3000 W. Alameda Ave.
Burbank 91523
www.kvea.com

CHANNEL 58–KLCS (213) 625-6958
1061 W. Temple St.
Los Angeles 90012
www.klcs.org

CHANNEL 7–KABC (818) 863-7777
500 Circle Seven Dr.
Glendale 91201
www.kabc.com

CHANNEL 9–KCAL (323) 467-9999
6121 Sunset Blvd.
Los Angeles 90028
www.kcal.com

CHELSEA STUDIOS, INC. (310) 492-6500
451 N. La Cienega Blvd.
Los Angeles 90048
www.chelseastudios.com

Only submissions from agents are accepted. Primarily does commercial casting. An appointment is required.

COLE AVENUE STUDIOS (323) 463-1600
1006 N. Cole Ave.
Hollywood 90038
www.coleavestudios.com

This facility is used by several casting directors and an appointment is required for admittance. Drop-offs are accepted but casting files are not maintained here. There is street parking.

THE CULVER STUDIOS (310) 836-5537
9336 W. Washington Blvd. FAX (310) 202-3272
Culver City 90232
www.theculverstudios.com

Submissions are accepted by mail or drop-off and must be addressed to a specific casting director, however drop-off delivery is not guaranteed. An appointment is required for admittance into the studio. There is no parking on the lot and street parking is limited so allow plenty of time.

WALT DISNEY COMPANY (818) 560-1000
500 S. Buena Vista St.
Burbank 91521

Submissions are accepted by mail and should be addressed to either Disney Casting, Touchstone, or a specific casting director. They do not accept drop-offs. Drive-on and walk-on passes are required. There is plenty of street parking.

GMT STUDIOS (310) 649-3733
5751 Buckingham Pkwy. FAX (310) 216-0056
Culver City 90230
www.gmtstudios.com

A rental lot for independent producers only, there are no casting

offices. Mailed submissions are preferred but drop-offs are accepted. All submissions must be addressed to a specific casting director or company. No clearance is required to enter the studio.

HOLLYWOOD CENTER STUDIOS (323) 860-0000
1040 N. Las Palmas
Hollywood 90038
www.hollywoodcenter.com

A rental lot for independent producers only, there are no casting offices. They do not accept drop-offs and an appointment is required for admittance. Street parking is available.

MGM/UNITED ARTISTS (310) 449-3000
10250 Constellation Blvd.
Los Angeles 90067

These are the offices of MGM, Inc., there is no filming. Mailed submissions should be addressed to Casting, they do not accept drop-offs. Actors are admitted to the parking structure by appointment.

NBC (818) 840-4444
3000 W. Alameda Ave.
Burbank 91523

Mailed submissions and drop-offs must be addressed to a specific casting director or office. An appointment is required for admittance into the studio and a pass is needed to park on the lot. There is street parking and there are several lots nearby.

NOHO ACTOR'S STUDIO (818) 309-9439
5215 Lankershim Blvd.
North Hollywood 91601
www.nohoactorsstudio.com
stagerentals@aol.com

This 45 seat theatre is available for rent and also has 2 rehearsal/class spaces. Piano, hardwood floors, parking.

OIL FACTORY, INC (310) 432-2900
9100 Wilshire Blvd., Ste. 100W
Beverly Hills 90212

Mailed submissions only to a specific person.

PARAMOUNT PICTURES (323) 956-5000
5555 Melrose Ave.
Los Angeles 90038

Mailed submissions and drop-offs are only accepted if addressed to a specific person. Drop-offs are not recommended. An appointment is required for admittance into the studio and parking is not available on the lot. Street parking is difficult but there is public parking nearby.

PROMENADE PLAYHOUSE (310) 656-8070
1404 Third Street Promenade FAX (310) 656-8069
Santa Monica 90401
www.pierodusa.com
info@pierodusa.com

Equity approved, 65-seat theatre ideal for small and large productions, showcases, video/film shoots, screenings, workshops, seminars and castings. Located in the heart of Santa Monica's renowned Third Street Promenade, by the beach with plenty of parking. Also available for rent are The Soho Stage and The Actors Box, all quality venues providing a creative home for a new generation of artists. Call for appointment to view. SEE AD ON PAGE 297.

RALEIGH STUDIOS (323) 466-3111
5300 Melrose Ave.
Los Angeles 90038
www.raleighstudios.com

Primarily a rental lot. Submissions are accepted by mail only and must be addressed to a specific company. They do not accept drop-offs. There is limited parking on the lot with a pass and there is some street parking available.

REN-MAR STUDIOS (323) 463-0808
846 N. Cahuenga Blvd. FAX (323) 465-8173
Hollywood 90038

Sound stages. Drop-offs are accepted at the receptionist's desk when addressed to a specific casting director. A clearance is required for admittance and parking is available on the lot with a pass or on Cahuenga Blvd.

ROBERTSON CASTING STUDIO (310) 556-2444
1551 S. Robertson., Ste. 202
Los Angeles 90035

Mailed submissions are accepted only if addressed to a specific person.

SCREENLAND STUDIOS (818) 508-2288
10501 Burbank Blvd. FAX (818) 753-8953
North Hollywood 91601

Two studios with Neo-Shok suspended hardwood floors. The large studio is 30x70 with 14' ceilings, surround sound, and a production office. There is an easy loading area.

SESSIONS WEST STUDIOS (310) 450-9228
2601 Ocean Park
Santa Monica 90405

Various casting directors located here. Submissions must be addressed to a specific casting director.

SONY PICTURES
STUDIOS AND ENTERTAINMENT (310) 244-4000
10202 W. Washington Blvd. FAX (310) 244-2626
Culver City 90232

Only mailed submissions are accepted and these must be addressed to a specific casting director, show, or production company. Drop-offs are absolutely not accepted. An appointment is required for admittance into the studio. There is parking on the lot with a pass or nearby public parking.

SUNSET-GOWER STUDIOS (323) 467-1001
1438 N. Gower St.
Hollywood 90028

Mailed submissions are accepted and must be addressed to a specific company, no drop-offs. An appointment is required for admittance into the studio. There is no parking on the lot without a pass. Street parking is possible but difficult.

UNIVERSAL STUDIOS (818) 777-1000
100 Universal City Plaza
Universal City 91608
www.universalstudios.com

Submissions addressed to a specific casting director are accepted. Drop-offs are also accepted, but there is no guarantee of delivery. An appointment is needed for admittance into the studio. Parking on their lot is by appointment only. Street parking is difficult.

VILLAGE STUDIO (310) 656-4600
519 Broadway FAX (310) 656-4610
Santa Monica 90401

They do not accept drop-offs. An appointment is required for admittance. There is metered street parking.

KATY WALLIN CASTING, CSA
MYSTIC ART STUDIOS (818) 563-4121
1918 Magnolia Blvd., Ste. 206 FAX (818) 563-4318
Burbank 91506
www.katywallin.com
katy@katywallin.com

Four fully equipped casting studios are available 7 days a week by appointment only. The facility is used by Katy Wallin. They rent space to other casting directors, producers and directors and it is also available for rehearsal space and table reading. Office hours Monday through Saturday 9:30 am to 6 pm.

WARNER BROS. STUDIOS (818) 954-6000
4000 Warner Blvd.
Burbank 91522

Submissions are accepted by mail or at the main gate for each individual feature casting call and must be addressed to a specific casting director. Admittance to the lot is by appointment only. A parking pass is needed to park on the lot, street parking is available.

SAMUEL WARREN & ASSOCIATES (619) 264-4135
2244 4th Ave., Ste D
San Diego 92101
www.samuelwarrenandassociatescasting.com

A theatrical and commercial casting facility. Mailed submissions and drop-offs accepted and kept on file for 6 months. No phone calls. There is parking on the street and also in the lot.

WESTSIDE CASTING STUDIOS (310) 820-9200

Was in the process of finding a new location at press time. Try the number for a forwarding message. Only submissions addressed to a specific casting director are accepted.

WHITEFIRE THEATRE (818) 687-8559
13500 Ventura Blvd.
Sherman Oaks 91423
www.whitefiretheatre.com
stagerentals@aol.com

99 seat theatre for rent on Ventura Boulevard's restaurant row, available daily, hourly or weekly.

CASTING SERVICES & EXTRA CASTING

If you've never been on a set, doing extra work is a great way to go to 'film school' for a day or so and get paid for doing it. And, with SAG having jurisdiction over extra work on film, you can possibly get your SAG card directly from doing extra work. But pursue extra work on a continual basis? Not if you want to act.
—"Your Film Acting Career" by M.K. Lewis and Rosemary R. Lewis

ACTOR'S ACCESS/SHOWFAX (310) 385-6920
2140 Cotner Ave.
Los Angeles 90025
www.showfax.com
info@showfax.com

Since 1993, the professional actor's resource for Sides and audition material. Via fax or download from our website, Sides always available to non-members as well as members.

ASCEND CASTING (818) 508-9881
12001 Ventura Pl., #203 FAX (818) 508-9885
Studio City 91604
www.ascendcasting.com

Founded by casting directors to build a service the facilitates the casting process. Effectively bridges the gap between the Producer and Casting Director seeking talent, and the Agent/Manager and actor seeking work.

CENTRAL CASTING (818) 562-2700
220 Flower St.
Burbank 91503
www.ep-services.com

Casts extras for features, commercials, industrials, and TV. SAG and AFTRA actors of all types. Submit P&R. They do not guarantee work. Also has a non-union division casting extras for features, commercials, industrials, and TV. Will only see people 18 years and older. P&R may be sent to the above address. In-person registration is Monday, Wednesday and Friday for non-union, and Tuesday and Thursday for union both for one hour from 10:30 to 11:30 am. Bring proof of American citizenship or right-to-work document plus a picture ID. Registration costs, $25 cash only. Complete info available on website.

CREATIVE EXTRAS CASTING (310) 391-9041
(310) 203-7860
2461 Santa Monica Blvd., #501
Santa Monica 90404

Vanessa Portillo casts extras primarily for TV and film. Mailed pictures and resumes are accepted, but no phone calls, faxes or drop offs, please. Hotline: (310) 203-1459.

BILL DANCE CASTING (818) 725-4209
(818) 771-8450
4605 Lankershim Blvd., Ste. 401
North Hollywood 91602
www.billdancecasting.com

Casts union and non-union extras, for feature films commercials and videos. Open registration at noon Tuesday and Wednesday only. $25 cash only to register.

EXTRAS AND MODELS (818) 995-3342
15720 Ventura Blvd., Ste. 608
Encino 91436
www.extrasandmodels.com
info@extrasandmodels.com

Online exposure of actor members to over 200 casting directors. For a low annual fee they create an online portfolio with photos, details and special skills. Casting Directors search the site daily looking for talent. The Casting Notices page allows you to submit yourself for work with the click of a mouse. Used for movies, music videos, commercials, print, and TV.

EXTRAS CASTING GUILD (310) 289-9400
400 S. Beverly Dr., Ste. 307
Beverly Hills 90212
www.extrascastingguild.com

Publishes guides for legitimate casting resources and operates a subscription-based online casting service for talent, producers and casting agencies.

EXTRAS MANAGEMENT (818) 972-9474
207 S. Flower St.
Burbank 91502

Casts union and non-union extras of all types age 18 and up. Reviews unsolicited pictures, resumes, and snapshots. A call-in service for registered union and non-union extras of all ages and types. They do not guarantee work for clients. Their registration fee pays for first and last month of service plus the photo charge.

HOLLYWOOD–MADISON GROUP (818) 762-8008
11684 Ventura Blvd., Ste. 258 FAX (818) 762-8089
Studio City 91604
www.hollywood-madison.com

Offers celebrity endorsement, talent casting, personal appearance and Hollywood tie-in services to advertisers, marketers and event planners. The firm's clients have included the National Hockey League, Pizza Hut, and Tokyo Broadcasting System. Specialists in the acquisition of celebrity talent. Has a comprehensive celebrity computer database.

MAGIC CASTING (805) 688-3702
1660 Cougar Ridge Rd.
Buellton 93427

Casts extras and principals in all types of projects. SAG, AFTRA, and non-union extras. They will review P&R and snapshots are acceptable. They look for professional, reliable actors. A small fee is required to register for extra work.

MYBREAKDOWN.COM, LLC
P.O. Box 54363
Irvine 92619
www.mybreakdown.com
bhoagland@mybreakdown.com

Premier online casting service featuring: membership-specific casting searches, electronic submission capabilities, and state of the art security. The working actor's one-stop marketing resource. Visit the website for more information.

JEFF OLAN CASTING INC. (818) 285-5462
14044 Ventura Blvd., Ste. 209
Sherman Oaks 91423
www.jeffolancasting.com

Jeff Olan, Gil Espinosa and Whitney Dunlap cast SAG, AFTRA, and non-union extra talent 18 and older of all types for features, commercials, videos, industrials, and TV. Reviews pictures and resumes. Open registration is Monday through Friday, 11 am to 2 pm. Everyone must bring a current 3x5 color snapshot photo, union members should also bring an 8x10. There is a one time fee of $25 for non-union people and a small fee for computer imaging for union members. If you need a photo they will shoot one for a $5 charge.

PRODUCERS CASTING AGENCY (310) 454-5233
P.O. Box 1527 FAX (310) 459-0229
Pacific Palisades 90272

Contact Virginia Barber casts commercials and SAG extras only. All types. There is no fee but there will be a $35 charge for pictures. Call office for registration information.

LYNN REINSTEIN CASTING (310) 965-2278
5225 Wilshire Blvd., Ste. 405
Los Angeles 90036
www.lessallcasting.com

Open to receiving pictures and resumes via mail only.

SMITH AND WEBSTER DAVIS (310) 364-3521
4924 Balboa Blvd., #431
Encino 91316
www.smith-websterdaviscasting.com

Tammy Smith and Dixie Webster-Davis cast union and non-union adults 18 and over for features, commercials and television. They are open to reviewing unsolicited pictures and resumes.

RON SMITH'S LOOK-ALIKES (323) 467-3030
928 N. San Vicente Blvd., Ste. 210
West Hollywood 90069
www.entertainmentforhire.com

Casts SAG, AFTRA, and non-union extras, also hires actors for personal appearances. Reviews pictures and resumes, snapshots are acceptable. They need more celebrity look a likes. No fee required.

STILETTO ENTERTAINMENT (310) 957-5757
8295 La Cienega Blvd. FAX (310) 957-5771
Inglewood 90301
www.stilettoentertainment.com

Stiletto Entertainment casts experienced singers and dancers for production shows aboard Holland America's luxury liners. Six-month contracts cruise the Caribbean, Panama Canal, Mexico, Alaska, Europe, Hawaii, New England, and South America. Performers receive competitive salary, onboard accommodations, medical/dental benefits and discount cruises after paid rehearsals in Los Angeles with travel and accommodations provided. All applicants must be 18 or older to work at sea. During auditions, singers will learn songs from their shows and a short dance combination. Dancers will learn a short challenging combination from their shows. Acting skills are required for all singers and acting and gymnastics are a plus for dancers. They also accept video auditions.

STRONGEYECONTACT.COM
www.strongeyecontact.com
derekc@strongeyecontact.com

Online casting notice service. Open a free account and begin or continue your career with the most technically advanced functionality available. They have a "Talent to Agent" submission feature online to increase the chances of call-ins for auditions and bookings by putting you in front of the casting director and in front of agents looking for talent.

STUDIO PHONE (310) 202-9872
P.O Box 661669 FAX (310) 842-8362
Los Angeles 90066
bkgrndxtrastudio@aol.com

This is a union phone-in and information service that works for the actor and has contact with several casting agencies, they give the agencies your availability info and help you get work. Union members. Call for an appointment to register. There is a monthly fee.

SYNERGY SUBMISSIONS (888) 952-1540
15030 Ventura Blvd., #863
Sherman Oaks 91413
www.synergysubmissions.com
hbranch@synergysubmissions.com

Designed to save you the time of self-marketing, Synergy scours all available casting resources and then submits their actors by courier. $69 per month gets your materials where you want them: in the hands of casting directors and producers.

WICKED TALENT (818) 237-5477
www.wickedtalent.com

Wicked Talent is the oldest and most respected modeling and movie extra referral service for alternative talent in the world. They offer goths, glam, pierced, punk, tattooed and all around circus-freaks to the entertainment industry. Not an agency, Wicked Talent is a not for profit company. They do not charge casting or booking fees to utilize their site nor do not they take percentages of talent work and do not interfere in your work. Through networking events year-round, Wicked Talent is helping to build relationships and set new standards for professionals.

DANCE COMPANIES

ANGELITA'S CONCIERTO FLAMENCO (562) 941-3925
11622 Marqudt Ave.
Whittier 90605

Artistic Director: Angelita. Works with professional level dancers. There is no apprentice program. The company has a dance studio and offers classes in flamenco technique. Company members are chosen from their dance school.

BALLET PACIFICA (949) 851-9930
1824 Kaiser Ave. FAX (949) 851-9974
Irvine 92614
www.ocartsnet.org/ballet_pacifica

Artistic Director: Ethan Steifel. A classical and contemporary ballet company for over 35 years. Professional level dancers.

BEACON STREET DANCE PROJECT (323) 633-0466
beaconstdance@earthlink.net

Artistic Director Jennifer Seigle. A modern dance theatre company comprised of dancers, actors and musicians of various backgrounds. The company specializes in collaborative fusion performance works. Company class is held weekly and is open to non-company dancers. Auditions are held as needed. Email for further information.

BETHUNE THEATREDANSE (DRC) (323) 874-0481
3342 Barham Blvd. FAX (323) 851-2078
Los Angeles 90068
www.bethunetheatredanse.com
zbethune@aol.com

Administrative Director: Pamela Bermudez. Artistic Director: Zina Bethune. A contemporary ballet/multimedia company. They accept pictures and resumes. There are 8-12 members in the company and they have a Dance Outreach education program of Bethune Theatredanse for disabled children to learn how to perform dance. They are always looking for new teachers.

CAL ARTS DANCE ENSEMBLE (DRC) (661) 255-1050
24700 McBean Parkway FAX (661) 291-3013
Valencia 91355
www.calarts.edu

Dean: Cristyne Lawson. This is the resident modern dance program for the California Institute of The Arts. There is no apprentice program.

FELIX CHAVEZ (818) 692-7828
www.felixdancetango.com
info@felixdancetango.com

Felix Chavez specializes in latin dance salsa, cha-cha, tango, rumba, bolero and ballroom dancing is also available. Exhibitions, shows, instruction for social dancing, training for competition, wedding routines.

JAZZ TAP ENSEMBLE (DRC) (310) 475-4412
1416 Westwood Blvd., Ste. 207 FAX (310) 475-4037
Los Angeles 90024
jtensemble@aol.com

Artistic Director: Lynn Dally. Managing Director: Gayle Hooks. An international touring ensemble that uses live jazz music and contemporary tap dancers. The time commitment varies. Submit a picture and resume to audition and they will call you if interested. There is an apprentice program. The company teaches tap classes, masters classes, and has a Christmas workshop from December 26-31.

THE JOFFREY BALLET (312) 739-0120
70 E. Lake St., Ste. 1300
Chicago, IL 60601
www.joffrey.com

Founder: Robert Joffrey. Founder/Artistic Director: Gerald Arpino. An American classical ballet and contemporary company. To audition for the main company send a video and resume with a cover letter. To audition for the Nutcracker Children, kids age 9-13 call in August for the September audition date. Contact Adam Sklute regarding auditioning at extension 42.

LORETTA LIVINGSTON & DANCERS (213) 627-4684
1318 E. 7th St., Ste. 201 FAX (213) 627-5875
Los Angeles 90021
www.livingstondance.com
dplett@pacbell.net

A modern dance company directed by Loretta Livingston, producing her concert dance works, improvisational works, and other special performance projects.

LOS ANGELES CHAMBER BALLET (DRC) (310) 453-4952
1060 20th St., Studio 18 FAX (310) 829-5049
Santa Monica 90403
www.raifordrogers.com

Artistic Director: Raiford Rogers. The company specializes in contemporary ballet. There is no apprentice program. The company is project driven and new members are chosen by audition.

LOS ANGELES CHOREOGRAPHERS AND DANCERS (DRC) (213) 385-1171
351 S. Virgil Ave.
Hollywood 90020
www.lachoreographersanddancers.org

Artistic Directors: Louise Reichlin and Alfred Desio. This non-profit organization has two professional dance companies: Louise Reichlin and Dancers, and Zapped Taps™/Alfred Desio. Company members are not required to be in both companies. There is an apprentice program. They practice 9 hours weekly working with professional level dancers. Company auditions are listed in the trades. Call for an audition appointment.

MARTIN DANCERS (818) 752-2616
11401 N. Chandler Blvd. FAX (213) 386-6299
North Hollywood 91601

Artistic Director: Shirley Martin. Dance drama and rhythm vocals are performed using the Horton technique and style. The company works with professional level dancers. There is a 6 month-1 year time commitment required for apprentices, and a 2 year commitment required for company members. Auditions are ongoing for company B. Dance classes are available. They hold musical improvs on Sundays with dancers performing to music. A children's company with scholorships is available. Call for audition information.

VALENTINA OUMANSKY DRAMATIC DANCE ENSEMBLE (323) 850-9497
3433 Cahuenga Blvd. West FAX (323) 876-9055
Los Angeles 90068

Artistic Director/Choreographer: Valentina Oumansky. A non-profit organization with a cast of actor/dancers who tour Southern California schools and communities throughout the year. All members can participate in the story form videos and membership is open to all ages. Valentina offers one free dramatic dance class to all newcomers. Ballet on Saturdays. Also teaches children.

PASADENA CIVIC BALLET, INC. (626) 792-0873
25 S. Sierra Madre Blvd. FAX (626) 356-0313
Pasadena 91107
www.pcballet.com
inforequest@pcballet.com

Formed in 1980, the Pasadena Civic Ballet Company (PCB) is a not-for-profit organization of pre-professional and professional dancers from ages 10 and up. These are serious, talented ballet students who are accepted by audition or judgment of the director. Referred to as the "Company", the PCB has four divisions: Junior, Teen, Senior, and Chamber Ensemble. The Junior and Teen divisions are for dancers ages 10-15. The members must have a minimum of three classes and one rehearsal per week. The Senior division is for dancers ages 13 and above, and requires at least four technique classes each week; at least three ballet (including Pointe) and one in character, jazz, hip hop or tap. Seniors also have at least one rehearsal per week. The Chamber Ensemble is for selected Senior dancers and older graduates or professional dancers that perform together with the Company and for special engagements. Company members have the opportunity of performing in major productions before large audiences. The Company's original presentations have included "A Christmas Carol", "Hansel and Gretel," and "Cinderella" as well as numerous other presentations. These performances provide a wonderful showcase for all of the dancers, with ensemble and solo opportunities. Dancers also perform in our annual "Solo Fete" and the PCB Center Showcases, as well as invitational events, charity groups, in-studio concerts, and guest appearances.

RHAPSODY IN TAPS (DRC) (562) 428-6411
4812 Matney Ave. FAX (310) 649-2409
Long Beach 90807
www.rhapsodyintaps.com

Artistic Director: Linda Sohl-Ellison. Rhythm tap with live jazz music. The company performs locally in Orange County at an annual performance in October at the Aratani Japan America Theatre, and also tours. The company performs both traditional and innovative choreography. All professional level dancers. There are 7 tap dancers plus 6 musicians.

SYNTHESIS DANCE STUDIO (818) 754-1760
4200 Lankershim Blvd. FAX (818) 754-1781
Universal City 91602
www.synthesisarts.com
dance@synthesisarts.com

Ballet, jazz, hip-hop, modern, ballroom, Salsa, Arg. Tango for dancers and entertainers. There is a special program for children. All instructors at Synthesis are professionals with extensive and distinguished careers as a performers, choreographers and teachers. Great location for rentals. Rental space available for private lessons, auditions, rehearsals, workshops, music video, filming, etc.

UCLA WORLD ARTS & CULTURE (310) 825-3951
124 Dance Bldg., Box 951608 FAX (310) 825-7507
Los Angeles 90095
www.ucla.arts.edu

A World Arts and Culture Department with a complete dance curriculum. Masters of fine art with specialization in cross cultural dances whose members are recruited from students in the dance school and some visiting artists. They perform concerts annually.

LULA WASHINGTON'S DANCE THEATRE (323) 292-5852
(323) 678-6250
3773 S. Crenshaw Blvd. FAX (310) 292-5851
Los Angeles 90016
www.lulawashington.com
luladance@aol.com

Executive Director: Erwin Washington. Artistic Director: Lula Washington. A modern dance, hip hop, jazz, ballet, African, and contemporary company that performs locally and on tour. The time commitment varies. There is an apprentice program. Works with all levels of dancers starting at age 5. To audition, fill out an application, and they will contact you. Rehearsal space is available for rent.

WESTSIDE BALLET (310) 828-2018
1709 Stewart St.
Santa Monica 90404
www.westsideballet.com

Director: Yvonne Mounsey. Business Manager: Kay Wade. The company performs ballet, tap, jazz, and modern dance. There is an apprentice program. Call for audition information.

Looping & Voice Over Groups

SANDY HOLT VOICE CASTER **(310) 271-8217**

Put your money where your mouth is. Sandy does weekend looping voice over seminars for film and TV. The seminar focuses on two-day workshop in a professional recording studio includes: breaking into looping, marketing yourself, playing different characters for film and TV shows and how to make a professional demo tape. Sandy Holt does voicecasting for the major studios including Dream Works, Disney and Warner Bros. Sandy says, 'The best way to learn is by doing.' Bring picture/resume/tapes/CDs. Sandy produces demo tapes/CDs custom made for your talents. Her clients work. SEE AD ON PAGE 51.

Miscellaneous

CREW CALL, INC. **(310) 673-2700**
1803 Mission St., Ste. 405 **FAX (800) 770-2595**
Santa Cruz 95060
www.crewcall-jobs.com

Voice mail delivery of information for actors regarding new film and TV projects. Often has information before any casting has been done. Applicant pays the fee. Call for information.

MURDER MYSTERY PLAYERS, INC. **(214) 630-6301**
P.O. Box 165087 **FAX (214) 630-6303**
Irving, TX 75016-5087

4656 Bancroft St., #D
San Diego 92116
www.murdermysteryplayers.com

MMP is a professional group based in Dallas which performs in all Dave and Buster's locations across the country. Actors must be skilled in over-the-top comedy, good with audience interaction and willing to portray wacky characters and get paid for it! Send your resume and headshot. Contact: Claudio Raygoza.

Online, CD ROM & Computerized Services

2b3 PRODUCTIONS **(310) 260-3157**
P.O. Box 3531 **FAX (419) 831-1297**
Santa Monica 90408
www.2b3pro.com
info@2b3pro.com

Market yourself on the Internet www.YourName.com – put your headshots/resume and everything else to showcase who you are. They can help set you up, host and design your site. Very affordable. Call about other marketing packages.

THE ACADEMY PLAYERS DIRECTORY ONLINE **(310) 247-3058**
1313 N. Vine St. **FAX (310) 550-5034**
Hollywood 90028
www.acadpd.org

The Academy Players Directory is available online as well as in a printed version. Known as the "Industry Standard" since 1937, The Players Directory is a cooperative service to the players and producers of Hollywood. To be a part of the Players Directory Online, an actor must be a member of an actor's union. The Players Directory Online is updated continually. It includes your photo(s), name, representation and resume. Casting directors can search for an actor by name, special skills, categories and various other attributes. The cost to be in the Player's Directory Online is $75 per year for one photo and includes your information in the printed version as well as the Now Casting Electronic Submission System. Extra photos online are an additional cost of $10 each. For more information, please contact the Academy Players Directory.

ACTOR SITE CREATOR **(888) 583-2499**
www.actorsitecreator.com
brooke@actorsitecreator.com

ActorSiteCreator is a website system that will allow you, the actor, to have an inexpensive, yet professional website that you maintain yourself. Your ActorSiteCreator website can display your headshots, resume, demo reel, contact information and much more. ActorSiteCreator is a simple and easy way to market yourself. $9.95/month.

ACTORS WEBMASTER **(818) 763-9991**
11684 Ventura Blvd., #999
Studio City 91604
www.actorswebmaster.com
ellen@actorswebmaster.com

Complete website design and hosting (free updates) service specializing in actors.

ACTORS WEB **(818) 256-5556**
4804 Laurel Canyon Blvd., Ste. 328
Valley Village 91607
www.actors-web.com
info@actors-web.com

Creates websites for actors to make them easily accessible to casting directors. Post your resume, headshot, demo reel, bookings, agent/manager contact information and photo gallery.

CASTINGCONNECTION.COM **(415) 647-8810**
3288 21st St., #155
San Francisco 94110
www.castingconnection.com
molly@castingconnection.com

An online casting service for indie filmmakers, playwrights, photographers and independent producers. Providing work opportunities to actors in San Francisco, Los Angeles, and New York.

CASTNET **(407) 244-3400**
127 W. Church St., Ste. 300
Orlando, FL 32201
www.castnet.com
castnet@castnet.com

Castnet enables actors, aspiring actors, agents, and casting directors to exchange casting information and to communicate on a confidential basis through a dedicated Intranet. Castnet replaces the acknowledged archaic casting system currently used in the Industry. Castnet consists of several interactive databases allowing casting directors and talent agents to exchange script breakdowns and agency submissions, schedule auditions, and view actors' headshots with audio and visual scenes in Hollywood and New York and anywhere in the acting world. Casting Directors and Talent agents acknowledge that migration to a computer based system is inevitable. Casting directors can execute a talent search by specifying a number of different search categories such as age, sex, height, hair color, eye color, special abilities, and experience. Castnet will then return a graphic compilation of alphabetically sorted actors with thumbnail-size photos and brief biographical information. This information can be clicked on with a computer mouse to produce a full-sized photo, detailed resume, and video and audio profiles of the actor in action. Castnet has been designed to enable casting directors and talent agents to transact many of their day-to-day business needs electronically, such as scheduling auditions, determining actor availability, obtaining and distributing audition scripts (sides) and manipulating an actor's headshot.

DIGITAL DESIGN L.A. INC. **(818) 845-2038**
3406 W. Burbank Blvd. **FAX (818) 841-6222**
Burbank 91502
www.digitaldesignla.com
barbara@digitaldesignla.com

Specializes in resumes for entertainers. Also web design and all graphic services are available.

INSITEFUL.ORG **(310) 359-2536**
5118 De Longpre Avenue
Los Angeles 90027
www.insiteful.org
admin@insiteful.org

Fast, reliable, interesting and up-to-date, Insiteful is the place to find great web design and site management for creatives who want to build and manage a successful online presence. Actors, writers, theatre companies have all found their services useful in creating clear, high impact pages that succinctly display CV, photographs, demo reels and business details in one place – often cutting down on, or even eliminating the need to send out expensive headshots. Competitive rates.

THE INTERNET MOVIE DATABASE **(206) 266-3408**
705 5th Avenue South, Rm. 463B
SeattleWA 98104
www.imdb.com

The Internet Movie Database (IMDb), one of the most popular online entertainment destinations features IMDb Publicity Photo Services, which allow the over 500,000 actors listed in the IMDb to add headshots and photo galleries to their IMDb web pages. By submitting a photograph to the IMDb, actors now have a powerful and highly-regarded avenue for promoting themselves to the thousands of casting directors, producers and directors who use the IMDb's searchable filmographies to research and cast their new film projects. For many actors, the site has replaced the need for a resume. IMDb Publicity Photo Services charges a $35 fee to post a headshot (via e-mail), with additional portfolio photos costing $10 each, and no annual maintenance fees. Already, hundreds of actors have taken advantage of IMDb Publicity Photo Services, including Oscar-winner Marlee Matlin ("Children of a Lesser God"), Forest Whitaker ("Ghost Dog," "The Crying Game"), Todd Field ("In the Bedroom"), and Alex Winter ("Bill and Ted's Excellent Adventure"). Visit www.imdb.com for more details.

MODIFIED STUDIOS **(310) 562-1961**
www.modifiedstudios.com
greg@modifiedstudios.com

Offers quality graphic and web design services at an actor's rate. Specializing in websites, resumes, zed cards and any marketing materials.

NOW CASTING **(818) 841-7165**
60 E. Magnolia Blvd.
Burbank 91502
www.nowcasting.com
info@nowcasting.com

Services include a private networking group focused on the business of acting where you can ask questions and share your knowledge about the business with other actors; the most up-to-date, fully searchable casting director database including likes, dislikes, assistants, associates, current and past projects and more; an agency database and at-a-glance chart to make submissions easier; mailing labels for casting directors and agencies; member recommended acting and voiceover resources; a fully searchable photographer database with sample headshots to make finding the right photographer a snap; member websites and much more.

ONLINE TALENT DIRECTORY.COM **(800) 501-1624** **(323) 785-2504**
1149 N. Gower St., Ste. 290
Los Angeles 90038
www.onlinetalentdirectory.com
info@slingblade.com

List your acting website for free on the world's largest online talent directory. Visit the website for more info.

PROTALENTPERFORMER SOFTWARE
623 Eagle Rock Ave. #101
West Orange, NJ 7052
www.protalentperformer.com
info@protalentsoftware.com

ProtalentPerformer 1.5 is Total Career Management Software for Performers. Mac and Windows. Created by performers for performers, protalentPERFORMER is designed to keep your busy life and career organized. protalentPERFORMER is designed to finally fill the long-standing need for total, paperless career management all in one simple tool.

SLINGBLADE DIGITAL **(323) 785-2504**
1149 N. Gower St., Ste. 290
Los Angeles 90038
www.slingblade.com
info@slingblade.com

Slingblade Digital offers custom web design, domain registration, hosting, video compression for your demo reel for the Internet and more. Working one-on-one with clients to present their unique image on the Internet. Post your headshots, resume, and reel on the web for casting directors and producers to view 24/7. Professional and

Online, CD ROM & Computerized Services

affordable for all actors. No job too small. Call for more info.

STAND OUT SITES (323) 200-9047
www.stand-out-sites.com
sos@stand-out-sites.com

A full-service web design company specializing in highly affordable as well as high-end and e-commerce websites and demo reels for the entertainment Industry. Organized by artists to help fellow performing artists self-promote and self-publicize themselves. Special prices for websites and reels for performing and creative artists.

Opera, Light Opera & Musical Theatre

AMERICAN MUSICAL THEATRE OF SAN JOSE (408) 453-7100
255 Almaden
San Jose 95113

Business Address: (408) 453-7123
1717 Technology Dr.
San Jose 95110
www.amtsj.org
recept@amtjs.org

Executive Director: Michael Miller. Musical Theatre. Equity contract for 8 performances, the rest receive a flat fee. P&R accepted and they maintain casting files. Holds open auditions and lists casting information in Back Stage West. Also has a summer conservatory for young singers age 12-18 who perform in their 2,600 seat house. This is the largest subscribed musical theatre in the U.S. Season: September through May.

BAYVIEW OPERA HOUSE (415) 824-0386
4705 3rd St. FAX (415) 824-7124
San Francisco 94124

Mailing Address:
P.O. Box 24086
San Francisco 94124
www.bayviewoperahouse.org
sbbpr@pacbell.net

Executive Director: Olahan Webb. San Francisco's oldest theatre, founded in 1888 and seating 300. Non-union. Accepts P&R. Free classes youth and adults. Season: Fall-Spring.

BROADWAY/LA (323) 468-1700
Pantages Theatre FAX (323) 464-1457
6233 Hollywood Blvd.
Los Angeles 90028
www.nederlander.com

This is a James Nederlander Theatre. General Manager: Martin Wiviott. Major Broadway musicals. National touring companies. Continually in performance. Shows are at the Wilshire Theatre and the Pantages Theatre.

CALIFORNIA MUSICAL THEATER (916) 446-5880
1419 H St. FAX (916) 446-1370
Sacramento 95814

1510 J St., Ste. 200 (916) 557-1999
Sacramento 95814
www.calmt.com
bking@calmt.com

Artistic Director: Scott Eckern. Executive Producer: Richard Lewis. Musicals. Resident theatre with an ensemble group of actors for the season, casts on a show-by-show basis for principal roles. Has an internship for singers during the summer. P&R accepted and they maintain casting files. Lists casting info in Back Stage West and the Equity Hotline. 2,500 seat theatre. Equity, RMTA contract. Also has outreach and educational program.

CIVIC LIGHT OPERA OF SOUTH BAY CITIES (310) 372-4477
P.O. Box 1157
Redondo Beach 90278

1935 Manhattan Beach Blvd.
Redondo Beach 90278
www.civiclightopera.com

Producing Director: Steven Ullman. Musical Theatre. Equity and non-Equity. Accepts P&R. Holds open auditions and lists casting information in the trades. Performs year round in their 1,425 seat theatre, and their 500 seat Hermosa Beach Playhouse.

DOWNEY CIVIC LIGHT OPERA (562) 923-1714
8335 Firestone Blvd.
Downey 90241

Mailing Address:
P.O. Box 429
Downey 90241
www.downeyca.org

Musicals and light opera. Non-Equity. Holds open auditions and lists casting info. in Back Stage West and Variety. P&R and tapes accepted. Has a 750 seat theatre. Season: October through June.

FULLERTON CIVIC LIGHT OPERA (714) 526-3832
Mailing Address: FAX (714) 992-1193
218 W. Commonwealth
Fullerton 92632
www.fclo.com

Artistic Director: Jan Duncan. General Manager: Griff Duncan. Specializes in Broadway musicals. Works with professional singers. Equity and CLO contracts. Lists casting information in Back Stage West and has an audition list. Call to be placed on the list. P&R accepted at auditions. Has 13 performances of each show in their 1,300 seat theatre. Season: February through November.

HIDDEN VALLEY MUSIC SEMINARS (831) 659-3115
P.O. Box 116
Carmel Valley 93924
www.hiddenvalleymusic.org

General Director: Peter Meckel. A training institution that works with young singers in their 20s and 30s. Fellowships are available. P&R accepted and they maintain casting files. An application and audition are required, applicants are notified of auditions by mail. Lists casting information in Back Stage West, Variety, the local trades, Musical America and Opera News. They present full productions that include ensemble members in their 350 seat theatre.

LAMPLIGHTERS MUSIC THEATRE (415) 227-4797
469 Bryant St. FAX (415) 896-2844
San Francisco 94107

P.O. Box 77367
San Francisco 93607
www.lamplighters.org

Community Theatre specializing in Gilbert & Sullivan Comic, Opera and Operetta.

LYRIC OPERA SAN DIEGO (619) 231-5714 / (619) 239-8836
2891 University Ave. FAX (619) 231-0662
San Diego 92104
www.lyricoperasandiego.com

Formerly known as San Diego Comic Opera, Lyric Opera San Diego has been bringing accessible, affordable opera and musical theatre productions to San Diego since 1979. The company proudly performs operas and musicals from the European and American tradition, in English, presenting the finest young musical talent available with full orchestra and chorus accompaniment. Performances are at the Stephen and Mary Birch North Park Theater. The Outreach Department presents preview performances to students and social service organizations throughout San Diego County. Insight lectures about the productions are offered prior to all mainstage performances. Open auditions are held twice a year, generally in Fall and Spring. Dates are set yearly. Special auditions may be requested and are based upon staff availability. Pictures and resumes may be submitted in advance to the General Director: Leon Natker. Artistic Director: J. Sherwood Montgomery. Non-Equity, actors are paid a stipend. Accepts pictures and resumes. Auditions are by appointment, call to be placed on their audition mailing list. Season: March through November.

OPERA PACIFIC (714) 546-6000 / (800) 34-OPERA
600 W. Warner Ave.
Santa Ana 92707
www.operapacific.org

Operas and operettas. Works with all levels of singers and has an apprentice program. Performances are in the 3,000 seat Performing Arts Center in Orange County. Season: November through May.

OPERA SAN JOSE (408) 437-4456 / (408) 437-4450
2149 Paragon Dr. FAX (408) 437-4455
San Jose 91531
www.operasj.org

General Director: Irene Dalis. Musical Director: David Rohrbaugh. A program for emerging professionals and resident artists. The resident program houses 10 artists who rotate among roles during the season. Performs at various locales in the San Jose area and occasionally tours.

SAN DIEGO CIVIC LIGHT OPERA (619) 544-7800 / (619) 544-7827
P.O. Box 3519
San Diego 92163
www.starlighttheatre.org

President: Kimberly Layton. Producing Artistic Director: Brian Wells. Light opera and Broadway musicals. Has a training school within the company. Accepts P&R. Holds open auditions in late March and April. Actors are paid. Has a 4,000 seat theatre.

ORGANIZATIONS

A MINOR CONSIDERATION (310) 532-1345
14530 Denker Ave.
Gardena 90247
www.minorcon.org

A Minor Consideration (AMC) is a non-profit organization formed to give aid and support to child actors past, present and future. Some of the previous child actors have bonded together to try to support those who need help and to address the situations that lead up to any difficulties. Through the efforts of organization like AMC, people are recognizing the special needs of child actors.

ABUNDANCE BOUND, INC. (800) 768-0281
P.O. Box 46517
Los Angeles 90046
www.abundancebound.com

Abundance Bound was created to educate and inspire actors to take the steps necessary to develop financial security. Through the utilization of seminars and personal coaching, actors learn strategies to control their money, eliminate debt, increase cash flow and create passive income, giving them time and energy to focus on their acting careers.

ACADEMY OF MOTION PICTURE ARTS & SCIENCES (310) 247-3000
8949 Wilshire Blvd. FAX (310) 859-9351
Beverly Hills 90211
www.ampas.org
ampas@oscars.org

Their purpose is to advance the Arts and Sciences, to foster cooperation of creative leaders for cultural, educational, and technological progress, to recognize outstanding achievement, to cooperate on technical research and improvement of methods and equipment, to provide a community forum and meeting ground for various branches and crafts, to represent the viewpoint of actual creators of Motion Pictures, and to foster educational activities between the professional community and the public at large. Awards the Oscar each spring.

ACADEMY OF SCIENCE FICTION, FANTASY AND HORROR FILMS (323) 752-5811
334 W. 54th St.
Los Angeles 90037
www.saturnawards.org

A non-profit, tax-deductible organization founded in 1972. The purpose of the Academy is to recognize and honor the films and filmmakers who work within all areas of Science Fiction, Fantasy, and Horror. The Academy annually presents the Saturn Awards and presents monthly Golden Scroll Awards for outstanding achievement. They screen over 100 feature films in 3 genres free of charge for members and their guests. Membership is open to the public.

THE ACADEMY OF TELEVISION ARTS AND SCIENCES **(818) 754-2800**
5220 Lankershim Blvd. **FAX (818) 761-2827**
North Hollywood 91601
www.emmys.org

Devoted both to the advancement of television arts and sciences and to fostering creative leadership in the television industry. In addition to recognizing outstanding programs and individual and engineering achievements by the presentation of the annual Emmy Awards, sponsors student internships and filmmaking contests, and hosts luncheons, meetings, workshops, and conferences.

THE ACTORS' FUND OF AMERICA **(323) 933-9244**
5757 Wilshire Blvd., Ste. 400 **FAX (323) 933-7615**
Los Angeles 90036
www.actorsfund.org

Has offices in New York, Chicago, and Los Angeles and provides much needed assistance to entertainment professionals through its human services programs. Funds accumulate from private donations, benefit performances, and special events and are dispensed on vital medical and dental care, housing, elder care, the disabled, Alzheimers, and AIDS patients as well as supporting the Actors' Fund Retirement Home and Nursing Facility in Englewood, New Jersey. Client confidentiality is of paramount importance. This is a non-profit organization with open membership.

THE ACTORS' NETWORK **(818) 509-1010**
11684 Ventura Blvd., #757 **FAX (818) 509-0646**
Studio City 91604
www.actors-network.com
members@actors-network.com

Where the serious actor does business. A business networking group for pro-active actors offering a two-studio space of information and resources regarding auditions, projects, Industry players, and scams. Membership also offers actor Trades, periodicals, an in-house resource library, weekly Industry topical discussions, special guests, networking activities, and four monthly guest speakers which include agents, casting directors, managers, producers, and directors. The Actors' Network assists with an actors' game plan by creating and developing first short term then long term goals. It offers three free orientations per month. This is not an acting class or CD workshop.

ALCOHOLICS ANONYMOUS **(323) 936-4343**
4311 Wilshire Blvd., Ste. 104
Los Angeles 90010
www.aa.org

A non-profit support organization for alcoholics. Produces a monthly newsletter and literature on alcoholism. The above phone number is also a 24 hour hotline that can give Alcoholics Anonymous meeting information for the greater Los Angeles area.

ALLIANCE OF MOTION PICTURE & TELEVISION PRODUCERS **(818) 995-3600**
15503 Ventura Blvd. **FAX (818) 382-1793**
Encino 91436
www.amptp.org

A trade association that handles labor negotiations for management. Has an open membership and negotiable fees.

THE AMERICAN CINEMATHEQUE **(323) 466-3456**
1800 N. Highland Ave. **FAX (323) 461-9737**
Ste. 717
Hollywood 90028
www.americancinematheque.com
andrew@americancinematheque.com

The American Cinematheque is a non-profit, movie theater which offers the public rare opportunities to see films from all over the world and to meet the filmmakers and actors who created the work. Featuring everything from American classics to foreign films past and present; new American Independents and even music videos. The Cinematheque's Independent Film Showcase the Alternative Screen accepts year-round submissions of new independent features and documentaries for potential screening in their showcase.

AMERICAN FILM INSTITUTE (AFI) **(323) 856-7600**
2021 N. Western Ave. **FAX (323) 856-7600**
Los Angeles 90027
www.afi.com
info@afionline.org

An independent non-profit organization founded in 1967. Its purposes are to advance and preserve the moving image as an art form, to assure preservation of that art form, and to develop and encourage new talent. There is open membership. Offers a discount to AFI members for workshops and seminars which are open to the public. They have a 2 year accredited program in directing, producing, writing, and production design. Students can earn MFAs or a certificate. Students need not have a Bachelors degree as long as they have the equivalent in experience.

ASIFA HOLLYWOOD INTERNATIONAL ANIMATED FILM SOCIETY **(818) 842-8330**
721 S. Victory Blvd. **FAX (818) 842-5645**
Burbank 91505
www.asifa-hollywood.org

A membership organization of animation professionals, devotees and students pursuing a career in animation. $45 for general membership, $20 for students. Write for information.

BRITISH ACADEMY OF FILM AND TELEVISION ARTS **(310) 652-4121**
8533 Melrose Ave., Ste. D
West Hollywood 90069
www.baftala.org

As the only Anglo-American professional organization founded to promote and advance original work in film, television and interactive media, BAFTA/LA serves as the bridge between the Hollywood and British production and entertainment business communities. They provide members with a wide variety of activities – including screenings of about 45 new films from the UK and the USA, with Q&As with the filmmakers. There are major glamorous social events, such as the Annual Britannia Awards, the BAFTA Film Awards Brunch and the Annual Garden Party. For television members, they offer unique and informal breakfast sessions with visiting UK television leaders, as well as special screenings of award-winning programs.

GENE BUA ACTING FOR LIFE THEATRE & ORGANIZATION (818) 547-3268
3435 W. Magnolia Blvd.
Burbank 91505
www.genebua.com

Focuses on deep emotional work and allowing the soul to shine through. "Transformational acting and award winning productions for those who dare to become more powerful and spontaneous in their art and in their lives." Most parts in plays and films are cast directly from the student body. Call for further information and an appointment. The feature film which Gene directed "348," won the New York International Film Festival. His students Caia Coley, and Nino Simone, won Best Actress, and Best New Rising Star. See listing under ACTING in the TRAINING section for further information. SEE AD ON PAGE 5.

CALIFORNIA ARTS COUNCIL (916) 322-6555
(800) 201-6201
1300 I St., Ste. 930 FAX (916) 322-6575
Sacramento 95814
www.cac.ca.gov
agottleib@caartscouncil.com

Established to promote artist awareness and participation in California. It is a state organization which provides grants and technical assistance to artists of all types and non-profit artist's organizations. Grant applications are reviewed and rated by outside peer panels and receive final approval from the 11 member council. Formed in 1976.

CASTING SOCIETY OF AMERICA (323) 463-1925
606 N. Larchmont Blvd., Ste. 4B
Los Angeles 90004
www.castingsociety.com

Organization of casting directors. Non-profit. Will accept pictures and resumes for their members if no other address is available.

CITY HEARTS: KIDS SAY YES TO THE ARTS (310) 455-2898
P.O. Box 1314
Topanga 90290
www.cityhearts.org

Provides inner city abused and homeless children with free classes and performance experience in the performing and visual arts. A non-profit organization.

COMMERCIAL CASTING DIRECTORS ASSOCIATION (818) 782-9900
11340 Moorpark St.
Studio City 91602

An organization of commercial casting directors. Jeff Gerrard, President.

ELIZABETH GLASER PEDIATRIC AIDS FOUNDATION (310) 314-1459
2950 31st St., Ste. 125 FAX (310) 314-1469
Santa Monica 90405
www.pedaids.org

Founded in 1988 by Elizabeth Glaser, Susan De Laurentis, and Susie Zeegen this is a non-profit organization confronting problems unique to children with HIV and AIDS, and other serious and life threatening diseases. It is the leading national organization identifying and funding critically needed pediatric AIDS research. The foundation's administrative overhead is less than 6% and the remainder of the funds raised go directly to scientists around the world. The foundation is committed to raising public awareness about pediatric AIDS stressing knowledge, compassion, and action.

EMBODI ENTERTAINMENT CO. (818) 754-2559
15030 Ventura Blvd., #569 FAX (413) 451-3970
Sherman Oaks 91403
www.embodi.org
embodientco@aol.com

A supportive non-profit African-American female owned and operated entertainment company, specializing in theatrical productions that cater to the "Voice of the Black Woman". Seeking African-American actresses, directors, producers, stylists, technical support, and writers. They produce three productions per calendar year and conduct fundraisers and workshops within the organization. Screening, initiation fee and monthly dues required.

THE ENTERTAINMENT INDUSTRIES FOUNDATION (818) 760-7722
11132 Ventura Blvd., Ste. 401 FAX (818) 760-7898
Studio City 91604-3156
www.eifoundation.org

Founded in 1940 by Samuel Goldwyn so that entertainment industry employees could have a single organization through which they could donate to several charities. Currently supports more than 200 health and human service agencies. Members must be in the Industry. The organization will take direct contributions or arranged payroll deductions to support charities.

ENTERTAINMENT INDUSTRY DEVELOPMENT CORPORATION (323) 957-1000
(866) 633-7533
7083 Hollywood Blvd., 5th Fl. FAX (323) 962-4966
Hollywood 90028
www.eidc.com

A volunteer committee that acts as an advisor to the Mayor regarding how the city can improve responsiveness to the Industry.

FILM ADVISORY BOARD JANET STOKES (323) 461-6541
P.O. Box 9258 FAX (323) 469-8541
North Hollywood 91609
www.filmadvisoryboard.org
fabfamaoe@medione.net

A non-profit organization. Previews films and theatre. Luncheons are given with producers, directors, and celebrity guest speakers. Gives an annual Award of Excellence.

HANDICAPPED ARTISTS, PERFORMERS AND PARTNERS, INC. (H.A.P.P.I.) (310) 470-1939
10835 Santa Monica Blvd. FAX (310) 470-1795
Los Angeles 90024
www.ottofelix.com
ottoffelix@aol.com

A continuing program of workshops and classes to assist talented disabled artists seeking careers in film, motion pictures, television, radio and other areas of show business through training and guidance – and to provide a forum for such talent. Through HAPPI it is possible to establish a new awareness of the handicapped community of talent. HAPPI will prove to the members themselves and to the world that they are capable of working side by side in everyday society and in show business.

HOLLYWOOD ARTS COUNCIL **(323) 462-2355**
P.O. Box 931056 **FAX (323) 465-9240**
Hollywood 90093
www.hollywoodartscouncil.org

A non-profit organization incorporated in 1978 with the purpose of promoting, nurturing, and supporting the arts in Hollywood through a variety of community projects and special events including the Hollywood Children's Festival of the Arts, Hollywood Arts Affair, and Discover Hollywood, a festival of the arts campaign. They publish "Discover The Arts in Hollywood." Membership fees: students and seniors $15 annually, individuals $25, and business organizations $50.

HOLLYWOOD FILM ARCHIVE **(323) 933-3345**
8391 Beverly Blvd., PMB 321
Hollywood 90048

Compiles and publishes movie reference material which is available for purchase by mail order. Script and story consulting available.

HOLLYWOOD FOREIGN PRESS **(310) 657-1731**
646 N. Robertson Blvd. **FAX (310) 657-5576**
West Hollywood 90069
www.hfpa.org
info@hfpa.org

An organization for foreign correspondents that presents the annual Golden Globe Awards for motion pictures and TV in January. Prospective members must be accredited and cleared by the Motion Picture Association one year prior to applying and must reside in Los Angeles. Hollywood based correspondents who are working for foreign publications may join for $500.

(323) 874-4005
HOLLYWOOD HERITAGE **(323) 874-2276**
P.O. Box 2586 **FAX (323) 465-5993**
Hollywood 90078
www.hollywoodheritage.org

A non-profit private preservation organization that deals with the architectural styles of Historical Hollywood. They have restored the Wattles estate and it is now available for location shoots and events such as weddings. They also run the Hollywood Heritage Museum at 2100 N. Highland Ave. across from the Hollywood Bowl and produce the publication, 'Hollywood Heritage Newsletter.' Please write or call for membership fee or additional information.

HOLLYWOOD RADIO &
TELEVISION SOCIETY **(818) 789-1182**
13701 Riverside Dr., Ste. 205 **FAX (818) 789-1210**
Sherman Oaks 91423
www.hrts.org
hrts@aol.com

Non-profit association of West Coast broadcast and cable executives. Eight Newsmaker luncheons a year on Industry topics and holiday party in December. Sponsor of the International Broadcasting Award for the world's best radio and TV commercials. Bi-annual newsletter, membership roster and Awards Book. Affiliated with International Radio and Television Society in New York. Non-profit, $100 initiation fee, $185 per year membership fee.

INDEPENDENT FEATURE
PROJECT/WEST **(310) 432-1200**
8750 Wilshire Blvd., 2nd Fl. **FAX (310) 432-1203**
Beverly Hills 90211
www.ifp.org

A non-profit organization that supports independent feature filmmakers. Has a network and resource bank, publishes a monthly newsletter and a quarterly magazine, "Filmmaker," runs screenings, and maintains an active file of members.

INDEPENDENT FILM AND
TELEVISION ALLIANCE **(310) 446-1000**
10850 Wilshire Blvd., 9th Fl. **FAX (310) 446-1600**
Los Angeles 90024
www.ifta-online.org

The Independent Film & Television Alliance ("IFTA" or "the Alliance") was established in 1980 as the American Film Marketing Association ("AFMA"). Its first members were a group of distributors and sales agents whose main goal was to expand the independent film business by creating a world-class trade show, the American Film Market (AFM). Today, the association has evolved into the trade association for the independent film and television industry worldwide, while the AFM concurrently has become the largest international film market in the world. On July 1, 2004, the association formally adopted its new name, recognizing its now-global membership and its mission to promote the independent Industry throughout the world. IFTA's membership includes 150 companies from 16 countries, spanning production, distribution and financing of independent film and television programming. Collectively, its members produce more than 400 independent films and countless hours of television programming each year and generate more than $4 billion in distribution revenues annually.

INTERNATIONAL ASSOCIATION OF
AUDIO VISUAL COMMUNICATORS **(760) 358-7012**
57 W. Palo Verde Ave. **FAX (760) 358-7569**
Ocotillo 92259
www.iaavc.org

A membership organization for audio visual professionals consisting of writers, directors, producers, and actors. Membership is $100. Non-profit. Presents the CINDY awards annually for films, videos, interactive, broadcast, and non-broadcast work.

ISLAND ARTISTS NETWORK
& ISLAND MEDIA ARTISTS **(310) 842-4188**
270 N. Canon Dr., Ste. 1587
Beverly Hills 90210

Motion picture production and entertainment education for minorities and others in the arts. No submissions. Non-profit organization.

LA STAGE ALLIANCE **(213) 614-0556**
644 S. Figueroa St.
Los Angeles 90017
www.theaterla.org
theaterla@aol.com

Formerly Theatre LA. A non-profit association of theatres and theatrical producers that supports theatre in greater L.A. by uniting, representing, and promoting the theatre community. They also administer the Ovation Awards program and host the annual event. Timetix in the Beverly Center offers 1/2 price tickets to actors. Individual memberships for $35 a year.

LOS ANGELES AREA CHAMBER OF COMMERCE (213) 580-7500
350 S. Bixel St. FAX (213) 588-7511
Los Angeles 90017
www.lachamber.org

Non-profit. The purpose is to promote business in the greater Los Angeles area through lobbying, services, committees, and council. Has an open membership and sponsors several awards including "Medici," which honors individuals who have made major contributions to the arts.

LOS ANGELES CINEMATHEQUE (323) 466-2020
6712 Hollywood Blvd.
Hollywood 90028

A non-profit service organization for filmmakers consisting of producers, directors, crew members, writers, and a few actors. Has workshops, discussions, and occasional productions within the organization.

LOS ANGELES COUNTY ARTS COMMISSION (213) 974-1343
500 W. Temple St., Ste. 374 FAX (213) 625-1765
Los Angeles 90012
www.lacountyarts.org

A 15 member commission which recommends grants to performing arts organizations. Contact this office for application.

MEDIA ACCESS (818) 409-0448
1255 S. Central Ave. TTY (818) 753-3427
Glendale 91204
www.disabilityemployment.org

Acts as a liaison and clearing house for disabled performers in the Industry. Offers a referral service and technical advice regarding set accessibility for the disabled, script consultation, and provides Industry training and workshops with an emphasis on auditioning. Also has a casting division.

MOTION PICTURE AND TELEVISION FUND (818) 876-1888 (800) 876-8320
23388 Mulholland Dr. FAX (818) 876-1781
Woodland Hills 91364
www.mptvfund.org

A service organization providing health care, social and charitable services, child care and retirement care. Provides assistance to all members of the Industry regardless of occupation. Operates an acute-care hospital, a skilled-nursing facility, a retirement facility and five outpatient health centers, each with access to a pharmacy, located in Hollywood, Woodland Hills, Santa Clarita, Toluca Lake and the West Side. MPTF offers a wide range of outpatient services including mammography, X-rays, rehabilitation, lab work and a child care center in West L.A. (Samuel Goldwyn Foundation Children's Center.) There are certain eligibility requirements such as length of time employed in the Industry, which vary for each service.

MOTION PICTURE ASSOCIATION OF AMERICA (818) 995-6600
15503 Ventura Blvd. FAX (818) 382-1799
Encino 91436
www.mpaa.org

A trade association that globally represents the major studios, serving as the voice and advocate of the American motion picture, home video and television industries, domestically through the MPAA and internationally through the MPA.

MUSICARES FOUNDATION (800) 687-4227
National Academy of Recording Arts & Sciences FAX (310) 392-2187
3402 Pico Blvd.
Santa Monica 90405
www.grammy.org

The MusiCares Foundation provides emergency financial assistance for HIV/AIDS treatment, critical illnesses, hospitalization, medical expenses and basic daily needs such as utilities and shelter for people in the music Industry. Through the Addiction Recovery Program, people can obtain treatment referrals, intervention opportunities and may be eligible for financial assistance to treat substance abuse and other addictions. Eligibility: Applicants are asked to document one of the following: at least five years of employment in the music Industry or at least 6 commercially released recording tracks or worked in at least 6 commercially or promotionally released music video selections.

NATIONAL ACADEMY OF RECORDING ARTS & SCIENCES, INC. (310) 392-3777
3402 Pico Blvd. FAX (310) 392-2778
Santa Monica 90405
www.grammy.com
master@grammy.com

A non-profit music industry organization that offers outreach programs to the music industry and its communities. Presents the annual Grammy Awards.

NATIONAL MICHAEL CHEKHOV ASSOCIATION (818) 761-5404
www.chekhov.net FAX (818) 761-5472
chekhovmic@aol.com

The Chekhov Theatre Institute held at the University of Southern Maine in conjunction with the National Michael Chekhov Association, usually in June. This program is an eight day intensive for actors or 9 days for the Teacher Certification Program and is team taught with International Master Chekhov Teacher Lisa Dalton, Chekhov Estate executrix, Hollywood Walk of Fame Honoree and long time personal friend/student of Mr. Chekhov, Mala Powers and Professor Wil Kilroy, co-founder of the National Michael Chekhov Association. Course may be taken for graduate, undergraduate, non-credit or ceu's.

NOSOTROS (323) 465-4167
650 North Bronson Ave. Ste. 102 FAX (323) 466-8540
Hollywood 90004
www.nosotros.org

An arts advocacy and entertainment organization founded in 1970 by Ricardo Montalban. Their mission is to improve the image of Latinos throughout the entertainment industry, to promote and expand employment opportunities as well as provide education and training for Hispanics in the performing arts. General Membership Meetings are held the first Wednesday of each month.

NOW CASTING (818) 841-7165
60 E. Magnolia Blvd.
Burbank 91502
www.nowcasting.com
info@nowcasting.com

Now Casting is run by actors who are dedicated to empowering Los Angeles actors to take control of their careers, increase their awareness of the business side of acting and share all information they gather in the process. Services include a private networking group focused on the business of acting where you can ask questions and share your knowledge about the business with other actors; the most up-to-date, fully searchable casting director database including likes, dislikes, assistants, associates, current and past projects and more; an agency database and at-a-glance chart to make submissions easier and the only online actor submission company in Los Angeles where you can submit yourself directly for high paying high profile jobs. Also includes mailing labels for casting directors and agencies; member recommended acting and voiceover resources; a fully searchable photographer database with sample headshots to make finding the right photographer a snap; member websites and much more.

SOUTHERN CALIFORNIA BROADCASTERS ASSOC. **(323) 938-3100**
5670 Wilshire Blvd., Ste. 1370 **FAX (323) 938-8600**
Los Angeles 90036
www.scba.com

A trade association and public service clearing house of radio and television stations. $35 fee for public service number, non-profit.

SOUTHERN CALIFORNIA MOTION PICTURE COUNCIL **(323) 931-8110** **(323) 953-6010**
1055 N. Kingsley, Space 244
Los Angeles 90029

A non-profit organization founded by Jean Doran in 1936. The purpose for SCMPC is to promote greater appreciation for movies and television and to promote and encourage "decent" family oriented films. They stress civic-minded, educational, and cultural programs. The selection of awards are for informative, entertaining, and uplifting films. They also award SCMPC Industry scholarships. Membership is only $15.

STUNTMEN'S ASSOCIATION OF MOTION PICTURES **(818) 766-4334**
10660 Riverside Dr. **FAX (818) 766-5943**
2nd Fl., Ste. E
Toluca Lake 91602
www.stuntmen.com
stuntmen@earthlink.net

Professional association for stuntmen.

STUNTS UNLIMITED **(818) 841-3555**
4421 Riverside Dr., #210
Toluca Lake 91505
www.stuntsunlimited.com
stuntsunlimited@aol.com

Fraternal organization of directors, second unit directors, stunt coordinators and stuntmen. Serving the Industry for over 25 years.

TALENT MANAGERS ASSOCIATION **(310) 205-8495**
4804 Laurel Canyon Blvd. **FAX (818) 765-2903**
 # 611
Valley Village 91607
www.talentmanagers.org

In 2001 the Conference of Personal Managers (COPM) changed their name to Talent Managers Association. A non-profit organization of personal managers with the goal to improve the business of personal managers. To join members must be reviewed by a code of ethics membership committee. Has a monthly networking meeting, seminars and speakers. The organization has existed for over 40 years.

THEATRE AUTHORITY **(323) 462-5761**
Theatre Authority West
Judy A. Bailey – Executive Director
6464 Sunset Blvd., #590
Hollywood 90028

Theatre Authority East **(212) 764 0156**
Wally Munroe – Executive Director
729 7th Ave. 11th Fl. **FAX (212) 764 0158**
New York, NY 10019

Theatre Authority is a non-profit charitable organization administering and regulating the free appearances of performers and providing assistance to members of the theatrical community. Either your agent or manager should check with the appropriate theatre authority office before committing yourself for an appearance. If you cannot check directly with theatre authority, call your local union office for assistance. Theatre Authority East has jurisdiction over all benefit performances east of Omaha, Nebraska. Theatre Authority West has jurisdiction over all areas west of and including Omaha.

UNITED STUNTWOMEN'S ASSOCIATION **(818) 508-4651**
4630 Laurel Canyon Blvd.
Studio City 91614
www.usastunt.com

A non-profit organization. Monthly dues and initiation fee required.

VARIETY, THE CHILDREN'S CHARITY **(323) 655-1547**
8455 Beverly Blvd., Ste. 501 **FAX (323) 658-8789**
Los Angeles 90048
www.varietysocal.org
variety25@aol.com

The purpose is to raise money for underprivileged and handicapped children. Affiliated with the Industry.

VOICE OF AMERICA **(310) 235-7227**
11000 Wilshire Blvd. **FAX (310) 479-3502**
Ste. C-300
Los Angeles 90024
www.voanews.gov

International radio that broadcasts worldwide in 47 languages.

WOMEN IN FILM **(310) 657-5144**
8857 West Olympic Blvd. **FAX (310) 657-5154**
Ste. 201
Beverly Hills 90211
www.wif.org

WIF's purpose is to empower, promote, nurture, and mentor women in the Industry through a network of valuable contacts, events, and programs including the Women In Film Mentor Program, the award-winning Public Service Announcement Production Program, and the Internship Program in association with the Fulfillment Fund. Additionally, they provide film finishing funds, scholarships, grants, advocacy, community outreach programs, monthly networking breakfasts, seminars, workshops, and a screening series with filmmakers. Founded in 1973 in Los Angeles, Women In Film is the leading nonprofit organization dedicated to women in the global entertainment industry. The Los Angeles chapter of Women In Film has over 2,400 women and men members. Women In Film increases the visibility of its members and recognizes their achievements through special awards ceremonies such as the Crystal Awards for outstanding achievement in film, the Lucy Awards for outstanding achievement in television, and the Martini Shot Mentor Awards which salute and honor those men who mentor women in the entertainment industry and help break through the glass ceiling.

WOMEN IN SHOW BUSINESS... FOR CHILDREN (310) 271-3415
P.O. Box 2535
Toluca Lake 91610

An organization of women and men employed in all areas of the Entertainment Industry. One of the causes they support is raising money for reconstructive and restorative surgery for needy children who have no resources.

WOMEN IN THEATRE (W.I.T.) (818) 763-5222
11684 Ventura Blvd., #444
Studio City 91604
www.nohoartsdistrict.com
womenintheatre@aol.com

A networking non-profit organization dedicated to the continuing education and development of all theatre professionals, including actors, directors, writers, producers and technical personnel. Monthly events include playreadings, workshops, mixers, and Industry speaker luncheons. Performance, expressions and job skills workshops round out the WIT programs for outreach into the community. In addition to quarterly membership meetings and a monthly newsletter, members are listed in a job referral database program for area theatres to access. Health and dental plans available as well as theatre discounts. Some of their best members are men.

PRODUCTION ACCOUNTING

ABC (818) 863-7777
4151 Prospect Ave.
Los Angeles 90027

AMBLIN ENTERTAINMENT (818) 733-7000
100 Universal City Plaza, Bungalow 5121
Universal City 91608
www.dreamworks.com

THE AUDIT TRAIL (818) 786-0825
5907 Noble Ave. FAX (818) 786-0829
Van Nuys 91411
www.audittrail.org

AXIUM PAYROLL SERVICES (818) 557-2999
300 E. Magnolia Blvd., 6th Fl. FAX (818) 557-0166
Burbank 91502
www.axium.com

CAST & CREW ENTERTAINMENT SERVICES (818) 848-6022
100 E. Tujunga Ave., 2nd Fl. FAX (818) 848-2695
Burbank 91502
www.castandcrew.com

CASTLE ROCK ENTERTAINMENT (310) 285-2300
335 N. Maple Dr., Ste. 135
Beverly Hills 90210
www.castle-rock.com

CBS TELEVISION CITY (323) 575-2345
7800 Beverly Blvd.
Los Angeles 90036

WALT DISNEY COMPANY (818) 560-1000
500 S. Buena Vista St.
Burbank 91521

E.M.K. MANAGEMENT (818) 766-3353
4632 W. Magnolia Blvd. FAX (818) 766-0858
Burbank 91505

ENTERTAINMENT PARTNERS (818) 955-6000
2835 N. Naomi St. FAX (818) 845-6507
Burbank 91504
www.epservices.com

FILM AUDITORS, INC. (213) 413-0033
849 N. Occidental Blvd. FAX (213) 413-0088
Los Angeles 90026
www.filmauditors.com

MEDIA SERVICES (310) 440-9600
500 S. Sepulveda Blvd., 4th Fl. FAX (310) 472-9979
Los Angeles 90049
www.media-services.com

NBC (818) 840-4444
3000 W. Alameda Ave.
Burbank 91523

NETPAY INCORPORATED (818) 487-1704
12509 Oxnard St., Ste. E FAX (818) 487-1756
North Hollywood 91606

12881 Knott St., Ste. 206 (714) 379-6891
Garden Grove 92841
www.netpayinc.com

PARAMOUNT PICTURES (323) 956-5000
5555 Melrose Ave.
Los Angeles 90038

PAYDAY, INC. (818) 995-4358
(323) 872-2152
13400 Riverside Dr., Ste. 204 FAX (818) 788-0430
Sherman Oaks 91423

PES PAYROLL (818) 729-0080
(800) 301-1992
4000 W. Burbank Blvd. FAX (818) 295-3893
Burbank 91505
www.pesinc.com

Production Accounting

PRIME CASTING (323) 962-0377
6430 Sunset Ste. 425 FAX (323) 466-4166
Hollywood 90028
www.primecasting.com

SESSIONS PAYROLL MANAGEMENT, INC. (818) 841-5202
303 N. Glenoaks Blvd. FAX (818) 841-9112
Ste. 810
Burbank 91502
www.sessionspayroll.com

(310) 665-6411
SONY PICTURES ENTERTAINMENT (310) 244-4000
10202 W. Washington Blvd. FAX (310) 665-6418
Culver City 90232

Marilyn Katz – Senior Vice President, Residuals.

WARNER BROS. STUDIOS (818) 954-6000
4000 Warner Blvd.
Burbank 91522

Production Companies

7TH SHADOW (818) 653-2291
620 Camino de los Mares, Ste. E455
San Clemente 92673
www.7thshadow.com
actor4him@hotmail.com

7th Shadow is a live entertainment company, specializing in concerts, theatre performances, and special events. They accept headshots/resumes and band press kits, along with scripts for the stage and screen. Offices in San Clemente and North Hollywood.

ABC (310) 863-7777
4151 Prospect Ave.
Los Angeles 90027

American Broadcasting Company.

AERIAL FOCUS (805) 455-3142
8 Camino Verde FAX (805) 962-9536
Santa Barbara 93103
www.aerialfocus.com
aerialfcs@aol.com

Stunts; Stunt Coordinating; Aerial Photography; Production Companies; DP. Aerial Focus provides: Helmet camera cinematography of extreme sports, hang gliding, base jumping, skydiving, wing walking, and exhibitions.

ALLIANCE ATLANTIS COMMUNICATIONS CORP. (310) 899-8000
808 Wilshire Blvd., 3rd Fl.
Santa Monica 90401
www.allianceatlantis.com

Union. TV series and MOWs. No submissions.

ALPINE PICTURES (818) 333-3600
3500 Magnolia Blvd.
Burbank 91505
www.alpine-ent.com

Union and non-union. Currently producing. Maintains casting files. Submit P&R. No phone calls and no drop-ins.

AMBLIN ENTERTAINMENT (818) 733-7000
100 Universal City Plaza, Bungalow 5121
Universal City 91608
www.dreamworks.com

Union. Features and TV. Produced "Indiana Jones 4," "Flag of Our Fathers," "Monster House," "Jurassic Park IV" and "Munich." Co-produces the series, "ER." No submissions.

MARILYN ATLAS MANAGEMENT AND PRODUCTIONS (310) 278-5047
8899 Beverly Blvd., Ste. 704 FAX (310) 278-5289
Los Angeles 90048

Does not accept any unsolicited materials. Industry referral only. Has produced "Real Women Have Curves," "Echoes," "A Certain Desire" "Suburban Turban" and much more.

BELISARIUS PRODUCTIONS (323) 468-4500
1438 N. Gower, Box 25
Los Angeles 90028

Union. Features and TV. Produces the series "NCIS." No submissions.

BELL-PHILLIP TV PRODUCTIONS (323) 575-4138
7800 Beverly Blvd., #3371
Los Angeles 90036

Produces the TV soap, "The Bold and The Beautiful."

BOOM CHIC STUDIOS (323) 782-6813
Beverly Blvd.
Los Angeles 90048
www.boomchic.com
karen@ioproductions.com

Audio Post production services and music production services. Voice over recording, sound effects editing, ADR, film composing services, all on Pro Tools 24 mix plus hard disk non-linear system. Compatible with all video formats from 3/4 inch, to Digibeta and DV.

BRENTWOOD PICTURES INTERNATIONAL (818) 225-7424
3619 Via del Prado
Calabasas 91307
www.brentwoodpro.com

Commercials for Japanese TV.

CARSEY-WERNER MANDABACH PRODUCTIONS (818) 655-5598
4024 Radford Ave., Bldg 3 FAX (818) 655-6192
Studio City 91604
www.carsey-werner.com

Union. TV. Produces the series, "That 70's Show." P&R to the individual casting directors for each show.

CASTLE ROCK ENTERTAINMENT (310) 285-2300
335 N. Maple Dr., Ste. 135
Beverly Hills 90210
www.castle-rock.com

Union and non-union. Features and TV. Produced the features "A Mighty Wind" and "The Polar Express" and for TV, "Seinfeld," "Boston Common," and "The Single Guy." No submissions.

CBS ENTERTAINMENT (323) 575-2345
7800 Beverly Blvd.
Los Angeles 90036

Union. TV including MOWs and daytime. No submissions.

CINERGI PRODUCTIONS (310) 315-6000
2308 Broadway
Santa Monica 90404

Union. Features. Produced "Terminator III" and "Basic Instinct II." No submissions.

CINEVATIVE (323) 852-8903
8271 Melrose Ave., Ste. 203 FAX (323) 852-0128
Los Angeles 90046
www.cinevative.com
production@cinevative.com

A production company specializing in corporate marketing, digital features, shorts, actor demo reels and music videos. Includes full production package, professional lighting, sound, camera, dollies and cranes, etc. Can process your project to give it a 35mm film look.

COLUMBIA PICTURES (310) 244-4000
10202 W. Washington Blvd.
Culver City 90232
www.sonypictures.com

Union. Features. No submissions. Produced "Spiderman II," "Dick and Jane."

COLUMBIA PICTURES TELEVISION (310) 202-1234 (310) 244-4000
9336 W. Washington Blvd.
Culver City 90232

TV. Produced the series "Just Shoot Me," "King of Queens," "Married...with Children," "Malcolm and Eddie."

CONCORDE/NEW HORIZON (310) 820-6733
11600 San Vicente Blvd. FAX (310) 207-6816
Los Angeles 90049
www.concorde-newhorizon.com

Union and non-union. Features. Produced "Baby Face, Dillinger and Capone" and "Black Rose of Harlem."

DAN CURTIS PRODUCTIONS (310) 395-9935
725 Arizone Ave., Ste. 301 FAX (310) 395-9936
Santa Monica 90404

Union. Features and TV. Produced the feature, "Me And The Kid" and the TV mini series, "War And Remembrance" "Winds of War" and "The Love Letter" (a Hallmark film). No submissions.

DIC ENTERTAINMENT LP (818) 955-5400
4100 W. Alameda Blvd. FAX (818) 955-5696
Burbank 91505

Union. TV animation. Produced the animated series "Action Man," "Siegfried and Roy," "Ultra Force," "Street Sharks" and "Gadget Boy and Heather." Accepts voice-over tapes and CDs, submit to Marsha Goodman.

DIGIMAX PRODUCTIONS LLC (818) 769-3333 (888) DIGIMAX
10061 Riverside Dr., #786
Toluca Lake 91602
www.digimaxproductions.com
info@digimaxproductions.com

DigiMax offers a broad range of digital video and post-production services including, digital video editing/shooting, tape duplication/transfers, DVD authoring and internet media solutions.

WALT DISNEY (818) 560-5151
500 S. Buena Vista St.
Burbank 91521

Union. Features and TV. Uses independent casting directors, no direct submissions. Produced the features "Eight Below," "Chronicles of Narnia," "Chicken Little," "Glory Road" and "Roving Mars."

THE ROBERT EVANS CO.
PARAMOUNT STUDIOS (323) 956-8800
5555 Melrose Ave. FAX (323) 862-0070
Lubitsch 117
Los Angeles 90038

Union. Features. Produced "Chinatown," "Godfather" and "The Out of Towners." Uses independent casting directors. No submissions.

EZTV (310) 829-3389
1629 18th St., Ste. 6 FAX (310) 453-4347
Santa Monica 90404
www.eztvmedia.com
eztvmedia@aol.com

An award-winning 25-year old production company with credits on Bravo, the BBC and PBS, always looking for good actors and performers for upcoming productions. Qualified talent may submit P&R.

FMS DIRECT (818) 708-7814
18618 Oxnard St.
Tarzana 91356
www.fmsdirect.com

Produces commercials. Send pictures and resumes to Rodney Buchser.

FOX PICTURES (310) 369-1000
P.O. Box 900
Beverly Hills 90213-0900

Union. Features. Produced "Thank You For Smoking," "Phat Girlz" and "Imagine Me & You." Casting is done through independent casting directors. No submissions.

FREMANTLE MEDIA (310) 255-4700
2700 Colorado Blvd., Ste. 450 FAX (310) 255-4800
Santa Monica 90404
www.fremantlemedia.com

TV. Produces the gameshows such as "Match Game" and "The Price is Right" and many more all over the world.

FUTURE AGENCY (310) 306-9202
8117 Manchester, #228
Playa Del Rey 90293

Event Producers.

LAWRENCE GORDON PRODUCTIONS (310) 264-4200
3000 W. Olympic Blvd., Ste. 2121
Santa Monica 90404

Union. Features. Produced "Lara Croft, Tomb Raider," "K-Pax," "Devil's Own," "Waterworld" and "Boogie Nights." No submissions.

GOTTA LAUGH ENTERTAINMENT (310) 828-0500
2461 Santa Monica Blvd., #332 FAX (310) 998-9114
Santa Monica 90404
got_a_laugh@yahoo.com

Produces uplifting feature films.

GRACIE FILMS/SONY CORP. (310) 244-4000
10202 W. Washington Blvd. FAX (310) 244-1530
Portier Bldg.
Culver City 90232

Union. Features. TV and Animation. No submissions. Projects include "The Simpsons" on TV and the features "Spanglish" and "As Good As It Gets."

GRUB STREET PRODUCTIONS (323) 956-4657
c/o Paramount TV
5555 Melrose Ave., Wilder Bldg., Ste. 101
Los Angeles 90038-3197

Union. P&R to Jeff Greenberg.

HOMELAND FILMS (818) 557-8284
3310 W. Burbank Blvd. FAX (818) 557-8348
Burbank 91505
www.homelandfilms.com
centralartists@centralartists.com

Production Company for Film and TV.

ISLAND ENTERTAINMENT GROUP, LTD. (310) 842-4188
270 N. Canon Dr., Ste. 1587
Beverly Hills 90210

Motion picture production, distribution and finance. They work with union and non-union actors and crew but only accept P&R when in production. Cast mostly with agents.

LCJ PRODUCTIONS (323) 877-4988
3841 Eureka Dr.
Studio City 91604

Union. TV, film, and independent CDs. Accepts P&R.

LIGHTSTORM ENTERTAINMENT, INC. (310) 656-6100
919 Santa Monica Blvd. FAX (310) 656-6102
Santa Monica 90401

Union. Features. Produced "Solaris," "Strange Daze" and "Titanic." Maintains casting files.

MANIFEST FILM CO. (310) 452-4403
2525 Main St., Ste. 206
Santa Monica 90405

Union. Features. Produced "Savior," "Dan Eldon" and "Victoria Woodhull." Uses independent casting directors. No submissions.

MGM/UNITED ARTISTS (310) 449-3000
10250 Constellation Blvd. FAX (310) 449-4100
Los Angeles 90067
www.mgm.com

Union. Produced the features "Out of Time" and "Good Boy". Uses independent casting directors. No submissions.

MORGAN CREEK PRODUCTIONS (310) 432-4848
10351 Santa Monica Blvd.
Los Angeles 90025
www.morgancreek.com

Union. Features. Produced "I'll Be There" and "Exorcist: The Beginning." Uses independent casting directors. No submissions.

NBC PRODUCTIONS (818) 840-7500
3000 W. Alameda
Burbank 91523
www.nbc.com

TV. Produces several series including "Will & Grace," "Coupling" and "E.R."

NEW LINE CINEMA (310) 854-5811
116 N. Robertson Blvd., Ste. 400
Los Angeles 90048
www.newline.com

Union. Features. Produced "Secondhand Lions," "Texas Chainsaw Massacre" and "Lord of the Rings."

PARAMOUNT (323) 956-5000
5555 Melrose Ave.
Los Angeles 90038
www.paramount.com

Union. Features and TV. Produced the features "Tomb Raider" and "The Sum of All Fears" and several TV shows including "Sabrina the Teenage Witch" and "Hey Arnold."

PSI, INC. (949) 261-6119
10817 H Skypark Circle FAX (949) 250-9018
Irvine 92614
www.psivideoinc.com
psivideo@worldnet.att.net

Uses both union and non-union actors for corporate videos and voice-over work. Accepts pictures and resumes.

JONI ROBBINS PRODUCTIONS (310) 288-8235
www.jonirobbins.com

Specializes in children's entertainment, animation, voice-over, TV, and children's Internet entertainment.

STU SEGALL PRODUCTIONS (858) 974-8988
4705 Ruffin Rd. FAX (858) 974-8978
San Diego 92123

TV. Produces the series "Veronica Mars".

SHANNON & COMPANY (949) 855-0844
23151 Plaza Pointe Dr. #100
Laguna Hills 92653

Rosenstrasse 7
Munich DL 8000
www.historyquestvideo.com
shannonandco@earthlink.net

This prestigious Motion Picture and Television production company with offices in Orange County and Bavaria Germany, specializes in docu-dramas and documentaries. Producers of "A Time For Heroes," "Order Castles of the Third Reich", "The Final Journey,", "The Missions of California", "Ruins of the Reich," "The White Rose" and "D-Day, the Race to the Rhine." Casting opportunities. Accepts submissions. Union/non union.

SPELLING TELEVISION, INC. (323) 965-5700
5700 Wilshire Blvd., Ste. 575 FAX (323) 965-5895
Los Angeles 90036

TV. Produces several series including "Charmed".

TOUCHSTONE TELEVISION (818) 560-1000
500 S. Buena Vista St.
Burbank 91421

Union. TV series. Produced "Lost," "Desperate Housewives," "Scrubs," and "Commander in Chief" among others. P&R to Disney Studios, TV Casting.

TRISTAR PICTURES (310) 244-4000
Jimmy Stewart Bldg.
10202 W. Washington Blvd.
Culver City 90232

Union and non-union. Features. Uses independent casting directors for each project. No submissions.

TWENTIETH CENTURY FOX (310) 369-1000
10201 Pico Blvd.
Beverly Hills 90213

Union. Features and TV.

UPN
UNITED PARAMOUNT NETWORK (310) 575-7000
11800 Wilshire Blvd.
Los Angeles 90025
www.upn.com

Union and non-union. "America's Next Top Model."

UNIVERSAL PICTURES (818) 777-1000
100 Universal City Plaza
Universal City 91608

Union. Features, TV, and animation. Produced "Just Shoot Me," "Monk," "The Producers," "Intolerable Cruelty" and "King Kong."

UNIVERSAL STUDIOS (818) 777-1000
(877) 804-2230
100 Universal City Plaza
Universal City 91609

VIACOM PRODUCTIONS, INC. (310) 446-6000
10880 Wilshire Blvd., Ste. 101
Los Angeles 90024
www.paramount.com

TV. Produces "Sabrina the Teenage Witch."

WARNER BROS. (818) 954-6000
4000 Warner Blvd.
Burbank 91522

Features and TV. Produced the features "Harry Potter," "Syriana" and "Poseidon" as well as numerous episodic shows.

Student Films

AMERICAN FILM INSTITUTE
SAG CONSERVATORY (323) 856-7736
2021 N. Western Ave.
Los Angeles 90027
www.afi.org

Actors must be paid up members of SAG and members of the SAG conservatory. AFI workshops and seminars are held October through May. Actors must call for application before submitting P&R.

CALIFORNIA INSTITUTE OF THE ARTS
SCHOOL OF FILM & VIDEO (661) 255-1050
24700 McBean Parkway
Valencia 91355
www.calarts.edu

Pictures and resumes sent by actors are posted on the casting bulletin boards at the school. They also list casting information in Back Stage West.

CALIFORNIA STATE UNIVERSITY, NORTHRIDGE
RADIO/TV/FILM DEPT. (818) 677-1200
18111 Nordhoff St.
Northridge 91330
www.csun.edu

Send picture and resume. The school maintains casting files. The students may also list casting information in The Hollywood Reporter, Back Stage West, and Variety.

COLUMBIA COLLEGE (818) 345-8414
18618 Oxnard St. FAX (818) 345-9053
Tarzana 91356
www.columbiacollege.edu

Will work with non-union talent. Send picture and resume. They maintain casting files. Casting information is also listed in Back Stage West and with some of the acting schools. They shoot 4 films and 3-4 videos a week from September to June and a few less during the summer. Actors receive a copy of their work.

LOS ANGELES CITY COLLEGE (LACC)
RADIO/TV/FILM DEPT.
CINEMA DIVISION (323) 953-4000 x2620
855 N. Vermont Ave. FAX (323) 953-4500
Los Angeles 90029
www.lacitycollege.edu

Send pictures and resumes, they maintain casting files.

LOS ANGELES VALLEY COLLEGE
CINEMA & MEDIA ARTS (818) 781-1200 x2354
5800 Fulton Ave. FAX (818) 785-4672
Van Nuys 91401
www.lavc.cc.ca.us

They film one minute public service announcements and, on occasion, longer sync-sound film projects including dramatic, comedic, and documentary works. They place ads in Back Stage West and they do maintain casting files. Send pictures and resume to Professor Joseph Daccurso.

STUDENT FILMS

LOYOLA MARYMOUNT UNIVERSITY
SCHOOL OF FILM AND TELEVISION (310) 338-2700
1 LMU Dr. FAX
Los Angeles 90045
www.lmu.edu

Actors may send pictures and resumes but they do not maintain casting files. They put casting information in Back Stage West and also on bulletin boards on the campus. There are a large number of student films shot each year.

UNIVERSITY OF CALIFORNIA
LOS ANGELES (UCLA) (310) 825-5761
FILM & TV DEPT. (310) 206-0426
405 Hilgard Ave. FAX (310) 825-3383
Los Angeles 90095-1622
www.ucla.edu

Casts union and non-union actors. Send P&R to the attention of Film and TV Department. They maintain casting files and can be approached anytime of the year. They also list casting information in Back Stage West. Send to the attention of Gary Bailord.

UNIVERSITY OF SOUTHERN CALIFORNIA (USC)
USC CINEMA SCHOOL
STUDENT PRODUCTIONS OFFICE (213) 821-2744
University Park
Los Angeles 90089-2211
www.usc.edu

Casts union and non-union actors. Send P&R with a note stating your intent to act in student films. They maintain a casting book which students refer to when casting projects. The students also list casting information in Back Stage West.

THEATRES

A "membership company" is a company of dues-paying actors who produce their own shows. A "resident theatre" is a group of people who are in residence at a theatre and produce their own shows, not necessarily a group of actors. A "production company" is a group of people who produce shows but do not have their own house and rent space as needed. Most theatres of 99 seats or less in Los Angeles County operate under the AEA 99 Seat Plan. In addition, some theatres operate under no plan at all. Actors should ask if the theatre is operating under an Equity plan at the time of the first audition, and, if so, which Equity Plan. Equity can answer questions about the theatre's validity. In most cases, the second listed phone number refers to ticket information and/or the box office. For information regarding musical theatres, please refer to the OPERA, LIGHT OPERA & MUSICAL THEATRE section.

2100 SQUARE FEET (323) 936-6807
5615 San Vicente Blvd.
Los Angeles 90019
www.2100squarefeet.com
2100sqft@earthlink.net

This Equity Waiver Theatre is dedicated to the support of producing new works. Multi-media offerings of theatre, dance, music and art. Accepts P&R and new playwrights year round. Artistic Director: Diana Castle. Producing Director: Steve Tietsort.

(323) 462-9707
2ND STAGE (323) 661-9827
6500 Santa Monica Blvd. FAX (323) 661-3903
Hollywood 90038
www.theblank.com

A resident theatre under the 99 Seat Plan. Directors cast the plays. Occasionally hold open casting calls. The 48 seat theatre is available for rent. 2nd Stage is owned and operated by The Blank Theatre.

A NOISE WITHIN (818) 240-0910
234 S. Brand Blvd.
Glendale 91204
www.anoisewithin.org
rasmussen@anoisewithin.org

Co-Artistic Directors: Geoff Elliott and Julia Rodriguez Elliott. A resident ensemble of classically trained actors. Operates under a special agreement with Equity and tours under a LORT D contract. Accepts P&R and holds open auditions. Offers conservatory classes. Their theatre has 144 seats.

ACME COMEDY THEATRE (323) 525-0202
135 N. La Brea Ave.
Hollywood 90036
www.acmecomedy.com

A state-of-the-art 99 seat theatre designed by renowned architect John Fischer that is host to a critically-acclaimed professional sketch comedy troupe managed by Producer/Director M.D. Sweeney. The Acme Improv and Sketch Comedy School offers classes on five levels beginning with an introduction to the basics of improvisation progressing through advanced sketch comedy writing and offering the potential of moving into Acme's professional performing company. In addition to sketch comedy Acme Comedy Theatre also hosts a wide array of comedy shows including improv, variety and solo performance. Study and perform comedy on the same stage as Wayne Brady, Ryan Stiles, Brad Sherwood, Fred Willard, Wil Wheaton, Adam Carolla, Alex Borstein and Upright Citizens Brigade. Company members who developed their writing skills at the Acme include Emmy-winning writer/producers "Friends," "The Simpsons," "Norm," "3rd Rock From the Sun" and Warner Bros. Animation.

ACTOR'S GANG (310) 838 GANG
9070 Venice Blvd. FAX (310) 838-4263
Culver City 90230
www.theactorsgang.com

Musicals, classics, and contemporary plays. A membership company operating under the 99 Seat Plan. Accepts P&R but they are not looking for new members at this time. Theatre has 99 seats.

ACTORS ART THEATRE (323) 969-4953
6128 Wilshire Blvd.
Los Angeles 90048
www.actorsart.com
actorsart@actorsart.com

A resident ensemble company. Not a membership company, no

dues. Accepts pictures and resumes and lists casting information in the Breakdowns. This 32 seat theatre is available for rent and rehearsals. See listing under ACTING in the TRAINING section for further information.

ACTORS CIRCLE THEATRE **(323) 882-8043**
7313 Santa Monica Blvd.
West Hollywood 90046

A 47 seat theatre with air conditioning and its own sound and lighting equipment. Available for rent Thursday through Sunday. SEE AD ON PAGE 3.

ACTORS CO-OP **(323) 462-8460**
Crossley Theatre **FAX (323) 462-3199**
Crossley Terrace Theatre
1760 N. Gower
Hollywood 90028
www.actorscoop.org

Producing Director, Marianne Savell. Artistic Director, Gary Lee Reed. Dramas and musicals involving the positive aspects of mankind with themes of freedom, hope, healing, and redemption. Operates under the 99 Seat Plan. Accepts P&R. Company auditions in spring. Both 99 seat theatres are on the grounds of the Hollywood Presbyterian Church. 14th season. 4 plays per season.

ACTORS FORUM THEATRE **(818) 506-0600**
10655 Magnolia Blvd. **FAX (323) 465-6898**
North Hollywood 91601
www.nohoartsdistrict.com
audsin@aol.com

Producing Artistic Director: Audrey Marlyn Singer. A membership company under the 99 Seat Plan. Company membership dues include workshops. An audition or recommendation is required. Company auditions are held 12:30 pm to 1:30 pm the last Saturday of each month, a scene or monologue is requested. Both company and open casting calls are held for productions. 49 seats. Theatre is sometimes available for rent which includes technical equipment.

ACTORS WORKOUT STUDIO **(818) 766-2171**
4735 Lankershim Blvd.
North Hollywood 91602
www.actorsworkout.com
info@actorsworkout.com

These 40 seat and 25 seat theatres operate under the 99 seat plan. The company is comprised of class members from the Actors Workout Studio but they cast outside the group when needed. Pictures and resumes are kept on file but submittals are only accepted for specific projects. Theatre is also available for rent.

AHMANSON THEATRE **(213) 972-7401**
(213) 365-3500
135 N. Grand Ave.
Los Angeles 90012
www.taperahmanson.com

Major professional productions of all types including Broadway musicals. Equity. Accepts pictures and resumes and has open calls or lists casting info in the Breakdowns, Back Stage West and on the SAG and AEA hotlines.

ALCAZAR THEATRE **(415) 441-6655**
(415) 441-4042
650 Geary St. **FAX (415) 441-9567**
San Francisco 94102

This is the theatre for Steve Dobbins Productions. They mount productions and will accept P&R. There are three theatres one with 800 seats and one with 500 seats, and another with 49 seats, all of which are available for rent.

ALEX THEATRE **(818) 243-7700**
(818) 243-2611
216 N. Brand Blvd. **FAX (818) 243-6468**
Glendale 91203
www.alextheatre.org

A multi-use facility for professional and community performing arts groups.

AMERICAN CONSERVATORY THEATRE (ACT) **(415) 834-3200**
(415) 749-2228
30 Grant Ave. **FAX (415) 834-3360**
San Francisco 94108
www.act-sfbay.org

Artistic Director: Carey Perloff. Managing Director: Heather Kitchen. An Equity LORT A contract theatre. They also have a full training program for actors. Attempts to cast locally for individual shows but also casts by invitation from NY and L.A. General auditions are listed on the AEA hotline. Accepts P&R, submit to the Casting Department.

ARLINGTON CENTER FOR PERFORMING ARTS. **(805) 963-4408**
1317 State St. **FAX (805) 966-4688**
Santa Barbara 93101

An Equity theatre. Strictly rental. This 2,000 seat theatre is available for 4-wall rental for concerts and movies.

BOB BAKER MARIONETTE THEATRE **(213) 250-9995**
1345 W. 1st. St. **FAX (213) 250-1120**
Los Angeles 90026
www.bobbakermarrionettes.com

Artistic Director: Bob Baker. Managing Director: Daniel Gonzalez. Non-Equity. A company of puppeteers with acting experience. A resident theatre and touring company. Accepts pictures and resumes, contact by phone weekdays for an audition appointment. Actors are paid hourly. This 200 seat theatre is the oldest marionette theatre in the U.S. Over 40 years in business.

BARNSDALL GALLERY THEATRE **(323) 644-6295**
4800 Hollywood Blvd.
Hollywood 90027

Mailing address:
433 S. Spring St.
Los Angeles 90013
www.culturela.org

This is a city-owned theatre with 299 seats that is strictly a rental facility. Call weekdays 9 am to 1 pm for rates.

BERKELEY REPERTORY THEATRE (510) 647-2900 (510) 647-2949
2025 Addison St. FAX (510) 847-2976
Berkeley 94704
www.berkeleyrep.org
info@berkeleyrep.org

Artistic Director: Tony Taccone. Managing Director: Susan Medak. Casting Director: Amy Potozkin. Classic and contemporary works. A resident theatre and touring company operating under the Equity LORT B contract. They have a parallel season of two plays both of which perform in the theatre and on tour. Accepts P&R and has open calls the third Monday of every month for out-of-town Equity and Equity eligible actors. Call for an appointment. They list casting info in Back Stage West, AEA hotline, and Callboard. They have a 401 seat theatre, and the RODA Theatre with 600 seats.

BEVERLY HILLS PLAYHOUSE (310) 855-1556
254 S. Robertson Blvd.
Beverly Hills 90211
www.katselas.com

A resident theatre operating under the 99 Seat Plan. They do in-house productions and this 99 seat theatre is available for rental.

BILINGUAL FOUNDATION OF THE ARTS (323) 225-4044
421 N. Avenue 19 FAX (323) 225-1250
Los Angeles 90031
www.bfatheatre.org

The Bilingual Foundation of the Arts is an organization that seeks to advance the Hispanic culture by developing, producing and presenting professional theatre in both Spanish and English for Hispanic and non-Hispanic audiences. BFA presents Hispanic and Hispanic American theatre in Los Angeles, brings new translation of Hispanic dramatic literature into English, develops and exposes Hispanic talent, offers residencies and workshops to new playwrights and directors and through its statewide tours brings the literature of the Hispanic world to many communities previously isolated from professional theatre. Artistic Director: Margarita Galban. Producing Director: Carmen Zapata. Managing Director: Lucia Cariaga. Spanish and English productions. A resident theatre under the 99 Seat Plan. Accepts P&R and maintains active casting files. Holds open calls for productions and lists casting info in the Trades. Actors are paid. Their theatre has 99 seats.

BLANK THEATRE COMPANY (323) 662-7734
1301 Lucile Ave. FAX (323) 661-3903
Los Angeles 90026
www.theblank.com

Artistic Director: Daniel Henning. This is an artist run theater production company established to further the vitality, stability, and development of live theatre in L.A. Artistis Producer: Noah Wylie.

GENE BUA ACTING FOR LIFE THEATRE (818) 547-3268
3435 W. Magnolia Blvd.
Burbank 91505
www.genebua.com

Artistic Director: Gene Bua. Producer/Head Writer: Toni Bull Bua. Primarily original productions including award winning shows such as "Pepper Street" and the "Second Wind." 99 Seat Plan. Usually casts from within the company for plays and films and holds 4 classes per week. Rents theatre on occasion. SEE AD ON PAGE 5.

BUFFALO NIGHTS THEATRE COMPANY (323) 969-4744
1050 Carmona
Los Angeles 90019
www.buffalonights.org
info@buffalonights.org

A producing company operating under the 99 Seat Plan. Started by UCLA alumni and students, emphasis is on producing quality theatre inspiring new perspectives. No dues. Will accept invitations to showcases, plays, and screenings.

CALIFORNIA REPERTORY THEATRE (562) 985-5357 (562) 985-5526
1250 Bellflower Blvd. FAX (562) 985-2263
Long Beach 90840
www.calrep.org

The professional graduate arm of the Theatre Department at CSULB. A multicultural company producing classics and new works from the international canon. A resident company.

CALIFORNIA SHAKESPEARE FESTIVAL (510) 548-3422
100 Gateway FAX (510) 843-9921
Orinda, CA 94563

Business address: (510) 843-9666
701 Heinz Ave.
Berkeley, CA 94710
www.calshakes.org

Artistic Director: Jonathan Moscone. Managing Director: Debbie Chin. An Equity theatre group operating under LORT D contract. Actors must audition to join. Accepts P&R and maintains active casting files. Holds open casting calls by appointment. Auditions are held in January. Lists casting info on Equity Hotline and in Callboard.

CALIFORNIA THEATRE CENTER (408) 245-2979
753 East El Camino Rd., Ste. B FAX (408) 245-0235
Sunnyvale, CA 94087

P.O. Box 2007 (408) 245-8977
Sunnyvale, CA 94087
www.ctcinc.org

General Director: Dr. Gayle Cornelison. A repertory touring theatre and production company. Non-Equity but will hire Equity actors under the guest artist plan. They usually produce original works. Submit P&R to Will Huddleston. Maintains casting files. Actors are paid. They have two seasons: September to July, plays for young audiences and June to August, adult shows in repertory.

CALIFORNIA YOUTH THEATRE (323) 461-7300
Ivar Theatre FAX (323) 461-7707
1605 N. Ivar Ave.
Hollywood 90038

Business address: (310) 657-3270
517 Westmount Dr.
Los Angeles 90048
www.cytivar.org

Artistic Director: Edward Wilson. Dedicated to teaching and producing work using young people up to age 25. The company performs musicals, original and dramatic plays. Non-Equity actors only. Holds open auditions and casting information is listed in Trades and Breakdown. Theatre available for rent.

CAMINO, CAMINITO
& CAMEO THEATRES (323) 953-4000 x2990
855 N. Vermont Ave.
Los Angeles 90029
www.lacitycollege.edu

These three theatres are part of the Theatre Academy on the campus of Los Angeles City College. The Caminito Theatre is on the 99 Seat Plan. They do not maintain casting files. The Academy has a full-time, audition/interview only, professional theatre training program in acting, technical theatre and costuming. Distinguished professionals and noted alumni are invited to perform in Academy productions. Departmental classes are also available. Auditions are held on a regular basis. Call for an application and further information.

CANDLELIGHT PAVILION (909) 626-1254
Bollinger Productions FAX (909) 626-6465
455 W. Foothill Blvd.
Claremont 91711
www.candlelightpavilion.com

Producer: Ben Bollinger. Musicals. A non-Equity dinner theatre. Usually does 8 shows per year, 6-12 weeks each. Open casting calls for each show are announced in Back Stage West. Tech positions are also open. P&R can be sent to Bollinger Productions but it is not recommended. They have 325 seats in their theatre.

CASSIOPEIA THEATRE COMPANY (323) 860-6585
643 Hill St., Ste. B
Santa Monica 90405
www.ctctheatre.com
cperoutka@aol.com

Founded in 2004 by five young actors, Cassiopeia Theatre Company (CTC) has grown into an impressive and highly respected ensemble comprised of actors, singers, dancers, directors, Olympic athletes, models, writers and other gifted artists. During its highly successful inaugural year, CTC was cheered by Backstage West as "a very promising theatre company" where the "acting is first-rate" and its members were "double-dipped in the gorgeous bucket." CTC produces four popular productions a year, including at least one original play, and hosts monthly parties and events. CTC holds open auditions for new members every three months.

CELEBRATION THEATRE (323) 957-1884
7051-B Santa Monica Blvd.
Los Angeles 90038

7985 Santa Monica Blvd. (310) 289-2999
Los Angeles 90046
www.celebrationtheatre.com
celetheatr@aol.com

Managing Artistic Director: Michael Matthews. Dedicated to producing plays by the gay and lesbian community under the 99 Seat Plan. Specializing in world premieres. Submissions accepted. Open casting calls are listed in Back Stage West and Breakdown. Actors don't need to be gay to work. Mostly produce their own work but occasionally do co-productions.

CELEBRITY CENTRE THEATRE (323) 960-3100
5930 Franklin Ave.
Hollywood 90028

Musicals, dramatic plays, original works, revivals, staged readings, and acting and vocal showcases. A resident theatre and production company operating under the 99 Seat Plan and a Special Production Contract. There are two theatres, the 50 seat theatre downstairs and the 400 seat auditorium. Theatres have state-of-the-art equipment and are available for rent.

CELTIC ARTS CENTER
AN CLAIDHEAH SOLUIS (818) 760-8322
4843 Laurel Canyon Blvd.
Studio City 91614
www.celticartscenter.com

Dramatic pieces, original works, and comedy revivals. A membership company under the 99 Seat Plan. To join the company an actor needs to call or attend one of their meetings. They cast from within the company and list casting information in Back Stage West if unable to cast a particular role from company membership. Active casting files are maintained. P&R are accepted.

CENTER THEATRE GROUP (213) 972-7542
KIRK DOUGLAS THEATRE (213) 628-2772
135 North Grand Ave
Los Angeles 90012
www.taperahmanson.com

General Manager: Doug Baker. The Center Theatre Group is primarily a producing theater company and often works at the Kirk Douglas Theatre operating under an Equity Production contract. Theatre has 318 seats and can be rented from time to time.

CERRITOS CENTER (562) 916-8501
FOR THE PERFORMING ARTS (562) 916-8500
12700 Center Court Dr. FAX (562) 916-8514
Cerritos 90703
www.cerritoscenter.com

A presenting organization whose mission is to present high quality music, dance, and theatre events. State-of-the-art moveable theatre.

DOROTHY CHANDLER PAVILION
BOOKING OFFICE (213) 972-7479
135 N. Grand Ave.
Los Angeles 90012

Taper Casting (213) 972-7374

Ahmanson Theatre Casting (213) 972-7382

An Equity theatre that is strictly a rental space with 3,197 seats. Rental includes space only.

THE CHANDLER STUDIO (818) 786-1045
12443 Chandler Blvd. FAX (818) 780-6517
North Hollywood 91607

Artistic Director: Michael Holmes. Original and classic works. Actors are chosen primarily from within the company. Holds open auditions and lists casting info in the trades. 99 Seat Plan. 33 seats. Theatre available for rental.

THE CHARLENS COMPANY. INC. (619) 528-9000
P.O. Box 40526 FAX 619-528-9000
San Diego 92104
www.thecharlenscompany.com
elizabethk@thecharlenscompany.com

Artistic Director: A. M. Charlens, Ph.D. This is a resident membership production company that was founded in 1971 in San Diego, but produces its plays in the greater Los Angeles area. Focuses primarily on Shakespeare, but puts up contemporary and new works each year. Lists casting information in Back Stage West.

CITY GARAGE (310) 319-9939
1340½ 4th St. (Alley) FAX (310) 396-1040
Santa Monica 90405

P.O. Box 2016
Santa Monica 90406
www.citygarage.org

Artistic Director: Frederique Michel. Managing Director: Charles Duncomde. A resident, membership company under the 99 Seat Plan that does avant-garde work. Seats 48. Casting is from within the company. P&R accepted for company auditions.

THE COAST PLAYHOUSE (323) 650-8509
8325 Santa Monica Blvd.
Los Angeles 90069

Producer: Don Fairbanks. 99 Seat Plan theatre. Usually does original works, musicals, and west coast premieres. No submissions. Lists casting info in Back Stage West. Rents space and technical equipment. Theatre has 99 seats.

THE COLONY/STUDIO THEATRE (818) 558-7000
555 N. 3rd St. FAX (818) 558-7110
Burbank 91505
www.colonytheatre.org

Producing Director: Barbara Beckley. A membership company operating under a HAT contract with LOA. Membership is by invitation only and open calls are held for each production. 276 seat theatre.

COMPANY OF ANGELS (323) 883-1717
2106 Hyperion Ave.
Silverlake 90027

P.O. Box 3480 (323) 666-6789
Hollywood 90078
www.companyofangels.org

This is the oldest membership company in Los Angeles. Operates under the 99 Seat Plan. When auditioning for new members they accept P&R. Dues paying company. They have a 50 seat theatre.

THE COMPLEX (323) 465-0383
6476 Santa Monica Blvd. FAX (323) 469-5408
Hollywood 90038
www.complexhollywood.com

Executive Director: Matt Chait. Resident theaters. There are five 99 Seat Plan theaters, up to 55 seats each, plus 5 rehearsal studios. Casting is done by the individual producers using the facility. The theatres are available for rent.

CONEJO PLAYERS (805) 495-3715
351 S. Moorpark Rd. FAX (805) 498-8065
Thousand Oaks 91361
www.conejoplayers.org

Executive Director: Richard Johnson. Board President: Doug Jocelyn. Two musicals, one dramatic play and two comedies in their season. A community non-Equity theatre. $1 charge to join theatre but you don't have to join to participate. They hold open auditions on the Sunday, Monday and Tuesday after the opening of the previous show. Lists casting info in Back Stage West and local papers. This state-of-the-art theatre has 188 seats. They also have the Conejo Afternoon Theatre at the same location. Two children's shows: May and September.

CORNERSTONE THEATER COMPANY (213) 613-1700
708 Traction Ave. FAX (213) 613-1714
Los Angeles 90013
www.cornerstonetheater.org
mail@cornerstonetheater.org

Cornerstone was begun in 1986 by artistic director Bill Rauch and founding director Alison Carey. They work alone as a professional ensemble and in collaboration with members of diverse communities across the country. Cornerstone works to help build an inclusive, community-based theater. In 1992, Cornerstone settled in Los Angeles to begin urban residency work. The company's community-based project includes collaboration with residents of Watts, Pacoima; and Arab-Americans citywide.

CORONET THEATRE (310) 657-7377 / (310) 652-9955
366 N. La Cienega Blvd.
Los Angeles 90048
www.coronet-theatre.com

Historic 284-seat theatre, used mainly for long-term commercial rentals. The home of Dee Gee Theatrical, a commercial theatre production company. Also the Studio Coronet with 99 seats and Upstairs at the Coronet which also seats 99. Available for rent.

COURT THEATRE (310) 652-4035
722 N. La Cienega Blvd. FAX (310) 854-5495
West Hollywood 90069

Artistic Director: Tom Astor. A 99 Seat Plan theatre. Accepts P&R on a per production basis, no active casting files. Holds open casting calls. Theatre has 90 seats.

COWELL THEATRE (415) 441-3400 / (415) 441-3687
Fort Mason Center FAX (415) 441-3410
Landmark Bldg A
San Francisco 94123-1382
www.fortmason.org

Director: Sharon Walton. This 437 seat theatre is primarily a rental facility. No submissions.

CYPRESS CIVIC THEATRE (714) 229-6796
5172 Orange Ave.
Cypress 90630

A non-Equity community theatre. Accepts pictures and resumes and maintains casting files. Holds open auditions and lists casting information in Back Stage West and the local papers. They have a 120 seat theatre. No rentals. Celebrating their 21st year in existence.

DEAF WEST THEATRE (818) 762-2998
5112 Lankershim Blvd. TDD (818) 762-2782
North Hollywood 91601
www.deafwest.org

Artistic Director: Ed Waterstreet. Operates under the 99 Seat Plan. Dedicated to producing plays using deaf or hard of hearing and hearing actors. Accepts P&R. All productions are both spoken and signed. It is not necessary to know sign language but it helps. This 99 seat theatre is available for rental.

DELL' ARTE COMPANY
DELL' ARTE SCHOOL OF PHYSICAL THEATRE (707) 668-5663
P.O. Box 816 FAX (707) 668-5665
Blue Lake, CA 95525
www.dellarte.com
dellarte@aol.com

Artistic Directors: Joan Schirle. Managing Director: Michael Fields. An Equity Letter of Agreement theatre. A membership company, "resident ensemble company committed to the actor as creator and developing relevant, experimental new plays." Also tours. Rarely holds open calls. Actors can join the company by first working in their training program, "the only school of physical theatre in the U.S." Home of the Mad River Festival.

DRAMA PROJECT (310) 497-5416
938 3rd St., #303
Santa Monica 90403
www.thedramaproject.com

99 seat plan. Produces classics through new works. Pictures and resumes accepted for specific projects. Lists information in Back Stage West.

DUCK'S BREATH MYSTERY THEATRE (800) 989 DUCK / (800) 989-3825
P.O. Box 22513
San Francisco 94122
www.drscience.com
steve@drscience.com

Original works and comedies. A theatrical collective production company and touring theatre. Accepts P&R but seldom casts from outside their group. If they are casting outside they will list info in Back Stage West and Callboard.

EAST COUNTY PERFORMING ARTS CENTER (619) 440-0372 / (619) 440-2277
210 E. Main St. FAX (619) 440-6429
El Cajon 92020
www.ecpac.com
jmayes@ecpac.com

Accepts road shows and they do their own productions as well.

EAST WEST PLAYERS YOUTH PROGRAM (213) 625-7000
120 North Judge John Asio FAX (213) 625-7111
Los Angeles 90012
www.eastwestplayers.org

Artistic Director: Tim Dang. The youth program of the East West Players. This touring company of adult actors does one act plays that deal with Asian Pacific folk tales for youth. Casting is done through East West Players. Call for audition information.

EAST WEST PLAYERS (213) 625-7000
120 North Judge John Asio FAX (213) 625-7111
Los Angeles 90012
www.eastwestplayers.org

Artistic Director: Tim Dang. Focus is on Asian-American works and talent. A resident theatre operating under the 240 Seat Plan. They present four mainstage performances each year including one musical and three dramas. They list casting information in Back Stage West.

EDGEMAR CENTER FOR THE ARTS (310) 399-3666
2437 Main St. FAX (310) 399-2898
Santa Monica 90405
www.edgemarcenter.org
paxjava@hotmail.com

A state of the art two theater and art gallery complex. 501(c)(3) non-profit. 99 Seat Plan Theater. Periodically hiring for following positions: Stage Manager, Usher, Box Office Manager, Technicians, Designers, Concessions. Writers, Actors, Directors and Producers are encouraged to submit themselves and their work.

EL CAMINO COLLEGE CENTER FOR THE ARTS
EL CAMINO COLLEGE **(310) 660-3748**
16007 Crenshaw Blvd. **FAX (310) 660-3734**
Torrance 90506
www.elcamino.cc.ca.us

Executive Director: Bruce Spain. Presentation house. Books a season, professional through management companies, and student productions. Marsee Auditorium seats 2,048, Campus Theatre seats 358 and the Haag Recital Hall seats 178. Casting notices for summer musicals in Back Stage West.

EL TEATRO CAMPESINO **(831) 623-2444**
705 4th St. **FAX (831) 623-4127**
San Juan Bautista, CA 95045

P.O. Box 1240
San Juan Bautista, CA 95045
www.elteatrocampesino.com

Artistic Director: Luis Valdez. Original Spanish and English works. A membership company and resident theatre operating under the Equity Small Professional Theatre contract. Accepts P&R and maintains casting files. They hold open casting calls. An actor joins by being cast in a show. The 150 seat theatre is available for rent.

EL TEATRO DE LA ESPERANZA
AT THE SAN FRANCISCO MISSION **(415) 240-9594**
P.O. Box 40578 **FAX (415) 255-8031**
San Francisco 94140-0578

2940 16th St.
San Francisco 94140

Artistic Director: Rodrigo Duarte Clark. Contemporary plays based on Latino mythology and culture in the U.S. A non-equity resident theatre located in San Francisco's Mission Area. A bi-lingual, bi-cultural production company. They cast on a show-by-show basis, accept pictures and resumes maintain casting files. They list casting information in Callboard. Actors are paid.

ELECTRIC LODGE THEATRE **(310) 306-1854**
1416 Electric Ave. **FAX (323) 306-1117**
Venice 90291
www.electriclodge.org

Founder and Artistic Director: Joel Shapiro. Operates under the 99 seat plan. Traditional experimental theatre, dance, music, screenings and performance art. The 1,500 square foot space is available for rent.

(805) 965-6252
ENSEMBLE THEATRE COMPANY **(805) 962-8606**
914 Santa Barbara St. **FAX (805) 965-5322**
Santa Barbara 93101
www.ensembletheatre.com

Artistic Director: Robert Grand-Weiss. Classical and contemporary drama. A resident theatre with a membership company operating under the Small Professional Theatre contract. There are no membership dues. To become a member of the company, actors must audition. They accept P&R and maintain casting files. They hold open casting calls and list casting info in the local paper as well as Back Stage West.

EUREKA THEATRE COMPANY **(415) 788-7469**
215 Jackson St. **FAX (415) 243-0789**
San Francisco 94107
www.eurekatheatre.org

Producing Executive Director: Torri Randall. A presentation house.

FIRST STAGE **(323) 850-6271**
First United Methodist Church **FAX (323) 850-6295**
6817 Franklin Ave.
Los Angeles 90028

P.O. Box 38280
Los Angeles 90038
www.firststagela.org

A resident, membership company operating under the 99 Seat Plan. Gives staged readings of new works written for screen and stage, no full productions. Readings are held on Monday nights at 7 pm. They need actors for readings and workshops. Accepts P&R and maintains casting files. Membership dues are $55 per quarter. Send pictures and resumes to the P.O. Box address and non-members are welcomed.

FOOTPRINT ON THE SUN **(310) 396-3680**
410 Lincoln Blvd., #249
Venice 90291

Powerhouse Theater
3116 2nd St.
Santa Monica 90405
www.footprintonthesun.org
adamsaunders@footprintonthesun.org

Footprint on the Sun is a Venice based resident theater company for an exceptionally talented and dedicated group of actors, writers, directors, and designers. Their focus is on craft and process. They cast actors "against" type, push their directors, designers and writers outside of their "comfort zones" and work in an extended rehearsal process to allow the work to realize its full potential. Weekly mandatory craft meetings to build a shared artistic vocabulary within which they can work. Their productions have been named Critics Choice in the Los Angeles Times, amongst many others. They are always looking to be inspired by new talents, so if you have an interest in working for the sake of the work, contact them via their website.

JOHN ANSON FORD THEATRE **(323) 871-4552**
2580 Cahuenga Blvd East **FAX (323) 464-1158**
Los Angeles 90068
www.fordamphitheatre.org

The Ford is a County regional park facility administered by the L.A. County Arts Commission. There are two theatres, one outdoor amphitheatre with 1,200 seats and one indoor with 90 seats. The amphitheatre operates May 1 through October 31. The County produces a twelve week series, "Summer Nights at the Ford" June through September. Applications for participation in "Summer Nights" are available from the Arts Commission in August. Rentals outside aforementioned time frame are negotiated on an individual basis. The 90 seat theatre, "Inside at the Ford," is used in conjunction with "Summer Nights." The space is available for other projects November 1 through April 30. Please contact the Arts Commission for information regarding the use of this space. The Arts Commission does not accept P&R.

THE FOUND THEATRE **(562) 433-3363**
599 Long Beach Blvd. **FAX (562) 433-3363**
Long Beach 90802
www.foundtheatre.org

Classics and original plays. A resident company of actors. There are no dues. To become a member submit P&R to Virginia DeMoss, they will keep you on file and call you to audition for a production. Active casting files maintained. They are very interested in new members. Call for casting information.

FOUNTAIN THEATRE (323) 663-2235
(323) 663-1525
5060 Fountain Ave. FAX (323) 663-1629
Los Angeles 90029
www.fountaintheatre.com

Producing Artistic Director: Deborah Lawlor. Managing Artistic Director: Stephen Sachs. World or west coast premieres. 99 Seat Plan. Accepts pictures and resumes and has open casting calls and lists information in Back Stage West for specific productions only. This is not a membership company. There are 78 seats in the Fountain theatre.

FULLERTON CIVIC LIGHT OPERA (714) 526-3832
(714) 879-1732
218 W. Commonwealth Ave. FAX (714) 992-1193
Fullerton 92832
www.fclo.com

Artistic Director: Jan Duncan, General Manager: Griff Duncan. Equity and CLO contracts. Lists casting information in Back Stage West and has an audition list. Call to be placed on the audition list. Pictures and resumes accepted at auditions. Has 13 performances of each show at their 1,300 seat theatre. Season: February through November.

GARDNER AND SIERRA STAGE (323) 876-1501
Gardner Stage
1501 N. Gardner St.
West Hollywood 90046

Sierra Stage
1444 N. Sierra Bonita Ave.
West Hollywood 90046

Managing Director: Jim Ingersoll. Rental theatres operating under the 99 Seat Plan. Gardner I has 32 seats, Gardner II is used as a studio for classes, and the Gardner III has 42 seats. The Sierra is an intimate 25 seat proscenium stage theatre. No submissions.

WILL GEER (310) 455-2322
THEATRICUM BOTANICUM (310) 455-3723
1419 N. Topanga Canyon Blvd. FAX (310) 455-3724
Topanga 90290
www.theatricum.com
theatricum@earthlink.net

Artistic Director: Ellen Geer. Classical, new, and musical works. A resident theatre operating under a LOA. Accepts pictures and resumes and maintains active casting files. Holds open casting calls in March for four productions and lists casting information on the Equity Hotline and in Back Stage West. See listing under ACTING in the TRAINING section for further information.

GEFFEN PLAYHOUSE (310) 208-6500
(310) 208-5454
10886 Le Conte Ave. FAX (310) 208-0341
Los Angeles 90024
www.geffenplayhouse.com

Producing Director: Gilbert Cates. Managing Director: Stephen Eich. Eclectic work that includes new plays, musicals, classics, etc. A resident theatre operating under a Equity LORT B contract. Accepts P&R, submit to Casting. Maintains casting files. Season is October-June. This 498 seat theatre is occasionally available for rent during the off-season. Affiliated with UCLA.

GLENDALE CENTER THEATRE (818) 244-8481
324 N. Orange St. FAX (818) 244-5042
Glendale 91203
www.glendalecentretheatre.com

Artistic Director: Tim Dietlein. Comedies, musicals, and children's theatre. Non-Equity. Accepts pictures and resumes and holds open casting calls. Lists casting information in Back Stage West. 440 seats.

GLOBE PLAYHOUSE
SHAKESPEARE SOCIETY OF AMERICA (323) 654-5623
1107 N. Kings Rd. FAX (323) 654-5627
West Hollywood 90069
www.shakespearesocamerica.com

Artistic Director: R. Thad Taylor. A resident theatre under the 99 Seat Plan. Almost exclusively Shakespearian productions. Directors of individual shows do their own casting. There are open calls. Lists casting information in Back Stage West. The 99 seat theatre is available for rent for most theatrical purposes including filming and has its own parking lot.

THE GLOBE THEATRES (619) 231-1941
(619) 239-2255
Old Globe, FAX (619) 231-5879
Cassius Carter Center Stage,
Lowell Davies Festival Theatre at Balboa Park
San Diego
P.O. Box 122171
San Diego, CA 92112
www.theglobetheatres.org

Artistic Director: Jack O'Brien. Executive Director: Louis G. Spisto. All styles of theatre. A resident theatre operating under Equity B, and C contracts. Open calls for Equity members are held several times a year. Actors are called to audition from submitted P&R and casting files are maintained. They have an MFA program for actors in collaboration with the University of San Diego. There are three Equity theatres, the Old Globe with 589 seats, the Cassius Carter Center Stage, 225 seats, and Lowell Davies Festival Theatre, 612 seats. Limited rental time is available.

GLORIOUS REPERTORY COMPANY
24TH STREET THEATRE (213) 745-6516
1117 24th St.
Los Angeles 90007
www.24thstreet.org

Artistic Director: Debbie Devine. Executive Director: Jay McAdams. Membership company and resident company of the 24th Street Theatre. Writes and perform original works. Has a children's wing, "The Glorious Players," that tours. Accepts P&R by mail.

THE GRACE PLAYERS (323) 464-1222
The Egyptian Arena
1625 N. Las Palmas
Hollywood 90028

Artistic Director, Natalija Nogulich. Classical works and new plays/playwrights. Also has a play reading series. A resident company operating under the 99 Seat Plan. Actors are drawn from Ms. Nogulich's acting class. Accepts P&R. This 99 seat theatre is available for rent.

GRANADA THEATRE (818) 363-6887
18167 Chatsworth St. FAX (818) 832-4959
Granada Hills 91344
www.granadatheatre.com

Executive Director: Jo Erickson. Performs a musical, 2 comedies, a mystery piece, and one other show per year. A community theatre. Non-Equity. Reviews pictures and resumes for specific productions only and lists casting information in Back Stage West and Breakdown. This is a 120 seat dinner theatre. Auditions for season productions are normally held from 7 pm to 9:30 pm at the theatre. Call or see website for additional information.

GREAT AMERICAN MELODRAMA & VAUDEVILLE THEATRE (805) 489-8523
1863 Pacific Blvd. Hwy. 1 FAX (805) 489-5539
Oceano, CA 93445

P.O. Box 1026
Oceano, CA 93445
www.americanmelodrama.com

Producer: John Schlenker. Turn-of-the-century melodramas, comedies of the 20s and 30s, musical theatre, and musical reviews. A resident non-Equity theatre. Three companies cast year round on a per season basis with options. Accepts P&R and maintains casting files. Holds open casting calls and lists casting info in New York, Chicago, L.A., San Francisco, Pittsburgh, local papers and Back Stage West. Actors are paid. Rental availability of their 265 seat theatre depends on their schedule. 31st year in operation.

GREAT LEAP, INC. (213) 250-8800
1145 Wilshire Blvd., Ste. 100-D
Los Angeles 90017
www.greatleap.org
greatleap@anet.net

Artistic Director: Nobuko Miyamoto. Interim Managing Director: Tarabu Betserai Kirkland. Professional arts organization which creates works that give expression to the Asian-American and multi cultural experience through music, dance, and workshop. A producing company.

GREENWAY COURT THEATER (323) 655-7679
544 N. Fairfax Ave. FAX (323) 655-7906
Los Angeles 90036
wwgaa@aol.com

Opened in January 2000, this theater is a non-profit organization, raising funds from the Trading Post which has been voted Best Market in Los Angeles and is open every Sunday on the corner of Fairfax and Melrose. These funds also benefit Fairfax High School. The theater also hosts the Actors Studio's Writers Group once a week; has hosted the Lincoln Center Theater's Director's Lab; there is a music program every Monday night; a Spoken Word program every Tuesday night and there is an ongoing after school digital video workshop for Fairfax Highschool students.

GROUNDLING THEATRE (323) 934-4747
(323) 934-9700
7307 Melrose Ave. FAX (323) 934-8143
Los Angeles 90046
www.groundlings.com

Executive Director Manager: Eric Venerbeck. A resident company of actors operating under the 99 Seat Plan. Company members are selected from The Sunday Company, the advanced group of actors in The Groundling's school.

GROUP REPERTORY THEATRE (818) 760-9368
(818) 769-7529
10900 Burbank Blvd.
North Hollywood 91601
www.lcgrt.com

Artistic Director: Lonny Chapman. A resident theatre and membership company operating under the 99 Seat Plan. To join submit a P&R, they will schedule an interview. They maintain active casting files but do not hold open auditions.

GROVE THEATER CENTER (714) 741-9555
12852 Main St.
Garden Grove 92640

1111B Olive Blvd. (818) 238-9998
Burbank 91505
www.gtc.org

Artistic Director: Kevin Cochran. All types of theatre. Diverse programming. Two theatres, GTC's Gem Theater with 172 seats and GTC's Festival Amphitheater with 550 seats. The Burbank Theatre has 98 seats. Open calls are listed in Back Stage West and auditions are held in L.A. and Orange County. Submissions should be made from listing in Back Stage West.

LORRAINE HANSBERRY THEATRE (415) 474-8800
620 Sutter St.
San Francisco 94102

Business address:
555 Sutter St., Ste. 305
San Francisco, CA 94102
www.lorrainehansberrytheatre.com
lhtsf@aol.com

Artistic Director: Stanley Williams. Managing Director: Quentin Easter. Premiere black theatre with original works and revivals. A resident theatre operating under the Small Professional Theatre contract. Accepts P&R and maintains casting files. Holds open casting calls and lists casting info in Back Stage West, Equity Hotline, and Callboard. The 300 seat theatre is available for rent.

HARMONY GOLD THEATRE (323) 851-4900
7655 Sunset Blvd. FAX (323) 851-5599
Los Angeles 90046
www.harmonygold.com

Executive Director: Frank Agrama. A 350 seat theatre.

HARRIET & CHARLES LUCKMAN FINE ARTS COMPLEX (323) 343-6610
California State University FAX (323) 343-6423
at Los Angeles
5151 State University Dr.
Los Angeles 90032
www.calstatela.edu.

Executive Director, Clifford Harper. A presenting house. Accepts P&R, and maintains casting files. 1,172 seat theatre, 7,000 sq. ft. art gallery. 50 seat amphitheatre and Street of the Arts comprise the complex.

HIGHWAYS (310) 453-1755
(310) 315-1459
1651 18th St. FAX (310) 453-4347
Santa Monica 90404
www.highwaysperformance.org

Artistic Director: Leo Garcia. Administrative Director: Mary Milelzcik. Original works. If requested to do so, actors can submit a 5 minute DVD or VHS tape which documents their performance art and dance. Please do not submit pictures and resumes. Write a letter explaining why you want to perform at Highways with background information on yourself. Call for further information.

HORTON GRAND THEATRE (619) 234-9583
444 4th Ave. FAX (619) 239-3823
San Diego 92101
www.tripleespresso.com

Strictly a 250 seat rental theatre. 1940s decor.

ELIZABETH HOWARD'S
CURTAIN CALL DINNER THEATRE (714) 838-1540
690 El Camino Real
Tustin 92780
www.curtaincalltheater.com

Artistic Director: John Ferola. Musicals. A non-Equity resident dinner theatre. Accepts P&R and maintains casting files. Holds open casting calls and lists casting information in Back Stage West. There are 300 seats in their theatre.

THE HUDSON MAINSTAGE/
HUDSON BACKSTAGE/ HUDSON GUILD/
HUDSON AVENUE THEATRE (323) 856-4249
6539 Santa Monica Blvd. FAX (323) 856-4252
Hollywood 90038
www.hudsontheatres.com

Artistic Directors: Elizabeth Reilly. Classics to contemporary works. The theatres are available for rent.

HUNTINGTON BEACH PLAYHOUSE (714) 375-0696
7111 Talbert Ave. FAX (714) 375-0698
P.O. Box 451
Huntington Beach 92648
www.hbph.com
hbplay@earthlink.net

Community theatre. Accepts P&R for specific productions only. Holds open auditions and lists casting information in Back Stage West and the local Trades.

INTERNATIONAL CITY THEATRE (562) 495-4595
300 E. Ocean Blvd.
Long Beach, CA 90802

Business address: (562) 436-4610
1 World Trade Center
P.O. Box 32069
Long Beach, CA 90802
www.ictlongbeach.com

Original and international works. Accepts pictures and resumes and maintains casting files. Holds open casting calls and lists casting information in Back Stage West and Breakdown. Has between 190 and 349 seats.

(415) 626-2787
INTERSECTION FOR THE ARTS (415) 626-3311
446 Valencia St. FAX (415) 626-1636
San Francisco 94103
www.theintersection.org

Program Director: Kevin Chen. Executive Director: Deborah Cullinan. Contemporary, Experimental works. A combination theatre/art gallery with a literary department. A resident non-equity theatre. No submissions. The 80 seat theatre is available for rent upon availability.

THE IVAR THEATRE (323) 461-7300
1605 N. Ivar Ave.
Hollywood 90028

A multi-functional, non-profit organization. No submissions, casts Equity and non-Equity actors and lists casting info in Back Stage West, Breakdown, the Trades, and the Equity Hot Line. 4 wall rental of this 284 seat theatre is available. For rental information contact the theatre manager.

JAPANESE AMERICAN CULTURAL (213) 680-3700
& COMMUNITY CENTER (213) 628-2725
244 S. San Pedro St. FAX (213) 617-8576
Los Angeles 90012
www.jaccc.org

A non-Equity presentation house. The 878 seat theatre is available for rent with a 4 hour minimum. Please do not submit P&R. Rates negotiable.

KNIGHTSBRIDGE THEATRE (626) 440-0821
1944 Riverside Dr. FAX (626) 440-0894
Los Angeles 90039
www.knightsbridgetheatre.com

Artistic Director: Joseph Stachura. Operates under the 99 Seat Plan. Accepts P&R and maintains casting files. Holds open casting for each production and lists information in Back Stage West.

L.A. CONNECTION
COMEDY REPERTORY THEATRE (818) 784-1868
13442 Ventura Blvd.
Sherman Oaks 91423
www.laconnectioncomedy.com

Founded in 1977 by Kent Skov, the company performs improvisational comedy, original plays, sitcoms, dramatic, improv, long form improv, sketch comedy and dubs old films in their 99 seat theatre. This is a membership company under the 99 Seat Plan and they cast entirely from within the company. Auditions for the company are held weekly and active casting files are maintained. Actors are paid 25% of the door profits. They also produce a TV show for syndication using company members and "Mad Movies" on Nickelodeon, and have developed shows for USA Network and the SCI FI Channel. Also has a development deal with Dick Clark Productions. They were nominated for cable's ACE Award for best comedy special in 1994. They perform for camps, corporations, industrials and trade shows throughout the country. Will rent theatre space. Some of their alumni are Mathew Perry, Sharon Laurance, Victoria Jackson, John Lovitz, Chris Kattan, Will Farrell and Taylor Negron. Continuous comedy shows 4 days a week.

L.A. THEATRE CENTER (213) 628-2772
514 S. Spring St.
Los Angeles 90013
www.culturela.org

Strictly a rental space. There are four theatres, one with 500 seats, one with 320 seats, one with 296 seats, and one with 99 seats. All inclusive in-house systems are available with rental. No submissions, incoming productions do their own casting.

(310) 827-0808
L.A. THEATRE WORKS (310) 827-0889
681 Venice Blvd. FAX (310) 827-4949
Venice 90291
www.latw.org
latworks@aol.com

A production company operating under Equity, AFTRA. No submissions, directors and producers of individual projects cast the plays. They have a radio series broadcast on KPCC. No scripts accepted. Actors may submit through agents only.

LA JOLLA PLAYHOUSE (858) 550-1070
2910 La Jolla Village Dr. FAX (858) 550-1075
La Jolla, CA 92037

P.O. Box 12039 (858) 550-1010
La Jolla, CA
www.lajollaplayhouse.com

Artistic Director: Des MacAnuff. Managing Director: Stephen Libman. A non-profit professional theatre operating under Equity LORT B, C, and D contracts. A resident company that offers internships. They cast non-Equity in minor roles. Holds open casting calls for productions and active casting files are maintained.

LA MIRADA THEATRE
FOR THE PERFORMING ARTS (714) 994-6310
14900 La Mirada Blvd. FAX (714) 994-5796
La Mirada, CA 90638

P.O. Box 1058 (562) 944-9801
La Mirada, CA 90637
www.lamiradatheatre.com

Dance, jazz, and musicals. A non-Equity resident theatre, although they are Equity for their McCoy Rigby Entertainment Season. Also a production company. Submit to McCoy Rigby Entertainment, 110 E. Wilshire Ave., #201, Fullerton, 92632. This 1,260 seat theatre is available for rent.

LAGUNA PLAYHOUSE (949) 497 ARTS
606 Laguna Canyon Rd.
Laguna Beach 92651

Mailing Address:
P.O. Box 1747
Laguna Beach 92652
www.lagunaplayhouse.com

Executive Director: Richard Stein. A non-profit resident theatre. Actors are paid. Accepts P&R and maintains casting files. Casts both Equity and non-Equity. Holds open auditions and lists casting info in Back Stage West. Actors may ask to be put on their mailing list for auditions. They also have a youth theatre company. This 418 seat theatre is available for rent on a daily basis.

LAMB'S PLAYERS THEATRE (619) 437-6050
1142 Orange Ave. FAX (619) 437-6053
Coronado, CA 92118

P.O. Box 182229 (619) 437-0600
Coronado, CA 92178
www.lambsplayers.org
lambsplaye@aol.com

Artistic Director: Robert Smyth. Classics and original works. A non-Equity repertory theatre with a full-time staffed repertory company. Actors are paid. Accepts pictures and resumes and maintains casting files. Holds open casting calls and lists casting information in Actor's Alliance Hotline. They have a 340 seat theatre.

LAURELGROVE THEATRE (818) 850-6328
FAX (818) 840-6913

Artistic Director: Jack Heller. Producing new playwrights. Call for further information.

(805) 962-1458
LOBERO THEATRE (805) 963-0761
33 E. Canon Perdido St. FAX (805) 962-4857
Santa Barbara 93101
www.lobero.com

General Manager: David Asbell. A 680 seat resident theatre available for rent only. Occasionally co-produces. No submissions.

LONG BEACH PLAYHOUSE
MAINSTAGE AND STUDIO THEA (562) 494-1014
5021 E. Anaheim St. FAX (562) 494-1616
Long Beach 90804

Box Office (562) 494-1616
www.lbphouse.com

Established in 1929, the playhouse houses two theaters: the 99 seat plan Actors Equity Studio Theatre and the 200-seat non-Equity Mainstage Theater. 16 productions are produced annually: eight in each theatre. Casts union and non-union actors. Pictures and resumes accepted at open calls. Also maintains acting classes for youth and adults, an annual Playwright's "New Works" project. Highschool outreach programs and internships for college students in scenic and costume design. This resident theatre also contains a curated art gallery.

LOS ANGELES DESIGNER'S THEATRE (323) 650-9600
P.O. Box 1883 FAX (323) 654-3210
Studio City 91614-0883
ladesigners@juno.com

Los Angeles Designers' Theatre was founded in 1970 and has produced over 400 productions consisting of over 5,000 performances and using the talents of over 5,000 actors, singers, dancers, directors, designers, choreographers, musical directors, composers and other personnel. They are not affiliated with any educational organization or government entity, but rather are a non-profit, tax-exempt theatre-producing organization serving the Los Angeles, Hollywood, Studio City, Beverly Hills, Universal City, Sherman Oaks, Burbank and Encino markets.

LOS ANGELES PLAYHOUSE
HOME OF THE OPEN FIST
THEATRE COMPANY (323) 882-6912
4712 Admiralty Way #557
Marina Del Rey 90292
www.openfist.org

Dramatic plays and original works. A membership company under the 99 Seat Plan. To join the company an actor must schedule an audition. They cast from within the company unless they cannot fill a particular role. Accepts pictures and resumes and maintains casting files.

LOS ANGELES REPERTORY COMPANY (323) 464-8542
6560 Hollywood Blvd., 2nd Fl. FAX (323) 464-6130
Hollywood 90028
www.larep.org

Managing Director: John Herzog. Dedicated to quality theatre, they have long rehearsal periods in order to fully develop plays. A production company. They are not a membership company and cast from the L.A. Theatre community at large. Maintains casting files.

LOS ANGELES WOMEN'S SHAKESPEARE CO. (310) 453-5069
1158 26th St., Ste. 399 FAX (310) 453-5069
Santa Monica 90403
www.lawsc.net

Artistic director: Lisa Walpe. Produces Shakespeare's plays with an all female ensemble of highly trained multi-racial artists. Operates under the 99 seat plan. Sometimes Equity LOA.

LOS FELIZ PLAYHOUSE (323) 953-2823
4646 Hollywood Blvd.
Hollywood 90027
www.ronburrus.com

Original and contemporary works. A resident theatre for Actors Platform (professional actors from Ron Burrus' Acting Studio). Maintains casting files. This 36 seat theatre is also available for rent. See listings for Ron Burrus under ACTING and COLD READING in the TRAINING section for further information. SEE AD ON PAGE 7.

LOST STUDIO FORMERLY LOFT STUDIO (323) 933-6944
130 S. La Brea Ave.
Los Angeles 90036
www.theloststudio.com
loststudio@yahoo.com

99 Seat Plan. The space is predominantly used for acting classes. Productions are cast from their classes although they cast from outside when needed. No submissions, they list auditions in the trades. The 70 seat theatre is available for rent for production or rehearsal.

MAGIC THEATRE (415) 441-8001, (415) 441-8822
Fort Mason Center, Bldg. D FAX (415) 771-5505
San Francisco 94123
www.magictheatre.org

Artistic Director: Chris Smith. Interim Managing Director: Rick Smith. New works and original plays and some revivals. An Equity resident theatre. Bay Area Regional Theatre. Accepts P&R and maintains casting files. Has two 160 seat theatres, both are available for rent. Call for rental information, (415) 441-4242.

MARIN THEATRE CO. (415) 388-5200, (415) 388-5208
397 Miller Ave. FAX (415) 388-0768
Mill Valley, CA 94941
www.marintheatre.org

Artistic Director: Lee Sankiwich. Managing Director: Gabriella Calicchio. A resident theatre with both Equity and non-Equity performers operating under the BAT contract. Accepts pictures and resumes and maintains casting files. Lists casting information in Callboard. Two theatres, the Mainstage with 250 seats and the Studio with 100 seats. Both are available for rent. 5 play season running from September through June.

MARINES MEMORIAL THEATRE (415) 441-7444, (415) 771-6900
609 Sutter St., Ste. 200
San Francisco 94102
www.marinesmemorialtheatre.com

A presenting house operating under an Equity production contract. No submissions. Casts Equity only and lists casting information on the AEA hotline and in the local trades. The theatre is 650 seats.

MARK TAPER FORUM (213) 972-7353
135 N. Grand Ave. FAX (213) 972-8051
Los Angeles 90012
www.taperahmanson.com

Under the artistic direction of founder Gordon Davidson, the Taper built a reputation for excellence in the development of new plays and voices for the theatre. Since 1967, the Taper has presented well over 350 plays ranging form the classics to contemporary European and American plays. Of these, more than 200 have been world or American premieres including Michael Cristofer's Pulitzer Prize-winning "The Shadow Box," Mark Medoff's "Children of a Lesser God," Luis Valdez's "Zoot Suit," "Jelly's Last Jam" and "Angels in America."

MARTIN ALLEY PLAYERS (818) 761-5404
110 Martin Alley FAX (818) 842-0947
Pasadena 91105
www.chekhov.net
chekhov@earthlink.net

Produces spiritually based plays and readings. Michael Chekhov based workouts are offered for members. Open auditions.

MASQUER'S CABARET THEATRE (323) 653-4848
8334 W. Third St. FAX (310) 392-6963
West Hollywood 90048
www.masquerscabaret.com

Dinner theatre. Call for more information.

MATRIX THEATRE (323) 852-1445
7657 Melrose Ave. FAX (323) 653-3279
Los Angeles 90046

The home of Matrix Theatre Company. Producer/Artistic Director: Joseph Stern. A resident, producing company under the 99 Seat Plan. This 99 seat theatre is available for rent.

MCCADDEN PLACE THEATRE (323) 463-2942
1157 N. McCadden Pl.
Los Angeles 90038

Produces new and published works. Has open casting calls and maintains casting files. This beautiful 50 seat, multi-level stage fully equipped theatre is available for rental. Reasonable rental rates.

THE SANFORD MEISNER THEATRE (818) 509-9651
5124 Lankershim Blvd. FAX (818) 769-5627
North Hollywood 91601
www.themeisnercenter.com

The Sanford Meisner Center is a 60 seat theatre developed for the use of Mr. Meisner's alumni. The Center is a dues-paying company composed of graduates of Mr. Meisners two-year program taught by Mr. Meisner or one his qualified teachers. Productions range from published to unpublished material.

THE MET THEATRE (323) 957-1152
1089 N. Oxford Ave. FAX (323) 957-1831
Los Angeles 90029
www.themettheatre.com

A non-profit theatre with two spaces. A 99 Seat Plan theatre upstairs and a 45 seat experimental theatre downstairs.

MARILYN MONROE THEATRE (323) 650-7777
7936 Santa Monica Blvd. FAX (323) 650-7770
West Hollywood 90046
www.strasberg.com
admissionsla@strasberg.com

Founder: Anna Strasberg. Resident 99 Seat Plan theatre with 99 seats. See listing for Lee Strasberg Creative Center in this section.

MORGAN-WIXSON THEATRE (310) 828-7519
2627 Pico Blvd.
Santa Monica 90405
www.morgan-wixson.org

A non-Equity community theatre. A membership company. Will accept submissions for specific productions. Holds open casting calls. Lists casting information in Back Stage West. Phone calls accepted Wednesday through Saturday 3 pm to 7 pm. The theatre has 201 seats.

MOVING ARTS (213) 622-8906
(213) 473-0640
514 S. Spring Street FAX (213) 622-8946
Los Angeles 90013
www.movingarts.org

Moving Arts has a national reputation for producing new plays by emerging playwrights. They have won numerous awards and garnered many rave reviews. They are a small membership company offering rehearsal, training, and workshops to company members.

NOHO ACTOR'S STUDIO (818) 763-5802
(818) 989-9146
5215 Lankershim Blvd.
North Hollywood 91601
www.nohoactorsstudio.com
stagerentals@aol.com

This 45 seat theatre is available for rent. Also has 2 rehearsal/class spaces. Located in the heart of the NoHo Arts District.

NORRIS THEATRE (310) 544-0403
27570 Crossfield Dr. FAX (310) 544-2473
Rolling Hills Estates 90274
www.norristheatre.org

A presenting 450 seat theatre. Accepts pictures and resumes for non-paid staged readings only. Submit to Playwright Development Project. Otherwise, please no submissions unless for specific project listed in Back Stage West.

NORTH COAST REPERTORY (858) 481-2155
(888) 776 NCRT
987D Lomas Santa Fe Dr. FAX (858) 481-0530
Solana Beach, CA 92075
www.northcoastrep.org
ncrt@northcoastrep.org

Artistic Director: David Ellenstein. the North Coast Repertory Theatre, a non-profit organization, has evolved into one of the area's leading performing arts organizations, recognized for the quality of its work and its commitment to excellence. Located in Solana Beach, in the heart of San Diego's Coastal North County, the theatre boasts an award-winning Mainstage season, with performances year-round to over 35,000 people in its intimate 194-seat setting. In addition, the theatre involves thousands of young people each year in the Theatre School – NCRT's education and outreach program. Audition information is announced on the website and on the audition hotline at (858) 481-2155 x 302 and the San Diego Actors' Alliance hotline at (619) 640-3333.

O.D.C. THEATRE (415) 863-9834
3153 17th St. FAX (415) 863-9833
San Francisco 94110

All performing arts. Will co-produce on occasion. There are two theatres including the 200 seat studio theatre. Theatre has sprung wood floor. Available for rent, evenings only.

ODYSSEY THEATRE ENSEMBLE (310) 477-2055
2055 S. Sepulveda Blvd. FAX (310) 444-0455
Los Angeles 90025
www.odysseytheatre.com

Three resident theatres operating under the 99 Seat Plan. A production company. Accepts P&R and holds open casting calls for productions. Lists casting info in the Trades. All three theatres have 99 seats and are available for rent.

ORANGE COUNTY (714) 556-2122
PERFORMING ARTS CENTER (714) 556-2787
600 Town Center Dr. FAX (714) 556-0156
Costa Mesa 92626
www.ocpac.org

A presentation and rental house only operating under an Equity contract.

P.L.A.Y. MARK TAPER FORUM (213) 972-7662
601 W. Temple Taper Annex
Los Angeles 90012

They produce theatre for young people and visit schools on occasion. They often do new work. Accepts pictures and resumes, lists casting information in Back Stage West and maintains casting files.

PACIFIC CONSERVATORY OF THE
PERFORMING ARTS (PCPA)
THEATRE FEST (805) 928-7731
P.O. Box 1700 FAX (805) 928-7506
Santa Maria 93456

800 S. College Dr. (805) 922-8313
Santa Maria 93454
www.pcpa.org

Classics, musicals, new, and experimental works. A repertory resident theatre operating under an Equity URTA contract. Also a conservatory and training center for students. Members of the company consist of professional artists in residence, members of their 2 year training program, and members of their one year actor's ensemble program. They also cast Equity actors. Accepts pictures and resumes and maintains casting files. Admission to the company is by audition and interview. The theatre holds a statewide audition tour covering all of California. Student members pay tuition, stipends are paid to the actor's ensemble, and Equity actors are on salary. There are three theatres, the 450 seat Marion Theatre, the 185 seat Severson Theatre, and the 700 seat Solvang Festival Theatre which is open in summer.

PACIFIC RESIDENT (310) 301-3971
THEATRE ENSEMBLE (310) 822 8392
P.O. Box 568 FAX (310) 301-3907
Venice 90294
www.pacificresidenttheatre.com
information@pacificresidenttheatre.com

Artistic Director: Marilyn Fox. Environmental staging of classic works and new American and world plays. 99 Seat Plan. A membership company. Has auditions twice a year and they accept pictures and resumes. They do not want any phone calls. They have an actor's conservatory with UCLA. The theatre is 50-99 seats and available for rent. Season: all year.

PALACE OF FINE ARTS THEATRE **(415) 563-6504** **(415) 567-6642**
3301 Lyon St.
San Francisco 94123
www.palaceoffinearts.org

Presenting house, rentals only.

PANTAGES THEATRE **(323) 468-1700**
6233 Hollywood Blvd.
Hollywood 90028
www.nederlander.com

A resident theatre operating under an Equity contract. Touring companies are booked through the Nederlander Organization. All casting is done through the private companies that book the theatre. This 2,705 seat theatre is available for 4 wall rental.

THE PASADENA PLAYHOUSE **(626) 792-8672**
39 S. El Molino Ave. **FAX (626) 792-7343**
Pasadena 91101

80 S. Lake St., #500 **(626) 356-7529**
Pasadena 91101
www.pasadenaplayhouse.org

The Pasadena Playhouse was organized in 1917 by Gilmore Brown, actor and director, as a non-profit educational corporation. The Playhouse became nationally known for presenting premiere performances of works by leading playwrights as well as plays by new dramatists. Today, the Pasadena Playhouse continues to be uniquely positioned as the only professional theatre in the San Gabriel Valley. A resident theatre operating under Equity LORT B+ contracts. Active casting files are maintained and they cast through a variety of casting directors. The theatre has 683 seats.

PIERCE THEATRE – PIERCE COLLEGE **(818) 710-4380**
6201 Winnetka Ave.
Woodland Hills 91371
www.piercecollege.com

The Performing Arts Building (PAB), with its 375-seat Main Stage Theater and 100-seat Arena Theater serves as an important cultural venue for all manner of Theater, Music, Dance and other community events. Under the direction of Chair Gene Putnam, the Department has developed a Musical Theatre program with appreciation and training courses and its top-quality summer musical productions, featuring the San Fernando Valley Symphony Orchestra. Auditions for all Pierce College Theater productions are open to the community. Auditions are normally held around the first week of each semester. All people who are cast in a production must apply to the college at the Admissions and Records Office and enroll as a student in the "Rehearsals and Performances" or "Play Production" courses. Cast members are, in most cases, expected to purchase their own stage make-up. If you are financially unable to afford the enrollment and health fees, please see the Financial Aid Office staff.

ROBERT CARNEGIE PLAYHOUSE WEST
SCHOOL AND REPERTORY THEATRE **(818) 881-6520**
4250 Lankershim Blvd.
North Hollywood 91602

PLAYHOUSE WEST THE SECOND STUDIO
10634 Magnolia Blvd.
North Hollywood 91601
www.playhousewest.net

Artistic Director: Robert Carnegie. A membership company based on mutual training that performs in repertory at both theatres. Operates under the 99 Seat Plan. No submissions. Reservation number: (818) 971-7191. See listing under ACTING in the TRAINING section for further information. SEE AD ON PAGE 9.

POWAY CENTER **(858) 748-0505**
FOR THE PERFORMING ARTS **(858) 679-4247**
15498 Espola Rd.
Poway 92064

Strictly a presentation house. Please, no submissions.

POWER HOUSE THEATRE **(310) 396-3680**
3116 2nd St. **FAX (310) 360-3494**
Santa Monica 90405
www.powerhousetheatre.com
info@powerhousetheatre.com

Located in the old Edison building, this theatre offers a variety of programming and performing opportunities. Visit their website or call for additional information.

PROMENADE PLAYHOUSE **(310) 656-8070**
1404 Third Street Promenade **FAX (310) 656-8069**
Santa Monica 90401
www.pierodusa.com
info@pierodusa.com

Equity approved, 65-seat theatre ideal for small and large productions, showcases, video/film shoots, screenings, workshops, seminars and castings. Located in the heart of Santa Monica's renowned Third Street Promenade, by the beach with plenty of parking. Also available for rent are The Soho Stage and The Actors Box, all quality venues providing a creative home for a new generation of artists. Call for appointment to view. SEE AD ON PAGE 297.

PUBLIC WORKS
IMPROVSATIONAL THEATRE **(323) 661-0524**
3724 W. Marcia Dr.
Los Angeles 90026
leeboek@hotmail.com

A small multi-cultural experimental ensemble that puts audiences in touch with contemporary political events and their immediate personal relevance. Ongoing performances and workshops. Contact Lee Boek.

JOHN RAITT THEATRE **(323) 871-8082**
6520 Hollywood Blvd.
Hollywood 90028
www.acmt.org
pgg@acmt.org

Artistic Director: Paul Gleason. A 99 seat theatre. Keeps pictures and resumes on file. Classics and originals. The American Center for Music and Theatre is dedicated to the development of professional performers and creators of American musical theater, as well as other types of artistic performance. They offer performances, production space, training, mentorship, and career opportunities to performers and production personnel.

PAUL E. RICHARDS THEATRE **(323) 257-2323**
2902 Rowena Ave.
Los Angeles 90027

Artistic Director: Paul E. Richards. Parking, A/C. This intimate adaptable space seats between 30-35. Traveling companies use the space or Paul casts productions from his classes.

THE ROAD THEATRE COMPANY **(818) 761-8838**
5108 Lankershim Blvd. **FAX (818) 761-1731**
North Hollywood 91601
www.roadtheatre.org
roadthtr@aol.com

Artistic Director, Taylor Gilbert. New works by established and new playwrights. Social, politically relevant plays. An acting company and volunteer group operating under the 99 Seat Plan. Accepts pictures and resumes. Rarely rents the 49 seat theatre.

ROYCE HALL UCLA **(310) 825-4401**
(310) 825-2101
405 Hilgard Ave.
Los Angeles 90024
www.ucla.edu

No submissions. A presentation house. Rentals only.

RUBICON THEATRE COMPANY **(805) 667-2900**
1006 E. Main Street, Ste. 300 **FAX (805) 667-2903**
Ventura 93001
www.rubicontheatre.org
rubicontheatre@earthlink.net

Artistic Directors: Jim O'Neill and Karyl Lynn Burns. Lists casting notices in Back Stage West. The Rubicon Theatre Company is a non-profit organization based in downtown Ventura's Cultural District. The mission of the company is to present high-quality professional theater for the entertainment, enrichment and education of the community.

SACRAMENTO THEATRE COMPANY **(916) 446-7501**
(916) 443-6722
1419 H St. **FAX (916) 446-4066**
Sacramento 95814
www.sactheatre.org
shannon@sactheatre.org

Artistic Director: Peggy Shannon. A resident theatre using both Equity and non-Equity performers operating under an Equity Letter of Agreement contract. Accepts pictures and resumes and maintains casting files. Holds open auditions and lists casting information with Breakdown. Has two theatres one with 300 seats and one with 90 seats. Season, September-May.

SAN DIEGO CIVIC THEATRE **(619) 615-4100**
(619) 570-1100
3rd & B St.
San Diego 92101

202 C St.
San Diego 92101
www.sdccc.org

A presentation house. Rentals only. No submissions.

SAN DIEGO JUNIOR THEATRE **(619) 239-1311**
(619) 239-8355
Balboa Park **FAX (619) 239-5048**
1650 El Prado Ste. 208
San Diego 92101
www.juniortheatre.com
info@juniortheatre.com

Education Director: Bethany Lockhart. Executive Director: Will Neblett. Non-Equity theatre that uses young performers ages 8-18. Also offers classes for ages 3-18 as well as giving performances.

SAN DIEGO REPERTORY THEATRE **(619) 231-3586**
(619) 544-1000
79 Horton Plaza **FAX (619) 235-0939**
San Diego 92101
www.sandiegorep.com
marketing@sandiegorep.com

Artistic Director: Sam Woodhouse. Managing Director: Karen Wood. Associate Artistic Director: Todd Salovey. Musicals, dramatic pieces, original plays, and revivals. A resident theatre operating under Equity Special Contract, Guest Artist, and LORT D contracts. Holds open casting calls for productions. They have two theatres available for rent, the Main Stage with 560 seats and the Lyceum with 250 seats.

SAN FRANCISCO MIME TROUPE **(415) 285-1717**
855 Treat Ave. **FAX (415) 285-1290**
San Francisco 94110
www.sfmt.org
office@sfmt.org

They are mimics, not pantomimics. Believing that all art is political, that art that does not challenge the status quo supports, they create plays and perform them to raise hell, to make people mad enough so that some day they will throw the bastards out! The chosen form is comedy, because laughter lowers people's defenses against unwelcome truths, combined with music, because music has the power to raise their hopes. All their comedies are serious, dramatizing the conflict between the presently powerful and the presently powerless. They work collectively and across racial, sexual, and generational lines to prove the possibility of the future; they exist as a challenge to despair.

SAN JOSE CENTER
FOR THE PERFORMING ARTS **(408) 277-5277**
255 Almaden Blvd. **FAX (408) 277-3535**
San Jose 95113
www.sjcc.com

A presentation theatre. Rentals only. No submissions.

SAN JOSE REPERTORY THEATRE **(408) 367-7266**
(408) 367-7255
101 Paseo de San Antonio **FAX (408) 367-7237**
San Jose 95109
www.sjrep.com
therep@vval.com

Artistic Director: Timothy Near. Non-profit organization. Drama and comedy with an occasional musical. A resident theatre operating under an Equity LORT C contract. There are open calls for productions. They accept pictures and resumes and maintain casting files. Their theatre has 532 seats.

SANTA MONICA PLAYHOUSE (310) 394-9779
1211 4th St. FAX (310) 393-5573
Santa Monica 90401
www.santamonicaplayhouse.com
smp@primenet.com

Artistic Director: Evelyn Rudie and Chris De Carlo. Original works. Resident theatre company performs in the Main Stage under the 99 Seat Plan. Casting files are maintained. General auditions held once a month and casting information is listed in Back Stage West. Rents space in the other three venues: The Other Space (70 seats), The Artist's Entrance Work Space (25 seats) and The White Box Theatre (15 seats). See listing under ACTING in the TRAINING section for further information.

SECRET ROSE THEATRE (818) 766-3691
11246 Magnolia Blvd. FAX (818) 766-3691
North Hollywood 91601
www.secretrose.com
kaz@secretrose.com

Artistic Director: Mike Rademaekers. Managing Director: Kaz Mata-Mura. 60 seats. Large stage with full lighting and sound system, follow spot and piano. Available for rent. Parking lot. Also, in-house productions including musicals, multi-cultural, youth programs, workshop, classic and new works. For more information, please visit their website. SEE AD ON PAGE 19.

SHAKESPEARE FESTIVAL/L.A. (213) 481-2273
1238 W. 1st St.
Los Angeles 90026
www.shakespearefestivalla.org

A professional theatre company dedicated to nurturing a tradition of public theatre that is accessible to all people. Collection of food for the needy instead of tickets.

SHOWBOAT TROUPE INC. (818) 222-7239
505 Live Oak Circle Dr. FAX (818) 591-7343
Calabasas 91302

Artistic Director: Mike Monahan. The Showboat Youtheatre. Children performers. Accepts pictures and resumes.

SHUBERT THEATRE (310) 201-1500
(800) 447-7400
2020 Avenue of the Stars FAX (310) 201-1585
Century City 90067

An Equity presentation house with 2,129 seats. No submissions.

SIERRA REPERTORY THEATRE (209) 532-3133
(209) 532-3120
P. O. Box 3030 FAX (209) 532-7270
Sonora, CA 95370
www.sierrarep.com
srt@mlode.com

Producing Director: Dennis Jones. Artistic Director: Scott Viets. Managing Director: Sara Jones. This small professional theatre with Equity and non-Equity contracts produces 10-11 shows per year in two theatres in the California Gold Rush Region.

SKYLIGHT THEATER (310) 855.1556
1816½ N. Vermont Ave.
Los Angeles 90027
www.katselas.com
gabwag@earthlink.net

Available for weekend rentals. Classes also held there in conjunction with the Milton Katselas' Beverly Hills Playhouse. Call for more information on classes.

SOUTH COAST REPERTORY THEATRE (714) 708-5500
655 Town Center Dr. FAX (714) 545-0391
Costa Mesa, CA 92626

Mailing Address:
P.O. Box 2197
Costa Mesa, CA 92628
www.scr.org

Producing Artistic Director: David Emmes. Artistic Director: Martin Benson. Managing Director: Paula Tomei. Casting Director/Artistic Associate: Joanne DeNaut. Resident company founded in 1964 includes five founding members. An Equity theatre with 507-seat Segerstrom Stage (LORT B) and the 336-seat Argyros Theatre (LORT D) and the 95 seat Nicholas Studio. A 9 play subscription season of classics, contemporary plays, and world premieres, plus two annual holiday plays, and the educational touring production. Also a 4-play series, Theatre for Young Audiences. No membership dues. They generally accept pictures and resumes and maintain casting files. No open calls. General auditions are held twice a year, must submit picture and resume to be considered for auditions. Breakdowns are given to agents.

STAGE DOOR THEATRE (818) 889-5209
28311 Agoura Rd.
Agoura Hills 91301
www.logix.com/stagedoor

Artistic Director: Mike Monteleoni. Continuous theatre with 6 shows per year. Both contemporary and classical plays. Accepts pictures and resumes and maintains casting files. Lists casting information in Back Stage West and local newspapers. This 49 seat independent theatre is available for rent for classes.

STAGES THEATRE CENTER (323) 465-1010
(323) 463-5356
1540 N. McCadden Place FAX (323) 463-3904
Los Angeles 90028
www.stagestheatrecenter.com
askstageshollywood.com

Artistic Director: Paul Verdier. Original work and European plays including Ionesco interpretations. Often tri-lingual pieces in French/English/Spanish. A resident theatre operating under the 99 Seat Plan. Accepts pictures and resumes and maintains casting files. Open calls for the productions are listed in the trades. The 49 seat theatre is available for rent.

STARLIGHT MUSICAL THEATRE
AT THE STARLIGHT BOWL (619) 544-7800
2005 Pan American Plaza FAX (619) 544-0496
San Diego 92101

Mailing Address: (619) 544-7827
P.O. Box 3519
San Diego 92163-1519
www.starlighttheatre.org

Musicals. Equity Guest Artist contract. A resident theatre. Holds two auditions per year in early spring, and early winter. Casting information in Back Stage West and on the AEA hotline. Theatre rental is possible. Two seasons only with performances in the outdoor 4,324 seat theatre.

STOP-GAP THEATRE (714) 979-7061 (800) 381 8481
1570 Brookhollow Dr., Ste. 114 FAX (714) 979-7065
Santa Ana 92705
www.stopgap.org

Executive Director: Don Laffoon. Artistic Director: Finnuala Kenny. Interactive touring plays for schools and drama therapy workshops deal with social issues for all ages. Accepts pictures and resumes and maintains casting files. They cast both Equity and non-Equity.

LEE STRASBERG CREATIVE CENTER (323) 650-7777
7936 Santa Monica Blvd.
Los Angeles 90046
www.strasberg.com

Artistic Director: Anna Strasberg. Four resident theatres of the Lee Strasberg Creative Center, Inc. Under the 99 Seat Plan. The Marilyn Monroe Theatre has 99 seats, Theatre Stras and Stage Lee each have 49 seats and the Haven has 25 seats.

AUGUST STRINDBERG SOCIETY OF LOS ANGELES (323) 463-7525
P.O. Box 93806
Los Angeles 90093-0806
www.tassla.org
stbpatch@dslextreme.com

Artistic Director: David Patch. Plays by August Strindberg only. Production company operating under the 99 Seat Plan. No dues, become a member by writing a letter to the August Strindberg Society. Accepts pictures and resumes for particular shows only. Holds open casting calls and lists casting information in Back Stage West and Breakdown.

STUDIO THEATRE (323) 850-9497
3433 Cahuenga Blvd. West FAX (323) 876-9055
Los Angeles 90068-1329

Artistic Producing Director: Valentina Oumansky. Dramatic dance theatre, live concerts, and video productions. A performance art facility and resident theatre operating under the 99 Seat Plan. Gives junior youth classes in dance, improv and drama, as well as instructional entertainment video productions for beg-pro levels. This flexible theatre with 50 seats is available for rent for rehearsals, full productions, filming, concerts, dance, and classes. The Studio Theatre is now a historic and cultural landmark of Los Angeles.

TAMARIND THEATRE (323) 465-7980 (323) 465-7989
5919 Franklin Ave.
Los Angeles 90028
www.ucbtheatre.com

Musicals, dramatic productions, and original works. A resident theatre under the 99 Seat Plan. Accepts pictures and resumes and maintains casting files. Lists casting information in Back Stage West and Breakdown. For rental information on this 92 seat theatre contact Tony Beasle.

MARK TAPER FORUM CENTER THEATRE GROUP (213) 972-7353
601 W. Temple St.
Los Angeles 90012
Casting office (213) 972-7374
Casting hotline (213) 972-7235
www.taperahmancon.com

Artistic Director: Michael Ritchie. Managing Director: Charles Dillingham. Casting Director: Amy Lieberman. A resident theatre operating under Equity contracts, LORT A and B. Accepts P&R and maintains casting files. Has two theatres, the 750 seat Main Stage and the 317 seat Kirk Douglas Theatre in Culver City.

THE THEATRE IN OLD TOWN (619) 688-2494 (619) 688-2491
4040 Twiggs St. FAX (619) 688-0960
San Diego 92110
www.theatreinoldtown.com
admin@theatreinoldtown.com

An Equity SPC theatre operated by Miracle Theatre Productions. Accepts pictures and resumes. Theatre has 244 seats. Artistic Director: Paula Kalustian.

THEATRE 40 (310) 364-3606
P.O. Box 5401 FAX (310) 396-2325
Beverly Hills 90210

241 Moreno Dr. (310) 364-0535
Beverly Hills 90210
www.theatre40.org
theatre40web@yahoo.com

Founded in 1965, Theatre 40 is a professional acting company with a 99 seat theatre on the Beverly Hills High School Campus. The company has established itself as a successful creative force mounting over 100 critically acclaimed productions of classical plays, revivals of popular contemporary plays and, in recent years, West Coast premieres of major contemporary playwrights. Theatre 40 is one of the most innovative theatrical ensembles in Southern California with a well supported subscription season. In 1995 Theatre 40 was the recipient of the prestigious Margaret Harford Award for Excellence in the Small Theatre given by the Los Angeles Drama Critics Circle. In order to become a member an actor must present an audition for the Artistic Committee. Active members pay dues of $20 per month, and support the company by ushering at productions, fulfilling a job on a committee, and helping with the Adult Education Theatre Appreciation Classes.

THEATRE CRAFT PLAYHOUSE (323) 876-1100
7445 1/4 Sunset Blvd.
Los Angeles 90046

Artistic Director, Rick Walters. A resident theatre under the 99 Seat Plan. Acting classes are available. The 60 seat theatre is available for rent.

THE THEATRE DISTRICT (323) 957-2343
804 North El Centro
Hollywood 90038
www.thetheatredistrict.com
info@thetheatredistrict.com

Artistic Director: Macario Gaxiola. 99-seat plan.

THEATRE OF ARTS (EST. 1927) (323) 463-2500
1621 N. McCadden Place FAX (323) 463-2005
Los Angeles 90028
www.theatre-of-arts.com

Will rent the 880 seat theatre, technical equipment included. Rehearsal spaces also available for rent.

THEATRE OF NOTE (323) 856-8611
1517 N. Cahuenga Blvd.
Hollywood 90028
www.theatreofnote.com

New works, one acts, full length plays, also does classics. A resident company under the 99 Seat Plan. Membership company with monthly dues. They hold open company auditions 2 times a year and list information in Back Stage West. Actors will be asked to interview and perform two monologues. They have a 45 seat theatre available for rent. Send submissions to the attention of David Bickford.

THEATRE PALISADES **(310) 454-1970**
941 Temescal Canyon Rd.
Pacific Palisades 90272

P.O. Box 881
Pacific Palisades 90272
www.theatrepalisades.com

Books shows and musicals. A non-Equity community theatre that operates as its own production company. Active casting files maintained of actors who have auditioned at the theatre. Holds open casting calls for productions. All positions are filled on a volunteer basis. Theatre has 125 seats. 40 years old.

THEATRE/THEATER **(323) 422-6361**
5041 Pico Blvd.
Hollywood 90028
www.theatretheater.net
thtrethter@earthlink.net

Artistic Director: Jeff Murray. New works or, at least, new to L.A. A resident theatre operating under the 99 Seat Plan. Accepts pictures and resumes and maintains casting files. Holds open casting calls and lists information in the Trades. Theatre is available for rent.

THEATRE UNLIMITED **(818) 205-1680**
10943 Camarillo St.
North Hollywood 91602

A non-profit theatre operating under the 99 seat plan. The 53 seat theatre is a rental facility.

THEATRE WEST **(323) 851-4839**
(323) 851-7977
3333 Cahuenga Blvd. West **FAX (323) 851-5286**
Los Angeles 90068
www.theatrewest.org
theatrewest@theatrewest.org

Managing Director: John Gallogly. A membership company including writers and directors as well as actors operating under an Equity Letter of Agreement contract. A resident theatre, members pay $60 initiation fee and $40 per month dues. To join the company actors are auditioned, writers should submit, and directors are interviewed. No casting files. They cast outside of the company only when necessary. Their 168 seat theatre is available for rent.

THIRD STAGE **(818) 842-4755**
2811 West Magnolia Blvd. **FAX (818) 842-4267**
Burbank 91505
www.thirdstage.org
thirdstage@sbcglobal.net

An intimate 50 seat theater located in the Magnolia Park district of Burbank. Highly regarded by the press and Industry insiders alike. Complete services are available for rent. Contact: James Henriksen.

UNIVERSITY OF SOUTHERN CALIFORNIA (USC) THEATRES **(213) 740-8686**
University Park **FAX (213) 740-8888**
Los Angeles 90089-0791
www.usc.edu

Non-Equity. Undergraduate and graduate students only. There are two theatres, the DRC with 60 seats, the Scene Dock Theatre with 99 seats and the Bing Theatre with 551 seats. Theatres are available for rent.

THE BIG VICTORY AND THE LITTLE VICTORY **(818) 841-4404**
(818) 841-5421
3326-24 W. Victory Blvd. **FAX (818) 841-6328**
Burbank 91505
www.thevictorytheatres.com
victory@thevictorytheatrecenter.com

Artistic Directors: Tom Ormeny and Maria Gobetti. Original new plays. A resident theatre operating under the 99 Seat Plan. Active casting files are maintained. They hold open calls for productions. There are two theatres, one with 48 seats and one with 99 seats, both are available for rent. Their mission is to develop and produce original material by American playwrights and a selection of important revivals and to develop emerging new talent.

WADSWORTH THEATRE
UCLA/VETERANS **(310) 825-4401**
ADMINISTRATIONS GROUNDS **(310) 825-2101**
10920 Wilshire Blvd., Ste. 750
Brentwood 90024
www.cto.ucla.edu

Established productions. A resident theatre. This 1,378 seat theatre is available for rent.

WESTCHESTER PLAYHOUSE
KENTWOOD PLAYERS **(310) 645-5156**
8301 Hindry Ave.
Los Angeles 90045
www.kentwoodplayers.org
boxoffice@kentwoodplayers.org

A community theatre with 112 seats. Non Equity. Lists casting information in Back Stage West. Award winning plays and musicals for over 50 years, the Kentwood Players are a non-profit community theatre that produces 6 shows each year. All talents are needed: actors, singers, dancers, painters, carpenters, bookkeepers, etc. Members range from teens to seniors and meetings are on the third Wednesday of each month at 8 pm. Auditions are held the day following the opening night of the current production.

WHITEFIRE THEATRE **(818) 990-2324**
(818) 687-8559
13500 Ventura Blvd.
Sherman Oaks 91423
www.whitefiretheatre.com
stagerentals@aol.com

Artistic/Managing Director: Bryan Rasmussen. They occasionally have open calls for productions. Their 99 seat, large black box theatre is available for rent. On Ventura Blvd.'s restaurant row.

WILL & COMPANY **(213) 239-8777**
LATC, 514 South Spring Street **FAX (213) 489-3481**
Los Angeles 90013
www.willandcompany.com
home@willandcompany.com

Multicultural theatre group in residence at the Los Angeles Theatre

Center. In addition to Mainstage productions at LATC and El Capitan, Will & Company is known for its exciting 45 minute adaptations of classic works of literature that travel to area schools. Will & Company offers comprehensive residency programs in schools tying theatre to core school subjects.

WILSHIRE EBELL THEATRE (323) 939-1128
(323) 939-0126
4401 W. 8th St.
Los Angeles 90005
www.ebella.com/theatre

Rentals only. Books shows. No submissions.

THE YOUNG ARTISTS ENSEMBLE (805) 381-2748
(805) 381-1246
403 W. Hillcrest Ave. FAX (805) 375-1341
Thousand Oaks 91360
www.yaeonline.com
info@yaeonline.com

Children's theatre, teen drama, and Broadway musicals in the summer. For young actors age 10-19. This company produces plays in the Arts Council Facility.

ZEPHYR THEATRE (323) 852-9111
7456 Melrose Ave. FAX (323) 852-0031
Los Angeles 90046

An 82-99 seat theatre available for rent only. Operates under the 99 Seat Plan. Theatre is wheelchair accessible.

ZOMBIE JOE'S UNDERGROUND THEATRE (818) 202-4120
4850 Lankershim Blvd.
North Hollywood 91601
www.zombiejoes.com

44 seat non-Equity theatre. Repertory company. Casts on a show by show basis, usually from within the company. Open calls a couple times a year advertised in Back Stage West. Actors welcome to check them out in person or on the web. They are an experimental theatre company and originated progressive theatre in Los Angeles. Since 1992. Also children's shows.

THEATRES: OUT OF STATE

ALABAMA

ALABAMA SHAKESPEARE FESTIVAL (334) 271-5300
(334) 271-5353
1 Festival Dr. FAX (334) 271-5348
Montgomery, AL 36117
www.asf.net

Producing Artistic Director: Geoffrey Sherman. Shakespeare and the classics as well as some contemporary pieces. A repertory, resident company operating under Equity LORT B, C, and D contracts. Also a presentation house. They will cast outside the company. Auditions are arranged through a casting agent and are held in Montgomery and N.Y. Accepts P&R and maintains casting files. Casts Equity and non-Equity. They have an MFA program and use students in productions. There are two theatres, the Festival Stage with 750 seats, and the Octagon Stage with 225 seats.

ALASKA

PERSERVERANCE THEATRE (907) 364-2421 x8
(907) 364-2421 x35
914 3rd St. FAX (907) 364-2603
Douglas, AK 99824
www.perseverancetheatre.org
info@perserverancetheatre.org

Artistic Director: PJ Paparelli. A non-union house that presents original pieces and classics showing the diverse voices in the state. P&R accepted, maintains casting files. Works under LOA contract on occasion. Season: year round.

ARIZONA

ARIZONA THEATRE COMPANY TUCSON (520) 884-8210
Temple of Music & Art FAX (520) 628-9129
330 S. Scott Ave.
P.O. Box 1631
Tucson, AZ 85702

40 E. 14th St. (520) 622-2823
Tucson, AZ 95701
www.arizonatheatre.com
info@arizonatheatre.com

ARIZONA THEATRE COMPANY PHOENIX (602) 256-6899
(602) 256-6995
Herberger Theatre Center FAX (602) 256-7399
502 W. Roosevelt.
Phoenix, AZ 85003

Since 1966, Arizona Theatre Company has created world-class professional theatre in Arizona. One of the largest regional theatre companies in the southwest. Produces classics, musicals and award-winning contemporary dramas in both Tucson and Phoenix. Under LORT B equity contract. Open general season auditions are normally held in the spring. A resident theatre they accept pictures and resumes and maintain casting files. Casts Equity and non-Equity. Holds open auditions in Tucson, Phoenix, N.Y., and L.A. Lists casting info on the Equity hotline and in local Trades. L.A. casting submissions must made by an agent. Performs in both locations listed above. The Tucson theatre has over 600 seats, the Phoenix theatre has over 800 seats.

ARKANSAS

ARKANSAS REPERTORY THEATRE (501) 378-0445
601 Main St.
P.O. Box 110
Little Rock, AR 72201
www.therep.org

Producing Artistic Director: Bob Hupp. Has an eclectic season that includes musicals, classics, original works, and contemporary plays. Accepts P&R, send to Brad Mooy. Equity house. They have 2 stages, one with 354 seats and one with 99 seats. Year round season.

COLORADO

DENVER CENTER THEATRE COMPANY (303) 893-4000
1101 13th St.
Denver, CO 80204

1050 13th St. (303) 893-4100
Denver, CO 80204
www.denvercenter.org

Artistic Director: Kent Thompson. Classics and world premieres of American works. A resident theatre and repertory company under the Equity LORT B, C and D contracts. They will cast outside the company. Accepts P&R and maintains casting files. Equity and non-Equity. Holds open auditions in Denver in the spring and L.A. or N.Y. depending on their schedule. They have four theatres, The Stage with 700 seats, The Space with 427 seats, The Force with 200 seats, and The Ricketson with 250 seats. Season, September-June.

CONNECTICUT

NATIONAL THEATRE OF THE DEAF (860) 236-4193
139 N. Main
West Hartford, CT 6107
www.ntd.org
info@ntd.org

Artistic and Executive Director: Paul Winters PhD. Director of Education and Outreach: Betty Beekman. Classics, dramatic pieces, and original works. Operates under an Equity Guest Artist contract. A touring company, actors audition to join. Accepts P&R and audition tapes and maintains casting files. They have a professional school in the summer for the deaf, students may audition for the company after completing the school training. Auditions all year, call for more information.

O'NEILL THEATER CENTER (860) 443-5378
305 Great Neck Rd. FAX (860) 443-9653
Waterford, CT 6385
www.oneilltheatrecenter.org
info@oneilltheatrecenter.org

Executive Director: Amy Sullivan. Artistic Director for the National Music Theatre Conference: Paulette Haupt. Artistic Director for the O'Neill Puppetry Conference: Pam Arciero. Has several programs that use actors including The O'Neill Playwrights Conference in June under the Equity LORT C contract, the O'Neill Music Theatre Conference in August under an Equity contract, the O'Neill Puppetry Conference in June. Casts in May and June. Usually uses agents, but actors may submit directly to Beth Whitaker.

YALE REPERTORY THEATRE (203) 432-1518
1120 Chapel St. FAX (203) 432-1550
New Haven, CT 6520

P.O. Box 1257 (203) 432-1234
New Haven, CT 6505
www.yalerep.org
yalerep@yale.edu

Artistic Director: James Bundy. Managing Director: Victoria Nolan. Dramatic and original works. Operates on an Equity LORT C contract. Casts on a show-by-show basis. They also attend the LORT Lotteries. The theatre has 489 seats.

FLORIDA

(305) 442-2662
COCONUT GROVE PLAYHOUSE (305) 442-4000
3500 Main Highway FAX (305) 444-6437
Miami, FL 33133
www.cgplayhouse.com
alleras@cgplayhouse.com

Producing Artistic Director: Arnold Mittelman. National and world premieres and occasionally revivals with new interpretations. A resident theatre operating under the Equity LORT B and D contracts. All productions are produced and created locally. Accepts P&R. Casts on a per show basis. Holds open auditions at the beginning of the season. Casts in Miami, N.Y., and sometimes in L.A. Lists casting info on the Equity hotline and in the Trades.

(352) 373-5968
HIPPODROME STATE THEATRE (352) 375-4477
25 Southeast Second Pl. FAX (352) 371-9130
Gainesville, FL 32601
www.thehipp.org

Producing Director: Mary Hausch. Contemporary theatre, classics and new works. A resident theatre operating under a SBT10LOA contract. Cast Equity and non-Equity on a show-by-show basis and lists casting information on the Equity Hotline. Accepts P&R and maintains casting files. Holds auditions in N.Y., locally, and sometimes in other locations as well. The theatre has 267 seats. They also have a theatre for young adults which is primarily touring, sometimes in-house. This is one of four state theatres in Florida.

ILLINOIS

APPLE TREE THEATRE (847) 432-8223
595 Elm Pl., Ste. 210 FAX (847) 432-5214
Highland Park, IL 60035
www.appletreetheatre.com
khenry@appletreetheatre.com

Executive/Artistic Director: Eileen Boevers. Over 20 years of award-winning theatre—Apple Tree Theatre is committed to producing a diverse and challenging selection of both dramas and musicals, from new works to classics, all of which illuminate, the human condition, celebrate the tenacity of the human spirit, and expand the vision of artists and audiences alike culturally, intellectually, emotionally and spiritually as they connect with one another. Holding to rigorous artistic standards, Apple Tree Theatre is determined to make these productions accessible by virtue of our regional location and by sensitive accommodation to the physical limitations of audience members. There are performing arts workshops, programs for children and also a traveling troupe. Equity. General call during the summer and then casts on a per production basis.

COURT THEATRE (773) 702-7005
(773) 753-4472
5535 S. Ellis FAX (773) 834-1897
Chicago, IL 60637
www.courttheatre.org
info@courttheatre.org

Artistic Director: Charles Newell. Executive Director: Dawn Helsing. Casting Director: Cree Rankin. The classics and some world theatre. A resident theatre under the Equity LORT D contract. Accepts P&R and maintains casting files. Also cast non-Equity. Lists casting info in the trades. Casts on a show-by-show basis. Holds general auditions in May and submissions for this audition must be received by March. Non-Equity actors should submit P&R for auditions in January. Their mission is "To celebrate the immutable power and relevance of classic theatre."

ILLINOIS THEATRE CENTER (708) 481-3510
371 Artists Walkway FAX (708) 481-3693
Park Forest, IL 60466

P.O. Box 397
Park Forest, IL 60466
www.ilthctr.org
ilthctr@bigplanet.com

Producing Director: Etel Billig. Casting Director: Maggie Evans. Resident company under Equity CAT III contract. Maintains casting files and accepts P&R. Casting notices listed on the Equity Hotline and at Equity in Chicago. Theatre has 180 seats. Season: September-May.

INDIANA

THE PHOENIX THEATRE (317) 635-7529
(317) 635-PLAY
749 N. Park Ave. FAX (317) 635-0010
Indianapolis, IN 46202
www.phoenixtheatre.org
info@phoenixtheatre.org

Resident company under Equity SPT contract. Adult contemporary drama. P&R accepted, maintains casting files, has open calls, and lists auditions in the trades. Main Stage seats 130, the Underground Theatre seats 75. Season year round.

KENTUCKY

ACTORS THEATRE OF LOUISVILLE (502) 584-1265
(502) 584-1205
316-320 W. Main St. FAX (502) 561-3300
Louisville, KY 40202-4218
www.actorstheatre.org
sspeer@actorstheatre.org

Executive Director: Alexander Speer. Artistic Manager: Zan Sawyer-Dailey. Produces plays and musicals as well as The Humana Festival of New American Plays. Operates under Equity LORT B, C, and D contracts. Casts on a per show basis for specific productions. Casts Equity. Has three theatres, The Pamela Brown Auditorium with 637 seats, the Bingham Theatre with 318 seats, and the Victor Jory Theatre with 159 seats. Season is year round. A top priority in casting the non-union roles is always with the Actors Theatre apprentice company because of the tremendous contribution of time and effort they give throughout an entire season without compensation. Equity auditions are held in New York, Chicago or Los Angeles, depending on the needs of the production. Auditions are arranged through agent submissions, and scheduled by a casting director in that city. Actors are encouraged to send photo and resumes.

PUBLIC THEATRE OF KENTUCKY
THE PHOENIX THEATRE (270) 781-6233
545 Morris Ave.
Bowling Green, KY 41201
www.ptkbg.org
ptk@bowlinggreen.net

PTK is a non-profit organization. All programs, activities, and services are provided equally without regard to race, color, religion, national origin, age, sex, or disability. PTK is funded in part by the Kentucky Arts Council and by the contributions of its individual and business supporters. The theatre hosts a theatre day camp in June. Producing Director: Delia Brown. Casts for an entire season and maintains casting files.

MAINE

PORTLAND STAGE COMPANY (207) 774-1043
25A Forest Ave. FAX (207) 774-0576
Portland, ME 4101

P.O. Box 1458 (207) 774-0465
Portland, ME 4104
www.portlandstage.com
portstage@aol.com

Artistic Director: Anita Stewart. Committed to rediscovering the classics and presenting original works. A resident theatre under the Equity LORT D contract. Casts Equity and non-Equity on a per show basis. Accepts P&R and maintains casting files. Attends the Lort Lottery and holds open auditions in N.Y. and Portland. Has a 286 seat theatre.

MASSACHUSETTS

AMERICAN REPERTORY THEATRE (617) 495-2668
(617) 547-8300
Loeb Drama Center FAX (617) 495-1705
64 Brattle St.
Cambridge, MA 2138
www.amrep.org
info@amrep.org

Artistic Director: Robert Woodruff. Executive Director: Robert J. Orchard. New American plays, neglected works from past, and classic texts with new interpretations. A resident theatre with a rotating company of actors operating under an Equity LORT B contract. Actors can audition to join the company. Accepts P&R and maintains casting files. Attends LORT Lottery auditions. Casts Equity but will also cast non-Equity from their training program. Auditions are held in N.Y.

HUNTINGTON THEATRE COMPANY (617) 266-7900
(617) 266-0800
264 Huntington Ave. FAX (617) 353-8300
Boston, MA 2115
www.huntingtontheatre.org
htc@bu.edu

Artistic Director: Nicholas Martin. Managing Director: Michael Maso. The Theatre-in-residence at Boston University. Contemporary plays new to Boston and rediscovered plays by classic authors. A resident theatre under the Equity LORT B contract. Casts Equity and non-Equity on a show-by-show basis. Accepts P&R and maintains casting files. Holds open auditions in Boston and N.Y. and lists casting information on the Equity hotline. Theatre has 890 seats.

MICHIGAN

THE PURPLE ROSE THEATRE (734) 475-5817 (734) 475-7902
137 Park St. FAX (734) 475-0802
Chelsea, MI 48118
www.purplerosetheatre.org
purplerose@earthlink.net

Executive Director: Jeff Daniels. Artistic Director: Guy Sanville. Managing Director: Alan Ribant. Original works with an emphasis on midwestern themes. A resident theatre and production company operating under the Small Professional Theatre contract. Holds auditions in spring and during the year as needed for specific productions and lists casting info on the Equity hotline. The theatre has 168 seats.

MINNESOTA

THE GUTHRIE THEATER (612) 347-1100 (612) 377-2224
725 Vineland Pl. FAX (612) 347-1188
Minneapolis, MN 55403
www.guthrietheater.org

Managing Director: Tom Troehl. Artistic Director: Joe Dowling. Classics of world literature. Operating under Equity LORT A and D contracts. Join by audition. Depending on production needs they cast in-house and use independent casting directors. Accepts P&R and maintains casting files. Casts Equity. Holds open auditions around the country. Two theatres, the Guthrie has 1,309 seats and the Guthrie Theatre on First has 352 seats. The Guthrie will be moving in the summer of 2006 to a new location with three theatres. Check the website for additional information.

MIXED BLOOD THEATRE COMPANY (612) 338-0937 (612) 338-6131
1501 S. 4th St. FAX (612) 338-1851
Minneapolis, MN 55454
www.mixedblood.com
junior@mixedblood.com

Artistic Director: Jack Reuler. A contemporary, multi-racial company. A resident Equity company. Accepts P&R. Gives Generals once a year in the summer and also casts by recommendation. Lists casting information on the Equity hotline. Also a touring company. The theatre has 200 seats.

NEW JERSEY

MCCARTER THEATRE CENTER FOR THE PERFORMING ARTS (609) 258-2787 (609) 258-6500
91 University Pl. FAX (609) 497-0369
Princeton, NJ 8540
www.mccarter.org
admin@mccarter.org

Artistic Director: Emily Mann. Managing Director: Jeff Woodward. Contemporary and classical works. A regional theatre under Equity LORT B+ and D contracts. Accepts P&R and maintains casting files. Casts Equity and non-Equity. Attends the LORT Lotteries. Auditions are held in N.Y. in February and March. The Matthew Theatre has 1,100 seats and the Berlin Theatre has 300 seats.

NEW YORK

LINCOLN CENTER THEATRE (212) 362-7600
150 W. 65th St. FAX (212) 873-0761
New York City, NY 10023-6975
www.lct.org

Executive Producer: Bernard Gersten. Artistic Director: Andre Bishop. A resident theatre operating under the Equity LORT A and B contracts. Casts on a per show basis. Accepts P&R for specific projects only. Casts through agent submissions, at the LORT Lotteries, and holds open auditions once or twice a year. Lists casting information in the trades. Has two theatres, the Vivian Beaumont with 1,050 seats, and the Mitzi E. Newhouse with 299 seats.

NEW YORK SHAKESPEARE FESTIVAL (212) 539-8500
JOSEPH PAPP PUBLIC THEATRE (212) 260-2400
425 Lafayette St. FAX (212) 539-8505
New York City, NY 10003
www.publictheater.org

Producer/Artistic Director: Oskar Eustis. Managing Director: Michael Hurst. Operates under Equity LORT B and Off Broadway contracts. Casts on a per show basis from personal and agent submissions. Actors are chosen to audition on the basis of their resumes. Holds auditions 10 days per year for Equity principals in N.Y., they also use the LORT Lotteries. Accepts pictures and resumes and maintains casting files. Casts non-Equity for the ensemble in the park. They have five theatres in the Lafayette St. building, the Delacourt is the theatre in Central Park.

PAN ASIAN REPERTORY THEATRE (212) 868-4030
263 W. 86th St. FAX (212) 868-4033
New York City, NY 10012
www.panasianrep.org
panasian@aol.com

Founded in 1977 by Tisa Chang to celebrate the talent and creativity of professional Asian American theatre artists. The company specializes in interculture productions of Asian American new plays, Asian masterworks in translation, and innovative adaptations of Western classics such as "Shogun" and "MacBeth." Pan Asian Rep has become the largest professional Asian American theatre in the nation with a mainstage New York season, Theatre for Youth program, touring and residencies nationally and internationally, community outreach, a stage reading series, and an actor training workshop.

SYRACUSE STAGE (315) 443-4008 (315) 443-3275
820 E. Genesee St. FAX (315) 443-9846
Syracuse, NY 13210
www.syracusestage.org
syrstalge@fyr.edu

Producing Director: James A. Clark. Artistic Director: Robert Moss. This is the only professional theatre in central New York state. Operates under an Equity LORT C contract. Casts Equity on a show-by-show basis. Attends the LORT Lotteries and accepts pictures and resumes and maintains casting files. Casting is done in N.Y. Their Archbold Theatre has 499 seats. Season, October-May.

NORTH CAROLINA

NORTH CAROLINA SHAKESPEARE FESTIVAL (336) 841-2273
P.O. Box 6066 FAX (336) 841-8627
High Point, NC 27262

1014 Mill Ave. (336) 887-3001
High Point, NC 27260
www.ncshakes.org
pedro@ncshakes.org

Managing Director: Pedro Silva. Classics. A repertory company operating under an Equity LORT D contract. Actors may audition to join the company. They will cast outside the company. Casts Equity and non-Equity in N.Y. and locally by appointment. Attends the LORT Lotteries. Accepts P&R and maintains casting files. They work through agents, but actors may call theatre for audition information. The regular season, July-October and they also perform seasonal productions during the year. High Point Theatre has 1,000 seats.

OHIO

ACTORS' SUMMIT (330) 342-0800
86 Owen Brown St.
Hudson, OH 44236
www.actorssummit.org
info@actorssummit.org

Artistic Director: Neil Thackaberry. Holds open casting calls and both members of Actors' Equity Association and nonunion professional actors are encouraged to audition. All performers are compensated. Actors' Summit operates under a Small Professional Theatre contract with AEA, tier III. Actors' Summit is committed to Non-Traditional Casting. Except in cases where race, gender, age, or disability is essential to the play, all roles will be cast on the basis of talent.

THE BECK CENTER FOR THE ARTS (216) 521-2540
17801 Detroit Ave.
Lakewood, OH 44107
www.beckcenter.org

The Beck Center for the Arts is the largest cultural arts center in northeast Ohio serving Cuyahoga and Lorain counties. The Main Stage and Studio theaters entertain 12,000 theatergoers each season, and their Youth Theater is the oldest continuously operating Children's theater in the United States. Accepts pictures and resumes and maintains casting files.

CLEVELAND PLAYHOUSE (216) 795-7000
(800) 278-1CPH
8500 Euclid Ave. FAX (216) 795-7005
Cleveland, OH 44106
www.clevelandplayhouse.com

Artistic Director: Michael Bloom. Managing Director: Dean R. Gladden. Open call each spring. Pictures and resumes kept on file. General auditions held subject to staff availability. Has a program to develop new plays as well as classes for adults and children.

OREGON

OREGON SHAKESPEARE FESTIVAL (541) 482-4331
(541) 482-2111
15 S. Pioneer FAX (541) 482-0446
Ashland, OR 97520
www.osfashland.org
media@osfashland.org

Artistic Director: Libby Appel. Classical and some contemporary works. A resident theatre operating under an Equity AEA special LORT B contract. No open casting calls. Audition info by mail only, send P&R and mailing address. Has three theatres, the Elizabethan Stage with 1,194 seats, the Angus Bowmer Theatre with 601 seats, and the Black Swan Theatre with 250-350 seats.

TENNESSEE

TENNESSEE REPERTORY THEATRE (615) 244-4878
Tennessee Performing Arts Center
505 Deaderick St.
Nashville, TN 37219

Business address: (615) 782-4000
161 Rains Ave.
Nashville, TN 37203
www.tnrep.org

Executive Artistic Director: David Alford. American and world classical theatre plus musicals. Operates under an Equity LOA. Casts on a show-by-show basis and accepts P&R and maintains casting files, submit to David Alford. Casts in Nashville in April or May. Actors are notified within two weeks if they are under consideration for a role. They use the James K. Polk theatre with 1,000 seats and the Johnson theatre.

TEXAS

GALVESTON SUMMER MUSICALS (409) 316-0346
10000 Emmet F. Lowry Freeway, Ste 1246
Texas City, TX 77591
www.galvestonmusicals.com.
galvestonmusical@aol.com

Musicals. Accepts pictures and resumes and maintains casting files. Casts non-Equity and guest artists. Holds open auditions all over the U.S. Has a 1,749 seat outdoor amphitheatre.

UTAH

PIONEER THEATRE COMPANY (801) 581-6356
(801) 581-6961
Pioneer Memorial Theatre FAX (801) 581-5472
University of Utah
300 South 1400 East
Salt Lake City, UT 84112
www.pioneertheatre.org

Artistic Director: Charles Morey. Classical and contemporary works including 2 musicals. A resident theatre under the Equity LORT B contract. Attends the LORT Lotteries, accepts P&R and maintains casting files. Lists casting notices in Local 801 union newsletter. They have a 900 seat theatre and an intern company from the University of Utah. The largest professional theatre in the area. PTC holds auditions for each show in Salt Lake City and New York City. For Salt Lake auditions, check the website or call

(801) 585-3927. New York audition appointments are through agent submissions only.

VIRGINIA

BARTER THEATRE **(276) 628-2281**
133 W. Main St. **FAX (276) 619-3335**
Abingdon, VA 24210

P.O. Box 867 **(276) 628-3991**
Abingdon, VA 24212
www.bartertheatre.com
barterinfo@bartertheatre.com

Artistic Director: Richard Rose. Business Manager: Joan Ballou. Classic and contemporary theatre. A resident theatre operating under an Equity LORT D contract. A fellowship program for actors selected by audition. Attends LORT Lotteries and accepts P&R and maintains casting files. Cast Equity and non-Equity. Casting is done in N.Y. and Abingdon. This is the State Theatre of Virginia, the oldest professional residency theatre in U.S., started during the depression – the township bartered for actors services with food, etc. There are two theatres, the Barter Theatre with 507 seats and the Second Theatre with 167 seats.

THEATER AT LIME KILN **(540) 463-7088**
2 West Street **FAX (540) 463-1082**
Lexington, VA 24450
www.theateratlimekiln.com
limekiln@cfw.com

Artistic Director: John Healy. Producing straight plays and an annual musical, Stonewall Country, from May – August in unique outdoor venues. Touring Resident company August to May. Concert series from May to October. Annual auditions in March but some individual auditions. Maintains casting files.

WASHINGTON

(206) 292-7660
A CONTEMPORARY THEATRE (ACT) **(206) 292-7676**
700 Union St. **FAX (206) 292-7670**
Seattle, WA 98101
www.acttheatre.org

Artistic Director: Kurt Beattie, Managing Director: Jim Loder. Contemporary American and European theatre and original works. A resident theatre operating under an Equity LORT C contract. Accepts P&R and maintains casting files. Holds auditions October-January in Seattle, L.A., Chicago, and N.Y. and lists casting information on the Equity hotline and in the local trades. Has two theatres each with 390 seats.

(206) 269-1901
INTIMAN THEATRE COMPANY **(206) 269-1900**
2nd Ave. North & Mercer St. **FAX (206) 269-1928**
Seattle, WA 98109
www.intiman.org
groups@initman.org

Artistic Director: Bartlett Shear. Managing Director: Laura Penn. Classics and contemporary work, emphasis is on the actor. A resident theatre under the Equity LORT C contract. Uses casting directors for out of town actors. Cast Equity and non-Equity. Holds open general auditions in January and lists casting information on the Equity hotline and in the local trades. The Initman participates in the annual general auditions organized by Theatre Puget Sound (TPS) which organizes two rounds of local generals per year. For more information, check out the website. They maintain an active file of both local and out-of-town actors based on those auditions.

WISCONSIN

(414) 224-1761
MILWAUKEE REPERTORY THEATRE **(414) 224-9490**
108 E. Wells St. **FAX (414) 224-9097**
Milwaukee, WI 53202
www.milwaukeerep.com
mailrep@milwaukeerep.com

Artistic Director: Joe Hanreddy. Classics and contemporary works. A resident theatre under Equity LORT A, B and D contracts. Cast Equity and non-Equity on a show-by-show basis. Accepts P&R and maintains casting files. Holds open Equity auditions in N.Y., Chicago, and L.A. Has three theatres, the Powerhouse with 720 seats, the Steimke with flexible seating (usually 215), the Stackner Cabaret Theatre with 116 seats. They have an intern program and interns can earn Equity points.

UNIONS

THE 4 As
ASSOCIATED ACTORS
& ARTISTS OF AMERICA

The 4 As is composed of 5 branches, including Actors' Equity Association (AEA), American Federation of Television & Radio Artists (AFTRA), American Guild of Variety Artists (AGVA), American Guild of Musical Artists (AGMA), Screen Actors Guild (SAG).

AEA

ACTORS' EQUITY ASSOCIATION (AEA)
Alan Eisenburg – Executive Director
John Holly – Western Regional Director
Museum Square **(323) 634-1750**
5757 Wilshire Blvd., Ste. 1 **FAX (323) 634-1777**
Los Angeles 90036

165 W. 46th St. **(212) 869-8530**
New York, NY 10036 **FAX (212) 718-9815**
www.actorsequity.org

Actors' Equity Association is the labor union encompassing all actors and stage managers in the legitimate theatre in the United States.

HISTORY

The union was founded by 112 actors on May 26, 1913 in New York City. For the preceding 20 years, exploitation had become a permanent condition of employment for the actor. There was no standard agreement; each manager drew his own conditions, and few actors were able to stand against them. The Actors Society of America formed the "Plan and Scope Committee" which in May, 1913 drafted the Constitution and By Laws for what is now called Actors' Equity Association.

In 1919 the strike against the Producing Managers Association occurred. The main issue of the dispute was recognition of Equity as the actor's bargaining agent. When the strike ended, the managers signed a 5 year contract, which included practically all of Equity's demands, and union membership had increased from 2,700 to about 14,000.

In 1924 Equity established an Equity shop and won bonding agreements, under which managers must post enough money to guarantee actor's salaries and transportation. They formed regulations to control the importation of alien actors (1928), protect the actor from exorbitant commissions by franchising theatrical representatives (1929), and in 1933 actors at least were assured a minimum wage. In 1935 the first payment of rehearsal expense money was won – $15 per week.

Some of Equity's other achievements include: organization of the industrial shows field; resident, children's and dinner theaters; overhaul of rules governing talent agents, improved working conditions, including an enforceable backstage safety and sanitary code.

The most controversial achievement was the establishment of a welfare fund and pension plan. In 1964 a "Principal Interview" clause was negotiated to guarantee that members of Equity would be seen by producers.

Equity has been in the forefront of the civil rights movement. In 1961 the League of New York Theaters and Equity agreed that no member of Equity shall be required to perform in any theater or other place of performance where discrimination is practiced against any actor or patron by reason of race, creed or color.

Equity is governed by an elected and non-salaried Council of 75, plus 8 officers. Actors' Equity Association is a branch of the Associated Actors and Artists of America (Four As), the organization from which performer unions derive their jurisdictional charters.

NEW MEMBERSHIP POLICY

There are three ways to become a member of Equity:

1) EQUITY CONTRACT:

You are eligible to join the union simply upon signing an Equity contract with a producer in any branch of the union's jurisdiction. However, certain LOA, SPT, TYA and MINI contracts have additional requirements that must be met before applications can be accepted. Upon completing an application form that is filed with Equity together with payment of your initiation fee and applicable dues, a temporary membership card is issued. Your membership application is then submitted to the Council of Equity – the governing body of the union – and when approved, you will receive your permanent membership card.

2) SISTER CONTRACT:

To be eligible you must be a member in good standing of any union affiliated with the 4 As for at least one year. (Also known as the "sister unions"). The Four As – the Associated Actors and Artists of America – consists of seven branches: AEA, AFTRA, AGMA, AGVA, SAG, Italian Actors Union (IAU) and Hebrew Actors Union (HAU). You must have performed under the jurisdiction of the parent union as either a principal performer or have three days of work comparable to an extra performer on a non-waiver basis. Proof of membership under SAG, AGMA, or HAU is accepted by presenting a current membership card. If, however, the parent union is AFTRA or AGVA, additional proof of employment is necessary. Copies of employment contracts or a letter from the union certifying the type of contract worked under will be accepted, in addition to your paid-up membership card.

3) MEMBERSHIP CANDIDATE PROGRAM

THE PROGRAM:

The Membership Candidate Program allows non-professional actors and stage managers to credit their work at certain Equity theaters towards membership in Actors Equity Association. See your Equity office for further information.

INITIATION FEES AND CURRENT DUES:

Must be paid by certified check or money order. Payment must be paid in full. Partial payments will be accepted while a person is working under contract. The initiation fee as of April 1, 2004 is $1,100 with annual basic dues of $118. Dues are payable semi-annually on the first of May and the first of November. When you are working there is a 2.25% (of salary) working dues.

You will be asked to complete a membership application, and you are required to sign your name. Should the name you use professionally (real or assumed) be identical or similar to the name used by a performer who is already an Equity member, you may be required, as a condition of membership, to make some change in your professional name. Adding only a middle initial to your name to change it from a currently existing member's name is no longer acceptable.

If you were born outside the United States, proof of citizenship or Resident Alien status must be supplied (Green Card, U.S. Passport, birth certificate, etc.) If you are a non-resident alien in this country, you may only work in an Equity Production after obtaining special permission from AEA.

If you are under 18 years of age, a parent or legal guardian must also sign the application.

Also note that a person will not become eligible for inactive status until a minimum of 3 dues periods (18 months) have elapsed from the date of joining.

EQUITY HOTLINE (323) 634-1776

Equity auditions are announced on the Hotline which is a 24 hour taped message. The Hotline will also announce any event relevant to Equity members, such as membership meetings, blood drives, fund-raisers, free theater tickets, etc. Also check the Equity office bulletin board for casting, rentals, sales, and other notices.

THE EQUITY HOTLINE IS FOR THE USE OF EQUITY MEMBERS ONLY

PROBLEMS OR QUESTIONS

IN A PRODUCTION:
On the first rehearsal the cast meets and votes in an Equity Deputy to represent and speak for them. All problems or questions should then be directed to the elected cast member.

Major problems should be directed to your Equity Business Representative, who handles the contracts, at the Equity office.

AT AN AUDITION:

There is an Equity Representative present at all Equity auditions and interviews to answer questions or help with any problems.

All other questions or problems, call the Actors' Equity Association in your area.

EASTERN REGION/NATIONAL OFFICE (212) 869-8530
165 West 46th St. FAX (212) 718-9815
New York, NY 10036

WESTERN REGION (323) 634-1750
Museum Square FAX (323) 634-1777
5757 Wilshire Blvd. Ste. 1
Los Angeles, CA 90036

350 Sansome St., Ste. 900 (415) 391-3838
San Francisco, CA 94104

(312) 641-0393
CENTRAL REGION (312) 641-0418
125 S. Clark St., Ste. 1500 FAX (312) 641-6365
Chicago, IL 60603

ORLANDO (407) 345-8600
Actor's Equity Association FAX (407) 345-1522
10319 Orangewood Blvd.
Orlando, FL 32821

Casting Procedures:

Every theater or production, with the exception of Membership Theater Companies, shall hold one day of open casting for each production. All theaters shall individually or collectively with other producers, hold a minimum of two days of open general auditions per year.

AFTRA

AMERICAN FEDERATION OF TELEVISION
& RADIO ARTISTS (AFTRA) (323) 634-8100
Ron Morgan - Local President FAX (323) 634-8246
Mathis L. Dunn - Interim Exec. Director
5757 Wilshire Blvd. Ste. 900
Los Angeles 90036
www.aftra.org

AFTRA's jurisdiction covers live and taped television, radio, transcriptions, phonograph records, and non-broadcast recorded material. Actors, dancers, singers, newspeople, sportscasters, announcers, specialty acts, DJs and stunt people are all covered under this union's jurisdiction.

A performer may join AFTRA in Los Angeles by signing the application for membership and paying by cash, cashier's check, credit card or money order the full initiation fee and dues.

At the time of printing, the initiation fee was $1,300 and minimum dues were $63.90 semi annually. Dues are payable semi-annually, May 1st and November 1st and are based on the performer's gross earnings under AFTRA's jurisdiction for the previous year.

If a performer elects to join AFTRA prior to securing a work commitment by an AFTRA signatory producer, a rider to be signed by the performer is attached to the application, in which the performer acknowledges AFTRA's advice that no work guarantee or access to membership in other 4 As unions is automatically provided through this membership.

In accordance with the Taft-Hartley laws, a performer is not obligated to pay the initiation fee to AFTRA when he/she first works under the union's jurisdiction. At the first AFTRA job, a performer is required to fill out a membership application. The performer is allowed a full thirty days working period, dating from the first engagement, before the initiation fee and dues are payable.

AFTRA was created by performers and broadcasters and is run by performers, and broadcasters. Through AFTRA you are eligible for life insurance, medical and hospital benefits, and pension, depending on your earnings under AFTRA.

Membership in AFTRA guarantees that 1) you will be paid the union fees for your work, 2) you will receive your pay promptly, 3) your health and retirement payments will be paid into the fund in your name by the signator, 4) residual payments will be collected for you when due, 5) you will have someone represent you in cases of dispute with your employer, 6) sick and benefit funds may now be obtained, 7) you may be a member of the AFTRA Credit Union, 8) you can utilize AFTRA member services, showcases, workshops, seminars and committees.

SOME RULES and REGULATIONS

AFTRA scale is the minimum fee established by AFTRA for each performer. You may not accept employment under AFTRA's jurisdiction for less than AFTRA scale.

In most instances, payment for work must be paid in full within twelve (12) working days of employment. In TV programs, the payment period varies, so check with your AFTRA office.

You may not: accept a check for less than scale; defer any part of payment due; accept goods, services, interest in property, etc. in place of AFTRA scale wages.

Many performers negotiate over-scale fees, however, over-scale contracts can become under-scale because of extra rehearsals. You must specify the number of rehearsal hours originally contracted for, and contract for any additional hours at not less than AFTRA scale.

Only deductions provided by law, such as social security, may be made from AFTRA scale wages.

A performer may now pay commission out of scale on National Non-Broadcast/Industrials and National Television Commercials. Category exemptions to this rule are singers, dancers, and extras. No other scale payments are commissionable.

This doesn't mean that all contracts will not include scale plus commission, but that it is possible to pay out of scale in some instances now.

A Voice Test, a competitive test to determine which of several performers will be hired, is the only thing you may do without pay.

You may not accept employment from employers who are not signatory to the AFTRA Codes and Fair Practice Agreements, or from employers who have been declared unfair by AFTRA. You are subject to fines for working for a non-signatory or an Unfair Producer. These fines can be avoided by checking with AFTRA in advance of working.

Benefit Performances: A clearance must be obtained from Theater Authority to appear in a Benefit performance. Theater Authority is an organization serving all talent unions as a nonprofit charitable organization administering and regulating the free appearances of performers. All charity and benefit functions must be cleared through them.

Payments for the following must be sent by the producer directly to the AFTRA office:

1. Radio spots – sessions and residuals
2. Video-taped commercials – sessions and residuals
3. Replay fee for TV programs – domestic and foreign
4. Sound recordings
5. Non-broadcast recordings – film strips
6. Video-taped industrials

Please notify AFTRA if you receive a check for one of the above services directly from the producer.

Any infraction of the "payment within 12 working days of employment" rule must be reported to your AFTRA office.

Notify AFTRA's membership office of any changes in address, phone or agent.

Several AFTRA contracts are negotiated jointly with the Screen Actors Guild; for example, Network Prime Time television shows.

MEMBER REPORT FORMS

Member Report Forms are obtainable at the AFTRA office, and must be signed by you and your employer and filed with AFTRA within 48 hours after completion of the following jobs:

1. Commercial radio transcriptions
2. Commercial TV tapes
3. Audition spot recordings or demos
4. Live local TV commercials
5. All non-broadcast recordings such as film strips and videos
6. Taped industrials
7. Sound recordings

In addition to the Member Report, you must telephone AFTRA in advance of a sound recording date.

These Member Reports enable AFTRA to see that you are paid your proper fee within the specified time, that you are paid your proper residual fees, and receive proper credits in your Health and Retirement account. Failure to file a report will result in a fine.

You may not accept employment from employers who are not signatory to the AFTRA Codes and Fair Practice Agreements, or from employers who have been declared unfair by AFTRA. You are subject to fines for working for a non-signatory or an Unfair Producer. These fines can be avoided by checking with AFTRA.

CASTING INFORMATION LINE (323) 634-8263
www.aftra.org

A pre-recorded message with current casting information, auditions, negotiation updates, meeting information, and all on going member service events. Note: Producers provide the casting information to AFTRA for AFTRA jobs.

EXTRA CASTING FILE

Paid-up members of the Los Angeles AFTRA Local may submit their picture and resume to the Membership Department for this file. AFTRA producers call and request certain types for extra work. Name and home telephone numbers are given to the producers. This service is used frequently for AFTRA television programs. To submit send or drop off your picture & resume to EXTRA FILE c/o AFTRA.

FREE INFORMATIONAL SEMINARS, WORKSHOPS & CASTING SHOWCASES (323) 634-8100

Informational seminars are held approximately three times a year, and feature guest panels of agents, casting directors etc. These are very popular events for paid-up AFTRA members. The average attendance is over 1,000.

AFTRA HEALTH & RETIREMENT PLAN (212) 499-4800
261 Madison Ave., 8th Fl.
New York, NY 10016

5757 Wilshire Blvd. **(323) 937-3631**
Los Angeles 90028

Medical, dental and pension benefits based on eligibility requirements. Call the above number for details about eligibility/benefits information or (800) 562-4690.

MEMBERSHIP MEETINGS

Membership meetings are held four times a year. Agendas may include election procedures, contract approval, and other important issues to members. Check the website for additional information.

PUBLICATIONS

AFTRA produces AFTRA Magazine, Talent Agency News, Music Notes and Broadcast Bulletin. All publications are designed to provide information on job related issues.

AIPADA (800) 756-HOPE
ALCOHOL & DRUG ABUSE HOTLINE (323) 660-4344

Available to members and families. All calls confidential. A.A. meetings Fridays at 8:30 p.m. at SAG.

BULLETIN BOARD

There is a bulletin board in the AFTRA offices which posts casting notices, roommates wanted, apartments for rent, photographers and sales. You may post information if you are a union member.

CREDIT UNION

AFTRA-SAG FEDERAL CREDIT UNION (818) 562-3400
5757 Wilshire Blvd., #925
Los Angeles 90036

14118 Magnolia Blvd. **(818) 562-3400**
Sherman Oaks 91423

4100 Riverside Dr., Ste. A **(800) 826-6946**
Burbank 91505
www.aftrasagfcu.org

AFTRA-SAG Federal Credit Union is the only financial institution that focuses solely on the financial needs of the performer. The credit union provides low-cost, high quality financial services to the members of SAG, AFTRA, AGVA and their family and household members. This credit union and your savings are federally insured to $100,000 by the National Credit Union Administration. AFTRA-SAG Federal Credit Union provides many of the same conveniences as banks, but with low or no fees, including: Worldwide ATM and

Visa Debit Card access, ATM deposit capabilities at over 5,000 locations nationwide, free 24 hour Internet Home Banking and toll-free Bank-By-Phone, free residual deposit program, free overdraft protection from savings. Dividend bearing checking accounts at the credit union are available with no monthly service charge and no minimum balance to maintain. You must have a savings account to take advantage of other services. Coogan accounts for young performers are available and online setup is easy with a low $50 minimum balance, competitive yields, Coogan share certificates available with higher yields. Transfers from other financial institutions are easy. Lending policies are designed with the income irregularities of the working performer in mind. Credit union membership is open to members in good standing or on honorary withdrawal with SAG, AFTRA, or AGVA. For more information about membership call the credit union or visit their website.

AGVA

AMERICAN GUILD OF VARIETY ARTISTS (AGVA) (818) 508-9984
4741 Laurel Canyon Blvd., #208
North Hollywood 91607

The American Guild of Variety Artists was chartered by the 4 As, in 1939. AGVA's jurisdiction includes, but is not limited to, ice shows, nightclubs, theme parks, cabarets, casual and club date performances and variety shows of all kinds. There is a membership of approximately five thousand members. AGVA's national office is in New York City, there is a branch office in Los Angeles and representatives around the country. The union, in accordance with Industry standards, sets and enforces salary minimums as well as conditions of employment such as rehearsal hours, overtime, safe and sanitary theatre conditions and travel stipulations. AGVA requires that all producers post a salary bond through the Bonding Secretary before beginning rehearsals. In this way, each artist is insured his/her salary regardless of the financial state of the production. Many AGVA members are "Casual and Clubdate Performers". They are artists such as singers, comics, dancers, clowns and mimes who perform individually in clubs or private affairs. For any information or questions specifically pertaining to these engagements, please contact AGVA at the above number.

NEW MEMBERSHIP

Any artist may join. Applicant must present evidence of work and/or training in the variety arts field, e.g. contracts, resume, letter or recommendation, etc. The AGVA initiation fee is $750.

AGVA dues payments are based on yearly earnings under an AGVA contract. Members are billed three times yearly: April 1st, August 1st and December 1st.

Note: There are no dues assessments on expense monies and/or per diems.

Any artist whose parent union is AGVA and is a paid up member, is eligible for reduced dues fees from sister unions. One years' membership with AGVA qualifies artists to join Actor' Equity and SAG under their open admission policy if you have paid dues and can show that you worked under an AGVA contract.

Those artists who have been on honorary withdrawal from AGVA may become active members by paying one period of dues. If you have questions, send a letter of inquiry to the national offices at 363 7th Ave., 17th Floor, New York, NY 10001.

AGVA WELFARE TRUST FUND (212) 627-4820
363 7th Ave. 7th Fl.
New York, NY 10001

All performers employed under an AGVA contract are eligible to receive medical coverage, provided by the AGVA Welfare Trust Fund. To qualify for Plan A, an artist must accumulate three weeks employment. For Plan B, three days employment within 6 months is required. At the time eligibility begins each artist will receive notification and a medical card from the Welfare Trust Administrator. Supplemental aid is also available to any artist now covered under medicare. There is a monthly premium that must be paid. Additionally a Basic Plan B Coverage is available to members who have been in good standing for 5 or more years. This is offered at no cost to the member. Eligibility will continue for 6 consecutive months, and will be redetermined at the end of each 6 month period based upon covered employment under an AGVA contract during the eligibility period. Please note that various monthly premiums may apply to both Plan A and Plan B. Claim forms must be filed within 120 days of service.

MARGIE COATE SICK & RELIEF FUND (EAST & WEST)

There are two (2) Union Sick and Relief Funds.

AGVA SICK & RELIEF FUND – EAST
MS. MICHIKO TERAJIMA, ADMINISTRATOR (212) 675-1003
363 7th Ave., 17th Fl.
New York, NY 10001

AGVA SICK & RELIEF FUND – WEST
STEVE ROSEN, ADMINISTRATOR (818) 508-9984
4741 Laurel Canyon Blvd., #208
North Hollywood 91607

The major source of income for both AGVA Sick and Relief Funds stems form allocations given by Theatre Authority, Inc. This fund can pay a variety of bills such as rent, utilities, hospital, medical and dental.

Only unpaid bills will be eligible for payment. These monies are a grant, not a loan, and need not be repaid to the fund.

Any member may apply for assistance from the union's Sick and Relief Funds, provided the member establishes need of such assistance.

Theatre Authority monies belong to the performers and are earned by performers through telethons and other charity affairs, which must first be cleared by Theatre Authority, Inc.

The Sick and Relief Fund also provides grants for AGVA members by sponsoring shows for senior citizens and hospitals around the country. These shows are cast from dues-paying unemployed members.

DGA

DIRECTORS GUILD OF AMERICA, DGA (310) 289-2000
7920 Sunset Blvd.
Los Angeles 90046
www.dga.org

The work of the members of the DGA is represented in theatrical motion pictures, television (filmed, live or taped), radio, industrial, educational and government films and commercials.

DRAMATISTS GUILD

Ralph Sevush – Executive Director
John Weidman – President **(212) 398-9366**
1501 Broadway #701 **FAX (212) 944-0420**
New York, NY 10036
www.dramatistsguild.com

Any writer who has completed a dramatic script may become a member of the Dramatists Guild of America and receive a wide range of benefits: business affairs advice; contract review; a subscription to the Guild's bi-monthly magazine, The Dramatist; The Dramatists Guild Newsletter, and the Resource Directory.

SAG

SCREEN ACTORS GUILD (SAG) **(323) 954-1600**
Alan Rosenberg – President
5757 Wilshire Blvd.
Los Angeles 90036-3600
www.sag.org

SAG 24-Hour Recorded Information:

Agents List	**(323) 549-6733**
Commercial/Infomercials Music Videos	**(323) 549-6858**
Industrials/Educational/Interactive	**(323) 549-6858**
Film Society Hotline	**(323) 549-6657**
Production Services	**(323) 549-6811**
General Information on SAG casting seminars and showcases	**(323) 549-6540**
Information on How to Join SAG	**(323) 549-6772**
Television	**(323) 549-6835**
Theatrical Films	**(323) 549-6828**

OTHER SAG DEPARTMENTS:

Actors to Locate	**(800) 503-6737**
Affirmative Action	**(323) 549-6644**
Agency Contracts	**(323) 549-6745**
Casting Sem./Showcase Info	**(323) 549-6540**
Communications	**(323) 549-6654**
Dues Information	**(323) 549-6755**
Emergency Funds	**(323) 549-6773**
Report Sexual Harassment	**(323) 549-6644**
Legal Affairs	**(323) 549-6627**
Membership Services	**(323) 549-6778**
President's Office	**(323) 549-6675**
Receptionist	**(323) 549-6404**
Residuals	**(323) 549-6505**
Signatory Records	**(323) 549-6869**
SAG Foundation & Book Pals	**(323) 549-6709**

SAG represents 120,000 professional actors and performing artists working in motion pictures nationwide, including: film, industrials, television, commercials, music videos and video games.

SAG members work as principal performers, stunt performers, pilots, puppeteers and models, singers, dancers, extras, and voice-over performers ranging from newborn to 100 years of age.

SAG is a democratic union run by a National Board of Directors. Board members are all performers, elected on a proportional, regional basis. Two nationally elected offices are President and Secretary-Treasurer.

SAG's two major contracts with producers cover the fields of theatrical films and television, and commercials. Additional contracts include: industrial and educational films; student films; New York extra players; Spanish language commercials; Public Broadcasting System contracts; low budget features; and music videos.

The Guild's primary responsibilities include negotiating contracts which establish the minimum wage scale and working conditions for professional performers; enforcement of those contracts; processing residual payments to members (for re-use of films and TV shows); regulation and franchising of talent agents; membership record-keeping and communications.

SAG strives to protect actor's wages and working conditions through organizing and aggressive advocacy at the bargaining table; representation on motion picture sets and locations; and increasingly, through legislative lobbying at the local, state and national levels.

SAG does not secure employment for members. In 2002, 80% of SAG members earned less than $5,000. Only 3,500 (5%) of the members earned more than $50,000.

SAG is also concerned with its member's general welfare and quality of living. Qualified members are provided with medical insurance and a pension plan, established through collective bargaining with producers. The SAG – Producers Pension and Health Plan is jointly administered by labor and management, and has offices in Los Angeles, New York and Chicago.

SAG Rule One: Members are prohibited from working within SAG's jurisdiction for any producer who refuses to sign a collective bargaining agreement.

HISTORY

In 1933 a small but brave group of actors founded a new craft guild to represent the interests of performers in the rapidly growing film industry. More than 70 years later, the Screen Actors Guild is still representing actors and their interests in a worldwide entertainment industry that the Guild's founders could have never imagined. Although the business has changed dramatically, and new technological advancements assure continued changes, the goals and ideals of the founders of SAG are still being vigorously pursued by today's generation of union leaders for the benefit of members nationwide.

Membership in the Guild says that you are an experienced, professional actor. Guild members include the world's finest actors, stunt performers, singers, dancers, background actors, pilot, puppeteers and voice performers. As professionals, the guild has established certain minimum standards that must be met.

In 1937, after affiliating with the American Federation of Labor and the Four As, SAG's early members voted to strike if necessary to achieve union recognition. With 98% of the major stars of the time ready to strike, the producers acquiesced, and on May 9, 1937, SAG had its first contract governing wages and working conditions for actors in feature films.

Los Angeles has the largest membership with approximately 70,000 performers. New York has the second largest membership with almost 36,000 performers.

BULLETIN BOARD

There is a bulletin board at SAG offices. Casting, roommates wanted, apartments for rent, sales, jobs, etc. are posted.

NEW MEMBERSHIP

An actor may become eligible for SAG membership under one of the following conditions:

1. Upon presentation of a letter, not earlier than two (2) weeks prior to the beginning of filming, from a SAG signatory motion picture producer or his authorized representative, or from a signatory, film television or commercial company, stating that the applicant is wanted for a principal role or speaking part in a specific film.

2. Upon presentation of proof of employment by a SAG signatory motion picture production company or film, television or commercial company, in a principal role or speaking part, which states the applicant's name, the name of the production or the commercial (the product), the salary paid, and the specific dates worked.

Such proof of employment may be in the form of a signed contract, a payroll check and/or stub, or a letter from the company (on the company's letterhead stationery), provided it states all the necessary information listed above.

3. If the applicant is a current paid up member in good standing of an affiliated guild for a period of at least one year or longer and has worked as a principal performer in that jurisdiction at least once. (AFTRA AEA, AGVA, AGMA, ACTRA)

OR:

If the applicant has worked as a principal performer in the jurisdiction of an affiliated guild but has not fulfilled the one-year membership requirement, but does have a definite commitment for a principal role or speaking part in a motion picture, filmed commercial or filmed television show. Such application will not be accepted for membership earlier than two weeks prior to the beginning of filming of his/her part.

The rules applicable to SEG members applying for membership into SAG vary somewhat from the above, and will be clarified at the time of application to SAG.

The joining fee is $1,482, plus semi-annual dues. Payable in full by cashier's check or money order. For further information call membership at (323) 549-6769.

SAG will investigate all applications for membership to make sure your application is bona fide. The Guild is investigating "eligibility" schemes and holding up dubious applications so beware of these practices and make sure that your application is legal or it could inhibit your entrance into the Guild.

The first job as a principal can denote which guild is parent and which guild receives full initiation fee and dues.

ADDITIONAL INFORMATION

There is a $10 charge for each check returned by the bank.

Name change requests and address changes must be made in writing. It is the member's responsibility to keep the Guild notified of a current address at all times.

Checks must be payable in U.S. dollars.

Billing dates are May 1st and November 1st. Dues must be paid by personal checks, money orders, Visa, Master Card or online at www.sag.org.

Membership cards may not be picked up at the Hollywood office; they will be mailed to your current address.

SAG INFOCAST LINE (323) 937-3441

SAG has a casting information phone line and a bulletin board available to members. Because the InfoCast information precedes the start of production, SAG members still must check on the signatory status of any independent filmmaker before signing a contract and performing a role. New listings every Mon – Fri. THE INFOCAST LINE IS FOR THE USE OF SAG MEMBERS ONLY.

AFTRA – SAG
FEDERAL CREDIT UNION (818) 562-3400
14118 Magnolia Blvd.
Sherman Oaks 91423

Outside California (800) 826-6946

Inside California (800) 354-3728

SCREEN ACTORS GUILD
PRODUCERS PENSION &
HEALTH PLANS (818) 954-9400
3601 W. Olive Ave.
Burbank 91505

P.O. Box 7830
Burbank 91510

New York Office (212) 599-6010

Outside California (800) 777-4013

Eligibility for coverage in the Health Plan is established through covered employment with Producers who have signed Collective Bargaining Agreements with the Screen Actors Guild providing for the contribution to the Plans. Pension and Health benefits are governed by a Board of Trustees composed of equal numbers of actor's and producer's representatives.

HEALTH PLAN www.sagph.org

The minimum earning requirement for Health Plan coverage must be achieved within a four consecutive quarter earning period in order for eligibility to be established. When eligibility is established, your spouse and eligible dependent children are also covered.

ELIGIBILITY REQUIREMENTS

Plan I
Participants earning $28,120 or more.

Participants earning from $7,500 up to $14,499 who also have 10 years of previous earned eligibility.

Retiree Health Plan participants.

Plan II
Participants earning $13,790 (or 74 days of employment).

The benefits are different for each of the Plans. Generally, covered expenses for Hospital, Major Medical and Prescription Drug benefits are provided. Under Plan I, Dental and Life Insurance coverage is also included.

Individuals will be entitled to self-pay for at least 18 months of coverage at the Plan under which they re covered when their earned eligibility terminates.

PENSION PLAN

If you earn 10 years of Pension Credit, you will qualify for a pension from the Pension Plan. Prior to January 1, 1992, a year of Pension Credit is granted for each calendar year in which you had $2,000 or more in Screen Actors Guild employment. In 1996, SAG agreed to grant one year of Pension Credit for each calender year in which you have $7,500 or more in Screen Actors Guild employment. Starting January 1, 2003 you must earn $15,000 in a calendar year to earn a Pension Credit. You earn a Pension Credit under the Alternative Eligibility Program if you work 70 days of covered employment in a calendar year after January 1, 2003.

A full, unreduced Regular Pension is payable at age 65. Between ages 55 and 65, an Early Retirement Pension is payable but is reduced for each month you are younger than age 65 when you retire. A Disability Pension is also available. Currently the minimum pension is $220 per month and the maximum pension is $6,000 per month.

Complete benefit booklets are available free of charge from either of the Pension and Health Offices.

RETIREMENT COMMUNITY

As a retiree with 20 years of service, an Industry member (and spouse) may be eligible to retire to this facility. There is no preference shown with regard to classification or status of the applicant.

Should income not be sufficient to meet the costs, the individual continues to be eligible for assistance.

SAG HOLLYWOOD FILM SOCIETY (323) 549-6657 (323) 549-6658

Screenings are held at the Directors Guild, 7920 Sunset Blvd. The Film Society shows current films, as close to the theatrical release date as possible. The cost is $65 for one year for passes to a minimum of 26 motion pictures.

The purpose of the SAG Film Society is to observe other actor's performances in order to improve one's own skills, to make actors aware of the kinds of motion pictures being made, and to create a building fund which will eventually benefit all members.

The Film Society is a non-profit organization. You must be an active, paid up member of SAG to apply for membership in the Film Society. No member under 10 years of age may join or attend screenings. Children under 16 must be accompanied by an adult.

The membership is non-transferable, and permits the entrance of the member and one guest.

No one but the actual member will be able to use the membership card. If you allow someone else to use your card, your membership will be cancelled.

Screenings are generally held every other Friday and Saturday; Fridays at 6:30 pm and 9:30 pm; Saturdays, 12 noon, 3 pm, 6 pm, and 9 pm. Latecomers are not admitted. For recorded information on upcoming films, call the hotline number listed above.

AGENT SEMINARS AND SHOWCASES

During these evening sessions at SAG headquarters, members of the Association of Talent Agents (ATA) volunteer a couple of hours to talk with a room full of actors. There is no charge for these programs. Contact SAG for more information on when programs are scheduled.

TALENT AGENCY FRANCHISING

SAG provides protections for members who deal with SAG-franchised agents Nationwide, hundreds of agencies are currently regulated by the Guild and entitled to represent SAG's members. To secure a SAG franchise, talent agents must sign a 75-page agreement known as the SAG Agency Regulations. These rules require ethical conduct and state licenses (where applicable), among other conditions. One of the Guild's primary regulations strictly limits agent's commissions to 10% of actor's salaries. The SAG rules also allow members to terminate agency contracts for cause, and offer several other advantages not shared by non-union performers and unregulated agents. SAG agents cannot send Guild members on non-union auditions, nor can agents cast, produce or act in any SAG motion pictures.

PUBLICATIONS AND MERCHANDISE

The Guild publishes an award-winning national magazine, "Screen Actor," as well as regional branch newsletters to inform members about issues and events in their local markets and the Industry as a whole. In addition to these periodicals, the Guild produces a number of free booklets of interest to members, such as "The Young Performer's Handbook," "The Actor's Guide to California Unemployment Benefits," "On-the-Set Safety Bulletins" and more.

VOLUNTEER INCOME TAX ASSISTANCE (VITA)

The United States Internal Revenue Service trains volunteer Guild members to assist fellow performers in preparing and filing annual income tax returns. This free service, known as VITA, is offered to qualified members each year in New York, Hollywood and Chicago.

COLLEGE SCHOLARSHIPS

Through the independent, non-profit Screen Actors Guild Foundation, SAG members and their children can apply for a John Dale Scholarship to attend an accredited institution of higher learning. The Foundation is now developing several educational programs to benefit members and the acting profession in the future.

BENEVOLENT FUNDS AND SOCIAL SERVICES

The SAG Foundation also administers the Guild's Emergency Assistance Fund which helps qualified members in dire financial need. Guild members may also become eligible for financial assistance and other social services through the Actors Fund of America, the Motion Picture Players Welfare Fund and the Motion Picture and Television Fund.

SAG CONSERVATORY

The purpose of the SAG Conservatory is to provide actors a supportive environment where they can experiment, learn and practice their craft. Fellow performers and Industry professionals will lead on-camera workshops on auditions, cold reading, commercial technique, film technique, improv, voice-over, video-scenes, and more. The Conservatory also offers Casting Director seminars, business seminars and placement in the casting file for American Film Institute, DWW and DGA student films. Membership is only $20 for the entire October to May season.

THE MOTION PICTURE & TELEVISION FUND — **(800) 876-8320** / **(818) 876-1050**
23388 Mulholland Dr.
Woodland Hills 91364-2792
www.mptvfund.org

The Motion Picture & Television Fund (MPTF) is a service organization promoting the well-being of California's entertainment community. MPTF provides these services with compassion and respect for the dignity of the whole person: child care at the Samuel Goldwyn Foundation Children's Center; licensed Residential Care Facility for the Elderly (RCFE); geriatric services; wellness programs; social and charitable services; and health care. Our health care includes health insurance plans through The Industry Advantage Health Plans, which is anchored around an entertainment-exclusive provider network, The Industry Health Network, featuring the Motion Picture & Television Hospital and five MPTF Health Centers. You can visit MPTF's website at www.mptvfund.org to learn how to enhance your quality of life.

SOCIAL AND CHARITABLE SERVICES

1. Clinical services.
2. Community information/referrals.
3. Geriatric Programs and Services.
4. AIDS/HIV information, confidential testing, referral, and pre- and post-test counseling.
5. Residency application assistance.
6. Hospital discharge planning.

SAMUEL GOLDWYN FOUNDATION CHILDREN'S CENTER — **(310) 445-8993**
2114 Pontius Ave.
Los Angeles 90025-5726

The Samuel Goldwyn Foundation Children's Center (SGFCC) is managed by the Motion Picture and Television Fund. SGFCC offers child care and early childhood education services to children from ages eight weeks to six years and whose parents work in the entertainment industry. Located in West Los Angeles, the SGFCC is open year-round (except on holidays) on weekdays, 7 am to 7 pm. The Samuel Goldwyn Children's Center is geared toward the demanding work schedules of the entertainment industry.

Outpatient Services
Temporary Emergency Financial Assistance
Medical Care Assistance

To qualify for assistance from MPTF, an applicant must meet certain basic requirements. Please contact MPTF's social services Department at (323) 634-3800 to verify eligibility.

MOTION PICTURE and TELEVISION HOSPITAL

The Motion Picture and Television Hospital is a state-of-the-art, full service, fully licensed, 256-bed, acute-care hospital. Services include the George Burns Intensive Care Unit, laboratory services, outpatient services, surgical services, pharmacy services, radiology, respiratory care, cardiac services and transitional care including physical, occupational and speech therapy.

MPTF HEALTH CENTERS

MPTF operates five entertainment industry-exclusive Health Centers conveniently located in areas where Industry members live and work: Woodland Hills Health Center, Toluca Lake Health Center, Westside Health Center, Bob Hope Health Center and Santa Clarita Health Center.

On-site ancillary services such as lab, radiology and physical therapy are available, as well as free parking.

WGA

WRITERS GUILD OF AMERICA — **(323) 951-4000**
Patric Verrone – President — **FAX (323) 782-4800**
WGA West, Inc.
7000 W. Third St.
Los Angeles 90048

WGA East, Inc. — **(212) 767-7800**
555 West 57th St., Ste. 1230 — **FAX (212) 582-1909**
New York, NY 10019
www.wga.org

HISTORY

The history of the Writers Guild of America can be traced back to 1912. At that time, the Authors Guild was first organized as a protective association for writers of books, short stories, articles, etc. Subsequently, writers of drama formed a Dramatists Guild and joined forces with the Authors Guild, which then became the Authors League. In 1921, the development of another medium of expression for writers – the motion picture industry – brought about the formation of the Screen Writers Guild and became a branch of the Authors League.

In the period of 1921 to 1933, the Screen Writers Guild operated more as a club than a Guild. It had a clubhouse, for social activities, put on plays and exchanged professional information. However, the need for some kind of action for the protection of writer's rights and economic conditions became apparent during this period. In working toward better protection, the Guild was reincorporated in 1936 as an affiliate of the Author's League, rather than a branch. In 1937, the historical U.S. Supreme Court decision upholding the constitutionality of the National Labor Relations Act, gave those working for unification of the Screen Writers Guild an opportunity to call for an election and eventually certified the reincorporated Screen Writers Guild as the collective bargaining agent of all writers in the motion picture industry.

In 1939, collective bargaining with the producers commenced. A deal was finalized in 1941; the first contract was signed in 1942 for seven years. The Screen Writers Guild went through a period of internal political struggle from 1939 to 1947. During this time, the Radio Writers Guild had been organized as another branch of the

Author's League – in response to the development of that industry; and then television began appearing on the scene in 1949. The Screen Writers Guild had helped to organize the Radio Writers Guild and in 1950 began organizing a group of television writers within its own body – for protective purposes but with the thought of eventual autonomy for this group. A Television Writers Group was organized within the Author's League with the same purpose in mind. However, the practice of endless proliferation of branches became burdensome to the Author's League and, commencing in 1949, meetings took place in New York between representatives of the Author's League, Dramatist's Guild, Radio Writers Guild, Television Writer's Group and Screen Writers Guild to try to devise a simpler but stronger form of unification

Finally, in 1954, a revised organizational structure was set up and the Writers Guild of America was formed. The Writers Guild of America today is a labor organization representing all screen, television, and radio writers. It is made up of Writers Guild of America, East and West, with offices in Los Angeles. The Mississippi River is used as the dividing line for administrative jurisdiction between the Guilds.

As a result of the merger in 1954 between the Screen Writers Guild and the western branch of the Radio Writers Guild, the screen writers then became the Screen Branch of WGAW. The television and radio writers became the TV-Radio Branch of WGAW. On January 18, 1973, Guild membership approved the amalgamation of the branches, and the Screen and TV-Radio Branches disappeared into the parent body. WGAW is run by a Board of Directors of 16 members under a President, Vice President and Secretary–Treasurer. WGAE has a Council of 21 members under a President, Vice President, and Secretary–Treasurer.

The administration of Writers Guild East and West is carried out under the supervision of an Executive Director for each organization.

The Writers Guild of America East and West is the sole collective bargaining representative for writers in the motion picture, television, and radio industries.

The Guild represents writers primarily for the purpose of collective bargaining in the motion picture, television and radio industries.

They do not obtain employment for writers, refer or recommend members for writing assignments, offer writing instruction or advice, nor do they accept or handle material for submission to production companies.

Literary material should be submitted directly to the production company or through a literary agent.

REQUIREMENTS FOR ADMISSION TO THE WGA, WEST, INC.

Several membership categories are available. Contact the Guild for eligibility requirements.

WRITERS GUILD REGISTRATION SERVICE

Purpose:

The Guild's Registration Service has been set up to assist members and non-members in establishing the completion date and the identity of their literary property written for the fields of theatrical motion pictures, television and radio. It also accepts book manuscripts, stage plays and music lyrics.

The Guild does not accept book manuscripts, stage plays, music, lyrics, photos, drawings (story boards) or articles of public record for filing.

Registration does not confer any statutory protection. It merely provides a record of the writer's claim to authorship of the literary material involved and of the date of its completion. The Registration Office does not make comparisons of registration deposits to determine similarity between works, nor does it give legal opinions or advice. Questions regarding Copyright protection should be directed to the United States Copyright office in Washington, D.C. or an attorney specializing in that area of the law.

Registration does not take the place of registering the copyright on your material with the U.S. Copyright Office.

GUILD FUNCTIONS & SERVICES:

CONTRACTS

Negotiation of Basic Agreements in screen, television (live, tape and film), radio and staff agreements (news and continuity writers).

ADMINISTRATION OF AGREEMENTS:

1. Handling of writer claims.
2. Checking of individual writer contracts for MBA violations.
3. Enforcement of Working Rules.
4. Processing of Grievances.
5. Arbitrations under the MBA.
6. Collection and processing of television and motion picture residuals.
7. Pension Plan.
8. Health and Welfare Plan.

CREDITS

1. Receipt of tentative notices.
2. Arbitration of protests.
3. Maintenance of Credit records.
4. Distribution of Credits Manual.
5. Credit information to members and to producers and agents.

ORIGINAL MATERIAL

1. Registration Service.
2. Collaboration Agreements.
3. Settlement of disputes (Committee on Original Material).
4. Copyright information and legislation.

AGENTS

1. Negotiation of Basic Agreement with Agents.
2. Recording, filing, and administration of individual agreements between writers and agents.
3. Distribution of lists of authorized agents.
4. Arbitration function in dispute between writers and agents.

EMPLOYMENT

1. Compilation and distribution of TV Market Lists.
2. Compilation and circulation of motion picture and TV credits lists to producers and agents.
3. Compilation and circulation of statistical data regarding members where requested.

INFORMATION

1. Inquiries by producers re: member credits, agents and contract provisions.
2. Inquiries by members and non-members re: production data and contract provisions.

AFFILIATION AND COOPERATION

1. Writer's Guild of Great Britain.
2. Australian Writer's Guild.
3. Writer's Guild of Canada (French and English).
4. Motion Picture and Television Relief Fund.
5. Permanent Charities Committee.
6. American Film Institute.
7. Affirmative Action program.
8. Other Industry functions and services.
9. S.A.R.D.E.C.
10. Writer's Guild of New Zealand.
11. I.A.W.G.
12. North American Council.
13. Freedom of Expression Network.

PUBLIC RELATIONS

1. Publications – Written By.
2. Trade press.
3. TV forums.
4. Annual Awards Event.

CREDIT UNION

1. Loans.
2. Investments.
3. Life Insurance.

GROUP INSURANCE

1. Life Insurance.
2. Disability, hospitalization, major medical.

LEGISLATION

1. Copyright.
2. Censorship.
3. Taxation.
4. Unemployment Compensation.

FILM SOCIETY

WORKSHOP PROGRAMS

SUPPORT OF FREEDOM OF EXPRESSION

1. Litigation.
2. Press.
3. Other.

DIRECTORY

COMMITTEES

1. Writer Conference.
2. Social Activities.

WRITERS GUILD THEATER

1. Screenings.
2. Rental. For rental information call (323) 782-4520.

THEATRE AUTHORITY

THEATRE AUTHORITY
Theatre Authority East (212) 764-0156
Wally Munroe FAX (212) 764-0158
Executive Director
729 7th Ave. 11th Fl.
New York, NY 10019

Theatre Authority West (323) 462-5761
Judy A. Bailey
Executive Director
6464 Sunset Blvd., #590
Hollywood 90028

Theatre Authority is a non-profit charitable organization administering and regulating the free appearances of performers and providing assistance to members of the theatrical community. Either your agent or manager should check with the appropriate theatre authority office before committing yourself for an appearance. If you cannot check directly with theatre authority, call your local union office for assistance. Theatre Authority East has jurisdiction over all benefit performances east of Omaha, Nebraska. Theatre Authority West has jurisdiction over all areas west of and including Omaha.

ADDITIONAL ENTERTAINMENT INDUSTRY GUILDS AND UNIONS

AFFILIATED PROPERTY CRAFTSMEN LOCAL 44 (818) 769-2500
12021 Riverside Dr. FAX (818) 769-1739
North Hollywood 91607
www.local44.org

ALLIANCE OF MOTION PICTURE & TELEVISION PRODUCERS (818) 995-3600
15503 Ventura Blvd.
Encino 91436
www.amptp.org

AMERICAN CINEMA EDITORS (818) 777-2900
100 Universal City Plaza FAX (818) 733-5023
Bldg. 2352, Rm. 202
Universal City 91608
www.ace-filmeditors.org

AMERICAN FEDERATION OF MUSICIANS (213) 251-4510
3550 Wilshire Blvd., Ste. 900
Hollywood 90010
www.afm.org

AMERICAN GUILD OF MUSICAL ARTISTS (212) 265-3687
1430 Broadway St., 14th Fl.
New York, NY 10018
www.musicalartists.org

AMERICAN SOCIETY OF CINEMATOGRAPHERS (800) 448-0145
1782 N. Orange Dr.
Hollywood 90028
www.theasc.com

Unions

AMERICAN SOCIETY OF COMPOSERS, AUTHORS & PUBLISHERS A.S.C.A.P. (323) 883-1000
7920 Sunset Blvd., #300
Los Angeles 90046
www.ascap.org

ANIMATION GUILD (818) 766-7151
4729 Lankershim Blvd. FAX (818) 506-4805
North Hollywood 91602
www.mpsc839.org

ASSOCIATION OF INDEPENDENT COMMERCIAL PRODS. (323) 960-4763
650 N. Bronson FAX (323) 960-4766
Bungalow 223B
Hollywood 90004
www.aicp.com

ASSOCIATION OF TALENT AGENTS (310) 274-0628
9255 Sunset Blvd., #930 FAX (310) 274-5063
Los Angeles 90069
www.agentassociation.com

COSTUME DESIGNERS GUILD LOCAL 892 (818) 905-1557
4730 Woodman Ave., Ste. 430
Sherman Oaks 91423
www.costumedesignersguild.com

FILM & VIDEO TECH LOCAL 683 (IATSE) (818) 252-5628
P.O. Box 7429
Burbank 91510

INTERNATIONAL ALLIANCE OF THEATRICAL STAGE EMPLOYEES (818) 980-3499
10045 Riverside Dr.
Toluca Lake 91602
www.iatse-intl.org

MOTION PICTURE & EDITORS GUILD LOCAL 776 (323) 876-4770
7715 Sunset Blvd., Ste. 200 FAX (323) 876-0861
Hollywood 90046
www.editorsguild.com

MOTION PICTURE ASSOCIATION OF AMERICA (818) 995-6600
15503 Ventura Blvd.
Encino 91436
www.mpaa.org

MOTION PICTURE COSTUMER IA LOCAL 705 (818) 487-5655
4731 Laurel Canyon Blvd.
Valley Village 91607

MOTION PICTURE ILLUSTRATORS & MATTE ARTISTS LOCAL 790 (IATSE) (818) 784-6555
13245 Riverside Dr., Ste. 300A
Sherman Oaks 91423

MOTION PICTURE SET PAINTERS LOCAL 729 (IATSE) (818) 842-7729
1811 W. Burbank Blvd.
Burbank 91506
www.ialocal729.com

MOTION PICTURE STUDIO GRIPS LOCAL 80 (IATSE) (818) 526-0700
2520 West Olive
Burbank 91505
www.iatselocal80.org

MUSICIANS UNION LOCAL 47 (323) 462-2161
817 N. Vine St.
Los Angeles 90038
www.afm.org

NATIONAL ACADEMY OF RECORDING ARTS & SCIENCES (310) 392-3777
3402 Pico Blvd.
Santa Monica 90405
www.grammy.org

NATIONAL ASSOCIATION THEATRE OWNERS (818) 506-1778
4605 Lankershim Blvd., #340
North Hollywood 91602
www.natoonline.org

PRODUCERS GUILD OF AMERICA (310) 358-9020
8530 Wilshire Blvd., Ste 450 FAX (310) 358-9520
Beverly Hills 90211
www.producersguild.org

PUBLICISTS GUILD OF AMERICA LOCAL 600 (323) 876-0160
7715 Sunset Blvd.
Los Angeles 90046
www.cameraguild.com

SCENIC & TITLE ARTISTS LOCAL 800 (818) 762-9995
11969 Ventura Blvd., #200
Studio City 91604
www.artist816.org

SCRIPT SUPERVISORS LOCAL 871 (IATSE) (818) 509-7871
11519 Chandler Blvd.
North Hollywood 91601
www.ialocal871.org

SET DESIGNERS & MODEL MAKERS LOCAL 847 & 790 (818) 784-6555
13245 Riverside Dr., Ste. 300A
Sherman Oaks 91423

SOCIETY OF MOTION PICTURES & TV ART DIRECTORS (818) 762-9995
11969 Ventura Blvd., #200
Studio City 91604
www.artdirectors.org

UNIONS

SOCIETY OF STAGE DIRECTORS & CHOREOGRAPHERS (212) 391-1070
Barbara Hauptman – Executive Director
1501 Broadway, #1701 FAX (212) 302-6195
New York, NY 10036
www.ssdc.org

SONGWRITERS GUILD OF AMERICA (323) 462-1108
6430 Sunset Blvd., #705 FAX (323) 462-5430
Hollywood 90028

1560 Broadway #1306 (212) 768 7902
New York City, NY 10036

209 10th Avenue South (615) 329-1782
Ste. 534 FAX (615) 329-2623
Nashville, TN 37203
www.songwriters.org
www.songwritersguild.com

Established in 1931 as a protective and advisory agency for songwriters representing authors and writers all over the world, covering all phases of music. Full members must be published songwriters; associate members can be unpublished songwriters. The membership is also comprised of estates of deceased writers and offers songwriting contract instruction, lectures, a newsletter, royalty collection services, a collaboration service, group life and medical insurance, monthly ASK-A-PRO sessions and low cost workshops. Annual dues start at $60 for associate members and $84-$108 for full members, depending on royalties collected by the Guild.

STUDIO ELECTRICAL LIGHTING TECH LOCAL 728 (IATSE) (818) 891-0728
14629 Nordhoff St.
Panorama City 91402
www.iatse728.org

THEATRICAL STAGE EMPLOYEES LOCAL 33 (IATSE) (818) 841-9233
1720 W. Magnolia Blvd.
Burbank 91506
www.ia33.org

UNITED SCENIC ARTISTS LOCAL 829 (323) 965-0957
5225 Wilshire Blvd., #506
Los Angeles 90036
www.usa829.org

UNION PAY RATES

The following are minimum rates for acting categories negotiated by the named unions. These rates were calculated in 2003 and are subject to change, therefore, we have listed contact numbers for each of the unions. Also, information about rules and regulations, membership eligibility, fees and other pertinent information can be found in the WORKING section of this book. If you have questions, contact the appropriate unions. They are there to serve the membership.

Equity www.actorsequity.org

Contracts:
Joe Garber, John Lowe
Timothy Smith, Julie Eisenbeiss,
Michael Van Duzer (323) 634-1750

AEA CONTRACTS

Equity contracts fall into various categories, each one geared toward the specific type of theatre operation for which it was negotiated. Within each category work rules often differ and there are frequently several salary tiers, based on the size of the house and operating budget of the theatre. The following is by no means a comprehensive explanation, only a brief guide to Equity contracts. Equity members should contact AEA for rule books and salaries appropriate to a given category. Remember too, that some contracts are in almost constant fluctuation, particularly those dealing with small theatres.

BAT (Bay Area Theatres) – Used within San Francisco Bay area in seasonal, not-for-profit theatres with less than 400 seats which have not previously produced under an Equity agreement. 5 salary tiers based on gross box office formula.

CASINO – Covers employment in any theatre or other performance venue within a casino/hotel property. Based on seating capacity, there are 4 salary tiers covering both full-length and tab version shows. Pension and health benefits are provided, as well as housing and per diem for out of town actors.

CAT (Chicago Area Theatres) – Used in theatres with 900 or fewer seats within a 35-mile perimeter of the Chicago city limits. Covers commercial and not-for-profit theatres. A multi-tiered agreement based on combination of weekly performances, rehearsal hours and potential box office.

CORST, COST – see below, under STOCK.

DT (Dinner Theatre) – Agreements are negotiated separately for each theatre in each regional area and salary scales vary from theatre to theatre.

FNPTC (Funded Non-Profit Theatre Code) – (see SHOWCASE CODE)

GA (Guest Artist) – Used by not-for-profit educational or community theatres that occasionally employ professional actors. 3 salary tiers based on the number of regularly scheduled performances.

HAT (Hollywood Area Theatre) – Used in the county of Los Angeles for theatres with less than 500 seats. 4 salary categories based on seating capacity and 7 salary levels tied to gross box office receipts.

LOA (Letter of Agreement) – Used in developmental situations. Every LOA is individually negotiated and the terms vary from theatre to theatre and from season to season. Each LOA is referenced to a standard rule book for those provisions not specifically set forth in the LOA.

LORT (League of Resident Theatres) – Used by not-for-profit regional theatres throughout the country. 5 tiers, based on actual weekly box office gross averaged over 3 years.

99-SEAT – Showcase – type code developed specifically for use in the county of Los Angeles in theatres of 99 seats or less. (Note: Codes are not standard Equity agreements. Professional services are rendered without pay, there is no obligation to remain in a production and none of the benefits or protections of standard agreements exists.)

PRODUCTION – Equity's foremost contract, with the highest minimum salaries. Covers both musicals and plays for Broadway, national, international and bus and truck tours by commercial or not-for-profit producers.

SHOWCASE CODE – Available for use in New York City in theatres of 99 seats or less. There are two such codes: the Tiered Code for Funded Non-Profit Theatres (FNPTC) and the Basic Showcase Code used for single, commercial productions.

SPT (Small Professional Theatres) – Used in theatres of less than 350 seats outside of New York, Chicago and Los Angeles and is part of Equity's Developing Theatres Department 10 salary categories are determined by the number of performances and maximum weekly hours of work. May be used in commercial and not-for-profit situations for both seasonal operations and single productions.

STOCK – A Stock theatre is one that presents consecutive productions of different shows with no lay-off or hiatus between the productions. The five Stock agreements are: CORST (Council of Resident Theatres), COST (Council of Stock Theatres), Outdoor Dramas, MSUA (Musical Stock and Unit Attractions) and RMTA (Resident Musical Theatre).

TYA (Theatre for Young Audiences) – Covers plays expressly written, created or adapted to be performed for children through high school age. Two forms of contracts: weekly contract and per-performance contract.

URTA (University Resident Theatre Association) – Available to colleges and universities that employ professional actors and stage managers on a regular basis to perform with students. 4 minimums salary tiers based on weekly box office gross and number of performances.

WESTERN SPECIAL PRODUCTION – Used only with special permission of Equity for commercial and not-for-profit productions in theatres up to 899 seats. Touring is prohibited. Most rules are similar to the standard Production Agreement.

WCLO (Western Region Community Non-profit Musical Theatre) – Used in Western regional community non-profit musical theatres. Touring is permitted between WCLO theatres.

Minimum Basic Agreement:

At the time of publication, these rates were being negotiated and may soon change. If you have any questions, call Equity. The following are weekly pay rates for actors:

	Non-Tony Eligible	Tony Eligible
Special Production NY –	$902.00 –	$1,209.00
Off Broadway A	$493.00 minimum	
Off Broadway B	$574.00 minimum	
Off Broadway C	$665.00 minimum	
Off Broadway D	$765.00 minimum	
Off Broadway E	$857.00 minimum	
Dinner Theatre (depending on the number of seats)	$300.00 – $565.00	

League of Resident Theatres (LORT) as of 2/28/05

LORT Experimental	$427.00
LORT A	$800.00
LORT B+	$754.00
LORT B	$700.00
LORT C	$650.00
LORT D	$531.00
Cabaret (depending on # of seats)	$377.00 – $744.00
Small Professional Theatres (SPT) (based on weekly gross)	$170.00 – $502.00
HAT (based on weekly gross)	$311.00 – $687.00
BAT (based on weekly gross	$180.00 – $515.00
Non Resident Dramatic Stock (COST) COST (Small)	$557.00 – $797.00
Resident Dramatic (CORST)	$508.00 – $750.00
(RMTA) Resident Musical	$826.00
Musical Stock and unit attraction	$755.00
Business Theatre (2 weeks)	$518.00 (first day) $307.00 (each day thereafter)
University/Resident Theatre Agreement	$440.00 – $666.00
Theatre for Young Audiences (TYA) or	$397.00 minimum $62.00-$78.00 per performance and up
Guest Artists (7 days)	$290.00 – $490.00
Production Contract	$1,422.00 minimum and up
Western Special Production	$921.00
WCLO	$875.00 (based on actual weekly gross)

AFTRA:

Television Field Representative: Gloria Murphy

New York	**(212) 532-0800**
Los Angeles	**(323) 634-8100**

AFTRAPrime Time Dramatic Television rates are listed under SAG/AFTRA television.

Principal Performers – Dramatic Programs:
Single Program Performance

Over 15 to 30 minutes –	$690.00
Over 45 to 60 minutes –	$929.00

Serials

Over 15 to 30 minutes –	$619.00
Over 45 to 60 minutes –	$827.00

Principal Performers – Non-Dramatic Programs:
Single Program Performance

Over 15 to 30 minutes –	$704.00
Over 45 to 60 minutes –	$894.00

Multiple Performances in One Calendar Week
Over 15 to 30 minutes –

1 Performance	$705.00
2 Performances	$1,322.00

Performers Who Speak Five Lines or Less:
Single program performance –

Over 15 to 30 minutes –	$331.00
Over 45 to 60 minutes –	$410.00

Serials

Over 15 to 30 minutes –	$293.00
Over 45 to 60 minutes –	$360.00

Announcers Off-Camera:
More than 10 lines

Over 15 to 30 minutes –	$377.00
Over 45 to 60 minutes –	$527.00

Less than 10 lines

Over 15 to 30 minutes –	$264.00
Over 45 to 60 minutes –	$314.00

Specialty Acts:
Program Fees –

1 Performer	$1,129.00
2 Performers	$1,787.00
3 Performers	$2,264.00
Each Add'l	$ 565.00

Walk-ons and Extras:
Program Fees
(Other than Serials and Variety Shows):

Over 15 to 30 minutes (General)	$92.25
Over 45 to 60 minutes (Specialty)	$102.25

Serials

Over 15 to 30 minutes	$116.00
Over 45 to 60 minutes	$147.00

AGVA:

Vary by contract

SAG:

Theatrical Contracts	**(323) 549-6828**
Television Contracts	**(323) 549-6835**
Singers' Representative	**(323) 549-6864**
Signatory Status	**(323) 549-6869**
Main Switchboard	**(323) 954-1600**
Residual Info. & Claims	**(323) 549-6505**

Minimum Basic Agreement:

Day Performers –	$ 716.00
Weekly Performers –	$2,483.00

Singers (Theatrical on and off-camera)

Solo and Duo –	$ 773.00
Groups 3-8 –	$ 679.00

Singers
(Television on-camera)

Solo & Duo –	$ 773.00
Groups 3-8 –	$ 679.00

Singers
(Television off-camera)

Solo & Duo –	$ 773.00
Groups 3-8	$ 410.00

Term Performers:

10 – 19 weeks (per week) –	$2,130.00
20 or more weeks (per week) –	$1,774.00

Theatrical Extras:

General Extra Performer –	$115.00
Special Ability Extra Performer –	$125.00
Stand-In –	$130.00

Commercials (basic day fee without unit fee, residuals, or any other use fee).

Principals, on-camera:	$535.00
Principals, off-camera:	$402.00

Allowances:

Meal Allowances:

Breakfast	$ 12.00
Lunch	$ 18.00
Dinner	$ 30.00
Travel Allowance:	$ 80.00

SAG/AFTRA

SAG/AFTRA Television:
Prime Time Dramatic Programs:

Day Rates:
Actor & Singer

(1/2-hour & 1-hour shows)	$ 678.00
3-Day Rate:	$2,150.00
Weekly Rate:	$2,198.00

Multiple Pictures (weekly):
Performers
1/2-hour & 1-hour shows $1,741.00

1 1/2-hour show	$2,046.00
2-hour show	$2,414.00

Series (weekly):
1/2-hr. 13 out of 13 – $2,352.00

less than 13 –	$2,691.00
1-hr. 13 out of 13 –	$2,352.00
less than 13 –	$3,156.00
1 1/2-hour 13 out of 13 –	$3,767.00
less than 13 –	$4,268.00
2-hour 13 out of 13 –	$4,710.00
less than 13 –	$5,458.00

2 or More Series in Combined Format:

1-hour –	$3,691.00
1 1/2-hour –	$4,981.00
2-hour –	$6,308.00

Television Trailers:

On & Off Camera (per day)	$ 678.00

ACE EVENT PRODUCTIONS
ANIMAL CRACKERS **(949) 487-9296**
27221 Ortega Highway **FAX (949) 388-7790**
Ste. E #389
San Juan Capistrano 92675
www.animalcrackersent.com

Booking agents for all types of talent including vocalists, dancers, specialty acts, celebrity look-a-likes, musicians, and magic acts for singing telegrams, also street performers. Year round employment. Submit P&R, then contact Marsi Roberson.

BALLYS CASINO RESORT **(702) 739-4111**
LAS VEGAS **(888) 742-9248**
3645 Las Vegas Blvd. South
Las Vegas, NV 89109
www.ballyslasvegas.com

Hires vocalists, dancers, musicians, and all kinds of specialty acts. Auditions are held in January and they book variety acts year round. Company Manager: Fluff Le Coque. Call for more information.

(702) 734-0410
CIRCUS CIRCUS **(702) 794-3875**
2880 Las Vegas Blvd. South
Las Vegas, NV 89109-1120
www.circuscircus.com

Hires specialty acts such as circus performers, ring masters, strolling entertainers, magicians, high wire acts, and jugglers. Employment is year round with 6 month contracts. Submit P&R and video tape. Submit either directly or through an agent or manager. No drop-ins. Mail submissions to the attention of Mike Hartzell Director of Entertainment.

(800) 258-2633
CLUB MED **(888) 258-2633**

Hires entertainers that will also work resort jobs as instructors, attendants, bartenders, etc. Applicants must be at least 19 years of age, have a valid passport, and be able to relocate for 6 months at a time. Entertainers work at night in talent shows, games, etc. The work is hard and the hours are long and there are no positions available for those who wish to do nothing but entertain. Seasonal. Club Med now has 2 sailing ships which are staffed by personnel who have worked in a village for at least one season.

DISNEYLAND **(714) 781-3445**
1313 Harbor Blvd.
Anaheim 92803

P.O. Box 3232
TDA 329R
Anaheim 92803

Hires variety artists, vocalists, dancers, and musicians to work at Disneyland. Send P&R and demo tape. Tapes can be returned with an SASE but they prefer to hold them in their files for future reference. Send all submissions to the attention of Manager of Talent Casting and Booking, Greg Bell.

(702) 597-7150
EXCALIBUR HOTEL CASINO **(877) 750-5464**
P.O. Box 96778
Las Vegas, NV 89193-6778
www.excalibur.com

Has a stage a show with a medieval theme and hires a range of performers and musicians such as jousters on horseback, unicyclists, and country-western performers. They also have strolling entertainers. At least 100 performers appear weekly. Send P&R to the attention of Mike Hartzell. Also submit a video if you have an act. Auditions are held on rare occasions.

KNOTT'S BERRY FARM **(714) 220-5390**
Entertainment Dept.
8039 Beach Blvd.
Buena Park 90620
www.knotts.com

Seasonal employment. Hires variety acts, musicians, jugglers, magicians, artists, fortune tellers, etc. Entertainers perform for catered events as well as at the park site. Variety acts should send a demo package including a P&R, bio, and video tape to Entertainment department.

(818) 780-4433
LIVE WIRES ENTERTAINMENT **(800) 939-7737**
P.O. Box 260766 **FAX (818) 343-9250**
Encino 91426
www.entertainmentexpress.us
entexp@aol.com

Singing telegrams. They do private parties, grand openings, and almost any type of function. The customer chooses a character to deliver the telegram or the company will create a personalized character. They also hire all forms of variety entertainment for private parties and events as well as people with experience in balloon decoration. Year round employment. Submit P&R. Provides DJs, dancers, lookalikes and variety entertainment for special events. Artistic and creative individuals should send resume. Especially interested in strong MC personalities for Bar/Bat Mitzvahs and interactive hip-hop dancers. Currently looking for DJs and people with dancing experience to work with their DJs.

MAGIC CASTLE **(323) 851-3313**
7001 Franklin Ave.
Hollywood 90028
www.magiccastle.com

The Academy of Magical Arts, better known as The Magic Castle, will put you in touch with their magician members and/or magic consultants. Call before submitting P&R and demo tape.

MAGIC MOUNTAIN ENTERTAINMENT
ATTN JODY HUTCHINSON **(661) 255-4858**
P.O. Box 5500
Valencia 91385
www.sixflags.com

Send P&R and any related press material, if available. They keep an active casting file and check it before holding open calls. They usually hold open auditions once a year. They also list casting information in Variety and the local papers.

MEDIEVAL TIMES **(714) 523-1100**
7662 Beach Blvd.
Buena Park 90260
www.medievaltimes.com

Year round employment. Hires actors for knights, MC, count, countess, and squires. The knight characters joust on horseback and require advanced horse riding skills. Performers work on the site. Send P&R and any other pertinent material to the attention of Lorence Watley. They hold open auditions and list casting information in Back Stage West.

MULLIGAN MANAGEMENT (818) 752-9474
11824 Oxnard St. FAX (818) 752-9477
North Hollywood 91606
www.lookalikes.net
mullianmgmt@lookalikes.net

Represents look-alikes, variety spokesmodels, dancers, and actors with customized comedy roasts for corporate events, conventions, and overseas commercial bookings. Reviews pictures and resumes, and VHS tapes. Especially interested in celebrity, political, or historical look-alikes. Attends showcases but does not see acts in the office.

MUSICIANS NETWORK (323) 993-3174
ADMINISTRATOR (323) 462-2161 x174
817 Vine St.
Hollywood 90038
www.promusic47.org
network@promusic47.org

Professional Musicians Local 47. American Federation of Musicians. A referral network for union musicians. There are year round employment opportunities. Contact by phone. They also list casting information with the Musicians Union.

PRINCESS CRUISE LINES (661) 753-0000
ENTERTAINMENT (800) PRINCESS
24305 Town Center Drive.
Santa Clarita 91355
www.princesscruises.com

Hires vocalists, dancers, musicians, disc jockeys, and light technicians. Auditions are held periodically when openings are available. They list casting information in The Hollywood Reporter, Variety, and Back Stage West. P&R and CDs should be sent to the entertainment department, they do maintain a casting file.

RENAISSANCE PLEASURE FAIRE (626) 969-4750
Performing Arts Department FAX (626) 815-9495
P.O. Box 1550
Irwindale 91706
www.renfair.com

Hires vocalists, dancers, and musicians for seasonal employment, May-June in the Santa Fe Dam Recreation area. Go to the website to download application and procedures for participation. They have many volunteers but will pay per day for theme characters and musicians. Looking for new age/cirque entertainment for stage or street work.

ROYAL CARIBBEAN CRUISES, LTD. (305) 539-6000
1050 Caribbean Way FAX (305) 539-3938
Miami, FL 33132
www.royalcaribbean.com

Hires singers, dancers, guest entertainers, and variety acts of all kinds. They prefer that you send pictures and resumes, demo tape or CD, and background material to ShipBoard Human Resources and resumes can be faxed after 5 pm EST.

STILETTO ENTERTAINMENT (310) 957-5757
8295 La Cienega Blvd. FAX (310) 957-5771
Inglewood 90301
www.stilettoentertainment.com

Stiletto Entertainment casts experienced singers and dancers for production shows aboard Holland America's luxury liners. Six-month contracts cruise the Caribbean, Panama Canal, Mexico, Alaska, Europe, Hawaii, New England, and South America. Performers receive competitive salary, onboard accommodations, medical/dental benefits and discount cruises after paid rehearsals in Los Angeles with travel and accommodations provided. All applicants must be 18 or older to work at sea. During auditions, singers will learn songs from their shows and a short dance combination. Dancers will learn a short challenging combination from their shows. Acting skills are required for all singers and acting and gymnastics are a plus for dancers. They also accept video auditions.

TROPICANA HOTEL (702) 739-2222
3801 Las Vegas Blvd. South
Las Vegas, NV 89109
www.tropicanalv.com

Hires all kinds of performers, especially dancers and singers, year round. Will review P&R and they maintain casting files. Send to the attention of Ari Levin, Director of Entertainment. They do not hold open auditions but cast as needed.

UNIVERSAL STUDIOS, HOLLYWOOD
ENTERTAINMENT DEPARTMENT (818) 622-3851
100 Universal City Plaza
Universal City 91608

Hires vocalists, dancers, musicians, specialty acts, and stunt/actors for shows. Employment is full time, part time, or seasonal. Send P&R and CD to the Entertainment Department, Bldg. 5511-4. Holds open auditions in the spring and posts notices in Back Stage West or Variety.

Working Regulations For Children

The State and local regulations governing the conditions of children working in the entertainment industry are complex. Because we feel that it is important for the parents of working children to be as informed as possible regarding their rights and responsibilities, we have compiled the following information including an article by Barbara Shiffman, founder of the Hollywood Screen Parents Association. We strongly suggest that you get both of the following recommended books for complete details about child labor laws.

THE BLUE BOOK – The Employment of Minors in the Entertainment Industry
Compiled by the Studio Teachers, IATSE Local 884; $5, call or write:

IATSE Local 884 (310) 652-5330
P.O. Box 461467
Los Angeles, CA 90046

"CHILD LABOR LAWS IN CALIFORNIA"
Contains excerpts specific to working children from the California Labor Code, California Administrative Code, and the California Education Code. There is no charge, call or write:

DIVISION OF LABOR/ROBERT JONES (213) 620-6330
STANDARDS ENFORCEMENT (213) 576-6227
320 W. 4th Ste. 450
Los Angeles 90013

DIVISION OF LABOR (818) 901-5315
STANDARDS ENFORCEMENT (818) 908-4556
6150 Van Nuys Blvd., Room 206
Van Nuys 91401
www.dir.cagov/dlse/dlse.html

CHILDREN IN FILM (818) 901-0082
6539 Colbath Ave.
Valley Glen 91401
www.childreninfilm.com
casala@childreninfilm.com

Children In Film provides parents and entertainment professionals with information about the employment of minors in the entertainment industry and assists in obtaining employment permits for children and production companies. The CIF website includes summaries of both California Child Labor Law and British Columbia Employment Standards as well as a list of Department of Labor Offices for all 50 U.S. States. You can download necessary application forms and other important documents such as a Coogan Law summary and a list of banks where Coogan trust accounts can be obtained. Laws. Additionally, CIF's "Kidstart" program provides parents with information on how to get their children started in show biz and offers resources for agents and managers specializing in kids.

Child Labor Guidelines

The following are guidelines set by the Screen Actors Guild and the Los Angeles Division of Labor Standards Enforcement. They are incomplete here and only touch on a few of the most important points, so if you are the parent or guardian of a minor who has been approached to work or is interested in working as an actor, please contact the State of California Labor Commissioner at: www.dir.ca.gov/dlse/dlse.html

SAG CHILD ACTOR HOTLINE (323) 549-6030

Los Angeles (213) 620-6330

Van Nuys Branch (818) 901-5315

Young Performers/Coogan Law (323) 549-6639

Ask for a copy of Title 8 and a copy of the booklet, "Child Labor Laws in California." They will also be able to answer questions regarding your specific situation. These regulations apply to all working situations including small theatres.

A minor is a person under 18 years of age. Employers must have a permit to employ a minor. All minors must obtain an entertainment work permit unless they have graduated from high school or have a Certificate of California High School Proficiency. If they are still in school, minors must obtain proof that they satisfactorily meet their school district's requirements regarding age, school record, attendance, and health. While a current report card is usually acceptable, further information may be necessary. High school graduates are required to present a diploma or other proof of graduation. A work permit is valid for six months and is usually renewable by mail.

A parent or guardian of any minor under the age of sixteen must be present and accompany such a minor on the set or location and be within sight or sound of said minor at all times.
If the minor is over the age of sixteen, he/she may attend the work place alone. He/she must, however, bring proof of age.

At least 3 hours of schooling are required on the set daily during the school calendar year. The hours must fall between 8 am and 4 pm; at no time may periods of less than 20 minutes count toward the 3 hours. Breaks may not be counted toward the school hours. While the minor's regular school teacher shall prepare all assignments, the child is responsible to the studio classroom for these assignments and any necessary school supplies, i.e. pens, paper, pencils, crayons, etc.

An emancipated minor who has not finished high school must still have the requisite 3 hours of schooling each day, unless specifically exempt by the court from Title 8 of the Education Code. For minors over the age of sixteen a studio teacher is required for education only. Any minor who can show proof of completion of high school requirements is recognized as an adult and no longer requires a studio teacher.

Studio Teachers:

A studio teacher, within the meaning of these regulations, is a certified teacher who holds both California Elementary and California Secondary teaching credentials which are valid and current, and who has been certified by the Labor Commissioner.

A studio teacher will be on each call for minors from age fifteen days to their sixteenth birthday, and for minors from age sixteen to eighteen when required for the child's education. One studio teacher must be provided for each group of ten minors or any fraction thereof. On Saturdays, Sundays, holidays, or during school vacation periods, one studio teacher must be provided for each group of twenty minors or fraction thereof.

In addition to teaching, the studio teacher on the set shall also have responsibility for caring and attending to the health, safety and morals of minors. In the discharge of these responsibilities, the studio teacher shall take cognizance of such factors as working conditions, physical surroundings, signs of the minor's mental and physical fatigue, and the demands placed upon the minor in relation to the minor's age, agility, strength and stamina. If, in the judgment of the studio teacher, conditions are such as to present a danger to the health, safety or morals of the minor, the studio teacher may refuse to allow the engagement of a minor on a set or location and may remove the minor therefrom.

No minor may be sent to make-up, wardrobe, hairdressing, or any other form of employment without a studio teacher. If school is not in session, a parent or guardian may accompany the minor.

The remuneration of the studio teacher shall be paid by the employer.

Working Hours of Minors:

The amount of time minors are permitted at the place of employment within a 24-hour period is limited according to age as follows:

a) Babies between the ages of 15 days and 6 months may be permitted to remain at the place of employment for a maximum of 2 hours. The day's work shall not exceed 20 minutes and under no conditions shall the baby be exposed to light of greater than 100-foot candlelight intensity for more than 30 seconds at a time. Studio teacher and nurse requirements vary, as do the time periods when an infant may work, according to the age of your infant; for all questions about your individual infant call Roberta O'Con at the State of California (818) 901-5315. In any workplace where you bring your infant make sure that a clean, comfortable environment is provided.

b) Minors between the ages of 6 months and 2 years may be permitted at the place of employment for a maximum of 4 hours. This four hour period must not have more than 2 hours of work, and thus must be balanced with 2 hours of rest and recreation.

c) Minors between the ages of 2 years and 6 years may be permitted at the place of employment for a maximum of six hours. The minor shall work for no more than 3 hours, the remaining 3 hour period may consist of rest and recreation, and/or education.

d) Minors who are between the ages of 6 and 9 may be at the place of employment for a maximum of 8 hours. This work period shall consist of not more than four hours of work, at least 3 hours of schooling, when school is in session, and one hour of rest and recreation. When school is not in session, working hours may be increased to 6 hours.

e) Minors who are between the ages 9 and 16 may be permitted at the place of employment for a maximum of 9 hours. This work period shall consist of not more than 5 hours of work, at least 3 hours of schooling, and one hour of rest and recreation. When school is not in session, working hours may be increased to 7 hours.

f) Minors who are between the ages of 16 and 18 years may be permitted at the place of employment for a maximum of 10 hours. This work period shall consist of not more than 6 hours of work, at least 3 hours of schooling, and one hour of rest and recreation. When school is not in session, working hours may be increased to 8 hours.

g) Twelve hours must elapse between the minor's time of dismissal and time of call on the following day. If the minor's regular school starts less than 12 hours after his or her dismissal time, the minor must be schooled the following day at the employer's place of business.

h) Time spent traveling may count as part of the working day of a minor.

Meal Periods:

All hours for the minor at the place of employment are exclusive of the meal period.

Meal periods must be within 6 hours of the minor's call time, for a minimum of 1/2hour, and extend the minor's day by no more than 1/2 hour. In cases when the meal period exceeds 1/2hour, the remaining time is considered rest and recreation.

Additional Notes:

1) If a minor between the ages of 14 and 18 obtains permission to work no more than 2 consecutive school days during school hours, the minor's working hours may be extended to, but may not exceed, 8 hours in a 24-hour period.

2) Requests for working extensions must be directed to the Labor Commissioner, Los Angeles Division of Labor, and must be made at least 48 hours in advance.

3) The parent or guardian is ultimately responsible for the child's medical care in terms of injury or accident.

4) The phone number for information regarding obtaining or renewing entertainment work permits for your child: Van Nuys (818) 901-5315.

NOTES

A

Academy Players Directory 281
Accents 87
Accompanists 137
Acting Books 112
Acting Coaches & Teachers 2
Actor's Demo Tapes 107, 183
Actors' Equity Association 318
Advertising Agencies 238
ADR Groups 107
AEA 318
AEA pay rates 330
AFTRA 320
AFTRA Pay Rates 331
AFTRA/SAG Federal Credit Union 324
Agents 199
Agents Chart 192
Agents, Modeling 213
Agents, Talent 199, 216
Agents, Talent - San Diego 211
Agents, Talent - San Francisco 212
Agents, Talent - Specialty 216
AGVA 322
AGVA Pay Rates 332
Airchecks 183
American Federation of Television & Radio Artists 320
American Guild of Variety Artists 322
Answering Machines 126
Answering Services 106
Arrangers 138
Artists Representation 199
Associations 284, 318
Attorneys 218
Audio Demo Production 107
Awards 240

B

Ballet 72, 295
Ballroom Dancing 72
Beauty Supply Stores 131, 171
Beepers 106
Body Building 69
Bookkeeping 176, 221
Books 112
Box Offices 295
Breakdown Services 133
Broadcast Schools 37
Business of Acting Classes 37
Business Managers 221

C

Cameras, Video 183
Cards, Business 168
Career Management 225
Cartoon Voice Tapes 107
Casting Directors 254
Casting Directors Chart 244
Casting Hotlines 321, 324
Casting Facilities 274
Casting Services 277
Children's Training 40
Children's Work Regulations 335
Classical Training 48
Clipping Services 121
Cold Reading Workshops 50
Colleges & Universities 103
Combat 56
Comedy Training 57
Commercial Agents 199
Commercial Training 63
Composers 138
Composites 142, 146
Computers 121
Computer Software/Services 281
Consultants, Image 130
Consultants, Marketing 133
Copies, Video 183
Copy Centers 168
Cosmetics 171
Costume Sales & Rental 123
Costume Training 83
Counseling, Career 83
Crash Courses 68
Cruise Ship Work 333

D

Dance Classes 72
Dance Companies 279
Dance Shoes 126
Dance Training 72
Dancewear 126
Delivery Services 137
Demo Tapes, Audio 107
Demo Tapes, Video 183
DGA 322
Dialects 87
Dialogue Coaches 87
Directing Training 83
Directories 139
Directors Guild of America 322
Dramatists Guild, Inc. 323
Dubbing Groups 281

E

Electronics & Computer Equipment 121, 126
Envelopes 179
Equity 318
Equity Pay Rates 330
Exercise Clothes/Wear 123
Extra Casting 277

F

The 4 As . . . 318
FAX Machines . . . 128
FAX Services . . . 128
Fencing . . . 56
Film Classes, Production . . . 84
Financial Management . . . 221
Fire Arms Training . . . 70
French Language . . . 87

G

Game Shows . . . 129
Graphics . . . 168
Guilds . . . 318
Gun Training . . . 70

H

Headshots . . . 148
Horseback Riding . . . 70

I

Ice Skating Training . . . 71
Image Consultants . . . 130
Improv Classes . . . 57
Internet Related Services . . . 281
Investment Counseling . . . 221

J

Jazz Dance Classes . . . 72

K

Karate . . . 56

L

Language (Dialects & Speech) . . . 87
Language (Foreign) Training . . . 87
Leotards . . . 126
Letterhead . . . 179
Libraries . . . 180
Light Opera . . . 283
Literary Agents . . . 216
Lithographs . . . 168
Looping Groups . . . 281

M

Mail Boxes . . . 128
Make-up . . . 179
Make-up Artists . . . 131
Make-up Training . . . 76
Managers, Business . . . 221
Managers, Personal . . . 225
Marketing Info & Consultants . . . 133
Martial Arts . . . 56
Messenger Services . . . 137
Misc. Training . . . 83
Modern Dance . . . 72, 279
Modeling Agents . . . 213
Modeling Schools . . . 77
Motorcycle Training . . . 83
Movement . . . 77
Music . . . 80, 138, 283
Music Lessons . . . 79
Musical Services . . . 138
Musical Theatre Companies . . . 283
Musical Theatre Training . . . 80
Musical Training . . . 80

N

Newspapers . . . 139

O

Off-Air Recording . . . 101
Office Supplies . . . 179
Opera Companies . . . 283
Organizations . . . 284
Other Industry Training . . . 83

P

Pagers . . . 106
Paper Supplies . . . 179
Performance & Showcases . . . 178
Periodicals . . . 139
Personal Managers . . . 225
Photocopying . . . 168
Photo Duplication . . . 142
Photo Reproduction Labs . . . 142
Photo Retouchers . . . 146
Photographers . . . 148
Pianists . . . 138
Plays . . . 295
Press Agents . . . 233
Press Clipping Services . . . 121
Press Releases . . . 167
Print Modeling . . . 213
Printing, Lithographers . . . 168
Printing . . . 168
Processing, Photo . . . 142
Production Accounting . . . 290
Production Companies . . . 291
Production Training . . . 84
Publications . . . 139
Public Relations Representatives . . . 233

R

Recording, Demo Tape . . . 107
Recording, Off-Air . . . 107
Recording Studios . . . 107
Rehearsal Studios . . . 172
Rentals, Costumes . . . 123
Rentals, Halls . . . 172
Representation . . . 192
Reproduction Labs . . . 142
Research Libraries . . . 180
Resume Services . . . 176
Retouchers . . . 146
Roller Skating . . . 71

S

SAG . . . 323
SAG Pay Rates . . . 332
Screen Actor's Guild . . . 323
Script Analysis . . . 85
Script Writing . . . 85
Scuba Diving . . . 71
Secretarial Services . . . 176
Shakespeare . . . 48
Sheet Music . . . 178
Showcase Clubs . . . 178
Showcases . . . 50
Singing . . . 91
Skating, Ice . . . 71
Skating, Roller . . . 71
Social & Ballroom Dancing . . . 72
Software . . . 281
Songwriters Guild . . . 330
Specialty Agents . . . 216
Specialty Clothing . . . 126
Specialty Vehicles (Training) . . . 71
Speech . . . 97
Stand-up Comedy Clubs . . . 178
Stand-up Comedy Training . . . 57
Stationery Stores . . . 179
Student Films . . . 294
Studio Lots . . . 274
Studio Parking . . . 274
Studios, Access to . . . 274
Studios, Recording . . . 107
Studios, Rental . . . 172
Stunt Schools . . . 86
Stylists . . . 171
Sword Play . . . 56, 70

T

Talent Agents . . . 199
Tap Dance . . . 72
Tape, Air Checks . . . 183
Tape, Audio . . . 107
Tape Duplication . . . 183
Tape Production . . . 183
Teaching . . . 87
Technical Theatre Training . . . 83
Television Producers . . . 291
Television Stations . . . 274
Tennis . . . 72
Theatre Companies . . . 295
Theatres . . . 295
Theatrical Agents . . . 199
Theatrical Libraries . . . 180
Theme Park Jobs . . . 333
Trade Papers . . . 139
TV Stations . . . 274
Typesetting . . . 168
Typists . . . 176

U

Union Pay Rates . . . 330
Unions . . . 318
Universities & Colleges . . . 103

V

Variety Agents . . . 216
Variety Work . . . 333
Vehicles, Training . . . 71
Video Camera Rental . . . 182
Video Production Companies . . . 183
Video Tape, Airchecks & Duplication . . . 183
Voice, Accents & Dialects . . . 87
Voice Mail . . . 106
Voice, Singing Training . . . 91
Voice, Speech Training . . . 97
Voice-Over Groups . . . 281
Voice-Over Training . . . 101

W

Wardrobe . . . 123, 187
Website Design . . . 281
WGA . . . 326
Wigs . . . 188
Work Regulations for Children . . . 335
Writers Guild of America . . . 326
Writing Training . . . 85

X,Y,Z

ZED Cards . . . 168

Index To Advertisers

Actor's Circle Theatre 3
Stella Adler 6
Jill Andre 10
Joel Asher 1, 113
Back Stage West . . . . Back Cover
Adilah Barnes 7
BBs Kids 41
Gene Bua 5
Brad Buckman Photography 151
Ron Burrus 7
Karen Bystedt Photography 150
K Callan / Sweden Press . . . Training Tab
Beatrice Carroll 93
Carrie Cavalier 152
Louis Chamis 101
June Chandler 1, 43
Lilyan Chauvin 16, 255
Bob Corff 91
Claire Corff 90
Sara Corwin Photography 154
Del Mar Media Arts 67
Piero Dusa Acting Conservatory 21
Robert Easton 89
Kelsey Edwards 153
Final Print 143
Samuel French Booksellers . 201, Team Tab
Ellen Gerstein 8
Valerie Grant 147
Paul Gregory 149
Mary Grover 93
Wendy Hall 157
Marlon Hoffman 23
Sandy Holt 51
Mark Husmann . . . . Marketing Tab
Kimberly Jentzen 1
Anita Jesse 15
Janice Kent 12
Harvey Lembeck 59
M. K. Lewis 14
Beverly Long 65
Eric Morris 13
Norris Photo 159
Playhouse West 9
Elizabeth Prescott 95
Promenade Playhouse 297
Jean-Louis Rodrigue 4
Tim Sabatino/Sabastudio 161
Roman Salicki 155
Secret Rose Theatre 19
Smart Girls 177
Aaron Speiser 17
Judith Stransky 11
Carol Tingle 94
Doug Warhit 2
Wilshire Wigs 189
Tory Wolfe 148
Marta Woodhull 97